The Making of European Music in the Long Eighteenth Century

THE NEW CULTURAL HISTORY OF MUSIC

Jane F. Fulcher, Series Editor

Series Board Members:
Celia Applegate
Philip Bohlman
Kate van Orden
Michael P. Steinberg

Enlightenment Orpheus: The Power of Music in Other Worlds
Vanessa Agnew

Voice Lessons: French *Mélodie* in the Belle Epoque
Katherine Bergeron

Songs, Scribes, and Societies: The History and Reception of the Loire Valley Chansonniers
Jane Alden

Harmony and Discord: Music and the Transformation of Russian Cultural Life
Lynn M. Sargeant

Musical Renderings of the Philippine Nation
Christi-Anne Castro

The Sense of Sound: Musical Meaning in France, 1260–1330
Emma Dillon

Staging the French Revolution: Cultural Politics and the Paris Opera, 1789–1794
Mark Darlow

Music, Piety, and Propaganda: The Soundscapes of Counter-Reformation Bavaria
Alexander J. Fisher

The Politics of Appropriation: German Romantic Music and the Ancient Greek Legacy
Jason Geary

Defining *Deutschtum*: Political Ideology, German Identity, and Music-Critical Discourse in Liberal Vienna
David Brodbeck

Materialities: Books, Readers, and the Chanson in Sixteenth-Century Europe
Kate van Orden

Singing the Resurrection: Body, Community, and Belief in Reformation Europe
Erin Lambert

Electronic Inspirations: Technologies of the Cold War Musical Avant-Garde
Jennifer Iverson

Musical Solidarities: Political Action and Music in Late Twentieth-Century Poland
Andrea F. Bohlman

Cultivated by Hand: Amateur Musicians in the Early American Republic
Glenda Goodman

Sounding Feminine: Women's Voices in British Musical Culture, 1780–1850
David Kennerley

Socialist Laments: Musical Mourning in the German Democratic Republic
Martha Sprigge

Singing the News of Death: Execution Ballads in Europe 1500–1900
Una McIlvenna

What the Ballad Knows: The Ballad Genre, Memory Culture, and German Nationalism
Adrian Daub

The Cantigas de Santa Maria: Power and Persuasion at the Alfonsine Court
Henry T. Drummond

The Making of European Music in the Long Eighteenth Century
D. R. M. Irving

The Making of European Music in the Long Eighteenth Century

D. R. M. IRVING

OXFORD
UNIVERSITY PRESS

OXFORD
UNIVERSITY PRESS

Oxford University Press is a department of the University of Oxford. It furthers
the University's objective of excellence in research, scholarship, and education
by publishing worldwide. Oxford is a registered trade mark of Oxford University
Press in the UK and certain other countries.

Published in the United States of America by Oxford University Press
198 Madison Avenue, New York, NY 10016, United States of America.

© Oxford University Press 2024

All rights reserved. No part of this publication may be reproduced, stored in
a retrieval system, or transmitted, in any form or by any means, without the
prior permission in writing of Oxford University Press, or as expressly permitted
by law, by license, or under terms agreed with the appropriate reproduction
rights organization. Inquiries concerning reproduction outside the scope of the
above should be sent to the Rights Department, Oxford University Press, at the
address above.

You must not circulate this work in any other form
and you must impose this same condition on any acquirer.

Library of Congress Cataloging-in-Publication Data
Names: Irving, D. R. M., 1981– author.
Title: The making of European music in the long eighteenth century / D. R. M. Irving.
Description: [1.] | New York, NY : Oxford University Press, 2024. |
Series: New cultural history of music | Includes bibliographical references and index.
Identifiers: LCCN 2024002131 (print) | LCCN 2024002132 (ebook) |
ISBN 9780197632185 (hardback) | ISBN 9780197632208 (epub)
Subjects: LCSH: Music—Europe—18th century—History and criticism. |
Europe—Civilization—18th century. |
Orientalism—Europe—History—18th century. | Orientalism in music.
Classification: LCC ML240.3 .I78 2024 (print) | LCC ML240.3 (ebook) |
DDC 780.94/09033—dc23/eng/20240116
LC record available at https://lccn.loc.gov/2024002131
LC ebook record available at https://lccn.loc.gov/2024002132

DOI: 10.1093/oso/9780197632185.001.0001

The publisher gratefully acknowledges the support of the Margarita M. Hanson Fund of
the American Musicological Society, supported in part by the National Endowment for
the Humanities and the Andrew W. Mellon Foundation.

The manufacturer's authorised representative in the EU for product safety is
Oxford University Press España S.A. of El Parque Empresarial San Fernando
de Henares, Avenida de Castilla, 2 – 28830 Madrid (www.oup.es/en or
product.safety@oup.com). OUP España S.A. also acts as importer into Spain
of products made by the manufacturer.

To all my teachers (thus far)—especially students and colleagues, family and friends

Contents

Acknowledgments	ix
Note on Sources	xv

Introduction: Musics of Continents and Hemispheres	1
Adjectival Anachronism and "Conceptual Imperialism"	8
Querying "European" and "Western" Musics in the Academy	15
Approach, Sources, and Positionality	22
An Interpretive Itinerary around Ideas	29

PART I. "EUROPE" IN MUSIC, MUSIC IN "EUROPE"   33

1. Musical Constructions of Europe in Myth and Allegory	37
Envoicing Europa, in Music for Chamber and Stage	40
Europe in a Quartet of Continents	52
The All-Singing, All-Dancing Parts of the World	61
Europe as a Musical Community of Nations	68
2. Europe as Place: Music and the Imagined Extent of a Continent	71
Musicians' Contemplation of Continental Frontiers	77
Transcending Physical Space: The Republic of Music	86
Superlative Europe: Musicians and Intra-Continental Fame	90

PART II. "EUROPEAN MUSIC"   99

3. Europeans, "Franks," and "Their" Musics	107
Europe and Collective Identities	110
"Homo Europaeus" and Discriminatory Taxonomies of Humankind	114
"European Ears"	123
"European Musicians"	126
4. The Emergence of the "European Music" Concept	133
Jesuits and "European Music," from China to Paraguay	136
"European Music," Turkey, and "Oriental Music"	149
French Music and Europe	160
"One Music for Europe," from the Sixteenth to Late Eighteenth Centuries	163
External Comparisons: "European Music" in the Wider World	174

PART III. "MODERN EUROPEAN MUSIC" AND "WESTERN MUSIC" — 179

5. "Modern" Europe and "Ancient" Others in Musical Thought — 183
   Articulations of "Modern" Music's Ascendancy — 188
   Conflating Ancients with Others, and (Some) Europeans with Moderns — 196
   "Barbarism" in Musical Thought from the Fifteenth to Eighteenth Centuries — 201
   The Search for "Perfection" and "Progress" — 210

6. Accidental Occident: The Setting of "the West" in Music History — 217
   Is "East" East and "West" West? Always the Twain Are Intertwined — 220
   Historical Orientations of Christianity — 224
   "The West" and Music as Viewed in Eighteenth-Century Europe — 229
   The Rise of "Western Music" as a Cultural System — 237

Epilogue — 246

Bibliography — 249
Index — 305

Acknowledgments

I wish to thank many individuals and groups who represent the sine qua non of this project. In 2014, Reinhard Strohm offered me an International Research Visitorship on his Balzan Prize Research Programme in Musicology, "Towards a Global History of Music." During this stay, which I undertook at King's College London, I had the opportunity to collaborate with Estelle Joubert in organizing a workshop titled "Alterity and Universalism in Eighteenth-Century Musical Thought" at the University of Oxford. The essay emerging from that project acted as the springboard for this book. I am deeply grateful to Reinhard Strohm for enthusiastically supporting my entry into this area of investigation, and to Estelle Joubert for our in-depth and ongoing discussions on the topic.

From mid-2015 in Melbourne—often described as the most "European" city in Australia—I received great inspiration and encouragement from colleagues at the University of Melbourne and other institutions. In chatting about various aspects of this research in its early stages, I learned much from (in alphabetical order) Reuben Brown, Joe Browning, Michael Christoforidis, Barry Conyngham, Jane Davidson, Matthew Dolan, Véronique Duché, Stephen Grant, John Griffiths, Erin Helyard, Shelley Hogan, Margaret Kartomi, Elizabeth Kertesz, Frederic Kiernan, Sarah Kirby, Linda Kouvaras, Hannah Lane, Elly Langford, Shane Lestideau, Jenny McCallum, Gary McPherson, Kerry Murphy, Donald Nicolson, John O'Donnell, Melanie Plesch, Nicholas Pollock, Jessica Priestley, Madeline Roycroft, Jenny Spinks, Hannah Spracklan-Holl, Janice Stockigt, Nicholas Tochka, Peter Tregear, Sally Treloyn, Jason Varuhas, Ian Watchorn, Paul Watt, and John Weretka. I am grateful for the same reasons to scholars in other parts of Australia and in New Zealand, including David Black, Denis Collins, Sarah Collins, Bronwyn Ellis, Yasmin Haskell, David Larkin, Alan Maddox, Samantha Owens, Jason Stoessel, and W. Dean Sutcliffe.

Following my move to Barcelona in early 2019, the project continued, and Tess Knighton has been a source of great encouragement and wisdom as it developed. I must record my thanks to her and to other colleagues within ICREA (Institució Catalana de Recerca i Estudis Avançats), including

Rebekah Clements, Margarita Díaz-Andreu, and Joan-Pau Rubiés, for conversations about it. At the IMF (Institució Milà i Fontanals de Recerca en Humanitats), CSIC (Consejo Superior de Investigaciones Científicas), I have enjoyed discussions with Jon Arrizabalaga, María Gembero Ustárroz, Oliver Hochadel, Josep Martí Pérez, José Pardo, Emilio Ros-Fábregas, our director Lluís Calvo, and many others. I am grateful to librarian Marta Ezpeleta García for tracking down published literature that was often obscure. Joan-Lluís Palos, Diana Carrió-Invernizzi, Consuelo Gómez, and collaborators in the project Poder y Representaciones Culturales en la Época Moderna (PyRCEM) at the Universitat de Barcelona and UNED (Universidad Nacional de Educación a Distancia) have been wonderfully supportive. I thank the President, Fellows, and members of Clare Hall, Cambridge, for welcoming my research during a Visiting Fellowship there in 2021.

Nicholas Cook, María Gembero-Ustárroz, Sarah Kirby, Tess Knighton, Samantha Owens, Alexander Rehding, Wolfgang Schmale, Maria Semi, W. Dean Sutcliffe, Makoto Harris Takao, and Richard Wistreich read drafts of all or parts of the manuscript and provided expert feedback, for which I am grateful. Anonymous readers for Oxford University Press offered insightful comments and constructive suggestions, which helped shape this work in significant ways. Katherine Butler Schofield encouraged me and guided me toward pertinent source materials and theoretical areas. Joyce Lindorff and Jean-Christophe Frisch have been longstanding and inspirational collaborators in our exploration of intercultural music history and performance. Bettina Varwig motivated me through conversations and her writings. Thomas Irvine, whose recent research has explored the reflexive formation of "European" and "Western" musical identities in the contexts of sonic encounters with China around 1800, has been enormously supportive of this work since it began.

Peter Agócs, Sara Aguilar, and Jessica Priestley provided essential contexts and details regarding classical antiquity and ancient texts, and helped me with Greek and Latin terminology; Qingfan Jiang, Joyce Lindorff, and François Picard advised me on and translated Chinese sources; and Jacob Olley shared knowledge about Ottoman historical contexts and references to relevant literature. Bella Brover-Lubovsky and Marina Frolova-Walker translated and advised me on Russian texts, and Alexei A. Panov and Ivan V. Rosanoff responded to my queries about a French source located in St. Petersburg, on which they had published. David Black, Sarah Kirby, and Makoto Harris Takao pointed out important primary sources; Makoto and

Lester Hu introduced me to relevant secondary literature. Noel Malcolm sent me a reference to a fascinating seventeenth-century text, and Norman Davies authorized the reproduction of his conceptual map of Europe. Dario Scarinci provided scans of archival materials. Thomas Betzwieser, Christopher Dingle, Federico Lanzellotti, and Nathan Martin kindly permitted me to cite conference papers. Christopher Eanes and Rosalind Halton advised me on seventeenth- and eighteenth-century works in manuscript form, and Christopher sent me his edition of one of them.

Nabil Matar answered questions about Arabic travel accounts, and Ruth HaCohen and Edwin Seroussi pointed me to literature on Jewish music history. Olivia Bloechl offered helpful feedback and inspired me through her work on music and the idea of Europe. Elisabeth Le Guin and I had memorable chats about intercultural issues in music history. I likewise enjoyed conversations with Rebekah Ahrendt and Théodora Psychoyou about intra-European interactions in music. Julia Byl, Fabio Morabito, Jim Sykes, Benjamin Walton, and Richard Williams have all been enthusiastic interlocutors regarding diverse aspects of musical identity and music's global histories. I am particularly grateful to Jen-yen Chen for our extensive dialogues about intercultural representation in the historiography and historical study of early modern musics. In the realm of historical performance practice I thank Madeleine Easton, Jean-Christophe Frisch, Cyrille Gerstenhaber, Francis Knights, Joyce Lindorff, Joseph McHardy, Barnaby Ralph, Matthew Thomson, Oliver Webber, Masumi Yamamoto, the members of the Melbourne Baroque Orchestra, and many others, for illuminating discussions of seventeenth- and eighteenth-century musics and related cultural contexts.

During conferences, correspondence, video calls, collaborations, and chats over coffee, I have enjoyed communicating with and learning from scholars including (in addition to all mentioned above and below) Jóhannes Ágústsson, Robert Attenborough, Suresh Babu, Geoffrey Baker, Krishna N. Balasubramaniam, Alison Behie, Egberto Bermúdez, Francisco Bethencourt, Andrea Bombi, Rogério Budasz, Geoffrey Burgess, Anna Maria Busse Berger, Jeanice Brooks, Bruce Alan Brown, Patricia Caicedo, Melissa Calaresu, Camilla Cavicchi, Daniel Castro Pantoja, William Cheng, Daniel Chua, Maria Alexandra Iñigo Chua, Victor Coelho, Janie Cole, Denis Collins, Suzanne Cusick, Rebecca Cypess, Drew Edward Davies, James Davies, Nick Davies, Helen Deeming, Emily Dolan, Jacob Dunn, Katharine Ellis, Sarah Eyerly, Ferran Escrivà-Llorca, Mark Everist, Dinko Fabris, Cesar

Favila, Danielle Fosler-Lussier, Andrew Frampton, Kristin Franseen, Richard Freedman, Matthew Gelbart, Ben Givan, Austin Glatthorn, Jaime González Bolado, Howard Griffiths, Sean Gurd, Andrew Hicks, Peter Holman, John Irving, Elizabeth Eva Leach, Sylvain Lemoine, Pauline LeVen, Marcy Caton Lingold, Samuel Llano, Javier Marín, Miguel-Ángel Marín, Nicholas Mathew, Catherine Mayes, Ascensión Mazuela-Anguita, Ivan Moody, Peter McMurray, Michael Noone, Laudan Nooshin, Diane Oliva, Christopher Page, Rose Pruiksma, Esperanza Rodríguez, Stephen Rose, Maria Ryan, Christina Skott, Gabriel Solis, Arne Spohr, Martin Stokes, Mark Tatlow, Ruth Tatlow, Gary Tomlinson, Álvaro Torrente, David Trippett, Mikkel Vad, Philippe Vendrix, Alejandro Vera, Margaret Walker, Hanna Walsdorf, Naomi Waltham-Smith, Wayne Weaver, Bryan White, and Andrew Woolley. Of course, any mistakes that remain are my own.

A number of events during the writing of this book provided platforms to present and try out ideas. They included the workshop "Musicology or Ethnomusicology? Discussing Disciplinary Boundaries in Non-Western Art Music" at the Faculty of Music, University of Cambridge, organized by Vera Wolkowicz (March 2019); the symposium "Folk Music Research, Folkloristics, and Anthropology of Music in Europe: Pathways in the Intellectual History of Ethnomusicology" at the Universität für Musik und Darstellende Kunst Wien, organized by Ulrich Morgenstern and Thomas Nußbaumer (October 2019); a seminar at Brown University (October 2019); a colloquium for the Faculty of Music, University of Cambridge (March 2020); the American Musicological Society's Annual Meeting for 2020 (online); and a virtual seminar for the Center for European Studies at Rutgers University (March 2022), convened by Rebecca Cypess and Sadia Abbas. I greatly appreciated the ideas, advice, and correspondence emanating from all these events.

I would like to express my gratitude to Kate van Orden for many inspiring conversations and her wise counsel as this research has progressed. I sincerely thank Jane Fulcher, founder and editor of the series The New Cultural History of Music, for her welcome of a proposal for a book in this collection, as well as for her encouragement and guidance as thinking, research, and writing took place. Norm Hirschy, Executive Editor, Academic and Trade, at Oxford University Press, has been a wonderful support at all stages of the project. Thanks go also to Rachel Ruisard, Mary Pelosi, and Ganga Balaji for steering the book smoothly through production, and to Wendy Keebler for her expert copy-editing. I am grateful to the American Musicological Society for the award of a subvention toward the production of this book, provided generously by the Margarita M. Hanson Fund, and supported in part by the National Endowment for the Humanities and the Andrew W. Mellon Foundation.

Like many people, I found my perspectives on almost every part of academia changed rapidly and radically in the three years starting in February 2020. The Covid pandemic had practical impacts on our ways of doing music research, and the Black Lives Matter movement made us rethink, fundamentally, the very substance, nature, and structure of the disciplines. New conversations have begun, others have continued, and there have been positive moves in many directions. I hope this book can contribute in some small way to these discourses, although my voice is of course only one in 8 billion. Yet it is on that individual, subjective level that we experience the world and find our place in it. So finally, on a personal note, I am profoundly grateful to Sara Aguilar, Thirza Hope, John Morgan, my nuclear and extended family, and especially Marcio.

Note on Sources

Translations are mine except where noted. Where I have used standard published English translations for quotations from source materials (including many from the early modern period, to retain the flavor of the period), I have added references pointing to the original texts. In transcriptions, I have silently changed "v" to "u" (occasionally "j" to "i"), and vice versa, but otherwise retain the orthography of primary sources (including diacritics as they appear). For reasons of space, I have indicated the sources of original-language quotations rather than reproduce them in footnotes, except in a few special cases. Most of these primary sources are digitized and are easily accessible online.

Throughout the book, I give dates of birth and death, wherever known, for people who are no longer living, as it enables a reader to situate their actions at particular points of those individuals' lives. I give these dates only at the first mention of a person's name (in the main text, unless the name appears solely in the footnotes); the index can be consulted to locate each initial instance. Regarding work titles, I offer translations only the first time they occur in the text. Where it is helpful to do so, I mention the location of some of the rarer published source materials.

Some preliminary thinking on aspects of the topics treated in this book appeared in my essay "Ancient Greeks, World Music, and Early Modern Constructions of Western European Identity," published in *Studies on a Global History of Music: A Balzan Musicology Project*, edited by Reinhard Strohm (Abingdon: Routledge, 2018), 21–41. Sections from that work (for which the publisher attributed me the rights) are woven into various chapters of the present book, in significantly revised and expanded form.

Introduction

Musics of Continents and Hemispheres

Musicians and musicologists regularly speak in continental, hemispheric, and even planetary terms. They use labels such as "African music," "American music," "Asian music," "Australian music," "European music," "Western music," and "world music," usually without scare quotes. Some propose continental coherence in musical traditions, as Kofi Agawu has done for Africa, suggesting the concept of a singular "African music" rather than "African musics."[1] Composer and conductor Leonard Bernstein (1918–1990), for the theme of a 1958 Young People's Concert, famously questioned what was "American music," although he specifically meant the United States of America rather than the Americas as a whole, demonstrating how such labels can be claimed by a part of a continent.[2] The journal *Asian Music*, on its establishment in 1968, tacitly left the boundaries of its subject area open.[3] In my native continent, Graeme Skinner has traced "the invention of Australian music."[4] As regards "European music," Reinhard Strohm has written of how its compositional practices arose in the late Middle Ages and Renaissance, while Olivia Bloechl has shown how this continental category cannot be understood in isolation from processes of early modern colonialism.[5] Even the practice of human music in Antarctica—although not using, so far, the adjective "Antarctic"—has become a topic of scholarly interest.[6]

Adjectives relating to continents are finite in number, but other large regions are also labeled with single or compound adjectives. Subcontinental categories such as "Indian music" have coexisted with descriptions of

---

[1] Agawu, *The African Imagination in Music*, 15. See responses in Erlmann, "Resisting Sameness," and Pooley, "Continental Musicology." See also Agawu, *On African Music*.
[2] Bernstein, "What Is American Music?"
[3] Willard Rhodes (1901–1992) stated that the journal's intended readership would embrace "cultivated amateurs" as well as "professional musicians and scholars who have specialized in Asian Music." Rhodes, "To the Reader," 2.
[4] Skinner, "The Invention of Australian Music."
[5] Strohm, *The Rise of European Music*; Bloechl, *Native American Song*.
[6] Hince, Summerson, and Wiesel, *Antarctica*.

"Hindustani music" since the early twentieth century.[7] Pablo Palomino has pointed to the invention of "Latin American music."[8] Oceanic categories exist, too; "Pasifika music," for example, denotes the musics of Polynesia and the diasporas originating from there.[9] Musics thus connect continents, across vast bodies of water: researchers have spoken of "Music in the Pacific World" and studied musics of the Indian Ocean in terms of "Afro-Asiatic seascapes."[10] Zooming out, we can see that the emergence of "world music" and its discourses to denote something distinct from "Western music" has also long provoked and stimulated debate.[11] More recently, the music of space and even "alien listening" have become subjects of exomusicological contemplation.[12]

Of course, the use of any term that joins a large-scale adjective to a concrete noun risks imposing an essentializing homogeneity and reductivism on the resulting compound. The conceptual labels emerging from this union are also potentially anachronistic in their application to different historical periods, if used in a timeless sense and without critical reflection or careful qualification. "European music" and "Western music" are perhaps among the two most prominent offenders in that sense, and they are the focus of this book. How did they arise within musicological literature produced by writers who self-identified (implicitly or explicitly) as being part of, or at least connected to, the traditions they denoted?

My two main claims are that "European music"—by which I specifically mean the adjective and noun appearing consecutively, rather than more general contextual references—was invented during the long eighteenth century (1670s–1820s) and that "Western music" had different meanings before and after 1800. In studying these concepts, I do not seek to deny the meanings and realities that people have imputed to them, whether in their ubiquity today

---

[7] Sourindro Mohun Tagore (1840–1914) used the term "Indian music" in the title of his book *Six Principal Ragas, with a Brief View of Indian Music*. The two terms "Indian music" and "Hindustani music" are used in the full title of a 1913 book by Sir Ernest Clements (b. 1873), *Introduction to the Study of Indian Music: An Attempt to Reconcile Modern Hindustani Music with Ancient Musical Theory and to Propound an Accurate and Comprehensive Method of Treatment of the Subject of Indian Musical Intonation*. Regarding the history of the term "Hindustani music," see Schofield, *Music and Musicians*, 7.

[8] Palomino, *The Invention of Latin American Music*.

[9] See, for example, Televave and Zemke, "Pasifika R&B Divas."

[10] "Music in the Pacific World: Change and Exchange through Sound and Memory," first conference of the IMS Study Group on the Global History of Music, Taipei, October 14–17, 2021, program at https://gim.ntu.edu.tw/ims-study-group-ghm2021-2/; Sykes and Byl, *Sounding the Indian Ocean*.

[11] See Nettl, "On World Music."

[12] Chua and Rehding, *Alien Listening*.

or their less frequent use in earlier times, but rather to probe their meanings in writings by Europeans over the course of the long eighteenth century and to identify their historiographical emergence in time and place. Through a close reading of selected primary sources, I additionally investigate how ideas of "progress" and "modernity" have been frequently applied to these two categories. As a necessary contextual foundation, I explore how early modern musicians and thinkers engaged with the origin myths that gave rise to the continent's name, the way they understood Europe as a physical place and an abstract space, and how the sense of being related to it became gradually expressed, embodied, and essentialized in identity categories such as "European ears" and "European musician."

The adjective "European" dates back to antiquity, but almost two thousand years passed before it was written alongside the noun "music." Why is this the case? There seem to be two sets of reasons. First, there was a looseness of a collective pan-European identity, geographical notions of Europe that were constantly evolving, and relative rarity of the terms "Europe" and "European" in texts of the Middle Ages and the early modern era.[13] Second, within a world that was still predominantly enchanted, the cosmological dimensions of music obviated the need for supranational terminological designations, since music was considered a metaphysical art.[14] Believed by most to have divine origins, music could not be tied down to a place. Rather, it simply existed in space, or the cosmos, in general. The need for the expression of a collective continental identity seemed to suggest itself only when representatives from diverse parts of Europe came into contact with societies elsewhere. Even so, for some writers on music, the descriptor "European" often referred to only a part of the continent. They excluded lands under Ottoman rule or certain regions where Orthodox Christianity predominated, even though those areas were understood to be geographically part of Europe. Owing to increased global exchange and expanding knowledge of "others" in large-scale regions known to Europeans in broad terms as China, India, Turkey, and Arabia, or even "the Indies," a number of writers from Europe—who frequently and mistakenly imagined each of those other civilizations to be culturally

---

[13] See the seminal article of 1980 by Peter Burke, "Did Europe Exist before 1700?" Klaus Oschema has more recently (2013) traced the use of the terms in medieval sources. See his book *Bilder von Europa im Mittelalter* and also his video "How Does Medieval Historians' Use of the Notion of 'Europe' Compare?"

[14] By "enchanted," I refer inversely to the Weberian notion of "the disenchantment of the world." For a review and critique, see Walsham, "The Reformation and 'the Disenchantment of the World' Reassessed."

monolithic and internally unified—began, self-consciously, to refer to an opaque and undifferentiated macro-category of "European music." This new concept coexisted with but also transcended the national musical styles of their own continent.

The term "European music," with the adjective and noun used contiguously (in whichever order), had its initial glimmers in the late seventeenth century. Research to date shows the first authors to use it in published works before 1700 were three members of the Society of Jesus (known as Jesuits), who will be introduced in the core of this book. The first example—in Latin, as "musicâ Europaeâ"—seems to have been first printed in a treatise on astronomy produced in the German-speaking lands in 1687 and written around eight years earlier by a Flemish Jesuit based in Beijing.[15] The following year, it appeared in French ("la musique Europeane") in a study of recent Chinese history by a French Jesuit in Paris.[16] A third example, this time in German ("*Europaei*sche Music"), was given by a Tyrolean Jesuit writing from Paraguay, in an edition of his letters issued in Nuremberg in 1696.[17] "European music" was then used only occasionally as a term and concept by writers in western European languages for the next seventy years. Significantly, it was used almost exclusively in contexts of comparison with cultures in other parts of the world, as a form of oppositional self-definition.

Over the course of the eighteenth century, people who called themselves "Europeans" began to construct a discourse that endowed their own sonic arts with senses of essentialism, exceptionalism, and superiority. This process took place within the conceptual space of what they called the "Republic of Music," a clear analogue of the "Republic of Letters." The emergence of "European music" based on intercultural comparisons coincided with struggles for supremacy between French and Italian styles in a number of domains of music. That story is well known, and a musicological view that focuses entirely on the spaces of musicking in Europe itself might consider those contexts as the sole crucible in which "European music" was forged.

---

[15] Verbiest, *Astronomia europaea*, 89. Its East Asian contexts were not without precedent: as discussed in chapter 4, a Jesuit publication of 1590—printed in Macau, for Japan—had anticipated this continental cultural identity in making a reference to "European singing" (although not "music" per se), making a contrast between contrapuntal vocal polyphony and Japanese styles. Sande, *Japanese Travellers in Sixteenth-Century Europe*, 155. Original text in Valignano and Sande, *De missione legatorum Iaponensium*, 110.

[16] Original text in Orléans, *Histoire*, 301. This example predates significantly a claim by a prominent historian that the adjective "européen[ne]"—in general terms, not specifically referring to music—was first used in French in 1721. Le Goff, *The Birth of Europe*, 3.

[17] Sepp and Böhm, *RR. PP. Antonii Sepp ... Reißbeschreibung*, 266. Original emphasis.

However, as the data presented in this book suggest, the term and concept seem to stem predominantly from reflexive self-fashioning within a global frame, rather than dialectical resolution of aesthetic disputes within the continent itself.

Following a century of relatively sporadic usage, "European music" rose to discursive prominence from the 1770s onward. It entered regular and continuous discourse as a fully fledged idea only from that decade, apparently first in England. Through repeated use in languages including English, French, German, Italian, and Spanish, the term became normalized and naturalized. "European music" simultaneously demonstrated the transcendence, and to some extent the dissolution, of certain ideas about national style and intra-European difference. It is tempting to speculate that its increasing appearance in written records (and presumably speech acts) is indexically linked to an accelerating tendency for standardization across Europe of music theory, music technology, and social frameworks for musicking—as well as dimensions such as instruments, printing, spaces for performance, and so on—in large-scale processes of innovation, reform, and adaptation that enabled increased transnational circulation and undoubtedly contributed to the growing sense of a collective continental music culture.[18]

The rise of "European music" as a common trope took place during the same decades in which, as Matthew Gelbart has shown, the ideas of "art music" and "folk music" were invented.[19] The entry of "European music" into popular discourse is also, strikingly, coterminous with the advent of Orientalism in the late eighteenth century, according to the chronology proposed by Edward W. Said (1935–2003).[20] By the middle third of the nineteenth century, European colonial dominance over many parts of Asia ("the Orient") was at a high point. It is perhaps no coincidence that around this time, the term "European music" became conflated with "Western music" (or the synonymous term "Occidental music"), and used interchangeably with it. "Western music" subsequently took on meanings still familiar to many people today, as a "unitary concept" and a "unified system."[21] Yet

---

[18] This book focuses on the history of ideas; the consideration of material aspects in the making of "European music" awaits another study. Colonialism and the extraction of resources provided the material basis for the emerging industrialization and standardization of musical practice. For discussion of some of these themes, see Irving and Joubert, "Introduction," 33–36.

[19] See Gelbart, *The Invention*.

[20] "Taking the late eighteenth century as a very roughly defined starting point Orientalism can be discussed and analyzed as the corporate institution for dealing with the Orient . . . as a Western style for dominating, restructuring, and having authority over the Orient." Said, *Orientalism*, 3.

[21] For a definition offered in 1985, see Nettl, *The Western Impact*, 5, 11.

this was a new sense of the term. Before the nineteenth century, "Western music" had referred specifically to Christian liturgical singing in Catholic (and then Protestant) practice, to denote its differentiation from practices of the "Eastern" churches.[22] It was only from the 1830s that "Western music"—again with the adjective and noun used contiguously—began to emerge as a monolithic and homogeneous concept and one unrelated to the earlier definition.

Europe's fascination with Asia was focused largely on China, and it is perhaps unsurprising that in the broad processes of "European" and "Western" self-fashioning from the sixteenth to nineteenth centuries, the Middle Kingdom played a significant role. Early-seventeenth-century intellectual exchanges in its imperial court involving missionaries and diplomats from Europe generated notions of "the West" that merged Chinese and European conceptualizations of geography.[23] These were occasionally applied to musical themes.[24] Even so, it took time for that terminology to make a tangible impact widely on musical discourse in Europe. It was predominantly in the late eighteenth and early nineteenth centuries that, "through its encounter with China"—and increased intensity of exchange between geographical extremes of Eurasia—"the West remade itself in sound," as Thomas Irvine has so memorably put it.[25] The early 1900s saw another development (in English, at least): "Western music" began to be used with the qualifying internal adjective "art" to create "Western art music." The earliest example identifiable so far seems to date from 1915 and is by an Australian American composer (to be introduced later), although he hyphenated the last two words.[26] It seems pertinent to note that this development can be attributed to someone whose origins lay outside of Europe (just as two of the Jesuits mentioning "European music" in the late seventeenth century were in Asia and South America).

Over the course of the twentieth and twenty-first centuries, there has been much naturalization and normalization of many large-scale categories of music, owing perhaps in part to the rapid expansion of musicology and music

---

[22] This binary opposition (based on culture, liturgical practices, and theology) dated back to antiquity in a loose sense but became especially pronounced from the point of Christianity's Great Schism of 1054. For a study of music in Western churches until the eleventh century, see Page, *The Christian West and Its Singers*.
[23] Morar, "The Westerner."
[24] Jiang and Irving, "Cultural Practices."
[25] Irvine, *Listening to China*, 1.
[26] Grainger, "The Impress of Personality," 417.

education. In the writing of music history, the terms "European music" and especially "Western music" have been frequently used in titles of scholarly works and as conceptual categories.[27] In certain academic constituencies in the nineteenth and twentieth centuries, they became so ubiquitous that the adjective "Western" even came to be believed unnecessary; as Christopher Small (1927–2011) pointed out, "scholars of Western music . . . quietly carried out a process of elision by means of which the word music becomes equated with 'works of music in the Western tradition.'"[28] The present book, inspired in part by Small and many critics of "Western art music," examines the historiographical and discursive processes by which the terms arose and how they came to signify what they do. Specifically, it asks what these labels meant for eighteenth-century musicians and thinkers defining themselves as "European" (or, less often, "Western"), before the descriptors became essentialized, reified, and seemingly absolute. The case studies presented in the chapters that follow aim to complicate—productively, I hope—past and current musicological application of these labels to musics before around 1800.

Tracing the historiographical and conceptual evolution of terminology has diverse methodological antecedents and ontological implications, as can be illustrated by a revelatory analogy and instructive comparison from the origin story of another concept: "world music." This term, at least in its use as a commercial category, is said to originate from a meeting of recording-company executives in London in July 1987 (by sheer coincidence, three centuries to the year after the first identifiable appearance of "European music" in print). Musicologists and ethnomusicologists have accorded that event such historical significance that even the name of the pub where it took place is cited in academic and popular literature (it was then called Empress of Russia).[29] Yet the concept of "world music" already had multiple meanings, as Bruno Nettl (1930–2020) pointed out; he himself used it in the title of a book from 1985, and he later traced its history.[30] The term even appears in the text of a lecture given in 1935 by the well-known early-music

---

[27] For example, Strohm, *The Rise of European Music*; Haar, *European Music, 1520–1640*; Taruskin, *The Oxford History of Western Music*.
[28] Small, *Musicking*, 3.
[29] Frith, "The Discourse of World Music," 305; M. Stokes, "Music and the Global Order," 52. The pub in question is now named the Pearl and Feather and is at 360 St. John Street in Clerkenwell, London. See C. L. Smith, "'World Music' Is Invented." See also Stokes, "Globalization and the Politics of World Music," 107; Cook, "Western Music as World Music," 80.
[30] Nettl, *Nettl's Elephant*, 33–53; Nettl, "On World Music." For a study of "world music" as a popular category, see Taylor, *Global Pop*.

pioneer Arnold Dolmetsch (1858–1940), who used an initial capital for both words and insisted that the category must include "the Eastern and Ancient schools."[31] The concept of "world music"—like "Western music"—has undergone changes in meanings, with an observable threshold of transition. And as much as the term often implied a mutually exclusive binary of "Western" versus "world," the rigidity and opacity of its dividing wall have been thoroughly critiqued. Nicholas Cook, for instance, observed in 2013 that it is now even possible to think of "Western music as world music."[32]

Adjectival Anachronism and "Conceptual Imperialism"

Are there really any problems in retrospectively applying labels such as "European music," "Western music," or "European composer" to repertory that existed or composers who worked before these terms entered common usage? The issue is that these adjectives are not used as neutral markers of geography but that they can imply a coherent and monolithic hyperculture. They come with the ideological baggage of essentialism and exceptionalism, often implicitly denying elements of cultural hybridity—incorporated and naturalized over countless generations—within ways of life in Europe, which itself is an abstract physical space with boundaries that have been constantly changing. Tracing these descriptors' history also brings to light the frequent addition (or tacit implication) of "modern" to the compound term "European music," especially within contexts of colonialism. The adjective is always a relative rather than absolute term, and even when it was not added, it came to be almost implicit in later uses of "European music" or "Western music." A simple point I want to emphasize in these pages is that if we lack critical awareness about the use of "Europe," "European," "Western," or "modern" in relation to music discourse before and after 1800, we might easily overlook how profoundly all those concepts have changed in just a few centuries' worth of historiography.[33]

The eighteenth century was a period of considerable flexibility for these ideas. Over the following more than two hundred years, however, "European music" and "Western music"—sometimes with the qualifying terms "modern"

---

[31] Dolmetsch, "Ancient Welsh Music," 121.
[32] Cook, "Western Music as World Music." See also Taylor, *Beyond Exoticism*.
[33] Francesco Benigno has made similar points about other concepts, in "a plea for historical rethinking"; see his book *Words in Time*.

or "ancient/early," depending on context—gradually became hardened ideas. They have symbolized a purportedly perennial form of expression (while simultaneously demonstrating a diachronic panorama of "progress," seen frozen in its notated scores and reproduced in performances) and projected a desired collective culture of the musics' creators. Many triumphalist narratives in "European" or "Western" music history—particularly those written by Europeans in the nineteenth and twentieth centuries, whether in a scholarly or popular vein—emphasized a teleological trajectory that led to a supposed "uniqueness" and "special position" of the subject and in surveying the past often used adjectives anachronistically.[34] These narratives implied and bestowed on diverse musics internal to Europe a certain homogeneity on a supranational basis and, as already mentioned, were broadly understood to denote a unified cultural system, linked to essentialized identity. The practices they signify have also been projected and transplanted to other parts of the world as forms of "universal" or "global" culture, ostensibly accessible and relevant to all.

Many scholars, guided by taxonomic and philological impulses, have imposed adjectives, labels, and categories on the historical interpretation (in many senses) of musics from earlier times. This process, and the privileging of notated musical sources—the canon of "Western art music"—as a body of "timeless masterpieces," has distorted our historical view of how people thought about and produced musics before the nineteenth century.[35] According to Lydia Goehr, who has described the canon as an "imaginary museum of musical works," the production and consumption of music in Europe as a "work-concept" fundamentally changed the regulation of musical practice from around 1800.[36] This shift also impacted the way Europeans saw other musics. As Olivia Bloechl and Melanie Lowe have observed, "by 1800, literate Europeans commonly regarded their own cultivated music as inherently different from that of peoples in other places and times: not just because of their distinct morphologies, but, more fundamentally, because of a new transcendentist conception of music and

---

[34] See especially Tomlinson, "Musicology, Anthropology, History," 60; Bloechl and Lowe, "Introduction: Rethinking Difference," 11. For earlier literature on the purported "special position" of Western music, see Wiora, *The Four Ages of Music*. See also a response to Wiora's work in Nettl, *The Western Impact*, 3.

[35] Goehr, *The Imaginary Museum*, 247. Thanks to Alexander Rehding for discussion of this point.

[36] Goehr, *The Imaginary Museum*, esp. chapter 4 ("The Central Claim"), 89–119. See also critiques of Goehr's thesis in Talbot, *The Musical Work*, and Taruskin, "Is There a Baby in the Bathwater?," 171–172.

its concomitant aesthetics."[37] Along similar lines, philosopher Santiago Castro-Gómez has identified the emergence at the beginning of the nineteenth century of what he calls "the hubris of point zero."[38] By this he means the imaginary perspective by which an observer can observe from a position of supposed neutrality without being observed. He locates its origins in the imperial anthropological projects of the late eighteenth century and relates it to the heinous ancient Greek sin of arrogance.[39] This "point zero," although relating to ethnographic observation, seems to have parallels with Goehr's point about the regulative work-concept in a chronological sense and the exceptionalist attitudes held by Europeans about their musics, as Bloechl and Lowe describe.

Goehr argued that the view of music from the perspective of a romantic aesthetic—the dominant perspective since 1800 and a phenomenon she terms "conceptual imperialism"—fundamentally altered historical views of previous epochs. She states:

> It all began around 1800 when musicians began to reconstruct musical history to make it look as if musicians had always thought about their activities in modern terms. Even if it was not believed that early musicians had thought explicitly in these terms, the assumption was that they would have, had circumstances allowed them to do so. Reconstructing or rewriting the past was and remains one of the most characteristic ways for persons to legitimate their present, for the process aids in the general forgetfulness that things could be different from how they presently are.[40]

Music historians' acts of monumentalizing and eulogizing composers from previous centuries often meant thinking of them as outliers who were "ahead of their time," feeding into teleological narratives of "progress" and "change" in the history of "Western art music." This emphasis on "change over time" created a comparative perspective in a chronological sense.[41] There emerged a common notion in historical thinking that certain musicians of earlier periods must have been hampered or restricted by their material

---

[37] Bloechl and Lowe, "Introduction: Rethinking Difference," 11. See also Tomlinson, "Musicology, Anthropology, History," 60.
[38] Castro-Gómez, *La hybris del punto cero*.
[39] Castro-Gómez, *La hybris del punto cero*, 18.
[40] Goehr, *The Imaginary Museum*, 245.
[41] I am grateful to Kate van Orden for conversations on this point.

surroundings and that a full expression of an inevitable musical modernity was not yet possible, to paraphrase Goehr.

Historian and postcolonial theorist Dipesh Chakrabarty has trenchantly observed the presence of a certain Eurocentrism in the ways scholars from various academic disciplines think about prominent individuals from the past. He writes: "It is only within some very particular traditions of thinking that we treat fundamental thinkers who are long dead and gone as though they were our own contemporaries. In the social sciences, these are invariably thinkers one encounters within the tradition that has come to call itself 'European' or 'Western.'"[42] In other words, specific individuals—often the proverbial "dead white men" of history—are privileged at the expense of all others; they are considered closer in time to "us." As Goehr points out (in the passage quoted above) in relation to nineteenth-century views of musicians of the past, "the assumption was that they would have [thought in modern terms]" if they could have.[43] Thus the later application, by historians, of the adjective "European" to these figures from before 1800 bestowed on them, in intercontinental or global terms, a cultural significance and meaning that diverged from thinking of their own times. We could even say that the retrospective imposition of anachronistic concepts and terminology, especially essentializing adjectives, is a symptom of a chronophagic colonialism that has been characteristic of much research into "European" musics of the past since the nineteenth century: it devours both repertory and knowledge, absorbing them within a monolithic musical corpus that is then affixed with labels both large and small.

While I concentrate here on adjectives, critique of anachronism in major concepts of musicology is, of course, by no means new. In his study of the emergence of "folk music" and "art music," Gelbart also discussed this issue and asserted that "we cannot unproblematically apply the idea of art music without distorting history before the end of the eighteenth century, [but] we cannot ignore it (and its shaping of judgments and historiography) after the turn of the nineteenth century in some circles, and after the mid-nineteenth century anywhere."[44] Nineteenth-century attitudes toward "art music" had a powerful impact and continue to have a legacy on thinking about music, as Marcello Sorce Keller observes: "Romantic ideas about the arts never had

---

[42] Chakrabarty, *Provincializing Europe*, 5. For a classic overview of Eurocentrism, see Amin, *Eurocentrism*.
[43] Goehr, *The Imaginary Museum*, 245.
[44] Gelbart, *The Invention*, 274.

a firmer hold on popular consciousness (as opposed to scholarly discourse) [than] ... they do today. So firm is their grip that even scholars occasionally slip back into them, once they step off their role as intellectuals and act as normal people do in everyday life."[45] Similarly, Goehr states that "the direct result of seeing the world's music—including early music—through romantic spectacles [that is, drawing on nineteenth-century aesthetic frameworks and ideologies] is that persons have assumed that the various types of music can easily be packaged in terms of works."[46] These "packaged" works are often the stumbling block in trying to untangle the complex meanings of the broader concepts of "European music" and "Western music."

So how else can we think about the many centuries of recoverable musics from before 1800? Perhaps historians of "European" or "Western" musics, in thinking beyond "works," can keep in mind Small's observation that music is primarily a process (practice) rather than a product (works).[47] They can also draw from ethnomusicology, which stresses the importance of studying music in culture according to the terms of the culture that produces it. In other words, cultural relativism rather than comparativism. Examining the emergence of the concepts of "European music" and "Western music" in pre- and post-1800 historiography arguably involves thinking in relativistic rather than comparativistic terms. Just as ethnomusicologists seek to study living musics in their cultural contexts and relativistically—that is, on their own terms—it behooves the historical musicologist to approach earlier contexts of music, especially those of centuries past, according to time-bound concepts and not anachronistically. Needless to say, this is an impossible task to achieve in full and can only be an ontological aspiration, borne out with reflexive methodologies.[48] After all, to use the famous expression, "the past is a foreign country."[49] It is culturally different from "us," and it is often assumed that the more removed we are chronologically from an earlier moment or period, the greater the cultural gulf that this temporal separation creates. Ralph Locke has pointed out that earlier eras—even if involving evocation of the cultural antecedents from whom one claims heritage—can operate as a form of exoticism within a "then/now" binarism.[50] And as anthropologist

[45] Sorce Keller, *What Makes Music European*, xii.
[46] Goehr, *The Imaginary Museum*, 249.
[47] Small, *Musicking*, 2.
[48] This is the dilemma of "authenticity," and I am grateful to W. Dean Sutcliffe for discussion of this point. The classic text on the subject is Kenyon, *Authenticity and Early Music*. See also D. Fabian, "The Meaning of Authenticity."
[49] Lowenthal, *The Past Is a Foreign Country*.
[50] Locke, *Musical Exoticism*, 64–65.

Clifford Geertz (1926–2006) observed: "The truth of the doctrine of cultural (or historical—it is the same thing) relativism is that we can never apprehend another people's or another period's imagination neatly, as though it were our own."[51] Even so, a great deal of chronologically comparative thought is still implicit in historical musicology. The only antidote to that comparative view—the subjective observer masquerading as "objective"—is "reflexivity" and self-awareness, to mitigate its worst effects and move toward a chronological relativism.[52]

In thinking about the difference between the meanings of labels "then" and "now," the idea of "presentism" must also be taken into account. Recent debates on this notion in education and public discourse have raised urgent issues regarding the ways historical subjects are taught and researched.[53] Historian Alexandra Walsham writes that "at root it [presentism] is a term of abuse, a slur conventionally deployed to describe an interpretation of history that is biased towards and coloured by present-day concerns, preoccupations and values."[54] She also points out that there exists "the opinion that anachronism is the most heinous sin of the historian."[55] Yet anachronism can also be useful; thinking about the past in the here and now, for instance, is precisely how research questions are formed.[56] Following historian Miri Rubin, who writes of the potential utility of some of the anachronisms embodied within presentism, I acknowledge that research is unavoidably created in the present moment. Rubin writes that "we come to the past with the best we can offer—our cherished values and our skills, the legacy of insights learned from scholars who have come before us—and we begin a dialogue. We formulate questions, and put them to the traces of the past."[57] In this sense, and in the spirit of dialogue, I would aver that the empirical gathering of data from old texts can help sharpen our critical focus and that this act can replace the tendency to reproduce the reductivist

---

[51] Geertz, *Local Knowledge*, 44.
[52] See Irving and Maddox, "Towards a Reflexive Paradigm," 56.
[53] See an overview in Miles and Gibson, "Rethinking Presentism." David Armitage has recently defended presentism, in the context of "human flourishing," and has offered a five-fold typology of the concept (teleological, idealist, analytical, perspectival, and omnipresent). See Armitage, "In Defense of Presentism," esp. 68. His typology is given in tabular form in Miles and Gibson, "Rethinking Presentism," 512.
[54] Walsham, "Introduction: Past and... Presentism," 213.
[55] Walsham, "Introduction: Past and... Presentism," 213.
[56] Rubin, "Presentism's Useful Anachronisms," 236.
[57] Rubin, "Presentism's Useful Anachronisms," 242.

categories implied by large-scale essentializing labels. Like a number of social and intellectual processes (such as globalization), anachronism can be "top-down" or "bottom-up." Rather than imposing views of the present on the past ("top-down") we can bring thought from the past into the light of present-day analysis ("bottom-up").

Of course, "letting sources speak for themselves" still runs a clear risk. On the one hand, it could lead to the loss of "hindsight" (a notion typically understood to refer to wisdom gained through experience). On the other hand, if we do not look at prima facie evidence afresh, the perpetuation of secondary interpretations or conceptual categories that increasingly allow primary source material to fall out of the field of vision will, in any case, at some stage create a clear need to "go back to the sources." I write here as someone who has engaged with "early music" for all my adult life. My enthusiasm for "historically informed performance" inspires me to attempt to understand how original sources might have been read in their own times rather than looking at them solely through layers or filters applied by subsequent generations.[58] Inspired by Goehr's notion of "conceptual imperialism," I would comment that "adjectival anachronism"—especially in the formation of macro-identities—has fundamentally distorted our views of how music was conceptualized by peoples in Europe in the early modern period.

In the practice of music history, the term and concept of "European music" is both anachronistic and anatopic, if used in a totalizing and essentializing sense, before the 1670s (roughly the beginning of the "long" eighteenth century). "Western art music" and "Western music" as terms and concepts are also incongruous, if used in an essentialized and homogeneous sense, with the repertories and practices that predate the nineteenth century. Both "European music" and "Western music" are deictic terms and concepts; that is, their definitions depend on context. Such labels have the potential to imply degrees of homogeneity and essentialism that cannot be retrospectively projected, and so any subconscious or unreflexive discursive use of these compound terms requires further critique. Their seemingly opaque nature also brings to mind a warning by Serge Gruzinski about the ideas of "identity" and "culture": "everything covered by those two terms is constantly in danger of being fetishized,

---

[58] The literature is vast; for some recent overviews, see N. Wilson, *The Art of Re-Enchantment*; Kelly, *Early Music*.

reified, naturalized, and elevated to the status of the absolute."[59] They lead to comparisons with everything outside that "absolute."

David Porter has described contrasting dyads such as European/other and Western/other as "binary comparisons of sizable aggregates" which "readily slip into misleading essentialisms."[60] They have long been immense scholarly challenges, but they have also sparked exhilarating debates in the disciplines of historical musicology and ethnomusicology, inspiring research on cultural and political dimensions including "difference, representation, and appropriation in music," as Georgina Born and David Hesmondhalgh, among others, have shown.[61] Such work has inspired gradual reforms for positive change in the disciplines, and the present study is one more in a long line to signal this need, since musicology's "cultural turn" of the 1990s and its more recent "global turn," although its methodology is somewhat different.[62] Scholars of music have long critiqued "European music" and "Western music" in diverse ways, as broad categories of thought and practice. Before outlining this book's approach in tracing the emergence of specific terms and concepts, then, let us consider musicological work in this field over the last three decades, as the foundations on which the subsequent chapters will build.

Querying "European" and "Western" Musics in the Academy

The gestation and birth of "European music" were the subject of several studies in the 1990s. A workshop with the title "A European Music: Fact or Fiction" was held in 1992 at the Third Conference of the International Society for the Study of European Ideas, which had as its overall theme "European Integration and the European Mind." At this event, ten papers "explored diversity and unity in European musical styles and national traditions."[63] Six were later published in the journal *History of European Ideas* and variously explored the question of whether the notion of "European music" was

---

[59] Gruzinski, *The Mestizo Mind*, 26.
[60] Porter, "Sinicizing Early Modernity," 300. Thanks to Lester Hu and Makoto Harris Takao for pointing out this article.
[61] Born and Hesmondhalgh, *Western Music and Its Others*.
[62] For overviews of the "cultural turn," see Clayton, Herbert, and Middleton, *The Cultural Study of Music*; for a critical assessment of recent literature on global music history, see Takao, "Global Music History."
[63] Skyllstad, "Report from Aalborg," 104.

a reality or a myth, the idea of hybridity and mixing in eighteenth-century practice, historical aspects of integration and assimilation of national traditions in the Balkans, the political dimensions of national musics, and the question of singular music or plural musics.[64]

In 1993, Reinhard Strohm published his landmark monograph *The Rise of European Music, 1380–1500*, which examined how a shared language of contrapuntal polyphony emerged in western parts of the continent in the long fifteenth century. This work made a major impact in musicology, with its clear positioning of the notion of "European music" as a set of compositional and theoretical approaches and a coherent practice that could be understood in a particular place and time. In its introduction, Strohm nevertheless acknowledged that "the European nations did not yet exist as political entities (the rise of European music accompanies their making)."[65] This observation prompted interesting reactions and debates. A review by Christopher Page took it head-on, commenting that an alternative study could be titled *"Music in the Rise of Europe"* and asserting that the continent "began to be 'made' four hundred years before European music, as Strohm understands it, began to 'rise.'"[66] Lewis Lockwood, in another review, pointed to the emergence of printing as a major turning point in the dissemination and circulation of shared repertory.[67] In a response to both reviewers, Strohm reiterated his thesis "that in the period c. 1380–c. 1500 there arose (or 'rose', i.e. developed) something which can be called 'European music'" and clarified that it was "in contrast to the more regionally diversified musics—not the 'inferior' music—of earlier times."[68] Another critique came from Leo Treitler, who, in a 1996 article in the *Black Music Research Journal*, argued for "a desegregated music historiography" and wrote that "as a student of the musical practices of the Carolingian era, I see the threatening implication in Strohm's title that what I regard as the oldest European music to which we have access is either not European or it is not music (or indeed that it is neither)."[69] His comment suggests that the stakes of two fields of research, music and history, depended on the

---

[64] The published papers include Bergamo, "Europäische Musik"; Bimberg, "The Idea of European Music"; Gligo, "Integration vs Assimilation."
[65] Strohm, *The Rise of European Music*, 3.
[66] Page, "Towards," 128.
[67] Lockwood, "Review of *The Rise of European Music*," 152.
[68] Strohm, "The 'Rise of European Music,'" 1.
[69] Treitler, "Toward a Desegregated Music Historiography," 5. See also Treitler, "Inventing a European Music Culture."

conceptual force of an adjective and the full range of values and identities that it implied.

Other studies exploring the concept of "European music" include a 2006 volume edited by James Haar, using that term in its title. It aimed to cover "the musical culture of Europe in the sixteenth and early seventeenth centuries ... outlining the chronological development of this culture," from the *ars perfecta* of Heinrich Glareanus (1488–1563) to around the end of the career of Claudio Monteverdi (1567–1643).[70] Bloechl's 2008 monograph, *Native American Song at the Frontiers of Early Modern Music*—from which the present study draws much inspiration—explored in pioneering ways how French and English engagement with Indigenous and enslaved African populations in the Americas during the seventeenth and eighteenth centuries contemporaneously impacted the shaping of musical identities of "Europe" and "the West." She critiqued musicology's ideological focus on Europe and showed, moreover, how a focus on colonial contexts can bring the purported coherence of "European" and "Western" musical categories into serious question.[71] Page published in 2010 a magisterial study on singers of Christian sacred music in its "first thousand years," considering not only the art of these musicians but also the role they played in making a European identity, in a space defined as "the Christian West." He located the rise of "European music" or "Western European music" in the eighth century as a set of shared practices of liturgical chant.[72] In 2012, Marcello Sorce Keller asked "what makes music European" in a book that used those same four words as an affirmative title, calling for further engagement with the concept from ethnomusicological perspectives, especially in terms of thinking about cultural contexts and ideologies and "looking beyond sound."[73]

A workshop held in 2014 at the Berlin–Brandenburg Academy of Sciences and Humanities was titled "Music and European Integration" and focused on that topic by looking at contexts from the end of the Second World War onward; these contributions appeared in a volume of 2017.[74] That same year, a book edited by Otfried Höffe and Andreas Kablitz, *Europäische Music—Musik Europas* (*European Music—Music of Europe*), included contributions discussing the idea of the "musical artwork" and "absolute music" as typifying

[70] Haar, "Preface," vii.
[71] Bloechl, *Native American Song*; see esp. 22, critiquing "a coherent European cultural identity."
[72] See Page, *The Christian West and Its Singers*, esp. 304, 528–534.
[73] Sorce Keller, *What Makes Music European*.
[74] Riethmüller, *The Role of Music*.

notions of "European music" and included essays on Johann Sebastian Bach (1685–1750), Wolfgang Amadeus Mozart (1756–1791), Ludwig van Beethoven (1770–1827), and Richard Wagner (1813–1883).[75] Moving from concepts of Europe to "the West," the year 2017 also saw the conference "Branding Western Music" at Universität Bern, which explored and dissected issues of reification, commodification, institutionalization, and cultural politics in "homogenisation and globalisation of a corpus of musical practices labelled as Western."[76]

In an essay for the 2018 *Cambridge History of Medieval Music*, Strohm returned to the topic of a continental category by suggesting that the term "early European music" is more appropriate than "medieval music." Significantly, he argued for the inclusion of Byzantine, Jewish, Syrian, and Arabic traditions within this rubric, since "they were contemporaneous with the Western Middle Ages and contributed to the development of European music in their own right.... [W]ithout the rest of the world, Europe would not exist."[77] In this sense, he emphasized interdependence and relativized music called "European" within broader cultural-geographical contexts. In the five years preceding that publication, Strohm's Balzan Prize research program in musicology "Towards a Global History of Music" (2013–2017)—which involved collaborative work by scholars from around the world—produced diverse studies with a variety of approaches that not only illustrated this statement but also opened up numerous pathways into decentered ways of studying the musical past.[78] My own contribution to that project looked at early modern European writers' construction of analogies between "ancient" and "other" peoples and the way their comparative assessments of those two groups contributed to the making of a new kind of western European identity. Fused with notions of "modernity," this process distanced them increasingly from both antiquity and the rest of the world.[79] Although I was referring to some of the same primary sources as does this book, I did not at that time recognize the neologistic nature of the adjective "European" as applied to music in the texts themselves. Nor did I realize the complex historiographical relationship that "European music" had with "Western music."

---

[75] Höffe and Kablitz, *Europäische Musik—Musik Europas*.
[76] See "Branding 'Western Music.'"
[77] Strohm, "'Medieval Music' or 'Early European Music'?," 1188, 1197.
[78] See three edited volumes emerging from this project: Strohm, *Studies on a Global History of Music*; Strohm, *The Music Road*; Strohm, *Transcultural Music History*. For an outline of its program, see Strohm, "The Balzan Musicology Project."
[79] Irving, "Ancient Greeks."

From this rapid survey, it is clear that, despite being critiqued from diverse perspectives over several decades, the interrelated and overlapping superordinate concepts of "European music" and "Western music" remain dominant today. Regardless of the name used, they are generally considered to contain domains such as art music, folk music, and popular music. Regarding art music, the descriptors "European" and "Western" are often interchangeable, but in 2012, ethnomusicologists Philip V. Bohlman and Martin Stokes explained a shift from one to the other in the following way:

> During the twentieth century, as European empires collapsed and European nations engaged with one another in world wars, European music changed identities in response, retreating from Europe to claim the "West" in its entirety. The collectively singular concept of music underwent a name change, from European art music to Western art music.[80]

Despite this change, "European music," with or without the intermediary term "art," has remained a phenomenon that ethnomusicologists have continued to reckon with. Dafni Tragaki addressed the concept in her introduction to a 2013 volume of studies on the Eurovision Song Contest. Addressing the question "What is 'European music'?," she made the following observations about common perceptions of it:

> "European music" and, consequently, the essence of European "civilization," is to be found in the great works of the genius composers that brought the noble art of music to its highest degree of sophistication. This "European music" is both timeless and transcendental, a fixed canon of masterpieces that survives history as it is superior to it and has the power to reaffirm continuity with the past; it is, indeed an almost organic part of the glorious imperial past. As such, it invests the imaginary of a European community born in music, a European community united by a common cultural heritage where the contribution of "others" remains invisible.[81]

Tragaki gave this summary in order to contextualize studies of contemporary popular music that subscribe to the category of European musical identity,

---

[80] Bohlman and Stokes, "Series Editors' Foreword," viii.
[81] Tragaki, "Introduction," 4.

for which the touchstone is "classical music." Within the frame of her discussion, it reads—with irony clearly intended—like a literal account of prevailing beliefs in certain kinds of public discourse.[82] Nevertheless, it is worth noting that the conceptual use of "European music" as opposed to "Western music" in contexts such as Eurovision today might relate to Gayatri Spivak's notion of "strategic essentialism."[83] Although European cultural identity is rarely thought of as representing a minority, the performances in Eurovision could perhaps be seen collectively to resist or destabilize the hegemony of two larger and overlapping categories ("American popular music" and "Western popular music") in the global frame of popular music.[84]

Diverse forms of European popular music have long been the focus of much work of ethnomusicologists and sociologists, but over the last few decades there has also been an increase in ethnomusicological studies of Western art music. Projects involving fieldwork and thick descriptions of cultural contexts, such as a collection of studies edited by Laudan Nooshin, stand out.[85] Institutionalized divisions between historical musicology and ethnomusicology that were based on inherited notions of "Western art music" or "European music" have now long been challenged seriously through reassessments of what "Westernness" and "Europeanness" mean, especially from the fields of postcolonial musicology, diasporic music histories, other forms of critical musicology and ethnomusicology, and the emerging field of global music history.[86] The postcolonial, critical, and global turns in musicology (among others) have cumulatively challenged previous approaches to music scholarship that were undeniably circumscribed and self-limiting in a number of ways, although many scholars working in these fields have been (or are) located in the Global North.[87]

---

[82] Bloechl points out some strikingly similar tropes about "early music" and "European identity" in a speech made by a politician in 2013. See Bloechl, "Race, Empire, and Early Music," 105.

[83] For an overview of "strategic essentialism" in the thought of Spivak, see Morton, *Gayatri Spivak*, 124–126.

[84] As Derek Scott has pointed out, performers in Eurovision from smaller competing states sometimes employ a kind of auto-exoticization—often on a local or regional level—in direct counterpoint to "mainstream" ("American" or "Western") popular music. See Scott, "'I Changed My Olga.'"

[85] See Nooshin, *The Ethnomusicology of Western Art Music*.

[86] The literature is vast, but some key anthologies include Bohlman, Blum, and Neuman, *Ethnomusicology and Modern Music History*; Solie, *Musicology and Difference*; Clayton, Herbert, and Middleton, *The Cultural Study of Music*; Bloechl, Lowe, and Kallberg, *Rethinking Difference*. See also Takao, "Global Music History."

[87] I am grateful to W. Dean Sutcliffe for discussion of this point. See also Chua, "Global Musicology."

Long-standing disciplinary gulfs between historical musicology and ethnomusicology—dating back to the mid-twentieth century and still institutionalized by academic societies, universities, and the job market—have diminished considerably, with many bridges built.[88] In the early 2000s, Cook asserted that "we are all (ethno)musicologists now," and a number of scholars proposed ideas of "the new (ethno)musicologies."[89] Within a 2008 volume dedicated to that latter theme, Jim Samson inquired, "How did European music become global? How did European music become European?" and asserted that "this is an excellent instance of ethnomusicology and musicology addressing two questions that almost boil down to one, and hardly an unimportant one."[90] The same year, Bloechl asked:

> How might music historical narratives change if colonial "outposts" of European musical activity were understood not as diversions from the "real" flow of music historical events in Europe, but as an eddying and rebounding of that flow that turned back a continuous music historical time, and with it a coherent cultural entity known as "Europe" (or "Spain," "France," or "England")?[91]

Decentering the history of music, and its historiographical focus, in an increasingly global framework involves grappling with such issues and interrogating any "coherent cultural entity," to use Bloechl's term. The changes in approaches to historical narratives speculated on by Bloechl have already become apparent as a result of the work that she and other scholars have been doing, such as the collaborative projects of Strohm and of Katherine Butler Schofield (the latter with her European Research Council project "Musical Transitions to European Colonialism in the Eastern Indian Ocean," 2011–2015).[92]

In this book, I seek to address these various questions through a diachronic tracing of the ideas and labels of "European music" and "Western music."

---

[88] See reflections by Nettl about his experiences of how the relationship between the disciplines changed over the course of his career (some sixty years). Nettl, "Have You Changed Your Mind?," esp. 54.
[89] Cook, "We Are All (Ethno)musicologists Now"; Stobart, *The New (Ethno)musicologies*.
[90] Samson, "A View from Musicology," 25.
[91] Bloechl, *Native American Song*, 25; see also 22.
[92] See Schofield, "Musical Transitions"; King's College London, "Musical Transitions." I was fortunate to work on this project as a postdoctoral research associate and then a visting fellow and have continued to learn much from collaboration with team members.

I am motivated by and indebted to the work of scholars just mentioned, as well as thinkers about musical exoticism including Locke and Timothy D. Taylor.[93] Looking across disciplinary divides—in a manner that is already beginning to intersect with similar thought emerging from the discipline of music theory, especially the work of Philip Ewell[94]—it is time to excavate deeper ideas of "Europe," to de-essentialize and de-exceptionalize the ways in which the adjective "European" is applied to the noun "music" in a global context, and to acknowledge the internal heterogeneity of the concepts of "European music" and "Western art music."

Approach, Sources, and Positionality

A major influence on my approach has been the work of organologist Jeremy Montagu (1927–2020).[95] In the introduction to his 2007 monograph *Origins and Development of Musical Instruments*—a summation of many decades of authoritative hands-on organological research—he made a comment about his chosen terminology that is worth quoting here at length:

> We shall use frequently in these pages such phrases as "in our culture" or "in our music." They are used in place of the meaningless terms "Western music," "European orchestras," and so forth. Possible alternatives are "international culture" and "international music," for "our" music has become international. We cannot talk of "Western" music when "our" sort of music is played worldwide; the Tokyo Philharmonic, for example, is eastern relative to Berlin, but western from Los Angeles. Nor can we legitimately speak of "European" when, for example, since the seventeenth century (even since the sixteenth, south of the Rio Grande), "our" music has been composed and played in the Americas.[96]

---

[93] Works of Bloechl, Samson, and Cook are cited above. On exoticism, see Taylor, *Beyond Exoticism*; Locke, *Musical Exoticism*; Locke, *Music and the Exotic*; Revuluri, "On Anxiety and Absorption."

[94] See, for example, Ewell, "Music Theory and the White Racial Frame"; Rehding, "Can the History of Theory Be Decentered?"

[95] See Wells, "Jeremy Montagu." In 2009, I had the opportunity of a lengthy visit with Montagu at his house, full to the rafters with instruments from around the world, where we talked about a diverse range of topics.

[96] He continues: "When saying *our*, I write as someone brought up in England and trained first in America and then in England, but it implies no value judgment—all musics are music. It is only because 'Western' and 'European' are without meaning in this context that we must have available *some* word to distinguish between 'ours' and that of people brought up and trained in different musics from mine." Montagu, *Origins and Development*, 2–3.

Montagu rightly points out the "meaningless" nature of some of these terms, even though they continue to have meaning for many people. My way of thinking is inspired by Montagu's but differs from it in that I will mostly write about such musics in the long eighteenth century (and two earlier centuries) in the third person. When I use "we," "our," or "us," I refer not to my musical background, nor yours, but to our joint journey in looking at primary sources and thinking about the history of ideas.

In the chapters that follow, I aim for a relativistic and reflexive study of European-language terms regarding "European" musics and how they are used in European-language historiography, based on European-language materials produced by Europeans in Europe, or in European colonies (and other outposts), for European readership. Whereas I do this using Europeans' own writings, recent studies have demonstrated the value of using extra-European sources to critique, from an external perspective, these same music cultures. David Urrows and Jen-yen Chen, among others, have produced revelatory work on early modern Chinese sources that describe the practices of Europeans from an etic perspective.[97] The reasons I choose my scope of European texts are not only my limitations as an individual trying to find a pathway through a dense forest of sources but also the question of who can speak for others today. Over the past few years, there has been a necessary re-evaluation of positionality and extractivism in musical research and practice, especially in studies related to colonialism and race that are made from etic perspectives.[98] Even the idea of representing "our heritage," emically, in historical terms, is not without problems. If "European music" is to be studied relativistically and reflexively, or "on its own terms," it must be considered what those "terms" were (in all senses) and how different that culture was from the researcher's present reality. As mentioned above, in terms of anachronism, the distant past of one's own culture can itself be considered "exotic." Studies of early modern ethnographic texts have shown us that the European description of other cultures in that period tells us more

---

[97] Urrows, "The Wind Qin"; Chen, "European Sounds." In a youthful essay, I sketched out some preliminary thinking about this topic; see Irving, "Interpreting Non-European Perceptions and Representations."

[98] See, for example, the call for researchers to "reorient themselves toward more equitable and resurgent world-making projects *with*, *by* and *for* Indigenous Peoples" in Perea, *Sound Relations*, 31. See also discussion of extractivism in Robinson, *Hungry Listening*, 113–147, esp. 119–121, and an introduction to a special journal issue on the topic in E. Clark, "Introduction: Audibilities of Colonialism and Extractivism." Increasing discussion of identity and positionality is indicated by a session on "Musical Whiteness and the Researcher's Racial Positionality," chaired by Ritwik Banerji, at the American Musicological Society Annual Meeting in New Orleans on November 11, 2022.

about their writers than the peoples who were observed.[99] In similar ways, perhaps our investigation of previous generations will simply result in our greater self-awareness.

In broaching this topic, I have been painfully aware of the vast number of primary sources and secondary literature on the idea of "Europe" itself and on music in or related to the continent. To tackle, let alone acknowledge, an evenly spread representative sample in a compact monograph is a sheer impossibility. What I offer here is instead an avowedly subjective reflection based on my individual training and experience (thus far) as an archival researcher, woven through with references to relevant scholarship. I am certain that there are many gaps in my bibliography that I did not recognize or about which I did not know whom to ask—I apologize in advance for lacunae—and primary sources that I did not see. The book is in part a thought experiment and in part an etymological and philological journey that takes specific words as its focal points. I locate these in a handful of western European languages, identified as those in which the bulk of literature on music was published by presses in Europe in the long eighteenth century.

My study relies on tiny observations accumulated over around six years, including many specks of archival gold glimpsed against the mesh of digital search engines and databases (such as Google Books, Gallica, and the Biblioteca Digital Hispánica, among others). The global Covid pandemic and local lockdowns from 2020 made this approach not just an option but a necessity. Of course, there are multiple methodological and epistemological issues that arise from the fact that these powerful search capacities sidestep and compress the amount of time and physical labor involved in archival research. The lure of being able to access and use an "irresistible nugget of historical detail" unearthed almost instantaneously from the mire of centuries of information involves, as Benjamin Walton has pointed out, a certain "shame" on the part of the researcher; it fundamentally changes readers' and audiences' perspectives on the degree of toil invested by the scholar and also brings into question their knowledge of contexts surrounding that information.[100] I share that sentiment. Nevertheless, this study would not be possible without these digital tools and their capability for the rapid and convenient accumulation of so many small pieces of data. If some of the evidence seems fragmentary, that is simply because it is; before the late eighteenth century,

---

[99] See Bohlman, "Missionaries," 5.
[100] Walton, "Quirk Shame," 122–123.

notions of pan-continental Europeanness in musical contexts were seldom articulated in such terms.

I thus write within the constraints of the primary sources I have been able to access. Taking my own linguistic limitations into full account and knowing the impossibility of taking a fully "global" approach, I frame my argument mainly in terms of critiquing "adjectival anachronism" (a different take on Goehr's "conceptual imperialism") in the historiography of "European" or "Western music." In other words, I aim to see how many early modern texts are silent or inconsistent about notions of "European" and "Western," even though musicologists today use the terms habitually, as if they are self-evident. I look at musical representations of Europe in myth and allegory, music's role in the construction of the continent as a space, and the eighteenth-century emergence of the notions of "European ears" and "European musicians." We will see from travelogues, histories, ethnographies, studies, reports, reference works, and a range of other texts how these writers constructed ideas of "European music" and "Western music," leaving in this process traces of their formation. I focus on critiquing these homogenized macrohistorical identities, which have long run risks of ethnocentric essentialization. As a study of the kind of language used in primary sources—including vocabulary that still has legacies in our writing of music history today—the book aims to contribute to the history of ideas. I hope it will also align with established and emerging decolonial methodologies, by questioning notions of pan-continental identity in musics from early modern Europe, and by highlighting relevant data to this end.

Engaging with primary sources that are written for, by, and about people who explicitly defined themselves using the term "European" and who wrote about "European music," the book undeniably presents a disproportionately large number of quotations from white men of the long eighteenth century, not to mention the periods before and after.[101] In my search for texts on these topics from the long eighteenth century, that has been the reality, and often the extent, of the search results. Such writings certainly reflect the hegemonic masculinity that was becoming increasingly dominant in eighteenth-century European culture.[102] I ask for your tolerance and patience in this regard: I

---

[101] However, for a challenge to male-centered perceptions of Europe, see Schmale, *Gender and Eurocentrism*.

[102] Thanks to Wolfgang Schmale for discussion of this point. In his book *Gender and Eurocentrism*, he observes: "Without naming it as such, the Enlightenment developed the concept of hegemonic masculinity, which would situate masculinity in relation to Europe in a manner quite different than before" (13).

do not cite "dead white male" authors to extol or valorize them but rather to show how a critique of these texts and an exploration of the inconsistencies within them are among the ways by which historiographical fictions and essentialisms can be identified and perhaps even taken apart. My approach differs from that of Bloechl, who observed in 2015:

> Better historical knowledge, compelling as it is, will not in itself displace the perceived whiteness of early European music, because this perception is not really based on a literal absence of race or racialized people in Europe. It rests instead on a modern correlation of power and prestige with whiteness and a libidinal projection of that racial structure onto the musical past.[103]

While concurring with this statement, I would perhaps add that an increased *historiographical* awareness can potentially help to disrupt and destabilize this "perceived whiteness" (or "absence of race"). This is because subjecting relevant early modern sources to a renewed diachronic critique might allow us to dismantle the discursive constructions that have underpinned that perception. We can potentially reveal their internal contradictions and paradoxes and also attempt to identify incipient examples of anticolonial and decolonial thinking.[104]

Some readers may find this book undertheorized; others the opposite. I am cautious about the imposition of theory—often generated from the analysis of a sharply delimited amount of data—when there is still so much unexamined primary evidence lying (sometimes in both senses of that word) in various archives. As Katherine Schofield once suggested to me, "the best theory arises from the sources you are working with."[105] In this book, I thus prefer to present texts straight from the proverbial "horses' mouths" and think afresh about what they might mean, rather than try to fit them into preexisting theoretical frameworks. Those readers looking for or expecting an analysis of musical notes themselves might be disappointed; this is the history of cultural signifiers rather than of the organized sounds that they signified. (All the same, the discussion of a range of compositions, especially in chapter 1, may point the reader to interesting experiences of reading, listening, and even performing.) I hope, nevertheless, that we can find a middle

---

[103] Bloechl, "Race, Empire, and Early Music," 79.
[104] Mignolo points out that decolonial thinking can be traced back to the early modern period. Mignolo, *The Darker Side of Western Modernity*, xxiv.
[105] Schofield, personal communication, December 22, 2022.

ground. Energized by current debates about research in the humanities that point to a multitude of possible ways forward, especially in contexts of "the global," I have gravitated toward my original love of close readings of primary sources and the tracing of small words, inspired in many ways by the approach demonstrated by historian Peter Burke in 1980.[106] As mentioned earlier, this approach also links directly to my inner voice as an "early music" performer, in the sense of going back to the sources and seeing what they show and imagining what this meant to readers at the time.

Focusing on small words in a smattering of references additionally leads to analogies with listening for silences between musical notes (or other sounds) and the contribution of this process to a growing awareness or alertness. Awareness is a central part of reflexivity, which Joel Kahn (1946–2017) once described as "the implications of the 'discovery' by anthropologists and their critics that the knowledge which anthropology produces is not innocent— that it is not a simple reflection of a pre-given social and cultural reality out there in the world."[107] In this same spirit of reflexivity, I acknowledge explicitly my own positionality in this project.[108] Although I am based in Europe, I was born and raised on a different continent.[109] Nevertheless, my physiognomy and many of my cultural traits and preferences probably suggest to an observer that I am "derived" from Europe. By an accident of birth and genes, a white face bestows an unfair advantage and usually unspoken privilege in often enabling its bearer to be absorbed (almost) seamlessly into many cultural frameworks and hierarchical structures in Europe, as well as in places that were constructed or have been impacted by European colonialism. By contrast, members of the global majority face structural racism and discrimination on a daily basis. I am increasingly conscious of both white privilege and male privilege within musicology, and academia at large, and do not doubt that I have benefited from many forms of structural discrimination. Fortunately, more light is being shone onto this pervasive form of inequality as movements to decolonize academic disciplines gain pace.[110]

---

[106] P. Burke, "Did Europe Exist."
[107] Kahn, "Anthropology and Modernity," 654.
[108] For a recent discussion of reflexivity in music history research, in this case relating to colonial Australia, see Irving and Maddox, "Towards a Reflexive Paradigm."
[109] The theme of being "in but not of Europe" was discussed by Stuart Hall in an essay of the same name, although his position was profoundly different from my own. Hall, *Selected Writings*, 374–385. For a range of recent perspectives on the idea of "belonging" in modern-day Europe, see Lerman, *Do I Belong?*
[110] For example, Ayana O. Smith has recently shared personal perspectives on her own professional experience as an African American scholar working on seventeenth- and eighteenth-century music. See Smith, "Editorial."

British activist Hamja Ahsan, in his recent book *Shy Radicals*, points to positive roles that can be played by shy white men, among other introverts, in allyship with people of color and others in moves for social justice and equality.[111] White male musicologists, by dint of sheer numbers, have disproportionately dominated the discipline in living memory, but their increasing participation in movements for change has the potential to mitigate further this historical (and current) representational imbalance.[112]

Like many people born in Australia, I am a descendant of waves of colonialists who, over fewer than ten generations, dispossessed the populations of approximately five hundred Indigenous nations within the continent (the geographical area of which is slightly less than that of the United States of America but more than that of the European Union). While the work of reconciliation is a long-standing and ongoing process, there is still much to do, as illustrated in October 2023 by the negative result of the national referendum on recognizing the Indigenous nations of the continent by creating a governmental "Aboriginal and Torres Strait Islander Voice."[113] Australia is also acknowledged by some (but not all) observers today, along with New Zealand, as part of the Global North, despite these countries' geographical location in the southern hemisphere.[114] To add a further layer of complexity, I remember in the 1990s being taught in classrooms—and hearing frequently in the public sphere—the idea that Australia was part of Asia. This notion and debates that surround it date back to the 1960s.[115] They were cultural, geographical, and economic in nature and also fed into music. In 1967, Australian composer Peter Sculthorpe (1929–2014) stated in an interview that he did not "believe in nationalism in music" but considered himself "intensely Australian," going on to articulate his views on "European music": "We are part of the Asian world now and so should Australian music be. For me, at least, *European music is dead*. I would rather listen to the Beatles

---

[111] Ahsan, *Shy Radicals*, 138–143.
[112] I am inspired in this comment by a remark made by Carolyn R. Bertozzi, 2022 Nobel laureate in chemistry, on the BBC program *Nobel Minds 2022* (December 18, 2022), hosted by Zeinab Badawi, regarding the position of women in science.
[113] National Indigenous Australians Agency, "Referendum."
[114] See a critique of Australia's relationship with notions of Global North and South in Collyer, "Australia and the Global South." See also discussion of non-Indigenous inhabitants of Australia, New Zealand, and South Africa contrasted with the Global South in Appiah, *The Lies That Bind*, 191. Given the discussion of the Eurovision Song Contest above, it is worth noting that Australia has participated in this competition since 2015 and is currently the only nation in the southern hemisphere to do so.
[115] See the 1964 article by Usha Mahajani, "Is Australia a Part of Asia?"

than to a large part of nineteenth-century music" (emphasis added).[116] It is interesting to note the mutually exclusive categories enunciated here: the Beatles, despite their origin, are not considered part of "European music." Rather, in this context, Sculthorpe appears to equate the notion of "European music"—probably implying "art music"—with "nineteenth-century music." The latter term is not given its own proper adjective, as if it were assumed that "nineteenth-century" aesthetic contexts are synonymous with "European." This statement, by such a prominent figure in the making of a national or continental music in Australia, adds further weight to the observation of Sorce Keller (quoted above) and others regarding romantic attitudes being ingrained in popular ideas about music.

An Interpretive Itinerary around Ideas

In the chapters that follow, I trace the construction not only of "European music" and "Western music" in the long eighteenth century but also concepts relevant to them, including "progress," "perfection," and a variety of superlatives, as well as "modernity," "civilization," and "barbarism." However, there are no claims to comprehensiveness, and the findings offered in these pages remain provisional. I will be both fascinated and delighted if and when fresh evidence emerges to prove me wrong about the chronologies I present, and I look forward to feedback on my interpretation of sources, welcoming dialogue and critique. A truly "global" perspective on the topic must await the collaborative work of scholars who have skills that are different from mine.[117] All this said, I hope that the data and discussion contained here will be surprising, revelatory, and useful for future research.

The book is split into three parts, each containing an introduction and two chapters. Part I looks at eighteenth-century representations and constructions of "Europe" as a notion and a space (physical and conceptual); part II examines the idea of "Europeans" as people and the emergence of the "European music" concept; and part III analyzes the way older ideas about "the West" and "modernity" were periodically recycled and reformulated in their application to music in early modern discourse. At the outset, it is

---

[116] In Skinner, *Peter Sculthorpe*, 482. Thanks to Nicholas Cook for highlighting this comment to me. See discussion in Cook, *Music, Encounter, Togetherness*, chapter 8.
[117] On collaboration, see Bloechl, Schofield, and Solis, "The Value of Collaboration."

necessary to establish context about notions of continents in regard to place, people, and identity. Chapter 1 thus looks at the way Europe was represented by and to people called Europeans through musical settings of origin myths and continental allegories. Chapter 2 surveys the changing physical and conceptual geographies of the continent and considers how these were perceived by certain musicians and travel writers. Chapter 3 examines the definitions of Europeans as people who heard and made music that would eventually be described as "European," "Western," and/or "modern." The key concepts and terms of "European music," "modernity," and "Western music," as they emerged in primary sources, are examined in Chapters 4, 5, and 6, respectively. If readers want to focus on just one chapter of this book, I suggest the fourth, containing the core findings about "European music."

Let me stress that I categorically do not intend to imply any form of universalism in regard to the main terms and concepts discussed here. Rather, I seek to reassess the ways musicologists (myself included) have used or still use them uncritically. Although my methodology involves occasionally sketching out the diachronic emergence of concepts as part of the history of ideas, I want to highlight that there is nothing inevitable or predetermined about the invention of "European music."[118] It was a messy process that went hand in hand with colonialism and the global extraction of wealth and knowledge, as well as the emergence of the kind of thought we consider part of "the Enlightenment."[119] By subjecting archival traces of the long eighteenth century to critical and contextual readings, in dialogue with the recent work of inspirational colleagues, I hope to contribute to the dismantling of teleologies that emerged not only during that time but also in the nineteenth century and beyond.

In the midst of current and recent threats to European integration, stability, and peace—due to diverse forms of cultural, political, and economic rupture, as well as military aggression—it seems timely to note that the long eighteenth century, the era in which "European music" emerged, saw decisive

---

[118] James Miles and Lindsay Gibson rightly warn that attempts to avoid presentism may lead to a belief "that people in the past can only be judged by the ethical standards of their time, not the present," and to the assumption that "past injustices were inevitable, that most people at the time supported these injustices, and that the injustices were justifiable." They comment that "making reasoned ethical judgments involves reflecting on and understanding a range of perspectives about social action" and also reflecting on the full spectrum of attitudes, norms, and values at the time. Miles and Gibson, "Rethinking Presentism," 523.

[119] For a view of multiple kinds of Enlightenments, see Bohlman, "Musical Thought in the Global Enlightenments."

moves toward political cooperation and peaceful alliances, and proposals for a European parliament.[120] I want to encourage us to look through and beyond perceived cultural and political boundaries to understand the internal and external processes by which the concept was first formulated. The development of "European music" was, of course, not unproblematic; it often involved value judgments and prejudice but at other times openness and empathy. Perhaps further understanding of the diverse human actions that surround music—or "musicking," to use Small's term—will aid with current objectives to deploy music as a means of social betterment, human flourishing, and social justice.

If anything ties together the abstract concept of a long eighteenth century for Europe, that so-called *siècle des Lumières* (century of enlightened philosophers, usually glossed as the Age of Enlightenment), it is the emergence of "European music" as a term and idea, as a touchstone for oppositional self-definition, and as a set of practices and repertories. The chronology of this process spans from the term's first identifiable articulations in the 1670s to its coalescing with, and subsumption by, "Western music" in the 1830s. All this took place against a backdrop of colonialism. Truly "global" histories of these concepts, involving a collaborative polyphony of authorial voices, are either in progress or remain to be written, and I await them with eager anticipation. In the meantime, I offer here this small—and, I hope, reflexive and relativistic—piece of the larger puzzle, a puzzle that is without boundaries, one with edges that are continually changing shape, contracting in places and expanding in others.

---

[120] See discussion of this point in chapter 4.

PART I
"EUROPE" IN MUSIC, MUSIC IN "EUROPE"

Writers, composers, artists, and performers of eighteenth-century Europe frequently used music to create new or perpetuate old concepts of the continent. Their processes involved the making of allegories in image, sound, and text to create a system of representation known as the "four parts of the world," specifically, Europe, Asia, Africa, and America. Personifications of them—usually (but not always) gendered as female—were painted and sculpted, embodied and animated; they sang and danced as characters in processions, operas, and ballets, and roles with those names even featured in sacred oratorios. Visual artists, moreover, produced other kinds of visual allegories, abstract and without anthropomorphosis, that illustrated the continents with a range of symbols. In both traditions, embodied or not, a clear Eurocentrism emerged: Europe was depicted with features (including musical elements) that not only distinguished it but also set it atop a global hierarchy.[1]

Some composers and writers reached back to origin myths to create musical and musico-dramatic works about the legendary figure from whom the continent's name is derived. This was Europa, a Phoenician princess who in most Greco-Roman versions of the story was abducted and raped by Zeus or Jupiter (also Jove in English or Giove in Italian), the king of the gods.[2] Musical settings of this troubling narrative present a range of approaches to its plot: some highlight Europa's grief, while others seem to downplay the assault; almost all reinforce patriarchy. Most of these works do not explicitly include the detail of how the continent came to be named (it exists in only

---

[1] Bethencourt, *Racisms*, 65–82; Schmale, Romberg, and Köstlbauer, *The Language of Continent Allegories*; Horowitz, "Introduction (1): Rival Interpretations," 1.

[2] March, *Dictionary of Classical Mythology*, 188–189; Passerini, *Il mito d'Europa*.

some versions of the myth); however, the etymological link was probably considered assumed knowledge and something of a cliché.

Personifications aside, whether allegorical or eponymous and mythological, continents were challenging entities to conceptualize. In 1793, Johann Gottfried Herder (1744–1803) described Europe in his *Briefe zu Beförderung der Humanität* (*Letters for the Advancement of Humanity*) as "merely a figment of the mind, that we piece together somewhat on the basis of the location of its countries, their common features, interests and intercourse."[3] Similarly, many eighteenth-century musicians understood Europe as the space in which diverse national styles and tastes coexisted.[4] In other words, they evoked, characterized, or mimicked specific cultural traits and musical practices of diverse national communities. A musical and cultural rivalry—sometimes friendly, often denigrating—between the internal "nations of Europe," enacted mostly by their creative artists and performers, became explicit. This sense of competition sometimes extended, in comparative terms, to nations of other parts of the world, in line with growing geographical and ethnographic knowledge, and involved both stereotyping and cultural appropriation. In constructing "Europe" as a continent, then, some musicians and artists concentrated on its internal components to feature individual nations. The surprisingly few works of music from the long eighteenth century that feature the word "Europe" in their titles do exactly that.

Ideas of cultural difference within the continent seemed more important than the question of distance. Allusions to the limits of this physical space also became a regular discursive trope. A distinctive form of expressing Europe's conceptual geography, defined by shared practices and experiences, began to appear in texts—and, presumably, in much speech that went unrecorded—through the use of superlatives, turns of phrase that described individuals or ensembles as possessing "the greatest" or "the best" musical skills "in Europe." In this way, musicians' identities, stories of their origins, and impressions of their wide-ranging fame began to be transformed in the public imagination. Individual musicians were normally described in records as being from a town, city, or region (and occasionally a nation state). When they reached a certain level of public recognition, they might be represented within a continental frame, as being "of" or "in" Europe. Nevertheless, as

---

[3] Translation in Drace-Francis, *European Identity*, 86. Original text in Herder, *Briefe zur Beförderung der Humanität*, Vol. 2, 15–16.

[4] For an overview of the period 1600–1750, see Schott, "National Styles"; Rose, "The Musical Map of Europe," 11–23.

part II of the book shows, the proper adjective "European" (as in "European musician" or "European composer") was rarely used in this intra-European sense during the eighteenth century. It was only when comparisons with other parts of the world were made that "European" was joined to "music," "musician(s)," and "instrument(s)" in a contiguous adjective-noun or noun-adjective combination.

Spatial awareness, on a continental or a global scale, was more conceptual than physical. A musical Europe could not be represented cartographically with any precision, especially as opinions on and definitions of the continent's eastern and northeastern boundaries changed over the course of the century.[5] Yet a sense of an international musical community could be imagined and implied through discourse. Various thinkers who wrote about music in French, English, German, Italian, and Spanish began to refer to a "Republic of Music," clearly analogous with the "Republic of Letters."[6] Transcending place, this republic implied a number of things: a growing network of musical communities across the continent, the links of thought and exchange between them (mediated by letters and publications), and, more specifically, the elite spaces of specialized music making within them, together with the kinds of audience reactions that they elicited. This Republic of Music suggested a political framework and evoked Platonic notions of good order, as well as music as a way to influence morals, the rule of law, and the participatory musicking of citizens.[7]

The long eighteenth century was thus a pivotal time for new concepts of "Europe." In a seminal essay of 2015, historian Wolfgang Schmale studied many of the processes through which these were formed.[8] Looking at the processes of Europeanization in that time and the move to "define Europe as a singular culture," Schmale focused on five key themes: (1) relations with antiquity, (2) the attempts to define "Europe" in works by prominent philosophers of the time, (3) geographical definitions, (4) emerging anthropological and racial classifications of Europeans in relation to peoples of other continents, and (5) the production and propagandization of allegorical iconography of the continents, which positioned Europe as "superior" to the others.[9] There is perhaps a sixth category (relating to the other five): music, in

---

[5] For a variety of primary texts, see excerpts translated in Drace-Francis, *European Identity*.
[6] For a description in German-speaking contexts, see Chapin, "Counterpoint," 381–382, 391.
[7] On legal aspects surrounding music in the period, see Ahrendt, "Politics," esp. 83–85, 98–99.
[8] Schmale, "Europe," 83.
[9] Schmale, "Europe," 79–94.

all its forms of practice, and its conceptualization by people who self-defined as "Europeans."

In this part of the book, I address two questions: How did musicians in the long eighteenth century refer to concepts of "Europe" in their work? At the same time, how did geographers, historians, and other writers attempting to define Europe invoke or refer to music in this process, if at all? In chapter 1, I look at representations in works of music and art, discussing musical settings of the Europa myth and the allegorization of the four continents, as well as the characterization of national styles of which a musical Europe was made up. Chapter 2 then turns to issues of the continent's space: musicians' ideas of physical geography, the rise of the Republic of Music, and the emergence of discourse about superlative musical skills "in Europe." Primary sources are immense, and so what follows is a selective analysis of case studies and examples that illustrate specific sides of this multifaceted field, highlighting the diversity of thought within it. Let us begin with the question of a name and its supposed origins.

1
Musical Constructions of Europe in Myth and Allegory

In Greek and Roman mythology, Europa was a Phoenician princess, daughter of King Agenor of Tyre or Sidon (in what is now Lebanon).[1] She was abducted by the god Zeus (Jupiter in Roman culture) in the form of a bull and trafficked to the island of Crete. After transforming into his regular self, the king of the gods raped her, in an act of violence that has been described by John T. Hamilton as "a founding myth of the West in every sense."[2] Europa subsequently bore three sons fathered by Zeus—Minos, Rhadamanthys, and Sarpedon—and became the wife of Asterion (Asterius), king of Crete, who raised the boys as his own.[3] In the fifth and fourth centuries BCE, the Greek tragedian Euripides (c. 480–c. 406 BCE) and the comic poets Hermippus (dates unknown) and Plato (fl. 410–391 BCE; not the philosopher) set this story in their plays.[4] Moschus (fl. 150 BCE) gave the "most complete account of the myth" in an epyllion (narrative poem) titled "Europa."[5] Some texts highlight the distraught expressions of Europa, as she lamented her fate. Roman poet Horace (65 BCE–8 BCE) relates in one of his odes how the goddess Venus abruptly told Europa to cease her sorrows and realize her fortune, saying that "a region of the world will bear your name."[6] Horace's contemporary Ovid (43 BCE–17/18 CE), in his *Fasti*, addresses Europa directly: "thou, Sidonian damsel, wast got with child by Jupiter, and a third part of the earth doth bear thy name."[7]

---

[1] In some early texts, she is described as the daughter of Phoinix (Phoenix). See a discussion of sources in Gantz, *Early Greek Myth*, 209–210.
[2] Hamilton, "Torture," 151. For an outline of the myth see Reeves, "The Rape of Europa," 27–29.
[3] See citations of diverse sources in March, *Dictionary of Classical Mythology*, 188–189; Grimal, *The Penguin Dictionary*, 147; Gantz, *Early Greek Myth*, 210; Robertson, "Europe I," 76.
[4] Reeves, "The Rape of Europa," 34. On other early works, see Robertson, "Europe I," 76; Gantz, *Early Greek Myth*, 208–212.
[5] Ginestet, "'She, Whom Jove Transported,'" 153. For the complete text, see Moschus, "Europa."
[6] Original text: "tua sectus orbis / nomina ducet." Horace, *Odes and Epodes*, 208 (Latin), 209 (translation) (Book 3, Ode 27, lines 75–76).
[7] Original text: "te, Sidoni, Iuppiter implet, / parsque tuum terrae tertia nomen habet." Ovid, *Fasti*, 306 (Latin), 307 (translation) (no. 5, section 14, lines 617–618). See also Markey, "Stradano's

Following treatments of the story by various Roman authors, Europa retreats quietly into the background in ancient literature and is referred to only obliquely and intertextually.[8]

Like most ancient myths and origin stories, this tale must have arisen orally, and among the earliest written traces of it there are already variations. When Herodotus (c. 484 BCE–c. 425 BCE) recounted it at the beginning of his *Histories*—centuries earlier than Moschus, Horace, or Ovid—he rationalized the plot by replacing the abductor Zeus with a band of Greeks, whom he presumes to have been Cretan.[9] He was, moreover, skeptical about Europe having being named for the princess, writing that "the origin of its name is . . . uncertain (as is the identity of the man who named it), unless we say that it is named after Europa from Tyre, and that before her time the continent was after all as nameless as the other continents were."[10] Herodotus also provides an intriguing detail, which disrupts any kind of essentialism in the narrative of the continent's original name, when he adds pointedly: "it is clear that Europa came from Asia and never visited the land mass which the Greeks now call Europe."[11] This anomalous aspect of eponymy was highlighted by Jamaican British sociologist Stuart Hall (1932–2014), who critiqued the use of Europa in political representation, asking: "If she represents Europe, why is she from 'elsewhere'?"[12] Emphasizing the hybridities involved in the creation of this origin myth, Hall went on to comment that "it is by common consent many centuries after the era of classical Greece before anything vaguely resembling Europe or a 'European identity' begins to make itself felt."[13] There are clearly paradoxes involved. Nevertheless, the story was pervasive and long-lived, and the trope of Europa on a bull became a common piece of iconography.[14] Political scientist Eszter Salgó comments that although the image

---

Allegorical Invention," 423, 425. The detail of naming, however, is not part of the more famous version of the story in Ovid's *Metamorphoses*. See Ovid, *Metamorphoses*, 118–121 (Book II, 833–875).

[8] I am grateful to Peter Agócs for discussions about Europa. For a detailed overview of the myth's passage through ancient literature, see Reeves, "The Rape of Europa." A concise summary of the Europa myth and versions of it is given in Pagden, "Europe: Conceptualizing a Continent," 33–34.

[9] Herodotus, *The Histories*, 3 (Book 1, § 2). Anthony Pagden notes that the Christian theologian Lactantius (c. 250 CE–c. 325 CE) promoted this version, since it was removed from supernatural "erotic fantasies from the ancient world." Pagden, "Europe: Conceptualizing a Continent," 34.

[10] Herodotus, *The Histories*, 250 (Book 4, § 45).
[11] Herodotus, *The Histories*, 250 (Book 4, § 45).
[12] Hall, *Selected Writings*, 378.
[13] Hall, *Selected Writings*, 379.
[14] For a catalogue and commentary on classical depictions, see Robertson, "Europe I."

"was pushed to the background in the Middle Ages, it regained its popularity during the Renaissance and has maintained its attractive power ever since."[15] It is reproduced today in a number of places as symbolic imagery of the European Union, being featured as a sculpture made in 1997 by Léon de Pas, *Europe en avant* (*Forward, Europe*) outside the Justus Lipsius building (headquarters of the Council of the European Union) in Brussels.[16] Europa and the bull also appear on some identity cards, on a series of euro banknotes, and on Greece's two-euro coin.[17]

Famous paintings of the scene of abduction produced prior to the long eighteenth century include those by Titian (c. 1490–1576) from 1559–1562, copied by Peter Paul Rubens (1577–1640) around seventy years later, and a 1632 work by Rembrandt (1606–1669).[18] All portray the bull rushing into the sea with Europa. While many visually evoke the sounds of distress, especially the cries from Europa's companions, one of the few to include a specifically musical element is a c. 1725 painting by Giovanni Battista Tiepolo (1696–1770), *Il ratto di Europa* (*The Rape of Europa*, figure 1.1).[19] Portraying an earlier part of the story, here the divinity of the god-disguised-as-bull is symbolized with an eagle (beside which Cupid urinates from a cloud), while in the background is a female companion playing a large frame drum, looking away from the group, and seemingly oblivious to the imminence of the next event.[20] In line with Hall's comments on hybridity, it is worth noting that Tiepolo includes among the retinue of Europa a dark-skinned youth, whose dress and posture suggest a male figure. This is a rare depiction of Blackness in iconography of the story. However, it follows stereotypical condescending characterizations common in other European art of the eighteenth century, as this youth appears to be in a position of service or enslavement, holding out a platter.

---

[15] Salgó, *Images from Paradise*, 54.
[16] Wintle, *Europa and the Bull*, 22.
[17] Salgó, *Images from Paradise*, 51–70.
[18] For a recent survey, see Oakley, "Changing Stories." The painting by Titian is in the Isabella Stewart Gardner Museum, Boston (P26e1); it can be viewed online at https://www.gardnermuseum.org/experience/collection/10978. The Rubens is in the Museo del Prado, Madrid (P001693); online at https://www.museodelprado.es/coleccion/obra-de-arte/el-rapto-de-europa/a136a9c4-3a2f-44bd-ab8a-97fd47c30d7e. The painting by Rembrandt is in the J. Paul Getty Museum, Los Angeles (95.PB.7); online at https://www.getty.edu/art/collection/object/103QS8.
[19] See Gallerie Accademia, Venezia, "Ratto di Europa: Giambattista Tiepolo"; Fondazione Giorgio Cini, "Tiepolo Giambattista—Ratto di Europa."
[20] For a commentary on this painting, although it does not mention the instrumentalist, see Fehl, "Farewell to Jokes," 775–777. See also Wintle, *The Image of Europe*, 110.

Figure 1.1. Giovanni Battista Tiepolo, *Il ratto di Europa* (c. 1720–1725). Gallerie Accademia, Venice, 435. Purchased from Count Francesco Agosti a Belluno. © Galleria dell'Accademia di Venezia/Su concessione del Ministero della Cultura.

Envoicing Europa, in Music for Chamber and Stage

The story of Europa, like other narratives from classical antiquity, became the basis for diverse pieces of music and music drama in early modern Europe.[21] Many sources are lost, which is perhaps why there has not yet been a full-scale critical survey of works on the theme. I will briefly discuss here a range of examples—which vary in scope and settings and in the amount of scholarly attention they have so far attracted—in order to demonstrate their place in musical constructions of Europe. Remarkably, almost all date from the seventeenth and eighteenth centuries and fade away from the record after the first decade of the nineteenth. Perhaps this is because the increasing imperial arrogance of Europeans in global contexts of colonialism was no longer

---

[21] Some are described in Gommers, *Europe*, 137, 141. For a creative take on the transit through several centuries of the representations of Europa in music drama, see Schmale, "Ihr redet Euch die Geschichte schön!"

compatible with the story of their continent's eponym being represented as a defenseless and vulnerable victim.[22] It may also reflect the increasing dominance of maleness in European culture from the eighteenth century onward.[23]

In Mantua in 1608, a year after Alessandro Striggio the younger (c. 1573–1630) and Monteverdi produced their *L'Orfeo* (*Orpheus*), Jupiter's rape of Europa was the subject of an intermedio with text by Gabriello Chiabrera (1552–1638) and music by Giovanni Giacomo Gastoldi (c. 1554–1609). It was performed during festivities for the marriage of Francesco Gonzaga (1586–1612) and Margherita of Savoy (1589–1655).[24] As Bonnie Gordon has discussed, the performance of Europa's lament "Cari paterni regni" ("Dear paternal lands") caused the audience to cry.[25] Relatively little is known of this early work, but it was soon followed by other settings of the tale. Performed at the palace of Millefonti (Turin), at the wedding of Vittorio Amedeo I (1587–1637) and Christine Marie of France (1606–1663), it had a realistic element as it involved actual water: "a canal of prodigious grandeur," as related in a publication of 1715. It featured a ballet scene described as follows: "Then Jupiter appeared, mounted on a bull crowned with flowers, which represented the abduction of Europa, crossing the canal with a group of nymphs, who performed a second musical *récit* appropriate to the subject."[26] This musical

---

[22] Despite the lack of musical settings in the nineteenth and twentieth centuries, the myth does not recede from European public discourse; if anything, visual representations of it became more prevalent, and, as noted above, its imagery is ubiquitous today.

[23] See Schmale, *Gender and Eurocentrism*.

[24] Harrán, "Madama Europa," 207–208; Gordon, *Monteverdi's Unruly Women*, 47, 84; Gordon, "Nuptial Voices," esp. 356. See also T. Carter, *Monteverdi's Musical Theatre*, 76–78. Recently, Gordon has drawn renewed attention to the acts of sexual violence that underlie the stories staged in the Mantuan festivities of 1608 and has outlined ways of teaching and interpreting the musical events in combination with an analysis of paintings and social awareness. In Cusick et al., "Sexual Violence in Opera," 235. For further engagement with the topic, see Renger and Ißler, *Europa—Stier und Sternenkranz*; MacNeil, "Weeping at the Water's Edge," 414.

[25] The chronicler Federico Follino (dates unknown) described the soprano "singing with sweetest harmony these grieving notes that tears of pity arose in the audience." Translation in MacNeil, "Weeping at the Water's Edge," 408. Original text in Follino, *Compendio*, 84. See also Cusick, "'There Was Not One Lady'"; Gordon, "Nuptial Voices," 356. It has been suggested that the part of Europa was possibly sung by Europa Rossi (fl. 1630), a famous singer at the court who was the sister of Salomone Rossi (c. 1570–c. 1630), resulting in the nickname being given to her. That claim has been contested, however, since there is evidence that she had that name much earlier, as Don Harrán has pointed out; even so, he comments that she was a likely candidate for a part, and perhaps her name led to her being considered for the title role. Harrán, "Madama Europa," 207–210. The fact of this symbolic and prominent stage name being held by a Jewish singer in Mantua nevertheless points to the cultural and religious plurality of professional musicians working in elite contexts in early modern Europe. For recent studies displacing and disrupting notions of whiteness in seventeenth-century Italian performance, see Wilbourne, "Little Black Giovanni's Dream"; Wilbourne, "'. . . La curiosità del personaggio.'"

[26] Original text in Bonnet-Bourdelot, *Histoire de la musique*, 365–366.

setting, apparently lost, was performed within the drama *Arione (Arion)*, which Giovanni Capponi (1586–1629) had written for the occasion.[27] Similar examples are an intermezzo titled "Europa rapita da Giove cangiato in toro" ("Europa Raped by Jupiter in the Form of a Bull") with music (now lost) by Ottavio Vernizzi (1569–1649) and text (extant) by Silvestro Branchi (dates unknown), performed in Bologna in 1623.[28] In 1653, festivities for yet another elite wedding included a *dramma per musica* (play for music) titled *Il ratto d'Europa* (*The Rape of Europa*), with a musical setting (which no longer survives) by Francesco Manelli (c. 1595–1667) to a libretto (which does) by Elvezio Sandri (Paolo Emilio Fantuzzi, d. 1661).[29]

These seventeenth-century intermedios in Italy had relatively short texts, and the duration of the music is unknown. Being staged for the higher echelons of society, they likely had a limited yet highly localized impact on popular constructions of Europe. Nevertheless, some people of lower status (relative to the elite) who were in close proximity or who were associated with the works' production—and thus, to use Small's term, musicking—were no doubt aware of them. Most being intended for weddings, these music dramas took as their priority the symbolic association of male rulers' power and might with the omnipotence of Jupiter. Alongside a conspicuous display of the renaissance of classical knowledge, the principal idea they evoked is clearly one of male domination and patriarchy, all amid and in spite of Europa's distress and lamentations. Within them, the question of her connection to a continental toponym remains unstated and implicit; it was probably assumed knowledge. This pattern continues in the earliest setting for which notated music survives, *L'Europa* (*Europa*) by Alessandro Melani (1639–1703). A *festa teatrale* (theatrical festive piece) dating from c. 1667, it is in sixteen movements and is scored for three voices, five string parts, two recorders, and continuo.[30] Its plot elaborates on the original myth; the

---

[27] Fantuzzi, *Notizie degli scrittori bolognesi*, Vol. 3, 92, 95–96. Bonnet-Bourdelot notes that "this festive work [*fête*] was the composition of Jean Capponi [Giovanni Capponi], [a] celebrated musician." Original text in Bonnet-Bourdelot, *Histoire de la musique*, 366.

[28] Roche, "Vernizzi." See Branchi, *Europa rapita da Giove*, 12–15, for the libretto of the "Intermezzo Primo" featuring Europa.

[29] Whenham, "Manelli." For the libretto, see Sandri and Manelli, *Il ratto d'Europa*.

[30] Weaver, "Melani Family (Opera)." Thomas Höft describes it as "a large-scale serenata" and notes that the identity of the librettist is not known. Höft, "L'Europa: Una festa teatrale." The manuscript is held in Vienna at the Österreichische Nationalbibliothek, Musiksammlung, Mus.Hs.18740 MUS MAG. Only one performance was documented at the time, but the work was revived in 2007. A recording of the work was made by Hermann Max and Das Kleine Konzert in 2008; see Melani, *L'Europa; Sacred Works*. For further context on Melani, see also Weaver, "Melani Family (Opera)"; Weaver, "Materiali per le biografie," 294.

character of Cupid plays a vital part in the action, and his interventions result in Europa's eventual love for her captor.

Later that century, there are further examples of the story being set for performance in elite contexts. A short masque by Huguenot writer Peter Anthony Motteux (1663–1718), *The Rape of Europa by Jupiter*, with music by John Eccles (c. 1668–1735), was performed in London "by their Majesties Servants" in 1694.[31] Three years later in the same city, a work invoking Europa was produced at Drury Lane for the celebrations surrounding the Peace of Ryswick. A song for the character of Jupiter, played by Richard Leveridge (1670–1758), specifically mentions Europa and acknowledges her "shrill, shrill cryes" alarming "the Regions of the Gods."[32] Little is known about the stage work, but it is interesting to note that the decontextualized publication of this song, within a collection of diverse vocal pieces, includes the stage direction of Jupiter descending "on his Eagle" and not taking the form of a bull. Although its dramatic function in the presentation of a story involving Europa is unclear, it clearly describes Europa's cries, which frighten the gods "in their heav[']nly abodes."

Besides such works produced for affairs of state and international events, the story moved into a more popular genre for quotidian performance, described by Sir John Hawkins (1719–1789) in 1776 as "a strange conjunction of opera and pantomime, the highest and lowest species of dramatic representation."[33] In commenting on such a form, Hawkins mentioned the contribution of composer John Ernest Galliard (c. 1666/1687–1747) to works that included the 1723 pantomime *Jupiter and Europa*.[34] This work

---

[31] The part of Europa was played by Mrs. Bracegirdle (Anne Bracegirdle, 1671–1748). [Motteux], *The Rape of Europa*, "The Names of the Persons that Sing," n.p. Three songs from it—including one for Europa, "Still, Still I'm Grieving," and another for the nymph Algaura, "Give Then Royal Maid Your Sorrows O're," which in their texts appear somewhat reminiscent of the dialogue of Dido and Belinda at the beginning of the libretto of *Dido and Aeneas* by Nahum Tate (1652–1715)—were published the following year and are extant. Hudgebut, *Thesaurus Musicus*, 9 ("Appear All," sung by Mrs. Hudson [Mary Hodson, c. 1673–after 1718]), 10 ("Still, Still I'm Grieving," sung by Mrs. Bracegirdle), 11 ("Give Then, Royal Maid," sung by Mrs. Cibber [Catherine Cibber, c. 1669–1734]).

[32] The song for Jupiter, "What Wou'd Europa Whose Shrill, Shrille Cryes," composed by Mr. Morgan (Thomas Morgan, fl. 1691–1699) and published in 1697, is described as being "sung by M:ʳ Leveridge in yᵉ Musick of the Peace [of Ryswick]." Morgan, *A Collection of New Songs*, n.p. On Morgan, see Spinks, "Morgan, Thomas." The title suggests an association with a major work produced for this political occasion, *Europe's Revels for the Peace of Ryswick*, with music by John Eccles. See Lowerre, "A *Ballet des nations*," 420. However, Michael Burden notes that this song and two others by Morgan are not included in the play's publication and that "it is possible that they were performed in some other work celebrating the Peace of Ryswick." See his edition of Eccles, *Europe's Revels*, 82.

[33] Hawkins, *A General History*, Vol. 5, 189–190.

[34] It also contained music by a Mr. Cobston (fl. 1723) and Richard Leveridge. Galliard, Cobston, and Leveridge, *Jupiter and Europa*.

was revived in 1736 as *The Royal Chace, or Merlin's Cave*.[35] Notably, some of its songs were published, suggesting the entry of some Europa-related works into domestic practice.[36]

The French royal court and the theaters in Paris are renowned as the locations of some of the most elaborate music dramas of the seventeenth century, and one wonders about the presence of the Europa myth on their stages. Jean-Baptiste Lully (1632–1687) represented Europa and Jupiter explicitly in a court ballet of 1665, *La naissance de Venus* (*The Birth of Venus*), the plot and text of which are attributed to Isaac de Benserade (1613–1691).[37] The first entrée of the second part portrays the abduction, with the part of Europa danced by a man, Monsieur de Souville (dates unknown).[38] No character or performer is listed in the part of Jupiter; one might speculate that the god was represented as a prop or machine in the form of a bull. In the music score, only three instrumental movements for this entrée survive, but Benserade's libretto gives a description of the scene:

> He [Jupiter] gets up, reveals himself in the view of the other nymphs, and going to the sea with such a sweet cargo, carries her to *one of the parts of the world that takes her name*; meanwhile her companions are distressed, and for the sorrow of the loss, break the crowns [of flowers] and bouquets with which they had arrayed themselves.[39] [emphasis added]

Here, unlike in the early-seventeenth-century examples, we see the geographical name of the continent being explicitly connected to the princess. This is a direct—albeit relatively brief—representation of Lully's story of Europa's abduction. Lully later composed music for works that allegorized the continent in other ways (within the symbolic framework of the four parts of the world, as we will see).

It is perhaps surprising that Europa is not the central topic of any high-profile *tragédies en musique* (musical tragedies, the most prominent form of French opera) that Lully created with librettist Philippe Quinault

---

[35] See also Baldwin and Wilson, "'Reviv'd by the Publisher,'" 9–10; Fiske and King, "Galliard, John Ernest."

[36] For example, the song "With Early Horn" was included in Walsh (the younger), *The British Musical Miscellany*, Vol. 5, 122–124.

[37] Lully, "La naissance de Venus." A manuscript copy is held at the Staatsbibliothek zu Berlin–Preußischer Kulturbesitz, Musikabteilung, Am.B 322 (2), ff. 33r–80v.

[38] Benserade, *Ballet royal de la naissance de Venus*, 35–36.

[39] Original text in Benserade, *Ballet royal de la naissance de Venus*, 35.

(1635–1688), many of which drew from Greek mythology. However, their *Isis* (1677) contained some subtle allusions to and analogies with the tale.[40] It was apparently not until the late 1730s that the first full-scale French *tragédie en musique* on the myth was composed, by Jean Laurent de Béthizy (1702–1781): *L'enlèvement d'Europe* (*The Abduction of Europa*).[41] Both music and text are lost, but the periodical *Mercure de France* (*French Mercury*) reports that the prologue and first act had a kind of preview performance on June 6, 1739, at the Concert de la Reine (the Queen's Concert) in Versailles, noting that "it has not yet been given to [performed for] the public."[42]

There does nevertheless survive more extensive evidence of another attempt, not fully realized, at a full-scale *tragédie en musique*, for which the entire text is extant. In 1760, Louis César de La Baume Le Blanc (1708–1780), Duke of La Vallière, observed in a catalogue of "ballets, operas, and other lyric works" that a libretto titled *Europe* (*Europa*), by Antoine-Louis Le Brun (1680–1743), had been published in 1712 but written at an unknown earlier date; he went on to comment that it had "never been set to music."[43] Le Brun's extant printed text consists of the regular *tragédie* structure of a prologue and five acts.[44] Its plot is set in a later period of Europa's life, with the assumption of a preexisting love between her and Jupiter. Europa's father, Agenor, is arranging for her to marry Narbal, a Phoenician prince who has been victorious in battle. However, Jupiter ultimately takes Europa for himself, in Act 5, Scene 2, abducting her from a "rustic temple dedicated to Love" ("Love" presumably being Aphrodite/Venus) at the point of the wedding, under cover of a darkness of night that spreads across the theater.[45] With the lack of evidence of a musical setting, then or now, one can only imagine how this *tragédie* might have been rendered by composers active at the time. Its text invites further examination.

---

[40] As Georgia Cowart suggests, "[i]n *Isis*, Quinault conflates European and Egyptian mythology to identify Isis, a central figure in the Egyptian pantheon, with Io, the nymph abducted by Jupiter/Louis as Europa. The opera thus subordinates the matriarchal eastern goddess to the European patriarchal ideal." Cowart, *The Triumph of Pleasure*, 124.

[41] Gommers, *Europe*, 141; Earhart, "Béthizy."

[42] Original text in *Mercure de France*, Vol. 2, 1435. See also Charlton, *Opera in the Age of Rousseau*, 14. If a staging of other acts and/or the work as a whole took place, references to it have yet to emerge.

[43] Original text in La Baume Le Blanc, *Ballets, opera*, 148.

[44] It is published in Le Brun, *Théatre lyrique*, 269–318.

[45] The description reads: "Une épaisse nuit se répand sur le Théatre, Jupiter dans l'obscurité enleve Europe." Le Brun, *Théatre lyrique*, 311; the temple is described on 309.

A mid-century French music drama on the myth for which there exist both a manuscript score and a printed libretto is *Jupiter et Europe* (*Jupiter and Europa*), a "new entertainment in one act" ("Divertissement nouveau en un Acte"), created in 1749. The text, by Louis Fuzelier (1672–1752), is set by two composers: the first is anonymized in the source, and the second is listed simply as "Dugué, ordinaire de la Musique du Roy." Their identities have been proposed as Nicolas Duport (1690–1773) and Alexandre Julien Dugué (1714–1780).[46] According to both sources, it was "performed before the king [Louis XV (1710–1774; reigned from 1715)] in the theater of the *petits Appartemens* of Versailles." The libretto gives the names of all the performers, some of whom were elite. Among the leading roles, Europa was sung by Madame de Pompadour (Jeanne Antoinette Poisson, 1721–1764)—who famously had a close relationship with the king—and Jupiter by the Marquis de La Salle (Marie-Louis Caillebot, 1716–1796).[47] They were accompanied by a star-studded orchestra, including "Le Sr. Blavet" (Michel Blavet, 1700–1768) on flute and "Le Sr. Mondonville" (Jean-Joseph Cassanéa de Mondonville, 1711–1772) as the leader of the first violins. There was even a royal element among the instrumentalists, with the "Prince de Dombes" (Louis Auguste de Bourbon, 1700–1755), grandson of Louis XIV (1638–1715; reigned from 1643), listed as playing bassoon.[48]

In this production, then, in a celebrated royal court, noble musicians and elite professional performers engaged directly with Europe's foundation myth. In Fuzelier's text, the naming of the continent is acknowledged by the character of Jupiter himself, at the end of the fifth and penultimate scene, where he sings of his desire "that even the future shares the care of celebrating the excess of my love"; he goes on to state that "we reveal to the eyes of Europa a shining image of the peoples that her name must one day bring together."[49] There follows directly the final scene (see figure 1.2), which is set by the side of "the principal rivers of Europe" and involves Jupiter, Europa, and "Genies in the form of different peoples who must dwell in Europe."[50]

---

[46] Fuzelier, *Fragmens*. See Cyr, "Duport"; "Alexandre Julien Dugué." La Baume Le Blanc lists just Dugué. La Baume Le Blanc, *Ballets, opera*, 222. For the music score, see Duport and Dugué, "Jupiter et Europe," manuscript.

[47] Fuzelier, *Fragmens*, [6]. See also La Baume Le Blanc, *Ballets, opera*, 222. For discussion of the Marquis de La Salle, see Rosow, "Lully's *Armide*," 182.

[48] Fuzelier, *Fragmens*, [3].

[49] "Que l'avenir même partage / Le soin de célébrer l'excès de mon amour; / Qu'on trace aux yeux d'Europe une brillante image / Des peuples que son nom doit rassembler un jour." Fuzelier, *Fragmens*, 19–20; Duport and Dugué, "Jupiter et Europe," 51–52.

[50] Original text in Duport and Dugué, "Jupiter et Europe," 53.

Figure 1.2. Nicolas Duport, Alexandre Julien Dugué, and Louis Fuzelier, "Jupiter et Europe," Bibliothèque Nationale de France, Département de la Musique, RES VMA MS-1241, 53.

It consists of a "March of the Genies," a chorus that they sing, and a number of dance movements: passepieds and then an "Air for the Italians." Europa sings a *cantatille* (little cantata), which is followed by a "march for the Spaniards" and then an allemande (with no role indicated but clearly referencing Germans through the name of the genre). Although the French are not named here, they are perhaps are implicitly represented by the passepied, a dance with French origins. This is clearly a Europe of nations, with their distinct characteristics.

Besides works intended for elaborate staging, there exist various cantatas on the theme of Europa in Italian, French, and English. The earliest traceable example, a work for solo voice and continuo, is attributed to two different composers—Alessandro Scarlatti (1660–1725) and Lelio Colista (1629–1680)—in the two surviving sources.[51] Titled *Europa rapita da Giove in forma di toro* (*Europa Abducted/Raped by Jove in the Form of a Bull*), it is set for solo voice and continuo and begins, "Era già l'alba e in cielo" ("It was already dawn and in the sky"). Although the text makes no explicit connection between Europa and the continent's name, it brings the ancient princess into more recent chronological contexts, mentioning "the unfaithful Arab" and "the Turkish herds," thus referring to some political and religious concerns of the time.[52]

Three French cantatas published between 1703 and 1745 set the story of Europa: *Jupiter et Europe* (*Jupiter and Europa*, 1703, republished 1745) by Nicolas Bernier (1664–1734) with text by Jean-Baptiste Rousseau (1671–1741); *Europe* (*Europa*, 1728) by Michel Pignolet de Montéclair (1667–1737); and *Europpe* [sic] (*Europa*, 1729) by François Collin de Blamont (1690–1760).[53] The same is true of a work titled *Concert françois: Europe et Jupiter* (1715) by a "Mr. Alexandre" (identified as Alexandre Pasquier, dates unknown); set for two voices (soprano and bass), flutes, violins, and continuo,

---

[51] Scarlatti, "Europa rapita da Giove," manuscript. Colista, "Europa rapita," manuscript. Thanks to Rosalind Halton for her helpful discussion of these sources.

[52] Scarlatti, "Europa rapita," ff. 173v, 175r-v.

[53] [Bernier], *Cantates françoises*, 88–125; Bernier, *Cantates françoises*, 88–125. A translation of Rousseau's text for Bernier's cantata is given in Gommers, *Europe*, 137–138. For an analysis of a segment from the first duo of this cantata, see Gjerdingen, "Partimento, que me veux-tu?," 99–100. For information on the attribution of the text and its sources, see Berton, "Bernier." Montéclair's work is for solo voice and continuo with a violin or flute. Montéclair, *Cantates a une et a deux voix avec simphonie*, 76–90. For a recent edition by Cedric Lee, see Montéclair, *Europe*. The text is by Ignace François de Limojon de Saint-Didier (1669–1739) and appears to be from his novel *Le voyage du Parnasse* (1716). Limojon de Saint Didier, *Le voyage du Parnasse*, 160–161. Collin de Blamont's "Europpe" is set for "voix seule & symphonie" (solo voice and symphony), the latter implying an accompanying ensemble indicated as flute or viol and harpsichord. Collin de Blamont, *Cantates françoises a voix seule*, 36–67; Gommers, *Europe*, 141; Anthony, "Collin [Colin] de Blamont."

it is the most extensive, with a score of fifty-five pages.[54] The cantata's plot begins after the abduction. Its text blatantly praises Jupiter and urges Europa to share in the glory of union with him, but she sings of her fears. Jupiter makes her immortal, and eventually—in this predictably coercive narrative—the two sing a duet wishing that "love alone" be "the master" of their happiness.[55] None of these French chamber works explicitly connects Europa with the geographical name of the continent, although they may allude to contemporaneous political events at court.[56]

Another cantata does explicitly narrate the aspect of eponymy: an English work for solo voice and continuo titled *Jupiter and Europa*, composed by William Hayes (1708–1777), professor of music at the University of Oxford, and self-published in 1742.[57] Hayes's setting of the story was probably meant to display his erudition in classical themes as much as his skills in musical composition. It is a short work structured as recitative–aria, recitative–aria. The text of the last movement is in the voice of Venus (she is described in its preceding recitative as "the Queen of Love"), who exhorts Europa to stop grieving and embrace joy as she realizes her position as the "Wife of Jove." In the B section of the concluding aria, she sings: "where will be your Country[']s shame, when half the world receives your name."[58] The text of this aria and its preceding recitative seem to be paraphrased from Horace's *Odes* (Book 3, Ode 27)—although Hayes leaves out the description of Venus "smiling deceitfully" ("perfidum rides") just before speaking to Europa.[59] Again, Jupiter's assault of the princess is downplayed.

From mid-century, examples decline in number, but four works based on Europa can be highlighted: a ballet, an opera, and two cantatas. In 1776, a *pantomime héroïque* (heroic pantomime) titled *L'enlèvement d'Europe* (*The Abduction of Europa*), with music by Jean-Baptiste Rochefort (1746–1819), was performed in Paris; a catalogue of 1785 elaborates that it was a ballet written for a group described as "grands Danseurs de corde" (great tightrope walkers and acrobats).[60] Such a label is likely a reference to the Grands

---

[54] [Pasquier], *Concert françois*. A copy is held in the Bibliothèque Nationale de France, Département de la Musique, D-12568. Pasquier's surname is inscribed by hand on the title page.
[55] "Que de nôtre bonheur l'Amour seul soit le Maître." [Pasquier], *Concert françois*, 44.
[56] Thanks to Jean-Christophe Frisch for discussion of this point.
[57] W. Hayes, *Vocal and Instrumental Musick*, Part II, 31–34; Heighes, *The Lives and Works of William and Philip Hayes*, 118–121.
[58] Hayes, *Vocal and Instrumental Musick*, 34.
[59] Horace, *Odes and Epodes*, 208 (Latin), 209 (translation) (Book 3, Ode 27, line 67).
[60] *Les spectacles de Paris*, Vol. 34, 210. See also Gommers, *Europe*, 141.

Danseurs et Sauteurs du Roi, a group founded and directed by Jean-Baptiste Nicolet (1728–1796), which in 1772 attracted the admiration of the king and received from him the royal part of its name.[61] Rochefort's composition appears to have remained in the repertory for several years. The newspaper *Chronique du Paris* (*Chronicle of Paris*) for November 19, 1789, advertises the work to be performed that day—incidentally taking place little more than four months after the storming of the Bastille—as "the second encore of *The Abduction of Europa by Jupiter in the Form of a Bull*, pantomime with large [stage] machines, in four acts."[62] Its score is lost, but music by Rochefort for other ballets may give an idea of the kind of musical style that he espoused. Even so, one wonders about the ways in which the story was paced, narrated, and represented and especially how the abduction scene of the plot was physically enacted, given that it involved tightropes.

In 1778, musical representations of Europa entered a new phase and the center stage of opera history. She became the subject of the inaugural performance in a new theater in Milan: the Nuovo Regio Ducale Teatro alla Scala, now known as La Scala. This was *Europa riconosciuta* (*Europa Recognized* or *Europa Revealed*), a two-act work with music by Antonio Salieri (1750–1825) and libretto by Mattia Verazi (c. 1730–1794).[63] An extravagant production with a star-studded cast, the opera was so specific and demanding in its performance requirements that it was not produced again that century and, in fact, was not revived until 2004.[64] The role of Europa, which demands a wide vocal range, was performed by soprano Marina Balducci (c. 1758–after 1784), who could sing up to g^3.[65] Some of her parts involved virtuosic coloratura at impressively high tessituras, and John Rice notes that the writing for her reaches a top F sharp, remarking that "hers is quite possibly the highest vocal line in any of Salieri's operas."[66]

Instead of presenting the story of Europa's abduction and rape by the god-disguised-as-bull, the librettist imagines another episode in her life, when she is married to Asterio (Asterion/Asterius), king of Crete.[67] Caroline Neubaur has observed that Verazi demythologized the subject, removing the violent acts of

---

[61] Isherwood, "The Festivity of the Parisian Boulevards," 297.
[62] Original text in "Spectacles," 352.
[63] Gommers, *Europe*, 141. For a recent study of music for this opera, see E. Stokes, "Antonio Salieri's Musical Recycling."
[64] Rice, *Antonio Salieri*, 267; Toscani, "Europa riconosciuta," 27.
[65] Verazi, *Europa riconosciuta*, 11; Libby, "Balducci."
[66] Rice, *Antonio Salieri*, 264.
[67] For a summary of the plot, see Rice, *Antonio Salieri*, 259.

Zeus/Jupiter; Claudio Toscani writes that the plot comes from the *Genealogie deorum gentilium* (*On the Genealogy of the Gods of the Gentiles*) of 1360 by Giovanni Boccaccio (1313–1375).[68] The title of the opera itself may reflect new cultural sensibilities surrounding the figure of Europa. Neubaur suggests that the "recognition" of Europa was an allegory for the legitimacy and authority of the rule of Empress Maria Theresa (1717–1780; reigned from 1743) over Lombardy.[69] Salieri was also seen to achieve a certain French-Italian stylistic synthesis in the music, as Marita P. McClymonds has highlighted, contributing to the sense of Europeanness as cultural integration or fusion.[70]

There are few examples that postdate this singular opera, a (literally) high point of works based on Europa. Two cantatas return to the conventional plot of the myth, involving Zeus/Jupiter. One is an unpublished setting by Francesco Bianchi (c. 1752–1810) with multiple instruments, titled—like earlier Italian examples—*Europa rapita* (*The Rape of Europa*); it is dated 1792, when the composer was based in Milan.[71] The text treats the serene setting in which Europa and her companions relaxed, the arrival of the bull, the abduction, and Europa's lament, with no consoling conclusion. The other comes from the first decade of the nineteenth century: *Europa in Creta* (*Europa in Crete*), with text by Luigi Prividali (1771–1844) and music by Ferdinando Paer (1771–1839). In this cantata's plot, the assault has already occurred, and Europa narrates how she is left alone and trembling on the beach, seeking help but not daring to move. It appears to have been originally intended for diegetic performance within a larger work: a "dramatic composition" titled *Arianna consolata* (*Ariadne Consoled*), dated 1803. In its Part 1, Scene 7, Pane (Pan) requests that the character Siringa (Syrinx) sing "Europa in Creta" to comfort Ariadne (who was, in Greek mythology, the daughter of Minos and thus the granddaughter of Europa).[72] Also published in Leipzig as an independent piece in 1810, *Europa in Creta* is the latest work on the topic that has so far emerged.[73] From that point onward, there seem to be few

---

[68] Neubaur, "*Europa riconosciuta*," 64; Toscani, "Europa riconosciuta," 22.

[69] Neubaur, "*Europa riconosciuta*," 64.

[70] McClymonds, "Salieri and the Franco-Italian Synthesis," 77–88. See also Stokes, "Antonio Salieri's Musical Recycling."

[71] Francesco Bianchi, "Europa rapita," manuscript.

[72] Prividali and Paer, *Arianna consolata: Accademia per musica* (1803), 28–29. A slightly different version of the diegetic performance as a whole appears in the printed text Prividali and Paer, *Arianna consolata: Accademia per musica* (1806); "Europa in Creta" appears on 16–17 in Part 1, Scene 5. Paer's score for *Arianna consolata* is in the Biblioteca del Conservatorio di Musica Luigi Cherubini, Florence (I-Fc), 2 vols., F.P.T.342.

[73] Paer, *Europa in Creta*.

musical traces of the Europa story. As mentioned earlier, one might speculate that this decline is related to an increasing hesitancy to highlight on the stage or in a concert setting a shameful element of evolving European identity, in a time of otherwise increasingly triumphalist discourse on Europe.[74]

Europe in a Quartet of Continents

Besides the princess Europa, an allegorical personification of the continent—sometimes conflated with the princess but more often not—was also represented onstage, usually alongside Africa, Asia, and the Americas.[75] In visual representations, there was a hierarchy of continents at play, with some details influenced by a normative manual of symbols in art written by Cesare Ripa (1555–1622), his *Iconologia*. First published in 1593, this treatise had a lasting legacy; it was reissued and translated on numerous occasions in the seventeenth and eighteenth centuries.[76] In the first illustrated edition of 1603, Ripa advised artists to depict Europe with a crown, "to show that Europe has always been superior, and queen of all the world," and recommended the inclusion of a horse, as well as a range of arms, an owl, and musical instruments.[77] Although the last element is not prominent in the 1603 print, the relevant plate of the 1613 edition shows Europe with a lute to her right, representing arts and rational order (figure 1.3).[78] In an English translation of 1778, the text on Europe states that "the trophies, the owl upon the books, and the musical instruments and other things lying at her feet, denote her superiority above all other parts of the world, with respect to arms, to literature, and all the liberal arts."[79] Musical instruments and, later, images of notation

---

[74] European identity was moving more toward hegemonic masculinity. See Schmale, *Gender and Eurocentrism*.

[75] Literature on the allegorical conceptualization of the four continents, or "four parts of the world," is vast, but there have been recent major studies that have combined the approaches of art history with the perspectives of anthropology, literary criticism, and global history. See Bethencourt, *Racisms*, 65–82; Horowitz and Arizzoli, *Bodies and Maps*; Schmale, Romberg, and Köstlbauer, *The Language of Continent Allegories*. See also Shirley, "Allegorical Images of Europe."

[76] Ripa, *Iconologia* (1593). However, the first edition did not include an entry for Europe.

[77] Original text in Ripa, *Iconologia* (1603), 332. See also Pagden, "Europe: Conceptualizing a Continent," 51 (he cites a 1611 edition published in Padua).

[78] Ripa, *Iconologia* (1613), Part 2, 63. The illustration of 1603, which does not show musical instruments, is at Ripa, *Iconologia* (1603), 333.

[79] Translation in Drace-Francis, *European Identity*, 32. From Ripa and Richardson, *Iconology*, Vol. 1, 30.

MUSICAL CONSTRUCTIONS OF EUROPE 53

DONNA ricchiſſimamente veſtita di habito Regale di più colori, con vna corona in teſta, & che ſieda in mezzo di due cornucopia incrociati,l'vno pieno d'ogni ſorte di frutti, grani,migli,panichi, riſi,& ſimili,e l'altro d'vue bianche, & negre. con la deſtra mano tiene vn belliſſimo tempio, & con il dito indice della ſiniſtra mano, moſtri Regni, Corone diuerſe, Scettri, ghirlande, & ſimili coſe, che gli ſtaranno da vna parte, & da l'altra vi ſarà vn cauallo con trofei, ſcudi,& più ſorte d'armi, vi ſarà ancora vn libro, & ſopra di eſſo vna ciuetta, & à canto diuerſi inſtromenti muſicali, vna ſquadra, alcuni ſcarpelli, & vna tauoletta, laquale ſogliono adoperare i pittori con diuerſi colori ſopra, & vi ſaranno anco alquanti pennelli.

Figure 1.3. Allegorical depiction of Europa, crowned, with lute and owl to her lower right. Cesare Ripa, *Iconologia di Cesare Ripa perugino* (Siena: Matteo Florimi, 1613), Part 2, 63, CC-BY. Image belonging to the holdings of the Biblioteca Nacional de España.

were accorded exclusively to Europe but denied to the other continents. We see a musical Eurocentrism personified.

The allegorical system of the "four parts of the world," highly popular throughout the seventeenth and eighteenth centuries, has been studied in detail by art historians and historians in a number of recent projects, including a detailed survey and analysis of examples in the southern parts of the Holy Roman Empire.[80] The Jesuits were particularly prominent in making use of the genre, which is perhaps unsurprising, given the rapid geographical expansion of their mission to each of these continents from the 1540s onward. As a form of propaganda and as part of their aims to universalize their religious message, they implemented this iconographic program in many of their churches. One of the most famous examples is the fresco completed in 1694 by Andrea Pozzo (1642–1709) on the ceiling of the church of Sant' Ignazio in Rome, titled *Gloria di Sant'Ignazio* (*Glorification of St. Ignatius*), celebrating the founder of the Society of Jesus, Ignatius of Loyola (1491–1556); Makoto Harris Takao describes it as "a representational configuration of the geography of Catholicism."[81] Pozzo created the illusion of a dome on a flat surface, as Luke Clossey notes, and the four painted continents appear to be supported by "each of the great vault's abutments."[82] The "four parts of the world" theme adorned many Jesuit churches throughout their provinces and, more generally, became common in popular Catholicism of the southern German-speaking lands.[83]

Probably the best-known eighteenth-century example of these painted allegories is an enormous fresco above the main staircase in the residence of the prince-bishop of Würzburg (figure 1.4a).[84] Completed by Tiepolo in

---

[80] See a database of examples from the south of the Holy Roman Empire at https://erdteilallegorien.univie.ac.at, produced as part of the project "A Discourse and Art Historical Analysis of the Allegories of the Four Continents in the South of the Holy Roman Empire and Its Documentation in a Hypermedia Environment" (2012–2016), funded by the Austrian Science Fund (FWF). For descriptions and outputs, see Romberg, "Continent Allegories in the Baroque Age"; Schmale, Romberg, and Köstlbauer, *The Language of Continent Allegories*. Other recent scholarship includes Shirley, "Allegorical Images of Europe," and the collection of essays in Horowitz and Arizzoli, *Bodies and Maps*. See also Spira, "Allegories of the Four Continents." For a study of depictions of Europe, see Wintle, *The Image of Europe*. For sixteenth-century representations of America, see Markey, "Stradano's Allegorical Invention." See also Rife, "The Exotic Gift," 149n40.

[81] Sterba, "From Conversion to Adoration," 176, 234 (fig. 47); Takao, "Encounters in the Glocal Mirror," 240, also 1–2.

[82] Clossey, *Salvation and Globalization*, 85–86.

[83] Horowitz, "Introduction (1): Rival Interpretations," 7–8; Sterba, "From Conversion to Adoration"; Ferlan, "A Global Context"; Schmale, "Continent Allegories"; Romberg, "Continent Allegories in the Baroque Age."

[84] For analyses of this painting, see Ashton, "Allegory, Fact, and Meaning"; Schmale, "Continent Allegories," 38–40.

Figure 1.4a. Staircase with fresco (completed 1753) by Giovanni Battista Tiepolo in the Würzburg Residence. DI016543 Treppenhaus, Blick Richtung Süden, R. 3, Würzburg, Residenz und Hofgarten. © Bildarchiv Foto Marburg/ Bayerische Schlösserverwaltung/Achim Bunz (CbDD).

Figure 1.4b. Detail of figure 1.4a, showing the allegorical figure of Europe with musicians. DI016543 Treppenhaus, Blick Richtung Süden, R. 3, Würzburg, Residenz und Hofgarten. © Bildarchiv Foto Marburg/Bayerische Schlösserverwaltung/Achim Bunz (CbDD).

1753, it depicts the four continents in an explicit hierarchy. Schmale, in his detailed analysis of the work, notes that its allegorical language points to a stadial and teleological view of human history, with the four parts of the world depicted with different levels of "civilization" (America, Africa, Asia, then Europe). This idea is reinforced by viewers' experience of seeing the work as they ascend the staircase, since Europe is the final continent to become visible; with her accoutrements and retinue (including musicians; see detail in figure 1.4b), she is represented as "the pinnacle of the history of civilization."[85] A smaller study made in advance of the fresco, now in the Metropolitan Museum, shows the whole scheme in a single view (figure 1.5).[86] In each of these images, the figure of Europe is enthroned, with a white bull—a Zeus/Jupiter who is possibly now depicted as domesticated—by her side, whereas the other continents sit on animals: respectively, a crocodile, a

---

[85] Schmale, "Continent Allegories," 38–40, 43. See also Pagden, "Europe: Conceptualizing a Continent," 51.

[86] The image can be viewed online (with capacity to zoom in) at https://www.metmuseum.org/art/collection/search/437790.

MUSICAL CONSTRUCTIONS OF EUROPE 57

Figure 1.5. Giovanni Battista Tiepolo, *Allegory of the Planets and Continents* (1752), oil on canvas. The Metropolitan Museum of Art, 1977.1.3. Gift of Mr. and Mrs. Charles Wrightsman, 1977. Public Domain (CC0).

camel, and an elephant.[87] Music appears only in association with Europe and not with Africa, America, or Asia; in both versions of the painting, Europe is accompanied by a singer and players of string and wind instruments.[88] Schmale observes that "Europe stands for the *telos* of History . . . and it was relatively 'easy' to express this message using the continent allegory: Instead of reading 500 pages or several volumes of a learned book, one needed only to look at a fresco in a palace or church."[89]

Beyond palaces or churches, these allegories also entered into domestic contexts and more popular consciousness. A number of artists produced paintings or tapestries with four sections, or four individual paintings in a series, that presented allegorical personifications or representations of the "four parts of the world." For example, in Mexico, a *biombo* (a painted folding screen based on a Japanese model) by Juan Correa (c. 1645/1650–1716) depicted the four continents.[90] In Europe, porcelain figurines and other three-dimensional sculptures became popular in the eighteenth century.[91] The trope reached to more ubiquitous and everyday objects for personal use. For example, an engraved design for a fan from the mid-1790s demonstrates the extent to which this program had been internalized but also diversified (figure 1.6). Here Europe—holding hands with Asia—has an open music score before her, while the border above includes a lyre.[92] Again, music is linked exceptionally with Europe.

Some painters created non-anthropomorphized allegories in which the continents were represented through an abstract gathering of objects and implied themes. In one such work, a painting of 1722 by French artist Jean-Baptiste Oudry (1686–1755) titled *L'allégorie de l'Europe* (*Allegory of Europe*), the viewer's attention is immediately commanded by a monkey, frozen in an animated pose, which clasps a violin and bow (figure 1.7).[93] A bust that seems to be of Minerva, Roman goddess of wisdom, faces the other direction, while the foreground is completed by an array of musical instruments

---

[87] Pagden, "Europe: Conceptualizing a Continent," 51; Schmale, "Continent Allegories," 39. Apart from Asia, these are divergences from Ripa, who recommended a horse for Europe, a lion for Africa, and a reptile for America. See Spira, "Allegories of the Four Continents."

[88] Anthony Rowland-Jones has observed that the musicians in the fresco correspond to three figures painted on a harpsichord lid, which is in turn based on Tiepolo's painting *Minuetto con Pantalone e Colombina* (c. 1756). Rowland-Jones, "The Minuet," 415, 422–423.

[89] Schmale, "Continent Allegories," 43.

[90] Hernández Araico, "El código festivo," 86.

[91] There are examples in the National Gallery of Victoria, Melbourne; see "The Four Continents (c. 1770)."

[92] "[Allégorie des quatre continents]," engraving from 1794–1798.

[93] For further details of this artwork, see https://emuseum.mfah.org/objects/18445/allegory-of-europe.

Figure 1.6. Engraved design for a fan with an allegory of the four continents (1794–1798). "[Allégorie des quatre continents]," in "Recueil d'éventails de la fin du XVIIIe siècle," Vol. 1, "VL38.18" [ESTNUM-19423]. Bibliothèque Nationale de France, Département Estampes et Photographie, LC-13-FOL. Sourced from gallica.bnf.fr.

Figure 1.7. Jean-Baptiste Oudry, *Allegory of Europe* (1722). The Museum of Fine Arts, Houston, BF.1987.2. Sarah Campbell Blaffer Foundation, Houston.

and sheet music as well as a parrot and a pot of variegated red and green foliage. The instruments—violin, musette, recorder, guitar—and sheet music embody the assumed reification of the arts, while Minerva's serene countenance implies the purported transcendence of European wisdom. These are complemented by the natural impulses of the small primate, whose direct attraction to the violin and bow seems to suggest homage paid by nature itself to European culture, with nature's imitative instincts naturally drawn to the music. Imitation was a key component of the French eighteenth-century approach to arts, and it is significant that both the animals depicted here are known for their mimetic acts.

Humans are represented by their absence and in the remnants of their material culture: instruments and scores, inanimate objects that become musical only when animated by their players. Like plants, these artifacts are vulnerable to the vicissitudes of time and the natural processes of decay. In Oudry's painting, the artifice of culture and the serenity of wisdom could be seen simultaneously to transcend nature as well as being subject to its laws. It is interesting to note that the two animals and the plant bring other continents into the frame of this allegory (although all likely involve some artistic license): the monkey resembles a tufted capuchin (*Sapajus apella*) or maybe a golden-bellied capuchin (*Sapajus xanthosternos*) from South America; the bird is likely an African gray parrot (*Psittacus erithacus*); and the plant's appearance suggests the "devil's backbone" (*Euphorbia tithymaloides*), native to the Americas but long cultivated as an ornamental plant in Europe, Africa, and Asia.[94] One wonders whether the botanical representation here alludes to Asia.

The All-Singing, All-Dancing Parts of the World

Besides frozen visual representations, the continents were brought to life through performance, a practice that has attracted scholarly attention over the past century. Research into this remarkable phenomenon can trace its impetus back to the efforts of James Hazen Hyde (1876–1959), a wealthy art connoisseur who collected many iconographical examples of the four continents (the bulk of which he bequeathed to the Metropolitan Museum of Art) and who published in 1926–1927 a pioneering two-part article on "The Four Parts of the World as Represented in Old-Time Pageants and Ballets."[95] In more recent times, some scholars have studied representations of individual continents, especially America, in festivals in Europe.[96] Others have considered all four continents' personifications in music and dance, with studies including those by Ellen R. Welch, a specialist in French literature

---

[94] Thanks to Robert Attenborough, Suresh Babu, Krishna N. Balasubramaniam, Alison Behie, Nick Davies, Jacob Dunn, Howard Griffiths, and Sylvain Lemoine for their expert advice in matching Oudry's depictions to species.

[95] Hyde, "The Four Parts of the World Part I"; Hyde, "The Four Parts of the World Part II." See also Hyde, "L'iconographie." On Hyde's collection, see Spira, "Allegories of the Four Continents"; Cooper Union Museum for the Arts of Decoration, *The Four Continents*.

[96] See, for example, Boorsch, "America in Festival Presentations"; Bloechl, *Native American Song*, 154–172 (including a table of Lully's works representing "Indians," "Americans," or "savages" on 156–159).

and theater, and Colombian musicologist Egberto Bermúdez.[97] In this section, I follow the example of Bermúdez in connecting iconography of the four parts of the world to their animation in performance.

In France, the continents were represented at a number of court festivals through costume, dance, and song, although their evocation was not so common as to become ubiquitous.[98] The *Ballet du grand bal de la douairière de Billebahault* (*Ballet of the Grand Ball of the Dowager of Bilbao*) of 1626 is one of the most prominent early examples.[99] The published libretto, containing verses by René Bordier (died c. 1658), poet of Louis XIII (1601–1643; reigned from 1610), gives descriptions and rubrics that clearly indicate the four parts of the world, along with other regions such as Greenland.[100] In 1669, the *Ballet royal de Flore* (*Royal Ballet of Flora*), with text by Benserade, involved dances by representations of the four continents and by troupes of dancers representing Europeans, Africans, Asians or Persians, and Americans, in honor of Louis XIV.[101] Lully's musical setting of this work includes a *récit* (sung declamation) by the character of Europe, two instrumental movements titled "Air pour l'Europe" ("Air for Europe"), and two choruses "des quatre parties du monde" ("of the four parts of the world").[102] Nothing in the music for the continents was stylistically differentiated from conventional Lullian forms; rather, the distinctive forms of representation were found in the visual elements of costuming.

The all-singing, all-dancing parts of the world also appeared in many places besides France. In Lisbon in 1610, for example, they were represented in festivities for the beatification of Ignatius of Loyola, as related by Jesuit Claude François Ménestrier (1631–1705) in the 1682 treatise *Des ballets*

---

[97] Welch, *A Theater of Diplomacy*; Bermúdez, "'Las cuatro partes del mundo.'"
[98] Welch, *A Theater of Diplomacy*, 101.
[99] Powell, *Music and Theatre*, 90; Whaples, "Exoticism in Dramatic Music," 18–19; Whaples, "Early Exoticism Revisited," 7. See also discussions in Pisani, *Imagining Native America in Music*, 25–27; and Bloechl, *Native American Song*, 1–2. It has been referred to by the title of *Ballet des quatre parties du monde*. See Hyde, "The Four Parts of the World Part II," 27.
[100] Bordier, *Grand bal de la douairière de Billebahault*. Thanks to Rose A. Pruiksma for sharing her expertise on this work.
[101] Welch, *A Theater of Diplomacy*, 147. Benserade, *Ballet royal de Flore*, 34. Bloechl notes that the king performed the character of "a European." Bloechl, *Native American Song*, 155. See also her discussion of iconographic representations of the continents honoring Louis XIV in Bloechl, *Opera and the Political Imaginary*, 37.
[102] See Lully, "Ballet royal de Flore," manuscript, 39 ("récit de l'Europe"), 41–45 ("Choeur des quatre parties du monde"), 46–47 ("[Marche] Pour les 4. Parties du monde"). For a reduced version, see Lully, "Partition des huit divertissemens des vieux ballets," manuscript, 44 ("Prelude des 4 parties du monde"), 45 (corresponding but unlabeled *récit* for Europe), 48–50 (corresponding chorus of the four parts of the world), 50–51 ("Air pour l'Europe" and "2e air"). For a recording, see Lully, *Lully: Ballet Royal de Flore*.

anciens et modernes selon les regles du theatre (*Of Ancient and Modern Ballets, According to the Rules of the Theater*).[103] This author stresses the connections between Ignatius and the ambassadors representing the continents, stating that

> to recognize the benefits that all the Parts of the world had received from him, [they] came to pay homage to him, and to offer him gifts, with the respects of the kingdoms and dependent provinces from each of these Parts. . . . Subsequently the peoples of diverse nations, each group dressed in the style of their country, performed a very agreeable ballet, consisting of four groups or quadrilles for the four Parts of the World.[104]

A few decades later in Naples, celebrations that followed news of the birth of the Prince of Asturias Felipe Próspero (1657–1661) included a representation "of the Empire that the new Prince would inherit, with four triumphal carriages bearing musicians and costumed figures for the four continents of the Spanish Empire: Europe, America, Asia, and Africa," as Louise Stein has noted.[105] In 1709, Augustus II (1670–1733), elector of Saxony (from 1694) and king of Poland (from 1709), presented "a procession and *Carrousel of the Four Nations of the World*" on the occasion of a state visit by king Frederik IV of Denmark (1671–1730; reigned from 1699).[106] Across oceans, the continents were also represented in festivities within colonies of Spain and Portugal.[107] In the Philippines, for example, Jesuit Pedro Murillo Velarde (1696–1753) described one such representation of 1748 in vivid detail.[108]

---

[103] Ménestrier, *Des ballets*.

[104] Original text in Ménestrier, *Des ballets*, 104–105.

[105] Stein, "Festivity and Spectacle," 279.

[106] Bowles goes on to note that the group representing Asia included "an ensemble of a dozen musicians performing *Türckischer musique* on five shawms, three large field drums, three pairs of timpani and cymbals." Bowles, "The Impact of Turkish Military Bands," 547–548.

[107] Bermúdez, in his extensive survey and analysis of this phenomenon, offers examples of cases in cities such as Potosí, Goa, Bahía, Santa Fé (Bogotá), and Popayán. Bermúdez, "'Las cuatro partes del mundo,'" 32–39. Bermúdez also points out that the vogue for the theme continued into the nineteenth century. He has critically examined some remarkable painted fragments from a mural in a house in the small town of Palmas del Socorro, in northeast Colombia, dating from the early nineteenth century, which were mostly lost when the building collapsed in 2014 (but fortunately photographed two years earlier); surviving snippets of text accompanying the images of the continents indicate that Europe was depicted in typical fashion with musical elements: violin and guitar. Bermúdez, "'Las cuatro partes del mundo,'" 11–14, 39–53 (see discussion of Europe on 48).

[108] Murillo Velarde, *Historia de la Provincia*, ff. 218v–219r; Brillantes-Silvestre, "Literatura, música y cultura." For the context surrounding these celebrations, see Irving, *Colonial Counterpoint*, 220–221.

If Jesuits played a prominent role in popularizing this theme in the seventeenth and eighteenth centuries, so did some of their former students. In 1659, the last full year of the Commonwealth period of Puritan rule in England, the Jesuit-educated English writer Richard Fleckno (died c. 1678) published his masque *The Mariage of Oceanus and Brittania: An Allegoricall Fiction, Really Declaring Englands Riches, Glory, and Puissance by Sea*.[109] It involved dancers who represented Asia, Africa, America, and Europe. Fleckno was perhaps more qualified to write about the four continents than his peers in London; he had traveled widely and in 1654 had even published a voyage account that listed the four parts of the world in its title.[110] His work's musical settings (also by him) are lost, but the libretto provides much detail about the performance. Given the nationalistic themes that the title indicates, it is perhaps unsurprising that the allegorical figures of Britannia and the Ocean prevail over all others. The continents are invited to pay homage to Britannia:

> *Come* Europe, *swarthy* Affrica,
> *Rich* Asia *and* America
> *Bring your treasures all away*
> *Tributo* [sic] *to pay*
> *Unto* Brittanias *Throne*
> *Come quickly come*.[111]

Fleckno goes on to give this description of staging: "Here the four parts of the World enter. *Asia* in *Turkish* habit, *Affrica* in Moorish, and all black, *America*, swarthy in a featherd garment; and *Europe* fair and richly clad. And daucing first severally their entrance they deliver their riches to *Oceanus*, who presents them to *Brittania*, in this following Song."[112] The subsequent vocal number refers to Asia bringing silk, Europe fruit, and Africa "all its wealth to boot"; America brings "no lesse precious things then [sic] they." Directions for action then indicate that they "all do reverence to Brittania, and daunce with Castanietes."[113] Such a scene provides a rare example of Europe being

---

[109] Fleckno, *The Mariage*. On this work, see Wiseman, *Drama and Politics*, 135–136.
[110] Fleckno, *A Relation of Ten Years Travell*. Most mentions of music in this travelogue occur during his time in Europe, although there is one discussion of a performance of fiddles and dancing aboard ship and a reference to "an excellent set of Trumpets," during his voyage from Lisbon to Brazil (see 63; it refers to events in 1648).
[111] Fleckno, *The Mariage*, 32–33.
[112] Fleckno, *The Mariage*, 33.
[113] Fleckno, *The Mariage*, 34.

represented on the same hierarchical stratum as the other continents. In using castanets, which were a marker of exoticism, she participates in dance on an ostensibly equal level with her counterparts. Even so, her character is described as visually distinctive, having a "fair" appearance and being dressed in clothes that are implied as superior to those of the others, as mentioned above.[114]

Following the restoration of the British monarchy, such representations continued. From December 1674, the masque *Calisto: Or, the Chaste Nimph* was staged at the court of Charles II (1630-1685; reigned from 1660), twenty to thirty times over a period of two months, with performers including nobles as well as court musicians.[115] The libretto was by John Crowne (1641-1712), who, like Fleckno, had crossed oceans. Early in his life, he had lived in Nova Scotia and Boston (studying at Harvard between 1657 and 1660).[116] The music, only some of which survives, was by Nicholas Staggins (d. 1700), who had been appointed Master of the King's Musick just a few months earlier in September 1674 (and a decade later became the first professor of music at the University of Cambridge).[117] The prologue of this work included four singers personifying the four continents, each with four attendants (singers and/or instrumentalists) who were clothed according to ideas of those places (Europe's fourth attendant was dressed in a "Roman habitt").[118] These singers were all cast as male, a decision that Crowne recognized was unusual. He writes in his preface "To the reader" that "I have in the *Prologue* represented the River *Thames* by a Woman, and *Europe* by a Man, contrary to all Authority and Antiquity. To that I answer, I know of no Sexes in Lands and Rivers, nor of any Laws in Poetry, but the fundamental one to please; they who do that, follow the highest Authority, and agree with the best Antiquity."[119] He continues:

> And *Thames, Peace* and *Plenty*, being represented by Women, I was necessitated (in spite of the Lady that bestrid the Bull) to make *Europe* a Man, and to call it not *Her* but—*His fair Continent*—Otherwise I must

---

[114] Fleckno, *The Mariage*, 33.
[115] A. White, *John Crowne*, 77, 82.
[116] For the libretto, see Crowne, *Calisto*. On Crowne's life in North America, see A. White, *John Crowne*, 14-15, 26-27.
[117] For studies of the surviving music from the masque, see Holman, *Four and Twenty Fiddlers*, 366-373. On his life, see Shaw, "Staggins."
[118] Walkling, "Masque and Politics," 43, 47, 48. For an analysis of the intended messages of this work, see Jenkinson, "John Crowne."
[119] Crowne, *Calisto*, "To the reader," n.p.

either have spoiled the Figure, and made three parts of the World Men, and one a Woman; or worse, by representing 'em all by Women, have spoiled the Musick, by making it consist all of Trebles.[120]

Historian Michael Wintle has observed that the convention of gendering continents as female in their allegorical personifications may relate to the gendering of place names as feminine in most Indo-European languages, although he qualifies that it is difficult to give an explanation for this phenomenon.[121] The ambiguity of the English language in this regard may go some way to account for Crowne's artistic license, and it is striking to note that he felt the need to defend or at least explain his decision in flouting this tradition, a feature that perhaps indicates widespread awareness of the female stereotype.

The staging of *Calisto* was extravagant, as the surviving bills for costuming and other expenses show.[122] Local performers took the roles of people from other parts of the world: two English ladies acted the part of "Two African Women, or Blacks," and the costumes prepared included those for the "Emperour of America," "4 African Kings," and six enslaved Africans.[123] In the prologue of the work, the four continents make a brief appearance, with brief dialogue that highlights the contemporary attitude with which they were viewed by the audience. In the opening of the prologue, they make their offerings to a nymph "representing the River *Thames*, attended by two Nymphs, representing *Peace* and *Plenty*: Near Her are the four Parts of the World, seeming to make Offerings to Her." The embodied (male) continents each speak one brief line, collectively pointing clearly to extractive colonialism and enslavement:

> Euro[pe]. *Thou shalt in all my noblest Arts be skill'd.*
> Asi[a.] *My Jewels shall adorn no Brow but Thine.*
> Amer[ica]. *Thy Lovers in my Gold shall shine.*
> Afri[ca]. *Thou for thy Slaves, shalt have these*
> *Scorched Sons of mine.*

It is worth noting that whereas Asia, America, and Africa offer jewels, gold, and enslaved human beings, respectively, Europe is exceptionalized, represented as alone possessing "Arts" (and therefore cultural capital, as

---

[120] Crowne, *Calisto*, "To the reader," n.p.
[121] Wintle, "Gender and Race," 49. There was not, however, any expectation of an exclusively female identity for continental allegories; thanks to Wolfgang Schmale for discussion of this point.
[122] Walkling, "Masque and Politics," 43–48.
[123] Walkling, "Masque and Politics," 38, 43, 44.

distinct from natural resources for mining or inhabitants for exploitation). The representation of the four continents seen here was, at the same time, subsumed within a colonialist sense of Britain's aspirations for ascendancy and programs for hegemony, with the "Genius of England" also playing a prominent role in the prologue.[124]

While these decidedly secular works all invoked many elements of Greco-Roman mythology, some compositions on Christian sacred themes—performed in religious contexts—also personified the continents and gave them voice. In Rome, a *concerto musicale* (a generic label for a cantata-like work) titled *Il mondo riparato* (*The World Repaired*), with words by Leonardo Mariano Sorba (dates unknown) and music by Giuseppe Ottavio Pitoni (1657–1743), was performed for Christmas celebrations in 1693 at "the apostolic palace," presumably in the presence of Pope Innocent XII (1615–1700; reigned from 1691). While the music is lost, the surviving text demonstrates that the four continents and the sun, together with a narrator, sang about the birth of Jesus Christ and the effects of this event on the world.[125] The voice types for the five roles—presumably, Pitoni had the singers of the papal choir at his disposal—are soprano for both the sun and for Europe (probably sung by castrati), contralto for Asia, tenor for America, and bass for Africa. One wonders whether a quasi-cosmological hierarchy may be implicit in this disposition, with higher-pitched voices perceived as being closer to the heavens and Europe placed again at the top of the hierarchy. Another example from almost a century later is for female voices. In 1776, Baldassare Galuppi (1706–1785) composed the oratorio *Mundi salus* (*The Salvation of the World*) in Venice for the Ospedale degl'Incurabili, a charitable hospital and religious institution well known for its musical activities. This work names the four continents as its interlocutors.[126] Europe, Asia, and Africa are set in soprano clef, but America is in alto. Although this difference in tessitura may simply reflect the choice of singers to perform the roles, one could speculate that it may indicate the geographical separation of the Americas compared with the contiguous nature of the other three continents. Further research may uncover multiple layers of meaning implicit in this work.

---

[124] Crowne, *Calisto*, "Prologue," n.p.
[125] Gianturco, "'Cantate spirituali e morali,'" 9, 17. The libretto was published as Sorba and Pitoni, *Il mondo riparato*. As Gianturco indicates (17), copies are held at the Biblioteca Casanatense, Rome, Vol. Misc. 1210/1, and at the Biblioteca Apostolica Vaticana, Vatican City, Misc. H. 103 (int. 31). However, the music appears to be lost.
[126] The score is in Paris; Galuppi, "Mundi salus," manuscript. It was revived in 2014 by Christopher Eanes, whom I thank for sharing with me his edition of it.

Europe as a Musical Community of Nations

The personification of Europe as an individual within the four "parts of the world" tradition did not necessarily extend to imply internal assimilation of the continent's internal populations into a unified homogeneous and monolithic culture. Inhabitants of Europe clearly understood this part of the world to be made up of diverse nations, many interrelated through aspects of music theory but differentiated through performance styles (a theme explored in chapter 4). Ideas about distinct nations' cultural characteristics were often reflected in the most visible forms of performance, especially their respective types of dances, which were practiced in courts across the continent.[127] As with stage works evoking the four "parts of the world," there was sometimes in the display of nations a sense of hierarchy and inequality. France, for instance, set itself as "first among equals" within its own court ballets.[128] The genre of the *ballet des nations* (ballet of the nations), which Marie-Claude Canova-Green describes as "the ritualized parade of foreigners on the court stage," became popular there from the 1620s onward.[129] Welch observes, moreover, that "the performance of nationality on the ballet stage enacted, and asked spectators to reflect upon, assumptions about national differentiation."[130] A prominent example in that sense is the 1670 *comédie-ballet* (a genre combining comedic theater, spoken or sung, and ballet) *Le bourgeois gentilhomme* (*The Middle-Class Gentleman*), with text by Molière (1622–1673) and music by Lully, which depicts and lampoons social and cultural mores of both France and Turkey, inspired by controversial diplomatic interactions of the previous year.[131]

Much has been written about the cultural complexities that emerge from staged representations of nations and peoples in music and dance.[132] Rather than re-rehearse those debates here, I want to make a small but significant point to bring this chapter to a close: whether in dramatic or instrumental works, the name of Europe as a continent was very rarely employed in titles of works that framed allegorical and symbolic representations of

---

[127] Marina Nordera observes that from the early sixteenth century, "courtly dancing . . . enriched itself with elements taken from the popular traditions of various countries. As a result, an international language surfaced, introducing a shared terminology transcending regional differences." Nordera, "The Exchange of Dance Cultures," 314.

[128] Rentsch, "Europa als künstlerische Suggestion."

[129] Canova-Green, "Dance and Ritual," 395.

[130] Welch, *A Theater of Diplomacy*, 62.

[131] See Walsdorf, *Ritual Design*; Whaples, "Early Exoticism Revisited," 11–14.

[132] See, for example, Taylor, "Peopling the Stage"; Taylor, *Beyond Exoticism*; Locke, *Musical Exoticism*; Bloechl; *Native American Song*; Locke, *Music and the Exotic*.

its internal nations. François Couperin (1668–1733), for instance, when he characterized national differences in a collection of chamber music published in 1726, simply called his suite *Les nations* (*The Nations*), not "Europe."[133] When "Europe" did appear—here I mean the geographical concept, as opposed to the mythical figure of Europa—it was exceptional. This term, in whichever language, appears to have been first used in that continental sense in the titles of two works of 1697. One was *L'Europe galante* (*Gallant Europe*), considered the first example of the opera-ballet genre, with a text by Antoine Houdar de La Motte (1672–1732) and music by André Campra (1660–1744).[134] Based on national stereotypes of love, the nations that are chosen for the plot are France, Spain, Italy, and Turkey. Librettist La Motte wrote that their selection was made on the basis of contrasting cultural characters and the opportunity for theatrical play; he stated that "we have followed the ordinary ideas that one has about the genius [characteristics] of their peoples," going on to describe their qualities.[135] These ideas were represented in ways that were entertaining for audiences of the times. The other work of that year was *Europe's Revels for the Peace of Ryswick*, produced in London, with a text by Motteux and music by Eccles. This production contained dances representing the Spanish, Dutch, French, and English.[136] While *Europe's Revels* was created for a specific political occasion, La Motte and Campra's *L'Europe galante* entered a repertory of repeated works. According to La Baume Le Blanc, writing in 1760, it was revived periodically; he gives precise dates of six revivals every eight to twelve years until 1755.[137] The score was also reprinted in many editions.[138]

[133] See Sadie, "Devils and Archangels," 156–157.
[134] Anthony, "Europe galante, L." For the first edition of the score, see Campra, *L'Europe galante*.
[135] Original text in La Motte, *L'Europe galante*, 8. These qualities are for the first three nations "fickle, indiscreet, and coquettish" (France); "faithful and romantic" (Spain); and "jealous, perceptive, and violent" (Italy). For Turkey, La Motte describes the expression ("as much as the theater has been able to permit it") of "nobility [or haughtiness] and sovereign nature" of the sultans and "anger" of the sultanas.
[136] Lowerre, "A *Ballet des nations*," esp. 428. For an edition of this work, see Eccles, *Europe's Revels*. Kathryn Lowerre, pointing out the contemporaneity of the two works, has suggested that Motteux based his framework on late-seventeenth-century *ballets des nations* from his native country; she also notes that other roles described in the cast list (although apparently represented by local performers) are an Irish rapparee and a Savoyard who sing, as well as a "Chorus of *Britains* and other Nations." Lowerre, "A *Ballet des nations*," 424–425.
[137] La Baume Le Blanc, *Ballets, opera*, 118. The son of an Ottoman ambassador reportedly saw a performance in Lyon in 1721 and requested a repeat performance of the Turkish *entrée* (act), apparently expressing delight. Mehmed Çelebi and Veinstein, *Le paradis des infidèles*, 208. It is interesting to note that *L'Europe galante* provides the majority of results in the Répertoire International des Sources Musicales catalogue (https://rism.info) when searching for "Europe" in the titles of works for this period.
[138] Anthony, "Printed Editions," 54–73.

There is a later well-known work that was clearly modeled on *L'Europe galante*; Roger Savage suggests that it was conceived as a sequel.[139] This is the *ballet héroïque* ("heroic ballet," but really an opera) *Les Indes galantes* (*The Gallant Indies*) of 1735/1736 by Jean-Philippe Rameau (1683–1764), which sets a libretto by Fuzelier.[140] The four "Indies" represented here are Persia, Turkey, Peru, and North America. If it was indeed intended to correlate with Campra's work (which seems likely), it is striking to note that here Turkey has been symbolically removed from Europe and conceptually relegated to the category of "the Indies." Nevertheless, Turkey returned to the conceptual fold of Europe in a mid-century Italian adaptation of La Motte's text of *L'Europe galante* by Leopoldo de Villati (1701–1752), with the Italian title *L'Europa galante*; this was set to music by Carl Heinrich Graun (1703/1704–1759) and performed at the Hofoper in Berlin as a *festa teatrale* on March 27, 1748.[141] The libretto included a German translation titled *Das galante Europa*.[142] These translations do not only speak to the cross-cultural popularity of the work; they also suggest an increasing desire for equivalence and competition in theatrical display.

We see considerable fluidity in musical constructions of Europe: its characterization could be about the cultural diversity of its internal populations or could involve comparisons of the continent as a whole with other parts of the world. The earliest representations of "Europe" in music drama focused on the tragic story of the mythological princess Europa as a survivor of abduction and sexual assault. Later allegorizations of the continent moved away from that story (although occasionally the personified Europe was interpreted as or conflated with Europa), and some were elaborated into celebrations of the specific characteristics of individual nations. Cultural contrasts between nations, however, could be overridden by similarities that outweighed differences, such as love. At the heart of musical-dramatic representations of diverse peoples, there arguably lay questions of what it meant to be human, with examples coming from different parts of the world. As we see in the next two chapters, the ideas of geographical origins and the ways music could mediate the connections of peoples to places—particularly "Europeans" to Europe—were issues that became increasingly prominent in discourse of the long eighteenth century.

---

[139] Savage, "Rameau's American Dancers," 450.
[140] On this work, see also Taylor, *Beyond Exoticism*, 51–57; Locke, *Musical Exoticism*, 97–105.
[141] Henzel, "Graun."
[142] [Villati], *L'Europa galante, festa teatrale . . . = Das galante Europa, ein Singespiel*.

2

Europe as Place

Music and the Imagined Extent of a Continent

Since antiquity, to use that hazy starting point, spatial awareness of Europe and cartographic representations of it have undergone radical transformations.[1] For much of this time, the link between place and name, however, was quite vague: as Peter Burke has asserted, "for nearly two thousand years, from the fifth century B.C. to the fifteenth century A.D., the term 'Europe' was in sporadic use without carrying very much weight, without meaning very much to many people."[2] Klaus Oschema has shown that the notion of Europe held a wide range of meanings in its transit through medieval sources.[3] To most people who thought about the continent in geographical terms, it was simply one of the three parts of the world—Asia (the largest of these), Europe, and Libya (Africa)—with the nexus of the triad located in the eastern parts of the Mediterranean. The resulting tripartite world was famously depicted in the T–O (*orbis terrarum*) maps introduced by Isidore of Seville (c. 560–636). These showed "the world as a disk surrounded by an encircling ocean," in which "three bodies of water, the Nile, the Mediterranean, and the Tanais (the River Don) created a T inside the O, slicing the world into three clearly differentiated segments."[4] Jerusalem, revered as a holy city and the seat of the biblical king David, was at the center of this representation.

Certain regions that straddled two or three of the continents were simultaneously under the rule of one or more polities, especially the Roman, Byzantine, and Ottoman Empires. Besides Jerusalem, a focal point of desire was Constantinople, founded in 324 by Roman emperor Constantine (c. 227–337; reigned from 306), who in 330 made this eponymous city his

---

[1] See, for example, Wintle, *The Image of Europe*; Kivelson, "The Cartographic Emergence of Europe?," 37–69. See also the special issue of *Belgeo* 3–4 (2008), devoted to this theme, beginning with Bodenstein, "Editorial," 241–244.

[2] P. Burke, "Did Europe Exist," 22, 23.

[3] Oschema, *Bilder von Europa*. See also Oschema, "How Does Medieval Historians' Use of the Notion of 'Europe' Compare?."

[4] Kivelson, "The Cartographic Emergence of Europe?," 39–40.

capital. It was a "new Rome," positioned at what was considered the easternmost point of the Balkan Peninsula—and thus one of the outer edges of Europe.[5] Constantine had converted to Christianity in 312, instituting it as a state religion throughout the territories he ruled, and Constantinople became a major religious center. In the late fourth century, well after his death, the empire of the Romans split into two administrative regions, east and west.[6] The western half fell in 476, but the Byzantine Empire—as its eastern counterpart was subsequently known—continued to flourish, with Constantinople remaining its capital. Both Latin and Greek were spoken there, but primarily Greek from the seventh century onward.[7] The ecclesiastical Schism of 1054 further entrenched within Christendom a binary of Greek (Orthodox) East and Latin (Catholic) West, with two separate Christian confessions. In the course of the Fourth Crusade—the ostensible aim of which was to capture Jerusalem and the Holy Land—the Latins did not hesitate to sack Constantinople in 1204, resulting in the division of the Byzantine Empire itself.[8]

Two and a half centuries later, the capture of Constantinople by Ottoman forces in 1453 symbolically extinguished the final political vestiges of the eastern Roman Empire.[9] Sultan Mehmed II (1432–1481; reigned 1444–1446 and 1451–1481), then just twenty-one years old, claimed the title of emperor of "Rome"—or "Rûm," as the former lands of the Byzantine Empire were known in Turkish.[10] In Rome itself, Italian humanist Silvio Piccolomini (1405–1464), who became Pope Pius II in 1458, popularized in his short reign a concept of "Europe" in his exhortations to resist further Ottoman expansion. As John A. Marino observes, he "is often seen as the thinker most responsible for putting the word 'Europe' into common usage."[11] The conceptual boundaries of the Christendom to which Pius II had referred gradually shrank to leave most of the Greek lands behind (except for certain Venetian colonies in the archipelago), forming a cultural sphere that was increasingly defined by political, religious, and cultural frameworks based on a derivative Roman identity.[12]

---

[5] Grig and Kelly, *Two Romes*.
[6] Sarris, "The Eastern Roman Empire," 26, 36–38.
[7] Kaldellis, "From Rome to New Rome," 396.
[8] Reinert, "Fragmentation," 250.
[9] Hobson, *The Eastern Origins*, 135–136, 308.
[10] Pagden, *The Pursuit of Europe*, 92. See also Oschema, "No 'Emperor of Europe,'" 432.
[11] Bisaha, *Creating East and West*, 86; Marino, "The Invention of Europe," 141.
[12] For a perspective on the "secondarity" or "derivativeness" of western European culture, see Brague, *Eccentric Culture*.

Anthony Pagden states that the Greeks under Ottoman rule were "fully absorbed into Asia."[13] From the sixteenth to eighteenth centuries, there was uncertainty and debate among "western" Christians over the extent to which people living in lands occupied by the Ottoman Empire could be considered culturally part of Europe, despite their physical location on the continent. Travelers and musicians going in all directions also contributed to growing notions farther north of an "eastern Europe" and complicated ideas about the East and the West.[14]

These are, of course, cultural definitions; what of geography and geology? To think about how all these notions intersected, it is helpful to see how Europe was conceptualized cartographically at the beginning of the eighteenth century. In 1700, the three-volume *Nouvelle geographie, ou, Description exacte de l'univers* (*New Geography, or Exact Description of the Universe*) by Denis Martineau du Plessis (b. 1651), richly illustrated with maps and depictions of peoples of the different parts of the world, was published in Amsterdam by Georges Gallet (died c. 1724). Europe (figure 2.1) is labeled as being drawn "according to the most modern authors," and in lieu of a cartouche, it has an illustration of a woman—clearly Europa—riding a bull bedecked with flowers.[15] It is framed by a border containing twenty coats of arms of all the self-contained political units, including both "Moscovie" (Muscovy, featuring Saint George and the dragon) and "Turquie" (Turkey, with an Islamic crescent). These heraldic emblems contribute to a symbolic view of Europe as a community of nation states.[16] This was a top-down vision of Europe that is in stark contrast with the bottom-up approach of ethnographically based studies emerging later in the century, such as those by Herder.[17]

There are two labels for Turkey: "Turquie" in the Balkan Peninsula, with Constantinople at what appears as its easternmost point, and "Turquie en Asie" ("Turkey in Asia") for Anatolia (or "Natolie," as inscribed below it).

---

[13] Pagden, "Europe: Conceptualizing a Continent," 35.
[14] See Bracewell, "The Limits of Europe." This point is discussed further in chapter 6.
[15] Whether intentional or not, it is striking that this image from an ancient story irrupts between the syllables of the word "modern," perhaps implicitly contesting that notion.
[16] By contrast, Asia and the Americas—the latter presented as North and South, in two separate maps—in Martineau du Plessis's work are not given any such heraldic emblems, whereas Africa does contain some coats of arms for the northern regions. See his *Nouvelle geographie*, plates in Vol. 2 at 262 (Asia) and Vol. 3 at 1 (Africa), 178 (North America), and 283 (South America).
[17] For discussion of Herder's ethnographic thinking, see Bohlman, "Johann Gottfried Herder"; Herder and Bohlman, *Song Loves the Masses*.

Figure 2.1. "L'Europe selon les Auth[eurs]. les plus Modernes" ("Europe according to the Most Modern Authors"). Map in Denis Martineau du Plessis, *Nouvelle geographie, ou, Description exacte de l'univers* (Amsterdam: George Gallet, 1700), Vol. 1, plate at 78. Bibliothèque du Musée de l'Homme, Réserve A 200 189. Sourced from gallica.bnf.fr, Bibliothèque Nationale de France.

EUROPE AS PLACE 75

Muscovy is represented cartographically as the largest region; it also the one with the fewest details, although the city of Moscow is clearly marked. The map was produced three years before the foundation of St. Petersburg, Russia's soon-to-be capital. That city's location is nevertheless indicated with the name of Saint Nicholas, whose patronage would be given to a grand cathedral constructed there in the middle of the century. Meanwhile, "Partie d'Afrique" ("Part of Africa") and the Mediterranean Sea appear to the south. The "Ocean Atlantique ou Occidental" ("Atlantic or Western Ocean")— along with several seas marked in large lettering: the "Mer Britannique" ("British Sea"), the "Mer de Danemark" ("Sea of Denmark"), and the "Mer de Moscovie" ("Sea of Muscovy")—create the sense of continental limits to the west and north, with the British Isles, Iceland, and part of Greenland included across the water. The boundaries to the east are more vague, however. As Martineau du Plessis describes in the accompanying text, they involve geographical features such as the (Greek) archipelago, the Bosphorus, a series of rivers, the city of Kazan, Siberia, and the River Ob.[18] Such places are implied as physical boundaries that symbolically split cultural worlds. On the other hand, other cartographic conceptualizations of Europe in the first half of the eighteenth century present cultural overlaps between continents, such as the map *Europa polyglotta* (*Polyglot Europe*) of 1741 by the German linguist Gottfried Hensel (1687–1745). In this he used colored shading to indicate the diffusion of the languages he considered to stem variously from the three sons of the biblical Noah, showing continuities across the perceived border between Europe and Asia (such as Greek extending from the Balkan Peninsula through Anatolia and Turkish in what is now Romania and Bulgaria).[19]

Imagining a frontier between Europe and Asia—and between Asia and Africa—mixed together conceptual-cultural and geographical boundaries, all of which were frequently porous.[20] Those of Europe are ambiguous where land is concerned. As Jürgen Osterhammel has pointed out, whereas voyages by ship gave an unambiguous sense of continental change in traveling from Europe to other continents, arrival in Asia by land was less clearly defined

---

[18] Martineau du Plessis, *Nouvelle geographie*, Vol. 1, 79.
[19] Schmale, "Europe," 88. A copy is held in the Division of Rare and Manuscript Collections, Cornell University Library, in the P. J. Mode Collection of Persuasive Cartography (8548). It is accessible online at https://www.jstor.org/stable/community.3293755.
[20] For recent studies on this topic, see essays in Rossi, *The Boundaries of Europe*.

for a number of early modern travelers; for some, "'Asia' begins where steeples give way to minarets and the muezzin's call to prayer replaces the tolling of church bells."[21] While such a notion problematically and reductively conflates Europe with Christendom and Asia with the world of Islam, seemingly on a mutually exclusive basis, it also represents how structures of political control and ideas about religious demographics became gradually tied to far-reaching notions of continental frontiers. It goes without saying, of course, that the constant movement of people, and the way sound travels with them, challenges any idea of immutable musical borders, as numerous scholars have stressed.[22] What interests me in this chapter is the way in which geographical definitions intersected or conflicted with cultural conceptions of Europe in literary works about or related to music. In critiquing some select examples, I want to highlight the shifting meanings that were prevalent in notions of Europe as a physical space. I also emphasize that Turkey and Muscovy (Russia) were seen as "bicontinental," spanning both Europe and Asia, and that their place in Europeans' conceptual geographies of music was complex and uncertain during this period.[23] I then look at the rise of the "Republic of Music," which transcended physical space to create a new conceptual dimension of common musicking, and consider how descriptions—or boasts—of individual musicians' skills and their fame contributed to a sense of Europe as a place for musical expression.

Musicians' Contemplation of Continental Frontiers

How did musicians of the long eighteenth century engage with the limits of Europe? To address this question, let us first consider a liminal figure whose life and work took him across multiple borders and transported him through many different categories of identity. The Moldavian *voivode* (prince) and renowned musician Dimitrie Cantemir (1673–1723) described the physical boundaries of Europe as follows in his history of the Ottoman Empire

---

[21] Osterhammel, *Unfabling the East*, 39. Christopher Page has made a similar observation in medieval contexts, although with reference to the withdrawal of Christian Crusaders from occupied territories in Palestine and Syria. See Page, "The Geography of Medieval Music," 320.

[22] See, for example, Stokes, "Introduction"; Stoessel, "Editor's Introduction," esp. 6–7.

[23] See Kivelson, "The Cartographic Emergence of Europe?," 56–58; Piccardo, "Lorsque la Russie 'entra' en Europe," 94; Koller, "Europe and the Ottoman Empire."

(written in Latin around 1720 and published in English translation in London in 1734–1735):

> Europe... or the *European Parts, Rumi-li* or simply *Europe, Rum,* is bounded with *Syria* by the *Arabians,* so that they who at this day go to *Aleppo* the Metropolis of *Syria,* are said to enter into the *European* Parts. But the *Turks* own the same Bounds to *Europe* as we do, namely, the *Bosphorus* of *Thrace, Tanais,* and the *Nile* [*Turcae autem communes nobis Europae terminos agnoscunt, Bosphorum Thraciae, Taniam et Nili ostia*].[24]

There is much detail to draw out from this short passage. First, it is significant to note that Cantemir uses the collective pronoun (*nobis*) in writing "as we do," thus identifying himself (for his intended readership) unambiguously as a European; of course, at the time of writing, he was in exile in and allying himself with Russia, which was in the process of Europeanizing (as discussed below).[25] Second, he points to the popular idea in Ottoman thought of Europe (Rum) being a cultural zone that stretched through Anatolia and as far as Aleppo.[26] Third, in writing of "the same Bounds to *Europe*," he was quoting a long-standing idea that had its origins in the T–O maps (mentioned above).

In London half a century earlier, we see that the division between Europe and Asia was also depicted strikingly in a book made and sold by the Playfords, a family famous for their production of music scores. This work was advertised as "*A Late Voyage to* Constantinople, by *Joseph Grelot*, a Baron of *France*, and newly Translated into English."[27] Printed and published in 1683 by John Playford junior (c. 1655–1685), nephew of John Playford senior (1623–1686/7), this book seems unique as the only travel account known to have been produced by their business. It was advertised for sale in some of their music scores, and it in turn contained advertisements for music.[28] It was apparently an innovative project, according to a boast on

---

[24] Cantemir, *The History*, Vol. 1, 4n.8. Original text in Cantemir and Cândea, *Creşterile şi descreşterile Imperiului Otoman*, 585. The original manuscript, "Incrementa et decrementa othmanici imperii," is in the Houghton Library, Harvard University, MS Lat 224.
[25] Popescu-Judetz, *Prince Dimitrie Cantemir*, 31–36.
[26] On the history of how the term "Rum" was applied to these regions, see Kafadar, "A Rome of One's Own," 7–25. Thanks to Jacob Olley for pointing out this reference.
[27] Grelot, *A Late Voyage*.
[28] The travelogue was available for purchase from Henry Playford (1657–c. 1707) at the shop founded by his father, John Playford senior. Advertisements for Grelot's book appeared in the third

its title page (in bold Gothic type): "The like never done before."[29] Two of the collaborators in this production—John Phillips (1631–1706), the translator of the French text, and Frederick Hendrick van Hove (c. 1628–1698), the engraver of illustrations—had previously worked with the Playfords on a number of musical publications.[30] Thus, this travel account was the joint production of craftspeople who had a track record of providing materials for the literate musical public. Its appearance as a commodity in London, where it was advertised and sold among music books, could be said to represent the consumers' intersecting interests in music making on a local level and knowledge about the wider world. Playford junior, clearly proud of the publication, wrote in the preface that "though many Travellers have written Books on this Subject, yet I assure thee none ever came into the world with more Authority than that of this Author."[31] Such a bold assurance by a member of a prominent music-publishing family attracts today's music historian to explore its iconography and various passages of sonic description within it, to see the kind of information available to readers in London, Paris, and beyond in the late seventeenth century.

The author, Guillaume-Joseph Grelot (born c. 1630), was a French painter who had accompanied the more famous traveler Jean Chardin (1643–1713) on one of his journeys.[32] Grelot's original book, *Relation nouvelle d'un voyage de Constantinople* (*New Account of a Voyage to Constantinople*), had been published in Paris in 1680.[33] It included engravings of his artworks that were renowned at the time for their apparent accuracy, and these were reproduced

---

book (1686) of *The Theater of Music* and the famous volume *Harmonia sacra* (1688), both published by Henry, and in *The Second Book of the Pleasant Musical Companion* (2nd ed., 1686), published by his father, John Playford. See J. Playford, *The Theater of MUSIC*, n.p., facing p. 1; H. Playford, *Harmonia sacra*, n.p. at end of volume; J. Playford, *The Second Book*, n.p., facing first page of music. See also Grelot, *A Late Voyage*, "Advertisements."

[29] Grelot, *A Late Voyage*, title page.

[30] Phillips's polemical text "Duellum musicum" ("Musical Duel") had been published by the Playfords in 1673. Lee, "Phillips, John." Van Hove had collaborated with the Playfords on a number of music books; he engraved the portrait of John senior that was reproduced in several editions of his treatise *A Brief Introduction to the Skill of Musick* from 1670 and the illustration for the title pages of Henry Playford's collection *Deliciae musicae* of 1695–1696. See the engraved portrait in Playford, Campion, and Simpson, *A Brief Introduction*, opposite the title page. See the title pages of H. Playford, *Deliciae musicae*, Vol. 1; H. Playford, *Deliciae musicae*, Vol. 2, Book 1; H. Playford, ed., *Deliciae musicae*, Vol. 2, Book 2.

[31] Grelot, *A Late Voyage*, "The Publisher to the Reader," n.p. Playford junior's detailed enthusiasm in this preface suggests that he had read Grelot's text thoroughly.

[32] See Longino, *French Travel Writing*, 108–128.

[33] Grelot, *Relation nouvelle*.

Figure 2.2. Depiction of the division between continents at the Hellespont. Engraving by Frederick Hendrick van Hove, after Guillaume-Joseph Grelot, in *A Late Voyage to Constantinople*, translated by John Phillips (London: John Playford, 1683), between 2 and 3. © The British Library Board (978.d.4). Copy belonging to Sir Joseph Banks (1743–1820).

in the Playford publication.[34] The first plate depicts with apparent preciseness the division of the continents at the Hellespont (Dardanelles), with two fortresses labeled, respectively, as being on the Asian and European sides (figure 2.2). Grelot describes this strait with great momentousness in the opening chapter of the book: "It is a great satisfaction at one and the same time, with one glance of the Eye to behold *Europe* and *Asia* so nearly joyn'd together, as if they had a desire to embrace and unite under one and the same Conquerour, or that they did only separate there to open him a

---

[34] In the preface to the English translation, Playford junior praises the engravings by van Hove as such precise reproductions that "you may fancy you see the Originals themselves." Grelot, *A Late Voyage*, "The Publisher to the Reader," n.p.

passage, and facilitate his generous Enterprises."[35] In commenting on the name "Constantinople," he observes that it "has been of longest continuance, as well among the *Latins*, as other *Christians* of *Europe*; but as for the *Turks* and other People of *Asia*, *Africa* and *Europe*, they all give it the name of *Stamboll*."[36] In this way, he emphasizes the convergence of three continents at and in the city.

Writing of the Ottoman capital, Grelot notes the absence of bells and the presence of muezzins, as well as mentioning other elements of Islamic religious sound.[37] Elsewhere, he comments further on campanological topics, observing: "the *Turks* spoyl'd all the Steeple-Music in the *Greek* Church. Instead of which, a certain Instrument call'd a *Simandron*, serves turn, which is a long narrow piece of Board, upon which the Officer rattles with a wooden stick, till he make the Board groan again; the noise of which assembles the poor Christians together."[38] One can imagine that the interest of Playford junior, as a printer of music, may have been piqued at a passage that mentioned the staff notation of Europe—or at least its absence—on the Greek island of Chios. Grelot, in writing of Orthodox worship in the town of Nenita, remarked that the vocal ensemble was in disarray and stopped midperformance. He considered the lack of notated scores to be part of the cause:

> It was near an hour before the Service began, and there was already such a horrid noise and confusion, that the *Calonarchi*[39] not being able to raise their Voices to be heard by those that were to take the Tune from their Notes, and the *Chanters* not having their books before them prick'd and rul'd as in *Europe*, the Music which was not in very good order was forc'd to cease; so that the *Protopsalti* or Rector of the Quire grew angry, and at length his patience forsaking him, after he had struck several blows upon the Bench

---

[35] Grelot, *A Late Voyage*, 16 (he also discusses the Hellespont on 2–17); original text in Grelot, *Relation nouvelle*, 19. There is also an engraving of "The City of Constantinople," with "The Bosphorus of Thrace" clearly labeled but without inscribing the terms "Asia" or "Europe." See Grelot, *A Late Voyage*, between 56 and 57; Grelot, *Relation nouvelle*, between 82 and 83.

[36] Grelot, *A Late Voyage*, 63; original text in Grelot, *Relation nouvelle*, 73.

[37] See Grelot, *A Late Voyage*, 186. He goes on to point out that there are so many muezzins that they do not collectively need to use their full voices to have the desired sonic effect.

[38] Grelot, *A Late Voyage*, 148; original text in Grelot, *Relation nouvelle*, 179. (For a description and depiction of this instrument, termed "Campana delli Greci" (bell of the Greeks), see Buonanni, *Gabinetto armonico*, 145–146 and plate CIX.) It is interesting to note here the gloss that the translator, Phillips, added to this passage, as neither the verb "groan" nor the adjective "poor" appears in Grelot's French text. Thus, although the illustrations had been reproduced from the French publication with particular accuracy, certain license had been taken with the textual descriptions.

[39] He defines "the *Calonarki* [sic]" as those "that name the Anthems and Songs, and set the Tunes." Grelot, *A Late Voyage*, 149.

where he sate with his *Dekaniki* or Deans staff of Authority, he turn'd to the people and cry'd out as low'd as he could bawl, *Sopotate Theocatarati; Curst of God, will ye never hold your Clacks?*[40]

Chios, the home of an Orthodox community but also under Ottoman rule along with most of the Greek-speaking lands, clearly lay outside Grelot's conception of the continent—although its being an island may also have contributed to this notion—as the singers did not have "books before them prick'd and rul'd [with staves] as in *Europe*."[41] "Europe" was apparently, for him, the domain of music scores in staff notation.

The limits of the inclusive category of a musical "Europe" can thus be inversely defined by what it excluded. Many Christian communities of the Orthodox faith were originally denied membership in a musical Europe, although some—such as societies in Crete, with a mixture of confessions—entered into it.[42] Orthodox societies thus occupied a liminal conceptual space. External observers assumed that the patterns of Turkish influence on Greek culture might apply to other Balkan nations under Ottoman rule, disqualifying many societies from membership in what we could call the "imagined musical community" of "Europe" until the late eighteenth century.[43] Musicologist and composer Ivan Moody has pointed out that within the complicated historical analyses of the Balkans' cultural position in the region, "there is the idea that Greece is perhaps not Europe at all."[44] Such a view was also held by some eighteenth-century Greek scholars themselves. For example, Romanian-born Iosipos Moisiodax (c. 1730–1800), in a publication made in Venice in 1761, exhorted fellow Greeks to "imitate Europe," with the last term implying that Greece was external to it.[45] However, in some parts of the Balkans, musical tastes were apparently changing in the latter part of the eighteenth century. As Carsten Niebuhr (1733–1815) reported in an

---

[40] Grelot, *A Late Voyage*, 151; original text in Grelot, *Relation nouvelle*, 183.
[41] For his description of the circumstances surrounding his visit to Nenita, Chios, see Grelot, *A Late Voyage*, 150; original text in Grelot, *Relation nouvelle*, 182.
[42] Théodora Psychoyou observes that "Crete became part of the European learned community." Psychoyou, "Latin Musical Practices," 91.
[43] See Irving, "Ancient Greeks," for a discussion of the conceptual exclusion of Greece from early modern notions of the musical boundaries of Europe. For more details of the musical implications of this phenomenon in the Balkans, see Romanou, *Serbian and Greek Art Music*; Sandu-Dediu, "The Beginnings of Romanian Composition." See also Samson, *Music in the Balkans*. I adapt the term "imagined musical communities" from the work of Anderson, *Imagined Communities*.
[44] Moody, "The Compass Revisited," 201. Moody cites discussion of this point (which relates more to nineteenth- and twentieth-century contexts) in Todorova, *Imagining the Balkans*, 42–45.
[45] In Drace-Francis, *European Identity*, 74–77.

account of his travels as part of a Danish expedition to Arabia (1761–1767), "the Bulgarian shepherds have already some taste for the music of Europe."[46] The sense of "Europe" and the Balkans as distinct zones was still reflected in 1821 by Athanase Thamyris (d. 1828), who, in an introduction to a manual of reformed Greek ecclesiastical music notation published in Paris (to where he had been sent from Constantinople), encouraged his peers to "not confine yourself to our music only, but study European as well."[47]

Russia, or Muscovy, was another predominantly Orthodox space that occupied an equivocal position in relation to "Europe."[48] Like Turkey, it spanned Europe and Asia.[49] From the perspective of some scholars in the western parts of Europe, it was different from other major sites of intercultural encounter, such as the Americas. Lara Piccardo has observed that whereas the Americas became integrated with Europe by means of the actions of "transplanted and transformed" colonialists from the end of the fifteenth century onward, Russia represented a form of "Eurasian 'bicontinentalism' that demarcated it from Europe, as an independent and unknown entity, viewed squarely as a 'non-Europe.'"[50] According to Janet Hartley, "[i]t is only at the end of the seventeenth century that the word for Europe is attested in Russian, and then only as a purely geographical term in translated geographical works which existed in only a few manuscript copies."[51] For ideas of both "Russia" and "Europe," then, the eighteenth century again looms large as a period in which conceptual transformations took place in several scholarly traditions.

Seventeenth-century Russia had its own distinctive musical traditions, which flourished in court and church (and instruments were banned in the latter).[52] Peter I (1672–1725), who reigned from 1682 and became known as "the Great," initiated programs of modernization and "Europeanization" of the country, with significant musical implications.[53] A fascinating insight into this period of transition is given by Italian castrato Filippo Balatri (1682–1756) in his autobiographical account of his stay in Muscovy (a term he uses instead of "Russia") between 1698 and 1701. Jan Kusber and Matthias Schnettger note that "it was in the wealthy houses of the *sloboda* [the

---

[46] Niebuhr, *Travels through Arabia*, Vol. 1, 135–136. See also Hansen, *Arabia felix*, 350.
[47] In Romanou, "The Music of the Modern Greeks," 272, 274.
[48] Hartley, "Is Russia Part of Europe?," 369.
[49] See Bassin, "Russia between Europe and Asia"; Masoero, "Russia between Europe and Asia."
[50] Original text in Piccardo, "Lorsque la Russie 'entra' en Europe," 94.
[51] Hartley, "Is Russia Part of Europe?," 369.
[52] Jensen, *Musical Cultures in Seventeenth-Century Russia*; on the prohibition of instruments in churches, see 79.
[53] Ritzarev, *Eighteenth-Century Russian Music*, 37.

residential area for foreigners in Moscow] that Russian nobles and the tsar himself came in contact with western European music and it was here and in the Golitsyn-palace, where Balatri performed his singing, Italian Arias, but also Russian (folk) songs in an Italian style."[54] In 1712, the tsar established his court at St. Petersburg.[55] Part of a flourishing maritime trade network in the Baltic, this city was a full participant in the transnational flow of musicians and other artists.

As Hartley has remarked, Russia's aspirations to be "part of 'Europe' ... essentially meant being accepted as one of the community of civilized, modern nations."[56] This aim and the transformations it involved resulted in political recognition of this new status elsewhere; for instance, the list of states in the French *Almanach royal* (*Royal Almanac*) included Muscovy after Poland in 1717.[57] In two rapid leaps, the process continued: in 1721, Peter I proclaimed Russia an empire and himself an emperor, and in 1730, the geographical boundaries of Europe moved east as the Ural Mountains were proposed as a geological and "natural" frontier with Asia in a publication by Swedish military officer Philipp Johann von Strahlenberg (1676–1747).[58] This enlargement of Europe's area would lay the foundations for an increased sense of "western" and "eastern" zones within it, although much of what we now think of as "eastern" was also regarded in the eighteenth century as "the North."[59]

According to Jean-Benjamin de La Borde (1734–1794), writing in 1780, the first formal concert ("concert en forme") was given in Russia by twelve German musicians in the retinue of Charles Frederick, Duke of Schleswig-Holstein-Gottorp (1700–1739), who came there to marry Anna Petrovna (1708–1728), the eldest daughter of Peter I. La Borde notes that this ensemble's performances, which started around 1724, attracted the interest of the tsar and that "he made them perform concerts regularly, twice per week, and that he attended almost always."[60] Marina Ritzarev has observed,

---

[54] Kusber and Schnettger, "The Russian Experience," 245.
[55] On this court, see Keenan, *St Petersburg*.
[56] Hartley, "Is Russia Part of Europe?," 369.
[57] Parker, "Europe: How Far?," 285.
[58] Following his capture in the 1709 Battle of Poltava, Strahlenberg had been imprisoned in Russia for thirteen years, during which time he devoted himself to the study of geography. See Schmale, "Europe," 87; Parker, "Europe: How Far?," 285–286. For an eighteenth-century English translation of the relevant text see Strahlenberg, *An Histori-Geographical Description*, 105–126.
[59] See Wolff, *Inventing Eastern Europe*; Karnes, "Inventing Eastern Europe," 108. On the transformation from "North" into "East," see Stråth, "The Conquest of the North," 102.
[60] La Borde, *Essai*, Vol. 1, 390–391, including note (c).

however, that "the genre most indicative of a 'level of Europization' [sic] was opera" and goes on to comment that "Peter did not establish opera as an institution, though he would have probably considered it to be a suitable European genre for his country."[61] Following the brief reign, from 1727, of his grandson and successor Peter II (1715–1730), it was only in the 1730s that Italian operas began to be performed in St. Petersburg; this phase took place during the rule of Peter I's niece, the Tsarina Anna (1693–1740; reigned from 1730).[62]

The subsequent reign of Peter III (1728–1762), although it lasted only six months before he died, saw additional steps in the project of cultural integration; La Borde asserted that this tsar "attracted to his court the most celebrated musicians of Europe."[63] On the same page, the French music historian referred to the theater of St. Petersburg as "one of the most brilliant of Europe," attributing its status to Italian musician Tommaso Traetta (1727–1779), in the service of Catherine the Great (1729–1796; reigned from 1762), widow of Peter III.[64] The Prussian-born tsarina continued her late husband's desire to Europeanize; in 1767, she declared that "Russia is a European state."[65] This statement came within her *Grand Instructions* to Russian lawmakers, a text that was additionally published in French, German, and English translations (the last in 1768), thus broadcasting her policies to western parts of Europe.[66] Valerie Kivelson observes that its emphatic declaration "betrayed some lingering ontological uncertainty" about the place of Russia in Europe; nevertheless, she also notes that "[t]hrough cultural reform, relentless image-making, and strategic mapping, Russia deliberately moved itself into Europe in the eighteenth century."[67] During Catherine's reign, opera productions at St. Petersburg included a wide range of Italian works by composers such as Galuppi, Giovanni Paisiello (1740–1816), Domenico Cimarosa

---

[61] Ritzarev, *Eighteenth-Century Russian Music*, 37.
[62] Ritzarev, *Eighteenth-Century Russian Music*, 39; Kusber and Schnettger, "The Russian Experience," 250; L. Hughes, *Russia in the Age of Peter the Great*, 246; Taruskin, *Defining Russia Musically*, xi.
[63] La Borde, *Essai*, Vol. 1, 392.
[64] La Borde, *Essai*, Vol. 1, 392.
[65] Hartley, "Is Russia Part of Europe?," 370; Catherine II, *The Grand Instructions*, 70; Drace-Francis, *European Identity*, 77.
[66] Catherine II, *The Grand Instructions*, 70; Drace-Francis, *European Identity*, 77.
[67] Kivelson, "The Cartographic Emergence of Europe?," 59, 64. Taruskin also notes that "[i]t was only the spread of Europeanized mores and attitudes beyond the precincts of the court, and the increased Russian presence in Europe following the Napoleonic wars, that really rooted European high culture in Russian urban centers and led beyond receptivity to actual Russian productivity in the European arts." Taruskin, *Defining Russia Musically*, xi.

(1749–1801), and Spanish-born Vicente Martín y Soler (1754–1801).[68] The empress also wrote the libretto of a work that represented Russia's imperial aims of reclaiming the lost glory of Byzantium.[69] A desire to continue integrating with the musical cultures of lands to the west is demonstrated by the production or planned publication by Russian presses of translated treatises by Paisiello, Leopold Mozart (1719–1787), Pier Francesco Tosi (1654–1732), and others.[70] The eighteenth century was thus a formative period for the inclusion of Muscovy or Russia—or at least the westernmost parts of it—in the musical idea of "Europe," by people on all sides of this complex relationship.[71]

Transcending Physical Space: The Republic of Music

The cases of Turkey's and Muscovy's bicontinentalism—and the ambiguity of boundaries between Europe and Asia from the Balkans to the Baltic—show that there was no sense of a monolithic musical space that filled the entire geographical area of the continent. Although the proper adjective "European" was used in the long eighteenth century to refer to intercontinental comparison of musics (as chapter 4 demonstrates), most discourse used the terminology "of Europe" and "in Europe" to imply a shared musical culture within Europe itself. This culture operated by means of a complex network of practitioners, creators, and consumers, through which musicians, objects, and ideas circulated.[72] There emerged a conceptual community, transcending political, ethnolinguistic, and geographical boundaries, interconnected through common musical activities: it was known as the "Republic of Music" and, in Rebekah Ahrendt's words, was "based on shared values and laws." [73]

Clearly an analogue of the "Republic of Letters," the Republic of Music overlapped with its model but at the same time was distinct from it.[74]

---

[68] Many of them traveled there via Warsaw; see Żórawska-Witkowska, "Eighteenth-Century Warsaw," 183–189. See also Bonner, "Catherine the Great," esp. 256–260 (a list of operas performed at St. Petersburg).
[69] Brover-Lubovsky, "The 'Greek Project'"; Frolova-Walker, "Inventing Ancestry," 9–13.
[70] See Jensen, "A Theoretical Work," 326–328.
[71] See also Taruskin, *Defining Russia Musically*.
[72] For recent research on networks of communication in early modern Europe, see Ahrendt and Van der Linden, "The Postmasters' Piggy Bank." On migration, see recent studies in Guzy-Pasiak and Markuszewska, *Music Migration*; Katalinić, *Music Migrations*; Nieden and Over, *Musicians' Mobilities*.
[73] Ahrendt, "Politics," 99.
[74] Chapin, "Counterpoint," 382. On the Republic of Letters in French contexts, see Goodman, *The Republic of Letters*.

As Keith Chapin has explained, "by the beginning of the eighteenth century, numerous writers on music emphasized their identity as musicians and implicitly acknowledged their differences from other humanists, addressing themselves specifically to a 'musical republic.'"[75] This notion was built on social events such as collaborative music making (for instance, in a *collegium musicum*, a local musical ensemble usually tied to a center of higher learning); outside immediate face-to-face contact, though, it was mediated through written genres.[76] Chapin points out additionally that the Republic of Music concept became known in German-speaking circles in the early eighteenth century and cites uses of the term by Georg Philipp Telemann (1681–1767) in 1717, Johann David Heinichen (1683–1729) in 1728, and Johann Adolph Scheibe (1708–1776) in 1749.[77]

In French, however, the term and concept can be traced earlier, to at least the beginning of the century.[78] The lexicographer and scholar of music Sébastien de Brossard (1655–1730), in his *Dictionnaire des termes* (*Dictionary of [Musical] Terms*) of 1701—published two years later with its better-known title *Dictionnaire de musique* (*Dictionary of Music*)—mentions "la Republique Musicale" ("the Musical Republic") toward the end of this volume, within a supplementary treatise on how to pronounce words in Italian "and other languages, especially Latin and French, for the use of people who sing."[79] He states that "there has never been more taste, nor more passion for Italian Music than there is currently in France" and emphasizes the importance of singers knowing how to pronounce the language, given that it "supplies the Musical Republic with an infinite amount of excellent pieces."[80] However, he does not gloss that term, and it was probably regarded as a self-explanatory elaboration of the Republic of Letters. A few decades

---

[75] Chapin, "Counterpoint," 381.

[76] Chapin, "'A Harmony or Concord,'" 240.

[77] Chapin, "Counterpoint," 381–382. Additional examples of contexts in which the German term "musikalische Republik" has been used can be seen in Heckmann, "Mann und Weib," 21; Menzel, "Senatoren," 13–19.

[78] By way of context, it is worth noting that in a definition from the well-known dictionary published in 1694 by the Académie Française, the term "republique" itself was defined simply as a "state governed by many [people]" ("Estat gouverné par plusieurs"). The entry goes on to say that "one calls, figuratively, *the republic of letters*, the literati in general, considered as making up a group," and gives the example "*Is there something new in the Republic of Letters?*" Original text in Académie Française, "Le Dictionnaire de l'Académie Française" (1694), Vol. 2, entry for "Republique."

[79] Brossard, *Dictionnaire des termes*, 324. Thanks to Alexei A. Panov and Ivan V. Rosanoff for confirming the details about this source. See their article "Sébastien de Brossard's Dictionnaire of 1701"; a comparison of the pagination of the different sources appears in table 2 on 424–426. For the 1703 edition, see Brossard, *Dictionnaire de musique*, "Traité de la maniere de bien prononcer les Mots Italiens," n.p.

[80] Brossard, *Dictionnaire des termes*, 324.

later, Couperin wrote in the preface to his suite *Les goûts-réünis* (*The Reunited Tastes*), published in Paris in 1724, that "for a long time, Italian taste and French taste have divided [or shared] the Republic of Music (in France)."[81] It seems possible that Couperin's placement of "in France" in parentheses indicates his opinion that the "Republic of Music" transcended national or political categories.[82]

The internationalism of the concept is demonstrated by its use in other contexts. An English example comes from "A Critical Discourse upon Opera's in England," published in London in 1709, a work attributed to Galliard.[83] The text makes a harsh critique of pasticcio operas on the English stage and continues: "I'm of the Opinion the *English* will in time grow more refined in their Taste for Musick, and won't stand in need of my Exhortations to quell this Pest that annoys the Republick of Musick, with as much Bravery as their Ancestors heretofore destroy'd the Wolves that had for a long time infested the Nation."[84] In the same city, another writer averred in 1720 that the absence of a singer from the opera "must disconcert the measures of the *Musical Republick!*" thus implying that the republic's "citizens" had clear expectations.[85] It was thus a fragile community built on habitus, to use the concept of Pierre Bourdieu (1930–2002), in the sense of internalized dispositions created through shared social experiences of music.[86]

There are also specimens of the term in Italian, reflecting further the cosmopolitan nature of the notion. In 1752, Francesco Provedi (c. 1710–after 1755) used the term in his treatise *Paragone della musica antica, e della moderna: Ragionamenti IV* (*Comparison of Ancient and Modern Music: Four Arguments*), with the observation that some authors had not brought the "advantages" to the "Republic of Music" ("Repubblica della Musica") that

---

[81] Original text: "Le goût Italien et le goût François, ont partagé depuis longtems, (en France) la République de la Musique." Couperin, *Les goûts-réünis*, "Préface."

[82] Mitchell Cohen, on the other hand, observes that Couperin's invocation of this imagined political entity "referred to culture and taste, but he was not living in an apolitical world, and it lends itself to speculation that his ideas may not always have been strictly musical, even when composing." Cohen, *The Politics of Opera*, 171.

[83] In Raguenet and [Galliard], *A Comparison*, 83. For the suggestion of Galliard as the author, see Lincoln, "J. E. Galliard," 349–352.

[84] [Galliard], "A Critical Discourse," 81–82, 83–84 (quotation).

[85] In W. Weber, "Redefining the Status of Opera," 509. William Weber also acknowledges the emergence of a shared set of cultural practices among wealthy patrons and the toleration of a range of tastes within their set but suggests that "deviation from this framework of assumptions and practices was tantamount to rebellion, threatening to destroy the bonds that held the Republic of Music together." W. Weber, "Redefining the Status of Opera," 510.

[86] For twenty-first-century perspectives on culturally inflected ways of listening to music, see Becker, "Exploring the Habitus of Listening," esp. 128–130.

their works had promised.[87] Provedi's treatise was reprinted in Venice in 1754.[88] This latter publication received a review the same year within a series significantly titled *Novelle della repubblica delle lettere per l'anno . . . (News from the Republic of Letters for the year . . .)*; its mention there is significant for linking the "Republic of Music" explicitly to the idea of the "Republic of Letters."[89] Another late-eighteenth-century example in Italian is by Spanish Jesuit Antonio Eximeno y Pujades (1729–1808), who uses the term "tutta la Repubblica musicale" ("all the musical republic") in his music history of 1774; this work was translated into Spanish and published in 1796.[90]

It becomes clear from these examples that the eighteenth-century Republic of Music was a conceptual space spanning multiple nations and languages and mediated by numerous translations. Within it, writers made critical evaluations and set out opinions (albeit "top-down") for general dissemination. The republic functioned as a discursive space in many ways. For instance, it could be the backdrop against which novelties were foregrounded for assessment, as seen when Christian Friedrich Daniel Schubart (1739–1791) described the pantaleon—a hammered dulcimer named for its inventor, Pantaleon Hebenstreit (1668–1750)—as an instrument that is "forever unable to set the tone in the musical Republic."[91] It had potential for controversy: Charles Burney (1726–1814) mentions in 1789 how *La serva padrona (The Servant Mistress)* by Giovanni Battista Pergolesi (1710–1736) "set the musical republic in a flame which has not yet been extinguished."[92] Its cosmopolitan community of citizens moreover constituted a purportedly autonomous democracy, in which robust debate took place. At the same time, though, some strong opinions within it could be characterized as tyranny. In October 1791, an anonymous review (attributed to Burney) of a book by William Jackson (1730–1803) published earlier that year excoriates Jackson for his criticisms of symphonies by composers whom he had left unnamed.[93] The reviewer sarcastically writes that if Jackson "had gone a little

---

[87] "Di qui è avvenuto, che le Opere loro sono tenute per sofisticherie, e per ciò non hanno recato alla Repubblica della Musica quel vantaggio, che promettevano sì copiosi Volumi." Provedi, *Paragone*, n.p.

[88] Provedi, "Paragone"; the term "Repubblica de Musica" appears at 446.

[89] The review is in *Novelle della repubblica delle lettere*, volume for 1754, 395.

[90] Eximeno [y Pujades], *Dell'origine e delle regole della musica*, 458; Eximeno [y Pujades], *Del origen y reglas de la musica*, Vol. 3, 245.

[91] Original text in Schubart, *C. F. D. Schubart's Ideen zu einer Ästhetik der Tonkunst*, 289. Stewart Pollens, who writes that this posthumous publication reflects the author's thinking in the 1780s, translates "der musikalische Republik" as "the musical public." Pollens, *A History of Stringed Keyboard Instruments*, 372.

[92] Burney, *A General History of Music*, Vol. 4, 609.

[93] R. Hughes, "Dr. Burney's Championship of Haydn," 93–94.

farther, and had assumed the *title*, as well as the style, of SUPREME DICTATOR in the republic of music, what would he have told us that we do not already know?"[94] This exaggerated epithet, clearly meant as an insult, may point to the desire for a politics within the Republic of Music that was participatory and not autocratic.

In generally assuming a democratic system of thought, the Republic of Music played a key part in the formation of the musical canon. Matthew Head describes oratorio performances in England in the last two decades of the eighteenth century as "expressing, doubly, a cult of the composer . . . and—related to this—a sort of musical Republic represented by the public concert beyond ecclesiastical and monarchic control."[95] References to the works of deceased musicians in the context of the Republic of Music also appear in London periodicals around this time. For instance, a laudatory tribute (in October 1798) to the late William Boyce (1711–1779) concludes with the words that his surviving works would "extort new applause from the republic of music."[96] Similarly, Samuel Wesley (1766–1837), in a letter of 1808 to organist Benjamin Jacob (1778–1829), invoked the "Republic of Musick" in arguing for the increase of knowledge and practice of the music of J. S. Bach.[97] It is evident that over the course of the eighteenth century, the Republic of Music shaped thought and became gradually acknowledged as a social network through shared theory, practice, aesthetics, and aspects of performance and economic culture. In music criticism, it also contributed to the emergence of new hierarchies of appreciation and implied a far-reaching frame of reference. If a musical Europe could not be defined geographically, it could at least be delineated conceptually, intellectually, and creatively through the mediation of regular correspondence and the circulation of music, musical knowledge, and musicians.

Superlative Europe: Musicians and Intra-Continental Fame

Within the broader context of critical reception in Europe of the long eighteenth century, writers also began to describe certain musicians

---

[94] "Review of *Observations on the Present State of Music*," 199.
[95] M. Head, "Music with 'No Past'?," 210.
[96] "Memoirs of the Late Dr. Boyce," 253.
[97] In Olleson, *Samuel Wesley*, 80.

in superlative and hyperbolic terms that used a continental scale. Such superlatives suggested a common aesthetic framework within the imagined boundaries of the community and contributed to musical constructions of Europe (although certain writers even used "the world" as their scope). An early example prefiguring the Republic of Music is by Athanasius Kircher (1602–1680) in his 1650 treatise *Musurgia universalis* (*Universal Composition*). Discussing theoretical issues regarding the treatment of the fourth as a consonant interval, he at one point appeals rhetorically to "the most skilled musicians of all Europe."[98] Another concerns Johann Heinrich Schmelzer (c. 1620–1680), who was described by Johann Sebastian Müller (1634–1708) in a travel diary of 1660 (published in 1714) as "the famous and nearly most distinguished violinist in all Europe."[99] Arcangelo Corelli (1653–1713) also received such an accolade. In 1701, the medical doctor Ellis Veryard (1657–1714)—who traveled widely in France, Italy, Spain, Malta, and several parts of the Ottoman Empire—gave a detailed description of his stay in Rome, writing: "the most famous Musician, especially for the Violin, is *Arcangelo Corelli*, commonly call'd *il Bolognese*: a Man so well known throughout all *Europe*, that I need not enlarge in his praise, but must acknowledge the great Civility he shew'd us when we went to visit him."[100] Despite Corelli being described as "so well known" across the continent, it is significant to note that the sobriquet by which he was best known, "the Bolognese," as quoted by Veryard, referred specifically to his city of birth. Nevertheless, other writers also commented on Corelli's fame stretching farther afield: Hawkins asserted in 1776 that "the proficiency of Corelli on his favourite instrument, the violin, was so great, that the fame of it reached throughout Europe; and [Johann] Mattheson [1681–1764] has not scrupled to say that he was the first performer on it in the world."[101]

Other musicians of the early eighteenth century were praised in similar terms by their contemporaries. Georg Muffat (1653–1704), whose writings were published in four languages—German, French, Italian, and Latin—stated in his *Florilegium secundum* (*Second Bouquet*) of 1698 that Lully's manner of playing the violin was "admired and praised by the most

---

[98] Kircher, *Musurgia universalis*, Vol. 1, 627.
[99] Brewer, *The Instrumental Music*, 64. Original text in Müller and Scheutz, "Reiße-Diarium von Johann Sebastian Müller," 71; Müller, "Reiße-Diarium," 178. See also P. Nettl, "Die Wiener Tanzkomposition," 123. Schmelzer was also discussed in the periodical *Diarium europäum* (*Journal of Europe*) in 1667, as P. Nettl points out. The title of this periodical implies a continental reach.
[100] Veryard, *An Account of Divers Choice Remarks*, 199.
[101] Hawkins, *A General History*, Vol. 4, 309–310.

accomplished musicians of the world," but in the French version, the word "Europe" was used for this last spatial category.[102] Similar continental superlatives were given by Évrard Titon du Tillet (1677–1762) in his compilation of biographies *Le Parnasse françois* (*The French Parnassus*), published in 1732, where he mentioned an "Italian named *Balthazarini* [the nickname for Balthasar de Beaujoyeux, originally Baldassare de Belgioioso (c. 1535–c.1587)], one of the best violins [violinists] of Europe."[103] Titon du Tillet described the French ensemble of the Vingt-quatre Violons du Roy (Twenty-four Violins of the King) as "the most famous in Europe," yet in a different part of the text, he also acknowledged Italy as "the first source of good music, which has spread throughout the different countries of Europe."[104]

While Europe provided the spatial scope within which musicians could shine, certain nations were still pinpointed. In many ways, questions of continental excellence in music were linked to the rivalry of French and Italian styles. In 1715, the *Histoire de la musique et de ses effets, depuis son origine jusqu'à present* (*History of Music and Its Effects, from Its Origin to the Present*)—compiled and completed by Jacques Bonnet-Bourdelot (1644–1723) from earlier work by his brother Pierre Bonnet-Bourdelot (1654–1708) and his uncle Pierre Bourdelot (1610–1685)—referred to the operas of Lully and Quinault as attracting "the admiration of all Europe."[105] Significantly, the examples just discussed distinguish between the use of a proper adjective for the national origin of musicians (such as "French" or "Italian") and the description of musicians as being "from" or "of" Europe. There can be seen a mix of expressions, even within the same sentence. For instance, Bonnet-Bourdelot writes first of "Italian music," then "French musicians," before mentioning "the most famous musicians of Europe."[106] Even though translations from French today might render "de l'Europe" as "European," the proper adjective "European" ("européen/ne" or other forms, discussed

---

[102] Muffat and Wilson, *Georg Muffat on Performance Practice*, ix, 31.
[103] Titon du Tillet, *Le Parnasse françois*, "Remarques sur la poësie et la musique," xlii. On this musician, see MacClintock and Fenlon, "Beaujoyeux [Beaujoyeulx], Balthasar de."
[104] Original text in Titon du Tillet, *Le Parnasse françois*, 393, and "Remarques sur la poësie et la musique," liii.
[105] Original text in Bonnet-Bourdelot, *Histoire de la musique*, 341.
[106] The complete original passage reads: "[T]elles sont les Cantates & les Sonates composées avec toute la force & tous les agrémens de la Musique Italienne, ce qui nous fait voir que les Musiciens François pourroient faire assault de Musique, de quelque nature qu'elle puisse être, contre les plus fameux Musiciens de l'Europe, & même en remporter le prix." Bonnet-Bourdelot, *Histoire de la musique*, 341–342.

in chapter 4) is notably absent. Thus, translating it as "musicians of Europe" may reflect more clearly the authors' meaning and intention.[107]

The cases mentioned so far have been found within the dense interiors of texts. However, there are also more obvious external labels. From the late seventeenth century, some music publishers in London began to advertise the sale of sheet music containing works by composers they described as "the best," "most eminent," or "most celebrated" masters in "Europe." Such a claim was a common ploy in eighteenth-century marketing of musical products.[108] For example, Henry Playford issued in 1695 *A General Catalogue of all the Choicest Musick-Books in English, Latin, Italian and French, both Vocal and Instrumental. Compos'd by the Best MASTERS in Europe, that have been from these Thirty Years past, to this present Time.*[109] Some decades later, a 1731 catalogue issued by John Walsh (1665/6–1736)—who from 1695 began to pick up and then dominate the market in early-eighteenth-century London—bore the title *Choice Musick by the most Celebrated Authors in Europe*. Constituting an alphabetical list of works by composers (listed only by surname) from "Albinoni" (Tomaso Giovanni Albinoni, 1671–1750/51) to "Ziani" (probably Marc'Antonio Ziani, c. 1653–1713), it includes English musicians such as Henry Purcell (1659–1695) and Robert Woodcock (1690–1728), but Italian names predominate.[110]

Besides catalogues, published anthologies of compositions also used this formula in their titles. In 1705, Walsh employed a superlative to describe composers as "the Greatest Masters in Europe" in a collection of pieces he published with John Hare (d. 1725): *Select Preludes & Vollentarys for the Violin, being Made and Contrived for the Improvement of the Hand with Variety of Compositions by all the Greatest Masters in Europe for that Instrument.*[111] Within single-volume anthologies, the "masters" to which the titles alluded were usually listed by name inside the scores—but not always. A collection of church music from 1751, *New Church Melody*, made

---

[107] I am not qualified to speak of the semantic differences between these formulations in terms of linguistics. I simply point out that whereas the adjectival use of "European" has been ubiquitous in the nineteenth, twentieth, and current centuries, this was not the case in earlier times.

[108] See a list of vocabulary and phrases appearing in eighteenth-century British newspapers in McGuinness, "Gigs, Roadies and Promoters," 270.

[109] [H. Playford], *A General Catalogue*.

[110] Walsh (the elder), *Choice Musick*.

[111] Walsh (the elder) and Hare, *Select Preludes & Vollentarys*. I became aware of this source and its use of the wording "Greatest Masters of Europe" in its title thanks to seeing the volume discussed in a conference paper by Federico Lanzellotti, "Carlo Ambrogio Lonati, 'Inventor of Double Stops,' and His Reception in Britain (1676–1724)."

by William Knapp (1698/9–1768), promised on its title page that it included "an Anthem on Psalm cxxvii. by One of the Greatest Masters in Europe."[112] The anthology was popular enough to be published in multiple editions, but by the time of the fifth, in 1764, the "greatest master" was still not named.[113] Concordant sources suggests that it was composed by "Mr. Harris," possibly implying James Harris (1709–1780), although it is not clear why he would be described in that way and so prominently on the title page.[114] Across the Atlantic in Northampton, Massachusetts, Jonathan Benjamin (c. 1754–1800) published in 1799 a volume titled *Harmonia Coelestis: A Collection of Church Music*, described on its title page as being "Chiefly Collected From the Greatest Masters in Europe, and Never Before Printed in America."[115] In the prefatory "Advertisement" he mentions works by George Frideric Handel (1685–1759) as well as by "Giardina [*sic*; Felice Gardini, 1716–1796], Purcell, [Martin] Madan [1725–1790], Millgrove [Benjamin Milgrove, 1731–1810], [Samuel] Arnold [1740–1802], &c.," and adds that "there are a number of tunes of *American* composition in this work, but for certain reasons, the Authors have not credit for them."[116] His use of the proper adjective "American" has a certain ambiguity in appearing to refer both to the act of composition and to the unnamed composers.

These kinds of titles reflect the changes that took place more broadly in publishing, subscription, and the growth of music societies—as well as in the acceleration and intensification of the circulation of repertory—in many countries during the second half of the eighteenth century.[117] While the proliferation of social organizations for music is a topic too vast to treat here, it is clear to see how "Europe" was invoked in the description of musical works or activities. Geographical issues also come to the fore in descriptions of

---

[112] Knapp, *New Church Melody* (1751), title page.

[113] Knapp, *New Church Melody* (1764), title page, 79–87 (anthem).

[114] Concordant sources listed in Répertoire International des Sources Musicales include St. Paul's Cathedral Library (GB-Lsp), MS Alto 3, Tenor 4, Bass 3 (manuscript copy, 1700–1730); Lincoln Cathedral Library (GB-Ll), MS 2, ff. 77v–78r (manuscript copy, 1757–1762) and MS 18, ff. 61v–63r (c. 1763); British Library, Add. MS 30932, ff. 118r–20r (manuscript copy, 1680–1720); Minster Library, York (GB-Y), M. 8 (S), ff. 154v–58v, and M. 164/H, H2 (S). Harris was a close friend and associate of Handel; see Burrows and Dunhill, *Music and Theatre in Handel's World*. However, whether that had anything to do with the epithet "greatest master" remains unknown.

[115] Benjamin, *Harmonia Coelestis*, title page. On this work, see Osterhout, "Andrew Wright," 10, 11, 19.

[116] Benjamin, *Harmonia Coelestis*, "Advertisement."

[117] As Luca Aversano has pointed out, "from the 1770s onwards, the first musical societies, usually organized by amateurs, appeared in eastern countries [of Europe]. Examples are the *Muzykal'nyj klub* (1772–1777) and the *Novyj muzykal'nyj klub* (1778–1793), both in Saint-Petersburg." Aversano, "The Transmission of Italian Musical Articles," 146.

the logistics of circulation, as we see in a range of examples. For instance, a monthly music journal titled *L'écho, ou Journal de musique françoise, italienne, contenant des airs, chansons, brunettes, duo tendres ou bachiques, rondes, vaudevilles, contredances, etc.* (*The Echo, or Journal of French [and] Italian Music, Containing Airs, Songs, Brunettes, Tender or Bacchic Duos, Rondos, Vaudevilles, Contredanses, etc.*) published in Liège by Benoît Andrez (1719–1804) from 1758 to 1773—the title of which clearly distinguishes between French and Italian styles—was described as being available at certain shops in Paris but also "in all the post-offices of Europe, and at the best bookshops in the most important cities."[118] Burney, after visiting Leipzig in 1773, described Breitkopf as "the most considerable vender [sic] of musical compositions in Europe" and observed that the proprietor "has, for thirteen or fourteen years, furnished his own country, as well as other parts of Europe, with a prodigious quantity of music from his press, of all kinds, by the greatest composers of the present age."[119] Meanwhile, W. A. Mozart noted proudly in a letter of 1778 to his father that the performance of his "Paris" symphony at the Concert Spirituel had been reported on in the *Courier de l'Europe* (*Europe's Courier*), an Anglo-French periodical published in London.[120] In 1801, the publisher Leduc, producing scores of the symphonies of Joseph Haydn (1732–1809), printed the comment that these works "have been Europe's delight for many years already and they offer composers in all genres material for the most serious studies."[121]

In London, "Europe" could sometimes stand for "mainland Europe." As Simon Fleming has pointed out, composers from the latter could account for between two-thirds and three-quarters of music publications offered for sale in the late eighteenth century.[122] In 1786, the music firm Longman and Broderip highlighted the term in the title of its catalogue *A Complete Register of All the New Musical Publications Imported from Different Parts of* Europe *by Longman and Broderip* (emphasis in original). This list contained instrumental music, including concertos, overtures, and symphonies, as well as chamber works ranging from duos to quintets.[123] In networks that promoted new repertory, cities were unsurprisingly the key nodes of exchange. A 1780

---

[118] Original text in Wahnon de Oliveira, "Publishing and Selling Music," 109–110, quotation on 110. Wahnon de Oliveira quotes this description from the December 1762 issue.
[119] Burney, *The Present State of Music*, Vol. 2, 73.
[120] Mozart and Mersmann, *Letters*, 106; see the report in "France," 404.
[121] Translation in Antolini, "Publishers and Buyers," 214 (original text at 214n.257).
[122] Fleming, "Foreign Composers," 226. See also Burchell, "'The First Talents of Europe,'" 93–113.
[123] Longman and Broderip, *A Complete Register*.

catalogue of music offered for sale by Johann Michael Götz (1740–1810) included "editions from nineteen European cities," which included London.[124] Works published in Naples from 1786 onward by Luigi Marescalchi (1745–1812) include the wording on their title pages that they are available "for all the major cities of Europe, at the usual addresses where printed music is sold."[125] Another factor that created an impression of cultural coherence and musical synchronization in the Republic of Music at the end of the eighteenth century was the rise of "simultaneous publishing" across cities and nations, with the aim of preventing piracy or breaches of copyright.[126]

In the second half of the eighteenth century, the superlatives being used to describe individual musicians or groups within Europe became popular to the point of cliché. Schubart uses the term "all of Europe" many times to report the influence of a musician or qualify the level of a musician's skill.[127] In 1764, the child W. A. Mozart was written up in a London newspaper as "the greatest prodigy that Europe or that even Human Nature has to boast of."[128] The letters of Mozart and his family mention on several occasions various instrumentalists and singers as "the best in Europe."[129] Jean-Jacques Rousseau (1712–1778) made a comparative assessment of the orchestras of Europe in his *Dictionnaire de musique* of 1768: he cited that of Naples as "the foremost orchestra in Europe" ("le premier *Orchestre* de l'Europe") for "the number and intelligence of the symphonists" ("le nombre & l'intelligence des Symphonistes"), but he considered the best-trained and -organized ensemble to be the opera orchestra of Dresden, directed by Johann Adolf Hasse (1699–1783).[130] On the other hand, "of all of Europe's orchestras" ("de tous les *Orchestres* de l'Europe"), he found that of the Opéra at Paris, despite being "one of the largest" ("quoiqu'un des plus nombreux"), to be the one with "the least effect" ("le moins d'effet").[131]

In 1773, Burney wrote of Domenico Ferrari (1722–1780), Pietro Nardini (1722–1793), and Antonio Lolli (c. 1725–1802) as "three of the greatest

---

[124] Quotation from Antolini, "Publishers and Buyers," 214. For a list of cities, see S. Adams, "International Dissemination of Printed Music," 29.

[125] For examples of the original wording, see his editions of Giuseppe Tartini (1692–1770), *L'arte dell'arco*; Federigo Fiorillo (1775–after 1823), *Studio per il violino diviso in trentasei capricci*, both undated. Copies are available on the International Music Score Library Project (IMSLP) at https://imslp.org.

[126] Guillo, "Legal Aspects," 134–136.

[127] DuBois, "Christian Friedrich Daniel Schubart's *Ideen zu einer Ästhetik der Tonkunst*."

[128] *The Public Advertiser*, June 1, 1764; reproduced in Deutsch, *Mozart*, 35.

[129] See examples in W. Mozart, *The Letters of Mozart and His Family*, 437, 485.

[130] Rousseau, *Dictionnaire de musique*, 359. Some copies of 1768 have different pagination.

[131] Rousseau, *Dictionnaire de musique*, 360.

performers on the violin in Europe"; in 1789, however, he went one step further and called Felice Giardini "the greatest performer [on violin] in Europe."[132] He also considered the "whole band of vocal and instrumental performers" at the Berlin Opera in 1752—based on his retrospective reading of the annals—as having been "the most splendid in Europe."[133] It seems that Burney occasionally implied continental Europe and not the British Isles when he used the term "Europe"; this distinction is apparent in his statement about the dispersal of the Dresden Opera orchestra (at the beginning of the Seven Years War), where he writes that "almost every great city of Europe, and London among the rest, acquired several exquisite and favourite performers."[134] Burney by no means intended to imply that England was not part of Europe, though. In his 1785 account of the Handel commemorations in Westminster Abbey (which had taken place the previous year), he observed that "there is, perhaps, *no country in Europe*, where the productions of old masters [composers] are more effectually preserved from oblivion, *than in England*" (emphasis added), going on to give examples of cathedral repertory and public concerts of old music.[135] For Burney, pan-continental frameworks were clearly an essential factor in canon formation.[136] Burney's rival Hawkins also gives a long list of "performers in Italy" on instruments including harpsichord, violin, violoncello, and theorbo, who were "celebrated throughout Europe," including England.[137]

Comments about musical greatness within Europe also arose from the pens of visitors from other parts of the world. A compelling example concerns a musician who also migrated to Europe and engaged in that continent's "own" musical arts in the most elite social and cultural contexts. On May 17, 1779, American diplomat John Adams (1735–1826) was visiting Lorient, France. There he heard about Joseph Bologne, Chevalier de

---

[132] Burney, *The Present State of Music*, Vol. 1, 103–104; Burney, *A General History of Music*, Vol. 4, 521.

[133] Burney, *The Present State of Music*, Vol. 2, 101.

[134] Burney, *The Present State of Music*, Vol. 2, 52.

[135] Burney, *An Account of the Musical Performances*, Preface, v. See also discussion of this passage in H. White, *The Musical Discourse of Servitude*, 156.

[136] For more context, see W. Weber, *The Rise of Musical Classics*.

[137] Hawkins, *A General History*, Vol. 5, 131; Lanzellotti, "Carlo Ambrogio Lonati." Hawkins also writes of one of Corelli's contemporaries, the now-unknown cornettist Galletti, that he "was deemed the greatest performer in the world." Hawkins, *A General History*, Vol. 5, 131. In this description, however, he appears to be paraphrasing a footnote by the translator of a text by François Raguenet, referring to the instrumentalist as "the greatest Prodigy in Nature, and the most surprizing Performer that ever was in the World." Raguenet and [Galliard], *A Comparison*, 51. Broad statements such as these and the reproduction of discourse appeared to matter more than mere details.

Saint-Georges (1745–1799), the famous violinist and swordsman born in the French Caribbean colony of Guadeloupe, the son of an enslaved African woman and a French planter.[138] Adams noted in his diary that Bologne was "the most accomplished Man *in Europe* in Riding, Running, Shooting, Fencing, Dancing, Musick" (emphasis added).[139] Using "in Europe" incidentally evaded essentialism in certain ways, positioning musicians in space and place and not necessarily implying their ethnicity. Yet it also represented an absence of race or the "whiteness" of discourse, leading to later problematic assumptions about race in music, to which we turn in chapter 3.[140]

All these descriptions of musicians label them as being "in Europe" or "of Europe," not "European." As the next part of the book shows, the proper adjective "European" began to be applied to musicians only when comparisons were made within contexts related to other parts of the world. Within the conceptual field of "Europe," superlatives served to consolidate ideas of a coherent musical space, in which citizens of the Republic of Music operated. These terms in turn would become linked to ideas of "Europeans," "European musicians," and "European music," as we will go on to explore.

---

[138] For a biography, see Banat, *The Chevalier de Saint-Georges*.

[139] J. Adams, "Diary of John Adams, Volume 2," May 17, 1779. I became aware of this source thanks to a conference paper by Christopher Dingle, " 'The Most Accomplished Man in Europe': Musical Traits of Joseph Bologne, Chevalier de Saint-Georges."

[140] Bloechl has critiqued "a predominant conception of Europe and of early music history as lacking race, which . . . casts them as white in modern racial schemas." Bloechl, "Race, Empire, and Early Music," 78.

PART II
"EUROPEAN MUSIC"

Today "European music" is commonplace as both a term and a concept. It is used perhaps less regularly than its corollary "Western music" but often—depending on context—interchangeably with it. As a collective and convenient label, "European music" is frequently applied to diverse musics of several millennia, from the cultures of ancient Greece to the most recent forms of popular musical expression.[1] It has been identified as a supranational musical category, with a set of common structures, processes, tools, and techniques: genres, contexts of performance, materials, and methods of dissemination. A transportable cultural complex, it has also gone abroad; as Strohm observed in his 1993 book *The Rise of European Music*, a seminal study of the growth of a shared language of Renaissance-era contrapuntal polyphony, "today, the European language of music has developed into a world language, and the European attitude towards music has become a model all over the world."[2]

A quarter of a century later, in a volume on global histories of music edited by Strohm, Jin-Ah Kim observed: "It is an established fact that 'European' music is disseminated globally and informs a part of 'Asian,' 'Arabic,' 'African,' and 'American' music and others."[3] Kim's use of scare quotes is worth highlighting, as it indicates a certain wariness of essentializing and reifying these large-scale adjectives. Part of the reason for this caution is the need to acknowledge the processes of hybridity, circulation, and mixing that have taken place over multiple centuries across oceans, and over countless

---

[1] Although I use the term "culture" here, we must note that our idea of it is really from the late nineteenth century; for a brief overview, see Appiah, *The Lies That Bind*, 189–190. Rubiés observes that in early modern comparative writings, the terms "rites and ceremonies" or "manners and customs" were used to refer to what we might think of as "culture." See Rubiés, "Comparing Cultures," 117. A related concept that emerged in eighteenth-century France was that of *civilization*; see Mazlish, *Civilization and Its Contents*, 20–48.

[2] Strohm, *The Rise of European Music*, 2.

[3] Kim, "'European Music' outside Europe?," 177.

millennia within large contiguous landmasses. Of course, it is fundamentally different to speak of music that exists *in* a place or space, as opposed to music that is *of* or *from* a place.[4] The historical tendency to conflate geographical place with specific social groupings and cultural identities, giving emphasis to certain stories and traditions that mediate those relationships, is a major factor in multiple histories of nationalisms and ethnonationalisms, in the connection of music to ideas of race, and in political, social, or religious movements that transcend the physical boundaries of geocultural regions or nation states.[5] Using any geographical adjectives as if they have clear conceptual boundaries runs not only the potential risk of internal cultural homogenization but also that of exclusion.

As mentioned in this book's introduction, the compound term "European music" appears to arise in the 1670s, and only a smattering of uses appear over the next seventy years. Its use in the title of a text on music (in this case, a manuscript treatise) is first seen in 1751—albeit with a misspelling and correction of the crucial adjective "European," which itself indicates a degree of unfamiliarity with the written term—and it only enters into common published discourse two decades later. My observations are inspired by the provocative question that heads a short but seminal article of 1980 by Peter Burke, "Did Europe Exist before 1700?" and his tracing of "Europe" and "European" as nouns, which have in many ways inspired and informed the chapters that follow.[6] They chime with the work of Klaus Oschema, who has considered the difference between academic conceptions of "Europe" today and the way these diverge from the term's use in the Middle Ages.[7]

It is worth noting that adjective-noun compounds of other continents' musics also seem to emerge in European languages in the eighteenth century; for example, an early instance of "*African* Musick" in English appears in 1733—intriguingly with reference to a janissary band.[8] "La Musique

---

[4] The title of a 2022 conference in Tours, France, on music in Africa and its diaspora 1300–1650 avoided the catch-all adjective "African," and discussions included debates about the conceptual category of "African music," given the enormous cultural diversity across the continent. Camilla Cavicchi, Janie Cole, and Philippe Vendrix organized "La musique en Afrique et sa diffusion dans le monde à l'époque moderne (1300–1650)," Centre d'Études Supérieures de la Renaissance, Tours, June 27–July 1, 2022. For a discussion of how a proper adjective for a national music can apply to contexts of cultural mixing and syncretism, see Kendall, "This Is Not Filipino Music."

[5] See Stokes, *Ethnicity, Identity, and Music*. For studies on race and music, see Radano and Bohlman, *Music and the Racial Imagination*; Julie Brown, *Western Music and Race*; Bloechl, "Race, Empire, and Early Music."

[6] P. Burke, "Did Europe Exist."

[7] Oschema, "How Does Medieval Historians' Use of the Notion of 'Europe' Compare?" See also Oschema, *Bilder von Europa im Mittelalter*; Oschema, "L'idée d'Europe."

[8] Proctor, *A Short Journal*, 24.

Asiatique" (Asian music) is used in French in 1749, in a text by historian Félix de Juvenel de Carlencas (1679–1760). He contrasts it with "European music" ("la Musique Européane"), which he deems to be "in its most flourishing state," and writes of "Asian music" that to consider it "in all its luster, it is necessary to go back to the tenth century"; he does so by citing a discussion by Al-Farabi (d. 950) of music in the court of "Seifeddoulat" (Sayf al-Dawla, 916–967) at Aleppo.[9] A satirical letter of 1770—published in London and York in a compilation of correspondence from newspapers—mentions "American music" in discussing a character named "Furioso, a musician of very extraordinary talents" who demonstrated "the Indian war-hoop" but disliked German musical style; later, he underwent an aesthetic conversion, after which he was supposedly convinced "that all the American music was composed upon German grounds."[10] These examples variously demonstrate the relatively loose sense in which these continental categories were employed.

In 1752, all four continents' musics were put into dialogue with each other in a single paragraph, with the proper adjective used for each, by Lübeck-based musician Caspar Ruetz (1708–1755), in his treatise *Widerlegte Vorurtheile von der Beschaffenheit der heutigen Kirchenmusic und von der Lebens-Art einiger Musicorum* (*Refutation of Prejudices Concerning the Nature of Contemporary Church Music and the Life Style of Some Musicians*).[11] This is the earliest example so far found of a concise passage mentioning all of them in immediate comparison. It also indicates a certain hardening of attitude. Ruetz writes:

> We are no longer indebted to [ancient] Hebrew music, since it is no longer available. Rather, we are much more indebted to European music since we have access to it and not to others. I can therefore sit back and be bold, because this is now the very best and most perfect in the world, against which all Asian music (from which even Chinese music is not excluded) falls away like chaff since it is barbaric. African and American music do not even enter into consideration. It is therefore the present-day European music which we have at hand to use in the service of God,

---

[9] Juvenel de Carlencas, *Essais sur l'histoire des belles lettres*, Vol. 2, 330. This passage seems to appear only in this "new augmented edition," not earlier versions.

[10] In Ramiger, "Number CLXXIV," 433 [*sic*; = 435].

[11] See discussion of this source, and its significance for the history of performance in Lübeck, in Snyder, *Dieterich Buxtehude*, 55.

and in fact in the highest degree that it has reached today, with all its art and beauty.[12]

The Eurocentrism of this statement and the sense of superiority with which Ruetz discusses "European music" are in clear evidence. At first glance, this passage may seem to conflate Europe with Christendom, but that is not necessarily a given. Still, Ruetz at least considers musics of other continents as possibilities for worship, even if he does so simply as a rhetorical device (we do not know whether he heard them).

Comparison with other continents, with an increasing tendency to denote "European music" as "superior," was the most dominant force in shaping discourse about an idea of a coherent category of identity and practice. The emergence of the supranational "European music" concept thus cannot be considered apart from the broader intercontinental contexts in which it was embedded. Mediated by travelers, merchants, diplomats, colonialists, and missionaries, "European music" was established largely within travel writing and related genres, whose intended readership transcended national and linguistic boundaries and proliferated in translation (and mistranslation), influencing other kinds of writing, including works on music. The transnational reading of travelogues by numerous generations in early modern Europe forged what Mary Louise Pratt—drawing from Gayatri Spivak—has termed "the 'domestic subject' of Euroimperialism."[13] Travel writing and its contribution to the rise of comparative ethnology played a key part in the making of the Republic of Letters in the seventeenth and eighteenth centuries.[14] Within this canon of literature, "European" was a convenient collective term that encapsulated multiple identities, especially given the transnational diversity of the membership of voyages, expeditions, and missions.

Ideas about Europe generated by thinkers within the continent itself were often predicated on a set of shared characteristics that combined notions of geography and religion.[15] Yet there was not necessarily a sense of a monolithic political—and especially not economic—"Europeanness" in the context of colonialist activity in the early modern period. As Kumkum Chatterjee and Clement Hawes have pointed out, "no early modern European power acted on behalf of a unified 'Europe' as such."[16] Nevertheless, in various parts

---

[12] Thanks to Estelle Joubert for this translation. Original text in Ruetz, *Widerlegte Vorurtheile*, 10.
[13] Pratt, *Imperial Eyes*, 4, 228n.3.
[14] See Rubiés, "Comparing Cultures," esp. 171.
[15] See, for example, E. Burke, *Two Letters*, 110–111.
[16] Chatterjee and Hawes, "Introduction," 8.

of the world in the sixteenth century, diverse people from Europe were initially viewed as a coherent cultural group by external observers, as Sanjay Subrahmanyam has shown in the case of South Asia.[17] Subrahmanyam also observes that although elite South Asian people visited Portugal in the seventeenth century, "not a single description of Europe [by them] emerges from all of this"; he notes that "as the English, Dutch, and eventually the French came to add their presences in India to that of the Portuguese, it is clear that the complexity of internal divisions in Europe became apparent to courtiers and rulers all over, from Calicut and Golconda to the Mughal empire."[18] Thus, as people in other parts of the world expanded their knowledge of the various nations of Europe, so did they become increasingly aware of cultural distinctions between those nations. Observations of a single nation at a vast geographical remove—represented by an often motley crew of envoys, opportunists, and exiles—provided ample opportunity for cultural critique and admiration or denigration of its mores. As Katrina Gulliver has pointed out with reference to colonialists from Europe in Southeast Asia, the "behaviour in colonies was seen to exemplify the essential national characteristics of each European group (in the eyes of their observers, particularly rival European nations)."[19]

As far as music goes, the most commonly contrasted national styles within Europe itself, which were sometimes also noted by observers in other continents, were "French" and "Italian."[20] Their differences extended to numerous structural, physical, and theoretical aspects, including forms of notation (with void notation and the use of the G1 or "French violin" clef), scoring (for five-part rather than four-part ensembles), and especially the bow hold used for playing violins and violas (with the thumb on the hair), which changed aspects of timbre and articulation and therefore the entire sounds of orchestras. Some composers in the first part of the century, such as Couperin, attempted to promote stylistic cohesion through instrumental music.[21] However, opera and other vocal genres remained resolutely distinct

---

[17] Subrahmanyam, "Taking Stock of the Franks."
[18] Subrahmanyam, "On the Hat-Wearers," 67.
[19] Gulliver, "Intercultural Exchange," 250.
[20] The literature on national styles is vast; for a concise overview, see Rose, "The Musical Map," 11–23; Cowart, *The Origins of Modern Musical Criticism*, 87–113 (specifically looking at French and Italian styles). On issues in performance practice, see Schott, "National Styles," 409–416. On the fusion of tastes, see especially Zohn, *Music for a Mixed Taste*.
[21] Couperin, for example, promoted the fusion of French and Italian tastes in a 1724 collection, *Les goûts-réünis*, which contained his programmatic work *Le Parnasse, ou L'apothéose de Corelli, grande sonade en trio* (*Parnassus, or the Apotheosis of Corelli, [a] Grand Trio Sonata*), as a French homage to that Italian composer. Couperin, *Les goûts-réünis*, 60–76. The following year, he published another

and over several decades became a space for great controversy; arguments rose to fever pitch in the early 1750s. The rivalry of French and Italian styles in that arena are undoubtedly a contributing factor to the slow rise in general use of the term "European music," which became common only from the 1770s. Considering national styles within Europe is important for our inquiry into the emergence of the "European music" concept mainly because of a curious paradox. If the differences of national styles were still relished and debated up to the mid-eighteenth century, but the term and concept of "European music" had already emerged in the 1670s, then what did the latter really refer to?

In this part of the book, I attempt to trace the rise of a collective "European" sense of shared musicality within the context of global intercultural convergence since the sixteenth century. In chapter 3, I discuss internal and external perceptions of the people known as "Europeans" or "Franks," first taking a rapid backward glance that spans from antiquity to the late Renaissance. I then go on to consider how Europeans, over the course of the seventeenth and eighteenth centuries, became one half of a binary that was pitted unequally with peoples from all other parts of the world. It was linked especially to dubious notions and uncertain descriptions of skin color that were linked with the "four" continents (in a still tentative way) from 1735 and then hardened and reified in that context by the late eighteenth century. I also scrutinize embodied notions of "the European," the "European ear," and the "European musician." In chapter 4, I focus on the rise of the term "European music" itself. Looking at writings produced by self-defined Europeans during the long eighteenth century, I highlight its early emergence in East Asian contexts and explore how its conceptual trajectory was shaped—predominantly for a "pan-European" readership—through intercultural encounters and comparisons. Taking a tour through Turkish contexts, I dwell on a French treatise of 1751 (alluded to above) that compares "Oriental music" with "European music." Despite being well known, this work has an interesting feature that has so far been passed over: I suggest that it is the earliest identifiable text of music theory to use both those specific terms in its title. Finally, I examine the rise of "European music" as a term of common discourse from the last third of

---

programmatic work that depicted both Corelli and Lully and contrasted their respective styles, his *Concert instrumental sous le titre d'Apothéose composé à la mémoire immortelle de l'incomparable Monsieur de Lully* (Ensemble Piece Titled Apotheosis[,] Composed to the Immortal Memory of the Incomparable Mr. Lully). Each movement has a descriptive heading, and in one, Apollo, the Greco-Roman god of music, persuades both musicians that "the union of French and Italian tastes must bring about perfection in music." Couperin, *Concert instrumental*, 12.

the eighteenth century, including its appearance in notable histories of music that were published in English, French, and German. Despite the prominence of such works, the "European music" concept is still characterized by a certain rarity right up to the 1830s, as I show in a liberal sprinkling of published examples from the tail end of the long eighteenth century.

By performing a conceptual archaeology of relevant terms and their application in primary sources as well as subsequent scholarship, I hope to tease out some of the ambiguities and paradoxes that are inherent in their use. We will see links across oceans and continents, since the invention of "European music" has origins from beyond Europe. It seems that the first known description of "European music" comes from China, the first ensemble named "European" was based in India, and the first publication of self-proclaimed "European" sheet music was made in America. All these neologistic phenomena emerged during the long eighteenth century, many in the contexts of encounters with other cultures. Examining their histories helps to de-essentialize and decenter the concept of "European music."

3
Europeans, "Franks," and "Their" Musics

The idea of "Europeans" as people has a long historiographical trajectory of shifting meanings. In the fifth century BCE, Greek historian Herodotus wrote of the separation of his world into Asia, Europe, and Libya (Africa).[1] He mentioned divisions between Asia and Europe at the Phasis (Rioni) and Tanais (Don) rivers, and bridges on which armies crossed the Bosphorus.[2] Writing of Persians and Greeks, he cited a longstanding binary that linked them to Asia and Europe respectively.[3] He also noted that Phrygians "were called Briges for as long as they lived in Europe," with their name changing only after they moved to Asia.[4] Another text from the ancient Greek world, the Hippocratic treatise *Airs, Waters, Places* (a work that discusses how climate and geography impact health and culture), used the substantive term "Europeans" to mean people living in the physical place called "Europe."[5]

The Romans also used the term "Europeans" (*europeenses*) for armies.[6] The notion of this word implying a military context persisted for centuries after the fall of their western empire. A famous reference to people with this term is found in a description by a Christian writer of the Battle of Tours and Poitiers in 732 CE, titled the *Mozarabic Chronicle* or *Continuatio hispanica* (written 754 CE).[7] Here it is used in contradistinction to their

---

[1] Herodotus, *The Histories*, 247–250 (Book 4, §§ 36–45).
[2] Herodotus, *The Histories*, 249–250 (Book 4, § 45), 264–265 (Book 4, §§ 87–89), 273 (Book 4, § 118); Guénoun, *About Europe*, 14–16. Herodotus, incidentally, was born in Halicarnassus (now Bodrum in Turkey) and therefore in Asia but maintained his Greek identity. See Appiah, *The Lies That Bind*, 192.
[3] Herodotus, *The Histories*, 4 (Book 1, § 4); P. Burke, "Did Europe Exist," 22.
[4] Herodotus, *The Histories*, 432 (Book 7, § 73). Thanks to Jessica Priestley for pointing this out and for her insights on this issue.
[5] Hippocrates, *Ancient Medicine*, 118–119, 136–137. I am grateful to Jessica Priestley and Peter Agócs for advice on this source. For a discussion of this text in relation to emerging racial identities, see Painter, *The History of White People*, 9–12.
[6] P. Burke, "Did Europe Exist," 23; he cites Heer, *The Intellectual History of Europe*, 7. Heer noted the use of the term "europeenses exercitus" ("European armies") in the *Historia Augusta* (*Augustan History*).
[7] Burke sees this specific instance of the word in the eighth century being used "in its traditional military context." P. Burke, "Did Europe Exist," 23. For an English translation of the relevant part of the text (attributed here, as it sometimes is, to eighth-century bishop Isidore of Beja), see Drace-Francis, *European Identity*, 11–12. See also discussion in Appiah, *The Lies That Bind*, 193–194.

The Making of European Music in the Long Eighteenth Century. D. R. M. Irving, Oxford University Press.
© Oxford University Press 2024. DOI: 10.1093/oso/9780197632185.003.0004

Muslim adversaries. The collective identity of "Europeans" was thus a form of oppositional self-definition, for which the presence of cultural others was intrinsic to the articulation of a label that suggested a homogenizing supranational identity. In this text, the term appears interchangeably with "Frank," "Christians," and "Men of the North"; meanwhile, words used for the Muslim forces are "Arabs," "Saracens," or "Ishmaelites."[8] Yet Isabella Walser-Bürgler has made an important qualification regarding this well-known source, writing: "While many over-enthusiastic interpreters have seen in this expression [Europeans] an ideological meaning, it seems to have been used merely as a pseudo-collective auxiliary term for all the different soldiers of European origin involved."[9] In this sense, it was what we could call an umbrella term. She points out, moreover, that the chronicler highlights the return of soldiers to their places of origin and remarks that "notions of a cultural, political, or ideological solidarity among the European army could not be more blatantly missing."[10] Even so, at the end of that century, Charlemagne (747–814; reigned from 768) was dubbed "the father of Europe" (*pater europae*).[11] He was also the king of "the Franks," and the decades around his coronation on Christmas Day in 800—launching the Holy Roman Empire—is the period in which "the curtain goes up" in one recent major history of "Western music," which cites the significant impact of the Carolingian dynasty on music notation and the formation of a literate repertory in western Europe.[12]

The word "Frank," in cognate forms, became well known in the Islamic world and adjacent territories as a term for Christians from Europe, particularly during the era of the Crusades. Studies of Islamic historiography have nevertheless revealed the multiplicity of its meanings; Daniel König states, for instance, that the label "never reached the status of an uncontested generic term for all Christian peoples of Western Europe."[13] Still, the lands of Europeans were referred to in many Islamic societies as "Frangistan."[14]

---

[8] Drace-Francis, *European Identity*, 12.
[9] Walser-Bürgler, *Europe and Europeanness*, 30.
[10] Walser-Bürgler, *Europe and Europeanness*, 31.
[11] P. Burke, "Did Europe Exist," 23. This notion, however, had a complex relationship with the development of ideas about Europe as a political space in the Middle Ages; see Oschema, "No 'Emperor of Europe.'"
[12] Taruskin, *The Oxford History of Western Music*, Vol. 1, 1–4. See also Page, *The Christian West and Its Singers*, 304, 323–326.
[13] König, *Arabic-Islamic Views*, 221, 230.
[14] On "Frangistan," see P. Burke, "Did Europe Exist," 23. Rifa'a Al-Tahtawi (1801–1873), an Egyptian scholar of geography and politics, wrote in 1831 on this concept as seen by the Ottoman Empire: "the Ottomans restrict the term *Ifranjistān* to mean Europe without the territories held by them, which they refer to as 'the lands of the *Rūm*.' Nevertheless, they also generalize the term *Rūm*

A number of Muslim observers also made references to an undifferentiated music of the Franks in a general and homogenized sense. For example, as Schofield has observed, Mughal theorist Ala-ud-din Barnawi (1598–1677) mentioned in a 1665 discussion of the Indo-Persian *thath* fretting system (which set particular temperaments) "that when the *thath* was set up, any style of music could be played in it—Persian, Hindustani, Afghani, Kashmiri, and startlingly even European (*firangi*) music."[15] Numerous references to Muslim travelers' views of music in and from Europe have also been uncovered in studies of their writing by Nabil Matar and Bernard Lewis, among others.[16] While lying outside the scope and approach of the present study and necessitating extensive collaboration across many languages and several disciplines, that vast topic presents fertile fields for further research.[17]

In ascribing continental labels to diverse and variegated groups and projecting them back in time, historians need, of course, to proceed with caution. As Kate Lowe has written, "[i]t is ... absurd to treat black Africans as a homogeneous group in the fifteenth and sixteenth centuries, just as it is absurd to talk of Europeans in the Renaissance period. These concepts only have value as oppositional or contrasting terms."[18] Yet the process of macro-differentiation that intercontinental comparisons entailed could often, in the eyes of the beholder, result in forms of exceptionalism that emphasized a perceived superiority of certain continents' people(s) over others. Katharina Piechocki has noted that Pope Pius II, for instance, asserted in the fifteenth century that "the inhabitants of Asia are always considered inferior to the inhabitants of Europe."[19] Observing that Renaissance humanists constructed "Europe as an autonomous continent and a new epistemological category," through discourse and new forms of vocabulary, Piechocki proposes the term "*europoiesis*" to describe this phenomenon.[20] Concepts and tropes

---

inasmuch as they use it to mean the lands of the Franks as well as some Asian countries under their rule." In Drace-Francis, *European Identity*, 119–120.

[15] Schofield [Brown], "Evidence." Barnawi is also mentioned in Joshi, *Uttar Pradesh District Gazetteers*, 283, and I have sourced his dates from there.
[16] Matar, *In the Lands of the Christians*; Matar, *Europe through Arab Eyes*; Matar, *An Arab Ambassador*; Lewis, *The Muslim Discovery of Europe*. See recent research in Diyāb and Muhanna, *The Book of Travels*. This source was discussed in a conference paper by Thomas Betzwieser, "French Opera through the Eyes of a Syrian Traveller."
[17] For two collections that include studies approaching this issue, see Schwartz, *Implicit Understandings*; and Chatterjee and Hawes, *Europe Observed*.
[18] Lowe, "Introduction," 2.
[19] Piechocki, *Cartographic Humanism*, 11.
[20] Piechocki, *Cartographic Humanism*, 12.

within literary traditions thus created the idea of the continent as much as any cartographic innovations, geographical discoveries, or political turning points. These gradually applied to music, but they were first established in other fields.

Europe and Collective Identities

In the extant textual records of early modern Europe, there can be seen a quantifiable rise over time in the use of both the nouns "Europe" and "European."[21] Burke summarizes three main contexts in which they appear: first, the perceived threat of the Ottoman Empire; second, discourse about invasions of other parts of the world; and third, "political conflict within Europe itself."[22] To these categories there can be added another dimension: the term's use to affirm belief in Europe's "superiority" over other cultures (as just seen in the statement of Pius II), an attitude that was based as much on the accumulation of material wealth as on racist ideology.[23] In the early sixteenth century, scholars including Jean Lemaire de Belges (1473–1524) began to speak of "our Europe," as a means of expressing solidarity among Christian nations in facing the Ottoman Empire.[24] Francis Bacon (1561–1626) referred to "nos Europaei" ("we Europeans") in his *De augmentis scientiarum* (*Partitions of the Sciences*) of 1623, implying Christian Europe, and a tendency for expressing a collective identity in this way continued in the seventeenth century.[25]

Members of the Society of Jesus, founded in 1540 (and suppressed in 1773), were prominent in promoting ideas of Europe, in all "four" parts of the world. When Jesuits first arrived in China, they were perceived as Buddhist scholars who had come from India.[26] Jesuits commonly presented themselves in China as people "from the West"; they were described in Chinese

---

[21] Burke states that "from the late fifteenth century on, we can at last stop counting instances of the word ['Europe'] on our fingers." See P. Burke, "Did Europe Exist," 23.

[22] P. Burke, "Did Europe Exist," 24–25.

[23] On the idea of European arrogance, see Osterhammel, *Unfabling the East*, 1–4. See also Schmale, "Europe," 89.

[24] Cowling, "Introduction," 8.

[25] P. Burke, "Did Europe Exist," 24, 28; Pagden, "Europe: Conceptualizing a Continent," 33. A collection of studies relevant to Europe's continental identity in that period is Schmale et al., *Studien zur Europäischen Identität*.

[26] Morar, "The Westerner," 17. See also Bertuccioli, "Europe as Seen from China," 19–28; Jiang and Irving, "Cultural Practices." I am grateful to Qingfan Jiang for her insights on this topic and for introducing me to the work of Morar.

sources, as Floran-Stefan Morar has pointed out, as "'people from the Great Western Ocean' (*Daxiyang ren* 大西洋人), often shortened to 'Ocean people' (*yang ren* 洋人) or 'Western people' (*xi ren* 西人)."[27] However, they soon became aware that they were called *folangji* (Franks) by local Muslims and that stories of Portuguese colonialism and conquest in Melaka and parts of India had preceded them.[28] Jesuits in China wanted to differentiate themselves from the conceptual legacy of Crusaders, embodied in the term "Frank," and to distinguish Europe geographically from Muslim regions that lay to the west of the Middle Kingdom (China).[29] In 1599–1601, Matteo Ricci (1552–1610) preceded his name in print with a continental descriptor, as "the European Matteo Ricci" (*Ouluobaren Limadou* 歐羅巴人 利瑪竇), which Morar has observed "was highly unusual, both for his Chinese audience and in Europe itself, [the latter being] more comfortable with the broader concept of Christendom."[30] Morar goes on to comment that "in using this label, Ricci made Europe into something unrecognizable at the time, a unified cultural and political entity."[31]

In 1602, Ricci printed the world map "Complete Geographical Map of Ten Thousand Countries" (*Kunyu Wanguo Quantu* 坤輿萬國全圖) on the orders of the Wanli emperor (1563–1620; reigned from 1572).[32] This cartographic representation of the world included in its detailed annotations notions of unity in Europe, with the comment that "the continent of Europe has over thirty countries. All adopt the political system of the ancient kings. They adhere to no heterodox doctrines, and all follow the holy faith of the Lord of Heaven."[33] In this map, the names of some individual countries are given. As Morar and Qiong Zhang have shown, one caption explained that Muslims had "erroneously" given the name "*Fulangji* 拂朗機" to Portugal and included a transliteration of the latter name; subsequent versions simply listed the transliteration as "Boerdowaer 波爾杜瓦爾" ("Portugal").[34] Part of the Jesuits' reasoning for presenting the unity of their continent, as

---

[27] Morar, "The Westerner," 14.
[28] In Melaka, as recorded in the fifteenth-century chronicle of Malay history *Sejarah melayu* [*Malay History* or *Malay Annals*], Europeans were also called *feringgi*, but on the first encounter, some people in Melaka said, "These are white Bengalis!" See Reid, "Early Southeast Asian Categorizations," 275.
[29] Zhang, *Making the New World Their Own*, 303; Morar, "The Westerner," 22; Jiang and Irving, "Cultural Practices."
[30] Morar, "The Westerner," 25. Thanks to Qingfan Jiang for advice on the Chinese terminology.
[31] Morar, "The Westerner," 25.
[32] I use the English translation of Ricci's map given by Zhang in *Making the New World Their Own*, 22.
[33] Translation in Zhang, *Making the New World Their Own*, 78.
[34] Morar, "The Westerner," 22; Zhang, *Making the New World Their Own*, 304–312.

Zhang has suggested, was undoubtedly to create the image of a power that rivaled China.[35] In their geographical discussions with Chinese scholars, the Jesuits promoted notions of Europe as a cultural and political entity in an image-making process that Timothy Brook has dubbed "Europaeology."[36] Ultimately, however, with the promotion of "the West" by Ricci and other Jesuits, it was the adjective "Western" that would be applied to musical elements of their activities in China (as discussed in chapter 6).[37]

The idea of Europe as a coherent entity vis-à-vis China was popularized in Europe itself through the publication of a number of Jesuit writings, especially a book of 1615—based on writings of Ricci—by Nicolas Trigault (1577–1628): *De christiana expeditione apud Sinas suscepta ab Societate Jesu* (*On the Christian Mission to the Chinese Undertaken by the Society of Jesus*).[38] Trigault, who had worked in China from 1611 and 1613, traveled around Europe in 1614–1618 in order to raise money and support for the mission. Clossey asserts that "Trigault attempted to work around national loyalties [in Europe] by creating a world polarized between China and Europe" but notes that he "held no illusions about Europe's unity."[39] Considering the reception of these interactions in Europe helps us to understand the entry of continental notions into common discourse and, later, into the historiography of music. The Jesuits were instrumental not only in changing the idea of "Frank" into "European" in China but also in promoting there an idea of a unified Europe. Even so, the term "Frank" persisted for many generations; for instance, British trader John Meares (c. 1756–1809) noted its use at Canton (Guangzhou) in the late 1780s.[40]

In the eighteenth century, people from Europe who lived or traveled in other parts of the world began to be conscious of being labeled by others with a single rubric. This sense of collectivity could be attributed in some ways to a growing sense of "diasporic intimacy"—to apply a concept of Svetlana Boym (1959–2015)—that transcended national difference, particularly where

---

[35] Zhang, *Making the New World Their Own*, 78. Dominic Sachsenmaier also observes that "Ricci's famous world map did not refer to the homelands of Islam, so his purpose was not to provide a global view of the spread of religions." Sachsenmaier, *Global Entanglements*, 130.
[36] Brook, "Europaeology?"
[37] Examining this conflation of ideas about Europe and "the West" in China at this time, Brook states that "the habit of speaking of Europe, and later of the Americas as well, as the West derives from this early moment of contact." Brook, "Europaeology?," 265.
[38] Ricci and Trigault, *De christiana expeditione apud Sinas*.
[39] Clossey, *Salvation and Globalization*, 63.
[40] He commented that "the Chinese call an European a Fanqui [sic]," in Meares, *Voyages*, lxxviii.

social music making was concerned.[41] In a study of musical culture by a community of diverse expatriates in Aleppo, Syria, Bryan White has noted that "the French were most numerous, but there were also Italians, Dutchmen, and occasionally Germans; all were known collectively as 'Franks,' and for the most part, they lived together harmoniously, making their entertainment among themselves."[42] Two brief examples of international musical collaboration among these "Franks" are worth highlighting. First, in around 1690, English Protestant merchant Rowland Sherman (1662/1665–1747/1748) played keyboard for sacred motets by Henry Du Mont (1610–1684) to perform them with French Catholic missionaries (Capuchins), on the occasion of social visits.[43] Second, the Swedish naturalist Fredrik Hasselquist (1722–1752), a student of biologist Carl Linnaeus (1707–1778), traveled to Turkey in 1749 and gave an account of festivities in "Budgia" (Buca, near İzmir), where he later died. He used both the terms "Franks" and "Europeans" when writing about musical activities.[44]

"Frank" was apparently accepted and embraced by the very people to whom it pertained. Explaining the term, Scottish doctor and naturalist Alexander Russell (c. 1715–1768) wrote in his famous study *The Natural History of Aleppo* (1756) that "the *Europeans*, or *Franks* (as they are generally called), residing in *Aleppo*, are chiefly *English* and *French*"; even so, he made a distinction in terms of religious confession, referring to Catholics as "*Franks* of the *Romish* religion."[45] The second, enlarged edition of this work—revised and expanded by Russell's half-brother Patrick (1726–1805) and published in 1794—gives a considerably larger explanation of "Europeans or Franks," mentioning specific nations: "The Europeans, or Franks, residing at Aleppo, are English, French, Venetian, Dutch, and Tuscan, or Imperial, subjects."[46] The text also quotes a French missionary on the topic, who pointed out the reflexive views that shaped this category: the "French, English, Italians and Dutch, in respect to the people among whom they dwelt, considered themselves as persons of the same country, and, in

---

[41] I am grateful to Alan Maddox for introducing me to the concept of "diasporic intimacy," on which see Boym, "On Diasporic Intimacy."
[42] B. White, "'Brothers of the String,'" 537. I thank Bryan White for discussions of his research in this area.
[43] B. White, "'Brothers of the String,'" 565.
[44] Hasselquist, *Voyages and Travels in the Levant*, 22.
[45] Russell, *The Natural History of Aleppo, and Parts Adjacent*, 132.
[46] Russell, *The Natural History of Aleppo: Containing a Description*, Vol. 2, 1. On the production of this second edition, see B. White, "'Brothers of the String,'" 540.

that light, were viewed by the natives, who, without distinction, reckoned them all Franks."[47]

"Homo Europaeus" and Discriminatory Taxonomies of Humankind

Scottish philosopher David Hume (1711–1776) also wrote about Europeans as "Franks" in his essay "Of National Characters," first published in 1748. He stated:

> Where several neighbouring Nations have a very close Communication together, either by Policy, Commerce, or Travelling, they acquire a Similitude of Manners, proportion'd to the Communication. Thus all the *Franks* appear to have a uniform Character to the Eastern Nations. The Differences among them are like the particular Accents of different Provinces, which are not distinguishable, except by an Ear accustom'd to them, and which commonly escape a Foreigner.[48]

The use of an aural analogy to refer to identification of cultural differences is striking, especially given the later emergence of a pan-continental "European ear" (discussed below). Hume observes the emergence of a cultural "similitude" through "very close communication." At the same time, he notes that it is a question of appearance and suggests that it is only an observer who becomes more knowledgeable—just as a foreigner's ear becomes gradually accustomed to different accents of the same language—who might distinguish cultural difference.

This was no benign essay, however. In a new edition five years after its original publication, Hume appended a footnote partway through, stating that Africans—for whom he used a pejorative term—and "all the other species of men (for there are four or five different kinds)" were "naturally inferior to the whites," adding the startling claim that nonwhites had "no ingenious

---

[47] Russell, *The Natural History of Aleppo: Containing a Description*, Vol. 2, 13–14. It is worth noting that in the course of the nineteenth century, as John Morgan O'Connell has pointed out, the terms "alaturka" (the Turkish adoption of the Italian term "alla turca" in Italian, to signify Turkish style) and "alafranga" (its opposite in an emerging binary, to denote practices of "European" origin) were used by social and cultural reformers among the Ottoman elite. O'Connell, "In the Time of Alaturka," especially 184–187. I am grateful to Maria Semi for highlighting the pertinence of this issue.

[48] Hume, *Three Essays*, 15.

manufactures amongst them, no arts, no sciences."[49] Aaron Garrett and Silvia Sebastiani have observed of this infamous comment that "it is disturbing, both in its content and in the fact that it was the persistent, and one assumes considered, view of a philosopher who was and is an avatar of Enlightenment and who is often looked upon as a secular saint and a model of character."[50] In mid-2020, in the midst of the international protests following the murder of African American man George Floyd (1973–2020), students highlighted this quotation afresh at the University in Edinburgh, where a prominent building bore a name honoring Hume. Their activism resulted in an official acknowledgment of the distress and offense caused by this philosopher's statement and the renaming of the edifice.[51]

Hume's views did not go unchallenged in his own times, either. In 1776, another Scottish writer, James Beattie (1735–1803), critiqued and directly contradicted him.[52] Beattie's essay "On the Nature and Immutability of Truth, in Opposition to Sophistry and Scepticism" included a description of the ingenuity of enslaved Africans in Europe "notwithstanding their unhappy circumstances," followed by the observation that "they become excellent handicraftsmen, and practical musicians, and indeed learn every thing their masters are at pains to teach them, perfidy and debauchery not excepted."[53] French priest and scholar Henri Jean-Baptiste Grégoire (1750–1831), a famous abolitionist (usually known as the Abbé Grégoire), also admonished and refuted Hume in his 1808 work *De la littérature des nègres, ou Recherches sur leurs facultés intellectuelles, leurs qualités morales et leur littérature* (*On the Literature of Black People, or Research into Their Intellectual Capabilities, Their Moral Qualities, and Their Literature*).[54] In this book, he provided many examples of Black individuals prominent in the arts and sciences—including the celebrated violinist and composer Joseph Bologne, chevalier de Saint-Georges—as well as discussing African and African diasporic practices of music and dance more widely.[55]

One of the figures highlighted by Grégoire was Ignatius Sancho (c. 1729–1780), born on a slaving ship to a mother who had been kidnapped

---

[49] Hume, *Essays and Treatises*, 291n.
[50] Garrett and Sebastiani, "David Hume on Race," 31. See also Sebastiani, "National Characters and Race." Thanks to Maria Semi for pointing out these references.
[51] "Equality, Diversity and Inclusion."
[52] Beattie, *Essays*, 310.
[53] Beattie, *Essays*, 311.
[54] Schaub and Sebastiani, *Race et histoire*, 456.
[55] Grégoire, *De la littérature des Nègres*. For discussion of Abbé Grégoire, see Appiah, *The Lies That Bind*, 115–118.

and enslaved; he was orphaned at the age of two. Taken to England, Sancho later found refuge and patronage in the household of John Montagu (1690–1749) and Mary Montagu (1689–1751), Duke and Duchess of Montagu.[56] A respected musician and writer, he published letters and compositions.[57] Notably, on the title page of his first collections of music, Sancho's name does not appear; rather, he is referred to with a continental label, as "an African" (and not, significantly, any prejudice-loaded contemporaneous term meaning "black"). Later, his last two music publications—*Cotillons &c.* (1776) and *Twelve Country Dances for the Year 1779*—list his name alone. Observing this transition, Rebecca Cypess has suggested that "Sancho's changing position in society may have led him to withhold his name in the earlier publications and reveal it in these latter two."[58] The term "African" also appears alongside his name in a collection of letters published in 1782, after his death; the preface states that the editor's motivations included her "desire of shewing that an untutored African may possess abilities equal to an European."[59]

This conceptual segregation along the lines of continental origin demonstrates that even though many people of color lived in major cities of Europe and were engaging in the same kinds of music that were esteemed by the elite, they were denied by patrons the identity category of "European," on essentialist terms. Writers in Europe who conflated North Africa with sub-Saharan Africa often employed the term "moor" to refer to Black musicians. As Arne Spohr has demonstrated, the German word *Mohr* (moor) was applied to Black trumpeters in German-speaking lands, contributing to constructions of the idea of Blackness in complex ways; similarly, we learn from the recent research of Emily Wilbourne that Giovanni Buonaccorsi (fl. 1651–1674), an enslaved person and operatic singer of African origin in seventeenth-century Italy, was known as "il moro."[60] The discriminatory terms "*pardo*" (in Portuguese) and "mulatto" (in several languages)—meaning people of mixed race, specifically of African descent—were used to

---

[56] Grégoire, *De la littérature des Nègres*, 252–253.
[57] Sancho, *Letters*. For a facsimile edition of his known musical works, see Sancho and Wright, *Ignatius Sancho (1729–1780)*. For a recent study on Sancho, see Cypess, "Notation, Performance, and the Significance of Print."
[58] Cypess, "Notation, Performance, and the Significance of Print," 201.
[59] Sancho, *Letters*, i–ii.
[60] Spohr, "'Mohr und Trompeter'"; Wilbourne, "'. . . La curiosità del personaggio,'" 134. See also Wilbourne, *Voice, Slavery, and Race*. Tess Knighton has pointed out examples in Iberia. See Knighton, "Instruments," 115–118.

describe the well-known free musicians Vicente Lusitano (d. after 1561) and Joseph Bologne, respectively.[61]

Sometimes, unless iconography or textual descriptions make their ethnicity evident, musicians' diverse origins and cultural identities can go unnoted in the historiography of music in early modern Europe, as well as in colonial contexts.[62] In 2015, Bloechl presciently proposed that "establishing the archive of race—including the presence and creative activity of racially marked people—in early music history is the most immediate way to begin countering the field's 'white mythology' and one of its most detrimental consequences: the marginalization of 'non-white' actors or aspects of their history."[63] In following this call to a focused engagement with this question in primary sources, we need also to keep in mind the chronological specificity of particular kinds of terminology and how notions based on color terms have changed over time. Spohr, for instance, points out how German perspectives on Africans "slowly shifted from religious interpretations of blackness to pseudoscientific race theories that emerged in late eighteenth-century Germany."[64] There were similar patterns in other parts of Europe regarding other racial signifiers based on other color terms, and the eighteenth century was a crucial period of transition, as we now go on to see.

It goes almost without saying that the use of any kind of reductive national, continental, or other labels in order to deny or downplay the creative abilities of different peoples is a long-standing feature in the history of racism.[65] In the eighteenth century, this form of categorical discrimination became enmeshed in emerging systems of biological and cultural taxonomies, some of which are widely recognized as being among the roots of later "scientific racism."[66] In his *Systema naturae* (*System of Nature*) of 1735, Linnaeus famously proposed a fourfold notion of the varieties of humankind ("Homo") as European, American, Asian, and African, clearly based on the "four" continents.[67] Linnaeus himself did not use the word "race," rather writing of "varieties" of humankind; nevertheless, his ideas were later subsumed

---

[61] Blackburn, Schumann, and McHardy, "Lusitano"; Banat, *The Chevalier de Saint-Georges*, 40.
[62] See also my discussion of how Spanish names can mask the identity of Indigenous musicians in archival documents from the Philippines, in Irving, *Colonial Counterpoint*, 159.
[63] Bloechl, "Race, Empire, and Early Music," 106. She outlines a program for research on 106–107. See also A. Clark, "Uncovering a Diverse Early Music."
[64] Spohr, "'Mohr und Trompeter,'" 619.
[65] For context, see Bethencourt, *Racisms*.
[66] For an overview, see Painter, *The History of White People*, 59–90; Bethencourt, *Racisms*, 252–270.
[67] In the tenth edition (1758), he added two more categories: "Ferus" (wild) and "Monstrosus" (monstruous). Charmantier, "Linnaeus and Race."

into thinking about races.[68] As historian of science Staffan Müller-Wille has persuasively argued, legacies of the theory of the humors and the enduring idea of the "four parts of the world" were evident in Linnaeus's categorization. Linnaeus applied the colors of the four humors—red blood, yellow bile, black bile, and white phlegm—to describe the skin color of people from each continent.[69]

If Linnaeus was drawing from ancient humoral theory of the Hippocratic tradition for his color categories, then it seems possible that his descriptions of color also followed classical thinking by referring to shades rather than specific hues.[70] He initially referred in 1735 to the skin colors of humans in this way: Europeans as "whitish" (in Latin, "albesc[ens]"), Americans as "reddish" ("rubesc[ens]"), Asians as "tawny" ("fuscus"), and Africans as "blackish" ("nigr[iculus]").[71] Linnaeus was not alone in using terms that approximated colors, rather than reifying them. In the early eighteenth century, Jesuits François-Xavier de Charlevoix (1682–1761) and Joseph-François Lafitau (1681–1746) also wrote the terms "olive-colored" ("olivâtre") and "reddish" ("rougeâtre") to describe people from Asia (1715) and America (1724), respectively.[72] Linnaeus's use of color terms later became less tentative in his tenth edition of *Systema naturae* of 1758, which Christina Skott has described as "an almost completely new work."[73] According to Müller-Wille, they are listed there as "red (*rufus*), white (*albus*), pale yellow (*luridus*), and black (*niger*), indicating both a hardening and, in the case of *luridus*, a more judgmental distinction."[74] This change represents a gradual move from the relative to the absolute, in conceptual terms, and a certain transition toward the conflation of color and racial classification. Later, in 1758, Linnaeus applied the temperaments of each humor—sanguine (red blood), choleric (yellow bile), melancholic (black bile), and phlegmatic (white phlegm)—to the four continents but mixed them up: for him, "white" Europeans were

---

[68] Müller-Wille, "Linnaeus," 194; Charmantier, "Linnaeus and Race."
[69] Müller-Wille, "Linnaeus."
[70] Thanks to Maria Semi for this insight. See also A. Clements, "Colour."
[71] Müller-Wille, "Linnaeus," 196.
[72] Keevak, *Becoming Yellow*, 29. For an example, see Charlevoix, *Histoire*, Vol. 1, 6. Lafitau, in using the word "reddish" (*rougeâtre*) rather than "red" (*rouge*) to describe the skin tone of Indigenous Americans (with whom he lived), attributed this fact of nature not to climate but to a metaphysical reason—"the imagination of mothers, who find beauty in this color"—as well as the practice of painting the body with *rocou*, a red paint prepared from the shrub *Bixa orellana*. Original text in Lafitau, *Moeurs des sauvages ameriquains*, Vol. 1, 29.
[73] Skott, "Linnaeus and the Troglodyte," 144.
[74] Müller-Wille, "Linnaeus," 200. Keevak translates the word *luridus* as "'lurid,' 'sallow,' or 'pale yellow.'" Keevak, "How Did East Asians Become Yellow?," 205.

"sanguine," "red" Americans "choleric," "pale yellow" Asians "melancholy," and "black" Africans "phlegmatic."[75]

As historians Michael Keevak and Rotem Kowner have shown, certain East Asians (Chinese and Japanese) had been frequently described as "white" in texts by writers from Europe well before the work of Linnaeus, especially by Jesuit missionaries in the late sixteenth century.[76] Yet this notion soon changed. Engelbert Kaempfer (1651–1716), for example, called the Japanese "brown" ("braune" in German), even though in the first publication of his popular *History of Japan*—an English translation that appeared in 1727—the word was rendered as "tawny."[77] Keevak observes that for early modern European scholars, "it had become necessary to ensure that Asians were safely distanced from a whiteness that only the West was allowed to embody—and a whiteness that was beginning to be defined at exactly the same time."[78] Even so, this porousness of the category continued in later decades; Schmale points out, for instance, that "according to [Immanuel] Kant [1724–1804], the 'white race' included not only Europeans but also Arabians, Turks and many others."[79]

The eighteenth century was a period of considerable change in thought about whiteness. An early example of the shifting meanings of "white" can be found in a novel of 1726, *The Voyages and Adventures of Captain Robert Boyle: In Several Parts of the World*, by Anglo-Irish writer William Rufus Chetwood (d. 1766).[80] Its text is in travelogue style and has a number of musical references; the narrator meets a fictionalized William Dampier (1651–1715), who apologizes for the lack of "*Italian* Musick" but has an "*English* Eunuch" (castrato) in his retinue.[81] The story includes an episode in Salvador, Brazil, where, as the protagonist recounts: "There may be about 20000 Whites (or I should say *Portugueze*, for they are none of the whitest,) and about treble that Number of Slaves."[82] In this statement, a stark binary

---

[75] Müller-Wille qualifies that "it cannot be emphasized enough how fanciful Linnaeus's color scheme actually is, if judged in terms of the humoral doctrine." Müller-Wille, "Linnaeus," 206.
[76] Keevak, *Becoming Yellow*, 27–30, 38–39; Kowner, *From White to Yellow*, 81, 84.
[77] Keevak, *Becoming Yellow*, 29.
[78] Keevak, *Becoming Yellow*, 38–39.
[79] Schmale, "Europe," 90. See also Bonnett, "Who Was White?"; Rubiés, "Were Early Modern Europeans Racist?," 61.
[80] "White, Adj. (and Adv.)"; Chetwood, *The Voyages and Adventures*. Chetwood's middle name, coincidentally, means "red."
[81] Chetwood, *The Voyages and Adventures*, 163. Dampier was an English privateer and naturalist who sailed around the world and visited the west coast of Australia, among other places. For discussion of his description of certain intercultural interactions in music, see Irving, "Exchange."
[82] Chetwood, *The Voyages and Adventures*, 197.

and power imbalance are immediately in evidence, and Boyle does not even mention the color of "slaves," leaving it for the reader to assume. With his description of the Portuguese as "none of the whitest," however, he is either referring to a spectrum within Europe or implying interracial unions within the Portuguese colonial empire and the people descended from them.

This author's cursory comment raises a significant point to consider, since Brazil plays a prominent role in the early history of eighteenth-century color schemes. Müller-Wille speculates that one of the sources consulted by Linnaeus was the *Historia naturalis brasiliae* (*Natural History of Brazil*) by Georg Marcgrave (1610–1644), published posthumously in 1648 (a copy of which was owned by the academic landlord with whom Linnaeus lodged in his student days). The work "notes with a modicum of surprise" the use of the term "Europeans" in Brazil to refer to people of Portuguese, Dutch, German, French, and English origin.[83] In it, Marcgrave also describes the emergence of a racially mixed society, with people born to parents of different backgrounds. According to Müller-Wille, this part of the text constitutes "one of the earliest accounts of a classification system known as *las castas*."[84] The *casta* (caste) system became prevalent in the multiethnic societies of the Portuguese and Spanish colonies of the Americas.

In Spanish territories, it resulted in a taxonomy of sixteen racialized categories. These were codified and represented in a genre of the visual arts, particularly in eighteenth-century Mexico, known as "*casta* painting."[85] A complete series conventionally contained sixteen images, each of which presented a heterosexual couple and their child, with individual labels, in a formula such as "from a Spaniard and an Indigenous person there comes a *mestizo*"; some examples include musical iconography.[86] These categories had legal import in Spain's American colonies, dictating aspects such as obligation to pay tribute (tax or compulsory labor) as well as the privilege to enter into specific professions. Related to the concept of *limpieza de sangre* (purity [literally cleanliness] of blood) emanating from fifteenth-century Spain, the *sistema de castas* "was tied to a colonial concern for restricting the political and economic claims of non-Spaniards, or rather, for delimiting who could claim to be Spanish," as Jesús Ramos-Kittrell has observed.[87] Identity

---

[83] Müller-Wille, "Linnaeus," 197. For the original source, see Piso and Marcgrave, *Historia naturalis brasiliae*, 268.
[84] Müller-Wille, "Linnaeus," 197.
[85] Katzew, *Casta Painting*.
[86] Ramos-Kittrell, *Playing in the Cathedral*, 70–71.
[87] Ramos-Kittrell, *Playing in the Cathedral*, 60–61.

was, however, based not only on descent but also on a set of attributes including "the individual's education, institutional affiliations, corporate memberships, and circle of social connections," in other words, "perceptions of an individual's social profile rather than . . . exact knowledge of his or her origins."[88]

Bloechl has pointed out that "the 'whiteness' of early modern Europe is a libidinal and political, as well as historical construct, and as such demands critical approaches that are guided, but not bound by historicity."[89] Schofield and Taylor have also noted how Linnaean thought (coalescing color, continents, and characteristics) impacted musical thinking of people who self-defined as Europeans in the eighteenth century.[90] At this time, prejudice and discrimination were gradually becoming normalized, over many decades, through discourse and cultural belief; as Schmale has observed, "the self-image of the *homo europaeus* was completely internalized," accompanied by a belief (for many Europeans) that "they were already culturally-racially encoded and therefore superior to others, as demonstrated by countless eighteenth-century texts with reports or narratives from various regions throughout the world."[91] Adding further complexity to the overlapping notions surrounding colors, some impinged on timbre, although they were not (yet) necessarily linked to race. For example, Burney pointed out in 1782 a white/black binary, also referring to "brown . . . *fusca*," thus using three of the four colors mentioned by Linnaeus: "The [ancient] Greeks indeed have the expression of a *white voice*, for a voice that is clear; and of a *black* voice, for the contrary: as the Romans talk of a brown voice, *fusca vox*, as that of Nero [37–68; reigned from 54] is called by Suetonious [c. 69–after 122]."[92] The significant intersections of timbre with race in the field of historical performance practice today have been highlighted by Melanie Marshall.[93]

Historian Nell Irvin Painter has discussed how other racial categorizations were proposed later in the eighteenth century by Johann Joachim Winckelmann (1717–1768) and Johann Friedrich Blumenbach (1752–1840), with the latter coining the term "Caucasian" and publishing it in

---

[88] Ramos-Kittrell, *Playing in the Cathedral*, 37. Although the term used in this system was "español" rather than "white," the latter term was also used generically in discourse of the time. See, for example, Ramos-Kittrell, *Playing in the Cathedral*, 66.
[89] Bloechl, "Race, Empire, and Early Music," 79.
[90] Schofield [Brown], "Reading Indian Music," 8–9; Taylor, *Beyond Exoticism*, 47–48.
[91] Schmale, "Europe," 89.
[92] Burney, *A General History of Music*, Vol. 2, 418n.(c); "White, Adj. (and Adv.)."
[93] See Marshall, "*Voce Bianca*"; Marshall, "The Sound of Whiteness"; Bloechl, "Race, Empire, and Early Music," 105n.83.

1795.[94] Although the term "Caucasian" does not appear to have been applied directly to music before 1800, a binary of "blacks" and "whites" in thinking about music was certainly articulated in North America by Thomas Jefferson (1743–1826) in his book *Notes on the State of Virginia* of 1782, questioning their respective musical abilities, in a form of scientific racism that has been recently examined by Gordon.[95] More generally, a binary of white/other was emerging in the minds of Europeans and European-descended people in the Americas. This way of thinking replaced an earlier religion-based binary of Christian/other and gradually hardened into a reductive racial categorization with a lasting impact.[96] Taylor refers to the decade of the 1770s as a threshold for this new perspective, pointing to the diminishing role of religion from this time as a factor of difference, since nonwhite people who had undergone conversion could also be fellow Christians. He remarks that "by the end of the eighteenth century and into the nineteenth, ... skin color and conceptions of race were ... entering the debates, in ways that are somewhat familiar today."[97] Even so, it must be observed that the new binary was not accepted wholesale by all Europeans. As Kwame Anthony Appiah has pointed out, the Abbé Grégoire admonished Jefferson, sending him a copy of his work *De la littérature des nègres*.[98]

We see that despite protests by thoughtful scholars, whiteness was frequently conflated with "European music" in subsequent centuries of European (and Euro-American) historiography.[99] Yet it is worth noting again that the eighteenth century itself presents a period of transition in which continental categories of humanity and the colors assigned to their inhabitants gradually moved from relatively loose to hard-and-fast concepts. In the

---

[94] Painter, *The History of White People*, 60–64, 72–77.
[95] Gordon, "What Mr Jefferson Didn't Hear," 109, 120–123. See also Eze, *Race and the Enlightenment*, 99.
[96] Taylor, *Beyond Exoticism*, 48.
[97] Taylor, *Beyond Exoticism*, 48.
[98] Appiah, *The Lies That Bind*, 115.
[99] This was especially evident in the kind of discourse used in some writings from comparative musicology. Curt Sachs, for instance, wrote of that discipline's methodology in 1943 that "primitive music must not be compared with the music of white men" (although he also commented that "the white musician must set aside not only his music but his very self, with all his tradition and prejudice"). Sachs, *The Rise of Music*, 25–26. Such a binary, typical of discourse in the early twentieth century, ignored and implicitly denied the contributions of people of color over countless millennia to the evolution of the inherently hybrid entities that would eventually fall within the categories of music labeled as "European music" and then "Western music." It also avoided discussion of transculturation and the contemporaneous practice by people of color of "the music of white men." With the application of such a racialized (and gendered) label as "the music of white men," there is the troubling implication that this category of music is being practiced only by such people and the fallacious sense of it being an exclusive cultural possession. Such labels ignored the reality of cultural practices that were created and shared by diverse communities.

midst of this process, the musics associated with peoples called "Europeans" and the language used to describe musics of other peoples became increasingly racialized. In looking for reasons for the historiographical emergence of the constructed (and embodied) connection and correlation between the Linnean notion of "homo europaeus" and music, we must go to examples of the concepts "European ear" and "European musicians." They are terms that appear in sharp relief, although still somewhat infrequently, in texts of the seventeenth and (especially) eighteenth centuries.

"European Ears"

This trope began to appear in literature with a global ambit, and transnational collectivity in experiencing musics outside Europe was a factor that contributed to its emergence. An early example comes from Samuel Purchas (1575–1625), a prominent London-based publisher of travel accounts. In 1625, clearly reflecting on his reading of multiple voyages in diverse parts of the world, he wrote:

> What eares but *European*, have heard so many Musicall Inventions for the Chamber, the Field, the Church? as for Bells, *Europe* alone bears the bel, and heares the Musicall consort thereof in the Steeples diversified, yea thence descending to Birds and Squirrells?[100]

The focus of this passage is evidently the geographically and culturally specific soundscapes experienced by people in Europe. Yet even at this early point in the century, the notion of "European ears" (hearing and aural perception) is surrounded by a certain cultural exceptionalism, which appears to arise directly from comparative ethnographic thinking in travel literature. Although it is difficult to see in this quoted passage how the well-read Purchas meant the complete absence of bells in other cultures—since many of the works he published referred to bells and metallophones of various kinds—it seems likely that he meant steeples containing an ensemble (or "consort") of bells of different sizes, operated by teams of bell-ringers. The animals mentioned here, "Birds and Squirrells," cannot be considered

---

[100] Purchas, *Purchas his Pilgrimes*, Vol. 1, 93 (original orthography). I encountered this text in Drace-Francis, *European Identity*, 35, where a modernized version of the text appears.

exclusive to Europe. Perhaps Purchas was making the exceptionalist claim that there were particularly "European" ways of listening to and interpreting their sounds or that these noises called for great acuity of hearing.

Purchas's comment seems to be a rare instance of "European ears" in English-language sources until the early eighteenth century. From that time onward, several more examples can be found in texts set in China and Turkey. Scottish doctor John Bell (1691–1780), a medical attendant to Russian ambassadors (who was sent with them successively to Persia, China, and Turkey), mentions the "European ear" in the 1763 account of his travels to China in the years 1719–1721. Interestingly, he was accompanied by an Italian and—in the context of an audience in 1721 with the Kangxi emperor (1654–1722; reigned 1661–1722)—writes of both the "Italian ear" and the "European ear" on the same page of his travelogue. He thus seems to imply them as categories that were overlapping and compatible, not mutually exclusive. Bell attributes the words "European ear" to the emperor: "The Emperor told the ambassador, that he knew well their musick would not please an EUROPEAN ear; but that every nation liked their own best."[101] Bell's paraphrase of this observation by Kangxi, shortly before the end of his long reign, suggests that the notion of a "European ear" was probably by then common in China. "European ears" ("oreilles Européanes") were also mentioned in the four-volume *Description géographique, historique, chronologique, politique, et physique de l'empire de la Chine et de la Tartarie Chinoise* (*Geographical, Historical, Chronological, Political, and Physical Description of the Empire of China and of Chinese Tartary*) of 1735 by Jesuit Jean-Baptiste Du Halde (1674–1743), referring to European listeners' reactions to Chinese music, in a passage about musical exchange (discussed in chapter 4).[102]

Another writer who mentions the reactions of "an *European* ear" with reference to Chinese music was John Brown (1715–1766), author of *A Dissertation on the Rise, Union, and Power, the Progressions, Separations, and Corruptions, of Poetry and Music*, published in 1763; it seems tempting to ponder whether he may have read Bell's text of the same year (although he specifically footnotes Du Halde at this point).[103] Yet not all Europeans considered "their" ears to be superior to those of others: as Lester Hu has

---

[101] Bell, *Travels from St. Petersburg*, Vol. 2, 63. I encountered this text via Gong, "Review of Ching-wah Lam."
[102] Original text in Du Halde, *Description*, Vol. 3, 266.
[103] J. Brown, *A Dissertation*, 168. On this source, see Davison, "John Brown's *Dissertation*"; Kassler, "Brown." Interestingly, the 1769 German translation of Brown's text glosses this as "the hearing of a European," but the Italian translation of 1772 translates "European ear" directly. Brown, *Dr. Brown's Betrachtungen*, 264–265; Brown, *Dell'origine*, 143.

pointed out, French Jesuit Jean-Joseph-Marie Amiot (1718–1793), based in China from 1751, wrote in a letter sent to Paris in 1780—in a section that was censored before its publication—that "the auditory nerve of European ears is to that of the ears of the Chinese, Egyptians, Greeks, and others of all peoples of the universe, both ancient and modern, what a belt strap is to the chanterelle of a violin."[104] Amiot, who lived most of his life in China and eventually self-identified as culturally Chinese, was clearly dubious about the capacities of the European ear to hear any subtleties.[105]

Transculturation is an important factor that underpins observations on listening. Charles Fonton (1725–1793/1795), a French interpreter who lived for most of his career in the Ottoman Empire, wrote in Constantinople in 1751 that "Oriental music" must be judged on its own terms and that long exposure to it would be required of "Italian or French ears," which would initially be hard to do.[106] Using the analogy of the eye to say how an Indian or Chinese person would find nothing to compare to the sexual attractiveness (at least in visual terms) of people from their own countries, Fonton invokes the collective eye of his continent of origin to make the pejorative comment that those same objects of admiration would not please a European. Yet he then becomes intensely relativistic, saying that the eye only finds something beautiful when it is seen according to the "genius" ("génie," which I would gloss as "creative disposition") of each nation and continues: "Now, it is the same in music; our ear, little used to certain foreign sounds, will find itself injured the first times that it hears them, then it imperceptibly becomes accustomed to it, and that which had at first offended it then flatters it agreeably."[107] Later in the treatise, he writes of the "effeminacy" of some "oriental airs" and comments on the short attention span of European listeners, writing that "for European ears the most powerful impressions, the strongest and most energetic sounds, less melancholic, and more joyful, are necessary."[108] In the same decade but in

---

[104] Original text in Hu, "Chinese Ears," 506, 506n.29, 507 (facsimile). Hu is quoting Amiot's letter to Henri Bertin, July 26, 1780, Paris, Bibliothèque Nationale de France, Bréquigny 3, f. 46v. "Chinese ears" were also considered by a number of scholars in Europe, including Herder, Burney, and Forkel. See Irvine, *Listening to China*, 44–48, 106, 167–171, esp. 169.

[105] On Amiot's self-identification as a Chinese mandarin, see Jiang, "In Search of the 'Oriental Origin,'" 128.

[106] Original text in Fonton, "Essay," manuscript (1751), 3–4. See also Shiloah, "An Eighteenth-Century Critic," 186.

[107] Original text in Fonton, "Essay," manuscript (1751), 8.

[108] He writes: "Il faut pour des oreilles européenes des Impressions plus fortes, des sons plus mâles, et plus nerveux, moins de melancolie, et plus de gayeté." Fonton, "Essay," manuscript (1751), 44.

contexts farther east, the "European ear" is mentioned in the 1794 edition of Russell's *The Natural History of Aleppo* but with some skepticism about the extent to which a transition in taste could occur: "The vocal music, to an European ear, seems at first not less uncouth than the Arabic language, and it seldom happens that time, which by degrees reconciles the language, goes further in music than to render it merely tolerable."[109] These eighteenth-century descriptions of transcultural listening are very different from the kinds of culturally specific sounds that Purchas wrote about in 1625.

"European Musicians"

From the embodied notion of "European ears," it was only a short step to the concept of a "European musician." That label has been used in certain musicological studies over the past few decades with reference to specific individuals of the seventeenth through nineteenth centuries, including Johann Jakob Froberger (1616–1667), Christoph Willibald Ritter von Gluck (1714–1787), Beethoven, and Carl Arnold (1794–1873).[110] Yet the compound term "European musician" appears quite rarely in literature of the eighteenth century. Since antiquity, it had been common to speak of one's origins in terms of specific communities; as shown in chapter 2, musicians within Europe itself instead described themselves as coming from cities or regions (Corelli, for example, was known as "il Bolognese").[111] The second edition (1808) of the biography of W. A. Mozart by Franz Xaver Niemetschek (1766–1849) describes its subject as a European by stating that Mozart's music had reached "the most distant parts of the world, where the name of

---

[109] Quoted in A. White, "'Brothers of the String,'" 540.

[110] Morrier, *J. J. Froberger*; Springer-Dissmann, "Gluck the Wanderer"; Gerstmeier, "Beethoven"; Kinderman and Miller, *Beethoven the European*; Herresthal, *Carl Arnold*. An exception is a study by Peter Wollny, who has written an essay describing J. S. Bach in the title as "a European" but stops short of using the proper adjective to call him a "European musician" or "European composer." See Wollny, "Johann Sebastian Bach."

[111] In a roll of the orchestra at the court of Dresden in c. 1717, for instance, most musicians listed their birthplaces as a town or city, and sometimes a region, rather than giving a "national" designation—with the exception of one musician from Spain, which was perhaps seen as sufficiently distant from Dresden to warrant a monolithic label. (Two musicians' birthplaces are also listed as Venice and Luxembourg, names for cities but also larger entities.) See Stockigt, "The Court of Saxony-Dresden," 39–40. Even though Italy and Germany were not unified nation states until the late nineteenth century, the adjectives "Italian" and "German" were in use before then, but musicians nevertheless preferred to give more specific (usually urban) locations of origin. Thanks to Janice Stockigt for discussion of this point.

the most famous Europeans hardly penetrates."[112] The author referred to a report of a performance in the Philippine Islands, which was apparently "heard with delight."[113] However, the compound term "European musician" is still not used.

When "European musician" does appear, it is sometimes in the context of a gloss by translators, pointing to the accretions of new ideas and concepts in the circulation of information in the Republic of Letters and the Republic of Music. An early example in this sense can be found in the 1731 English translation of a work by German scholar Peter Kolb (1675–1726). This man undertook a voyage from 1705 to 1712 during which he traveled to the Cape of Good Hope, principally for astronomical research. In 1719, he published his travelogue in German; as Pratt observes, it "was translated into Dutch (1721), English (1731), and French (1741), and remained one of the main print sources on southern Africa through the first half of the century."[114] In this work, he described two instruments he called *gom gom* and recounted, with admiration, a performance on an ensemble of these instruments by two "Hottentot" (Khoikhoi) musicians.[115] He writes that he initially thought that the players were Europeans and that he was "surpris'd" to discover their true identity.[116] The text goes on to include the following pejorative comment:

> The Reader may think of my Taste for Musick as he pleases, but I cannot help declaring it as my Opinion, that the *Gom Gom*, as insignificant a Piece of Work as it is, was it to be studied by a judicious *European* Musician, would be found to have as fine Musick in it as any Instrument we have, and be as much admir'd.[117]

---

[112] Original text in Niemetschek, *Lebensbeschreibung*, 64–65. I am grateful to David Black for pointing out this reference. It is also discussed in Keefe, "Across the Divide," 669.

[113] Original text in Niemetschek, *Lebensbeschreibung*, 65. He cites the "botanist Haenke"; this was Thaddeus Xaverius Peregrinus Haenke (1761–1816), who had accompanied the Spanish expedition to the Pacific led by Alessandro Malaspina (1754–1810). Incidentally, Handel's music was also reported in the Philippines, in a travelogue published in 1790. Although it does not use the term "European music" to describe the performance, the travelogue does mention "European ships" elsewhere. Meares, *Voyages*, 39 (ships), 44 (Handel). See also Irving, *Colonial Counterpoint*, 68–69.

[114] Pratt, *Imperial Eyes*, 41.

[115] Mugglestone points out that Kolb's descriptions of two distinct instruments, both of which he terms *gom gom*, refer to the *gora*—"an unbraced mouth-resonated musical bow peculiar to South Africa . . . organologically unusual in that it is a blown chordophone"—and the "grand" gom-gom. Mugglestone, "The Gora," 94. On the *gora* see also Agnew, *Enlightenment Orpheus*, 149–150.

[116] Kolb, *The Present State*, Vol. 1, 272–273.

[117] Kolb, *The Present State*, Vol. 1, 273. The second English edition of 1738 repeats this wording. Kolb, *The Present State* (2nd ed.), Vol. 1, 275.

This seems to be the earliest (so far) traceable published use of the term "European musician" in English. It appears, however, to be an invention of the English translator Guido Medley (dates unknown), since the original German text does not mention it. The relevant sentences instead refer to what ethnomusicologist Erica Mugglestone, in her extensive study of Kolb's description of these two instruments, has rendered as follows: "Provided, moreover, that more artistically skilled hands than those of the Hottentots should come across the instrument and have a natural affinity for it, its charm would not only be greatly increased, but also this instrument would, in the course of time, attain a greater perfection."[118] Dutch and French editions of 1727 and 1741, respectively, do not use the term, either, although the latter mentions "skilful Europeans" ("adroits Européens").[119] Historian Anne Good also notes that in 1745, the French version was translated back into German, "indicating that the original, though very popular, was just too long-winded for many readers."[120] This cycle of textual transmission is a pertinent example of how contemporaneous translations in Europe could result in quite different readings and concepts in the eighteenth century.[121]

In the following decades, there are still surprisingly few examples of "European musician(s)" identifiable in published works. In 1779, a descriptive text about Rome as a city mentions the term "Musici Europei."[122] Its author, Dominique Magnan (1731–1796) writes about the Maronite College (S. Giovanni del Collegio de' Maroniti) in Strada Nuova, one of the principal institutions for Eastern Christianity in Rome, where "the Divine Office was celebrated according to the Syriac Rite," attracting onlookers who were pleased to see their ceremonies "so different from those of the Latins [Catholics], and especially to hear their chanting, mixed with the sound of many singular instruments, unknown to European musicians."[123] This

---

[118] Mugglestone, "The Gora," 97. Original text in Kolb, *Caput Bonae Spei hodiernum*, 528.

[119] Kolb, *Caput Bonae Spei hodiernum*, 527–528. Kolb, *Naaukeurige en uitvoerige beschryving van de kaap de Goede Hoop*, Vol. 1, 106. Kolb, *Description du Cap de Bonne-Espérance*, Vol. 1, 209–210.

[120] Good, "The Construction of an Authoritative Text," 91. However, some two decades later, the text of Medley appears to have been incorporated within the *Histoire universelle*, Vol. 25, 18. For the English version, see *The Modern Part of the Universal History*, Vol. 15 (published 1760), 506, which states: "Our author . . . believes the grand Gom-gom worthy of the study of the most judicious *European* musician."

[121] Joan-Pau Rubiés has called Medley's translation "idiosyncratic" and further observes that "Medley felt free to summarize and re-arrrange the material, and despite praising Kolb for his factual accuracy, he introduced a more negative moral evaluation of the Hottentots." Rubiés, "Ethnography, Philosophy," 119.

[122] Original text in Magnan, *La città di Roma*, Vol. 1, col. 51.

[123] Original text in Magnan, *La città di Roma*, Vol. 1, cols 50–51.

Italian text is a translation of a work in French that had been published in Rome the previous year, but it is significant to note that the original version states "musicians of Europe" ("Musiciens de l'Europe") rather than using the proper adjective "European."[124] Like Magnan, La Borde in his *Essai sur la musique ancienne et moderne* (*Essay on Ancient and Modern Music*) of 1780 does not mention "European musicians" ("musiciens européens") but instead writes "musicians of Europe" or "Europe's musicians" ("musiciens de l'Europe").[125] Amiot, in his *Abrégé chronologique* (*Chronological Summary*) of 1788, uses the term "European musician" in giving an anonymized retelling of the demonstration of staff notation by a Jesuit in 1679 (a famous case discussed in chapter 4), as a corrective to what he considers to be inaccurate accounts of China.[126]

In Spanish, the equivalent term "músico europeo," in the singular, appears in the mid-1790s, with reference to a performance of African music that "would not flatter the ears of a European musician"; this anecdote was translated into Portuguese (with the term "Musico Europeo") in 1800.[127] The Spanish version quotes, in translation, the work of a Swedish naturalist—another student of Linnaeus—"Mr Sparmann [sic]" (Anders Sparrman, 1748–1820), although it does not cite the precise publication from which it comes.[128] The label "European musician" is thus introduced in the context of intertextuality and in a chain of translation; the Swedish text makes no mention of that term, nor does the German, English, or French translation.[129] Another Spanish example of "musicos europeos," this time in the plural, comes from the context of revolutionary Latin America in the 1820s. The fourth article in a treaty of August 3, 1823, following the surrender on July 24 of the Spanish army at Maracaibo, Colombia, allows for the safe passage

---

[124] Original text in Magnan, *La ville de Rome*, Vol. 1, col. 52.

[125] La Borde, *Essai*, Vol. 1, 392; Vol. 3, 511, 512, 523. However, he does mention a "Tambour Européen" (European drum) and gives a depiction of it—alongside drums labeled as Chinese, Persian, African, and Lapp (Sami)—as well as "military kettledrums" ("Tymballes militaires"). La Borde, *Essai*, Vol. 1, plate facing 286.

[126] "Le Musicien Européen, après avoir tracé sur son *album* quelques lignes parallelles, la notoit à mesure, afin de pouvoir la jouer ensuite avec autant de facilité que s'il l'eût apprise par coeur." Amiot, "Abrégé chronologique," 138.

[127] Laporte, *El viagero universal*, Vol. 7 [1796], 319. For the Portuguese, see Laporte, *O viajante universal*, Vol. 9 [1800], 310.

[128] Laporte, *El viagero universal*, Vol. 7, 298.

[129] The Swedish original is in Sparrman, *Resa till Goda Hopps-Udden*, 421. Thanks to Christina Skott for translating the relevant sentence and offering advice. The German (1784), English (1785), and French (1787) versions of this passage are located, respectively, at Sparrman, *Reise nach dem Vorgebirge der guten Hoffnung*, 355; Sparrman, *A Voyage to the Cape of Good Hope*, Vol. 2, 29; and Sparrman, *Voyage au Cap de Bonne-Espérance*, Vol. 2, 217.

of "European troops" leaving the territory, on the proviso of their future non-aggression against the new republic, and adds: "The European musicians are included in this article."[130] The use of the continental term here may suggest the transnational origins of musicians from Europe among the troops, with not all originating from Spain.

A few decades earlier, an intra-European frame of reference for "European musicians" appeared when Burney used the term in the third volume of his *General History of Music* (1789), with comparative reference to Spain. He writes: "It seems as if the Spaniards were placed lower among European musicians at this time [the sixteenth century] than in equity they ought, by those who imagine [Cristóbal de] *Morales* [c. 1500–1553] to have been the *first* practical musician of eminence in that country, and [Francisco de] *Salinas* [1513–1590] the *only* theorist that was produced there during the sixteenth century."[131] It seems possible to read into his rare use of the proper adjective "European" that he was differentiating—and exoticizing—Spaniards within that category. As Emilio Ros-Fábregas has pointed out, the exclusion of Spain from the "concert of Europe" was a common tendency in mid-twentieth-century music historiography produced outside Spain, while nationalist arguments for Spanish musical exceptionalism were also made in Spain until relatively late in the twentieth century.[132] However, seeds of that idea appear to have been already sown in the eighteenth.

In 1792, Johann Nikolaus Forkel (1749–1818) referred specifically to "European composers" ("europäischen Componisten") when mentioning in an annotated bibliography a catalogue of musical works published by Walsh (probably John the younger, 1709–1766); he cites Walsh's work as "A Catalogue of Music: containing all the Vocal and Instrumental-Music, printed in England," but does not give a date.[133] It is likely a publication of c. 1741, which has the main title as listed by Forkel. On checking that source itself, it is interesting to note that its subtitle does not mention Europe, although it does refer to music printed in foreign countries: "For John Walsh. Where May Be Had, Variety of English, and Italian Songs, Also Musical Instruments of All Sorts, and Variety of Curious Pieces of Musick Printed Abroad."[134] Thus, if this

---

[130] Original text in *Coleccion de documentos*, Vol. 3 [1826], 292.
[131] Burney, *A General History of Music*, Vol. 3, 289. This comment is repeated in the section "History of the Music of Spain" in the entry "Spain" for the thirty-third volume of *The Cyclopaedia* that was published by Abraham Rees (1743–1825) in 1819. Burney, "Spain," n.p.
[132] Ros-Fábregas, "Cristóbal de Morales," 229–231.
[133] Original text in Forkel, *Allgemeine Litteratur der Musik*, 197.
[134] Walsh (the younger), *A Cattalogue [sic] of Musick*, title page.

document is the same, then it appears that the gloss of "European composers" in the bibliography of 1792 originates from Forkel himself.

Beyond the geographical boundaries of Europe (however defined), the term "European" as applied to groups of musicians began to denote a sense of segregation and racialized difference in the late eighteenth century. Raymond Head has observed that in the 1790s, the ensemble in Bengal known as the "Calcutta Band" changed its name to the "European Band"; he comments that this "change of name [was] indicative of the gradual separation of the British and the Indian populations."[135] The same term was also used by Sir George Staunton (1737–1801) in his description of the British embassy led by Lord Macartney (George Macartney, 1737–1806) to the Qianlong emperor of China (1711–1799; reigned 1735–1796). Here, however, it is not a specific name of a performing group but a more generic usage: a mention of "the European band of music, which performed a concert every evening in the Embassador's [sic] apartments."[136]

Other examples of the English term "European musicians" relate to court and military contexts in Islamic states. The July 1807 issue of the *European Magazine, and London Review* includes a tribute to the late Ottoman emperor Selim III (1761–1808; reigned 1789–1807) by the pseudonymous reporter Constantinopolitanus, who writes: "When he came to the throne, he greatly encouraged music, and often had European musicians to play before him, on instruments unusual to the Turks."[137] In the eighth volume of the *Asiatic Annual Register*, for November 1805 (published 1809), there is mention of "the garrison band of European musicians" who occupied one boat among five for the reception of Mohammed Nubbee Khan (sic; Moḥammad Nabi Khan, dates unknown), ambassador from Fatḥ-ʿAli Shah (1798–1834; reigned from 1797) of Persia.[138] Condescending comparisons between different groups of musicians playing common repertory also appear in reports of the early nineteenth century. For example, a reference to a military troupe of Arab musicians in Alexandria—newly arrived from Cairo—who performed works by Gioachino Rossini (1792–1868) in a manner "as well as the best European musicians" was published in French in the periodical *Courrier de Smyrne* (*Smyrna Courier*) in 1829.[139] It was also printed in

---

[135] R. Head, "Corelli in Calcutta," 551. An advertisement listing the group as such appears in the *Calcutta Gazette* of October 20, 1796. Shilsbury, "R. Shilsbury."
[136] Staunton, *An Authentic Account*, Vol. 2, 340.
[137] Constantinopolitanus [pseudonym], "Selim III," 4.
[138] Campbell and Samuel, *The Asiatic Annual Register*, Vol. 8, 93; Mahdavi, "Jukes, Andrew."
[139] Original French text in "Turquie," 95.

translations in Spanish and German publications, disseminating this comment further.[140]

A few decades into the nineteenth century, then, it is possible to see in music historiography a chain of intertextuality regarding "Europeanness," as well as the retrospective projection of the term "European(s)" onto musicians of centuries past (as seen in the case of Burney's comment on Morales). The notions of "European ears" and "European musicians" had become racialized—and the latter often denied to prominent musicians from elsewhere such as Sancho, who was described as "African"—but also related to cultural notions of the continent. Yet "the music itself" that came to be called "European" could nevertheless transcend continental boundaries and be appreciated, practiced, rejected, or ignored by people in other parts of the world, as we now go on to see.

---

[140] Original Spanish text in "Noticias extrangeras," 499; original German text in "Türkei," 994.

4
The Emergence of the "European Music" Concept

An early comparative text that hints at a collective European identity in music, contrasted with that of another culture, is the 1585 treatise written in Japan by Portuguese Jesuit Luís Fróis (1532–1597), *Tratado em que se contêm muito sucinta e abreviadamente algumas contradições e diferenças de costumes entre a gente de Europa e esta província de Japão* (*Treatise in Which Is Contained, Most Briefly and Succinctly, Some of the Contradictions and Differences in the Customs of the People of Europe and This [Jesuit] Province of Japan*).[1] At first glance, one notices that its title mentions "the people of Europe" rather than "Europeans."[2] Within the text, each comparison is structured as a simple contrast, in the sense of "we do this, but they do that." Fróis refers to "our" customs and customs "among us," sometimes qualifying his observations by citing "the nations of Europe." This last term implies a European community—despite internal differences in cultural practice— that contrasts as a whole with Japan. Yet rather than applying the proper adjective "European" to categories such as "women" or "dances," he uses the structure "women of Europe" or "dances of Europe." For example, in the section on music, Fróis includes entries such as the following dubious contrast: "Among the nations of Europe all [singers] use *garganta* [glossing or vocal ornamentation]; among the Japanese none use it."[3]

Five years later, in the Jesuit publication *De missione legatorum iaponensium ad romanam curiam* (*On the Mission of the Japanese Ambassadors to the Roman Court*) by Jesuits Duarte de Sande (1547–1599) and Alessandro Valignano (1539–1606), the term "European singing" is used, denoting polyphony. This publication consists of a set of dialogues between Japanese

---

[1] For an edition, see Fróis and Schütte, *Kulturgegensätze Europa-Japan*.
[2] Fróis, incidentally, like Francis Xavier and other early Jesuits in Japan, described Japanese people as "white" ("alvos"). Kowner, *From White to Yellow*, 81–83, esp. 82.
[3] Fróis and Schütte, *Kulturgegensätze Europa-Japan*, 246. For translations of many other comparative statements from this treatise relating to music and dance, see Harich-Schneider, *A History of Japanese Music*, 478–479.

interlocutors about customs in Europe, based on experiences there in the late 1580s; it was printed in Macau in 1590 as a Latin primer for students in Jesuit missions in Japan.[4] The authors are presumed to be Valignano and Sande (the latter translated it into Latin), based on the journals kept by four Japanese youths: Mancio Itō Sukemasu (c. 1569–1612), Miguel Chijiwa Seizaemon (c. 1569–1633), Martinho Hara (1569–1629), and Julião Nakaura (1568–1633), envoys in the "*Tenshō shōnen shisetsu* 天正少年使節" ("Tenshō era boys' embassy").[5] These youths had studied, in Japan, the musical practices of Europe. Taken by the Jesuits to Europe on a voyage lasting from 1582 to 1590 as part of an embassy to raise support for the mission in Japan, they had a diverse range of musical experiences in Portugal, Spain, and Italy (1584–1586) and gave performances that have been well documented and studied; they also brought instruments from Europe back to Japan.[6]

In the eleventh dialogue of the 1590 book, a character named Linus (Lino)—based on Ōmura Suminobu (dates unknown), who was a cousin of Miguel Chijiwa Seizaemon—comments to his interlocutor Michael (Miguel) that he was not yet able to perceive the "sweetness" of the foreign musical styles performed by the youths who had returned from Europe.[7] Michael replies as follows:

> You are not yet used to European singing and harmony [*Europeo cantui et symphoniae*], so you do not yet appreciate how sweet and pleasant it is, whereas we, since we are now accustomed to listening to it, feel that there is nothing more agreeable to the ear. But if we care to avert our minds from what is customary, and to consider the thing in itself, we find that European singing [*Europeum cantum*] is in fact composed with remarkable skill; it does not always keep to the same note for all voices, as ours does, but some notes are higher, some lower, some intermediate, and when all of these are skilfully sung together, at the same time, they produce a certain remarkable harmony. Add to these what they call the falsetto voice, and those which are higher than the normal note, all of which (whether observing the rule or, sometimes, raised above it) together with the sounds

---

[4] Harich-Schneider, *A History of Japanese Music*, 467.

[5] See Moran, "The Real Author"; Pelliccia, "Representing Catholic Europe"; see also a summary of this issue by Derek Massarella in Sande, *Japanese Travellers*, 1, 20–21.

[6] For details of the musical aspects of the embassy, see, for example, Harich-Schneider, "Renaissance Europe through Japanese Eyes"; Harich-Schneider, *A History of Japanese Music*, 463–467; Waterhouse, "Southern Barbarian Music," 360–363; Kambe, "Viols in Japan," 52–60.

[7] On the identity of Lino, who had not left Japan, see Sande, *Japanese Travellers*, 9, 30, and 39.

of the musical instruments, are wonderfully pleasing to the ear of the listener.[8]

Referring to the shaping of taste through experience, this passage represents a remarkable and inventive way of explaining vertical harmony and contrapuntal polyphony within a transcultural framework. Harich-Schneider notes that "Michael seems to refer to strict vocal polyphony in contrast to florid parts or coloratura, maybe vocal improvisation. Anyway, one feels everywhere the editing hand of Father de Sande, or Valignano."[9] Despite the mysteries surrounding its authorship, the text presents what seems to be a unique published instance of the compound term "European singing" in the sixteenth century, unless further examples emerge.[10]

Yet writers of that time had already begun to refer collectively to "our Europe" and "we Europeans," as we saw in chapter 3. From at least the early seventeenth century, this formula gradually extended to descriptions of music. When acknowledging musical contrasts with other parts of the world, European scholars began to write of "our music." For example, Salomon de Caus (1576–1626) used it in 1615, discussing the differences between "the music of the East and West Indies" and "our music."[11] Marin Mersenne (1588–1648), writing to Nicolas-Claude Fabri de Peiresc (1580–1637), mentioned the same term in 1634 in a comparative context when stating that he and "the most able musicians" apparently found little difference between a "Turkish air" (perhaps referring to a French performance from a transcription of a Turkish melody) and "our music."[12] Peiresc, in a letter of the same year to his agent in Cairo, acknowledged receipt of a music treatise in Arabic, and in return offered to send to two musicians there—if they were "curious"—"books of our music of Christendom [*notre musique de Crestienté*] . . . some of the most melodious, both of Paris and of Rome."[13] Such wording seems to imply a collective identity in music based on a common religious confession, although it simultaneously distinguishes between French and Italian styles, by mentioning two major cities.

---

[8] Translation from Sande, *Japanese Travellers*, 155. Original text in Valignano and Sande, *De missione legatorum Iaponensium*, 110.
[9] Harich-Schneider, *A History of Japanese Music*, 469n.68.
[10] On questions of authorship, see Sande, *Japanese Travellers*, 20–21.
[11] Caus, *Institution harmonique*, Part 1, f. 23r. See also Wright, "Turning a Deaf Ear," 156.
[12] Original text in Mersenne, Larroque, and Coste, *Les correspondants*, 88. It is unclear whether by "our" Mersenne meant "French music" or a supranational "European music," but it seems likely to be the latter, given his work within a universalist paradigm of numerically based rationality and order.
[13] Quoted in Miller, *Peiresc's Mediterranean World*, 123 (original text at 496n.387).

Jesuits and "European Music," from China to Paraguay

The term "European music" appears to have emerged in the Jesuits' China mission in the 1670s (if earlier, sources have yet to be identified). The manuscript of their Annual Letter for 1678–1679, held in the archive of the Society of Jesus in Rome, reports on the musical acts of Portuguese Jesuit Tomé Pereira (1645–1708) before the emperor and includes two uses of the term "our European music."[14] However, the earliest printed use of this term so far identified in a European language appears to come from the book *Astronomia europaea* by Flemish Jesuit Ferdinand Verbiest (1623–1688), which was written in China, sent to Europe, and published in Dillingen in 1687 (figure 4.1). Verbiest, well known as an astronomer and mathematician, arrived in China in 1658 and remained there for the rest of his life. He was one of the many missionaries involved in the introduction of the theory of "European music" to the imperial court and its reception and study there under the patronage of the Kangxi emperor—a complex phenomenon on which there is an extensive corpus of musicological studies.[15] In what follows, both relying and building on established work, I will consider specifically the entry of "European music" as a term and a concept into European-language historiography.

Verbiest came into contact with Kangxi through their discussion of diverse academic topics. His published mention of "European music" appears as follows in chapter 25, "Music" (see figure 4.2 for a facsimile of the original passage):

> When in 1676 [*sic*; 1679] the Emperor had me brought into the inner rooms of his Palace, together with Father Filippo Grimaldi [1638–1712] and Father Tomé Pereyra [Pereira], he ordered the latter to play an organ and a European harpsichord which we once had presented to him, and he took much delight in the European music [*& plurimùm musicâ Europaeâ oblectatus est*]. Soon, he had his own musicians perform a Chinese song

---

[14] In Archivum Romanum Societatis Iesu, JapSin 117, the term is given in Latin as "musicae nostrae Europaeae" and "musicâ nostrâ Europaeâ" on the same page (on ff. 167r and 187r, which are copies of the same text). See discussion in Golvers and Verbiest, *The* Astronomia Europaea, 313.

[15] I refer the reader to experts in those fields. See, for example, among others, Gild [Gild-Bohne], *Das Lü Lü Zheng Yi Xubian*; Gild, "The Introduction of European Musical Theory"; Gild, "Mission by Music"; Picard, "Music"; Picard and Thoraval, "*Musica mecanica*"; Allsop and Lindorff, "Teodorico Pedrini"; Lindorff, "Pereira's Musical Heritage"; Yu, "The Meaning and Cultural Functions"; Jia, "The Dissemination of Western Music"; Jiang, "In Search of the 'Oriental Origin'"; Hu, "A Princely Manuscript"; Hu, "From Ut Re Mi to Fourteen-Tone Temperament."

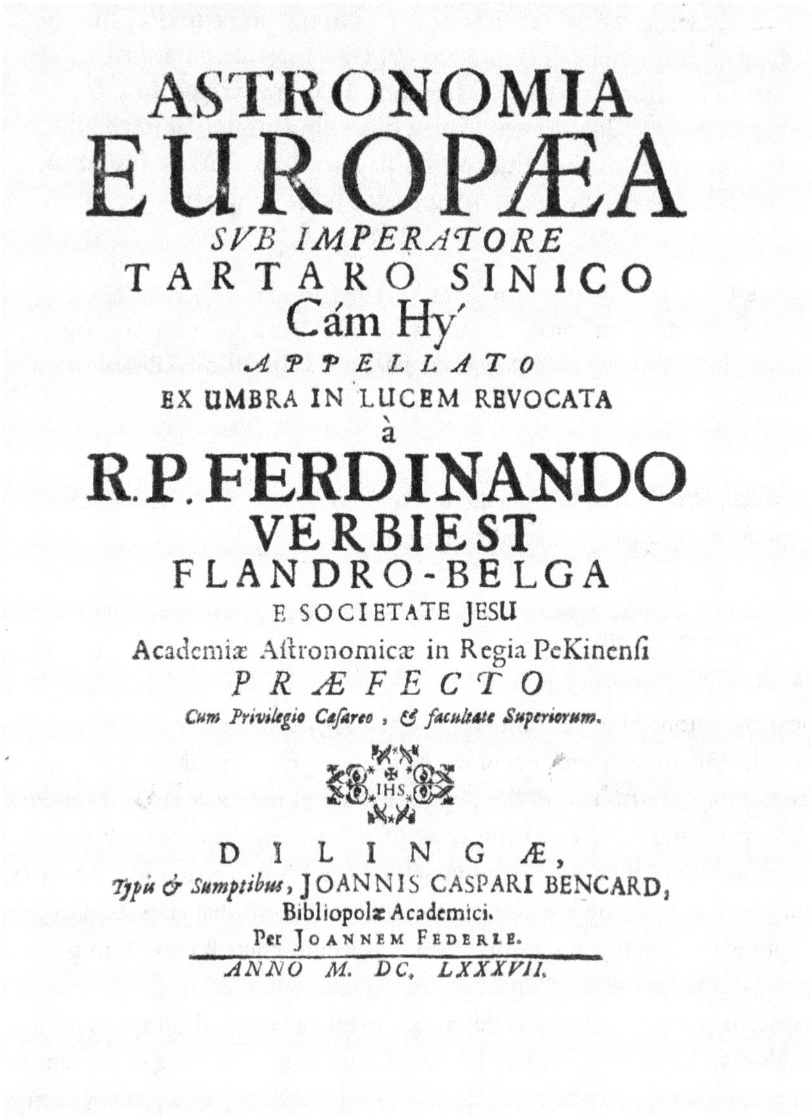

ASTRONOMIA EUROPÆA

SVB IMPERATORE
TARTARO SINICO
Cám Hý
APPELLATO
EX UMBRA IN LUCEM REVOCATA
à
R. P. FERDINANDO VERBIEST
FLANDRO-BELGA
E SOCIETATE JESU
Academiæ Aftronomicæ in Regia PeKinenfi
PRÆFECTO
Cum Privilegio Cæfareo, & facultate Superiorum.

DILINGÆ,
Typis & Sumptibus, JOANNIS CASPARI BENCARD,
Bibliopolæ Academici.
Per JOANNEM FEDERLE.
ANNO M. DC. LXXXVII.

Figure 4.1. Ferdinand Verbiest, *Astronomia europaea sub imperatore tartaro sinico Cám Hý appellato* (Dillingen: Joannis Caspari Bencard, 1687), title page. © The British Library Board (530.d.22).

> Anno 1676. Imperator, cùm me unâ cum P. Philippo Grimaldi, & P. Thoma Pereyra ad interius palatium suum introduci mandâſſet, P. Thomam Pereyra organum, & clavicymbalum Europæum, quod olim obtulimus, pulſare juſſit, & plurimùm muſicâ Europæâ oblectatus eſt. Mox ſuos muſicos cantilenam Sinicam proponere juſſit, quam ipſe Imperator,

Figure 4.2. The earliest-known (so far) printed use of the adjective-noun compound "European music" ("musicâ Europaeâ") in a European language. Excerpt from Verbiest, *Astronomia europaea*, 89. © The British Library Board (530.d.22).

> which, after having had practised it for a long time the Emperor himself performed perfectly on another musical instrument.[16]

Verbiest's narrative goes on to recount the story of Pereira transcribing Chinese music with what was called "our musical notes or European *characters*" (European staff notation) and repeating it flawlessly after one hearing, astonishing the emperor.[17] This anecdote became something of a favorite tale in eighteenth-century historiography of music in Europe, and its retelling contributed to the popularization of the neologistic compound "European music." Nevertheless, as Qingfan Jiang has recently noted, a corroborating Chinese description of the event is yet to be found.[18] Verbiest's chapter concludes by mentioning that Pereira was at that stage building an organ with an automatic mechanism that would make it play "European as well as Chinese music" ("musicam Europaeam simul & Sinicam").[19] In this sense, he put the two large-scale categories into a balanced comparison.

Noël Golvers has persuasively shown, based on his reading of contemporaneous sources, that the year 1676 displayed in the chapter is probably a misprint for 1679.[20] He dates the event to "a period shortly before or after January

---

[16] Translation from Golvers and Verbiest, *The* Astronomia Europaea, 125. Original text in Verbiest, *Astronomia europaea*, 89–90.

[17] Golvers and Verbiest, *The* Astronomia Europaea, 125. Thanks to Joyce Lindorff for introducing me to the work of both Verbiest and Golvers.

[18] Jiang, "In Search of the 'Oriental Origin,'" 145.

[19] Urrows, "The Pipe Organ," 30; Golvers and Verbiest, *The* Astronomia Europaea, 126 (translation), 439 (facsimile of original, at 91).

[20] Golvers and Verbiest, *The* Astronomia Europaea, 312–313n.8.

1679 and, at the latest ... the first half of that year."[21] If that is the case, and given that Verbiest completed his draft manuscript of *Astronomia europaea* on March 1, 1680, he would thus have had a relatively fresh memory of what had happened.[22] Golvers has demonstrated that much of the treatise was compiled and re-edited from earlier material that had circulated but that the chapter on music was "newly composed."[23] He also points out that Verbiest's book as a whole contains 187 words that are neo-Latin neologisms.[24] One is the term "musica" as applied to an ensemble of musicians (here specifically "the Emperor's music band"), which had been commonly used in that sense in vernacular languages—as "musica" or cognate forms—since at least the mid-sixteenth century but was new in Latin.[25] It is perhaps not surprising, then, that this text is also the location of the earliest known published use of the neologism "European music."

The three Jesuits involved in Verbiest's story were, respectively, Flemish, Italian, and Portuguese. An allusion to their art as "European" was a convenient way of describing them collectively and reflecting their "diasporic intimacy" or shared membership in a supranational Christendom based in western Europe.[26] The harpsichord and organ introduced to the court by the missionaries were also described as "European."[27] Despite the lack of a Chinese source on this event, we may wonder: was the first published articulation of the term "European music" as a conflation of nonspecified national musics actually derived from the emperor himself? (Recall Kangxi's 1721 description of a "European ear," discussed in chapter 3.) Or was it from the missionaries' desire to use music as a unified "European" science, as part of their mission?

Beyond court contexts, we can glimpse a layperson's view of the Jesuits' domestic life in the Chinese capital, and "European" musical practices in it, given by Italian traveler Giovanni Francesco Gemelli Careri (1651–1725), who stopped there in 1695 during his voyage around the world. He writes

---

[21] Golvers, "Ferdinand Verbiest on European Astronomy," 79.
[22] Golvers, *Ferdinand Verbiest*, 161.
[23] Golvers, *Ferdinand Verbiest*, 159. See also Golvers, "Ferdinand Verbiest on European Astronomy," esp. 79.
[24] Golvers, *Ferdinand Verbiest*, 60–72.
[25] Golvers, *Ferdinand Verbiest*, 77, 79. For the original context, see Golvers and Verbiest, *The Astronomia Europaea*, 76 (translation), 374 (facsimile of the original, at 26).
[26] See Boym, "On Diasporic Intimacy."
[27] Urrows, "The Pipe Organ," 30; Golvers and Verbiest, *The Astronomia Europaea*, 125 (harpsichord), 126 (organ), 437 (facsimile of the original, at 89, "clavicymbalum Europaeum"), 438 (facsimile of the original, at 91, "Organum illud Europaeum").

that he immediately went to introduce himself to Grimaldi, who told him that he must seek an audience with and present himself to the emperor before any accommodation could be offered by the Jesuits. His account goes on to say (I quote the English translation of 1704) that there were "two of his [the emperor's] Pages in the House, who learn'd Musick of F. Pereira, after the *European* manner [*la musica alla maniera della nostra Europa*], [and] it would be hard to Conceal my coming from him [the emperor], because those Pages were Spies, who told the Emperor all they saw."[28] Thus, Chinese musicians were explicitly noted to engage in "European" practices—although the proper adjective is not used in the original Italian wording, which would be more directly translated as "music in the manner of our Europe."

Regarding Pereira's performance before Kangxi, and particularly the demonstration of notating melodies by ear, we see that various eighteenth-century references to "European music" in French, English, Spanish, and Italian—and no doubt other languages—are found in the reiterations of this story or in reports of the subsequent work of Pereira in music theory that was commissioned by the emperor.[29] Probably its most well-known retelling is that found in one of the most famous accounts of China published in early-eighteenth-century Europe, Du Halde's *Description géographique, historique, chronologique, politique, et physique de l'empire de la Chine et de la Tartarie Chinoise* of 1735. The author prefaces the tale by stating that "European music [*la Musique Européane*] does not displease them [the Chinese], provided that they hear only a single voice singing, accompanied by some instruments"; he describes how "European airs" ("airs d'Europe") were played by Grimaldi and Pereira and in discussing the emperor's reaction refers twice to "Europe's

---

[28] Gemelli Careri, "A Voyage," Vol. 4, 316. Original text in Gemelli Careri, *Giro del mondo*, Vol. 4 (1700), 113. The double role of the students as imperial informants is unsurprising, given the strict control of foreigners residing in China, but the Jesuits' description of them highlights the diplomatic delicacy of the missionaries' position there and also the mediating role of the study of musical practice and theory. Later extolling the scholarly accomplishments of Kangxi, Gemelli Careri describes the music taught by Pereira as one of the *"European* Sciences," along with mathematics (and astronomy) taught by Verbiest and the Euclidian mathematics taught by another Jesuit, Jean-François Gerbillon (1654–1707). Gemelli Careri, "A Voyage," Vol. 4, 394. Original text in Gemelli Careri, *Giro del mondo*, Vol. 4, 437.

[29] For instance, in Prévost, *Histoire générale*, vol. 6 (1748), 288 (the same page refers to "La Musique de l'Europe," in terms of practice, and "la Musique Européenne," with reference to the works of music theory produced by Pereira); La Borde, *Essai*, Vol. 1, 360, 361. For an example in English, see Winterbotham, *An Historical, Geographical, and Philosophical View*, 429. In Italian: Prévost, *Storia generale de' viaggi*, Vol. 22, 281; Foresti, *Del mappamondo*, 350 (mentioning Pereira's teaching of Kangxi in general terms); Napoli Signorelli, *Storia critica*, Vol. 1, 24 (referring only to theory, not the incident). A Spanish reference also refers to Kangxi's enthusiasm for "European songs [*canciones Europèas*]"; "Historia general de los viages," 5852; thanks to María Gembero-Ustárroz for pointing out this source.

music" ("la Musique d'Europe").³⁰ Following this anecdote, Du Halde mentions Kangxi's proposal to establish "an Academy for Music" and also the production of four volumes of music theory, to which was added "a fifth on the elements of European Music [*la Musique Européane*], made by Father Pereira."³¹ Thus, European music was considered by the emperor a distinct art yet one that was nevertheless complementary to Chinese knowledge.

Still, Du Halde's well-known text was not the first in which the term "European music" ("la musique européane") appeared in French. The earliest identifiable example (so far) is from the late seventeenth century, and it also concerns Pereira. It was produced in Paris by another Jesuit: a history of the Manchu conquest of China by Pierre-Joseph d'Orléans (1641–1698), published in 1688. The author simply states that "two years ago the emperor brought the fathers Verbiest and Grimaldi to Western Tartary, and this year he brought Father Pereira, to learn from him, en route, European music [*la musique Europeane*]."³² A letter from Verbiest to the Jesuit superior in Canton, Francesco Saverio Filippucci (1632–1692), dated June 23, 1685, corroborates this story, mentioning that "the king [emperor] appears to want to learn the rules of European music" ("o Rey parece querer aprender a regra da muzica Europaea").³³ Pereira's own account of the journey also relates that already on the third day, the emperor was engaging in study of "the principles of our music" ("os principios de nossa musica").³⁴ Another letter by Verbiest from August that year, this time in Latin, refers to the same trip and describes the subject as "the art of our European music" ("artem musicae nostrae Europaeae"); intriguingly, it also mentions Verbiest's plan to translate sections of Kircher's *Musurgia universalis* into Chinese (although Golvers notes that this is the last to be heard of that project).³⁵

Verbiest died in 1688 and Pereira in 1708. From 1711, the Lazarist missionary Teodorico Pedrini (1671–1746) assumed Pereira's role as the chief exponent of European music theory at the Chinese imperial court. According to him, Kangxi was certainly aware of differences in French and Italian approaches to music theory. As Peter Allsop and Joyce Lindorff have

---

[30] Original text in Du Halde, *Description*, Vol. 3, 266.
[31] Original text in Du Halde, *Description*, Vol. 3, 266.
[32] Original text in Orléans, *Histoire*, 301. For a nineteenth-century English translation, see Orléans, *History*, quotation at 96. The same volume includes as an appendix a translation of Pereira's letter from on the road, 132–148; music is mentioned on 132–134.
[33] Verbiest and Golvers, *Letters of a Peking Jesuit*, 640.
[34] Pereira, *Tomás Pereira: Obras*, Vol. 2, 23.
[35] Golvers and Verbiest, *The Astronomia Europaea*, 311; see also Verbiest and Golvers, *Letters of a Peking Jesuit*, 647, 874.

shown, Pedrini writes in a letter describing his first audience with Kangxi that the emperor referred to the method of adding a seventh solmization syllable to the hexachord; even though he mistakenly called it "French" instead of "Italian," he indicated his knowledge of the two systems.[36] Like the Jesuits a few decades earlier, Pedrini also mentioned "our European music" ("n[ost]ra Musica Europea") in a letter of 1714.[37] Pedrini was commissioned by Kangxi to complete a treatise (in Chinese) on European music theory, which had been left unfinished by Pereira; this was published in 1723.[38] In the following decades, other references to "European music" emanating from Chinese contexts continued in a number of writings by missionaries. For example, Jesuit Murillo Velarde, based in Manila, observed in 1752 that he had seen reference in a 1745 letter from Beijing to progress in "European music of instruments and voices."[39] From the range of examples discussed here, it is clear that for the first seventy years of the emergence of the "European music" term and concept within European-language music historiography, a major role was played by China and by Catholic missionaries.

On another continent, another reference to "European music" that predates 1700 can be found in writings from the Jesuit missions to the Guaraní (in current-day Paraguay, Argentina, and Uruguay). The Guaraní became famous in eighteenth-century Europe for their transcultural adoption of musical arts of that continent, introduced to them initially by the missionaries but then sustained and developed by them on their own terms. In their lands, the "reductions"—the name for missions, from the Spanish verb *reducir* ("to reduce" or bring to obedience)—began in 1610, and by the time of the Jesuits' expulsion from Spanish territories in 1767, there were thirty such communities with a combined population of just under 90,000 inhabitants (including around eighty Jesuits).[40] Each reduction had its own ensemble of singers and instrumentalists.[41] There were also workshops for making musical instruments and producing music scores. One of the most famous reductions for this kind of activity was Nuestra Señora de los Santos Reyes del Yapeyú (now Yapeyú, Argentina); its florescence in this respect owes much to the work of Tyrolean Jesuit Anton Sepp von Reinegg

---

[36] Allsop and Lindorff, "Da Fermo," 78–79.
[37] In Allsop and Lindorff, "Da Fermo," 83.
[38] Jami, "Tomé Pereira," 194.
[39] Murillo Velarde, *Geographia historica*, Vol. 7, 150.
[40] Sarreal, *The Guaraní and Their Missions*, 85, 239.
[41] Early Jesuit music teachers included Jean Vaisseau (1583–1623) and Louis Berger (1597–1639). Herczog, *Orfeo nelle Indie*, 33–41.

(1655–1733).⁴² The earliest known example of "European music" from Paraguay comes from him.

Before discussing that, it is worth examining Sepp's early career—he was evidently a proficient musical performer, instrument maker, composer, and teacher—since it provides context for his writing about music and "Europe" in the missions. Born in Kaltern, Tyrol, Sepp sang as a child in the choir of St. Stephen's Cathedral (Stefansdom) in Vienna, and at some stage in his youth apparently traveled to England, probably in the capacity of a musician.⁴³ As was usual for the time, he learned a range of instruments. His later texts show that they included viol, theorbo, flute, trumpet, shawm, keyboards, and trumpet marine.⁴⁴ He entered the Society of Jesus in Landsberg at the age of eighteen, in 1674; for the next two years, he was a student of rhetoric there and then logic and metaphysics for a further two years in Ingolstadt.⁴⁵ From letters sent later from Paraguay, it appears that at some stage he also studied the rules of music as set out by the Swiss-born composer Johann Melchior Gletle (1626–1683), *Kapellmeister* (chapel master) of Augsburg cathedral.⁴⁶

From 1679, Sepp taught grammar and music at Landsberg and then humanities in Lucerne; he applied in the latter city in 1682 to go on overseas missions.⁴⁷ In May 1687, he was ordained as a priest in Augsburg. Leaving Trent, he went via Genoa (where he took his final vows) to Spain in 1689, and after staying in Seville an entire year, he departed Cádiz on January 17, 1691.⁴⁸ He traveled to South America in a group of forty-four missionaries "of divers Nations," describing them as "*Spaniards, Italians, Flemmings* [sic], *Sicilians, Sardinians, Genoeses, Milaneses, Romans, Bohemians*, and *Austrians*" and identifying himself as "a Native of *Tyrol*."⁴⁹ This was a remarkably mixed group, coming from several regions of Catholic Europe (except France). Non-Spaniards were generally prevented by Spanish authorities from traveling to the colonies in the Americas (especially during the War of the Spanish Succession), although exceptions were made, and Sepp noted

---

⁴² A recent study of Sepp's work is in Toelle, "'Was michs kostet.'"
⁴³ Furlong, *Antonio Sepp*, 8; Sepp and Hoffmann, *Relación de viaje*, 12–14. Another source lists Innsbruck as his birthplace; see Furlong, *Antonio Sepp*, 11; Pastells and Mateos, *Historia*, Vol. 4, 237.
⁴⁴ Sepp and Hoffmann, *Relación de viaje*, 13.
⁴⁵ The biographical details here and above are drawn from Sepp and Hoffmann, *Relación de viaje*, 11–19; Caraman and McNaspy, "Sepp von Reinegg."
⁴⁶ Stöcklein, *Der neue Welt-Bott*, nos. 48, 55.
⁴⁷ His letter of application (dated September 19, 1682) is transcribed in Hernández, *Misiones del Paraguay*, Vol. 1, 573; it is this source that refers to his time in England. See discussion in Sepp and Hoffmann, *Relación de viaje*, 13, 15.
⁴⁸ Sepp, "An Account," 637.
⁴⁹ Sepp, "An Account," 637.

that "the *Spaniards* [made] no difference betwixt the Nations of the several Provinces of *Germany*."[50]

Much of what is known of Sepp's work in the missions comes from letters written by him to his family members and other recipients. In 1696, his brother Gabriel (dates unknown) published in Brixen and Nuremberg a selection from this correspondence, constituting what appears to be the earliest German-language printed source to include the term "European music" ("*Europaei*sche Music").[51] In this publication, Sepp alludes to the work of missionary music teachers who preceded him: first some Jesuits from the Low Countries who "taught the Indians to sing," without music notation and "through oral transmission," and then a Spanish Jesuit who "composed Masses, Vespers, Offertories and Litanies, though all in a style as ancient as the Old Testament or Noah's Ark."[52] Condescending about these early attempts and eager to update the styles of music being taught, Sepp details his labors in producing multipart works for local use; he composed and copied all the materials for use but also remembered and recycled some parts of works by Gletle that he knew "almost by heart." He begs to be sent the published works of his late teacher, especially "the Masses, short, shorter and very short Vespers, and also, for the love of Mary, the Litanies"; he says he does not require the motets but will "accept them if they were brought to me."[53] In return, he promises along with half a dozen of his priestly colleagues to say "sixty holy Masses for each person, be he priest or layman, who shall defray those costs" as well as twenty for a priest who would send them.[54]

Here the gift economy melds with a spiritual economy, but this request also seeps into more worldly concerns such as a musician's fame, extending across continents. It is here that Sepp mentions "European music":

> It is right that Herr Glettle [sic] should flourish in America also, exactly as in Europe, where I have always treasured him most highly, and also for the good reason that this would relieve me of the unspeakable trouble and work

---

[50] Clossey, *Salvation and Globalization*, 149–152; Sepp, "An Account," 649.

[51] The work's title page describes Gabriel's selection and redaction of the texts, but the extent to which he intervened editorially is unknown. On Sepp's siblings, see Sepp and Hoffmann, *Relación de viaje*, 12.

[52] Translation in Harrison, *Time, Place and Music*, 109; original in Sepp and Böhm, *RR. PP. Antonii Sepp*, 253–255.

[53] Translation in Harrison, *Time, Place and Music*, 110; original in Sepp and Böhm, *RR. PP. Antonii Sepp*, 258–259.

[54] Translation in Harrison, *Time, Place and Music*, 110–111. Original text in Sepp and Böhm, *RR. PP. Antonii Sepp*, 59.

which composing entails for me. What it has cost me to instruct the Indians in our European music [*in unser* Europaei*schen Music*] is known to the dear God alone.[55]

The reason for the continental adjective appears to be a reflection of the two parts of the world that have just been discussed—America and Europe—in mentioning the fame of a musician who had influenced him profoundly. He also evokes "European music" as a system of practice that he aimed to instill in (or impose on) local musicians. It seems that Sepp's request for scores may have had the result he desired. In 1723, a German Jesuit, Matías Strobel (Matthäus Ströbel, 1696–1769), wrote of Yapeyú that the musicians used "music books brought from Germany and Italy," which Timothy D. Watkins has suggested were "doubtless the music sent by Sepp's friends."[56]

Sepp clearly considered Gletle's works to be at the vanguard of new musical styles. Gletle himself had given a uniform title to his five major opuses of liturgical music, *Expeditionis musicae* (*Musical Expeditions*); he numbered them with classes one through five, and his prefaces make analogies with oceangoing voyages, including that of Jason and the Argonauts.[57] The third opus, *Expeditionis musicae classis III* (Augsburg, 1670), contained eight concerted masses (seven for five solo and five ripieno voices, with five concertante instruments and basso continuo, and one for eight voices, with seven instruments and basso continuo), as well as a concluding motet.[58] This was at the top of Sepp's list of impassioned musical requests. The collection survives (in Germany and Sweden) only as an incomplete set of part books—too few to reconstruct the score without a major process of recomposition.[59] Yet even the most cursory look at the few extant prints demonstrates that they involved the kind of elaborate writing for liturgical music that was then emerging from Italian-influenced centers and would have required high levels of instrumental and vocal skill for their performance.[60]

---

[55] Translation in Harrison, *Time, Place and Music*, 112. Original text in Sepp and Böhm, *RR. PP. Antonii Sepp*, 266. In later editions, the phrase appears as "in unserer Europaeischen Music."
[56] Watkins, "Musical Instruments," 303.
[57] For example, see an English translation of dedication text from the second set (Augsburg, 1668) in Lukin, "Johann Melchior Gletle's *Expeditionis musicae classis II*," 102–103.
[58] Gletle, *Expeditionis musicae classis III*.
[59] It is listed in the RISM catalogue as RISM A/I G 2618.
[60] See discussion of Gletle's compositional style in Lukin, "Johann Melchior Gletle's *Expeditionis musicae classis II*," esp. 24–25.

Teaching the techniques and expression needed to perform this kind of repertory—given that they were profoundly different from the older musical styles that Sepp encountered on his arrival in Paraguay—would likely also have entailed intense periods of instruction. Sepp appears to have engaged in this process, as he relates:

> All the missionaries, one here, another there, for a hundred miles around, send me their musicians so that I may instruct them in this art, which seems to them a completely new one, as different as day is from night from the way of the old Spanish teachers which they still retain. They know nothing about time-signatures or a regular beat, nor about the different triple metres, nor about such indications as 7–6 or 4–3 in figured bass. The Spaniards, as I observed in Seville and Cadiz, even to this day have no solmisation and no quarter-notes—much less triplets. Their notation is all in white notes—whole notes, half-notes and plainsong note-forms, to wit, very ancient music, in worthless old books like those that the choir-directors in the German Province have whole chests-full, and which are useful only for binding the work of more recent composers. This is why I have to begin from the beginning with my bearded, hoary choir-chaps the musical scale *ut, re, mi, fa, sol, la*, which I quite willingly do for the love of God.[61]

Despite these complaints, Sepp's claim about the purported absence of solmization or note divisions can probably be dismissed as a form of rhetorical hyperbole. Solmization was a mainstay of music education (by religious institutions and in other contexts) in early modern Spain, and Seville in the 1680s was home to composers such as Diego José de Salazar (1659–1709), *maestro de capilla* (chapel master) at the cathedral from 1685, who worked with styles involving figured bass and complex metrical divisions.[62] Of course, outside elite institutions, it is likely that there were musicians in Spain with different kinds and levels of experience, and perhaps Sepp was referring to them.

The 1696 publication of Sepp's writings appeared in a number of subsequent reprints and editions. As far as translations go, the only candidate seems to be an abridged English version, issued by Awnsham Churchill (1658–1728) and John Churchill (c. 1663–c. 1714) in 1704 (and reprinted several times).[63]

---

[61] Translation from Harrison, *Time, Place and Music*, 112–113.
[62] See Álvarez Martínez, "Salazar."
[63] Harrison writes that the Churchill version "seems to be the only version in another language." Harrison, *Time, Place and Music*, 97. See the relevant passage on music in Sepp, "An Account," 658.

THE EMERGENCE OF THE "EUROPEAN MUSIC" CONCEPT   147

However, that text omits the the passage mentioning "European music." Unlike the case of Verbiest, Sepp's use of "European music" appears not to have entered into intertextual relationships with works by other authors. Nevertheless, his same letter was printed in another version in 1726, in *Der neue Welt-Bott* (*The New World-Messenger*), a German-language collection of "edifying" Jesuit correspondence.[64] Although this recension again makes no mention of "European music," it does include discussion of Indigenous skills in "European arts and sciences," emphasizing music as one of these.[65] Sepp also indicates his desire to introduce "German and Roman" styles to the missions.[66] Thinking about intertextuality raises the question of Sepp's possible knowledge of Verbiest's *Astronomia europaea*. A direct documentary link remains to be identified, but the possibility that Sepp was inspired by the reference to "European music" from Verbiest's famous "notation story" cannot be ruled out. Sepp's ordination had taken place in May 1687 in Augsburg, only a day's walk away from Dillingen, where Verbiest's book had been printed earlier that same year. The Jesuit communities were tight-knit and in regular communication and discourse, and the possibility of Sepp's contact with this source is theoretically feasible.

Another hint of the potential influence of Verbiest is Sepp's mention in the 1696 publication of a "European organ" ("Europäische Orgel"), a term that appears rarely in early modern sources but which both these Jesuits use.[67] Sepp relates that there were two organs in the mission, one imported from Europe and another made locally by the Guaraní with such exactitude that he thought the latter was the European instrument ("Europäische Orgel").[68] He states elsewhere that an organ had been bought in the Netherlands for the mission, and he differentiates between the various qualities of German and Spanish instruments.[69] Of course, the Iberian traditions of organ building (involving, for instance, a split keyboard with different registers below

---

[64] In Stöcklein, *Der neue Welt-Bott*, nos. 48, 40–60. On this source, see Strasser, "*Welt-Bott*." Both of the published texts are ostensibly based on the same letter by Anton Sepp dated June 24, 1692, written in Yapeyú. Lenke, "Heil und Heilung," 42–43.
[65] Pelizäus, "Musikalische Mission," 22.
[66] Leonhardt, "El P. Antonio Sepp," 371. Original text in Stöcklein, *Der neue Welt-Bott*, nos. 48, 55.
[67] Sepp and Böhm, *RR. PP. Antonii Sepp*, 292.
[68] Sepp and Hoffmann, *Relación de viaje*, 215; Sepp and Böhm, *RR. PP. Antonii Sepp*, 292.
[69] Harrison, *Time, Place and Music*, 112; Sepp and Hoffmann, *Relación de viaje*, 206; original in Sepp and Böhm, *RR. PP. Antonii Sepp*, 264. It is worth noting, as an aside, that his teacher Gletle was one of the ten composers who are known to have written works specifically for the trumpet marine and that Sepp had such an instrument made in Cádiz to take with him to Paraguay. Sepp, "An Account," 648; Sepp and Hoffmann, *Relación de viaje*, 164, 206; original in Sepp and Böhm, *RR. PP. Antonii Sepp*, 151, 264. See also Adkins, "Trumpet Marine."

and above middle C) are significantly different from styles in other parts of Europe, and this could be another reason for the distinctive "European" adjective applied here.[70] This sense would echo the distinction between older Iberian styles of music and the newer "European" styles that he had introduced to the missions. However, perhaps it also refers to being imported rather than locally built.

In his *Continuatio laborum apostolicum* (*Continuation of the Apostolic Work*)—a sequel to his original account which was published in a Latin and a German version in 1709 and 1710, respectively—Sepp mentions being ordered by the Jesuit provincial (Lauro Núñez, 1632-1719) to build an organ "in the European style" ("Organum Europaeo modo"; "ein . . . Orgl [sic] auf Europaeische Weiß und Manier"). He constructed this instrument in the mission of Itapúa (Paraguay).[71] Not having enough tin to make the larger pipes, Sepp substituted thin strips of local cedar wood glued together with parchment for the lower registers, and in his writings, he describes the delight with which the success of the process was met by Indigenous observers when the pipes were first activated.[72] Sepp speculates that leading "European organists" ("Europäische Herrn Organisten") would be able to appreciate how the sound of the organ could mix with cornetts, trumpets, bassoons, and shawms.[73]

We have seen so far that the first three published examples of "European music" before 1700—in Latin, French, and German—can all be attributed to Jesuits. Given the popularity of the allegorical scheme of the "four parts of the world" in the institutions of the Society of Jesus and their style of propaganda (discussed in chapter 1), it is not surprising that the sense of continental categories seeped deeply into their discourse about cultural practices. We now go on to consider how the concept continued to travel through historiography in the long eighteenth century, with examples that seem to show broader awareness of these early uses.

---

[70] It is interesting to note that the Jesuits did not build Iberian-style organs in China. See Urrows, "The Pipe Organ," 39. Verbiest mentioned a "European organ" ("Organum illud Europaeum") in his *Astronomia europaea*; see Golvers and Verbiest, *The Astronomia Europaea*, 126 (translation), 439 (facsimile of the original, at 91).

[71] Sepp and Hoffmann, *Continuación*, 138-139; original in Sepp and Sepp, *Continuation*, 87-88. A shorter account is given in the Latin version: Sepp, *Continuatio*, 30-33. See also discussion in Watkins, "Musical Instruments," 302; Nawrot, *Indígenas y cultura musical*, 39.

[72] Sepp and Hoffmann, *Continuación*, 138; original in Sepp and Sepp, *Continuation*, 89.

[73] Sepp and Hoffmann, *Continuación*, 139; original in Sepp and Sepp, *Continuation*, 91. See also Nawrot, *Indígenas y cultura musical*, 39.

"European Music," Turkey, and "Oriental Music"

China and Paraguay were distant "others" to early modern Europeans, but Turkey was a near neighbor. Considerably more travelers from Turkey than from China arrived at the capitals of western Europe.[74] Some visits took place in contexts of state diplomacy, certain acts of which invariably involved music. In 1721, an unnamed writer in Paris reported how an Ottoman ambassador to France discussed first the difference between "their" (that is, Turkish) music and that of France and Italy.[75] This episode included another "notation story": in this case, there was an offer by a French host to the ambassador to transcribe whatever Turkish air he would like, after just two hearings, and to see it performed on the spot by voices and instruments of his choosing. Such a dare seems to reflect the hubris surrounding Pereira's story from the Chinese court (and perhaps indicates knowledge of that tale). It is also striking to note in this anecdote that in the conversation about the comparison of styles, French music and Italian music were clearly differentiated and not conflated as "European."

However, a report published in 1739 of another diplomatic encounter, referring back to an episode from 1665 in a French embassy to the Ottoman Empire, used the term "European" in place of either "French" or "Italian":

> The *Caïmacan* [*kaymakam*, a term for an elite Ottoman official] displayed much pleasure in hearing European music [*témoigna beaucoup de plaisir d'entendre la Musique Européenne*], and most of all in seeing and hearing the playing of a small organ in the chapel of the ambassador; he was very happy with this, and appeared to understand well the difference between European music and their music [*& témoigna bien comprendre la différence de la Musique Européenne, & de la leur*].[76]

This report comes from the volume titled *Le ceremonial diplomatique des cours de l'Europe* (*Diplomatic Ceremonial of the Courts of Europe*), a normative manual for diplomacy setting out precedents and current practice, which also contains a collection of treaties. If the original source from

---

[74] There was constant interaction with people from Turkey, as discussed in Holm and Rasmussen, *Imagined, Embodied and Actual Turks*. Compare this with the apparently rarer direct interface with Chinese music in eighteenth-century Europe itself; an example is discussed in Clarke, "An Encounter with Chinese Music."
[75] Original text in "Journal de Paris," 166.
[76] Original text in Dumont and Rousset de Missy, *Le ceremonial diplomatique*, Vol. 2, 705.

150 "EUROPEAN MUSIC"

1665—on which this story was based—survives, and if it also uses the specific term "European music," it has yet to be uncovered. With its discussions of etiquette, it would go on to have far-reaching influence in the continuing codification of diplomatic protocol.[77] The events and ceremonies surrounding embassies were important conduits, flowing in both directions, for all parties' knowledge of other cultures and customs.

Certain descriptions of Ottoman musical practice emanated from elite individuals who occupied liminal positions between cultures. Two such characters who come into the story of the "European music" concept in Turkish contexts are Cantemir and Fonton (mentioned in chapters 2 and 3, respectively). Cantemir, a *voivode* (local governor) of Moldavia under Ottoman rule, possessed an insider's perspective on life under Ottoman rule. Besides occupying a political role, he was a scholar, composer, and performer; he invented a new notation system and left many scores of Ottoman court music.[78] Cantemir's large-scale work in Latin, "Incrementorum et decrementorum aulae othman[n]icae sive aliothman[n]icae historiae a prima gentis origine ad nostra usque tempora deductae libri tres," was first published in 1734–1735 in an English translation titled *The History of the Growth and Decay of the Othman Empire*.[79] In this work, Cantemir uses the binary of Turkish and European music to make this comparative assessment:

> I may certainly venture to say, that the *Turkish* Musick for metre and proportion is more perfect than any *European*, but withal so hard to be understood, that in the spacious City of *Constantinople*, where resides the greatest Court in the World, among so many Musicians and Lovers of Musick, you will scarce find three or four, who thoroughly understand the grounds of this Art.[80]

---

[77] For an overview of this work, see H. Scott, "Diplomatic Culture," 79–80.

[78] For recent research on Cantemir, see Neubauer, "New Light on Cantemir," 3–21. For his notations, see Cantemir and Wright, *Demetrius Cantemir* Part 1; Cantemir and Wright, *Demetrius Cantemir* Vol. 2.

[79] Monica Vasileanu points out that the Latin manuscript (in the Houghton Library, Harvard University, MS Lat 224) was identified by Virgil Cândea in 1984 and notes the surprise its discovery occasioned, since its content differed strikingly from the known translations. She renders the original title as "The History of the Increase and the Decrease of the Othman or Alothman Court, carried out from the very beginnings of the nation until our times, in three books." Citing Cândea, she notes that the 1734–1735 translation, made by English clergyman Nicholas Tindal (1687–1774), has been criticized for redesigning and reordering the work, as well as omitting many parts. Vasileanu, "What Was a Relevant Translation?," 82.

[80] Cantemir, *The History*, Vol. 1, 151–152n.14. The original text reads: "Id certe audacter asserere possumus, Turcicam Musicam metro vocumque proportione omni Eur[o]paea esse perfectiorem, at simul adeo captu difficilem, ut Constantinopoli, in Urbe tam ampla, Aulae totius orbis maximae receptaculo, Orientis concilio, inter tot Musicos et Musicae amatores, vix tres aut quatuor, qui

Although the word "music" (or "Musick") is absent after "*European*" in the English version, it is implied, and "any" suggests plurality. In the original Latin text, the term "omni Eur[o]paea" ("all European") seems to denote an overarching category of musics, but it still allows for the idea of heterogeneity. In mentioning the "grounds of this Art" in regard to Turkish music, on the other hand, he gives the impression that there is a singular system, despite referring to the intricacies of Turkish music theory.

There is a striking mix here of praise for Turkish music (as "more perfect" than the musics of Europe) and skepticism regarding the extent of theoretical knowledge of it. Of course, in this history, Cantemir was clearly writing for a "European" readership, as Jordi Savall—who has done much to disseminate knowledge of this composer's music—has recently pointed out.[81] Cantemir commented that "it will perhaps seem strange to the *European* Reader to see the study of so noble an art [that is, music] prais'd by me in a Nation accounted barbarian by all *Christendom*."[82] His mention of the "*European* Reader" ("Lectori Europaeo") signals that he was reflexively aware of his relational position as an author writing from an emic Ottoman perspective but addressing external readers; at the same time, he was a complex figure who occupied a liminal position across several cultures.[83] As much as we might project back current-day definitions of "Europeanness" to embrace Cantemir (who, as we saw in chapter 2, self-identified as being among "Europeans") and his music, it is worth remembering that in the eighteenth century, his art was apparently considered, by Europeans and Ottomans alike, "Oriental" or "Eastern." This idea is echoed in the work of Fonton (born a few years after Cantemir's death), who pointed out that "Oriental" listeners would be "insensible as rocks" to the music of "the Lullys and the Tartinis"

---

interiores eius artis rationes perspectas habeant, reperiantur." Cantemir, *Demetrii principis Cantemirii*, 367. In discussing this passage, Eugenia Popescu-Judetz names some of the experts in Turkish music at the time as Hafiz Post (c. 1630–1694), Buhurî-zâde Itrî (c. 1640–1712), and Nayî Osman Dede (c. 1652–1730). Popescu-Judetz, *Prince Dimitrie Cantemir*, 22–23.

[81] Savall, "Istanbul: Dimitrie Cantemir," 128.
[82] Cantemir, *The History*, Vol. 1, 151n.14. The original text reads: "παράδοξος [parádoxos] forte videbitur Lectori Europaeo, si in ea gente tam nobilis artis studium a me laudatum observaverit, quae totius reipublicae Christianae suffragiis pro barbara habetur." Cantemir and Cândea, *Creșterile și descreșterile Imperiului Otoman*, 367.
[83] Michiel Leezenberg observes: "As a humanist, Cantemir was shaped by Orthodox and Ottoman traditions as much as by western European learning." He goes on to note that "one should be careful . . . to avoid projecting back present-day nationalist assumptions, or even the nineteenth-century categories of historical and comparative linguistics, onto earlier authors." Leezenberg, "The Oriental Origins of Orientalism," 259.

but that they would become "full of enthusiasm about an air of their famous Cantimir [sic]."[84]

Fonton's statement comes from his 1751 treatise titled "Essay sur la musique orientale compareé [sic] a la musique européene [sic]" ("Essay on Oriental Music Compared to European Music"), a work based on several years' experience of living within the Ottoman Empire; his autograph manuscript is held at the Bibliothèque Nationale de France.[85] Born in France to a family with a history of working in diplomacy, Fonton studied languages in Paris at the Jesuit college of Louis-le-Grand from 1737 to 1746; as a student there, it is likely that he was fully immersed in that institution's musical culture, where ballets and major stage works were regularly performed.[86] He moved to Istanbul in 1746 and continued his training (with the Capuchins), subsequently serving as a *drogman* (interpreter) in Aleppo, then Cairo (from 1759) and Smyrna (1774–1778).[87] Fonton's academic prowess is displayed in his production of scientific works and translations and adaptations of histories.[88] The "Essay" was apparently written to conclude his period of studies in the Ottoman capital, and it was dedicated to Antoine-Louis Rouillé (1689–1761), minister for the French navy.[89] While the manuscript is set out as if ready for publication, it was not printed at the time. However, an abridged edition appeared in 1838 in the journal *Revue et Gazette Musicale de Paris* (*Review and Musical Gazette of Paris*).[90] Thus, it seems that Fonton's

---

[84] Fonton, "Essay," manuscript (1751), 4. See also Shiloah, "An Eighteenth-Century Critic," 186.

[85] The complete title of the original manuscript by Fonton, dated Constantinople 1751, is "Essay sur la musique orientale compareé [sic] a la musique européene [sic] ou l'on tache de donner une ideé [sic] generale de la musique des peuples de l'orient, de leur gout particulier, de leur regles dans le chant, et la combinaison des tons, avec une notion abregeé de leurs principaux instrumens"; it is held in the Bibliothèque Nationale de France (Département des Manuscrits, NAF 4023; catalogue entry at https://archivesetmanuscrits.bnf.fr/ark:/12148/cc400578). All my citations from his original text come from this source, unless otherwise indicated. For a digital version of the manuscript, see https://gallica.bnf.fr/ark:/12148/btv1b52518530j. For a critical edition of the text by Eckhard Neubauer, see Fonton, "Essai sur la musique orientale comparée à la musique européenne [1751]." An accompanying study and index are provided in Neubauer, "Der *Essai sur la musique orientale*." The work has been translated into Turkish by Cem Behar; see Fonton, *18. yüzyılda Türk müziği*. It has also been translated into English by Robert Martin; see Fonton, "Essay Comparing" [Part 1]; Fonton, "Essay Comparing" [Part 2]. For discussions of this treatise, see Shiloah, "An Eighteenth-Century Critic"; Klotz, "Tartini the Indian."

[86] As Anne-Marie Touzard has pointed out, five ballets were staged during Fonton's time there. Touzard, "Un drogman musicien," 198–199. In those years, Campra wrote music for the college, and the dancer Jean-Georges Noverre (1727–1810) performed there. Demeilliez, "Campra maître de musique"; Demeilliez, "Noverre."

[87] Shiloah, "An Eighteenth-Century Critic," 183; Cler, "Fonton," 418; Touzard, "Un drogman musicien," 201–204.

[88] Cler, "Fonton," 418; Touzard, "Un drogman musicien," 204.

[89] Shiloah, "An Eighteenth-Century Critic," 183.

[90] Fonton, "Essai sur la musique orientale" (1838). In a brief introduction to that publication (on 421), an anonymous writer claims that the work was "intended to be printed" but admits lack of

work had some kind of circulation prior to the rediscovery of its significance in the late twentieth century.

In a 1991 study of Fonton's treatise, Amnon Shiloah (1928–2014) pointed out Fonton's "harsh and cogent criticism of what may be called ethnocentric European views," described his approach as "emic" (with his long exposure to Ottoman culture), and asserted that some of the ideas found in the work's introduction are "strikingly similar to the major concerns of modern ethnomusicology."[91] Fonton's work surveys the origins of music as seen by Ottoman theorists, examines the division of the octave through mathematical ratios, describes and compares scale systems, and discusses the qualities of various instruments and the affective power of musical performance. Yet apart from titles and headings, Fonton uses the specific term "European music" in the main text only four times (writing it thrice as "la Musique Européene" and once as "la Musique Europééne").[92] Toward the end of his preliminary discourse, he employs it specifically to write of his objectives in the essay: "I will attempt to make Oriental music known, such as it is today; and in order to outline a more distinct idea of it, I will put it in parallel with European music, less however to compare the beauties of it than to make the difference of it better felt."[93]

In the treatise's second article, he invokes a fluvial metaphor to compare the two kinds of music and propose a parallel:

> By its meanderings Oriental music is comparable to a peaceful and tranquil stream, whose sweet and flattering murmuring ensnares [or binds; *enchaîne*] the soul and sends it to sleep in the bosom of pleasure. If I may be permitted to express myself less exactly, I would say, to follow this comparison, that European music is a great and majestic river which ripples its waters with discernment, measures its course depending on the needs of the lands that it irrigates, and carries with it richness and abundance

---

knowledge about what prevented that plan; there then follows speculation that the many plates of music and engravings of instruments—as well as "a table of twelve pages in Turkish characters"—could have presented too much cost for booksellers to recoup if they had offered the work for sale to "a too-restrained public."

[91] Shiloah, "An Eighteenth-Century Critic," 182, 188.
[92] Fonton, "Essai sur la musique orientale" (ed. Neubauer), 281, 291, 292, 293; see original text in Fonton, "Essay," manuscript (1751), 10, 45, 49, 50.
[93] Original text in Fonton, "Essay," manuscript (1751), 9–10; modernized transcription in Fonton, "Essai sur la musique orientale" (ed. Neubauer), 281.

everywhere. I leave it to the connoisseurs to decide on the accuracy of the parallel.[94]

This idea of comparison—and even the word "parallel"—invokes two prominent publications of several decades earlier: the *Comparaison de la musique italienne et de la musique françoise* (*Comparison of Italian Music and French Music*) of 1705–1706 by Jean-Louis Le Cerf de la Viéville (1674–1707) and the *Paralele* [sic] *des Italiens et des François, en ce qui regarde la musique et les opéra* (*Parallel of the Italians and the French, as Regards Music and Operas*) by François Raguenet (c. 1660–1722).[95] It also prefigures the direct attack by Jean-Jacques Rousseau on French music, published in 1753.[96] Yet Fonton was careful with his expression. It is interesting to note that in the autograph manuscript, he had originally written the following wording for the beginning of the second sentence quoted above: "Therefore, to follow this comparison, we will say from our perspective that European music is . . ." ("Pour suivre donc la Comparaison, nous dirons de notre Cote, que la Musique Européene est . . ."). However, he then crossed out most of the words, adding insertions and an adjustment to give the more circumspect phrasing of the final text: "If I may be permitted to express myself less exactly, I would say, to follow this comparison, that European music is . . ." ("S'il m'etoit permis de m'exprimer moins exactement, je dirois pour suivre cette Comparaison, que la Musique Européene est . . .").[97] It seems that Fonton was unsure about making concrete statements, leaving room for a variety of interpretations.

Fonton mentions a number of peoples of Europe, referring specifically to four archetypal tastes: French, Italian, German, and English. Observing that each taste is different from another—for example, "the French differs in all ways from the Italian"—but that all claim to be good, he surmises that "it would be impossible to decide, since it would be necessary to belong to no country at all, and to appear on the earth without having been born in any of its four parts," these parts clearly denoting the "four parts of the world," or continents.[98] Later in the treatise, he writes of the difference of

---

[94] Original text in Fonton, "Essay," manuscript (1751), 45; modernized transcription in Fonton, "Essai sur la musique orientale" (ed. Neubauer), 291.

[95] See discussion of this point in Shiloah, "An Eighteenth-Century Critic," 183–184. Le Cerf de la Viéville, *Comparaison*; Raguenet, *Paralele*.

[96] Rousseau, *Lettre sur la musique françoise*.

[97] Fonton, "Essay," manuscript (1751), 45.

[98] He writes: "Il seroit impossible de decider, puisqu'il faudroit n'apartenir à aucun païs, et paroître sur la Terre, sans y avoir pris naissance dans aucune de ses quatre Parties." Fonton, "Essay," manuscript (1751), 5–6; modernized transcription in Fonton, "Essai sur la musique orientale" (ed. Neubauer),

"the Orientals": "Completely distanced from our manners and our customs, they do not come any closer to us in their music, which has no connection to that of any people of Europe."[99] (As is the case in earlier works, discussed above, Fonton writes about "peoples" of Europe and does not use the term "Europeans.") It is also worth noting that in his title, Fonton chooses the term "Oriental music" (that is, "Eastern music") to compare and contrast with "European music," rather than using "Asian music" to match the continental adjective given for Europe. The last term was certainly known in French at the time, although it was not widespread in use.[100] If we question why Fonton does not use the continental adjective "Asian" to balance "European," we could also ask why the hemispheric term "Western" is not used to correspond to "Eastern [*orientale*]." The likely reason for his choice, as explored in chapter 6, is that "Western music" before the nineteenth century referred specifically to Christian liturgical music, not to all kinds of music associated with "Europe."

Fonton's text is possibly the first to use "European music" in its very title.[101] The cover page of the autograph manuscript (f. Ar) has an intriguing feature: it exhibits some orthographic uncertainty surrounding the key adjective (figure 4.3). The word clearly appears as having been written originally as "Uropeéne," with a corrective "E" inserted above the first letter. Thus, we see "LA MUSIQUE ᴱUROPEÉNE [*sic*]" (with the acute accent appearing over the middle of the double "e"). If anything points to the relatively rarity of the adjective "European" in describing music in the eighteenth century, this incongruity could constitute a vital piece of evidence. The block lettering closely resembles Fonton's handwriting on the full title page (f. Br), in which he spells the word with the correct initial vowel (figure 4.4). These precede his signed dedicatory letter (ff. Cr–Dr), before the treatise begins. The apparent

---

280. Although Shiloah glosses "quatre Parties" as "four countries," referring back to France, Italy, Germany, and England ("An Eighteenth-Century Critic," 187), it would seem from Fonton's mention of "la Terre" and the use of a capital for "Parties" that he is referring to the "four parts of the world."

[99] "En tout eloignés de nos manieres, et de nos usages, Ils ne se raprochent pas plus de nous dans leur musique, qui n'a null raport avec celle d'aucun peuple de l'Europe." Fonton, "Essay," manuscript (1751), 38. See also Fonton, "Essai sur la musique orientale" (ed. Neubauer), 289.

[100] As mentioned in the introduction to part II of this book, an example of "Musique Asiatique" in comparison to "Musique Européane [*sic*]" was published in 1749. Juvenel de Carlencas, *Essais sur l'histoire des belles lettres*, Vol. 2, 330.

[101] Another early example (although not extant) comes from a reference made late in the next decade. According to Adam Parr, in 1768, Amiot sent to Armand-Jérôme Bignon (1711–1772), the librarian of the king of France, "a work entitled *Accord de la musique chinoise avec la musique européenne* (*The Concurrence of Chinese and European Music*)." Parr, *The Mandate of Heaven*, 260. However, that source does not seem to survive (I thank François Picard for his advice on this matter).

Figure 4.3. Misspelled and corrected adjective for "European" in the earliest known (so far) music treatise to use "European music" in its title. Charles Fonton, "Essay sur la musique orientale compareé a la musique européene," autograph manuscript dated Constantinople 1751, Bibliothèque Nationale de France, Département des Manuscrits, NAF 4023, cover page (f. Ar).

Figure 4.4. Charles Fonton, "Essay sur la musique orientale compareé a la musique europeéne," autograph manuscript dated Constantinople 1751, Bibliothèque Nationale de France, Département des Manuscrits, NAF 4023, title page (f. Br).

anomaly of "Uropeéne" on the cover page could, of course, be explained away as a simple scribal mishap, yet it nevertheless points clearly to the lack of orthographic standardization and even the author's unfamiliarity with writing it. The careful inscription of the larger capital letter "U" might even suggest some kind of cognitive connection with a specific vowel sound in the pronunciation of the word.

There is another possibility: perhaps this "error" points to Fonton's awareness of a certain theory that was widely known in French-language scholarship. In the famous *Encyclopédie ou Dictionnaire raisonné des sciences, des arts et des métiers* (*Encyclopedia or Systematic Dictionary of the Sciences, Arts and Crafts*) of Denis Diderot (1713–1784) and Jean Le Rond d'Alembert (1717–1783), the sixth volume (from 1756) includes an entry for "Europe" in the category of "Geography," written by Chevalier Louis de Jaucourt (1704–1779). He defines it as a "large inhabited region of the world," stating:

> The etymology which is perhaps the most convincing derives the word *Europe* from the Phoenician *urappa*, which in this language means *white face*; [this is an] epithet that one could have given to the daughter of Agenor, sister of Cadmus, but [one] at least which is suitable for the Europeans, who are neither swarthy [*basanés*] like the southern Asians, nor black [*noirs*] like the Africans.[102]

The "daughter of Agenor, sister of Cadmus" was, of course, none other than the mythical figure of Europa (discussed in chapter 1). This idea regarding the word "urappa" had been circulating in France within annotated translations of Horace by André Dacier (1651–1722), published in multiple bilingual editions since the 1680s, where in his "Remarks on Ode 27, Book 3," Dacier articulates the same etymology mentioned by Jaucourt.[103] Fonton likely read Horace during his studies at the college of Louis-le-Grand, where two editions of this work (1681–1689 and 1709) were listed in a catalogue of 1764.[104] It seems probable that he was directly or indirectly aware of Dacier's annotated editions and possible that he was influenced by this etymology.

---

[102] Original text in Jaucourt, "Europe," Vol. 6 (1756), 211–212. Sourced from Jaucourt, "Europe," online.

[103] For the original text in an early edition, see Horace and Dacier, *Remarques critiques sur les oeuvres d'Horace*, Vol. 3 (1683), 451. The third edition of this work, incidentally, was published by Ballard, of the famous music printing house, and likely known to many purchasers of music. Horace and Dacier, *Oeuvres d'Horace en latin et françois*.

[104] These were offered for sale in an auction of books following the suppression of the Jesuits in France in 1764. *Catalogue des livres*, 156 (nos. 2704 and 2705).

THE EMERGENCE OF THE "EUROPEAN MUSIC" CONCEPT 159

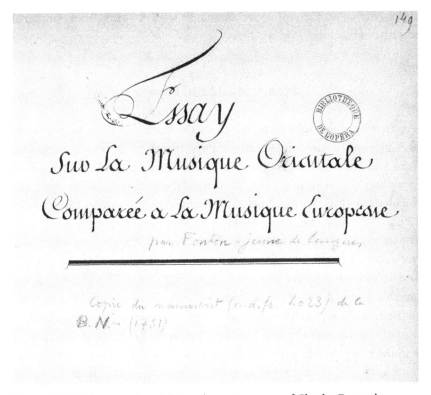

Figure 4.5. Title page of an eighteenth-century copy of Charles Fonton's "Essay," in Paul Louis Roualle de Boisgelou (1734–1806), "Recueil de diverses pieces sur la musique," Bibliothèque Nationale de France, Département Bibliothèque–Musée de l'Opéra, B-24 (1-10), f. 149r. Sourced from gallica.bnf.fr.

My attempts to account for Fonton's original spelling of "Uropéene" are, of course, no more than speculation. However, I feel that such a prominent quirk on the cover page of his thesis cannot be passed over without comment. At the same time, it must be acknowledged that his writing of "Uropéene" is an exceptional idiosyncrasy within the two eighteenth-century sources of this treatise. A contemporaneous copy, which was originally held in the Bibliothèque de l'Opéra, contains slightly ambiguous lettering in the headings (see figure 4.5) but nevertheless appears to use the spelling "Europeene" in the title and the text.[105] On the title pages of two manuscripts

---

[105] Fonton, "Essay sur la musique orientale comparée a la musique europeene," in "Recueil de diverses pieces sur la musique," Bibliothèque Nationale de France, f. 163r.

160 "EUROPEAN MUSIC"

of this famous work, then, we see alternative ways of writing the continental adjective at the time.

French Music and Europe

Diversity in orthography is a telling hint of the newness of the adjectival usage of "European" in mid-eighteenth-century French.[106] In a work produced three years after that of Fonton, Amiot also used the spelling "la Musique Européanne" in essay of c. 1754, "De la musique moderne des Chinois" ("On the Modern Music of the Chinese").[107] Pierre-Joseph Roussier (1716/1717–1792), on the other hand, uses the form "la Musique Européenne" in 1755.[108] The following decade, the Académie Française—the royally founded organization that arbitrated on matters of linguistic convention—included for the first time an entry for the adjective "EUROPÉEN, [EUROP]ÉENNE" in the fourth edition (1762) of its dictionary. The Académie defined the term laconically as "that which belongs to Europe" and went on to comment, perhaps a little emphatically, that "one does not say EUROPÉAN at all [*on ne dit point EUROPÉAN*]. It is for this reason alone that this word is placed in the Dictionary."[109] Note here the use of the verb "to say" rather than "to write"; such an observation may suggest changes in pronunciation, but it also implies that the word was inscribed so rarely that its lettering was unfamiliar. The last part of the definition—"for this reason alone"—also hints that the adjective had been considered almost not worth including in this official lexicon.

There is perhaps a direct catalyst for the entry: a publication from the previous year. Voltaire (François-Marie Arouet, 1694–1778) had produced a text using three spellings of the adjective consecutively; he did so probably deliberately to emphasize the lack of agreement surrounding the word. His "Rescrit de l'Empereur de la Chine à l'occasion du *Projet de paix perpétuelle*" ("Response of the Emperor of China on the Occasion of the

---

[106] Le Goff writes that it was first used in French in 1721. Le Goff, *The Birth of Europe*, 3. However, as shown earlier in this chapter, it was applied to music in 1688 by Pierre-Joseph d'Orléans in his *Histoire des deux conquerans tartares*, 301.

[107] Amiot, "De la musique moderne des Chinois," manuscript, 1. On this work, see also Jiang, "In Search of the 'Oriental Origin,'" 128.

[108] Roussier, *Observations*, 155. Here he writes of "all the nations that practice European music" ("Toutes les nations qui cultivent la Musique Europeenne"), with reference to diminutive intervals, inversely implying a global frame that includes other domains of music.

[109] Original text in Académie Française, "Le Dictionnaire de l'Académie Française," 4th ed. (1762), Vol. 1, entry for "Européen, éenne."

Project of Perpetual Peace"), was appended to Jean-Jacques Rousseau's 1761 commentary on the "Project to bring about Perpetual Peace in Europe," a treatise of 1713 by the Abbé de Saint-Pierre (Charles-Irénée Castel de Saint-Pierre, 1658–1743).[110] Voltaire satirically ventriloquized the emperor of China in this response to Rousseau. The text referred to various ways in which "perpetual peace" could be disrupted, such as aggressions between neighboring states—for example, "if the Grand Turk attacked Hungary"— or "if the Europain, or European, or Europeen Diet [*la Diéte Europaine, ou Européenne, ou Européane*] did not find itself to have sufficient money."[111] The three possible spellings, deliberately listed in sequence, are clearly a pointed comment by Voltaire on the novelty and unfamiliarity of the concept. The imagined Chinese emperor ends the letter by suggesting that he and Rousseau should become, jointly, "the first president of the Diet [that is, the European parliament]."[112] Such a remark seems to constitute approbation by Voltaire of Rousseau as a champion of political and social reform in Europe.

Given Rousseau's extensive thought on European peace and integration— not to mention countless aspects of European identity and the history of Europeans—it may seem somewhat curious that he himself does not appear to use the term "European music" in any of his writings (as far as I can ascertain). In his *Dictionnaire de musique* of 1768, for example, he hedges his bets by referring to "the peoples of Europe," to make distinctions between nations, and uses the term "Européens" (Europeans) only once, in his famous statement that the Europeans were the only people "of all the peoples of the Earth [*de tous les peuples de la terre*]" to use harmony (to which we return in chapter 5).[113] There seems to be a clear reason for this: for many decades of his active writing life, Rousseau was fully immersed in the battle between French and Italian styles. "European" was suggestive only in intercontinental contexts.

---

[110] Saint-Pierre, *Projet pour rendre la paix perpetuelle*. Beginning in 1756, just before the start of the Seven Years War, Rousseau made an in-depth and sympathetic study of Saint-Pierre; Frédéric Ramel has noted that both thinkers used the idea of "concert" in dialogue with international relations but in distinct ways. Ramel, "Perpetual Peace," 134.

[111] Original text in Voltaire, "Rescrit de l'empereur de la Chine," 81. (Of the three possible spellings for these words in English translation, I use "European" for the second spelling, "Européenne," rather than for its seemingly direct equivalent, "Européane," to reflect the orthography standardized by the Académie Française the following year.) A private reaction by Friedrich Melchior, Baron von Grimm (1723–1807) in May of that year also used two of those spellings: "la diète européenne ou européane." Grimm et al., *Correspondance littéraire, philosophique et critique*, Vol. 4, 398.

[112] Voltaire, "Rescrit de l'empereur de la Chine," 83.

[113] Rousseau, *Dictionnaire de musique*, 37 ("B fa si"), 187 ("Échelle"), 245 ("Harmonie").

Debates on the relative merits of French and Italian musics reached their zenith in 1752 with the *querelle des bouffons* (quarrel of the buffoons).[114] A primary cause for controversy that year was the presence of Italian opera in Paris, brought to a head by an Italian troupe's performance of the opera *La serva padrona* by the late Giovanni Battista Pergolesi. This was not merely an intellectual pamphlet war about the finer points of aesthetics or the politics of royal tastes in music. So much was at stake—especially national pride—that a level of epistemic violence ensued. An effigy of Rousseau was even publicly burned for his having dared to attack the central tenets of French musical identity, in his *Lettre sur la musique françoise* (*Letter on French Music*, 1753); he had concluded this text with an inflammatory paragraph stating baldly and boldly that the French did not have a music.[115] During and after this mid-century debate, the opinions of cultural outsiders were transformed into sources of evidence to support arguments about the strength of the Italian style over the French, as Vanessa Agnew has shown.[116] In experiments or as parts of stories that circulated in many forms of music discourse, people from Armenia, Greece, and Polynesia were invoked as ostensibly neutral arbitrators in the battle between French and Italian styles for aesthetic supremacy in Europe.[117]

The circumscribed idea of a homogeneous "European music" in the late eighteenth century—and also the conceptual exclusion of contemporary Greece from "Europe" (as described in chapter 2)—is seen in an anecdote recounted by Burney in 1773 about a Greek woman who had "never heard any European music" being taken to the opera in Paris. Here the concept of "European music" is extracted and disembedded from geographical notions, referring to an aesthetic category and a cultural practice shared among an imagined community of nations. It ends with her going to Venice, hearing Italian opera with "her uncorrupted ears," and preferring the latter.[118] As Burney points out, it resembles very closely a story told by Rousseau in his letter on French music about an Armenian man at the opera in Venice who, according to Rousseau, "had never heard any Music [*n'avoit jamais entendu de*

---

[114] See Higgins, "Old Sluts and Dangerous Minuets."
[115] Burney, *A General History of Music*, Vol. 4, 615. See Rousseau, *Essay on the Origin of Languages*, 174. Original text in Rousseau, *Lettre sur la musique françoise*, 92.
[116] Agnew, *Enlightenment Orpheus*, 57–58.
[117] The Armenian case is mentioned in Rousseau, *Lettre sur la musique françoise*, 27–29. The Greek and Polynesian (Tahitian) cases are mentioned in Burney, *The Present State of Music*, Vol. 2, 122–125. See also my discussion in Irving, "Exchange."
[118] Burney, *The Present State of Music*, Vol. 2, 122–123.

Musique]" (that is, music without a qualifying adjective) but ended up preferring Italian.[119] This story was doubted at the time, and recent scholarship has also suggested that Rousseau, who enjoyed wearing Armenian clothing, may have been referring to himself.[120] Yet the experience of the Greek lady was apparently not apocryphal, for Burney states that he later met her in Potsdam and conversed with her at a lunch. He does not mention her name, describing her rather as "the Grecian lady, who had been so offended with French music, and so pleased with Italian, upon her first arrival in Europe."[121] Although Burney reinforces the then-prevailing notion of Greece as "non-European" space by referring to her "arrival in Europe," further research may throw new light on the identity of this woman and her point of origin.

"One Music for Europe," from the Sixteenth to Late Eighteenth Centuries

The idea of a uniform space for music in Europe—although still often excluding the Balkans—was prominent in writings of the late eighteenth century. Scholars looked at common approaches to counterpoint across numerous nations, tracing them centuries earlier, but still contrasted these with local differences in performance styles. In 1776, Burney's rival, Hawkins, wrote about the "uniformity" of compositional rules across western Europe, locating this phenomenon in the mid-sixteenth century:

> The principles of music, and the precepts of musical composition, as taught in the several countries of Europe about the middle of the sixteenth century *were uniformly the same*; the same harmonies, the same modulations were practised in the compositions of the Flemish, the Italian, the German, the French, and the English musicians; and nothing characteristic of the genius or humour of a particular country or province, as was once the case of the Moorish and Provençal music, was discernible in the songs of that period, except in those of the Scots and Irish.[122] [emphasis added]

---

[119] Rousseau, *Lettre sur la musique françoise*, 27–29.
[120] See Arnold, *Musical Debate and Political Culture*, 104; Trottier, "L'Arménien de Venise." Thanks to Nathan Martin for his advice on this point, for referring me to the work of Trottier, and for sharing with me a copy of his conference paper "Figures of Alterity in Rousseau's Writings on Music."
[121] Burney, *The Present State of Music*, Vol. 2, 142.
[122] Hawkins, *A General History*, Vol. 4, 1. See discussion of this passage in Gelbart, *The Invention*, 37, 119.

This brief observation about theoretical similarities in composition anticipates Strohm's identification and detailed study of the emergence of common contrapuntal practices in fifteenth-century Europe, a phenomenon that he called "the rise of European music."[123] However, even in contrapuntal practice, it is clear that certain national tendencies existed, as indicated, for instance, by the name of the compositional style *contenance angloise* (English manner), exemplified by John Dunstaple (c. 1390–1453).

Before Hawkins, differences between the rates of change in the theoretical principles followed by different nations were noted by a number of theorists (a theme that is explored in more detail in chapter 5). For example, the idea of Spanish (or Iberian) conservatism in music theory, practice, and composition—in comparison with other European nations—was a theme that emerged in the *Mapa armónico práctico* (*Practical Harmonic Map*) of 1742 by Catalan composer and theorist Francesc Valls (1671–1747). He observed:

> [I]n older times there were common rules for all nations, as an inquisitive person can see in many printed books by Italian, Spanish, French and German authors, and various manuscripts that still exist amongst scholars of music. And yet, in our Spain, not only are the old rules maintained, but to these our predecessors added others which they thought necessary for the greater cleanliness of the old rules and for the best harmony, which were passed by tradition from teachers to students.[124]

Valls was making a rhetorical point; he argued the need for the synchronization of Spanish rules with those in other parts of Europe. In some ways, his comments here echo the pejorative statements made by Sepp (quoted above) regarding practices in Seville and Cádiz, although they were likely exaggerated.

Perceptions and stereotypes of Spanish musical conservatism became amplified in other parts of the world, where distinctions were often made between customs of different European nations, rather than Europeans being merged into one monolithic category. For example, Simon de La Loubère (1642–1729) in Siam (Thailand) in the 1680s referred to Siamese musicians having vocal genres and instruments similar to "the Spaniards'

---

[123] Strohm, *The Rise of European Music*.
[124] Original text in Valls, *Mapa armónico práctico*, 13.

chirimías [shawms]" and not meant in a flattering sense.[125] As noted earlier in this chapter, Sepp wrote to his family about the old-fashioned Spanish music theory (and, by implication, practice) followed in the South American missions and sought to introduce German and Roman styles.[126] In Mexico City, a violinist auditioning for the cathedral *capilla* (musical ensemble) in 1721 was criticized for having knowledge of Italian style but not Spanish.[127] National styles were thus distinguishable in the colonies in the early eighteenth century, even if later in the eighteenth century, a more cosmopolitan "European" set of categories reigned. Emic and etic perspectives alike thus embraced divergent views of Europeans, ranging from homogeneous to heterogeneous.

Within Europe from the Middle Ages, senses of musical variegation between nations related mostly to vocal style. Tropes about distinctiveness in various collective communities' manners of singing—some of which became ingrained in discourse through repetition over successive generations—can be identified in a range of examples. As Christopher Page has shown, Boncompagnus of Signa (c. 1165/1175–after 1240) compared Greeks with Latins (that is, the singing of Orthodox Christian liturgy versus its Catholic counterpart) and paraphrased the pejorative opinions of the French about Italian singing and of the Italians about French and German.[128] Jason Stoessel points out that writers in Europe from the thirteenth century onward used animal similes to describe the vocal-music practices of other peoples (including a French writer's memory of observing Mongols sing in 1247 and his account that "they bellow like bulls or howl like wolves").[129] In the fifteenth and sixteenth centuries, according to Chiara Bertoglio, music theorists including Franchinus Gaffurius (1451–1522), Andreas Ornitoparchus (1490–1520?), Heinrich Finck (1444/1445–1527), Pietro Aaron (c. 1480–c. 1545), and Johannes Tinctoris (c. 1430/1435–1511) listed diverse metaphors, clichés, and descriptions of national singing styles of the English, French, Spanish, Germans, and Italians.[130] Most general statements about nations' cultural characteristics in music were predicated more on performance than on compositional structure.

---

[125] La Loubère, *Du royaume de Siam*, Vol. 1, 208.
[126] Harrison, *Time, Place and Music*, 110–111.
[127] Marín López, "Tradición e innovación," 247.
[128] Page, "Around the Performance," 348.
[129] Stoessel, "Howling Like Wolves," esp. 202; see also 229–232 for transcriptions and translations of examples. See also Stoessel, "Voice and Song."
[130] See Bertoglio, *Reforming Music*, 143–144.

From the time of the new writings on harmony by Gioseffo Zarlino (1517–1590)—considered by some eighteenth-century writers, including Rameau, as the beginnings of "modern music"—contrapuntal rules became more or less standardized until they were challenged by exponents of *seconda pratica* (second practice), such as Monteverdi. Yet Zarlino himself recognized differences in national styles of performance practice despite this emerging conformity in composition. In his writings on modes, he states: "An Italian sings differently from a Frenchman, and a Spaniard sings in a manner different from that of a German, and of course different from that of the barbarian nations of infidels, which is obvious."[131] With his "of course," he implied that Italians were most stylistically distanced from "barbarian nations," compared with their neighbors in France, Spain, and the German-speaking lands. Colorful descriptions such as these (and those quoted above) were repeated and amplified in the seventeenth century by Jesuits Kircher and Ménestrier, among other writers. Kircher quoted in his *Musurgia universalis* an "old saying" that "the Italians bleat, the Spanish bark, the Germans bellow, the French warble."[132] In 1681, Ménestrier repeated this formula and commented additionally that "the English whistle and the Turks howl."[133] What, then, did "Europeans" do? As we saw at the beginning of this chapter, a Jesuit publication of around a century earlier suggested simply that they sang differently from the Japanese.

The idea of national style had a long legacy and was grounded in essentialist ideas. Kircher, after giving the clichés just mentioned, linked stylistic differences in music to environmental conditions ("the spirit of the place and natural tendency"), "or from custom maintained by long-standing habit, finally becoming nature."[134] Stephen Rose has observed, however, that "contrary to Kircher's assertion, foreign styles were often highly popular, particularly in England and Germany."[135] Nevertheless, questions of

---

[131] Zarlino, *On the Modes*, 6.
[132] Kircher, "From *Musurgia universalis*," 709. See also discussion in Irving, "Exchange."
[133] Translation in Kircher, "From *Musurgia universalis*," 709n.3. Original text in Ménestrier, *Des représentations*, 107.
[134] Kircher, "From *Musurgia universalis*," 709. He allowed that listeners who heard a particular kind of music for extended periods of time could end up preferring it.
[135] Rose, "The Musical Map of Europe," 15. Some decades later, J. S. Bach became a prominent example of a musician who composed in five national styles (German, French, Italian, English, and Polish). Even though there is no evidence that his music was called "European" in his own lifetime, his compositional output has nevertheless been considered the epitome of "European music"—or even of the musics of the entire earth, in a galactic context. One scientist claimed that transmitting Bach's music intergalactically would be "boasting." See Small, *Musicking*, 3; Chua and Rehding, *Alien Listening*, 123.

climate raised by Kircher referred not only to musical production but also to reception, and they remained points for consideration a century later. In 1748, Charles-Louis de Secondat, Baron de Montesquieu (1689–1755), wrote of different climates' influence on musical taste: "I have been at the opera in England and in Italy, where I have seen the same pieces and the same performers; and yet the same music produces such different effects on the two nations: one is so cold and phlegmatic, and the other so lively and enraptured, that it seems almost inconceivable."[136] The notion of climate having an effect in this sense continued to persist over the next few decades. In 1780, Scottish writer James Dunbar (1742–1798) wrote of both French and Italian styles, then generalized them as "European," pointing out that they were equally disliked, or "exploded," in Turkey, speculating on the effects of biology, the environment, and culture creating difference:

> The French music accordingly, as well as the Italian, is universally exploded among the Turks; and whether from the texture of their organs, or from climate, or from certain habitudes of life, possesses no power to ravish their ears with harmony, or to interest the passions. In general European music is disrelished, or exploded in the East.[137]

Ultimately, it seems that the opaque category of "European music" overrode questions of difference in national climates or cultural practices, when put into a kind of comparative critique with the musics of others. Thus, amid all the debates about aesthetic fusion that occupied music critics and theorists for many decades of the eighteenth century, "European music" was considered coherent in its ability to repel, or at least circumscribe, the appreciation of some people in other parts of the world.

Despite comments such as this, we see that from the 1770s, "European music" had begun to represent a cosmopolitan set of practices circulating within and beyond European nations, and it entered discourse more frequently. Gluck was among the key figures in this process.[138] In 1773, a year before moving to Paris, he wrote that he wished to collaborate with Rousseau in searching for melodies that appropriately reflected the prosody of languages and different national characters, creating the means "to produce

---

[136] Translation of 1755 by Thomas Nugent (c. 1700–1772), in Drace-Francis, *European Identity*, 52. Original text in Montesquieu, *De l'esprit des lois*, Vol. 1, 364.
[137] Dunbar, *Essays on the History of Mankind*, 114.
[138] See Waeber, "Opera and Ballet," 211–217; see also Darlow, *Dissonance in the Republic of Letters*.

a music suitable to all nations, and to get rid of the ridiculous distinction of national musical styles."[139] By "national musical styles," he was referring quite specifically to French and Italian opera. (This stated desire aside, however, the following year Gluck adapted his earlier Italian setting of the story of Orpheus and Eurydice to a French version, making alterations in casting, scoring, and length to suit the contexts and tastes of opera performance in Paris.)[140]

A more extensive elaboration of what a unified music for the continent could mean appeared in the 1780s. Michel-Paul Guy de Chabanon (1730–1792)—who was, incidentally, born in the French colony of Saint-Domingue (Haiti) and later studied at the Jesuit college of Louis-le-Grand in Paris, overlapping there for some years with Fonton—offered in 1785 what is possibly the first detailed description of the new idea of a singular supranational music "for all of Europe," although he did not use the conjunct term "European music." Perhaps his own early life in the Caribbean contributed to the shaping of his perspective, since he had first encountered Europe from outside. In his work *De la musique considérée en elle-même* (*Of Music, Considered on Its Own Terms*), he observed:

> In the state of civilization and mutual communication that all the peoples of Europe have among themselves, there exists for them a commerce of fine arts, of taste, of spirit and of philosophy, which ebbs and flows from one end of this continent to the other: the same discoveries, the same ideas, the same methods. In this free circulation of the arts, they all lose something of their *indigenous* character [emphasis original]; they are modified in dissolving together with other foreign characteristics. In this respect Europe can be considered like a mother-country, in which all of its arts are compatriots; they all speak the same language, they observe the same customs.
>
> In applying what I have just said specifically to music, one will find a degree of truth that remains incontrovertible. There remains only one music for all of Europe, ever since France got rid of the barriers of ignorance and of bad taste. From one nation to another, this universal language of our continent at most undergoes some differences in pronunciation—that is to say, in the manner of musical performance.[141]

---

[139] Original text in Gluck, "Lettre," 184. See discussion in Springer-Dissmann, "Gluck the Wanderer," 81.

[140] J. Hayes, "Orfeo ed Euridice."

[141] Thanks to Cyrille Gerstenhaber for her advice on translation. Given the significance of this passage, I reproduce the entire original text here:

A few pages later, he goes on to say: "Travel from Rome to London, and from London to Madrid; you will see different customs and prejudices, [but] you will have only heard the same music."[142]

In Chabanon's description of music of Europe as a "universal language of our continent," if "language" refers to music, then his analogy of "pronunciation" probably refers to performance practice.[143] His examples point specifically to major cities or metropolises (Rome, London, and Madrid, presumably taking Paris as a given), which coincidentally align—although not explicitly—with certain centers of the Republic of Music (discussed in chapter 2). Chabanon also adds a footnote directly after his words "this universal language of our continent," writing at the bottom of the page that "one considers here music as a perfected art."[144] In this passage, it is also interesting to note his italicized use of the adjective "indigenous" ("*indigène*"); this word had been included as a noun in the fourth edition of the *Dictionnaire de l'Académie Française* in 1762, with the definition "Thus are called the natives of a country."[145] In 1787, the *Dictionaire critique de la langue française* repeated this definition for the noun, elaborating that "this word is only used among the savants," but adding a horticultural example for the adjective: "[an] *indigenous* plant as opposed to an *exotic* plant."[146] One wonders if Chabanon's use of this adjective in French is among the earliest instances to be applied to music.

"Dans l'état de civilisation, & de communication mutuelle où sont entre-eux tous les Peuples de l'Europe, il existe pour eux un commerce de beaux Arts, de goût, d'esprit & de lumières, qui fait fluer & refluer d'un bout de ce continent à l'autre, les mêmes découvertes, les mêmes principes, les mêmes méthodes. Dans cette libre circulation des Arts, ils perdent tous quelque chose de leur caractère *indigène*; ils l'altèrent en le fondant avec d'autres caractères étrangers: l'Europe à cet égard peut être considérée comme une mère-patrie, dont tous les Arts sont concitoyens; ils parlent tous la même langue, ils obéissent aux mêmes coutumes.

"En appliquant spécialement à la Musique ce que je viens de dire, on y trouvera un degré de vérité plus incontestable encore. Il n'y a plus qu'une Musique pour l'Europe entière, depuis que la France a renversé les barrières de l'ignorance & du mauvais goût. Cette langue universelle de notre continent, subit, tout au plus, d'un peuple à un autre, quelques différences dans la prononciation, c'est-à-dire, dans la façon d'exécuter la Musique." Chabanon, *De la musique*, 96–97.

[142] "Passez de Rome à Londres, & de Londres à Madrid; vous aurez vu des moeurs & des préjugés différens; vous n'aurez entendu qu'une même musique." Chabanon, *De la musique*, 100.
[143] On the question of Chabanon and universals, see Guertin, "La reconstruction"; Guertin, "The Universal and the Particular."
[144] "On considère ici la Musique comme un Art perfectionné." Chabanon, *De la musique*, 97n.1.
[145] Académie Française, "Le Dictionnaire de l'Académie Française," 4th ed. (1762), Vol. 1, entry for "Indigène. Subst."
[146] Féraud, "Dictionaire critique de la langue française," entry for "Indigène."

The idea of universal taste in music—as distinct from a "universal language"—had also been discussed several decades earlier by Johann Joachim Quantz (1697–1773), who in his treatise on playing the flute wrote about the possibilities emerging from the mixing of Italian and French styles, a process that he described as being practiced especially by Germans. Setting out some ideals and guidelines for composers, he observed in the penultimate section: "if, I say, all these things are unanimously observed, in time *a good style* [sic; taste] *that is universal* can be introduced in music" (emphasis original).[147] In this way, he clearly articulated that the quest for pan-European unity in music was about establishing a "universal taste" or at least a music unmarked by national styles, involving the synchronization of the most current stylistic trends in multiple major urban centers.

It is likely no coincidence that "European music" and the idea of "a single music" for Europe began to be used consistently in published discourse at a time when scholars were making new statements about a sense of supranational European identity among western European nations. As historian Norman Davies has pointed out, thinkers including Rousseau and Edmund Burke (1729–1797) wrote of "Europeans" constituting a collective identity, seeing this as a new notion that supplanted earlier concepts of Europe as a major constituent part of Christendom.[148] For example, Rousseau opined in his essay *Considérations sur le gouvernement de Pologne* (*Considerations Regarding the Government of Poland*) of 1771–1772 (published in 1782): "There are no more Frenchmen, Germans, Spaniards, even Englishmen, nowadays, regardless of what people may say; there are only Europeans. All have the same tastes, the same passions, the same morals, because none has been given a national form by a distinctive institution."[149] In 1796, Burke stated that "no citizen of Europe could be altogether an exile in any part of it."[150] While the latter comment clearly related to the privileged cosmopolitan and educated strata of society who had the resources for mobility, a feedback loop of self-reflexivity generated a new collective identity of

---

[147] Quantz, *On Playing the Flute*, 342. Original German text in Quantz, *Versuch*, 333. The words I have emphasized here also appear in a larger font size in the original. For the original French text (which does not have an emphasis on those words), see Quantz, *Essai*, 335.

[148] Davies, *Europe: A History*, 7–8. Davies notes that "the Treaty of Utrecht of 1713 provided the last major occasion when public reference to the *Respublica Christiana*, the 'Christian Commonwealth,' was made" (7).

[149] Davies, *Europe: A History*, 8. I quote the translation from Rousseau, *The Social Contract*, 187–188; see original text in Rousseau, *Considérations sur le gouvernement*, 17.

[150] Davies, *Europe: A History*, 8. I quote the form of the text from E. Burke, *Two Letters*, 110–111.

"Europeanness," as well as contributing to Eurocentrism—especially in terms of making comparisons that were condescending toward other cultures.

In this context, it is worth mentioning Guillaume André Villoteau (1759–1839), who participated in 1798 in the expedition to Egypt of Napoleon Bonaparte (1769–1821; ruled in various capacities 1799–1815). In 1807, Villoteau stated in his *Recherches sur l'analogie de la musique avec les arts* (*Investigations into the Analogy of Music with the Arts*) his intention "to coolly observe and scrupulously examine, in the musics of most nations whose customs are entirely different from ours, all that appeared to me to diverge from our European music [*notre musique Européenne*]."[151] His implication that European music was a single, unified system is clearly in evidence. Other writers in Europe also began to claim that the fame of composers from their own continent extended across vast stretches of the earth to be received by people in other regions—as seen in the example of W. A. Mozart's music being performed in the Philippines in the 1790s (chapter 3)—and implied that "European music" was endowed with a sense of global "superiority." New waves of metropolitan musical influence emanating from Europe to other parts of the world simultaneously increased a sense of pan-European identity and differentiation from local practices.

A trope I want to call "competitive distancing" became popular in composer biographies or musical references within other works. For example, in 1812, Giuseppe Carpani (1751–1825) observed of the late Haydn that his music was heard "from Mexico to Calcutta [Kolkata], just as from Naples to London, [and] from Pera to Paris."[152] A similar formula was offered in 1824 by Stendhal (1783–1842) to describe the fame of Rossini, which extended "from Moscow to Naples, from London to Vienna, from Paris to Calcutta."[153] In 1815, the Handel and Haydn Society was founded in Boston, Massachusetts, to promote the works of the two composers for which it was named (as well as those of others), instituting an enduring organizational framework to canonize individual musicians from another continent.[154] The fame of composers, performers, and librettists from Europe and the classicization of their creative outputs were seen to cut across national and

---

[151] Original text in Villoteau, *Recherches sur l'analogie*, Vol. 1, 4.
[152] Original text in Carpani, *Le Haydine*, 3. On Haydn's international reputation, stretching from the Americas to parts of Asia, see Tolley, *Painting the Cannon's Roar*, 20–22.
[153] Stendhal, *Memoirs of Rossini*, xiii.
[154] Perkins, *History*.

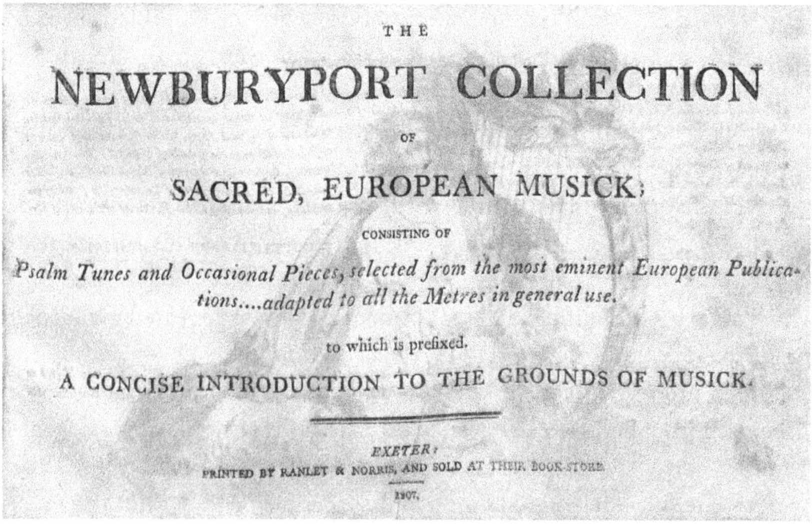

> THE
> # NEWBURYPORT COLLECTION
> OF
> ## SACRED, EUROPEAN MUSICK;
> CONSISTING OF
> *Psalm Tunes and Occasional Pieces, selected from the most eminent European Publications....adapted to all the Metres in general use.*
>
> to which is prefixed,
>
> A CONCISE INTRODUCTION TO THE GROUNDS OF MUSICK.
>
> ———
>
> *EXETER:*
> PRINTED BY RANLET & NORRIS, AND SOLD AT THEIR BOOK-STORE
> 1807.

Figure 4.6. An early example of printed music to mention "European music" in its title. Amos Blanchard, ed., *The Newburyport Collection of Sacred, European Musick* (Exeter, NH: Ranlet & Norris, 1807), title page. Special Collections, Wright Library, Princeton Theological Seminary.

continental boundaries; it was taken as a given that the geographical gulfs of oceans were merely seas to be crossed.

Conceptual distancing and competitive distancing contributed to the reification of the adjective and category "European" in musical terms. The earliest identifiable example of the precise term "European music" in the title of sheet music—distinct from descriptions of works by "the greatest masters of Europe," mentioned in chapter 2—comes from a publication in the young United States of America in 1807: *The Newburyport Collection of Sacred, European Musick* (figure 4.6).[155] Note that the title refers to "sacred, European music" and not "European sacred music" (as might be more commonly said in English today); the geographical adjective is placed directly next to the noun, emphasizing origin.[156] In another American publication, *The Boston Handel and Haydn Society Collection of Church Music* (1830),

---

[155] Blanchard, *The Newburyport Collection of Sacred, European Musick*. A slightly earlier example of a publication from the United States using "European," but in the sense of "European masters," is Benjamin, *Harmonia Coelestis*.

[156] If it were in French or Spanish, for example, we would usually refer to "la musique sacrée européenne" or "la música sagrada europea," but here "European" becomes privileged, and the term's equivalent would be "la musique européenne sacrée" or "la música europea sagrada."

THE EMERGENCE OF THE "EUROPEAN MUSIC" CONCEPT 173

the editor, Lowell Mason (1792–1872), mentions "European music" when explaining how the tenor clef was a C clef that could be used in different ways: "This clef is also in common use in European music for the Treble or Soprano, and when thus used it is placed upon the first line of the Staff."[157] From a transatlantic perspective, the nations of Europe were homogenized in a form of intercontinental comparison. Given that staff notation was part of Mason's own musical training and background, perhaps he simply meant that "European music" was a related tradition that intersected here with his American cultural identity, which was distinct and independent.

Thus, we see that "European" as applied to music was sometimes used to refer specifically to notation. Amiot used it in this sense in his *Mémoire sur la musique des Chinois, tant anciens que modernes* (*Dissertation on the Music of the Chinese, Ancient as well as Modern*), published in Paris in 1779, describing the French publication of a Chinese hymn as "notated in the European manner [*noté à l'Européenne*]."[158] Villoteau also employed the term "musique européenne" in his *Description de l'Égypte* (*Description of Egypt*, published in 1809) to refer to the device of staff notation, using it to represent pitches in an eighteen-fold division of the octave in Arabic music theory.[159] Rousseau described staff notation in his *Dictionnaire de musique* (1768) as "the musical and universal language of all Europe" ("la Langue Musicale & universelle de toute l'Europe") and even stated (erroneously) that "it is only the nations of Europe who know how to write their music" ("Il n'y a que les Nations de l'Europe qui sachent écrire leur Musique").[160] However, in his *Essai sur l'origine des langues* (*Essay on the Origin of Languages*), written from 1754 to 1761 and published posthumously, he noted the cultural specificity of European staff notation, as well as its limitations, remarking that it was unable to notate pitch "inflections" in the songs of Indigenous Americans.[161]

As noted earlier, Rousseau did not write the term "European music." In the large-scale music histories that began to emerge in the 1770s and 1780s, the adjective "European" appears rarely. It seems to be used only four times in Burney's *General History of Music* and never in the formulation "European music."[162] Hawkins does not mention "European music" in his *General History of the Science and Practice of Music*; in fact, he uses the

---

[157] Mason, *The Boston Handel and Haydn Society Collection*, viii.
[158] Amiot, *Mémoire*, 236nl.
[159] Villoteau, "De l'état actuel," 629.
[160] Rousseau, *Dictionnaire de musique*, 73 (notation), 74 (universal musical language).
[161] Rousseau, "Essai sur l'origine des langues," 425. See discussion in Irving, "Ancient Greeks," 31.
[162] Burney, *A General History of Music*, Vol. 2, 54; Vol. 4, 5–6.

adjective "European" only three times across the five volumes, to refer to "provinces," "colleges," and "churches."[163] La Borde does make references to "musique européenne" in his *Essai sur la musique ancienne et moderne*, but only three times. The first two examples are found in the story of musical exchange in the Chinese imperial court during the reign of Kangxi; the third is in reference to Rameau's "science of harmony" being essential to "European music."[164] Forkel uses the term "europäische Musik" in the first volume of his *Allgemeine Geschichte der Musik (General History of Music)*, issued in 1788, to make a contrast with modern Greek music. Using it twice in the same sentence, he claims that Greek informants had assured him of the difference between Greek and "European" intervals, saying that their melodies were dissimilar; he then comments disparagingly that the music of the modern Greeks was "a real howl" when compared with "European music."[165]

External Comparisons: "European Music" in the Wider World

Various references in German to "European music" ("europäische Musik") in the three decades on each side of 1800 refer to comparisons with perceived cultural others. The first passage that includes a discussion of musics of all four continents in a single paragraph was published by Ruetz in 1752 (as quoted in the introduction to part II of this book).[166] Relatively few additional examples of "European music" in German can be located so far in the late eighteenth century, but let us survey some here. The 1773 German translation of Burney's travelogue mentioning the anecdote about a Greek lady at the Paris Opera (discussed above) includes the term.[167] Franz Joseph Sulzer (1727–1791) observed in 1781: "Turkish composers have so little understanding of harmony that they in fact rely upon European music and swear that they can extract no melody from the multi-vocal texture."[168] Another Sulzer, Johann Georg (1720–1779), wrote in the early 1770s that "the

---

[163] Hawkins, *A General History*, Vol. 1, 419; Vol. 2, 29; Vol. 3, 445.
[164] La Borde, *Essai*, Vol. 1, 360–361; Vol. 3, 648n (b).
[165] Original text in Forkel, *Allgemeine Geschichte der Musik*, Vol. 1, 447. See also discussion in Romanou, "The Music of the Modern Greeks," 267.
[166] Ruetz, *Widerlegte Vorurtheile*, 10.
[167] Burney, *Carl Burney's der Musik Doctors Tagebuch*, Vol. 3, 86.
[168] Translation in Al-Taee, *Representations*, 97. Original text in Sulzer, *Geschichte des transalpinischen Daciens*, Vol. 2, 436.

Chinese have no ear for European music, while Europeans cannot bear to hear Chinese music."[169] In 1789, a German text by August Christian Borheck (1751–1815) mentions that the ruler of Morocco "is not only an amateur [*Liebhaber*] of music, but also a connoisseur [*Kenner*] of this art; however, European music is too artificial [or contrived; *künstlich*] for him."[170] These references to Turkish, Chinese, and Moroccan listeners are phrased in condescending ways that clearly reflect the Orientalist discourses emerging at the time.

In travel writing in other languages, the term "European music" was used in contexts stretching from South Asia to the eastern Pacific Ocean. It was mentioned with reference to taste but also in terms of comparing the structures of music. For example, Thomas Forrest (c. 1729–c. 1802) observed in the southern Philippines in 1779 (in a popular travelogue that was also translated into French): "the Bisayan slaves play often on the violin, and the Sooloos [the Tausug people of the Sulu Archipelago] are fond of European music."[171] In a publication of 1806, Sir John Barrow (1764–1848) stated that "the Cochin-chinese [inhabitants of Vietnam] had no ear for the soft and harmonious chords of European music," preferring their own styles.[172] William Mariner (1791–1853), a shipwrecked English sailor who lived in Tonga from 1806 to 1810, likened certain kinds of song to recitative and stated in his account—dictated to a medical doctor, John Martin (1789–1869), and published in 1817—that "others ... have a considerable variety of tone, and approach to the character of European music: such for example is the latter part of that which we have given the notation of."[173] These cases demonstrate

---

[169] Translation in Hoyt, "On the Primitives of Music Theory," 206.

[170] Original text in Borheck, *Neue Erdbeschreibung*, Vol. 1, 485. He is paraphrasing the account of Georg Høst (1734–1794), who traveled to Morocco in 1760–1768 and performed for Mohammed ben Abdallah (1710–1790; reigned from 1759) on a keyboard instrument that was a gift from the king of Denmark (it is described as "Clavesin" in the Danish original and "Flügel" in the German translation). See Høst, *Efterretninger om Marókos og Fes*, 246n.(z); Høst, *Nachrichten von Marókos und Fes*, 262–263n.(z); Høst, *Relations sur les royaumes de Marrakech et Fès*, 204–205. Jørgen Bæk Simonsen has recently given a summary of this travelogue and notes, incidentally, that "neither of Høst's books of 1779 and 1791, has been the subject of academic analysis." Simonsen, "Georg Hjersing Høst," 422–423.

[171] Forrest, *A Voyage to New Guinea*, 330. For the French translation of 1780 (using the term "la musique Européenne"), see Forrest, *Voyage aux Moluques*, 375.

[172] Barrow, *A Voyage to Cochinchina*, 297. Thanks to Makoto Harris Takao for pointing out this reference.

[173] Mariner and Martin, *An Account*, 1st ed., Vol. 2, 336 (the notations appear on 338–339). Thanks to Makoto Harris Takao for pointing out this reference. Interestingly, a definition of the Tongan style of singing called *híva*, which is sung without dancing, mentions that "they call European singing *híva*, because probably the *híva* is very seldom accompanied either with music [instrumental?] or clapping of the hands." Mariner and Martin, *An Account*, 1st ed., Vol. 2, 333. The second edition updates the end of the last clause to read, "such for example are some of those to which we shall directly give

the more frequent use of the term "European music" in travel literature and its contribution to the rise of a global comparative binary of European/other.

Sometimes the adjective "European" or the term "European music" was applied only in translations. An account of singing by an Aboriginal woman in Australia by François Péron (1775–1810) at the beginning of the nineteenth century, for instance, states in the English translation of 1809 that "it would be very difficult to give any idea of music, such as it was, so different from the general principles of any European music"; however, the original French refers to the "European" musical system as "la nôtre" (ours).[174] On the other hand, sometimes later publications omitted or redacted the term "European" in this context. An interesting example comes from accounts of the first Russian voyage of circumnavigation (1803–1806), commanded by Adam Johann von Kruzenshtern (1770–1846), in a section regarding experiences in "Nukihiwa" (Nuku Hiva) in the Marquesas Islands.[175] An instance of the term "European music" in Russian ("Европейская музыка") is identifiable in an 1818 Russian translation of an extract from Kruzenshtern's manuscript journal; this same extract had been previously published at St. Petersburg in a German almanac in 1810.[176] The editor of the earlier German version states that he had issued it with Kruzenshtern's permission; the editor of the Russian translation states that he was republishing these extracts because the official voyage accounts were expensive.[177]

The relevant sentence from Kruzenshtern's manuscript in Russian translation states: "Their singing is more like howling than any concordant combination of voices, and I doubt if our most pleasant European music [Европейская музыка], our Haydns and Rombergs, would bring them greater enjoyment [than their own]."[178] The use of "European music" reflects

---

expression according to the European system of notation," perhaps reflecting an increasing awareness of other kinds of notation. Mariner and Martin, *An Account*, 2nd ed., Vol. 2, 322.

[174] English translation in Péron, *A Voyage of Discovery*, 197. Original text in Péron, *Voyage de découvertes*, Vol. 1, 253. Thanks to Makoto Harris Takao for pointing out this reference.
[175] For a study of the expedition's visit there, see Govor, *Twelve Days at Nuku Hiva*. I use the now standardized orthography of Kruzenshtern's surname, but in early sources, it is also given as Krusenstern.
[176] [Kruzenshtern], "O zhiteliakh ostrova Nukagivy," 236; [Kruzenshtern], "Die Insulaner von Nukahiwa," 212.
[177] [Kruzenshtern], "Die Insulaner von Nukahiwa," 183; [Kruzenshtern], "O zhiteliakh ostrova Nukagivy," 191, footnote. Thanks to Estelle Joubert and Marina Frolova-Walker for translations of the relevant sentences.
[178] Translation by Marina Frolova-Walker. Original text in [Kruzenshtern], "O zhiteliakh ostrova Nukagivy," 236. I am grateful to Marina Frolova-Walker and Bella Brover-Lubovsky for their advice and guidance on this text.

THE EMERGENCE OF THE "EUROPEAN MUSIC" CONCEPT 177

the sense seen in other early-nineteenth-century voyage accounts quoted above. A distinct feature is the naming of specific composers, and in the plural (whereas the German original gives the singular).[179] One wonders if this expression in Russian could be meant in a general sense of "diverse composers" or if it could imply both Joseph Haydn and his brother Michael Haydn (1737–1806) and members of the Romberg family such as Andreas Jakob Romberg (1767–1821) and Bernhard Heinrich Romberg (1767–1841). Nevertheless, it is interesting to note that none of the official published voyage accounts—in Russian, German, Dutch, English, Italian, and French—mentions "European music" or names of composers. The German voyage account, published in 1811, mentions "the most beautiful music" rather than "European music"; in an English translation ("from the original German") of two years later, the sentence was rendered as follows: "Their singing is more like howling, than any regular concordant sound; yet they were satisfied with it, and I much doubt whether any Nukahiwer would be affected by the most beautiful music."[180] (The same expression, "the most beautiful music," appears in the Dutch translation of 1811, the Italian of 1818, and the French of 1821; all were made from German, with the last translated by Kruzenshtern himself.)[181]

Given the heightened sense of cultural difference in Russia regarding the cultures of "Europe," it is striking to note the choice of "European music" and the listing of named composers in place of "the most beautiful music." Even more notable is the fact that the first official voyage account, published in Russian in 1809, has distinct vocabulary for this passage: "Their singing resembles howling rather than a concordant combination of voices, but they enjoy it more than the most pleasant music of educated peoples." Here the "art music" of "Europe"—a geographical concept that had specific meanings in Russia of the long eighteenth century, as we saw in chapter 3—is equated with taste formed through education, which the reader could probably infer was linked to programs of

---

[179] The German version reads: "Their singing is more of a howl, rather than a regular joining of the voices; even so I doubt that our most beautiful European music, that of Haydn and Romberg, would bring them [any] greater pleasure." Translation by Estelle Joubert. Original text in [Kruzenshtern], "Die Insulaner von Nukahiwa," 212.

[180] Original text in Kruzenshtern, *Reise um die Welt*, Vol. 1, 254. English translation from Kruzenshtern, *Voyage round the World*, Vol. 1, 177.

[181] For the Dutch, see Kruzenshtern, *Reize om de wereld*, Vol. 1, 274–275; for the Italian, see Kruzenshtern, *Viaggio intorno al mondo*, Vol. 1, 205–206; for the French, see Kruzenshtern, *Voyage autour du monde*, Vol. 1, 238.

modernization and Europeanization that had been promoted by tsars and tsarinas over the long eighteenth century.[182]

As we have seen, comparison with musics of other parts of the world was the predominant context in which the adjective-noun compound "European music" appeared until around 1830. From that point onward, it would merge into synonymity with a reinvented idea of "Western music" (or "Occidental music"), as part III of this book goes on to outline. The conflation of "European music" and "Western music" was perhaps due to an apparent need to contrast it with increasingly monolithic notions of "Eastern music." Yet this is a complex transformation, since the idea of "Western music" had previously referred to other musical ideas. Until at least the end of the eighteenth century it referred to something else altogether: Christian liturgical chant, psalms, and hymns.

---

[182] Translation by Marina Frolova-Walker. Original text in Kruzenshtern, *Puteshestvie vokrug sveta*, Vol. 1, 215.

PART III

"MODERN EUROPEAN MUSIC" AND "WESTERN MUSIC"

The use of the contiguous adjective-noun compound "Western music"—or "Occidental music," which we can consider synonymous—to signify a totalizing system of musical practice cannot currently be traced in European languages any earlier than the 1830s. The term is older, but when it appeared in previous epochs, it was used specifically to denote contrasts between the liturgical music practices of different forms of Christianity: the "Eastern" (Orthodox) and the "Western" (initially Catholic alone and then also Protestant and nonconformist) branches of the religion, and usually plainchant. It did not mean the same as the sense in which we use it today. New notions about "Western music" in a relational and reified sense were initiated in the early nineteenth century, to make a contrast with emerging ideas about "Oriental" or "Eastern music."

When considering this difference in Western music's meanings, it is important to recognize that the gradually hardening binary of "East" and "West" was more porous before 1800. Earlier forms of music in the space we call Europe arguably had greater affinities with "other" musics than with later manifestations of "European music" or "Western art music." It is also worth noting that in the field of historical performance practice, a number of "early musicians"—from pioneers in the movement including Thomas Binkley (1931–1995) and David Munrow (1942–1976) to musicians active today such as Jean-Christophe Frisch and Jordi Savall—have worked with practitioners of "traditional cultures" to gain ideas of performance styles that many believe have not experienced ruptures or discontinuities, unlike earlier forms of "art music" in Europe.[1] Jonathan Shull has traced some of the processes by which early musicians have sought inspiration from "other" living traditions, and

---

[1] Frisch has recounted many of these exchanges in his book *Le baroque nomade*.

John Haines and Kirsten Yri have shown how the early work of Binkley and his Studio der Früher Musik in the 1960s and 1970s challenged notions of ethnic or cultural homogeneity in the performance styles of medieval music from Europe, looking especially at intersections with practices coming from Islamic cultures.[2]

There are historical precedents for these kinds of collaborations, although their contextual frames differ. One such example of cross-cultural continuity and fungibility can be seen in the visit of Sufi Muslims to a Franciscan convent in Jerusalem in the early seventeenth century. As Eugène Roger (fl. 1639–1644) recounted:

> When these [Sufi] dervishes arrive in Jerusalem to visit the holy places, their brethren bring them into our Convent of St. Sauveur, where they gather in the church to dance to the sound [*cadence*] of our organs or regals [*regales*], which our Religious play to display some sort of goodwill to them. For outside Constantinople, there are neither organs nor regals anywhere except among us in Jerusalem and Bethlehem. They consider these instruments something so admirable, that at the same time that they hear them, they enter into an ecstasy.... When they come to our convent to dance there, they bring flowers to adorn our altars.... When we go to visit them, they play their instruments in return, and dance to give us joyful greetings [*pour nous congratuler*].[3]

This description offers a relatively rare example of members of different religions "sharing sacred space" in a shared devotional act involving music in this place and time.[4] More examples of intercultural collaboration that surface from primary sources, referring to diverse parts of the world, will likely keep complicating and blurring the musical "boundaries" that have been reified over time through the constructions of ideas of "the West," some of which still linger in musicology.

In 2001, Kay Kaufman Shelemay asked directly, "Is 'Early Music' 'Western Music'?"[5] She discussed the way in which research into performance practice and also cross-cultural projects have served to connect or compare earlier

---

[2] Shull, "Locating the Past"; Haines, "The Arabic Style"; Yri, "Thomas Binkley."
[3] Original text in Roger, *La terre saincte*, 245. Thanks to Noel Malcolm for pointing out this reference.
[4] Limor, "Sharing Sacred Space," 220–222. For discussion of another example from the seventeenth century, see Irving, "Psalms, Islam, and Music," 53–54.
[5] Shelemay, "Toward an Ethnomusicology," 18.

repertories from Europe with other music cultures, stating that "period ensembles and repertories crossed what are in twentieth-century scholarship perceived as clear boundaries."[6] Citing musicologist and viol player Laurence Dreyfus, she considered how "early music" approaches can defamiliarize and exoticize listeners' experiences of canonic repertories.[7] By engaging with older musics, we see that the veneer of a monolithic "Westernness" that is also inherently "modern" becomes increasingly thin. This said, thinkers of the early modern period all described the notion of "modernity" in a variety of ways, constantly recycling and reinventing it. Their processes of revising narratives of the musical past also had other ramifications. With the hubris of the first age of colonialism dawning in the sixteenth century, self-defining Europeans speedily entered into a spiral of cultural amnesia about the Islamic impact—symbolic or otherwise—on their music, as well as other domains of life. The emergence of an essentialized "European" music culture in discourse was based in part on the systematic erasure of any evidence of Islamic—or Arabian or "Moorish"—cultural influence. Many writers also denigrated the music making of Jewish communities and marginalized their contributions to public musics in Europe.[8] These patterns continued in the eighteenth century and beyond.

Yri has observed that "the concept of the 'West' is one purged of Semitic and Arabic influences and is politically and ideologically motivated to assert Western superiority over the East."[9] She draws from the work of literary scholar María Rosa Menocal (1953–2012), who argued that the Arabic role in Spanish (and, more broadly, European) literary genres and practices had been systematically and deliberately suppressed by generations of scholars who sought to purge ideas of this cultural impact on Spain and Europe.[10] Nevertheless, there were some exceptions in the eighteenth century. As Alexander Bevilacqua has recently shown, scholars such as Simon Ockley (1678–1720) and Johann Jacob Reiske (1716–1774) already acknowledged the contribution of Islamic learning and actively sought "to incorporate Islamic history into the history of the revival of learning in the West that had begun in the Middle Ages, and which Europeans understood as the origin of the Renaissance and of their own modernity."[11]

---

[6] Shelemay, "Toward an Ethnomusicology," 19.
[7] Shelemay, "Toward an Ethnomusicology," 21.
[8] See HaCohen, *The Music Libel*.
[9] Yri, "Thomas Binkley," 275.
[10] Menocal, *The Arabic Role*.
[11] Bevilacqua, *The Republic of Arabic Letters*, 152.

In music, this same issue has been explored in similar ways by musicologists and performers over several generations in the twentieth century, especially by Henry George Farmer (1882–1965), who promoted the case for Arabian and Islamic influence on instruments and aspects of music theory and practice in Europe.[12] Treitler pointed out the ways in which Western music historiography has been inflected by nineteenth-century scholarship that downplayed and then disqualified the African and Semitic dimensions of ancient Greek culture (as famously studied by Martin Bernal in his *Black Athena: The Afroasiatic Roots of Classical Civilization*).[13] Don Harrán (1936–2016), among others, similarly demonstrated the contributions of Jewish composers, musicians, and thinkers to the making of music in early modern Europe.[14]

This part of the book continues our critique of the history of European and Western identities in music. Chapter 5 traces the rise of exceptionalist thought about "modernity" in discourse about musics of Europe (or "European music," as it gradually became in the long eighteenth century) through the diachronic analysis of early modern comparative thought that tied intercultural comparison to the binary of antiquity and modernity. It shows, in particular, that the notion of "barbarians" being outsiders was taken from ancient thought and reapplied in musical aesthetic thinking. For some eighteenth-century writers on music, "progress" involved moving away from the "ancient" to the "modern" and toward their concept of "perfection." By the early nineteenth century, the conflation of "Europe," "music," and "modernity," in a global comparative sense, had arisen within a Eurocentric epistemology. Chapter 6 attempts to chart changes in meanings of the concept of "Western music" in some of the dominant western European languages of musicology. It aims to demonstrate how this term—or its cognate "Occidental music"—was reinvented in the early nineteenth century, supplanting the use of the term and concept of "European music," which (as chapter 4 showed) emerged in European languages only in the long eighteenth century. "Western music" took on new resonances over the following two centuries, in line with changing ideas of "the West."

---

[12] Farmer, *Historical Facts*; Burstyn, "The 'Arabian Influence'"; Haines, "The Arabic Style."
[13] Treitler, "Gender and Other Dualities," 31–33; Bernal, *Black Athena*. See also discussion in Samson, *Music in the Balkans*, 133.
[14] See, for example, Harrán, *Salamone Rossi*; Harrán, *Three Early Modern Hebrew Scholars*.

5
"Modern" Europe and "Ancient" Others in Musical Thought

In the French learned circles from 1687 to 1715, an intense debate raged on and off as scholars argued whether modern learning had eclipsed the knowledge of the ancients: the *querelle des anciens et modernes* (the dispute of the ancients and moderns). Charles Perrault (1628–1703)—incidentally, author of the "Mother Goose" fairy tales (*Contes de ma mère l'Oye*), such as "Puss in Boots," "Little Red Riding Hood," and others—was firmly on the side of the Moderns. In 1692, he opined that "today the music of the Ancients is still the music of all the Earth, *with the exception of a part of Europe*. This is so true that even at Constantinople they do not yet know music in parts" (emphasis added).[1] Perrault's "part of Europe" referred to an imagined community of western European nations whose music shared a set of emerging common characteristics: vertical harmony, a compatible notation system, genre categories, and specific instruments. The exceptionalism he assigned to it was tied explicitly to notions of "modernity" in the music being practiced there, especially "music in parts." He implicitly acknowledged the otherness of regions beyond the imagined frontiers of this "exceptional" zone, including many Balkan nations under Ottoman rule.

This conflation of music, modernity, and "part of Europe" can thus be contextualized politically. Due to fear about Ottoman expansion into Europe over the previous centuries and the threats of perceived cultural and territorial loss, some European writers in the seventeenth and eighteenth centuries had begun to see the societies in which they lived as the sole guardians of an ancient musical heritage, which itself was referred to (rhetorically or otherwise) as being of divine origin. For instance, in 1615, Salomon de Caus stated: "it seems that the Muses have abandoned Greece, Egypt, and Israel—indeed, the rest of the Earth—to retreat to these parts of Europe, and while we

---

[1] Original text in Perrault, *Paralelle*, Vol. 4, 265–266. See also discussion in M. Stokes, "Globalization," 114–116.

cherish them, we must not doubt that they will diligently stay here."[2] Again we see the term "these parts of Europe." In the late eighteenth century, Schubart rearticulated this idea, referring more explicitly to Greek refugee scholars bringing knowledge to Italy: "out of Constantinople's ruins stepped forth the teachers of all the human race. The Muses fled to Italy."[3] Such genealogies of music—along with tales of exile and refuge—reveal sentiments of protectionism and salvage. Yet they also imply the subsequent and ongoing absence of the supernatural creators of music within the very lands to the south and east from which these beings had purportedly escaped.

Thus, even as writers from Europe began to conceive of their music as "different" and to develop incipient ideas of exceptionalism, they acknowledged the roots of their musical science and practice as originating from regions in the eastern Mediterranean, spanning Africa and Asia. Antiquity and modernity were interlinked in this sense, but modernity was reformulated as having a new conceptual home: "part of Europe," in time shortened to and generalized as "Europe." Although early modern scholars who were in or from that space still revered and extolled the ancients, some considered their own societies to have eclipsed ancient culture and to be the harbingers or possessors of modernity. For instance, Spanish Jesuit José de Acosta (1540–1600) described how his travel south from Spain, across the Atlantic and the equator, then into mountainous regions of Peru, made him realize something fundamental. He recognized that what ancient Greek "poets and philosophers" had written of the extreme heat of the "torrid zone" could not be borne out in his (and others') experience, and recorded that in this moment, he laughed. As he shivered in the cold and moved into the sun to warm himself, he thought risibly of the *Meteorology* and philosophy of Aristotle (384–322 BCE) and took them lightly.[4] This laughter of Acosta—whether a friendly chuckle or a derisive guffaw—is perhaps one of the most symbolic and significant moments in the reflexive realization of modernity in the late Renaissance: the surpassing of the thought and science of the ancients.[5] Mockery, or at least a feeling of superiority, began to be an identifiable part of intercultural comparisons of other musics from

---

[2] Original text in Caus, *Institution harmonique*, Part 1, f. 23v.

[3] He continues: "and also with them Polyhymnia, Urania's cordial sister." These two figures were respectively the Muses of sacred hymns and astronomy. DuBois, "Christian Friedrich Daniel Schubart's *Ideen*," 84.

[4] Grafton, *New Worlds, Ancient Texts*, 1; Rubiés, "The Discovery of New Worlds," 67. Original text in Acosta, *Historia natural y moral*, 102.

[5] I am grateful to Joan-Pau Rubiés for discussion of this point.

the European perspective. Although it did not always involve mirth, there were often many levels of condescension implicit.

As is well known, early modern Europeans frequently made comparisons and contrasts between ancient Greeks and Indigenous peoples around the world. While the resulting observations have often been seen as a kind of empathetic evaluation, they can also be regarded as being part of a process of double distancing, since the observers were simultaneously distinguishing themselves as "modern" as opposed to the "ancients" (of whom contemporaneous "others" reminded them).[6] This tendency increased over the course of the long eighteenth century and presaged an increased cultural "break" with antiquity. As observed by Kwame Gyekye, "the social and economic changes and the scientific and technological achievements of the post-seventeenth-century European generations provided the basis of their claim to the status of being modern. They must also have regarded their sociocultural traits and achievements as in many ways discontinuous with those of previous European societies and cultures."[7] People from other parts of the world, and their musics, were seen as "stuck in the past" and incommensurable with European modernity, a phenomenon that anthropologist Johannes Fabian famously called the "denial of coevalness," defining it as "a persistent and systematic tendency to place the referent(s) of anthropology in a Time other than the present of the producer of anthropological discourse."[8] Eighteenth-century western European writers on music engaged persistently with this way of thinking.

Through forms of critical engagement that Estelle Joubert has termed "analytical encounters," a number of travelers, missionaries, and scholars produced a wealth of comparative-ethnographic literature regarding music, including scales, instruments, and performance practices.[9] In this process, however, they positioned themselves at the top of a vertical hierarchy, which spanned from "savagery" to "barbarism" to "civilization," with implied relative positions along the way. The arrogance of self-defined Europeans toward others' musics came from a steadfast belief in their own modernity. From the sixteenth to late eighteenth centuries, discourse on music in the "part of Europe" to which Perrault had alluded (which some other writers glossed as "Europe") began gradually to reflect, quite self-consciously, a prevailing

[6] Irving, "Ancient Greeks," 26–32.
[7] Gyekye, *Tradition and Modernity*, 268.
[8] J. Fabian, *Time and the Other*, 31.
[9] Joubert, "Analytical Encounters."

confidence in this art form as "modern" and, by implication, different from and "superior" to other musics, even the renowned musics of ancient Greece and Rome.[10] With modernity came the attendant subtext and discourse of "progress," the idea that ancient and other musics were "static," whereas "European music" was innovative and constantly "improving."[11] Some scholars in Europe also saw their art music as a "universal" practice (or at least one with universalizing potential) and a "universal language"—a trope that has existed up to our own times.[12] They linked this belief in universality to ideas of modernity and superiority. As Arjun Appadurai has memorably stated, "modernity belongs to that small family of theories that both declares and desires universal applicability for itself."[13]

"Modernity" in music history can be seen either as a chronological period—for which historiographers have indicated many possible starting points—or as a constantly transforming disposition of relational thought and practice. Earlier uses of the term "modern" had often simply meant the opposite of but also the successor to "antiquity." Gyekye writes of its origins:

> Modernity is etymologically linked to the Latin *modernus*, a word that the medieval scholars derived from *modo*, meaning "just now," "recently," also "present" (*tempus modernum*: present, modern times). . . . Cassiodorus (c. A.D. 485–580), a scholar and statesman, for the first time distinguished between the "ancients" (*antiqui*), the masters of the ancient classical culture, and the "moderns" (*moderni*), their present heirs.[14]

This binary was loosely followed in the field of music, although theorists tended to disagree about the chronology of the "break" between ancient and modern. Writers on music in Europe from c. 1500 onward have identified many "moments" or "turns" of modernity; these range from the writings of Boethius (c. 480–524 CE), to the invention of the staff and solmization by Guido de Arezzo (c. 991/992–after 1033), to the contrapuntal regulation of Zarlino, to the new musics of Giulio Caccini (1551–1618) and the monodists or the C sharp of the opening theme of Beethoven's "Eroica" symphony.[15]

---

[10] Taylor, *Beyond Exoticism*, 8; Hoyt, "On the Primitives of Music Theory," 199.
[11] See G. Tomlinson, "Musicology, Anthropology, History," esp. 64–65.
[12] As mentioned in chapter 4, Chabanon described music as a "universal language." For discussion of Chabanon and universality, see Guertin, "La reconstruction," 274, and Guertin, "The Universal and the Particular."
[13] Appadurai, *Modernity at Large*, 1.
[14] Gyekye, *Tradition and Modernity*, 267–268.
[15] For the last example, see Chua, *Absolute Music*, 9. The other examples are referenced below.

Wherever it occurs, thinking about modernity or modernization is a process (sometimes reflexive) that involves a dialectical approach to the reform of old or new ways—or, on the other hand, complete desuetude.[16] This disuse is usually prompted by the widespread and continual introduction of new technologies or transformation or recycling of cultural practice.

If we apply the concept of recycling to modernity, we see a constant revolution from the early sixteenth to late eighteenth centuries rather than a watershed or threshold, such as that which we commonly associate with the period beginning around 1800, a technologically mediated moment of irreversible change.[17] In regard to the latter, Karol Berger has pointed to the late eighteenth century as the point at which music in Europe began to be seen within a linear rather than cyclical concept of time.[18] This is an epistemological point, but the shift also seems to have a striking parallel in musical structures: it has been noted that in the canon of "Western art music," the practice of the cyclical ostinato (for basslines) more or less fell out of use in the nineteenth century.[19] As Susan McClary observes, "over the course of the nineteenth and twentieth centuries, repetitive procedures in music acquired a singularly bad reputation."[20] In the work of many composers, cycles were replaced by direction-led impulses.

From the Renaissance onward, the revival or recycling of ancient knowledge in musical thought was sublimated into a "modern" project that aimed to eclipse earlier forms of musical expression. Yet composers, theorists, and historians nevertheless sought out cultural and aesthetic legitimacy from antiquity. The early intellectual forgers of a "modern" and "European" musical identity asserted their music's purportedly unbroken chain of descent from antiquity. In doing so, it was incumbent on them to paper over the fissures in the emerging binaries of East/West and ancient/modern and to fill the conceptual void between the religions of the self/other, in order to minimize the paradoxes at play. When theorists wanted to rhetorically emphasize a

---

[16] Anthony Giddens asserts that "the modern world is born out of discontinuity with what went before rather than continuity with it." Giddens, *The Constitution of Society*, 239. See also discussion in J. Tomlinson, *Globalization and Culture*, 35–39.

[17] I borrow the concept of recycling from Budasz, "Of Cannibals." On labels of periods and the "break" between "early modernity" and "modernity," see H. Scott, "Introduction," 10; Osterhammel, *The Transformation of the World*, 48; Janz and Yang, "Introduction," 24n.19. For a discussion of c. 1800 as the end of the "biological old regime," in which "virtually all human activity drew upon *renewable* sources of energy supplied on an annual basis by the sun," see Marks, *The Origins of the Modern World*, 40.

[18] See Berger, *Bach's Cycle, Mozart's Arrow*.

[19] Schnapper, *L'ostinato*.

[20] McClary, "Cycles of Repetition," 21. Repetitive forms of composition, of course, resurfaced in twentieth-century minimalism.

distinctiveness of practice in the making of musical genealogy, they did so sometimes by simply making qualifications about inherited conceptual legacies. For instance, Pietro Cerone (c. 1560–1625) stated in 1613 that music had "many inventors" in antiquity, citing a broad range of historical and mythological figures from Hebrew, Roman, and Greek traditions: Jubal, Mercury, Orpheus, Amphion, Pythagoras, Moses, and Boethius. However, he went on to deny a connection of this ancient music with modern practice: "from here we can more or less acknowledge that they did not invent our music [*la nuestra Musica*], but [rather] some principles that fall into the consideration of music."[21] For Cerone, modern music in theory and practice was related to ancient antecedents, but it was also distinct and disconnected from them.

In what follows, I trace how early modern western European writers linked notions of musical "modernity" to their idea of "Europe," through diverse forms of comparative thought. From the sixteenth century, they made contrasts with their ancient forebears, as well as with contemporaneous cultural "others," frequently conflating aspects of the two groups. Significantly, they took the notions of "barbarians" from ancient Greco-Roman thought and reapplied them in music-aesthetic discourse to refer to "non-normative" practices encountered not only in other parts of the world but also within Europe. These became the touchstones of "difference." Tropes of "progress" and "perfection" also entered into western European ideas on music in the course of the long eighteenth century. By the early 1800s, the merging of "European music" with "modernity"—against a backdrop of worldwide intercultural comparison—was more or less assumed by scholars in Europe (and elsewhere), and the idea of musical exceptionalism was an assumed part of Eurocentric epistemology. Some European writers began to combine the terms to describe their art music as "modern European music." Even when they only used the term "European music," its "modernity" was still implied.

Articulations of "Modern" Music's Ascendancy

The idea of modernity as a kind of "historical discontinuity" was related directly to engagement with the wider world, in thought or action (often colonialistic), by writers from Christian Europe. Knowledge of classical antiquity provided a convenient reference point for comparative observations

---

[21] Original text in Cerone, *El melopeo y maestro*, 226–227.

of other societies, and scholars identified what they believed to be similarities between ancients and others in numerous areas involving music: scale systems, performance practices, instruments, and so on. Some of them incorporated notions of ancient music within their theory and practice while simultaneously distancing themselves from it. It is pertinent in this light to highlight Strohm's observation that "[a]lthough some thin threads connect European music with the musical thought of the ancient Greeks and Romans, the alleged revival of antiquity in European music of the sixteenth century has never been much more than a self-legitimizing posture."[22] The breach with the ancient world was simultaneously mourned and celebrated in early modern discourse; it was a love-hate relationship.

Theorists and composers thus sought self-consciously to create something deliberately new. This turn in western European musical thinking might seem curiously at odds with the embracing of ancient theory by humanist scholars. However, it is important to note the differences between ideas of "newness" in the sixteenth century and our own.[23] The recycling of ancient practice into "modern" musical expression, which was essentially a dialectical process, was nothing unusual for Renaissance humanists. For thinkers on and practitioners of music, the rediscovery of ancient knowledge was not necessarily about its recreation but about how it "self-legitimized" modern practice. This perspective is reflected in the titles of sixteenth-century treatises such as *L'antica musica ridotta alla moderna prattica* (*Ancient Music Adapted to Modern Practice*) of 1555 by Nicola Vicentino (1511–1576) and the *Dialogo della musica antica et della moderna* (*Dialogue on Ancient and Modern Music*) of 1581 by Vincenzo Galilei (1520–1591).[24] Engagement between the antitheses of the ancient and the modern, particularly by the Florentine Camerata, produced a synthesis of musical practice.[25]

The sixteenth century saw the articulation of many notions of musical modernity. An example is readily observable in a statement about technological inventions: as Flora Dennis has pointed out, medical doctor Leonardo Fioravanti (1517–1588) described the clavichord and the harpsichord as "modern instruments, because they have been the most recent to come to light in the world."[26] Other writers identified the threshold of modernity

---

[22] Strohm, "The Difference of Early European Music," 382.
[23] I am grateful to Maria Semi for this observation.
[24] Vicentino, *L'antica musica*; Vicentino, *Ancient Music*; Galilei, *Dialogo*; Galilei, *Dialogue*.
[25] See Palisca, *The Florentine Camerata*.
[26] Dennis, "Musical Sound and Material Culture," 372.

in music by naming theorists. Galilei, for instance, gave a list of "modern" authors in his *Dialogo della musica antica et della moderna*, starting with Guido de Arezzo, then jumping ahead to Gaffurius and proceeding from there.[27] Thomas Morley (1557–1602) distinguished in 1597 between "Late Writers" (that is, recent theorists) and "Ancient Writers"; for the latter, he gave just five names: "Psellus [Michael Psellus (1018–after 1078)], Boëthius, Ptolemaeus [Ptolemy (83–161)], Aristoxenus [born c. 375–360 BCE], [and] Guido Aretinus [Guido of Arezzo]."[28]

Subsequent generations benefited from the accumulation of knowledge and, of course, developed increased hindsight. Bettina Varwig notes that Italian composer Marco Scacchi (c. 1600–1662) had a much more recent view of musical modernity and that he brought it into direct dialogue with colonialist expansion. In his *Breve discorso sopra la musica moderna* (*Brief Discourse on Modern Music*) in 1649, Scacchi saw the first half of the seventeenth century as a time of musical innovation, stating that "this modern style is more pleasing and better than the ancient"; he drew parallels between "modern musicians" and the westward journey of Christopher Columbus (1451–1506).[29] Although his analogy was between musical creativity and the exploration of unknown spaces, this conceptual interface created by Scacchi brings to mind an observation of Walter Mignolo, who writes that "'modernity' is a complex narrative whose point of origination was Europe; a narrative that builds Western civilization by celebrating its achievements while hiding at the same time its darker side, 'coloniality.' Coloniality, in other words, is constitutive of modernity—there is no modernity without coloniality."[30] Scacchi's comment is relatively unusual in the music theory of early modern Europe for making an explicit connection or analogy with a named navigator, but similar resonances in other texts may also be detectable the further we look.[31]

Eighteenth-century writers reflected on scholars of antiquity, the Middle Ages, and more recent eras to propose revised notions of modernity. Handel even commented on it in terms of "liberation" from practices of antiquity, opining in a 1719 letter to Mattheson: "Knowledge [of the Greek modes] is

---

[27] Galilei, *Dialogue*, 11.
[28] He makes the marginal note that the last three were "[c]ited by Franchinus" (Gaffurius). Morley, *A Plaine and Easie Introduction*, n.p. (last page). See also Weiss, "Vandals, Students, or Scholars?," 227.
[29] Varwig, *Histories of Heinrich Schütz*, 173.
[30] Mignolo, *The Darker Side of Western Modernity*, 2–3.
[31] For a late-twentieth-century example identifying such connections in the early sixteenth century, see Keyser, "The Character of Exploration."

doubtless necessary to those who want to practice and perform ancient music, which formerly was composed according to such modes; however, *since now we have been freed from the narrow bounds of the ancient music*, I cannot perceive what use the Greek modes have in today's music" (emphasis added).[32] Others took a considerably longer view of musical modernity's emergence. According to Leopold Mozart in his treatise of 1756 on playing the violin, "music remained essentially Grecian [by which he means ancient] until at last Guido d'Arezzo invented a so-called Newer Music in the year 1024."[33] Burney, extending this backward look by several more centuries, observed in 1782 that "BOETHIUS may be regarded as *the last ancient, and first modern* who established a dominion in the Scientific parts of the Musical Empire, to which all the learned in Europe were long unanimous in submitting" (emphasis added).[34] Despite his view of Boethius as the threshold between the ancient and the modern, he also comments (in another volume of his *General History*): "Music is a modern art with us, as it is only a few centuries since the present system is supposed to have been invented; whereas ancient music flourished and was cultivated some thousand years before that period."[35]

Burney's statement about the "few centuries" since musical modernity emerged appears to chime with a statement by Rameau in his *Traité de l'harmonie* (*Treatise on Harmony*, 1722). Rameau considered modern music as having existed since the work of Zarlino in the sixteenth century. He wrote: "If modern musicians (i.e., since Zarlino) had attempted to justify their practices, as did the Ancients, they would certainly have put an end to prejudices [of others] unfavourable to them."[36] Later in his preface, Rameau referred to "the perfection of our modern music," and with the collective possessive adjective "our," he seemed to imply continuity in "modern" European music since Zarlino.[37] Similarly, Jean Terrasson (1670–1750) wrote in his 1715 commentary on Homer's *Iliad* that "to teach oneself about the superiority of modern music over ancient music, one must read the *Istitutioni*

---

[32] In Lester, *Between Modes and Keys*, 126. Ruth Smith notes, however, that "Handel knew about the Greek modes and has been noted using them in later life in his pedagogic material." R. Smith, "Early Music's Dramatic Significance," 188n.35.
[33] L. Mozart, *A Treatise*, 22.
[34] Burney, *A General History of Music*, Vol. 2, 442–443.
[35] Burney, *A General History of Music*, Vol. 1, 27. However, Burney also noted elsewhere: "as to the superior [sic] or inferiour [sic] degree of excellence in the ancient music, compared with the modern, it is now as impossible to determine, as it is [impossible] *to hear both sides*." Burney, *A General History of Music*, Vol. 1, 3.
[36] Rameau, *Treatise on Harmony*, xxxiv. Original text in Rameau, *Traité de l'harmonie*, preface, n.p.
[37] Rameau, *Treatise on Harmony*, xxxv. Original text in Rameau, *Traité de l'harmonie*, preface, n.p.

harmoniche [*Harmonic Institutions*] of Zarlino, especially the second part."[38] Even Voltaire commented on this chronology, in his 1756 *Essai sur les moeurs et l'esprit des nations* (*Essay on the Customs and Spirit of Nations*): "Music was only cultivated [practiced] well from the dawn of the sixteenth century, but the strongest presumptions make [us] think that it is very superior to that of the Greeks, who have not left any monument from which one could suppose that they sang in parts."[39] With this pointed reference, Voltaire probably followed Rameau in considering Zarlino among the first proponents of this new kind of music.

Given this range of eighteenth-century opinion citing him, we may ask what Zarlino himself thought of the binary between antiquity and modernity. He certainly made a distinction between "musicians in the past" and "the best of the moderns" (among whom he surely counted himself).[40] Writing on modes, Zarlino commented: "modern music is practiced differently from ancient music, and because there is no example or vestige of ancient music which can lead us to a true and perfect knowledge of it."[41] He was cited by Giulio Cesare Monteverdi (1573–1639) in 1607 when the latter defended his brother Claudio's *seconda pratica*, a phenomenon that is often cited as an indicator of the beginning of "modern" music, even though G. C. Monteverdi claimed that *seconda pratica* dated back to Cipriano de Rore (1515/1516–1565).[42] G. C. Monteverdi quoted a statement from Zarlino's *Sopplimenti musicali* (*Musical Supplements*) of 1588: "It never was nor is it my intention to treat of the usage of practice according to the manner of the ancients, either Greeks or Latins, even if at times I touch upon it. My intention is solely to describe the method of those who have discovered our way of causing several parts to sound together and various modulations and various melodies."[43] G. C. Monteverdi pointed out that his brother sought to create a "second practice" based on melody, not a "new" practice that supplanted the "perfection" of composition as codified by Zarlino.

Toward the end of the sixteenth century, the Florentine Camerata experimented with the purported recreation of ancient reciting styles in the creation of opera. They knew they were modern. If they were really trying to

---

[38] Original text in Terrasson, *Dissertation critique*, Vol. 1, 220.
[39] Original text in Voltaire, *Collection complette*, Vol. 9, 370.
[40] Zarlino, *The Art of Counterpoint*, 55.
[41] Zarlino, *On the Modes*, 1.
[42] Monteverdi and Monteverdi, "Explanation of the Letter," 540.
[43] Translation in Monteverdi and Monteverdi, "Explanation of the Letter," 540–541 (quoting Zarlino).

recreate the actual practices of ancient Greece, then why did they not perform in ancient Greek rather than Italian? Certainly, they would have had the philological knowledge and expertise at their disposal. Commenting on the claims of ancient revival, McClary writes:

> Despite the humanistic red herrings proffered by [Jacopo] Peri [1561–1633], Caccini, and others to the effect that they were reviving Greek performance practices, these gentlemen knew very well that they were basing their new reciting style on the improvisatory practices of contemporary popular music. Thus the eagerness with which the humanist myth was constructed and elaborated sought both to conceal the vulgar origins of its techniques and to flatter the erudition of its cultivated patrons.[44]

Some of this "contemporary popular music" undoubtedly drew from diverse practices that existed within the multiethnic cosmopolitan port cities and inland commercial centers at the crossroads of trade. The extent of this process remains an open question; Kate van Orden has recently shown how Turkish language was incorporated into some sixteenth-century chansons.[45] Certainly, Francesco Rognoni (d. c. 1626) wrote in 1620, in a well-known passage, that some singers in Venice "have a way of making *gorgie* in the Moorish style, beating the diminutions in a certain way displeasing to all, singing *a a a*, so that it seems that they are laughing. These people perhaps resemble the Ethiopians or Moors."[46] This is clearly a reference to the emulation of contemporary, living practice rather than an imagined resuscitation of ancient styles, and Rognoni goes on to cite a popular travelogue on which he bases his comparison.[47] Seventeenth-century Venetians knew the performance techniques of cultural others through travel, trade, and regular maritime interactions in the eastern Mediterranean; they also saw and heard many forms of "other" musics produced by representatives of nations who visited or lived in the serene republic.[48]

If Italian humanists had really wanted to study performing practices of ancient Greece, Claude Palisca (1921–2001) asserted in 1985, they could have gone searching for vestiges of ancient practices among the living traditions

---

[44] McClary, "Afterword," 155.
[45] See van Orden, "Hearing Franco-Ottoman Relations."
[46] Translation in Wistreich, "'La voce è grata assai, ma,'" 15.
[47] See a transcription of Rognoni's original text and discussion of the travelogue in S. Carter, "Francesco Rognoni's *Selva*," 26.
[48] See Fenlon, "'Other' Musics."

of neighboring Greek islands.[49] If they had done so, however, they might have engaged in the type of experiential travel writing where "traversing geographical space meant travelling back in time," which, as Agnew pointed out in 2009, is "bad historiography and worse ethnomusicology."[50] For the few travelers who went from western Europe to Greece and the Ottoman lands in the sixteenth to eighteenth centuries, there was the expectation that they would find physical remnants of classical civilization. In 1553, Pierre Belon (1517–1564) opined: "Whoever would like to know something about the instrumental music of the ancients would be better off experiencing those that are seen in Greece and Turkey, as we find in written accounts."[51] This suggestion referred to comparison between sonic practices, but the search for correspondences also extended to material objects themselves. According to Lucy Pollard, the English scholar John Covel (1638–1722), who was in Constantinople in the 1670s as chaplain to the Levant Company, "explained Turkish musical instruments, bolsters, and coaches all in terms of classical origins, making it clear that he was not just comparing ancient with modern but assuming actual survival of classical types."[52] We see, then, that cultural practices and objects were considered (by some) to embody direct links with the distant past. Pollard adds that some seventeenth-century English travelers saw themselves, and not the contemporary Greeks, as heirs to antique Hellenic civilization.[53]

One eighteenth-century writer who did, however, see connections between ancient and modern Greek culture was Lady Mary Wortley Montagu (1689–1762). Being among the first elite English women to visit the Ottoman Empire, she lived there for two years with her ambassador husband. In correspondence that was later published, Montagu made comparisons between her ideas of ancient Greek culture and what she observed with her own eyes and ears, likening women performers especially to notions of ancient nymphs.[54] Noting Montagu's "frustrated desire to transcend history, to experience the past in the present," Efterpi Mitsi observes that this aristocrat's notion of " 'Greece' is related to a developing Eurocentric ideology, which assigned to modern Greeks the passive role of the living ancestors of European civilisation, without however incorporating them into Europe."[55]

---

[49] Palisca, *Humanism*, 23.
[50] Agnew, "Editorial," 159.
[51] Original text quoted in Wright, "Turning a Deaf Ear," 157n.46.
[52] Pollard, " 'Every Stone Tells a Story,' " 50.
[53] Pollard, " 'Every Stone Tells a Story,' " 62.
[54] M. Montagu, "From Letters of 1717–1718."
[55] Mitsi, "Lady Elizabeth Craven's Letters," 27.

Montagu also left some striking observations on musical instruments. In a letter dated April 1, 1717, written to Alexander Pope (1688–1744) from Adrianople (now Edirne), she described people "playing on a rural instrument, perfectly answering the description of the ancient *Fistula* [panpipe], being composed of unequal reeds, with a simple but agreeable softness in the sound."[56] Intriguingly, she went on to refer to the potential for research that we might today describe as applied archaeomusicology: "Mr. *Addison* might here make the experiment he speaks of in his travels; there being not one instrument of music among the Greek or Roman Statues, that is not to be found in the hands of the people of this country."[57]

This intriguing comment clearly refers directly to the published account of Joseph Addison (1672–1719) of his experiences in Italy during the years 1701–1703. In Rome, Addison had seen sculptures of mythological figures holding musical instruments and wrote that these "might certainly give a great Light to the Dispute for Preference between the Ancient and Modern Musick." He suggested taking (that is, reproducing) "all their Models in Wood, which might not only give us some Notion of the ancient Musick, but help us to pleasanter Instruments than are now in use."[58] Thus, he hinted at a twofold outcome for organological research, proposing the reconstruction of instruments with organic matter as well as referring to the absorption of ancient ideas and technological features into instruments of his own times. In the latter context, he valorized the potential sonic quality of ancient instruments, suggesting that they had higher degrees of euphony; he referred to the possibility of a dialectical process (echoing the title of Vicentino's 1555 treatise, mentioned above) in applying elements from them to instrument making, resulting in a greater capacity for "pleasantness." Nevertheless, he also pointed to the sheer absence in ancient iconography of bows for string instruments, the capabilities of which to sustain or swell sound "give so wonderful a Sweetness to our Modern Musick."[59] He doubted the propensity of ancient instruments to produce strong and "full and sonorous" sounds.[60]

Mentioning the "Syringa" (or syrinx, another term for panpipe)—which seems to be the element that inspired Montagu to think of his work—he described the variation in the number of pipes (from four to twelve). He

---

[56] M. Montagu, *Letters*, Vol. 2, 41.
[57] M. Montagu, *Letters*, Vol. 2, 41–42.
[58] Addison, *Remarks*, 321.
[59] Addison, *Remarks*, 321–322.
[60] Addison, *Remarks*, 322.

subsequently remarked on the variation in the make of harps and "Tibiae" (a Roman term for auloi) and criticized the tendencies of "Writers of Antiquities" to impose a standardized form or holotype on an object (whether instrument, urn, or household god) instead of acknowledging heterogeneity.[61] Nevertheless, Montagu's brief remark hinted at organological diversity. She equated the current examples of instruments around her with those of antiquity, such as the panpipes she saw and heard (which "perfectly answer[ed] the description of the ancient *Fistula*"). Yet opposing views also circulated. For example, Hasselquist (the Swedish traveler mentioned in chapter 3) recorded in Turkey in the middle of the century that he was unimpressed with instrumental performances that he saw. Writing that "in vain may we now look for an Orpheus among the Greeks," he then reported on a dance by women that purportedly harked back to antiquity—resembling ancient sculptures—but was skeptical about the music used to accompany it, which "did not appear to me to have been designed for it by the antients."[62] Such a comment echoes what Mitsi has additionally noted of eighteenth-century British travelers in Greek lands, that while they "(somewhat reluctantly) recognised modern Greeks as the remote descendants of the classical Hellenes, they argued that centuries of Ottoman rule had corrupted their culture."[63]

Conflating Ancients with Others, and (Some) Europeans with Moderns

From a range of vantage points, then, certain early modern writers self-identifying as European asserted their difference not only from their contemporaneous neighbors but also from antiquity. They appropriated a possession of the knowledge of classical civilization whose remnants they observed, while at the same time denying its cultural prestige and heritage to others. Even so, musical practices of the "modern" Greeks were occasionally considered symbols of ancient authority. Zarlino, for instance, cited the use of the consecutive fourths sung in the Greek church in sixteenth-century Venice—for him a locus of musical and religious

---

[61] Addison, *Remarks*, 321–323.
[62] Hasselquist, *Voyages and Travels in the Levant*, 22–23.
[63] Mitsi, "Lady Elizabeth Craven's Letters," 27.

alterity—as evidence for the acceptability of this interval as a consonance in the systems of harmony that he proposed.[64] Travelers from Europe to other parts of the world also reported on what they thought were vestiges of ancient music and dance. References to antiquity were commonplace for early modern ethnographers, many of whom attempted to construct historical genealogies that were consistent with a biblically based chronology and geography.[65]

The Americas were among the most prominent regions for this kind of thought, owing mainly to the need to situate these previously unknown continents within the contexts of ancient geographical knowledge.[66] Acosta, for instance, posited in the late sixteenth century that Indigenous Americans could be descended from peoples who had crossed the Bering Strait in the distant past (coincidentally a prescient hypothesis of the peopling of the Americas via northern Asia, which archaeological and genetic studies have since proven).[67] In the centuries that followed, numerous missionaries, travelers, and officials observed and discoursed on similarities between cultural practices of Indigenous Americans and ancient societies. Some comparisons have been interpreted as forms of empathetic ethnography, since they sometimes emphasized common humanity and the universality of certain cultural traits.[68] This empathy played a significant role in the formation of human rights: Bartolomé de Las Casas (c. 1484–1566), for example, employed certain analogies with antiquity in his political, theological, and juridical defense of Indigenous Americans and famously stated that "all humankind is one."[69] Humanist and pioneering essayist Michel de Montaigne (1533–1592) wrote in "Des cannibales" of the song of a group of Tupinambá from Brazil, whom he met at Rouen in 1562: "Now I know enough about poetry to make the following judgement: not only is there nothing 'barbarous' in this conceit [their poetry] but it is thoroughly anacreontic. Their language is . . . a pleasant one with an agreeable sound . . . and has terminations

---

[64] Zarlino, *The Art of Counterpoint*, 14. On Greek music in Venice, see Fenlon, "'Other' Musics," 468–470.
[65] See Pagden, *The Fall of Natural Man*; Rubiés, "The Spanish Contribution."
[66] See Grafton, *New Worlds, Ancient Texts*.
[67] Pagden, *The Fall of Natural Man*, 194; Rubiés, "The Spanish Contribution," 438. See also Oppenheimer, "Out-of-Africa, the Peopling of Continents and Islands."
[68] See Bohlman, "Missionaries."
[69] Las Casas, *Apologética historia de las Indias*, 128. See contextual discussion in Irving, "The Hearing of Humanity."

rather like Greek."[70] Here we see a strong sense of empathy and something of a cross-cultural aesthetic appreciation.[71]

Montaigne was probably one of the first in a long line of observers to accommodate others within ideas of the tradition of Anacreon (c. 582–c. 485 BCE), the ancient Greek lyric poet famed for his drinking songs. Bohlman observes that Montaigne "does not stop at observing the rational intent of the singer, but valorizes that intent by his 'Anacreontic' allusion and his remarks about a possible sonorous parallel with classical Antiquity, surely a deliberate choice in Renaissance Europe."[72] However, it was only in 1554—just eight years prior to the meeting of Montaigne and the Tupinambá—that the Anacreontic texts had been presented to the European public by the printer Henri Estienne (1528/1531–1598); as a young man in 1551, Estienne had encountered the unique manuscript of them.[73] His publication of the rediscovered source was highly significant: Patricia Rosenmeyer writes that "his *editio princeps* of 1554 deeply influenced three centuries of poets and scholars; it was the prototype for all subsequent editions until the mid-1800s."[74]

The enduring legacy and popularity of these texts in Europe could perhaps account in part for the musical connections that Europeans made with Anacreontic style in the second half of the eighteenth century. In 1768, for instance, the French navigator Louis Antoine de Bougainville (1729–1811) arrived at Tahiti (which he named "La Nouvelle Cythère" after Cythera in the Peloponnese, the birthplace of Venus) and made an Anacreontic analogy: "[A Tahitian man] then leaned towards us, and with a tender air he slowly sung a song, without doubt of the Anacreontic kind, to the tune of a flute, which another Indian blew with his nose."[75] It seems likely that the bibulous and erotic nature of Anacreontic texts and the perceived lack of sexual

---

[70] Montaigne, *The Complete Essays*, 240. Original text in Montaigne, *Essais*, Vol. 1, 326–327. For discussion of Montaigne's meeting with the Tupinambá, see Budasz, "Of Cannibals," esp. 1–2; G. Tomlinson, *The Singing of the New World*, 93–109.

[71] Writing of this incident, among others, Rogério Budasz notes that "different forms of interaction between Europe and Brazil were at play, motivated by a variety of factors, provoking a range of responses, and almost always featuring music as one of the primary cultural products to be borrowed, assimilated, or recycled." Budasz, "Of Cannibals," 3.

[72] Bohlman, "Representation and Cultural Critique," 137.

[73] Rosenmeyer, *The Poetics of Imitation*, 1. In fact, the sixty Anacreontic texts are now thought "to span almost six hundred years, from late Hellenistic or early Roman times to the Byzantine era." Rosenmeyer, *The Poetics of Imitation*, 3. Thanks to Peter Agócs for pointing out information about Anacreon.

[74] Rosenmeyer, *The Poetics of Imitation*, 4.

[75] Bougainville, *A Voyage round the World*, 223. Original text in Bougainville, *Voyage autour du monde*, 194. See discussion of context in Irving, "The Pacific," 209–210.

inhibitions among peoples observed there invited direct comparisons with the "Ancients," distancing "modern" Europeans from these practices and contributing (for some) to a sense of cultural "superiority."

Connections between "ancients" and "others" were also made through observations on dance. Thoinot Arbeau (1520–1595), in his *Orchésographie* (*Orchesography*) of 1589, gives a long list of biblical, historical, and mythological examples from antiquity to support the practice of dancing, but within this list he places two contemporaneous cases: "The [people of the] Indies praise the sun by dancing. And those who have traveled in new lands [*terres neufves*] report that the Savages dance when they see the sun rise."[76] These two examples are immediately preceded by another from ancient Rome ("Appius Claudius commended dancing after his triumph") and followed directly by one from Greece (Socrates, c. 470–399 BCE).[77] Ironically, the newness of the "new lands"—it is most probably the Americas that are implied here—is equated by Arbeau with the practices of Greco-Roman antiquity, a comparison that underscores the implied modernity of not only the writer but also his presumed readers. Whereas early modern Europeans were still part of lands that were not "new" in their eyes (the "Old World"), they self-consciously projected an identity that distinguished them sharply from ancient cultures. Arbeau's treatise, among other texts, represented a new codification—reified in print and disseminated widely—of performance genres that were deemed contemporary and modern.

Further comparisons over the next century reinforced the "modernity" and implied "superiority" of "European music" when pitted against the traditions of other parts of the world. Spanish colonialism throughout the Americas and the Philippines occasioned opportunities for ethnographers to differentiate between "old" (Indigenous) and "new"—introduced and gradually hybridizing—practices. For example, in the Philippines in 1668, Jesuit Francisco Ignacio Alzina (1610–1674) compared the music of Visayan people with that of the most "polished" (*política*) nations, pointing out what he saw as the absence of "science and scientific principles for music" (by which he probably meant intervallic ratios) while allowing that their singing "improved" when they were introduced to European modes.[78] The latter view—clearly condescending—had the aim of making Indigenous cultures

---

[76] Original text in Arbeau, *Orchésographie*, n.p.
[77] Arbeau, *Orchesography*, 13; original text in Arbeau, *Orchésographie*, n.p.
[78] Original text in Yepes and Alzina, *Una etnografía*, 24–25. See also Irving, *Colonial Counterpoint*, 90.

accessible and comprehensible for European readers but also represented an erosion of difference after many generations of colonial interaction.[79] Adapting a concept of Rogério Budasz, we can see that in this way, otherness was "recycled in European terms" and transformed into a sense of musical modernity for the observer.[80]

The conceptual conflation of the musics of the ancients with those of the rest of the world did not necessarily imply that they were exactly the same. Rather, it could suggest that they had comparable forms and structures or that they were similarly "distant" from the practices of "modern" Europe. This sense of analogy between antiquity and the wider world, and the observation of music as a ubiquitous practice throughout the earth were used in 1715 by Jacques Bonnet-Bourdelot (whose book incorporated earlier work by his late brother and late uncle) to attack the idea that the ancient Greeks were the "inventors" of music:

> Mr. H. . . . ship's lieutenant, who has made lengthy voyages in the East and West Indies, has assured me that he has found music established in all the places where he landed, but very different from the type [of music] practiced in Europe. Almost all the peoples of distant countries only know the four principal notes of music [Bonnet-Bourdelot states earlier that these are attributed to Mercury, and are *mi, fa, sol, la*], as in its [music's] origin, which proves absolutely that the [ancient] Greeks are definitely not the inventors of music, as they claim to be.[81]

The argument can be summarized as follows: it was previously thought that all music descended from the ancient Greeks, but given that foundational musical principles are found in distant territories located to the east and the west, this cannot be the case. Bonnet-Bourdelot's earwitness informant thus disputes the primacy of ancient Greece in the "invention" of music, while noting that the music currently "practiced in Europe" is "very different."

In 1724, Lafitau published a large-scale piece of comparative ethnography in his *Moeurs des sauvages américains comparées aux moeurs des premiers temps* (*Customs of the Indigenous Americans Compared to Those of the Earliest Times*). Bohlman discusses a plate that compared the instruments from each category and observes of Lafitau that he "was a remarkable experimenter

---

[79] G. Tomlinson, *The Singing of the New World*, 21.
[80] Budasz, "Of Cannibals," 4.
[81] Original text in Bonnet-Bourdelot, *Histoire de la musique*, 156.

with musical ethnography . . . demonstrating that such instruments possessed no less rational functions than similar instruments of the Greeks."[82] Yet a closer reading of the continuation of Lafitau's text reveals a disparaging assessment of American and Greek instruments alike:

> There is reason to believe that our Indians' turtle is the same as the poets' or Apollo's. [He then gives a description of Mercury finding the turtle on a river bank.] But if this turtle of the Indians is the same thing as Apollo's lyre, since the lyre, sistrum and rhombus of the ancients were exactly alike in sound and appearance, I may be permitted to say that, if this was Apollo's lyre, the poets have wasted their time in praising so highly its music, which was quite inferior to that of the poorest village fiddler. They are no less wrong in invoking it with its muses, if their songs of *hié, évohé* [*éuohé*],[83] etc. were none other than the *hé, hé, éoué*, drawn by our Indians from the depths of their throats, for certainly I do not know of more detestable music anywhere in the world.[84]

Lafitau's lack of empathy with the music he heard—or the way it distanced him from the idea of ancient Greek music through the assertion of the assumed "superiority" of contemporary music of the Europe of his times—appears unambiguous. He implicitly equated modernity with music from his own culture.

"Barbarism" in Musical Thought from the Fifteenth to Eighteenth Centuries

In these contexts of intercultural comparison, writers in early modern Europe sometimes described cultural others as "barbarians" and their musics as "barbarous." The pejorative stereotype of a barbarian as uncouth, uncivilized, and rough is, of course, a trope with an ancient pedigree, and the following analysis of barbarism in these writers' discourse on music needs to be contextually grounded with consideration of the literal origins of the term "barbarian." This word, as used by ancient Greeks, originally described a cultural outsider

---

[82] Bohlman, "Representation and Cultural Critique," 137. On Lafitau, see also Boch, "L'Occident."
[83] *Hié* is a ritual cry of Apollo (paean); *éuohé* is a cry of Dionysius (Bacchic cry). Thanks to Peter Agócs for this insight.
[84] English translation in Lafitau, *Customs of the American Indians*, Vol. 1, 153–155. Original text in Lafitau, *Moeurs des sauvages ameriquains*, Vol. 1, 216–218.

who spoke another language; it was an onomatopoeic label, ostensibly mimicking the repetitive syllabic utterances "bar bar" of the other.[85] Its application (for purposes of oppositional self-definition) in the fifteenth to eighteenth centuries is not surprising, for as we have seen, many viewed themselves as the heirs of Greco-Roman antiquity, even if they felt superior to it. For the first part of the early modern period, the trope of "barbarism" was used by a number of Christian writers to denigrate musics produced by people not of their religion, especially Turks. As Nancy Bisaha has noted, Renaissance humanist thinkers transformed the image of the Turk into "the new barbarian" following the Ottoman conquest of Constantinople in 1453.[86]

This concept soon entered music discourse. For instance, Tinctoris in the late fifteenth century described the Turks as "that most barbarous race" and mentioned hearing prisoners of war in Naples performing on the "tambura" pieces so wild that, as he asserts, they "emphasize[d] the barbarity of those who played them."[87] In a different region of the Mediterranean, the wars against Muslims in Spain in the fifteenth century also led to this trope being applied against their music. In the "Prologo segundo para el piadoso lector" ("Second Prologue for the Pious Reader") of his 1555 treatise *Declaracion de instrumentos musicales* (*Treatise on Musical Instruments*), Juan Bermudo (c. 1510–after 1559)—who was based for most of his life in Andalusia—presented a disclaimer in case his works were translated into Latin or other languages in the future. He complained of errors proliferating among some singers, who he claimed had taken "certain bad habits" from "the barbarians in the time of the wars" ("los barbaros que en el tiempo de las guerras avia, de adonde algunos cantantes tomaron ciertos malos resabios").[88] Here the term "barbarian" was applied to the non-Christian Other (often called "moors"), although Bermudo pointed out that their musical practices had been absorbed into local custom.[89]

---

[85] Boletsi, *Barbarism and Its Discontents*, 57.

[86] Bisaha, *Creating East and West*, 62. Bisaha cites the term "the new barbarian" from Schwoebel, *The Shadow of the Crescent*, 147.

[87] Baines, "Fifteenth-Century Instruments," 25. Tinctoris denigrated the instrument as "puny," relating it to his disparaging view of the culture that produced it (23).

[88] See a discussion of this passage in Stevenson, *Juan Bermudo*, 21. Original text in Bermudo, *Comiença el libro llamado declaracion de instrumentos musicales*, n.p. [f. 7r]. This passage constitutes an intriguing description of performance practice, but Owen Wright has acknowledged in his assessment of the history of music in Spain under Muslim rule "the stark fact that the music itself cannot be disinterred." Wright, "Music in Muslim Spain," 555.

[89] Not long after Bermudo wrote, "Moorish" dance-music forms such as *zambras* were still practiced by groups going by the same name in southern Spain, although their performance close to

In the German-speaking lands, Michael Praetorius (1571–1621) extended the trope of barbarism to even more distant cultures in the organological part of his treatise *Syntagma musicum*, published in 1619: "I have also thought fit to include illustrations of the barbaric folk instruments used in Muscovy, Turkey, and Arabia, and of those used in India and America, so that we Germans may become acquainted with them as well; not, of course, in the sense of using them ourselves!—simply of knowing what they look like."[90] Here he emphasizes cultural distance from the objects he discusses and intolerance for the societies that produced them. In a complete contrast to the 1553 opinion of Belon (discussed above)—who maintained the possibility of finding remnants of ancient instruments in Greece and Turkey—Praetorius appeared to blame Muslim expansion for the loss of them:

> There are in Palestine, Asia Minor, and Greece no surviving traces of ancient instruments, since Mahomet, in establishing his tyrannical régime, fiendish religion, and degraded inhuman barbarism, forbade throughout his whole domain not only the liberal arts, servants of civilized society, but anything at all that could make people happy, like wine or the music of strings. In place of these he ordained a satanic bell and drum, along with the buzz-chirp-wail of shawms. This music is highly esteemed among the Muslims, and is used at holidays and merrymakings, as well as in war.[91]

This was a statement built on prejudice and without clear indication of the sources of this information. Yet other uses of the trope of barbarism around this time did not have negative intentions. In 1627, Pietro della Valle (1586–1652), famous for his travels into Asia, published an account of the funeral ceremonies held in Rome for his deceased Syrian wife, Sitti Maani (al Jaïruda) della Valle (c. 1598–1621). Addressing her directly, he described her

---

Catholic religious contexts was carefully monitored. See Castillo-Ferreira, "Chant, Liturgy and Reform," 317–320. However, Spanish king Felipe II (1527–1598; reigned from 1556) made a decree in 1566 (put into effect two years later) that set in place a program of extirpation of Islamic cultural influence and heritage, eliminating performance practices and institutions such as bathhouses, as well as Arabic language and writings. See N. Malcolm, *Agents of Empire*, 97. On professional musicians and instrument makers of Muslim and Jewish origins working in sixteenth-century Spain, see Knighton, "Instruments." For context and documents on the Morisco population in Spain and their eventual expulsion by Felipe III (1578–1621; reigned from 1598) in 1609, see Zayas, *Los moriscos*.

[90] Praetorius, *Syntagma musicum*, II, 7.
[91] Praetorius, *Syntagma musicum*, II, 6.

"sweetness of singing, . . . smoothness of voice, and the gracefulness of the dances practiced in the Orient, [as well as] the skill with which you played diverse barbarous instruments [*diversi barbari strumenti*], which are customary in those lands [*che in quelle terre si costumano*]."[92] Della Valle famously loved Sitti, and here "barbarous" is not used in a pejorative sense but simply to accentuate—and probably revere—her cultural difference.

Zarlino also exhibited knowledge of other theoretical traditions and makes references to barbarians in these contexts. In his *Dimostrazioni harmoniche* (*Harmonic Demonstrations*) of 1571, he refers to a tripartite division of Greek, Latin, and "barbarian writers [*barbaro Scrittore*]," the last perhaps implying sources in Arabic characters that he could not read.[93] Here religious confession is conflated with the binary of self/barbarian. There was also respect for musical learning in these rival cultures: in the 1630s, Peiresc wrote about representations (diagrams) of ancient Greek music in an Arabic manuscript and "had never seen this in all the printed books and manuscripts which passed through my hands. This made us recognize that, among these barbarous peoples, there had to be truly liberated spirits."[94] In 1633, Giovanni Battista Doni (1595–1647) wrote to Mersenne: "I hope to have begun to illustrate the ancient music, and by that means to bring back ours to its ancient splendour from the barbarism in which it lies since the German and Arabic inundations."[95] For Doni, contemporary music of (southern) Europe is considered to be in a state of barbarism, a barbarism caused by multiple incursions into the ruins of the Roman Empire.

The terms "barbarian," "barbarous," and "barbarism" were thus applied quite indiscriminately to anyone who was considered to deviate from the cultural standards created and imposed by elite thinkers and critics, to denigrate (which is the case in the majority of instances) or to praise. The same charge of "barbarism" was leveled internally at musicians in Christian Europe, as we shall see. There was, however, crossover; in a possible early nod to the moves toward the *seconda pratica*, before it was even labeled as such, Galilei wrote in 1581: "to adorn their impertinent and vain designs they pronounce the words in the very unaccustomed way of some remote barbarian."[96] Galilei

---

[92] Original text in Rocchi, della Valle, and Zanetti, *Funerale*, 121.

[93] Original text in Zarlino, *Dimostrationi harmoniche*, 265.

[94] In Miller, *Peiresc's Mediterranean World*, 124. Miller points out there that Peiresc "had heard the Moors singing 'excellently well' in Rome, many years before." See also a similar comment at 111.

[95] In Harrison, "Observation, Elucidation, Utilization," 11.

[96] Translation adapted from Galilei, *Dialogue*, 223; it uses the word "exotic" instead of "remote." However, the original text ends that sentence with "alcuno remoto barbaro." See Galilei, *Dialogo*, 89.

thus compared singers' exaggerations in pronunciation to the imagined performance style of peoples distant to him. In another internal criticism of musical practices in Europe, Cerone in 1613 referred to "barbarous composers" ("barbaros Compositores") mixing modes (*tonos*) to the extent that "the ears of an old donkey would not be enough to suffer [endure] the enormous licences, continuing ignorance, and the diverse mix that they use."[97]

Many thinkers in eighteenth-century Europe promoted a three-part hierarchical structure of savage–barbarian–civilized, with Europeans placed at the "civilized" rung.[98] (Brown, on the other hand, added two higher levels in his 1763 treatise on poetry and music: "refined" and "corrupted.")[99] "Barbarism" was an ambiguous term with diverse meanings. Osterhammel has identified four types as being operative in eighteenth-century European thought. The first was the halfway point between a "savage" and a "civilized" state. (For example, Hawkins famously stated in 1776 that "the best music of barbarians is said to be hideous and astonishing sounds," although it is unlikely that he heard any performances of people he called "barbarians.")[100] The second referred to the "Berber lands" of North Africa and their piratical activities in the Mediterranean; the third to "inhumane cruelties of all kinds ... whether they were committed by Europeans or non-Europeans"; and the fourth was a generic label used to impute a notion of uncivilized behavior by an entire community, implying an idea of "deficiency."[101] Osterhammel points out that the charges of barbarism were frequently leveled against Europeans themselves: "Calling Europeans barbaric meant unmasking their claim to superiority as hypocrisy."[102] Using "barbarism" as an analogy within musical discourse could reflect any or all of these positions and also emphasized the privileged position of the writer.

Yet barbarism was not an immutable state for either the subject or the viewer. Lafitau observed in 1724 (I quote Brown's translation of this passage for its eighteenth-century flavor): "The Music and Dance of the *Americans*

---

[97] Cerone, *El melopeo y maestro*, 235. Also discussed in Harrán, "Tradition and Innovation," 118 n.60.
[98] See Muthu, *Enlightenment against Empire*, 33. On seventeenth-century concepts of "savagery" in music, see Bloechl, *Native American Song*.
[99] In discussing the need for an institution of "A Poetic and Musical Academy," he noted "how congenial the *poetic* and *musical* Arts are with the Frame and Faculties of Man: That in every Period of Manners, whether savage, barbarous, civilized, refined, or corrupted, their Influence hath been felt in every Nation of the Earth." J. Brown, *A Dissertation*, 240.
[100] Hawkins, *A General History*, Vol. 1, xix. See also Savage, "Rameau's American Dancers," 442.
[101] Osterhammel, *Unfabling the East*, 298–301.
[102] Osterhammel, *Unfabling the East*, 299.

have something in them extremely *barbarous*, which at first *disgusts*: We grow *reconciled* to them *by Degrees*, and in the *End* partake of them with *Pleasure*. As to the Savages themselves, they are *fond* of them even to *Distraction*."[103] We see, then, that the categories of savage, barbarous, and civilized had somewhat fluid boundaries. In other words, one did not have to be a "barbarian" to be "barbarous"—here "barbarous" is the intermediate point at which the "savage" performer and the (implied) "civilized" viewer could converge.

Another example of this plasticity, from a different perspective, is seen in the writing of Quantz, who in his flute treatise of 1752 used it in two different ways. He famously stated that "*except among barbarians* there is not a single nation that does not have something in its music that is more pleasing to it than to other nations" (emphasis added).[104] Yet he did not reserve the concept of barbarism exclusively for peoples from beyond Europe. Later, discussing French and Italian styles, he commented that "the Italians used to call the German style in music *un gusto barbaro, a barbarous style*," referring to the times that predated German composers' performances of their works in Italy.[105] This terminology reflects in general terms xenophobic ideas about crudeness, and it persisted for many decades. Such a use was echoed in 1814 by Stendhal, who wrote that "the amateurs throughout Europe, with the exception of the French, think the melody of a neighbouring nation jerking and irregular; at once, trailing and barbarous; and, above all, wearisome."[106] However, as Maria Semi has recently noted, late-eighteenth-century references to "barbarism" in the musics of other parts of the world sometimes represented a noble ideal of "simplicity."[107]

The intra-European criticism of musical barbarousness was also given a chronological dimension—perhaps an early example of Goehr's idea of "conceptual imperialism"—with some music historians of the eighteenth century considering people living in pre-Renaissance Europe as barbarians. Brown called the time of the Crusades—an epoch in which, incidentally, he claims the origins of the oratorio genre are to be found—a "barbarous Period."[108] Rousseau, in his *Dictionnaire de musique*'s entry on "plainchant," commented

---

[103] Brown, *A Dissertation*, 75. Original text in Lafitau, *Moeurs des sauvages ameriquains*, Vol. 2, 227.
[104] Quantz, *On Playing the Flute*, 320. See discussion of this quote in Shiloah, "An Eighteenth-Century Critic," 184–185.
[105] Quantz, *On Playing the Flute*, 341.
[106] Stendhal, *The Life of Haydn*, 165. Original text in Stendhal, *Lettres écrites de Vienne*, 145.
[107] Semi, "Writing about Polyphony," 17.
[108] Brown, *A Dissertation*, 215.

that the essence of chant as practiced by the ancient Greeks had lost all its beauty since passing through the hands of the (European) barbarians.[109] In 1775, English writer Richard Twiss (1747–1821) published an account of his travels in Spain, and in an appendix titled "Summary of the History of Spain," he commented on Islamic society a thousand years earlier: "About this time the Moorish gallantry, arms, and arts flourished, and they rendered Granada and Cordova [Córdoba] two of the most beautiful cities in Europe: thus the Barbarians were become the civilized inhabitants of Spain, and the Spaniards were changed into Barbarians."[110] Amiot, one of the last Jesuits in China from the first Society of Jesus (which had been suppressed by the pope in 1773), took a Sinocentric model of Chinese as civilized and non-Chinese peoples as barbarous, applying this latter adjective to the "peoples of the West" in his *Mémoire sur la musique des Chinois* (published in 1779).[111]

In the long eighteenth century, European writers could thus locate the barbarians as much within the imagined (and changing) boundaries of "Europe"—in contemporary and older times—as outside them. Burney used the term "barbarous" frequently in his four-volume *General History of Music*, at first in the sense known in classical antiquity (of the crude and uncouth manners of barbarians) but also in regard to the musical taste of his contemporaries; at one point, he refers to "those who think all Music barbarous but that of the present day."[112] In his two-page conclusion to the entire work, "barbarism" emerges as a central theme; he is apologetic about having mentioned "barbarous times and more barbarous Music" in such detail, acknowledging that "it may be thought a useless labour," and notes that "I have spoken of some musicians whose fame is so much faded, that it is perhaps the last time they will ever be mentioned."[113]

Harmony itself became a target for charges of "barbarism," even though histories of music produced in eighteenth-century Europe often regarded the emergence of harmony in teleological terms, seeing it as an indexical link to civilizational progress. Rousseau famously claimed in his *Dictionnaire de musique* that only Europeans, "of all the peoples of the earth," used vertical "harmony" in their music (which was also identified as an essential

---

[109] Rousseau, *Dictionnaire de musique*, 379.

[110] Twiss, *Travels through Portugal and Spain*, 356. On Twiss's writings on music during his travels in Spain, see also Lombardía, "From Lavapiés to Stockholm," 195–198.

[111] Original text in Amiot, *Mémoire sur la musique des Chinois*, 16. See also Jiang, "In Search of the 'Oriental Origin,'" 126–127.

[112] Burney, *A General History of Music*, Vol. 3, 149.

[113] Burney, *A General History of Music*, Vol. 4, 684–685.

characteristic of the French style, especially the kind championed by Rameau in his operas), but railed against its conflation with ideas of nature.[114] In his *Essai sur l'origine des langues*, Rousseau also underscored differences between ancient Greek and modern European conceptions of "harmony," claiming that some mockery was going on:

> Our harmony is known to be a gothic invention. Those who claim to find the system of the Greeks in our own [musical system] are making fun of us. The system of the Greeks had absolutely no harmony in our sense except what was required to tune instruments [in] perfect consonances.[115]

He elaborated on this question at great length in his *Dictionnaire de musique*, in a direct critique of the affective powers attributed to harmonic expression by Rameau and his followers. Pointing out its (purportedly) exclusive practice by Europeans and that "no animal, no bird, no being in nature, produces any other concord than the unison," Rousseau criticized "northern nations" of Europe for the prominence that they give harmony "as a foundation of all the rules in art" and concluded: "it is very difficult not to suspect that all our harmony is but a gothic and barbarous invention, which we should never have followed if we had been more sensible of the true beauties of art, and of music truly natural."[116]

Rousseau thus considered harmony to be a specifically northern European innovation, long postdating antiquity. By contrast, the science of harmonics was a mathematical art whose proportions were put to practical use in very different ways by ancient Greek musicians. All such observations underpinned Rousseau's enduring belief in the primacy of melody over harmony and the power of the melodic voice unconstrained by vertical harmony. However, as Agnew and other scholars have shown, Europeans' encounters with Indigenous harmony in the Pacific in the 1770s upset the theories of civilizational development in music (from simple to complex).[117] Polynesian peoples were often equated with the ancient Greeks, whose music

---

[114] Original text in Rousseau, *Dictionnaire de musique*, 245.

[115] Rousseau, *Essay on the Origin of Languages*, 327–328. Original text in Rousseau, "Essai sur l'origine des langues," 425.

[116] Rousseau, *A Dictionary of Music*, 191. Original text in Rousseau, *Dictionnaire de musique*, 245. Jacques Derrida (1930–2004) notes that "harmony according to Rousseau is a musical perversion that dominates Europe (Northern Europe) alone, and ethnocentrism consists of considering it a natural and universal principle of music." Derrida, *Of Grammatology*, 212. See also Agnew, *Enlightenment Orpheus*, 98–99.

[117] Agnew, *Enlightenment Orpheus*, 98–99, 114–115.

was believed to be monophonic, but eyewitness (or earwitness) reports of vertical harmony practiced in the Pacific led to heated debates—mostly among Burney, John Montagu (fourth earl of Sandwich, 1718–1792), and other interlocutors—about whether societies there could have developed a musical culture that was more "advanced" than that of the ancients.[118]

Although Rameau and Rousseau disagreed about the value of harmony as a constituent element of contemporary music practice, they both clearly acknowledged a breach between ancient and modern musics. Rousseau's skepticism about claims for continuities from ancient Greek to the music that he knew in Europe was made explicitly in his *Essai sur l'origine des langues*. He criticized Pierre-Jean Burette (1665–1747), a medical doctor and scholar of antiquity, for his reconstructions and performances of ancient Greek music at the Académie des Inscriptions et Belles-Lettres. Rousseau stated that the French orators, musicians, and academicians would have no more chance of performing and understanding this music than Indigenous Americans throwing musket balls with their hands and emitting noises with their mouths to reproduce the effects of firearms.[119] Burney, however, writing on the same experiments in 1776, had a different view. He commented: "with all the advantages of modern notes and modern measure, if I had been told that they came from the Cherokees, or the Hottentots [Khoikhoi], I should not have been surprised at their excellence."[120] In this roundabout comment, Burney is praising the musical qualities of these particular ancient Greek melodies but also implying that he would have been predisposed to expect less than "excellent" music from people lying outside the boundaries of his idea of civilization.[121] However, in the last paragraph of his entire history—at the end of the fourth and final volume, published in 1789—Burney qualifies that "many specimens of melody are given, not as models of perfection, but reliques [sic] of barbarism, and indisputable vouchers [evidence] that

---

[118] See Irving, "The Pacific," 210–211, 228–229; Agnew, *Enlightenment Orpheus*, 98–99. On the observation of panpipes in the Pacific, which resembled ancient Greek examples, see also Irving, "Comparative Organography," 384–385.

[119] See Rousseau, *Essay on the Origin of Languages*, 319. Original text in Rousseau, "Essai sur l'origine des langues," 409–410.

[120] Burney, *A General History of Music*, Vol. 1, 103. See discussion of this quotation in Semi, "Writing about Polyphony," 7–8, 8n.37.

[121] It is worth also noting Burney's oblique reference to some of the "four parts of the world" in his mention here of both America and Africa, although he does not cite Asia, which in this system of representation was considered closer to Europe (as discussed in chapter 1). As Semi shows, however, Burney mentions Asia, Africa, and America in his entry on "Arabian Music" for Rees's *Cyclopaedia*. See Semi, "Writing about Polyphony," 14.

mankind was delighted with bad Music, before good had been heard."[122] For Burney, musical perfection was clearly to be found closer to his own day.

The Search for "Perfection" and "Progress"

"Perfection" as an inert state but also as a process of gradual transformation toward this goal may have been seen either as the antithesis of or the means of escape from barbarism, whether this barbarism referred to the remnants of a past age or the practices of contemporaneous others. Fonton, in his "Essay sur la musique orientale compareé [sic] a la musique europeéne [sic]" of 1751 (discussed in part II of this book), writes about ancient connections in Turkish music as follows, referring to ideas of the preservation of music in its descent through time and the condition of stasis:

> We do not know enough about the music of the Ancients to be able to assure [ourselves] that it is absolutely the same. But at least there is a lot of scope to believe that if vestiges of it still remain in any place, this must be among the Orientals, among whom most arts are conserved, quite close to as they were in their origin, almost *without any progress nor any perfection*.[123] [emphasis added]

Fonton's description of Turkish music as "static"—as being among the arts "preserved in a state close to that of their origin"—implies the assumed modernity of the "European music" with which he compares it. His use of the word "perfection" even seems to echo Rameau, who, in the preface to his 1722 *Traité de l'harmonie*, had stated rhetorically that he aimed to support the claim that "our music has attained the last degree of perfection and that the Ancients were far from this perfection."[124] (Fonton was likely familiar with that well-known text; a copy was held at the Jesuit college in Paris where he studied.)[125] Yet in spite of the belief that vestiges of ancient practice might have existed among certain contemporary peoples, as Fonton states, such a hypothesis was not extended altogether to the modern Greeks, who, as

---

[122] Burney, *A General History of Music*, Vol. 4, 685.
[123] Original text in Fonton, "Essay," manuscript (1751), 38–39.
[124] Rameau, *Treatise on Harmony*, xxxiii. Original text in Rameau, *Traité de l'harmonie*, preface, n.p.
[125] *Catalogue des livres*, 134 (no. 2326).

mentioned earlier, were believed to have lost many aspects of their ancient forebears' music. He has reservations about their claim to have preserved "certain signs" ("certains signes") of ancient music notation, for instance.[126]

Some eighteenth-century scholars deemed the musics of Europe to have reached "perfection," thus being "superior" to their former incarnations as well as to all other musics of the world, whether ancient or contemporary. They believed that they had evolved to this point through a process of "progress," something they discursively denied to other peoples or attributed to the influence of other forces. For instance, Hawkins opined in 1776 that "the *slow progress of music in Spain* may in some degree be accounted for by the prevalence of Moorish manners and customs for many centuries in that country" (emphasis added).[127] And in 1788, pondering the earliest stages of human music and rhythmic "music consisting of single tones," Forkel wrote: "How long a people can tolerate this first crude state of music cannot be precisely determined. We do still find it today, however, among many Asiatic, African, and American peoples, whom we also know to *have made no progress* for millennia in other branches of culture" (emphasis added).[128] It is worth noting that Forkel even uses here the trope of the four parts of the world, implying that Europe has completed this evolutionary process of musical "progress."

There are exceptions to every discursive tendency, however. One example is the early-eighteenth-century adulation of the "perfect" music of the Hebrew king David and that practiced in the Temple of Solomon. As Ruth Smith has shown, one English commentator in 1738 discussed Handel's aim to use "sackbutts, timbrells and tubal cain's [*sic*]" in his oratorio *Saul* to evoke instrumental sounds from the time of David, when "musick was in its greatest perfection."[129] A description and depiction of Hebrew instruments, published by Antoine Augustin Calmet (1672–1757), also referred to them being in their greatest state of perfection in this time.[130] Meanwhile, Benedetto Marcello (1686–1739) considered that a "shadow" of ancient Hebrew instrumental practice remained in his own times but nevertheless attempted to incorporate ancient Hebrew melodies into his new settings of psalm texts, compositions that circulated widely. He owned property in

---

[126] Fonton, "Essai sur la musique orientale" (ed. Neubauer), 295.
[127] Hawkins, *A General History*, Vol. 3, 87n.
[128] Forkel, "From *A General History of Music*," 1019. Original text in Forkel, *Allgemeine Geschichte der Musik*, Vol. 1, 4. See also discussion in G. Tomlinson, "Musicology, Anthropology, History," 64–65.
[129] Quoted in R. Smith, "Early Music's Dramatic Significance," 173.
[130] R. Smith, "Early Music's Dramatic Significance," 173–174, 188n.36.

Venice close to the Ghetto and may have heard Jewish cantillation through his windows; Edwin Seroussi notes that Marcello was "the first non-Jewish western musician to become truly involved with the actual Jewish musical traditions of his time" and that "his innovation resided in the belief that extant oral traditions was an authentic source for the study of musical antiquity."[131] However, this idea of unchanging practice in oral traditions was also subjected to critique; Burney, for one, doubted the uniformity and continuity of tradition in the vocal music that Marcello had transcribed.[132] As noted earlier in this book, Ruetz in 1752 deemed ancient Hebrew music to be "no longer available," considering it distinct from the "present-day European music" accessible for (Christian) worship.[133]

A more material perspective came into play regarding the transmission from antiquity of musical instruments, their recycling in nations of Europe, and finally their "perfection." For example, in 1687, Jean Rousseau (1644–1699) wrote of the viol:

> It was transmitted from the Egyptians to the Greeks, from the Greeks to the Italians, and from the Italians to the English, who were the first to compose and play pieces of harmony [consort music] on the viol, and who took the knowledge of this to other kingdoms.... So the viol passed from the English to the Germans and to the Spanish, and we can say that we are the last who have played it, but also that *the viol owes its perfection to the French* [*c'est aux François à qui la Viole doit sa perfection*].[134] [emphasis added]

Here a clear sense of French national pride emerges with the mention of the instrument's "perfection." It is interesting to note that this genealogy omits any mention of Islamic contributions to the emergence of the instrument, even though it was a creation emerging from Muslim societies in Spain.[135]

Such a genesis was not beyond early modern writers' horizons of knowledge, although awareness of it may have been stronger in the sixteenth and the late eighteenth centuries than in intermediate times. Ian Woodfield notes that the viol's hybrid origins were inversely recognized by Silvestro Ganassi (b. 1492) in the *Regola Rubertina* (*Rubertine Rule/Method*), published in Venice in 1542,

---

[131] Seroussi, "In Search of Jewish Musical Antiquity," 171.
[132] Seroussi, "In Search of Jewish Musical Antiquity," 154.
[133] Ruetz, *Widerlegte Vorurtheile*, 10.
[134] Original text in Jean Rousseau, *Traité de la viole*, 17–18.
[135] On Islamic contexts for the instrument's emergence, see Otterstedt, *The Viol*, 20, 23; Woodfield, *The Early History of the Viol*, 37.

writing that "the first important viol tutor specifically rejected the use of any 'Moorish gesture' ('atto di moresca') in playing the viol, a considerable irony, since posture and playing method were the most significant contributions of the Moors to the development of the viol."[136] More than two centuries later, Hawkins did acknowledge these origins as an alternative narrative: "There are other writers who derive the viol itself from the Arabian Rebab, from whence perhaps Ribible and Rebec, the use whereof it is said the Christians learned from the Saracens in the time of the Crusades; but it is more probable, by reason of its antiquity, that it was brought into Spain by the Moors."[137] By the mid-1770s, this was in any case probably something of an academic point, since the viol (along with the lute, theorbo, recorder, and other previously popular instruments) was beginning to fall almost completely out of use.[138]

Instruments not embraced and adapted over time by nations in Europe were sometimes seen as remaining in a "static" form. Following a description of his attendance at a "concert" in Cairo in the 1760s and as part of a survey of instruments, Niebuhr wrote: "It should seem, from the simple construction of their musical instruments, that those are of a very ancient origin, and have been transmitted down, without undergoing any remarkable alteration."[139] Hawkins, on the other hand, wrote specifically of the alteration—albeit minimal, in his view—of one transculturally adopted instrument in terms of "improvement": "The Spanish guitar is no other than the Arabian Pandura a little improved."[140] Similarly, La Borde observed in 1780 of "the inhabitants of the coasts of Africa" that "they have invented many kinds of instruments that echo those of Europe, but they are *very far from the same perfection* [*fort éloignés de la même perfection*]. They have trumpets, drums, spinets, lutes, flutes, flageolets, organs, etc." (emphasis added).[141] "Perfection" in European discourse was apparently seen in the late eighteenth century as the endpoint of teleological "progress," a process that was considered to reside exclusively in the musics of Europe or the actions of Europeans.

By the beginning of the nineteenth century, the assumption that self-proclaimed "European music" was synonymous with a new kind of

---

[136] Woodfield, *The Early History of the Viol*, 37. By 1581, however, Galilei asserted that the Italians were the inventors of the viol. Galilei, *Dialogue*, 369.

[137] Hawkins, *A General History*, Vol. 1, lv ("Preliminary Discourse").

[138] For a study of repertory for the viol from its last period of popularity in the eighteenth century, see O'Loghlin, *Frederick the Great and His Musicians*.

[139] English translation from Niebuhr, *Travels through Arabia*, Vol. 1, 133.

[140] Hawkins, *A General History*, Vol. 3, 87n.

[141] Original text in La Borde, *Essai*, Vol. 1, 216.

"modernity" began to be a commonplace in discourse that linked these terms and concepts, whether explicitly or implicitly. Chapter 4 showed that the invention of "European music" was carried out gradually through a reflexive process of making contrasts with musics from around the world. It was in the decades around 1800 that the idea of "modern European music" became a coherent and yet opaque discursive concept that was differentiated not only from living practices throughout the world but also from earlier musics in Europe. For instance, Forkel wrote in the foreword to the second volume (1801) of his *Allgemeine Geschichte der Musik* of "the modern European art of music" ("der neuern Europäischen Music-Art").[142] Similarly, Villoteau made broad comparisons between "our modern European music" ("notre musique Européenne moderne") and "that of other ancient or modern peoples" ("celle des autres peuples anciens ou modernes") in his *Recherches sur l'analogie de la musique avec les arts* of 1807.[143]

In 1834, Raphael Georg Kiesewetter (1773–1850) published a history that brought together notions of Europe, the West, and modernity in its title: *Geschichte der europäisch-abendländischen oder unsrer heutigen Musik* (*History of Western-European or Our Contemporary/Modern Music*). Here he spelled out the breach of the music of which he wrote with that of antiquity:

> It is a preconceived opinion, as widely spread as it is deeply rooted, that modern Music was modelled on that of ancient Greece, of which it is in fact merely a continuation ... the truth is, that modern music flourished only in proportion as it began to separate and withdraw itself from the system laid down and enforced by the Greeks, and that *it reached a considerable degree of perfection only when it succeeded in completely emancipating itself from the last remnant, real or supposed, of the ancient Grecian.*[144] [emphasis added]

Here the conflation of "modernity" and new standards of "European music" appear clear, as does the complete shedding of this music's supposed—and previously prized—ancestry from ancient Greece, to reach "perfection."

Exceptionalism in discourse became even more apparent when "modern European music" was compared with other systems. For instance, writing of music in northern India in 1834 (coincidentally the same year as Kiesewetter's history), an anonymous English observer made reference to modes in music of

---

[142] Forkel, *Allgemeine Geschichte der Musik*, Vol. 2, iii ("Vorrede").
[143] Villoteau, *Recherches sur l'analogie*, Vol. 1, xlii.
[144] Kiesewetter, *History of the Modern Music*, 1–2.

Greek antiquity and "Gregorian canto fermo" (Gregorian chant), commenting that "these same modes exist in the Hindoo music, and therefore, many of them will not carry a regular modal harmony, such as distinguishes all *modern European music*, which contains only two modes" (emphasis added).[145] This writer was probably paraphrasing N. Augustus Willard (dates unknown) from his work of the same year, *A Treatise on the Music of Hindoostan*, which states that "the number of tones [in Indian music] is the same as in the modern music of Europe, but the subdivisions are more in the manner of the ancient enharmonic genus of the Greeks."[146] Similar comparisons with Arabic and Chinese music were made by Abbé Terence Joseph O'Donnelly (dates unknown)—a priest and scholar in Paris—in a book of elementary music theory published in 1841 (and in French translation the following year in Paris): "The distance between a tone and semitone, is the smallest interval perceptible in *modern European music*; I say in *modern European*, because the ancients distinguished quarter tones; and the Arabs, and Chinese employ them still, but to us, their use is unknown" (emphasis added).[147]

Discourse by Europeans about "their" musics developed a specific strand of thinking that essentialized its substance and promoted its self-proclaimed "modernity" and exceptionalism in global terms, denying connections or intersections with other cultures. Encounters with other music cultures had inspired European thinkers to reconceptualize their own art form in terms of divergence on a global scale. Theories about "superiority" and "progress" were supported by trends in thinking that foregrounded the mathematical elements of music, especially intervallic ratios and instrument design and especially the use of vertical harmony and part music. By 1869, François-Joseph Fétis (1784–1871) could assert: "Everywhere and at all times there have been popular songs and religious chants; *only among the modern Europeans* is there an art of music" (emphasis added).[148] This kind of statement was the assumption on which early comparative musicology was built, from the 1880s onward, with European or Western musical modernity regarded as the normative standard and the yardstick for comparison.[149]

---

[145] "Itinerant Musicians," 227.
[146] Willard, *A Treatise*, 25. Sir William Jones (1746–1794) had also referred to "the modern European scale" and "*European* modes" in his treatise of 1784–1792 "On the Musical Modes of the Hindus." Jones, "On the Musical Modes," 80, 84.
[147] O'Donnelly, *Academy of Elementary Music*, 11. For the French translation, see O'Donnelly, *Académie de musique élémentaire*, 23.
[148] Original text in Fétis, *Histoire générale de la musique*, Vol. 1, 5. See also discussion of this quotation in Osterhammel, *Unfabling the East*, 480–482. For more context on Fétis's thought, see Christensen, *Stories of Tonality*.
[149] On the rise of comparative musicology in the 1880s, see Nettl, *Nettl's Elephant*, 3–21.

Through their belief in claims to a monopoly on musical "modernity," with an essentializing posture formed through several centuries of intercultural comparison and distancing, the musically minded writers who self-defined as European thus constructed an idea of their art in which it was set apart from musics of "their" antiquity and all musics of other parts of the world. They described moving away from the "ancient" to the "modern" as "progress," and believed "perfection" to be its endpoint. Yet, as this chapter has shown, by analyzing the conceptual place of classical antiquity in the development of ancient/other analogies of musical practices throughout the world, we can throw new light on the complicated processes by which some early modern European writers asserted the purported "modernity" of their own musics in direct relation to those of others. By critiquing the ways in which a discourse promoting a western European musical identity emerged in parallel with many forms of colonialism around the world, we can identify how teleological narratives of European exceptionalism were generated within the historiography of music and develop a heightened awareness of the kinds of paradoxical language used in many primary sources.

6

Accidental Occident

The Setting of "the West" in Music History

The idea of "the West" is a long-standing concept, but historically it has had meanings quite different from what we regularly impute to it today.[1] Etymologically, the English terms "Orient" and "Occident" (from Latin) refer, respectively, to the rising and setting of the sun, as do "East" and "West" (from Germanic). The same solar connections are true of a number of other languages. Even the names for some whole regions reflect their relationship to dawn and dusk; examples are, respectively, Anatolia in Greek and Maghreb in Arabic. At its most reductive level, the geographical idea of "the West" is an astronomical concept.[2] The term "Western" also conjures up images of pre-heliocentric thinking, implying the sun's revolution around the earth. For as long as the globe was not circumnavigated and Africa-Eurasia defined the limits of the only continental landmass known to people there, "East" and "West" were relatively finite terms. But "Western" was a term that gained new meaning at the height of European imperialism, bringing with it the idea of endless expansion and hegemony.[3] From 1492, "the West" also implied the Americas.[4] After Ferdinand Magellan (c. 1480–1521) crossed the Pacific from east to west, parts of East and Southeast Asia were known in Spanish as "*Las Indias del poniente,* the Indies of the West, or, more poetically, the Indies of the Setting Sun," as Ricardo Padrón puts it.[5] Both Spain and Britain had tropes of their respective empires being global territorial configurations over which "the sun never set."[6]

---

[1] See Appiah, *The Lies That Bind*; Bonnett, *The Idea of the West*.
[2] Thanks to Andrew Hicks for discussion of this point.
[3] Walter Mignolo notes that "hemispheric partitions are a recent phenomenon in view of the age of the planet." Mignolo, *The Politics of Decolonial Investigations*, 289 (see also the chapter "Decolonial Reflections on Hemispheric Partitions," 287–313).
[4] For a discussion of this point in relation to eighteenth-century music, see Polzonetti, "Oriental Tyranny."
[5] Padrón, *The Indies of the Setting Sun*, 3.
[6] Irving, *Colonial Counterpoint*, 22; Jackson, *The British Empire*, 5.

"MODERN EUROPEAN MUSIC" AND "WESTERN MUSIC"

When issues of geography have come to the fore in the history of music, the location of "the West" has sometimes been explained as incorporating "America" as well as "Europe." This is, however, a loose description, as Richard Taruskin (1945–2022) pointed out in the opening of his six-volume *Oxford History of Western Music* (2005). He wrote that Europe and its later conjunction with America "is what we still casually mean by 'the West,' although the concept is undergoing sometimes curious change: a Soviet music magazine I once subscribed to gave news of the pianist Yevgeny Kissin's 'Western debut'—in Tokyo."[7] In 2010, Taruskin discussed the failure of musicologists to recognize the significance of a 1677 description of the circle of fifths published in Russia by Ukrainian musician Nikolay Diletsky (c. 1630–c.1680), as studied by Claudia Jensen, which predated a 1711 description of the same concept by Heinichen—long seen by many historians and theorists as its first expression—by more than thirty years.[8] Taruskin noted that "Russia, it seems, is not yet a part of 'Western Music' as imagined by most music historians," going on to assert that "the Cambridge histories of seventeenth- and eighteenth-century music . . . stop short at the Oder-Neisse line" (the frontier established in 1950 between what was then East Germany and Poland).[9] The "East-West" divide after the Second World War, not only in Europe but more globally, caused many societies that in the eighteenth century were thought of as part of the "Western hemisphere," in broad musical and cultural terms, to be part of "the Eastern bloc." For current generations of music scholars working within and parallel to "Western" societies—even those born after the fall of the Berlin Wall—it seems that internalized elements of language and attitudes of the Cold War have been projected retrospectively onto the music history of past centuries, whether consciously or not.

Another definition of a singular Western music in binary opposition to the "rest" of the world's musics is given by Born and Hesmondhalgh in their edited volume *Western Music and Its Others*. They state:

> We use "Western" to denote Europe and North America. Many people now prefer the divisions "North" and "South" as a means of referring to the division between relatively rich and poor areas of the world. But, given that

---

[7] Taruskin, *The Oxford History of Western Music*, Vol. 1, xiii.
[8] Taruskin, "Review," 295; Jensen, "A Theoretical Work."
[9] Taruskin, "Review," 295; Jensen, "A Theoretical Work."

this is a book about music, we need to refer to the longstanding concept of "Western music" while distancing ourselves from those traditions of analysis which have taken such a category for granted, or which have privileged it, or both.[10]

Looking at this definition, we see Europe and the Americas listed once more, but "North America" in the case of the latter. There is much to think about here. First, the designation of "North America" seems problematic, since in its anglophone (and anglocentric) sense, it excludes Mexico on cultural grounds.[11] Mexico is nevertheless geographically part of the North American continent and has strong cultural continuities with the United States of America. Second, many regions outside "Europe and North America" have their own traditions of art music that are sometimes interrelated with "Western" forms, or not.[12]

The exclusion of other regions—although imagined boundaries are constantly shifting and are not consistently applied—from some definitions of "the West" in music studies is arguably a repercussion due to the countless processes of colonial extractivism and exploitation that have taken place over the last half a millennium. As sociologist Aníbal Quijano (1928–2018) pointed out: "The 'Western' European dominators and their Euro–North American descendants are still the principal beneficiaries, together with the non-European part of the world not quite former European colonies, Japan mainly, and mainly their ruling classes."[13] The zones outlined by Quijano, along with Australia and New Zealand, generally make up what is called the "Global North."[14] Although the "Global North" could be considered in many ways synonymous with "the West," this category includes countries labeled "Eastern," such as Japan, which are home to communities that have played a major role in cultivating "Western music."

---

[10] Born and Hesmondhalgh, "Introduction," 47n.1.
[11] It is worth noting that Spain's relationship with the idea of "the West" has also been subject to critique. See Casares, Fernández de la Cuesta, and López-Calo, *España en la música de Occidente*.
[12] This topic was explored at the workshop "Musicology or Ethnomusicology? Discussing Disciplinary Boundaries in Non-Western Art Music," organized by Vera Wolkowicz and held at the University of Cambridge on March 22, 2019, supported by Cambridge's Faculty of Music and the Institute of Musical Research (Royal Holloway University of London). It featured a memorable keynote by Melanie Plesch titled "The West and the Rest: Some Reflections on Ex-centric Art Musics."
[13] Quijano, "Coloniality and Modernity/Rationality," 168.
[14] See also Appiah, *The Lies That Bind*, 191. However, this categorization is not always accepted; see discussion in Collyer, "Australia and the Global South."

Cook, writing about the place of "Western music" in the world, points out some potential pitfalls of essentialism that are inherent in large conceptual categories such as these:

> "Western music" refers to a classical tradition now most strongly rooted in Asia, and a popular tradition that is in reality a global hybrid. But these paradoxes are hardly surprising. The concept of "the West," at least as used in those parts of the world that have styled themselves that way, goes back no further than the late nineteenth century[.] . . . And as much as its antonym "non-Western," it [the word "Western"] is an essentializing term, suggesting a homogeneity that is largely spurious. The concept of "Western music" is then as much in need of scare quotes as "world music."[15]

Given that historical musicology and ethnomusicology appear to have long dispensed with the terms "Eastern music" or "Oriental music," is it justifiable to continue using the term "Western music" or "Occidental music," unless using it with scare quotes, as Cook suggests, or in relativistic terms that take account of its different meanings before and after 1800? In this chapter, I will first look at sources predating 1800 to see how ideas of "the West" and music coincided. Before the nineteenth century, "Western music" meant liturgical Christian music by Catholic and (later) Protestant Christians who defined themselves in opposition to Orthodox Christianity. I then go on to show that from around the 1830s, the same term began to be used to contrast a whole system of music (not just Christian liturgical practice and repertory) to the emerging ideas of "the East." Finally, I give a brief summary of the trajectory of the concept through musicological literature of the nineteenth and twentieth centuries.

Is "East" East and "West" West? Always the Twain Are Intertwined

The notion of a binarism and mutual exclusivity of East and West was made famous to the point of cliché by Rudyard Kipling (1865–1936), to whose memorable poetic pronouncement this subheading inversely refers.[16] If

---

[15] Cook, "Western Music as World Music," 89.
[16] In 1889, his poem "The Ballad of East and West" began with the line: "Oh, East is East, and West is West, and never the twain shall meet." For the full text of this poem, see Kipling, *Rudyard Kipling's Verse*, 233–236. Kipling's vision of eternal divergence toward the end of the nineteenth century is quite

Europe as an imagined whole (or part of it) became synonymous with "the West" (or part of it), this involved a gradual and complex transformation. So did the application of "Western" to the noun "music," a process that was equally (if not more) problematic. Jeremy Montagu highlighted the vagueness of the terminology: "To talk of Western music is silly—west of where? Istanbul? Los Angeles? Tokyo? To talk of European music is tactless."[17] The idea of "the West" is always relational. As pointed out in chapter 2, for many centuries of the last two millennia, it meant the western half of the Roman Empire, then Latin Christendom as opposed to the Byzantine Empire (the eastern Roman Empire, until 1453).

The fall of Constantinople has long been regarded as a significant "turning point" in the construction of a renewed "Western identity." However, John M. Hobson sees responses in western Christendom to both this event and the Ottoman capture of Athens in 1456—which in turn spurred on Portuguese transoceanic voyages—as a legacy of the Crusades.[18] The gradual Ottoman advance also had implications for western European (especially Italian) humanism's engagement with Greek literary and scientific texts from the ancient world. From 1397 to 1534, Greek scholars fleeing from Ottoman expansion poured into Italy, chiefly Venice, bringing with them a wealth of knowledge, and, in the words of classicist and musician Deno John Geanakoplos (1916–2007), "western Europe advanced in its knowledge of Greek from virtual ignorance of the language to the recovery and mastery of almost the entire corpus of Greek literature in the original."[19] The rediscovery of ancient sources inspired a new wave of interest in pagan classical civilizations and their musical thought (as noted in chapter 5), with major implications for music theory and practice. This involved not only renewed

---

different, however, from attempts at hybridity made by Johann Wolfgang von Goethe (1749–1832) some seventy years earlier. In 1819, Goethe published the *West-oestlicher Divan* (*West-Eastern Divan*), a collection of poems (not all by him) inspired by Persian forms. Goethe, *West-oestlicher Divan*. For an early English translation (published in 1877), see Goethe, *Goethe's West-Easterly Divan*. Thanks to Maria Semi for mentioning this work of Goethe in our discussions. Some of the poems from this collection were set to music by Franz Schubert (1797–1828). For a study of certain settings, see Boucher, "Goethe's 'Suleika.'"

[17] J. Montagu, "Why Ethno-organology?," 34.
[18] Hobson, *The Eastern Origins*, 135–136.
[19] Geanakoplos, *Greek Scholars in Venice*, 279. As Thomas J. Mathiesen observes, "until the end of the sixth century, both Greek and Latin were used and understood in Eastern and Western intellectual centers, but in the last quarter of the century, a linguistic fracture accelerated the separation of the intellectual tradition of the Eastern empire from the West. This fracture ... would not be even partially repaired until the so-called revival of ancient learning at the end of the Middle Ages." Mathiesen, "Hermes or Clio?," 6.

interest in the theory of music—looking especially at tuning systems and intervallic ratios—but also a fresh emphasis on the study of rhetoric and its application to music.[20]

In many ways, this humanist project can be seen as a deliberate and performative European act of reclaiming cultural ownership of knowledge from societies falling under Ottoman rule. Appiah, critiquing an exceptionalist "Western" identity, has referred to ancient Greek learning as a proverbial "golden nugget" on which it is based, highlighting the paradox that this knowledge was simultaneously shared with Islamic scholarship, also heir to the Greek classical tradition.[21] Comparative literature specialist Su Fang Ng has similarly argued that many other cultures have an equal if not greater claim to descent from ancient Greece. Ideas, stories, science, and cultural influence from ancient Greece spread to India—probably as a result of the conquests of Alexander the Great (356–323 BCE; reigned from 336 BCE)—and to Southeast Asia. In her study of the *Hikayat Iskandar Zulkarnain* (*The Story of Iskandar Dhu-l-Qarnayn*), the Islamic version of the Alexander romance and one of the masterpieces of Malay classical literature, she observes:

> The uncanny mix of familiarity and strangeness of the Islamic Alexander reminds us how much the notion of Western origins in Ancient Greece is a fictional construction. Indeed, [ancient] Greece was more properly part of the Hellenistic Orient and Near Eastern world, sharing much with its "eastern" neighbors and looking toward Persia with envy.[22]

It is difficult, if not impossible, to trace forms of music that were supposedly "pure" and that purportedly remained intact and unaffected by contact with the cultures that surrounded them. When ancient forms were "reclaimed" in Renaissance Europe, many were already inherently hybrid.[23] By way of a primary example, in one of the manuscripts of ancient Greek music theory that came to western Europe—in the collection that Cardinal Bessarion (1403–1472) donated to Venice—a "Turkish monochord" was used as an illustrative diagram.[24] The supposed cultural "purity" of this corpus of ancient literature

---

[20] Regarding rhetoric in western European music from the late fifteenth century onward, see Haynes and Burgess, *The Pathetick Musician*, 4–5.
[21] Appiah, "There is No Such Thing."
[22] Ng, "Global Renaissance," 300.
[23] See P. Burke, *Hybrid Renaissance*.
[24] Mathiesen, *Ancient Greek Music Theory*, 698 (see also 747). It appears in a copy of Ptolemy's *Harmonics*, on f. 163v of Gr. 322 (coll. 711) in the Biblioteca Marciana, Venice.

in its transit to "western" Europe and through time, and its exclusion of surrounding cultural contexts, is thus open to question.

From the late Middle Ages through the seventeenth century, the presence of diverse musicians in royal courts in Europe and Asia also indicates the porousness of "East-West" boundaries. The instrumental ensembles and courtly dancers of Tudor England or of Castile and Aragon under the Catholic monarchs arguably had many resemblances to what might be seen in Istanbul or Agra. Indeed, Henry VIII (1491–1547; reigned from 1509) of England sent for drummers from Vienna, "in the Hungarian manner," to emulate Ottoman grandeur and employed Sephardic Jewish viol players in his court.[25] In 1520, François I (1494–1547; reigned from 1515), king of France, sent a musical ensemble to Ottoman sultan Suleiman the Magnificent (1494–1566; reigned from 1520), along with a musical instrument, as reported by Praetorius.[26] Jewish musicians played in papal courts and Ferrara.[27] Black trumpeters were employed in many royal and noble houses.[28] Mughal emperor Jahangir (1569–1627; reigned from 1605) requested that English cornettist Robert Trully (dates unknown) teach one of his musicians to play that instrument (and ordered six copies made of it).[29] Another famous Islamic ruler, Shah Suleiman I of Persia (1648–1694; reigned from 1666), was noted by an English traveler in c. 1668 to have a French servant in Isfahan who played the violin.[30] It seems logical to assume that none of these musicians would have been sought out for or sent to these elite institutions, or gainfully employed in service of their patrons, if there had been no "use" for or appreciation of them.

Examples continue: Prince Cem (1459–1495), an exiled son of Ottoman sultan Mehmed II, is depicted as listening to a lutenist while dining in his house in Rhodes.[31] While this is a flourish of the engraver who illustrated the scene, it is entirely plausible; the playing of a plucked string instrument resembling the 'ūd (oud) would not have appeared in any way out of context for the exiled prince. Instrumentalists from far western parts of Europe also traveled to the eastern Mediterranean; for instance, a few decades earlier, the

---

[25] Wright, "Turning a Deaf Ear," 161; Prior, "Jewish Musicians."
[26] Praetorius, *Syntagma musicum, II*, 6. Wright, however, considers this story "clearly apocryphal." Wright, "Turning a Deaf Ear," 159. See elaboration of this point in Wright, "How French Is *Frenkçin*?"
[27] Otterstedt, *The Viol*, 23.
[28] Knighton, "Instruments," 115–118; Spohr, "'Mohr und Trompeter.'"
[29] Woodfield, *English Musicians*, 205–206.
[30] Woodfield, *English Musicians*, 245; Temple, "The Travels of Richard Bell," 125, 126.
[31] Caoursin, *Rhodiorum vicecancellarii*, n.p.

musician Juan Alfonso de Sevilla (dates unknown)—who served the royal court of Aragon as a lutenist—was greatly admired by Byzantine emperor John VIII Palaiologus (1392–1448; reigned from 1425) for his performances of romances in Castilian to the accompaniment of the lute.[32] Peiresc also states that in 1601, he witnessed in Rome a Persian emissary (whom he names elsewhere as a merchant) perform on a chordophone for Pope Clement VIII (1536–1605; reigned from 1592), who rewarded the musician with a gift.[33] In these contexts, there was certainly a sense of equivalence in the ways court music was patronized across supposed "East-West" boundaries, even if some of the performances almost certainly functioned also as representations of "the exotic."[34] It is not feasible to assume the complete incommensurability of "Western" and "Eastern" musics in this early period (a trope that arose in the late eighteenth, the nineteenth, and especially the twentieth centuries), although there were distinctions articulated within the context of the Christian church.

Historical Orientations of Christianity

Differences between "East" and "West" in Christendom were entrenched by divergences of Christian liturgical practice (not to mention theology). It is interesting to see how ancient comments about church musics from East and West were reinterpreted in Renaissance sources. For instance, Saint Augustine (354–430)—bishop of Hippo in northern Africa—made a comment in his *Confessions* about some "Eastern" practices of singing hymns and chants being adopted in Milan.[35] His observation was discussed by Tinctoris in the early 1480s in one version of his treatise *De inventione et usu musicae* (*On the Invention and Use of Music*), as follows: "Hence, witness Augustine, 'it was established *by the westerners* that hymns and songs should be sung according to the custom of eastern parts (lest the people pine away with the tedium of mourning)'" (emphasis added).[36] It is striking to note, however,

---

[32] Knighton, "Instruments," 122–123.

[33] Miller, *Peiresc's Mediterranean World*, 111, 490n.318.

[34] For a discussion of fungibility or interchangeability in the cross-cultural circulation and representation of musical practices, see Taylor, *Beyond Exoticism*, 20–22.

[35] Augustine, *Confessions*, Vol. 2, 28–31 (Book 9, 7:15). See also Page, *The Christian West and Its Singers*, 99, 133–134.

[36] English translation from Tinctoris, *De inventione et usu musice*. (As noted there, this comment was made only in the manuscript source of diverse chapters held in the Bibliothèque Municipale de Cambrai, not the Naples print of extracts.)

that the original text in Augustine's *Confessions* does not include the term "westerners" and only speaks of singing according to the custom of "eastern parts [*orientalium partium*]."[37] The gloss appears to have been added by Tinctoris, in whose text it seems to emphasize the geographical and ecclesiastical distinction. More than a millennium separates the two authors, and Tinctoris's choice of terminology probably reflected notions of Westernness in his time.

Christopher Page has traced the emergence of a medieval "Latin West" or "Latin Occident" within geographical boundaries that were gradually shrinking "by accident, or rather through major territorial losses"; he also points to a certain degree of liturgical and music-theoretical coherence within this space.[38] Its cultural and political connections across the Mediterranean Sea underwent a radical transformation, especially in the seventh and eighth centuries, as Islamic conquests spread across northern Africa and into the Iberian peninsula. Several centuries later, Christian Crusades attempted to claim territories to the east that had formerly been part of the Roman Empire(s) and to establish dominion over Jerusalem and surrounding lands. In around 1124, Fulcher of Chartres (c. 1059–c. 1128) wrote about the kingdom established in Jerusalem by the Crusaders, a few decades after the seizure of the city, in terms of West and East: "Consider, I pray, and reflect in our time God has transformed the Occident into the Orient. For we who were Occidentals have now become Orientals."[39] This statement suggests fluidity in the concepts of East and West as identity categories, pointing to the potential for transformation between them. Nevertheless, the binary probably reflects more clearly the long-standing divisions of the Roman Empire as well as of (part of) Christendom into the "Latin West" and the "Byzantine East," especially following the East-West schism of the churches in 1054.

The idea of a singular music of Latin Christendom gave a sense of coherence to those who saw it from an etic perspective, both before and after the Reformation. This book has so far mentioned several condescending descriptions of Orthodox music by Catholic or Protestant Christian writers, and it is revelatory and instructive to consider the reverse gaze. In the late 1430s, a Russian Orthodox delegate at the Council of Ferrara and Florence,

---

[37] Original text in Augustine, *Confessions*, Vol. 2, 30.
[38] Page, "The Geography of Medieval Music," 320. See also Page, "Towards"; Page, *The Chistian West and Its Singers*, esp. 499–500, 528–534. On the North-South and East-West dichotomies that contributed to the contraction of this physical space, see Brague, *Eccentric Culture*, 7–12; Guénoun, *About Europe*, 51–54.
[39] Quoted in Howard, *Venice and the East*, 33.

which sought and failed to bring the Eastern and Western churches back into a common communion, wrote of "Latins" in the following terms:

> What have you seen of worth among the Latins? They do not even know how to venerate the Church of God. They raise their voices as the fools, and their singing is a discordant wail. They have no idea of beauty and reverence in worship, for they strike trombones, blow horns, use organs, wave their hands, trample with their feet and do many other irreverent and disorderly things which bring joy to the devil.[40]

As can be seen from such a statement, divergences between the musical traditions of the Western and Eastern churches had become fundamentally different. At these councils, the Orthodox representatives were repelled by the local use of polyphony and instruments, as Daniel Glowotz has shown.[41]

Coincidentally, but significantly, the period between the split of the churches and their failed reunion is roughly coterminous with two key developments in the history of "Western music": first, the rise of the theory and practice taught by Guido of Arezzo from the eleventh century onward (the staff, the gamut, and solmization), and second, the rise of a common musical language, based on contrapuntal polyphony, and its spread throughout western Europe during the long fifteenth century (the process that Strohm described as "the rise of European music").[42] According to Dimitri Conomos, "[Greek] musicians in Constantinople and on Mount Athos were probably oblivious of the rise of polyphony in the West, particularly after the formal break between the two Churches in the eleventh century, which was preceded by a long period of increasing estrangement."[43] Orthodox Christendom's views on the kinds of music appropriate for worship reinforced its apparent alterity to Christians who followed Latin rites.

Still, there are surprisingly few mentions of "Western music" in western European languages in the sixteenth and seventeenth centuries, although there are allusions to the idea. Hieronymo Roman (1536–1597) refers to "chant in the Occident" ("el canto en Occidente") in his *Repúblicas del mundo* (*Republics of the World*) of 1575; notably, he describes this music as being "in" a place rather than using the proper adjective "Occidental."[44] Catholic

---

[40] In Zernov, *Moscow, the Third Rome*, 37. Quoted in Conomos, "Experimental Polyphony," 1–2.
[41] Glowotz, "Die musikalische Konfrontation."
[42] Strohm, *The Rise of European Music*.
[43] Conomos, "Experimental Polyphony," 1.
[44] Original text in Román, *Repúblicas del mundo*, f. 215v.

views of liturgical chant in Eastern (Orthodox) churches were patronizing; in 1588, when Francisco Guerrero (1528–1599), on his way to Jerusalem, heard a Mass celebrated by Greeks on the Ionian island of Zante (Zakynthos, which was then still under Venetian rule), he described their chanting as "very simple, and ignorant [unlearned]."[45] Kircher wrote in 1650: "The peoples of the East [*Orientis populi*]—Greeks, Syrians, Egyptians, Africans sojourning in Rome—could hardly endure the refined music of the Romans. They preferred their own confused and discordant voices (you would more truly call it the howling and shrieking of animals) to the said music from many parasangs away."[46] He likely based this comment on his own subjective earwitnessing of the voices he described. The common link of Christianity did not prevent pejorative assessment of national or confessional styles of vocalization in peoples grouped together monolithically under the rubric of "the East." Nevertheless, the quality of the "Eastern" voice was admired for its quality by some western European theorists, even in theory if they did not actually hear it. Mersenne wrote in 1636 of the climate of "Greece and other Oriental countries" having a beneficial effect on the voice, explicitly setting Greece among Eastern nations.[47] In this way, he anticipated the thinking of Montesquieu on climate's influence on people and customs (discussed in chapter 4).

Mersenne was, incidentally, part of plans for one of the most remarkable comparative projects of the early seventeenth century, which sought to examine chant traditions across the largest confessional divide in Christianity. He and Peiresc designed a plan to collect, in one fell swoop, data from numerous groups of Eastern Christians in the Church of the Holy Sepulchre at Jerusalem. The convergence of so many different confessions—from "East" and "West" alike—at one of the holiest sites of Christendom would provide an opportunity for the full diversity of religious liturgical and devotional expression to be experienced.[48] Historian Peter Miller describes the proposal

---

[45] Original text in Guerrero, *El viage de Hierusalem*, f. 13r–v.
[46] Translation quoted from Murata, "Music History," 195. Original text in Kircher, *Musurgia universalis*, Vol. 1, 544.
[47] Original text in Mersenne, *Harmonie universelle*, Book 1, 42.
[48] One wonders whether the descriptions given by Guerrero, mentioned above, may have been an inspiration for this project. Guerrero listed the Christians in Jerusalem as Latins, Jacobites, Greeks, Ethiopians, Armenians, Syrians, Georgians, and Maronites; in the Church of Holy Sepulchre, each group had "two or three religious distributed in the chapels of this holy church, who said Divine Office each one in their own style and language." Original text in Guerrero, *El viage de Hierusalem*, ff. 58v–59r. He reflected on how happy he was "at midnight to hear all these nations recite Matins, each one in their language and [style of] chant." Original text in Guerrero, *El viage de Hierusalem*, f. 67r–v.

of Mersenne and Peiresc as a comparative project on many levels: the intention was to transcribe all chants in staff notation to compare the Greek chants with those of the Copts, Armenians, Maronites, and Ethiopians and then to ask the informants to notate their chants in their own scripts.[49] As Peiresc wrote to Théophile Minuti (1592–1662) in 1633: "someone a little cognizant of our music ... could put in our musical notes the melody of these different songs of all these peoples and ... transcribe separately the notes of each according to their writing in order to compare them with ours."[50] How this ambitious project played out (if at all) is unknown, yet it is clear that the touchstone against which it would have assessed other traditions of chant was a kind of standardized Gregorian chant, which was certainly also present in Jerusalem.[51]

Intercultural interfaces elsewhere played a major role in the formation of ideas of "the West." The Jesuits in their mission to China—well known as the "Middle Kingdom"—actively sought to conflate "Europe" with preexisting Chinese notions of "the West" and to change those ideas.[52] To the Chinese, India was to the west, and many lands lay in the direction of what was called "Xiyang" or the Western Ocean.[53] As mentioned in chapter 3, Ricci and other Jesuits presented themselves to the Chinese as men "from the West." Ricci split China's notion of a Western Ocean into two: the Xiao Xiyang 小西洋 or "Small Western Ocean" (Indian Ocean) and the Da Xiyang 大西洋 or "Great Western Ocean" (the North Atlantic).[54] In the early seventeenth century, Trigault and Ricci reported the arrival of the first Jesuits in Beijing in 1601 (following a previous, aborted attempt of 1598), specifically mentioning "the Great Occident" (the West) to their readers in Europe: "Licin [a high-ranking eunuch, dates unknown] ... received them most graciously in the name of the King. He wanted to know what their purpose was in bringing presents to the King, and they told him they were foreigners *from the Great Occident, as the Chinese call Europe*" (emphasis added).[55] This report of the Jesuits' reception

---

[49] Miller, *Peiresc's Mediterranean World*, 108–111.

[50] Translation in Miller, *Peiresc's Mediterranean World*, 110 (for original French text, see 490n.315).

[51] Dinko Fabris has studied nineteen extant chant books held by the Franciscans in Jerusalem—dating from the thirteenth to seventeenth centuries, they are of Italian provenance—and writes that it could be simplistically concluded that "for almost four centuries the *Custodia francescana* in Jerusalem performed liturgical chant in the Church of the Holy Sepulchre exactly as at any European [Catholic] church and monastery." Fabris, "Urban Musicologies," 59.

[52] Morar, "The Westerner."

[53] Yang, "Music, China, and the West," 2.

[54] Mosca, *From Frontier Policy to Foreign Policy*, 50; Zhang, *Making the New World Their Own*, 207–208; Jiang and Irving, "Cultural Practices."

[55] Translation from Ricci and Trigault, *China in the Sixteenth Century*, 372–373. Original text in Ricci and Trigault, *De christiana expeditione apud Sinas*, 409.

at court was intended for readers in Europe, and thus, certain Jesuits were instrumental in shaping, not only in China but also in Europe, new ideas of "the West."

Ricci brought a keyboard instrument (probably a clavichord or harpsichord), which was called a *xiqin* 西琴 ("Western zither"), and by order of the emperor, he taught eunuchs to play. His *Xiqin quyi bazhang* 西琴曲意八章 (*Eight Songs for a Western String Instrument*), of which only the texts were published, became possibly the first printed work by a musician from Europe to proclaim in its title an explicit link to the idea of the "Western" (although this refers specifically to the instrument rather than the music).[56] One of Ricci's Jesuit successors in China, Giulio Aleni (1582–1649), wrote in Chinese that "[t]he general name of the land is Europe. It is situated in the extreme west of China; hence it is called the Great West, Far West, or Extreme West. With reference to the ocean, it is also called the Great Western Ocean (Country)."[57] In his *Hsi-fang ta-wen* 西方答問 (*Questions and Answers Regarding the West*), he also used *xiqin* 西琴 as the name for the stringed keyboard instrument from Europe.[58] These early-seventeenth-century Jesuit descriptions of "the West" were laudatory, but more than a century later, as noted in chapter 5, Amiot used "the West" in a pejorative sense in his treatise on Chinese music (sent to Paris, where it was published in 1779). As Jiang has discussed, Amiot defended the antiquity of Chinese knowledge, positing that Egypt and Greece learned from it and that it was then disseminated to "the barbarous peoples of the West" (in other words, the ancient inhabitants of Europe).[59]

"The West" and Music as Viewed in Eighteenth-Century Europe

Well before Amiot, other thinkers in eighteenth-century Europe saw "the East" as the source of many musical practices that "the West" had imbibed. At the end of the sixteenth century, Morley wrote of late classical scholar

---

[56] See discussion in Lindorff, "Missionaries," 405–406; see also Jiang and Irving, "Cultural Practices."

[57] Mosca, *From Frontier Policy to Foreign Policy*, 50.

[58] Mish, "Creating an Image of Europe," 9, 42. Thanks to Qingfan Jiang for her advice on this point and for identifying for me the relevant part of Aleni's text.

[59] Original text in Amiot, *Mémoire*, 16. For discussion of the context of this statement, see Jiang, "In Search of the 'Oriental Origin,'" 126–127.

Boethius that "that it may be justly said, that if it had not beene for him the knowledge of musicke had not yet come into our Westerne part of the world."[60] In 1721, Alexander Malcolm (1685–1763), a Scottish writer on music based in Edinburgh, described regions to the east of Egypt as "Fountains" of knowledge for the "Western World":

> *Greece* was the Country in *Europe* where Learning first flourished; and tho' we believe they drew from other Fountains, as *Egypt* and the more Eastern Parts, yet they are the Fountains to us, and to all the Western World: Other Antiquities we neither know so well, nor so much of, at least of such as have any Pretence to a greater Antiquity; except the *Jewish*; and tho' we are sure they had *Musick*, yet we have no Account of the Inventors among them, for 'tis probable they learned it in *Egypt*; and therefore this Enquiry about the Inventors of *Musick* since the Flood, must be limited to *Greece*.[61]

Malcolm, unlike some writers of his time, specifies Greece territorially as a "Country in *Europe*" and the conduit for knowledge coming from the East. It is strange, though, that he does not mention the biblical Jubal as an inventor of music among the ancient Hebrews. His use of the term "Western World"—in contrast to "Eastern Parts"—also suggests a hemispheric binary in terms of music. A corresponding example can be found in the English translation of Cantemir's history of the Ottoman Empire (published in 1734–1735 and discussed in chapters 2 and 3): "If God grant me life and leisure, I will explain in a separate Treatise the whole Art [of music] according to the opinion of the Eastern World."[62]

Another example that points to East-West transmission but also "improvement" comes from the 1727 lute treatise by Ernst Gottlieb Baron (1696–1760), who writes: "We have previously observed the origin of our noble instrument and its state of extreme simplicity under the Egyptians and Greeks. Now we turn our eyes and disposition to the Occident and witness the manner in which it came from the borders of Asia into magnificent and charming Italy."[63] It is worth noting that some of these observations

---

[60] Morley, *A Plaine and Easie Introduction*, 184. This passage was reproduced and discussed in Hawkins, *A General History*, Vol. 3, 343.
[61] A. Malcolm, *A Treatise of Musick*, 465.
[62] Cantemir, *The History*, Vol. 1, 152n.14. See also Popescu-Judetz, *Prince Dimitrie Cantemir*, 32–33.
[63] Baron, *Study of the Lute*, 34. Original text in Baron, *Historisch-Theoretisch und Practische Untersuchung*, 28.

(especially those of Malcolm and Baron) foreshadow by more than a century the famous proposal of Georg Wilhelm Friedrich Hegel (1770–1831) in his *Vorlesungen über die Philosophie der Weltgeschichte* (*Lectures on the Philosophy of World History*), published posthumously in 1837, that "world history travels from east to west; for Europe is the absolute end of history, just as Asia is the beginning."[64]

Even so, few notions of "Westernness" in texts before 1800 were tied adjectivally to music in the sense that "Western music" implies today.[65] The precise adjective-noun term appears rarely. One example is by Johann Gottfried Walther (1684–1748), who lists "musica occidentaria [sic]" ("Western music") in his *Musicalisches Lexicon* (*Musical Lexicon*) of 1732 (figure 6.1). His definition of it, as a historical concept, refers explicitly to ecclesiastical use and liturgical function: "the choral music used in the Western church" (that is, not Orthodox but the Roman Catholic and, later, Protestant churches).[66] Walther's mention of this term, although it appears in a volume that became a highly influential reference work, is not the first; he cites its appearance in a work by Paul Hachenberg (1642–1680), *Summi viri Germania media* (*The Greatest Men of Central Germany*), a dissertation presented at Heidelberg and first published in 1675.[67] There the music of the medieval Frankish church is described as "Occidental."[68]

Among the smattering of eighteenth-century references combining "the West" and music, one of the most intriguing and telling cases of its inconsistency comes from Quantz's 1752 treatise on playing the flute. Quantz writes (and I quote the English translation from a popular twentieth-century edition): "it is beyond all doubt... that in Occidental lands the Germans were the first to revive, if not to establish, the basic principles of the transverse flute as well as of many other wind instruments."[69] In the original German text (from which the English was translated), the geographical designation appears as

---

[64] Hegel, *Lectures*, 197.
[65] Hawkins, for instance, refers to "the West" in a variety of ways, as some select examples demonstrate: Charlemagne's domain (Vol. 1, 378); the "western church" (Vol. 1, 287); the "western parts of Europe" (Vol. 2, 302); the "western part of the world" (Vol. 1, 343, quoting Morley, as mentioned above).
[66] Original text in Walther, *Musicalisches Lexicon*, 434. For further context, see Page, *The Christian West and Its Singers*.
[67] Hachenberg, *Pauli Hachenbergi P.P. Germania media*. It was republished a number of times. I have been unable to access the original publication but cite the third edition (1709) in the next note.
[68] Hachenberg, *Pauli Hachenbergi summi viri Germania media*, 139.
[69] Quantz, *On Playing the Flute*, 29.

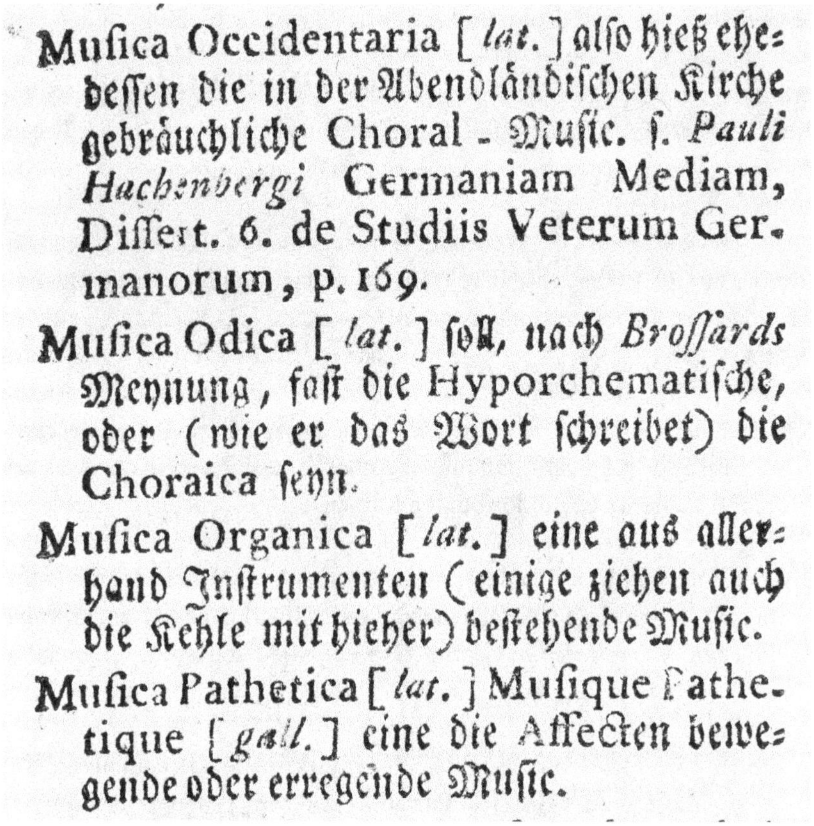

Musica Occidentaria [*lat.*] also hieß ehedessen die in der Abendländischen Kirche gebräuchliche Choral - Music. s. *Pauli Hachenbergi* Germaniam Mediam, Differt. 6. de Studiis Veterum Germanorum, p. 169.

Musica Odica [*lat.*] soll, nach *Broßards* Meynung, fast die Hyporchematische, oder (wie er das Wort schreibet) die Choraica seyn.

Musica Organica [*lat.*] eine aus allerhand Instrumenten (einige ziehen auch die Kehle mit hieher) bestehende Music.

Musica Pathetica [*lat.*] Musique Pathetique [*gall.*] eine die Affecten bewegende oder erregende Music.

Figure 6.1. Entry for "musica occidentaria [sic]," from Johann Gottfried Walther, *Musicalisches Lexicon: oder, Musicalische bibliothec* (Leipzig: W. Deer 1732), 434. © The British Library Board (1042.g.3).

"in den Abendländern" (figure 6.2).[70] However, it is important to note that Quantz's treatise was published in both German and French versions in the same year. The latter, also dedicated to King Frederick II "the Great" (1712–1786) of Prussia (whose language of preference at court was French, suggesting the greater social prestige ascribed to this version), states that the flute came not to Western regions but "to the North [*au Nord*]" (figure 6.3).[71] This last term, incidentally, is used by Rousseau to discuss the collective music culture of Europe that espoused the uses of harmony that he railed against.[72]

---

[70] Quantz, *Versuch*, 23. For an appraisal of and queries about the authorship of this treatise, see Jerold, "Quantz and Agricola."
[71] Quantz, *Essai d'une méthode*, 23.
[72] "Peuples du Nord." Rousseau, *Dictionnaire de musique*, 245.

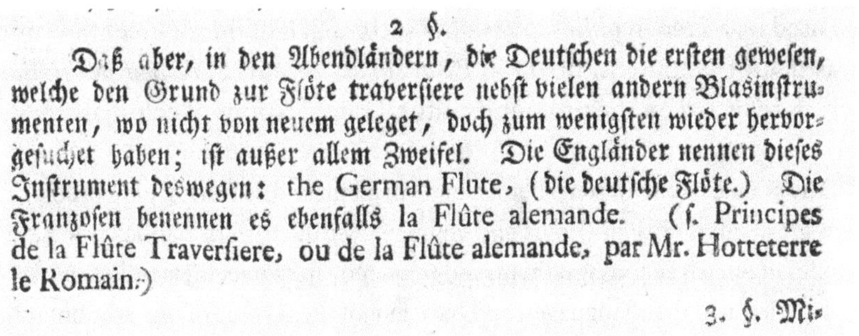

> 2 §.
> Daß aber, in den Abendländern, die Deutschen die ersten gewesen, welche den Grund zur Flöte traversiere nebst vielen andern Blasinstrumenten, wo nicht von neuem geleget, doch zum wenigsten wieder hervorgesuchet haben; ist außer allem Zweifel. Die Engländer nennen dieses Instrument deswegen: the German Flute, (die deutsche Flöte.) Die Franzosen benennen es ebenfalls la Flûte alemande. (f. Principes de la Flûte Traverfiere, ou de la Flûte alemande, par Mr. Hotteterre le Romain.)
>
> 3. §. Mi-

Figure 6.2. Johann Joachim Quantz, *Versuch einer Anweisung die Flötetraversiere zu spielen* (Berlin: Johann Friedrich Voss, 1752), 23. © The British Library Board (7895.ee.11).

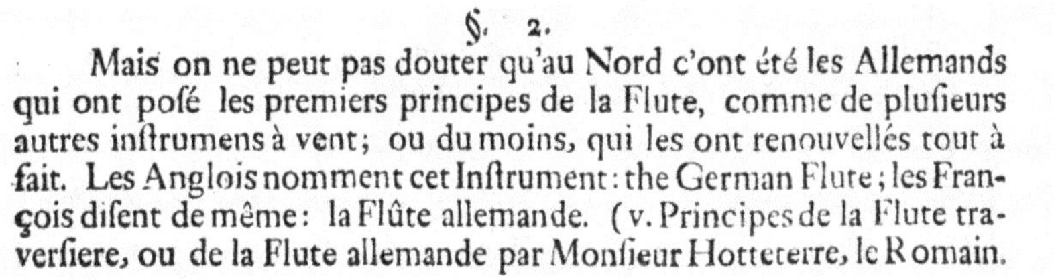

> §. 2.
> Mais on ne peut pas douter qu'au Nord c'ont été les Allemands qui ont posé les premiers principes de la Flute, comme de plufieurs autres inftrumens à vent; ou du moins, qui les ont renouvellés tout à fait. Les Anglois nomment cet Inftrument: the German Flute; les François difent de même: la Flûte allemande. (v. Principes de la Flute traverfiere, ou de la Flute allemande par Monfieur Hotteterre, le Romain.

Figure 6.3. Johann Joachim Quantz, *Essai d'une méthode pour apprendre à jouer de la flûte traversière* (Berlin: Chrétien Frédéric Voss, 1752), 23. Bibliothèque Nationale de France, Département de Musique, CG-97. Sourced from gallica.bnf.fr.

It is also worth observing that one of the most authoritative scholarly texts for the time, the *Encyclopédie*, gives both an astronomical and a geographical entry for "Occident" (in the eleventh volume, published in 1765). For geography, Jean le Rond d'Alembert (1717–1783) observes that "Occidental" is a relational term applying to countries situated at the setting of the sun in regard to other countries, and gives four examples. First, the Holy Roman Empire was called Occidental "as opposed to the Oriental empire, which was that of Constantinople"; second, the Roman church as Occidental in contrast to the Greek church (and other Orthodox churches); third, "the French, the Spanish, the Italians, etc. are called *western nations* with regard to the Asian [nations]"; and finally, the West Indies and the East Indies.[73] Yet what was perhaps the most significant binary of East-West to

---

[73] Original text in d'Alembert, "Occident," Vol. 11, 331.

be used by a French *philosophe* in the second half of the eighteenth century was that of Voltaire in his 1756 *Essai sur les moeurs et l'esprit des nations*, which reflected on the profound cultural ramifications of colonialism:

> The people of our western hemisphere, in all these discoveries, gave proofs of a great superiority of genius and courage over the eastern nations. We have settled ourselves amongst them, and frequently in spite of their resistance. We have learned their languages, and have taught them some of our arts; but nature hath given them one advantage which overbalances all ours; which is, that they do not want us, but we them.[74]

Voltaire and other contemporary thinkers thus reflexively recognized the imbalances of this relationship, acknowledging Europe's debt to Asia and other parts of the world, especially the Americas.[75]

Within the continent of Europe itself, there have long been notions of an East–West binary, which has been refracted in the musical past and in musicology in diverse ways. I mentioned at the outset of this chapter some of the Cold War legacies in musicological thought, as highlighted by Taruskin. The Cold War division of "East" and "West" is one political and conceptual boundary out of many, but as Davies has shown, there are multiple "fault lines" within the continent of Europe, from the Roman *limes* (frontiers) of antiquity to the Iron Curtain (figure 6.4).[76] In his conceptual configuration, other divisions are made on the basis of Catholic or Orthodox confessions of Christianity and the Ottoman advance into Europe. There is no clear single way to define "eastern" and "western" Europe.

A number of scholars have approached notions of "eastern Europe" in ways that shed considerable light on the complexity of the question.[77] For instance, Samson has documented in detail musical life in the Balkans, a vast southeastern region of the continent that incorporates many aspects

---

[74] English translation from Voltaire, *The Works*, Vol. 4, 179. Original text in Voltaire, *Collection complette*, Vol. 9, 506. Osterhammel uses this quotation as an epigraph at the opening of his monumental study *Unfabling the East*, 1.

[75] This notion was explored in depth in Raynal, *Histoire philosophique*. However, that work contains very few direct references to music.

[76] Davies describes the *limes* as "dividing Europe into one area with a Roman past and another area without it." Davies, *Europe: A History*, 27.

[77] For a discussion of "ambiguities" in defining eastern Europe, see Guénoun, *About Europe*, 51–53.

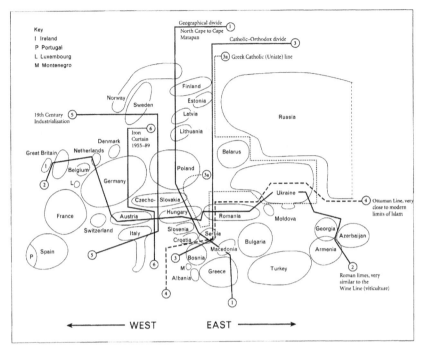

Figure 6.4. Map of "East–West Fault Lines in Europe." In Norman Davies, *Europe: A History* (Oxford: Oxford University Press, 1996), 18. Reproduced by kind permission of Norman Davies.

of musics from "Eastern" and "Western" traditions.[78] As Wendy Bracewell has pointed out in her detailed study of "East European" travel writing, "ecclesiastical divisions, above all, shaped the travellers' representations of the world: 'East' and 'West' most often referred to the eastern and western churches. 'Europe,' if it was used at all, remained a geographical term, not a synonym for a shared Christianity."[79] Larry Wolff similarly notes that some travelers in the eighteenth century had a sense of leaving "Europe" as they entered its eastern parts and writes that the uncertain boundaries between Europe and Asia "encouraged the construction of Eastern Europe

---

[78] Samson, *Music in the Balkans*. Ivan Moody has suggested new approaches to the study of "southern" Europe in "The Compass Revisited." For discussion of notions of "northern nations" in the eighteenth century, see Gelbart, *The Invention*, 63, 69, 241.

[79] Bracewell, "The Limits of Europe," 76.

as a paradox of simultaneous inclusion and exclusion, Europe but not Europe."[80] As much as people from "western Europe" fashioned ideas of "eastern Europe," the question of how populations in "eastern Europe" used the specific geographical term "western" to frame neighboring music cultures in the early modern period—beyond the scope of the exclusively self-referential sources examined for this book—suggests a fertile field for future research: what terms did they use? Of course, it must be remembered that in the eighteenth century, some thinkers described many parts of what we might call "eastern Europe"—and also parts of "western Europe," as the quotation from the French version of Quantz's treatise showed above—as "the North."[81]

Music played a major part in these multiple processes of oppositional self-definition. Kevin Karnes has noted the role of the descriptions of aural experiences by travelers, including Herder, in this respect; he also observes the prevailing belief that traveling east involved going "backward in time."[82] The perceived alterity of the vocal traditions of the eastern parts of Europe attracted particular attention from Herder in his published collections of *Volkslieder* (*Folk Songs*) in 1778–1779 and 1807.[83] Catherine Mayes also observes that the people whom Herder studied "were a highly abstract peasant class rooted in a utopian past whose vernacular he idealized seemingly because it corresponded to his own taste."[84] Although these communities were removed from lofty ideals of "art music," some of their musics were incorporated by composers in Vienna and other cities into accessible repertory—for example, in the form of "Hungarian dances"—for domestic performance by musicians who were even novices; as Mayes writes, these "evoked a world of primitive music-making in which an undoubtedly largely imaginary past had persisted into the present."[85] There was, in this way, a reinforcement for the elite of the "modernity" of the kinds of western European "art music" that shaped their aesthetic frameworks.

---

[80] Wolff, *Inventing Eastern Europe*, 7.

[81] See Stråth, "The Conquest of the North," 102.

[82] Karnes, "Inventing Eastern Europe," esp. 79.

[83] Bohlman notes that "the density of songs from Eastern European and Baltic sources increases as the individual books appear chronologically." Herder and Bohlman, *Song Loves the Masses*, 72. See also an assessment of Herder's influence in the coining of the folk-song concept in Gelbart, *The Invention*, 102–110.

[84] Mayes, "Eastern European National Music," 74.

[85] Mayes, "Eastern European National Music," 90.

The Rise of "Western Music" as a Cultural System

If "Western music" (or "Occidental music") was not understood in the eighteenth century in the way we think of it today, then to impose that term and concept—without careful qualification—on music from before c. 1800 is anachronistic. Its subsequent meanings referred not to Christian liturgical music of the "Western" church(es) but rather to a whole system of music that was synonymous with ideas of "modern European music" emerging in the late eighteenth and early nineteenth centuries. An early example of the term "Western music" that signals this latter totalizing sense appears in the famous German periodical *Allgemeine musikalisches Zeitung* (*General Musical Newspaper*) in 1833, referring to composers representing "images of the Orient" in works of "Occidental music."[86] Whereas Fonton in 1751 used the continental term "European music" in relation to "Oriental [Eastern] Music," as discussed in chapter 4, we now see here a hemispheric term that balances "East" with "West." Just a year later, a review of Willard's *Treatise on the Music of Hindoostan* (Calcutta, 1834) refers to "music of *the west* both ancient and modern" (emphasis added).[87] In French, however, the eventual conflation of the concept of "European music" with that of "Western music" seems to be almost a historiographical accident of translation. The title of Kiesewetter's 1834 publication *Geschichte der europäisch-abendländischen oder unsrer heutigen Musik* (*History of Western-European or Our Contemporary/Modern Music*) was described in French by Fétis in 1835 simply as "Histoire de la musique occidentale" ("History of Western Music").[88] While this is a simplification of the terminology, it also removes "European" from Kiesewetter's original compound adjective.[89]

Shortly thereafter, "la musique occidentale" was used by Edmond de Coussemaker (1805–1876) in his 1839–1840 study of the composer and theorist Hucbald of St. Amand (c. 850–930), which he prefaced with a "Historical

---

[86] "Mehre Tonsetzer beeifern sich jetzt, aus den Bildern des Orients eine Auswahl für occidentalische Musik zu treffen." "Kurzer Anzeigen," col. 387. Thanks to David Black for pointing out this reference.
[87] "Scientific Intelligence," 248. Thanks to Sarah Kirby for sharing this source. See discussion of Willard's treatise in chapter 5.
[88] Kiesewetter, *Geschichte der europäisch-abendländischen oder unsrer heutigen Musik*; Kiesewetter, *History of the Modern Music of Western Europe*. The translation of the title into French comes from Fétis, *Biographie universelle*, Vol. 1, cxcix.
[89] In English, however, it was translated by Robert Müller in 1848 as *History of the Modern Music of Western Europe*. Among the three languages (German, French, and English), there appears to be little semantic agreement on precise terminology at this stage.

Sketch of Occidental Music from the Origin of Christianity to the Tenth Century" ("Esquisse historique de la musique occidentale depuis l'origine du christianisme jusqu'au Xe siècle") and followed with three appendices (on ancient Greek music, the history and use of neumes, and the history of instruments).[90] Largely, the word "Occidental" accompanies "Europe" as an adjective—except, notably, in the work's title. In two instances, though, he specifically asserts that the bow for string instruments had Western origins, putting a broader "Occident" into a binary contrast with "Orient." He observes that there is no evidence for bows in either ancient Egypt or ancient Greece, arguing for an "Occidental origin" and citing the Welsh crwth.[91] However, in 1856, Fétis insisted on the bow's Eastern origins, in his study of bowed string instruments, stating twice on the same page: *"There is nothing in the West which has not come from the East. In many places of my writings I have stated this truth, and now again repeat it."*[92] Such a comment seems to align with the views of Hegel (mentioned above) regarding the move of cultures from east to west.[93] Other scholars at the time also acknowledged and embraced cultures to the east, seeing them as a source of musical origins. In 1864, Carl Engel (1818–1882) wrote about "the Eastern origin of our own music," stating that "most of our musical inventions and contrivances appear to have been in use, though less perfect, among ancient Asiatic nations."[94] Citing a range of resemblances in music theory, practice, and instruments, he declared: "Such coincidences, of which more might be cited, in whatever manner they may be explained, reveal a closer affinity between ancient Asiatic music and our own than is usually supposed to exist."[95]

Gradually, the idea of "European music" began to overlap with new uses of the term "Occidental music" or "Western music" (as translated into a variety of languages). Scholars including Alexander J. Ellis (1814–1890), August Wilhelm Ambros (1816–1876), Hermann von Helmholtz (1821–1894), Carl Stumpf (1848–1936), Guido Adler (1855–1941), and Curt Sachs (1881–1959) all used the term "Western music" or "Occidental music" in various ways; Adler, for instance, wrote of "europäisch-abendländische Musik" (translated

---

[90] Coussemaker, "Hucbald," 181–218. On Coussemaker, see Christensen, *Stories of Tonality*, 79–89.
[91] Coussemaker, "Hucbald," 213–214, 356.
[92] English translation from Fétis, *Notice of Anthony Stradivari*, 9. Original text in Fétis, *Antoine Stradivari*, 11.
[93] Hegel, *Lectures*, 197.
[94] Engel, *The Music of the Most Ancient Nations*, 363.
[95] Engel, *The Music of the Most Ancient Nations*, 365. This sentence opens the very final paragraph of his book.

as "European, Occidental music").[96] However, both Engel and Richard Wallaschek (1860–1917) avoided the use of the term "West" or "Western"—except in their strict geographical meanings—preferring instead "European," in their respective publications.[97]

In the early twentieth century, there emerged what would become a persistent trope about "Western [art] music": the idea of its exceptionalism in global terms. This was often linked to ideas of its "rationalization," as proposed by sociologist Max Weber (1864–1920). Weber connected music directly to his theories of "Western civilization," citing harmony, the "rational" design of instruments with resonating bodies made according to specific ratios, and tuning systems. In his famous work of 1905, *Die protestantische Ethik und der Geist des Kapitalismus* (*The Protestant Ethic and the Spirit of Capitalism*), Weber made claims for the uniqueness of music "in the Occident" as early as the fourth paragraph of his introduction, arguing for the singularity of musical ideas such as harmonic structures, instrumentation, notation, and genres. First pointing out some shared human practices in musical expression, he embarked on a Eurocentric definition that essentializes and exceptionalizes the practice of music in what he sees as Western capitalist society. He begins with an initially inclusive overview:

> The musical ear of other peoples has probably been even more sensitively developed than our own, certainly not less so. Polyphonic music of various kinds has been widely distributed over the earth. The co-operation of a number of instruments and also the singing of parts have existed elsewhere. All our rational tone intervals have been known and calculated.[98]

Weber then goes on to argue, erroneously, for the "uniqueness" of specific aspects of music "in the Occident":

> But rational harmonious music, both counterpoint and harmony, formation of the tone material on the basis of three triads with the harmonic third; our chromatics and enharmonics, not interpreted in terms of space, but, since the Renaissance, of harmony; our orchestra, with its string quartet

---

[96] Adler, "Umfang, Methode und Ziel," 8; Adler and Mugglestone, "Guido Adler's 'The Scope, Method, and Aim,'" 8.
[97] Engel, *The Music of the Most Ancient Nations*; Engel, *An Introduction*; Wallaschek, *Primitive Music*.
[98] M. Weber, *The Protestant Ethic*, 14.

as a nucleus, and the organization of ensembles of wind instruments; our bass accompaniment; our system of notation, which has made possible the composition and production of *modern musical works*, and thus their very survival; our sonatas, symphonies, operas; and finally, as means to all these, our fundamental instruments, the organ, piano, violin, etc.; *all these things are known only in the Occident*, although programme music, tone poetry, alteration of tones and chromatics, have existed in various musical traditions as means of expression.[99] [emphasis added]

Although quoted less often than text from Weber's music-focused work *The Rational and Social Foundations of Music* (published posthumously in 1958; an earlier version appeared in 1921 as *Die rationalen und soziologischen Grundlagen der Musik*), this passage is a clear credo of "Western" musical exceptionalism.[100] Ideas from it are not infrequently echoed in triumphalist narratives of "Western music" today or evoked in political speeches or ideological position statements.[101]

Weber used the simple term "Western music," but we can also trace the evolution of the three-word term "Western art music" (used mostly in English) from the early twentieth century onward. The earliest identifiable use, with a hyphenated adjective-noun combination for "art music," appears to be by Percy Grainger (1882–1961) in an article titled "The Impress of Personality in Unwritten Music," from the very first volume of the *Musical Quarterly* (published in 1915). Under the subheading "Primitive Music Is Too Complex for Untrained Modern Ears," he stated:

While so many of the greatest musical geniuses listen spellbound to the unconscious, effortless musical utterances of primitive man, the general educated public, on the other hand, though willing enough to applaud adaptations of folk-songs by popular composers, shows little or no appreciation of such art in its unembellished original state, when, indeed, it

---

[99] M. Weber, *The Protestant Ethic*, 14–15.

[100] See M. Weber, *The Rational and Social Foundations*. For a critique of this treatise, see Wierzbicki, "Max Weber and Musicology."

[101] See an example in a speech given in Warsaw on July 6, 2017, by US President Donald J. Trump, who stated: "if we don't forget who are, we just can't be beaten. Americans will never forget. The nations of Europe will never forget. We are the fastest and the greatest community. There is nothing like our community of nations. The world has never known anything like our community of nations. We write symphonies. We pursue innovation. We celebrate our ancient heroes, embrace our timeless traditions and customs, and always seek to explore and discover brand-new frontiers." Trump, "Remarks by President Trump"; also cited by Cheng in *Loving Music till It Hurts*, 11.

generally is far too complex (as regards rhythm, dynamics, and scales) to appeal to listeners whose ears have not been subjected to the ultra-refining influence of close association with the subtle developments of *our latest Western art-music*.[102] [emphasis added]

Grainger made this comment in the context of lauding the recent trends of composers being inspired by traditional musics from many regions. Yet, in case it appears triumphalist at the surface level, it is worth contextualizing and mitigating his statement by noting that in the same article, he described "Western civilization" as "ruthless"; observing the vulnerable status of many traditions, he also urged "composers and students" (of his own kind of music) to document them for posterity.[103]

Major studies of "Western art music" in the twentieth and twenty-first centuries have defined their scope in different ways, demonstrating simultaneously the reification and the vagueness of the concept. In the monumental study by Paul Henry Lang (1901–1991) published in 1941, *Music in Western Civilization*, the author at first appeared to take the scope of its study as being self-evident. Briefly referring to the infamous book of 1918 *Der Untergang des Abendlandes* (*The Decline of the West*) by Oswald Spengler (1880–1936), Lang wrote about debates concerning music of the twentieth century before referring to the geocultural locus of the art form as follows on the last page of his narrative: "The music of the new century will rise from the civilization of democracy and has, indeed, already sprung from the unspoiled and untapped energies of the New World and the countries of the peripheries of Europe, which heretofore were outside the main territory of Western civilization."[104] While mentioning its expansion, he defines "the West" in relation and in opposition to its global surrounds.

Nevertheless, a polarized view of the West and the proverbial "rest" was by no means shared by all scholars at that time. Others still acknowledged the porousness of supposed boundaries and the equivalences and analogous nature of practices from each "side." For example, German Jewish ethnomusicologist Robert Lachmann (1892–1939) stated in a radio broadcast in Jerusalem in 1937 that "for about a century"—quite coincidentally, Lachmann seems to mean a century since the 1830s, which we have already

---

[102] Grainger, "The Impress of Personality," 417.
[103] Grainger, "The Impress of Personality," 434–435.
[104] Lang, *Music in Western Civilization*, 1030. His mention of Spengler is on page 1029. On Spengler, see also Appiah, *The Lies That Bind*, 201.

seen was a decade of origin for new notions of "Western music"—"by far the greatest and most important part of the musical production in Central and Western Europe has been conceived independent of special occasions. The legitimate place for this kind of music is the concert hall with its neutral atmosphere where people assemble with the sole object of listening to music and of appreciating its intrinsic qualities. In contrast with this, applied music, i.e., music composed for definite social ends or events, has been pushed into the background."[105] He goes on to assert:

> It is of little help to insist on the contrast which exists between present day musical practice in East and West. This would easily lead to exaggerations and false generalities. *We had better remember that, a few centuries ago, the social functions of European music were not at all unlike those of Eastern.* At that time and even more when we go still farther back we find that in Europe as well music fell into groups vastly differing from each other according to their function in social life and to their distribution among different social classes. John [*sic*] Sebastian Bach's Cantatas, to mention one instance, were intended not to figure each as an item in some concert programme irrespective of time and place, but for immediate use at his own church on a particular Sunday.[106] [emphasis added]

Lachmann mentions a process of change since the eighteenth century. He says "European music" rather than "Western music"; although he certainly does refer to a binary of "East" and "West," it is in terms of emphasizing a sense of greater analogy between them in previous eras. Another German Jewish scholar, Sachs, took a different view, with a longer timescale of divergence. He combined the sense of Europe and "the West" while acknowledging the links with "the Orient," writing on the other side of the Atlantic in 1943: "The Orient has kept alive melodic styles that medieval Europe choked to death under the hold of harmony, and the Middle East still plays the instruments that it gave to the West a thousand years ago."[107] Such observations reflected and reinforced the ideas of Orientalism, emphasizing the idea of "the East" as ancient and timeless and Europe, or eventually in the nineteenth century "the West," as the locus of modernity and change.[108]

---

[105] Lachmann, *The Oriental Music Broadcasts*, 59.
[106] Lachmann, *The Oriental Music Broadcasts*, 59.
[107] Sachs, *The Rise of Music*, 29.
[108] Said, *Orientalism*.

After the Second World War, Walter Wiora (1906–1997), in his classic study *The Four Ages of Music* (1966; first published in German in 1961 as *Die vier Weltalter der Musik*), offered a global reading of the art form, identifying "Western music" as an outlier of human musical achievement.[109] For Wiora, the history of music could be divided into four ages, with fluid chronological boundaries: the first was the "Prehistoric and Early Period," the second was represented by "Music in the High Civilizations of Antiquity and the Orient," the third involved the emergence of "The Special Position of Western Music," while the fourth age is our own: "The Age of Techniques and of Global Industrial Culture." Partly in response to Wiora's fourth age, Nettl in 1985 examined the global impact of "Western music" on diverse music cultures around the world and gave a list of characteristics defining twentieth-century Western art music that "help to justify viewing Western music as a unified system."[110]

Looking back on his career in 2017, Nettl also recalled that during his student days, he "often had to defend the validity of what was then called comparative musicology"; he noted that "Western classical music became an enemy, and we came to call it, somewhat derisively, WEAM [Western European Art Music]. Later, the enmity between these camps receded, but coping with WEAM has always been and remains an issue in ethnomusicology."[111] Reflecting on mid-twentieth-century canons of ethnomusicology, Bohlman commented in 1992: "Western art music . . . [was] dismissed [by ethnomusicologists in the 1950s] . . . because it no longer was of particular interest to ethnomusicologists or because the long-awaited cross-influences just were not happening."[112] He made this observation in a volume in which many scholars from both ethnomusicology and historical musicology surveyed the fields, looking for common ground.[113] In line with this intra- and cross-disciplinary critique, Treitler coined another acronym, "WECT," to describe "the West European Classical Tradition," the idea of which he

---

[109] Wiora, *The Four Ages of Music*. Interestingly, the title of the original German publication could perhaps also be rendered in English as *The Four Global Ages of Music*. Although this subtle distinction was lost in translation, it is evident that Wiora aimed toward an all-encompassing and desegregated worldview of music history. One also wonders if his book's title was a reference to the 1816 song "Die vier Weltalter" ("The Four World-Ages," Op. 111, No. 3) by Schubert to a text by Friedrich Schiller (1759–1809).

[110] He continues: "they also can be related to a variety of characteristics of Western culture at large." B. Nettl, *The Western Impact*, 5.

[111] B. Nettl, "Have You Changed Your Mind?," 54. For a collection of recent ethnomusicological studies of Western art music, see Nooshin, *The Ethnomusicology of Western Art Music*.

[112] Bohlman, "Ethnomusicology's Challenge," 127.

[113] See a range of examples in Bergeron and Bohlman, *Disciplining Music*.

defined in 1996 as "a narration of the rise of Europe, of Western culture, of European music. It is history functioning as myth, providing criteria for the representation of music."[114] A few years earlier, he had additionally observed: "Music history is, among other things, a discourse of myth through which 'Western civilization' contemplates and presents itself."[115] The horizon of "the West" in music history seemed to be entering twilight.

Changes in scholarly paradigms do not occur uniformly across space and time, of course. In 1999, Ellen Koskoff described making comparisons in her musicology classes between the musical contexts of 1680s Italy and those of India, with the result that "soon, some students began to complain. They said I was infecting Western music with 'creeping multiculturalism.' They argued that other cultures' musics were irrelevant for them to learn because they would only be tested on Western music when applying to graduate schools."[116] Only a quarter of a century ago, it was still common for many musicologists and ethnomusicologists to consider "European music" or "Western music" as a culture system with boundaries that were (purportedly) clearly delineated, if a little frayed at the edges. Since then, however, this situation has been and is currently changing rapidly, especially with the rise of global music history (enthusiasm for which is shared within historical musicology, ethnomusicology, and music theory) and the burgeoning of research, publications, and new courses in that field.[117] Increasing visibility of diversity within the globally connected community of music scholars, increased democratization of the disciplines, and moves to increase access to scholarly resources are all contributing to positive transformations in the disciplines. In many ongoing discussions, the question of how to decenter many areas of music studies—in other words, transcend its traditional focus on "Western art music" (or, inversely, the non-consideration of it, in some areas of ethnomusicology)—has remained a persistent theme.[118]

---

[114] Treitler, "Toward a Desegregated Music Historiography," 3.
[115] Treitler, "Gender and Other Dualities," 23.
[116] Koskoff, "What Do We Want to Teach?," 557.
[117] See Strohm, *Studies on a Global History of Music*; Strohm, *The Music Road*; Strohm, *Transcultural Music History*; Law, Castro Pantoja, and Chang, "Teaching Global Music History"; Bloechl et al., "Colloquy"; Bloechl, "Editorial"; Takao, "Global Music History"; Takao, "Towards a Global Baroque."
[118] See, for example, Ewell, "Music Theory and the White Racial Frame"; Rehding, "Can the History of Theory Be Decentered?"; Walker, "Towards a Decolonized Music History Curriculum"; Janz and Yang, "Introduction."

One way, among many, of contributing to the decentering of knowledge is to look at the historical processes that created those centers. As this chapter has shown, a monolithic notion of "Western music" emerged through the essentializing power of the adjective referring to the abstract and changing notion of "the West." Yet the meanings evoked by the current notion of "Western music"—or "Occidental music"—cannot be traced in European languages any earlier than the 1830s. The term itself is older, but when it did appear in previous centuries (and rarely so), it was used to denote contrasts between the liturgical music practices of different forms of Christianity. It referred only to church music, and usually plainchant, not to a whole system of music. New notions about "Western music" in a relational and reified sense were initiated in the nineteenth century, largely as a counterpart to Orientalist ideas of "Eastern music." They evolved radically in the twentieth century, being marked especially by the "East-West" divide of the Cold War (which made many societies formerly considered "Western" to be part of the "Eastern bloc"). Our sweep through historiography shows that a significant number of these ideas and their attendant discourses of exceptionalism arose through direct European contact with the rest of the world and the reception in Europe of knowledge about the rest of the world. These notions emerged as part of broader patterns of colonialism and imperialism that projected a sense of assumed universality of "Western" culture while at the same time asserting political, cultural, and economic hegemony.

Epilogue

In the seventeenth and eighteenth centuries, musicians and artists engaged with the origin myths of the continent's name from diverse perspectives, bringing issues of gender, patriarchy, religion, and politics to the fore. They represented the continent allegorically in ways that contributed to the rise of Eurocentrism in thought and practice. These contexts gave rise to an understanding of Europe as a geographical place and a conceptual space, within which musicking occurred and a Republic of Music operated. People traveling from Europe to other parts of the world increasingly defined themselves or were described as "European," and the signifier became linked to musicians' ears and selves in thought and discourse. Over the long eighteenth century, the notion of "European music" as a category that transcended national difference gradually emerged through intercontinental comparison in other parts of the world. It simultaneously began to be applied to music within the continent itself from the 1770s, after the resolution of battles between national styles. By the early nineteenth century, people self-defining as "Europeans" had collectively constructed what they considered to be a "universal language" of music, transnational and polylocal, removable from its original contexts and transportable. "Modern European music," coalescing from the 1830s with the concept of "Western music," began to be seen as a coherent, homogeneous, and monolithic entity. Owing to the emerging standardization or at least equivalence of institutional, social, and technological frameworks, it could be reproduced at a far remove, as a polycentric art form.

The idea of "European music" as a homogeneous pan-continental music system was far from being concrete in the long eighteenth century, despite assumptions that have long been made to that effect and continue frequently to be made. Given the sporadic use of the term "Western music" before the nineteenth century and the specificity of its meaning (that is, Christian sacred musics that are not Orthodox), it seems potentially misleading to apply it retrospectively to pre-1800 repertory and practices, at least in the totalizing sense with which it has been used for almost two centuries of music scholarship. As regards the use of the adjective "modern" in the historiography of music, this is always deictic, and in the early modern period, it was often pejorative, frequently evoking "conceptual imperialism" in reference to the author's own perceived heritage or condescension when used in cross-cultural and colonialist senses. This term must be read in context and interpreted accordingly.

What, then, can we do? It seems to me important to recognize, reflexively, that problematic labels arose at specific points in time and, for diverse reasons, to choose to interpret them according to the conceptual circumstances and cultural prejudices that led to their use. (By way of comparison, and as mentioned in chapter 6, it is worth noting again that the terms "Eastern music" and "Oriental music" have fallen out of use in musicology, unless being quoted for critique.) We can also attempt not to project "European music" or "Western music" (as a cultural system) retrospectively on earlier periods—at least, not without careful qualification.[1] I hesitate to make any seemingly concrete recommendations, since I am just one voice among many, but I think that a recognition of the chronological frame of a concept is a powerful way to mitigate its effects. We can also think of music as a practice and a process rather than a product or a set of works, as Small suggested in the introduction to his concept of "musicking": "music is not a thing at all but an activity, something that people do."[2] I suggest that unless essentializing labels were used at the time—such as "French music" and "Italian music" in the eighteenth century—we ought to talk about music as being "in" or "of" a place and be increasingly careful about applying monolithic category names that have the potential to come across as homogenizing and essentializing. I am not necessarily advocating the avoidance of concepts and terms such as "European music" or "Western music" altogether but merely pointing out that in the context of documentary sources from western Europe in the long eighteenth century, they have very specific meanings that require acknowledgment.

As research and higher education in music face increasing challenges in their scope and methods, the need to rethink essentialized categories that have become reified through adjectival anachronism becomes more urgent.[3]

---

[1] Certainly, in my own writing from now on relating to music from the long eighteenth century (or earlier), I will aim to avoid using the adjective-noun compounds "European music" or "Western music" unless I am evoking the meanings they had at the time, based on the source materials from which they emerge, or critiquing the ways in which they have been interpreted since.
[2] Small, *Musicking*, 2.
[3] For a thoughtful reflection on the issue of "unpacking European exceptionalism," see Walker, "Towards a Decolonized Music History Curriculum," 13–16.

Discourse is a powerful tool with long-standing influences and implications, and it is clear today that ideas of "European music" and "Western music" are so thoroughly embedded within discursive practices of musicology and the language of the public sphere that they are not often questioned.[4] Yet the scrutiny of this kind of language remains essential to the decolonization of the mind, especially when contemporary movements of ethnonationalism, ethnoregionalism, and populist politics harness music history and aesthetics to support their ideologies. Currently, the disciplines of historical musicology and ethnomusicology are embarking on new global history paradigms that aim to "provincialize Europe," to use Chakrabarty's term, and re-evaluate music history accordingly. At this juncture, it becomes increasingly essential to critically analyze the constructs of "Europe," "European music," and "Western music." In such a way, we may further understand how certain cultural discourses, political underpinnings, and economic interests that surround these terms and concepts have long skewed the epistemological field of "Western" music history in their own favor.

---

[4] On taking labels in musical thought "for granted," see Gelbart, *The Invention*.

Bibliography

Archival Sources

"[Allégorie des quatre continents]." In "Recueil d'éventails de la fin du XVIIIe siècle." Engraving, 1794–1798. Bibliothèque Nationale de France, Département Estampes et Photographie, LC-13-FOL, Vol. 1, "VI.38.18" [ESTNUM-19423].

Amiot, Jean-Joseph-Marie. "De la musique moderne des Chinois." Manuscript, c. 1754 [1755–1780 in catalogue]. Bibliothèque Nationale de France, Département de la Musique, RES VMB MS-14.

Archivum Romanum Societatis Iesu. JapSin 117.

Bianchi, Francesco. "Europa rapita." Manuscript, [1791–1800]. Biblioteca del Conservatorio Statale di Musica Giuseppe Verdi, Milan, Mus. Tr. ms. 212.

Cantemir, Dimitrie. "Incrementa et decrementa othmanici imperii." Manuscript, c. 1720. Houghton Library, Harvard University, MS Lat 224.

Colista, Lelio. "Europa rapita," in "Villanelle spirituali et altri recitativi a una voce: Del P. Iac.º Caproli Romano." Manuscript, [1641–1660]. Biblioteca del Conservatorio di Musica S. Pietro a Majella, 33.4.14, Vol. 2, 259–280.

Duport, Nicolas, and Dugué, Alexandre Julien. "Jupiter et Europe, divertissement nouveau representé devant le roy sur le théatre des petits appartemens à Versailles. Les paroles sont du Sieur Fuselier. La musique est des Sieurs ** & Dugué, ordinaire de la Musique du Roy." Manuscript, 1749–1798. Bibliothèque Nationale de France, Département de la Musique, RES VMA MS-1241.

Fonton, Charles. "Essay sur la musique orientale comparée a la musique europeene." In Paul Louis Roualle de Boisgelou, "Recueil de diverses pieces sur la musique." Manuscript, 1751–1800. Bibliothèque Nationale de France, Département Bibliothèque–Musée de l'Opéra, B-24 (1-10), ff. 149r–190v.

Fonton, Charles. "Essay sur la musique orientale compareé [sic] a la musique européene [sic] ou l'on tache de donner une ideé [sic] generale de la musique des peuples de l'orient, de leur gout particulier, de leur regles dans le chant, et la combinaison des tons, avec une notion abregeé de leurs principaux instrumens." Manuscript (autograph), 1751. Bibliothèque Nationale de France, Département des Manuscrits, NAF 4023, first part (ff. A–D, pages 1–143).

"The Four Continents (c. 1770): Derby Porcelain, Derby (manufacturer)." Porcelain, c. 1770. National Gallery of Victoria, Melbourne, 382.1-4-D4. The Colin Templeton Collection, Gift of Mrs Colin Templeton, 1942.

Galuppi, Baldassare. "Mundi salus." Manuscript, 1776. Bibliothèque Nationale de France, Département de la Musique, Ms. 1889.

Lully, Jean-Baptiste. "Ballet royal de Flore: Dansé par sa majesté le mois de fevrier 1669. Recueilly et copiée par Philidor laisné [sic] en 1690." Manuscript copy by André Philidor, 1690. Bibliothèque Nationale de France, Département Centre Technique du Livre, RES-F-515, 38–58.

Lully, Jean-Baptiste. "Deuxieme Divertissement." In "Partition des huit divertissemens des vieux ballets mis en musique par Mr de Lully, sur-intendant de la Musique du Roy. Copiez par ordre exprés de son altesse serenissime Monseigneur le Comte de Toulouze, par M. Philidor l'aîné, ordinaire de la Musique du Roy, et garde de toute sa Bibliotheque de Musique, et par son fils aîné, l'an 1703." Manuscript copy by André Philidor, 1703. 2 vols. Bibliothèque Nationale de France, Département Centre Technique du Livre, RES-F-1710, Vol. 1, 30–57 [ff. 18–32].

Lully, Jean-Baptiste. "La naissance de Venus," in "Ballets de Lully, tom. 3." Manuscript copy, c. 1700. Staatsbibliothek zu Berlin–Preußischer Kulturbesitz, Musikabteilung, Am.B 322 (2), ff. 33r–80v.

Melani, Alessandro. "L'Europa." Manuscript, [seventeenth century]. Österreichische Nationalbibliothek. Mus.Hs.18740 MUS MAG. https://digital.onb.ac.at/RepViewer/viewer.faces?doc=DTL_4269951.

Paer, Ferdinand. "Arianna consolata." Manuscript copy, [1801–1810]. 2 vols. Biblioteca del Conservatorio di Musica Luigi Cherubini, Florence, F.P.T.342.

Ptolemy. *Harmonics*. Gr. 322 (coll. 711). Biblioteca Marciana, Venice.

Scarlatti, Alessandro. "Europa rapita da Giove in forma di toro. Cantata a voce sola del sigr. Alessandro Scarlatti." Manuscript, [eighteenth century]. Bibliothèque Nationale de France, Département de la Musique, D.11840 (8), ff. 165r–175v.

Other Sources

Académie Française. "Le Dictionnaire de l'Académie Française." Vol. 2. Paris: Coignard, 1694. ARTFL Project: Dictionnaires d'autrefois, 2022. https://artfl-project.uchicago.edu/content/dictionnaires-dautrefois

Académie Française. "Le Dictionnaire de l'Académie Française." 4th ed. Vol. 1. Paris: Brunet, 1762. ARTFL Project: Dictionnaires d'autrefois, 2023. https://artfl-project.uchicago.edu/content/dictionnaires-dautrefois

Acosta, José de. *Historia natural y moral de las Indias*. Seville: Juan de Leon, 1590.

Adams, John. "Diary of John Adams, Volume 2." *Adams Papers Digital Edition*, 2022. https://www.masshist.org/publications/adams-papers/index.php/view/ADMS-01-02-02-0009-0004-0010

Adams, Sarah. "International Dissemination of Printed Music during the Second Half of the Eighteenth Century." In *The Dissemination of Music: Studies in the History of Music Publishing*, edited by Hans Lenneberg, 21–42. Abingdon: Routledge, 2013.

Addison, Joseph. *Remarks on Several Parts of Italy, &c. in the Years 1701, 1702, 1703*. London: Jacob Tonson, 1705.

Adkins, Cecil. "Trumpet Marine." *Oxford Music Online/Grove Music Online*, 2001. https://www.oxfordmusiconline.com/grovemusic/view/10.1093/gmo/9781561592630.001.0001/omo-9781561592630-e-0000028494

Adler, Guido. "Umfang, Methode und Ziel der Musikwissenschaft." *Vierteljahrsschrift für Musikwissenschaft* 1 (1885): 5–20.

Adler, Guido, and Erica Mugglestone. "Guido Adler's 'The Scope, Method, and Aim of Musicology' (1885): An English Translation with an Historico-Analytical Commentary." *Yearbook for Traditional Music* 13 (1981): 1–21.

Agawu, V. Kofi. *The African Imagination in Music*. New York: Oxford University Press, 2016.

Agawu, V. Kofi. *On African Music: Techniques, Influences, Scholarship*. New York: Oxford University Press, 2023.

BIBLIOGRAPHY 251

Agnew, Vanessa. "Editorial." *Eighteenth-Century Music* 6, no. 2 (2009): 159–160.
Agnew, Vanessa. *Enlightenment Orpheus: The Power of Music in Other Worlds*. New York: Oxford University Press, 2008.
Ahrendt, Rebekah. "Politics: Music and the Law." In *A Cultural History of Music in the Age of Enlightenment*, edited by David R. M. Irving and Estelle Joubert, 81–99. London: Bloomsbury, 2024.
Ahrendt, Rebekah, and David Van der Linden. "The Postmasters' Piggy Bank: Experiencing the Accidental Archive." *French Historical Studies* 40, no. 2 (2017): 189–213.
Ahsan, Hamja. *Shy Radicals: The Antisystemic Politics of the Militant Introvert*. 4th ed. London: Book Works, 2020.
Alembert, Jean le Rond d'. "Occident [Géographie]." In *Encyclopédie, ou dictionnaire raisonné des sciences, des arts et des métiers*. University of Chicago, ARTFL Encyclopédie Project, Autumn 2017. https://artflsrv04.uchicago.edu/philologic4.7/encyclopedie0 922/navigate/11/1775
"Alexandre Julien Dugué (1714–1780)." *BnF Data*, 2022. https://data.bnf.fr/fr/14981932/ alexandre_julien_dugue/
Allsop, Peter, and Joyce Lindorff. "Da Fermo alla corte imperiale della Cina: Teodorico Pedrini, musico e missionario apostolico." Translated by Sara Dieci. *Rivista Italiana di Musicologia* 42, no. 1 (2007): 69–103.
Allsop, Peter, and Joyce Lindorff. "Teodorico Pedrini: The Music and Letters of an 18th-Century Missionary in China." *Vincentian Heritage* 27, no. 2 (2008): 43–59.
Al-Taee, Nasser. *Representations of the Orient in Western Music: Violence and Sensuality*. Farnham: Ashgate, 2010.
Álvarez Martínez, Ma. Salud. "Salazar, Diego José de." In *Diccionario de la música española e hispanoamericana*, edited by Emilio Casares Rodicio, José López-Calo, and Ismael Fernández de la Cuesta, Vol. 9, 574–575. Madrid: Sociedad General de Autores y Editores, 2002.
Amin, Samir. *Eurocentrism: Modernity, Religion, and Democracy: A Critique of Eurocentrism and Culturalism*. Translated by Russell Moore and James H. Membrez. New York: Monthly Review Press, 2009.
Amiot, Jean-Joseph-Marie. "Abrégé chronologique de l'histoire universelle de l'empire chinois." In *Mémoires concernant l'histoire, les sciences, les arts, les mœurs, les usages, etc. des Chinois, par les Missionnaires de Pékin*, 74–308. Paris: Nyon l'aîné, 1788.
Amiot, Jean-Joseph-Marie. *Mémoire sur la musique des Chinois, tant anciens que modernes*. Paris: Nyon l'Aîné, 1779.
Anderson, Benedict. *Imagined Communities: Reflections on the Origin and Spread of Nationalism*. Rev. extended ed. London: Verso, 1991.
Anthony, James R. "Collin [Colin] de Blamont, François." *Oxford Music Online/Grove Music Online*, 2001. https://www.oxfordmusiconline.com/grovemusic/view/10.1093/ gmo/9781561592630.001.0001/omo-9781561592630-e-0000006121
Anthony, James R. "Europe galante, L' ('Galant Europe')." *Oxford Music Online/Grove Music Online*, 2002). https://www.oxfordmusiconline.com/grovemusic/display/10.1093/ gmo/9781561592630.001.0001/omo-9781561592630-e-5000003642
Anthony, James R. "Printed Editions of Andre Campra's *L'Europe Galante*." *Musical Quarterly* 56, no. 1 (1970): 54–73.
Antolini, Bianca Maria. "Publishers and Buyers." Edited and translated by Rudolf Rasch. In *Music Publishing in Europe 1600–1900: Concepts and Issues, Bibliography*, 209–240. Berlin: Berliner Wissenschafts-Verlag, 2005.
Appadurai, Arjun. *Modernity at Large: Cultural Dimensions of Globalization*. Minneapolis: University of Minnesota Press, 1996.

252 BIBLIOGRAPHY

Appiah, Kwame Anthony. *The Lies That Bind: Rethinking Identity*. London: Profile Books, 2018.

Appiah, Kwame Anthony. "There Is No Such Thing as Western Civilisation." *The Guardian*, November 9, 2016. https://www.theguardian.com/world/2016/nov/09/western-civilisation-appiah-reith-lecture

Arbeau, Thoinot. *Orchésographie*. Langres: Jehan des Preyz, 1589.

Arbeau, Thoinot. *Orchesography*. Translated by Mary Stewart Evans. New York: Dover, 1967.

Armitage, David. "In Defense of Presentism." In *History and Human Flourishing*, edited by Darrin M. McMahon, 59–84. New York: Oxford University Press, 2022.

Arnold, R. J. *Musical Debate and Political Culture in France, 1700–1830*. Woodbridge, UK: Boydell Press, 2017.

Ashton, Mark. "Allegory, Fact, and Meaning in Giambattista Tiepolo's Four Continents in Würzburg." *Art Bulletin* 60, no. 1 (1978): 109–125.

Augustine. *Confessions*, Vol. 2: *Books 9–13*. Translated by William Watts. Loeb Classical Library 27. Cambridge, MA: Harvard University Press, 1912.

Aversano, Luca. "The Transmission of Italian Musical Articles through Germany and Austria to Eastern Europe around 1800." In *The Circulation of Music in Europe 1600–1900: A Collection of Essays and Case Studies*, edited by Rudolf Rasch, 143–156. Berlin: Berliner Wissenschafts-Verlag, 2008.

Baines, Anthony. "Fifteenth-Century Instruments in Tinctoris's *De Inventione et Usu Musicae*." *Galpin Society Journal* 3 (1950): 19–26.

Baldwin, Olive, and Thelma Wilson. "'Reviv'd by the Publisher of the Former Masks': The Firm of John Walsh and the *Monthly Mask*, 1717–27 and 1737–8." *Royal Musical Association Research Chronicle* 42 (2009): 1–44.

Banat, Gabriel. *The Chevalier de Saint-Georges: Virtuoso of the Sword and the Bow*. Hillsdale, NY: Pendragon, 2006.

Baron, Ernst Gottlieb. *Historisch-Theoretisch und Practische Untersuchung des Instruments der Lauten, mit Fleiss aufgesetzt und allen rechtschaffenen Liebhabern zum Vergnügen herausgegeben*. Nuremberg: Johann Friedrich Rüdiger, 1727.

Baron, Ernst Gottlieb. *Study of the Lute (1727)*. Translated by Douglas Alton Smith. Redondo Beach, CA: Instrumenta Antiqua, 1976.

Barrow, John Sir. *A Voyage to Cochinchina, in the Years 1792 and 1793: Containing a General View of the Valuable Productions and the Political Importrance of This Flourishing Kingdom; and Also of Such European Settlements as Were Visited on the Voyage; With Sketches of the Manners, Character, and Condition of Their Several Inhabitants*. London: T. Cadell and W. Davies, 1806.

Bassin, Mark. "Russia between Europe and Asia: The Ideological Construction of Geographical Space." *Slavic Review* 50, no. 1 (1991): 1–17.

Beattie, James. *Essays. On the Nature and Immutability of Truth, in Opposition to Sophistry and Scepticism. On Poetry and Music, as They Affect the Mind. On Laughter, and Ludicrous Composition. On the Utility of Classical Learning*. Edinburgh: William Creech, 1776.

Becker, Judith. "Exploring the Habitus of Listening: Anthropological Perspectives." In *Handbook of Music and Emotion: Theory, Research, Applications*, edited by Patrik N. Juslin and John A. Sloboda, 127–157. Oxford: Oxford University Press, 2010.

Bell, John. *Travels from St. Petersburg in Russia, to Diverse parts of Asia*. 2 vols. Glasgow: John Bell, 1763.

Benigno, Francesco. *Words in Time: A Plea for Historical Re-thinking*. Translated by David Fairservice. London: Routledge, 2017.
Benjamin, Jonathan. *Harmonia Coelestis: A Collection of Church Music, in Two, Three, and Four Parts. With Words Adapted to Each, Comprehending Not Only the Metres in Common Use, but the Particular Metres, in the Hartford Collection of Hymns;—The Tunes Correctly Figured for the Organ and Harpsichord.—With an Inttoduction [sic], to Music. Chiefly Collected From the Greatest Masters in Europe, and Never Before Printed in America*. Northampton, MA: Oliver D. & I. Cooke, 1799.
Benserade, Isaac de. *Ballet royal de Flore: Dansé par Sa Majesté, le mois de février 1669*. Paris: Robert Ballard, 1669.
Benserade, Isaac de. *Ballet royal de la naissance de Venus: Dansé par Sa Majesté, le 26. de Janvier 1665*. Paris: Robert Ballard, 1665.
Bergamo, Marija. "Europäische Musik—Fakt und Fiktion zugleich." *History of European Ideas* 20, nos. 1–3 (1995): 447–452.
Berger, Karol. *Bach's Cycle, Mozart's Arrow: An Essay on the Origins of Musical Modernity*. Berkeley: University of California Press, 2007.
Bergeron, Katherine, and Philip V. Bohlman, eds. *Disciplining Music: Musicology and Its Canons*. Chicago: University of Chicago Press, 1992.
Bermúdez, Egberto. "'Las cuatro partes del mundo': Canto y baile en Palmas del Socorro (Santander, noreste de Colombia) ca. 1810–1820." In *Iconografía musical na América Latina: Discursos e narrativas entre olhares e escutas/Iconografía musical en América Latina: Discursos y narrativas entre miradas y escuchas*, edited by Pablo Sotuyo Blanco, 11–72. Salvador: Editora da UFBA, 2019.
Bermudo, Juan. *Comiença el libro llamado declaracio[n] de instrume[n]tos musicales dirigido al illustrissimo señor el señor don Francisco de Çuniga [sic], Conde de Miranda*. Ossuna: Juan de Leon, 1555.
Bernal, Martin. *Black Athena: The Afroasiatic Roots of Classical Civilization*. 3 vols. New Brunswick, NJ: Rutgers University Press, 1987–2006.
Bernier, Nicolas. *Cantates françoises ou musique de chambre a voix seule avec simphonie et sans simphonie et la basse continüe . . . quatrième livre*. New ed. Paris: Madame Vanhowe, Mr. Poilly, Mr. Neuilly, 1745.
[Bernier], [Nicolas]. *Cantates françoises ou musique de chambre a voix seule et a deux avec symphonie et sans symphonie avec la basse continüe . . . quatrième livre*. Paris: Foucault, 1703.
Bernstein, Leonard. "What Is American Music?" *Leonard Bernstein Office*, 2022 [1958]. https://leonardbernstein.com/lectures/television-scripts/young-peoples-concerts/what-is-american-music
Bertoglio, Chiara. *Reforming Music: Music and the Religious Reformations of the Sixteenth Century*. Berlin: De Gruyter, 2017.
Berton, Nathalie. "Bernier, Nicolas (1665–1734): Jupiter et Europe (cantate française)." *Catalogue de l'oeuvre de Nicolas Bernier (1665–1734)*, December 2007. http://philidor.cmbv.fr/ark:/13681/308mqy4j71y13mxvqfmh
Bertuccioli, Giuliano. "Europe as Seen from China before the Arrival of the Jesuits." In *"Scholar from the West": Giulio Aleni S.J. (1582–1649) and the Dialogue between Christianity and China*, edited by Tiziana Lippiello and Roman Malek, 19–28. Brescia: Fondazione Civiltà Bresciana; Sankt Augustin: Monumenta Serica Institute, 1997.
Bethencourt, Francisco. *Racisms: From the Crusades to the Twentieth Century*. Princeton, NJ: Princeton University Press, 2014.

Betzwieser, Thomas. "French Opera through the Eyes of a Syrian Traveller: Hanna Diyâb in the Land of the Sun King." Paper presented at the American Musicological Society Annual Meeting, New Orleans, November 11, 2022.

Bevilacqua, Alexander. *The Republic of Arabic Letters: Islam and the European Enlightenment*. Cambridge, MA: Harvard University Press, 2018.

Bimberg, Guido. "The Idea of European Music in German Eighteenth[-]century Music Theory and Composition Practice." *History of European Ideas* 20, nos 1–3 (1995): 453–459.

Bisaha, Nancy. *Creating East and West: Renaissance Humanists and the Ottoman Turks*. Philadelphia: University of Pennsylvania Press, 2004.

Blackburn, Bonnie J., Garrett Schumann, and Joseph McHardy. "Lusitano, Vicente." *Oxford Music Online/Grove Music Online*, 2022. https://www.oxfordmusiconline.com/grovemusic/view/10.1093/gmo/9781561592630.001.0001/omo-9781561592630-e-0000017205

Blanchard, Amos, ed. *The Newburyport Collection of Sacred, European Musick; Consisting of Psalm Tunes and Occasional Pieces, Selected from the Most Eminent European Publications—Adapted to All the Metres in General Use. To Which Is Prefixed a Concise Introduction to the Grounds of Musick*. Exeter, NH: Ranlet & Norris, 1807.

Bloechl, Olivia A. "Editorial." *Eighteenth-Century Music* 17, no. 2 (2020): 173–176.

Bloechl, Olivia A. *Native American Song at the Frontiers of Early Modern Music*. Cambridge: Cambridge University Press, 2008.

Bloechl, Olivia A. *Opera and the Political Imaginary in Old Regime France*. Chicago: University of Chicago Press, 2018.

Bloechl, Olivia A. "Race, Empire, and Early Music." In *Rethinking Difference in Music Scholarship*, edited by Olivia Ashley Bloechl, Melanie Lowe, and Jeffrey Kallberg, 77–107. Cambridge: Cambridge University Press, 2015.

Bloechl, Olivia, Hyun Kyong Hannah Chang, Juliana M. Pistorius, Julia Byl, Hedy Law, Gabriel Solis, Choi Yu-jun, and Daniel F. Castro Pantoja. "Colloquy: Theorizing Global Music History." *Journal of the American Musicological Society* 76, no. 3 (2023): 831–872.

Bloechl, Olivia A., and Melanie Lowe. "Introduction: Rethinking Difference." In *Rethinking Difference in Music Scholarship*, edited by Olivia Ashley Bloechl, Melanie Lowe, and Jeffrey Kallberg, 1–52. Cambridge: Cambridge University Press, 2015.

Bloechl, Olivia A., Melanie Lowe, and Jeffrey Kallberg, eds. *Rethinking Difference in Music Scholarship*. Cambridge: Cambridge University Press, 2015.

Bloechl, Olivia, Katherine Butler Schofield, and Gabriel Solis. "The Value of Collaboration." *AMS Musicology Now*, March 20, 2017. https://musicologynow.org/the-value-of-collaboration/

Boch, Julie. "L'Occident au miroir des sauvages: Figures du païen chez Fontenelle et Lafitau." *Tangence*, no. 72 (2003): 75–91.

Bodenstein, Wulf. "Editorial: Formatting Europe—Mapping a Continent." *Belgeo: Revue belge de géographie* 3–4 (2008): 241–244. http://journals.openedition.org/belgeo/7653

Bohlman, Philip V. "Ethnomusicology's Challenge to the Canon; the Canon's Challenge to Ethnomusicology." In *Disciplining Music: Musicology and Its Canons*, edited by Katherine Bergeron and Philip V. Bohlman, 116–136. Chicago: University of Chicago Press, 1992.

Bohlman, Philip V. "Johann Gottfried Herder and the Global Moment of World-Music History." In *The Cambridge History of World Music*, edited by Philip V. Bohlman, 255–276. Cambridge: Cambridge University Press, 2013.

Bohlman, Philip V. "Missionaries, Magical Muses, and Magnificent Menageries: Image and Imagination in the Early History of Ethnomusicology." *World of Music* 30, no. 3 (1988): 5–27.
Bohlman, Philip V. "Musical Thought in the Global Enlightenments." In *Studies on a Global History of Music: A Balzan Musicology Project*, edited by Reinhard Strohm, 61–80. Abingdon: Routledge, 2018.
Bohlman, Philip V. "Representation and Cultural Critique in the History of Ethnomusicology." In *Comparative Musicology and Anthropology of Music: Essays on the History of Ethnomusicology*, edited by Bruno Nettl and Philip V. Bohlman, 131–151. Chicago: University of Chicago Press, 1991.
Bohlman, Philip V., Stephen Blum, and Daniel M. Neuman, eds. *Ethnomusicology and Modern Music History*. Urbana: University of Illinois Press, 1991.
Bohlman, Philip V., and Martin Stokes. "Series Editors' Foreword." In Marcello Sorce Keller, *What Makes Music European: Looking beyond Sound*, vii–ix. Lanham, MD: Scarecrow Press, 2012.
Boletsi, Maria. *Barbarism and Its Discontents*. Stanford, CA: Stanford University Press, 2013.
Bonner, Elise. "Catherine the Great and the Rise of Comic Opera in Late Eighteenth-Century St. Petersburg." PhD diss., Princeton University, 2017.
Bonnett, Alastair. *The Idea of the West: Culture, Politics and History*. Basingstoke: Palgrave Macmillan, 2004.
Bonnett, Alastair. "Who Was White? The Disappearance of Non-European White Identities and the Formation of European Racial Whiteness." *Ethnic and Racial Studies* 21, no. 6 (1998): 1029–1055.
Bonnet-Bourdelot, Jacques. *Histoire de la musique et de ses effets, depuis son origine jusqu'à présent*. Paris: Jean Cochart, Etienne Ganeau, Jacques Quillau, 1715.
Boorsch, Suzanne. "America in Festival Presentations." In *First Images of America: The Impact of the New World on the Old*, edited by Fredi Chiappelli, Michael J. B. Allen, and Robert Louis Benson, Vol. 1, 503–515. Berkeley: University of California Press, 1976.
Bordier, René. *Grand bal de la douairière de Billebahault. Ballet dansé par le roy, au mois de février 1626. Vers dudit ballet par le sieur Bordier, ayant charge de la Poësie pres de sa Majesté*. [Paris]: Imprimerie du Louvre, 1626.
Borheck, August Christian. *Neue Erdbeschreibung von ganz Afrika: Aus den besten ältern und neuern Hülfsmitteln gesammlet und bearbeitet*. 2 vols. Frankfurt am Main: Varrentrapp und Wenner, 1789–1791.
Born, Georgina, and David Hesmondhalgh. "Introduction: On Difference, Representation, and Appropriation in Music." In *Western Music and Its Others: Difference, Representation, and Appropriation in Music*, edited by Georgina Born and David Hesmondhalgh, 1–58. Berkeley: University of California Press, 2000.
Born, Georgina, and David Hesmondhalgh, eds. *Western Music and Its Others: Difference, Representation, and Appropriation in Music*. Berkeley: University of California Press, 2000.
Boucher, Cynthia. "Goethe's 'Suleika.'" *Musicological Explorations* 8 (2007): 65–96.
Bougainville, Louis Antoine de. *Voyage autour du monde, par la frégate du roi La Boudeuse et la flûte l'Étoile; en 1766, 1767, 1768 & 1769*. Paris: Saillant & Nyon, 1771.
Bougainville, Louis Antoine de. *A Voyage round the World. Performed by Order of His Most Christian Majesty, In the Years 1766, 1767, 1768, and 1769*. Translated by John Reinhold Forster. London: J. Nourse and T. Davies, 1772.

Bowles, Edmund A. "The Impact of Turkish Military Bands on European Court Festivals in the 17th and 18th Centuries." *Early Music* 34, no. 4 (2006): 533–559.

Boym, Svetlana. "On Diasporic Intimacy: Ilya Kabakov's Installations and Immigrant Homes." *Critical Inquiry* 24, no. 2 (1998): 498–524.

Bracewell, Wendy. "The Limits of Europe in East European Travel Writing." In *Under Eastern Eyes: A Comparative Introduction to East European Travel Writing on Europe*, edited by Wendy Bracewell and Alex Drace-Francis, 61–120. Budapest: Central European University Press, 2008.

Brague, Rémi. *Eccentric Culture: A Theory of Western Civilization*. Translated by Samuel Lester. South Bend, IN: St. Augustine's Press, 2002.

Branchi, Silvestro. *Europa rapita da Giove cangiato in toro, Il Trionfo della Fama, Angelica legata allo scoglio, liberata da Ruggiero, Rinaldo liberato da gl'incanti d'Armida, intermezi [sic]*. Bologna: Mascheroni e Ferroni, 1623.

"Branding 'Western Music.'" Institut für Musikwissenschaft, Universität Bern, 2017. https://www.musik.unibe.ch/forschung/tagungen/vergangene_tagungen/branding_western_music/index_ger.html.

Brewer, Charles E. *The Instrumental Music of Schmeltzer, Biber, Muffat and Their Contemporaries*. Farnham: Ashgate, 2011.

Brillantes-Silvestre, Ma. Patricia. "Literatura, música y cultura: Una traducción al inglés de unos documentos selectos en español sobre la música de Filipinas pre-hispánica e hispánica." MA thesis, University of the Philippines Diliman, 1998.

Brook, Timothy. "Europaeology? On the Difficulty of Assembling a Knowledge of Europe in China." In *Christianity and Cultures: Japan & China in Comparison, 1543–1644*, edited by M. Antoni J. Üçerler, 261–285. Rome: Institutum Historicum Societatis Iesu, 2009.

Brossard, Sébastien de. *Dictionnaire de musique, contenant une explication des Termes Grecs, Latins, Italiens & François les plus usitez dans la Musique*. Paris: Christophe Ballard, 1703.

Brossard, Sébastien de. *Dictionnaire des termes grecs, latins et italiens, dont on se sert frequemment dans toutes sortes de Musique, & particulierement dans l'Italienne*. Paris: Christophe Ballard, 1701.

Brover-Lubovsky, Bella. "The 'Greek Project' of Catherine the Great and Giuseppe Sarti." *Journal of Musicological Research* 32, no. 1 (2013): 28–61.

Brown, John. *Dell'origine, unione, e forza, progressi, separazioni, e corruzioni della poesia, e della musica*. Translated by Pietro Crocchi. Florence: Stamperia Bonducciana, 1772.

Brown, John. *A Dissertation on the Rise, Union, and Power, the Progressions, Separations, and Corruptions, of Poetry and Music*. London: L. Davis and C. Reymers, 1763.

Brown, John. *Dr. Brown's Betrachtungen über die Poesie und Musik: Nach ihrem Ursprunge, ihrer Vereinigung, Gewalt, Wachsthum, Trennung und Verderbniss*. Translated by Johann Joachim Eschenburg. Leipzig: Weidmanns Erben und Reich, 1769.

Brown, Julie, ed. *Western Music and Race*. Cambridge: Cambridge University Press, 2007.

Budasz, Rogério. "Of Cannibals and the Recycling of Otherness." *Music & Letters* 87, no. 1 (2006): 1–15.

Buonanni, Filippo. *Gabinetto armonico pieno d'istromenti sonori*. Rome: G. Placho, 1722.

Burchell, Jenny. "'The First Talents of Europe': British Music Printers and Publishers and Imported Instrumental Music in the Eighteenth Century." In *Concert Life in Eighteenth-Century Britain*, edited by Susan Wollenberg and Simon McVeigh, 93–113. Aldershot: Ashgate, 2004.

Burke, Edmund. *Two Letters Addressed to a Member of the Present Parliament, on the Proposals for Peace with the Regicide Directory of France.* London: F. and C. Rivington, 1796.

Burke, Peter. "Did Europe Exist before 1700?" *History of European Ideas* 1, no. 1 (1980): 21–29.

Burke, Peter. *Hybrid Renaissance: Culture, Language, Architecture.* Budapest: Central European University Press, 2016.

Burney, Charles. *An Account of the Musical Performances in Westminister-Abbey, and the Pantheon, May 26th, 27th, 29th; and June the 3d, and 5th, 1784: in Commemoration of Handel.* London: Musical Fund, 1785.

Burney, Charles. *Carl Burney's der Musik Doctors Tagebuch.* Translated by Christoph Daniel Ebeling (Vol. 1) and Johann Joachim Christoph Bode (Vols. 2–3). 3 vols. Hamburg: Bode, 1772–1773.

Burney, Charles. *A General History of Music: From the Earliest Ages to the Present Period. To Which is Prefixed, A Dissertation on the Music of the Ancients.* 4 vols. London: Charles Burney, 1776–1789.

Burney, Charles. *The Present State of Music in Germany, the Netherlands and United Provinces: Or, The Journal of a Tour Through Those Countries, Undertaken to Collect Materials for a General History of Music.* 2 vols. London: T. Becket, J. Robson, and G. Robinson, 1773.

Burney, Charles. "Spain." In *The Cyclopaedia; or, Universal Dictionary of Arts, Sciences, and Literature,* edited by Abraham Rees, Vol. 33, n.p. London: Longman, 1802–1819.

Burrows, Donald, and Rosemary Dunhill. *Music and Theatre in Handel's World: The Family Papers of James Harris, 1732–1780.* Oxford: Oxford University Press, 2002.

Burstyn, Shai. "The 'Arabian Influence' Thesis Revisited." *Current Musicology* 45, no. 4 (1990): 119–146.

Campbell, Lawrence Dundas, and E. Samuel, eds. *The Asiatic Annual Register, or, A View of the History of Hindustan, and of the Politics, Commerce and Literature of Asia.* 13 vols. London: J. Debrett, T. Cadell, W. Davies, 1800–1811.

Campra, André. *L'Europe galante, mis en musique.* Paris: Christophe Ballard, 1697.

Canova-Green, Marie-Claude. "Dance and Ritual: the *Ballet des nations* at the Court of Louis XIII." *Renaissance Studies* 9, no. 4 (1995): 395–403.

Cantemir, Dimitrie. *Demetrii principis Cantemirii incrementorum et decrementorum aulae Othman[n]icae sive Aliothman[n]icae historiae a prima gentis origine ad nostra usque tempora deductae libri tres. 1.* Critical edition by Dan Slușanschi with a preface by Virgil Cândea. Timișoara: Amarcord, 2002.

Cantemir, Dimitrie. *The History of the Growth and Decay of the Othman Empire.* Translated by N. Tindal. 2 vols. London: James, John, and Paul Knapton, 1734–1735.

Cantemir, Dimitrie, and Virgil Cândea. *Creșterile și descreșterile Imperiului Otoman: Textul original Latin în forma finală revizuită de autor.* Facsimile edition of the manuscript with an introduction by Virgil Cândea. Bucharest: Roza Vânturilor, 1999.

Cantemir, Dimitrie, and Owen Wright. *Demetrius Cantemir: The Collection of Notations, Part 1: Text.* London: School of Oriental and African Studies, University of London, 1992.

Cantemir, Dimitrie, and Owen Wright. *Demetrius Cantemir: The Collection of Notations, Vol. 2: Commentary.* Aldershot: Ashgate, 2000.

Caoursin, Guillaume. *Rhodiorum vicecancellarii: Obsidionis Rhodie urbis descriptio.* Ulm: Johann Reger, 1496.

Caraman, Philip, and Clement J. McNaspy. "Sepp von Reinegg, Anton." In *Diccionario histórico de la Compañía de Jesús: Biográfico-temático*, edited by Charles E. O'Neill and Joaquín María Domínguez, Vol. 4, 3555–3556. Rome: Institutum Historicum; Madrid: Universidad Pontificia Comillas, 2001.

Carpani, Giuseppe. *Le Haydine: Ovvero lettere su la vita e le opere del celebre maestro Giuseppe Haydn*. Milan: Candido Buccinelli, 1812.

Carter, Stewart. "Francesco Rognoni's *Selva de varii passaggi* (1602): Fresh Details Concerning Early-Baroque Vocal Ornamentation." *Performance Practice Review* 2, no. 1 (1989): 5–33.

Carter, Tim. *Monteverdi's Musical Theatre*. New Haven, CT: Yale University Press, 2002.

Casares, Emilio, Ismael Fernández de la Cuesta, and José López-Calo, eds. *Espāna en la música de Occidente: Actas del Congreso Internacional celebrado en Salamanca, 29 de octubre–5 de noviembre de 1985, "Año Europeo de la Música."* 2 vols. Madrid: Instituto Nacional de los Artes Escénicas y de la Musica, 1987.

Castillo-Ferreira, Mercedes. "Chant, Liturgy and Reform." In *Companion to Music in the Age of the Catholic Monarchs*, edited by Tess Knighton, 282–322. Leiden: Brill, 2017.

Castro-Gómez, Santiago. *La hybris del punto cero: Ciencia, raza e ilustración en la Nueva Granada (1750–1816)*. Bogotá: Pontificia Universidad Javeriana, 2005.

Catalogue des livres de la bibliotheque des ci-devant soi-disans Jésuites du Collége de Clermont, dont la vente commencera le lundi 19 mars 1764. Paris: Saugrain & Leclerc, 1764.

Catherine II, Empress of Russia. *The Grand Instructions to the Commissioners Appointed to Frame a New Code of Laws for the Russian Empire, Composed by Her Imperial Majesty Catherine II, Empress of all the Russias*. Translated by Michael Tatischeff. London: T. Jefferys, 1768.

Caus, Salomon de. *Institution harmonique divisée en deux parties: En la premiere sont monstrées les proportions des interualles harmoniques, et en la deuxiesme les compositions dicelles*. Frankfurt: Jan Norton, 1615.

Cerone, Pietro. *El melopeo y maestro: Tractado de musica theorica y practica*. Naples: Juan Bautista Gargano, y Lucrecio Nucci, 1613.

Chabanon, Michel-Paul Guy de. *De la musique considérée en elle-même et dans ses rapports avec la parole, les langues, la poésie et le théâtre*. Paris: Pissot, 1785.

Chakrabarty, Dipesh. *Provincializing Europe: Postcolonial Thought and Historical Difference*. Reissue, with a new preface by the author. Princeton, NJ: Princeton University Press, 2008.

Chapin, Keith. "Counterpoint: From the Bees or for the Birds? Telemann and Early Eighteenth-Century Quarrels with Tradition." *Music & Letters* 92, no. 3 (2011): 377–409.

Chapin, Keith. "'A Harmony or Concord of Several and Diverse Voices': Autonomy in 17th-Century German Music Theory and Practice." *International Review of the Aesthetics and Sociology of Music* 42, no. 2 (2011): 219–255.

Charlevoix, Pierre-François-Xavier de. *Histoire de l'etablissement, des progres et de la decadence du Christianisme dans l'Empire du Japon: Où l'on voit les differentes revolutions qui ont agité cette monarchie pendant plus d'un siecle*. 3 vols. Rouen: Jacques Joseph le Boullenger, 1715.

Charlton, David. *Opera in the Age of Rousseau: Music, Confrontation, Realism*. Cambridge: Cambridge University Press, 2012.

Charmantier, Isabelle. "Linnaeus and Race." Linnean Society of London, September 3, 2020. https://www.linnean.org/learning/who-was-linnaeus/linnaeus-and-race.
Chatterjee, Kumkum, and Clement Hawes, eds. *Europe Observed: Multiple Gazes in Early Modern Encounters*. Lewisburg, PA: Bucknell University Press, 2008.
Chatterjee, Kumkum, and Clement Hawes. "Introduction." In *Europe Observed: Multiple Gazes in Early Modern Encounters*, edited by Kumkum Chatterjee and Clement Hawes, 1–43. Lewisburg, PA: Bucknell University Press, 2008.
Chen, Jen-yen. "European Sounds and Their Chinese Listeners in the Sino-Western Contact Zone of Macau and Guangzhou, Southern China." In *Chinese Music and Musical Instruments*, edited by Énio Souza. Lisbon: Cientro Cientifico e Cultural de Macau, forthcoming.
Cheng, William. *Loving Music till It Hurts*. New York: Oxford University Press, 2019.
Chetwood, William Rufus. *The Voyages and Adventures of Captain Robert Boyle: In Several Parts of the World*. London: John Watts, 1726.
Christensen, Thomas. *Stories of Tonality in the Age of François-Joseph Fétis*. Chicago: University of Chicago Press, 2019.
Chua, Daniel K. L. *Absolute Music and the Construction of Meaning*. Cambridge: Cambridge University Press, 1999.
Chua, Daniel K. L. "Global Musicology: A Keynote without a Key." *Acta Musicologica* 94, no. 1 (2022): 109–26.
Chua, Daniel K. L., and Alexander Rehding. *Alien Listening: Voyager's Golden Record and Music from Earth*. New York: Zone Books, 2021.
Clark, Alice V. "Uncovering a Diverse Early Music." *Journal of Music History Pedagogy* 11, no. 1 (2021): 1–21.
Clark, Emily Hansell. "Introduction: Audibilities of Colonialism and Extractivism." *World of Music* 10, no. 2 (2021): 5–20.
Clarke, David. "An Encounter with Chinese Music in Mid-18th-Century London." *Early Music* 38, no. 4 (2010): 543–558.
Clayton, Martin, Trevor Herbert, and Richard Middleton, eds. *The Cultural Study of Music: A Critical Introduction*. 2nd ed. New York: Routledge, 2012.
Clements, Ashley. "Colour, Ancient Perception of." *Oxford Classical Dictionary*, March 7, 2016. https://oxfordre.com/classics/view/10.1093/acrefore/9780199381135.001.0001/acrefore-9780199381135-e-6980
Clements, Sir Ernest. *Introduction to the Study of Indian Music: An Attempt to Reconcile Modern Hindustani Music with Ancient Musical Theory and to Propound an Accurate and Comprehensive Method of Treatment of the Subject of Indian Musical Intonation*. London: Longmans, Green, 1913.
Cler, Jérôme. "Fonton, Charles." In *Dictionnaire des orientalistes de langue française*, rev. and expanded ed., edited by François Pouillon, 418–419. Paris: IISMM; Éditions Karthala, 2012.
Clossey, Luke. *Salvation and Globalization in the Early Jesuit Missions*. Cambridge: Cambridge University Press, 2008.
Cohen, Mitchell. *The Politics of Opera: A History from Monteverdi to Mozart*. Princeton, NJ: Princeton University Press, 2017.
Coleccion de documentos relativos á la vida pública del libertador de Colombia y del Perú Simon Bolívar, para servir á la historia de la independencia del Suramérica. 21 vols. Caracas: Devisme hermanos, 1826–1829.

Collin de Blamont, François. *Cantates françoises a voix seule sans Symphonie, et avec Symphonie Composée de differens Instrumens . . . Livre Second*. Paris: Le Sr. Boivin, Le Sr. Le Claire, 1729.

Collyer, Fran M. "Australia and the Global South: Knowledge and the Ambiguities of Place and Identity." *Journal of Historical Sociology* 34, no. 1 (2021): 41–54.

Conomos, Dimitri. "Experimental Polyphony, 'According to the . . . Latins,' in Late Byzantine Psalmody." *Early Music History* 2 (1982): 1–16.

Constantinopolitanus [pseudonym]. "Selim III: Late Emperor of the Turks [with a portrait]." *European Magazine, and London Review*, July 1807, 3–6 (and plate).

Cook, Nicholas. *Music, Encounter, Togetherness*. New York: Oxford University Press, 2024.

Cook, Nicholas. "We Are All (Ethno)musicologists Now." In *The New (Ethno)musicologies*, edited by Henry Stobart, 48–70. Lanham, MD: Scarecrow Press, 2008.

Cook, Nicholas. "Western Music as World Music." In *The Cambridge History of World Music*, edited by Philip V. Bohlman, 75–100. Cambridge: Cambridge University Press, 2013.

Cooper Union Museum for the Arts of Decoration. *The Four Continents: From the Collection of James Hazen Hyde*. New York: Cooper Union Museum for the Arts of Decoration, 1961.

Couperin, François. *Concert instrumental sous le titre d'Apothéose composé à la mémoire immortelle de l'incomparable Monsieur de Lully*. Paris: l'auteur, le Sieur Boivin, 1725.

Couperin, François. *Les goûts-réünis ou Nouveaux Concerts a l'usage de toutes les sortes d'instruments de musique augmentés d'une grande sonade en trio. Intitulée Le Parnasse ou l'Apothéose de Corelli*. Paris: l'auteur, le Sieur Boivin, 1724.

Coussemaker, Edmund de. "Hucbald, moine de St.-Amand et ses traités de musique." *Memoires de la Société Centrale d'Agriculture, Sciences et Arts du Département du Nord* (1839–1840): 171–394.

Cowart, Georgia. *The Origins of Modern Musical Criticism: French and Italian Music 1600–1750*. Ann Arbor, MI: UMI Research Press, 1981.

Cowart, Georgia. *The Triumph of Pleasure: Louis XIV and the Politics of Spectacle*. Chicago: University of Chicago Press, 2014.

Cowling, David. "Introduction." In *Conceptions of Europe in Renaissance France: Essays in Honour of Keith Cameron*, edited by David Cowling, 7–18. Amsterdam: Rodopi, 2006.

Crowne, John. *Calisto, or, The Chaste Nimph, the Late Masque at Court as It was Frequently Presented There, by Several Persons of Great Quality: With the Prologue, and the Songs Betwixt the Acts*. London: James Magnes and Richard Bentley, 1675.

Cusick, Suzanne G. "'There Was Not One Lady Who Failed to Shed a Tear': Arianna's Lament and the Construction of Modern Womanhood." *Early Music* 22, no. 1 (1994): 21–43.

Cusick, Suzanne G., Monica A. Hershberger, Richard Will, Micaela Baranello, Bonnie Gordon, and Ellie M. Hisama. "Sexual Violence in Opera: Scholarship, Pedagogy, and Production as Resistance." *Journal of the American Musicological Society* 71, no. 1 (2018): 213–253.

Cypess, Rebecca. "Notation, Performance, and the Significance of Print in the Music of Ignatius Sancho (c. 1729–1780)." *Journal for Eighteenth-Century Studies* 46, no. 2 (2023): 185–211.

Cyr, Mary. "Duport (Du Port), Nicolas." *Oxford Music Online/Grove Music Online*, 2015. https://www.oxfordmusiconline.com/grovemusic/view/10.1093/gmo/9781561592630.001.0001/omo-9781561592630-e-0002277523

Darlow, Mark. *Dissonance in the Republic of Letters: The Querelle des Gluckistes et des Piccinnistes*. Abingdon: Routledge, 2013.

Davies, Norman. *Europe: A History*. Oxford: Oxford University Press, 1996.

Davison, Alan. "John Brown's *Dissertation* (1763) on Poetry and Music: An Eighteenth-Century View on Music's Role in the Rise and Fall of Civilization." In *Late Eighteenth-Century Music and Visual Culture*, edited by Cliff Eisen and Alan Davison, 55–70. Turnhout: Brepols, 2017.

Demeilliez, Marie. "Campra maître de musique au Collège Louis-Le-Grand de la Compagnie de Jésus." In *Itinéraires d'André Campra (1660–1744): D'Aix à Versailles, de l'Église à l'Opéra*, edited by Catherine Cessac, 61–75. Wavre: Éditions Mardaga, 2012.

Demeilliez, Marie. "Noverre, jeune danseur au Collège Louis-le-Grand (1741–1742)." *Musicorum* 10 (2011): 15–38.

Dennis, Flora. "Musical Sound and Material Culture." In *The Routledge Handbook of Material Culture in Early Modern Europe*, edited by Catherine Richardson, Tara Hamling, and David Gaimster, 371–382. London: Routledge, 2017.

Derrida, Jacques. *Of Grammatology*. Translated by Gayatri Chakravorty Spivak. Corrected ed. Baltimore: Johns Hopkins University Press, 1997.

Deutsch, Otto Erich. *Mozart: A Documentary Biography*. Translated by Eric Blom, Peter Branscombe, and Jeremy Noble. Stanford, CA: Stanford University Press, 1965.

Dingle, Christopher. "'The Most Accomplished Man in Europe': Musical Traits of Joseph Bologne, Chevalier de Saint-Georges." Paper presented at the 58th Annual Conference of the Royal Musical Association, Durham University, September 8, 2022.

Diyāb, Ḥannā, and Elias Muhanna. *The Book of Travels*, Vol. 1. Edited by Johannes Stephan and Michael Cooperson. New York: New York University Press, 2021.

Dolmetsch, Arnold. "Ancient Welsh Music." ["Address delivered at Seaford House, Belgrave Square . . . on the 24th January, 1935."] *Transactions of the Honourable Society of Cymmrodorion*, Session 1933–34–35 (1936): 115–125.

Drace-Francis, Alex. *European Identity: A Historical Reader*. Basingstoke: Palgrave Macmillan, 2013.

DuBois, Ted Alan. "Christian Friedrich Daniel Schubart's *Ideen zu einer Ästhetik der Tonkunst*: An Annotated Translation." PhD diss., University of Southern California, 1983.

Du Halde, Jean-Baptiste. *Description géographique, historique, chronologique, politique, et physique de l'empire de la Chine et de la Tartarie Chinoise*. 4 vols. Paris: P. G. Le Mercier, 1735.

Dumont, Jean, and Jean Rousset de Missy. *Le ceremonial diplomatique des cours de l'Europe, ou collection des actes, memoires et relations qui concernent les dignitez, titulatures, honneurs et prééminences; les fonctions publiques des souverains, leurs sacres, couronnemmens, batêmes, & enterremens; les investitures des grands fiefs; les entrées publiques, audiences, fonctions, immunitez & Franchises des ambassadeurs & autres ministres publics; leurs disputes & démêlez de préféance; et en général tout ce qui a rapport au cérémonial et à l'etiquette*. 2 vols. Amsterdam: les Janssons à Waesberge, Wetstein & Smith, & Z. Chatelain; The Hague: P. de Hondt, la Veuve de Ch. Le Vier, & J. Neaulme, 1739.

Dunbar, James. *Essays on the History of Mankind in Rude and Cultivated Ages*. London: W. Strahan, T. Cadell, and J. Balfour, 1780.

Earhart, A. Louise H. "Béthizy, Jean Laurent de." *Oxford Music Online/Grove Music Online*, 2001. https://www.oxfordmusiconline.com/grovemusic/view/10.1093/gmo/9781561592630.001.0001/omo-9781561592630-e-0000002970

Eccles, John. *Europe's Revels for the Peace of Ryswick*. Edited by Michael Burden. Middleton, WI: A-R Editions, 2019.

Engel, Carl. *An Introduction to the Study of National Music: Comprising Researches into Popular Songs, Traditions, and Customs*. London: Longmans, Green, Reader, and Dyer, 1866.

Engel, Carl. *The Music of the Most Ancient Nations, Particularly of the Assyrians, Egyptians, and Hebrews; with Special Reference to Recent Discoveries in Western Asia and in Egypt*. London: John Murray, 1864.

"Equality, Diversity and Inclusion—An Update." University of Edinburgh, September 15, 2021. https://www.ed.ac.uk/news/students/2020/equality-diversity-and-inclusion-an-update.

Erlmann, Veit. "Resisting Sameness: À propos Kofi Agawu's *Representing African Music*." *Music Theory Spectrum* 26, no. 2 (2004): 291–304.

Ewell, Philip A. "Music Theory and the White Racial Frame." *Music Theory Online* 26, no. 2 (2020). https://mtosmt.org/issues/mto.20.26.2/mto.20.26.2.ewell.html

Eximeno [y Pujades], Antonio. *Dell'origine e delle regole della musica colla storia del suo progresso, decadenza, e rinnovazione*. Rome: Michel'Angelo Barbiellini, 1774.

Eximeno [y Pujades], Antonio. *Del origen y reglas de la musica, con la historia de su progreso, decadencia y restauracion*. Translated by Francisco Antonio Gutirrez. 3 vols. Madrid: Imprenta Real, 1796.

Eze, Emmanuel Chukwudi. *Race and the Enlightenment: A Reader*. Cambridge, MA: Blackwell, 1997.

Fabian, Dorottya. "The Meaning of Authenticity and the Early Music Movement: A Historical Review." *International Review of the Aesthetics and Sociology of Music* 32, no. 2 (2001): 153–167.

Fabian, Johannes. *Time and the Other: How Anthropology Makes Its Object*. New York: Columbia University Press, 2014.

Fabris, Dinko. "Urban Musicologies." In *Hearing the City in Early Modern Europe*, edited by Tess Knighton and Asención Mazuela-Anguita, 53–68. Turnhout: Brepols, 2018.

Fantuzzi, Giovanni. *Notizie degli scrittori bolognesi*. 9 vols. Bologna: Stamperia di San Tommaso d'Aquino, 1781–1794.

Farmer, Henry George. *Historical Facts for the Arabian Musical Influence*. London: W. Reeve, 1930.

Fehl, Philipp P. "Farewell to Jokes: The Last *Capricci* of Giovanni Domenico Tiepolo and the Tradition of Irony in Venetian Painting." *Critical Inquiry* 5, no. 4 (1979): 761–791.

Fenlon, Iain. "'Other' Musics in Sixteenth-Century Venice." In *Sleuthing the Muse: Essays in Honor of William F. Prizer*, edited by Kristine Forney and Jeremy L. Smith, 461–474. Hillsdale, NY: Pendragon Press, 2012.

Féraud, Jean-François. "Dictionaire critique de la langue française." Vol. 2 (E–N). Marseille, 1787–1788. ARTFL Project: Dictionnaires d'autrefois, 2023. https://artfl-project.uchicago.edu/content/dictionnaires-dautrefois

Ferlan, Claudio. "A Global Context for Communication Strategies in the Jesuit Colleges of Klagenfurt and Gorizia (17th–18th Centuries)." In *The Language of Continent Allegories in Baroque Central Europe*, edited by Wolfgang Schmale, Marion Romberg, and Josef Köstlbauer, 191–201. Stuttgart: Franz Steiner, 2016.

Fétis, François-Joseph. *Antoine Stradivari, luthier célèbre connu sous le nom de Stradivarius: Précédé de recherches historiques et critiques sur l'origine et les transformations des instruments à archet et suivi d'analyses théoriques sur l'archet et sur François Tourte, auteur de ses derniers perfectionnements.* Paris: Vuillaume, 1856.

Fétis, François-Joseph. *Biographie universelle des musiciens et bibliographie générale de la musique.* 8 vols. Paris: Librairie de H. Fournier, 1835–1844.

Fétis, François-Joseph. *Histoire générale de la musique depuis les temps les plus anciens jusqu'à nos jours.* 5 vols. Paris: Didot Frères, 1869–1876.

Fétis, François-Joseph. *Notice of Anthony Stradivari: Preceded by Historical and Critical Researches on the Origin and Transformations of Bow Instruments and Followed by a Theoretical Analysis of the Bow, and Remarks on Francis Tourte.* Translated by John Bishop. London: Robert Cocks, 1864.

Fiorillo, Federigo. *Studio per il violino diviso in trentasei capricci.* Naples: Luigi Marescalchi, n.d.

Fiske, Roger, and Richard G. King. "Galliard, John Ernest." *Oxford Music Online/Grove Music Online*, 2001. https://www.oxfordmusiconline.com/grovemusic/view/10.1093/gmo/9781561592630.001.0001/omo-9781561592630-e-0000010555

Fleckno, Richard. *The Mariage of Oceanus and Brittania: An Allegoricall Fiction, Really Declaring ENGLANDS Riches, Glory, and Puissance by SEA. To be Represented in Musick, Dances, and Proper Scenes. All Invented, Written, and Composed, by Richard Fleckno, Esq.* [London]: [n.p.], 1659.

Fleckno, Richard. *A Relation of Ten Years Travell in Europe, Asia, Affrique and America. All by Way of Letters Occasionally Written to Divers Noble Personages, from Place to Place; And Continued to This Present Year.* London: the author, 1654.

Fleming, Simon. "Foreign Composers, the Subscription Market, and the Popularity of Continental Music in Eighteenth-Century Britain." In *Music by Subscription: Composers and Their Networks in the British Music-Publishing Trade, 1676–1820*, edited by Simon Fleming and Martin Perkins, 221–241. London: Routledge, 2021.

Follino, Federico. *Compendio delle sontuose feste fatte l'anno 1608 nella citta di Mantova, per le reali nozze del serenissimo prencipe D. Francesco Gonzaga, con la serenissima infante Margherita di Savoia.* Mantua: Presso Aurelio and Lodovico Osanna, 1608.

Fondazione Giorgio Cini. "Tiepolo Giambattista—Ratto di Europa." https://arte.cini.it/Opere/393427.

Fonton, Charles. *18. yüzyılda Türk müziği: Şark musikisi (Avrupa musikisiyle karşılaştırmalı bir deneme).* Translated by Cem Behar. Istanbul: Pan Yayıncılık, 1987.

Fonton, Charles. "Essai sur la musique orientale comparée à la musique européenne [1751]." Edited by Eckhard Neubauer. *Zeitschrift für Geschichte der Arabisch-Islamischen Wissenschaften* 2 (1985): 225–324.

Fonton, Charles. "Essai sur la musique orientale comparée à la musique européenne." *Revue et Gazette Musicale de Paris* 5, nos. 43 (October 28, 1838): 421–429; 44 (November 4, 1838): 433–435.

Fonton, Charles. "Essay Comparing Turkish Music to European Music" [Part 1]. Translated by Robert Martin. *Turkish Music Quarterly* 1, no. 2 (1988): 1–8.

Fonton, Charles. "Essay Comparing Turkish Music to European Music" [Part 2]. Translated by Robert Martin. *Turkish Music Quarterly* 2, no. 1 (1989): 1–11.

Foresti, Antonio. *Del mappamondo istorico tomo settimo, parte prima: Che contiene le vite degl'imperatori della China.* Venice: Girolamo Albrizzi, 1716.

Forkel, Johann Nikolaus. *Allgemeine Geschichte der Musik.* 2 vols. Leipzig: Schwickertschen Verlage, 1788–1801.

Forkel, Johann Nikolaus. *Allgemeine Litteratur der Musik: oder, Anleitung zur Kenntniß musikalischer Bücher, welche von den ältesten bis auf die neusten Zeiten bey den Griechen, Römern und den meisten neuern europäischen Nationen sind geschrieben worden.* Leipzig: Schwickertschen Verlage, 1792.

Forkel, Johann Nikolaus. "From *A General History of Music* (1788–1801)." Translated by Wye J. Allanbrook. In *Strunk's Source Readings in Music History*, edited by Leo Treitler, 1012–1029. New York: W. W. Norton, 1998.

Forrest, Thomas. *Voyage aux Moluques et à la Nouvelle Guinée: Fait sur la galere la Tartare en 1774, 1775 & 1776, par ordre de la Compagnie angloise, par le capitaine Forrest.* Translated by Jean Nicolas Démeunier. Paris: Hôtel de Thou, 1780.

Forrest, Thomas. *A Voyage to New Guinea, and the Moluccas, from Balambangan: Including an Account of Magindano, Sooloo, and Other Islands . . . Performed in the Tartar Galley, Belonging to the Honourable East India Company, During the Years 1774, 1775, and 1776, by Captain Thomas Forrest.* London: G. Scott, 1779.

"France." *Courier de l'Europe* 3, no. 51 (1778): 403–404.

Frisch, Jean-Christophe. *Le baroque nomade.* Arles: Actes Sud, 2014.

Frith, Simon. "The Discourse of World Music." In *Western Music and Its Others: Difference, Representation, and Appropriation in Music*, edited by Georgina Born and David Hesmondhalgh, 305–322. Berkeley: University of California Press, 2000.

Fróis, Luís, and Josef Franz Schütte. *Kulturgegensätze Europa-Japan (1585): Tratado em que se contem muito susinta: e abbreviadamente algumas contradições e differenças de custumes antre a gente de Europa a esta provincia de Japão.* Tokyo: Sophia Universität, 1955.

Frolova-Walker, Marina. "Inventing Ancestry, Imagining Antiquity: Classical Greece in Russian Music." In *Musical Receptions of Greek Antiquity: From the Romantic Era to Modernism*, edited by Katerina Levidou, Katy Romanou, and George Vlastos, 2–34. Newcastle upon Tyne: Cambridge Scholars, 2016.

Furlong, Guillermo. *Antonio Sepp S.J. y su "gobierno temporal" (1732).* Buenos Aires: Ediciones Theoria, 1962.

Fuzelier, Louis. *Fragmens. Jupiter et Europe, divertissement nouveau. Les Saturnales, entrée du Ballet des Fêtes Grecques & Romaines. Zelie, divertissement nouveau. Représentés devant le roi, sur le théâtre des petits appartemens à Versailles.* [Paris]: Imprimés par exprès commandement de Sa Majesté, 1749.

Galilei, Vincenzo. *Dialogo della musica antica, et della moderna.* Florence: G. Marescotti, 1581.

Galilei, Vincenzo. *Dialogue on Ancient and Modern Music.* Translated by Claude V. Palisca. New Haven, CT: Yale University Press, 2003.

Gallerie Accademia, Venezia. "Ratto di Europa: Giambattista Tiepolo." https://www.gallerieaccademia.it/ratto-di-europa-1

[Galliard, John Ernest]. "A Critical Discourse upon Opera's in England, and a Means Proposed for Their Improvement." In *A Comparison Between the French and Italian Musick and Opera's. Translated from the French; with Some Remarks. To Which is added A Critical Discourse upon Opera's in England, and a Means Proposed for their Improvement*, by François Raguenet and [John Ernest Galliard], 62–86. London: William Lewis, 1709.

Galliard, John Ernest, Mr. Cobston, and Richard Leveridge. *Jupiter and Europa: A Masque of Songs.* London: J. Walsh and J. Hare, 1723.

Gantz, Timothy. *Early Greek Myth: A Guide to Literary and Artistic Sources.* Baltimore: Johns Hopkins University Press, 1993.

Garrett, Aaron, and Silvia Sebastiani. "David Hume on Race." In *The Oxford Handbook of Philosophy and Race,* edited by Naomi Zack, 31–43. New York: Oxford University Press, 2017.

Geanakoplos, Deno John. *Greek Scholars in Venice: Studies in the Dissemination of Greek Learning from Byzantium to Western Europe.* Cambridge, MA: Harvard University Press, 1962.

Geertz, Clifford. *Local Knowledge: Further Essays in Interpretive Anthropology.* New York: Basic Books, 2008.

Gelbart, Matthew. *The Invention of "Folk Music" and "Art Music": Emerging Categories from Ossian to Wagner.* Cambridge: Cambridge University Press, 2007.

Gemelli Careri, Giovanni Francesco. *Giro del mondo.* 6 vols. Naples: Giuseppe Rosselli, 1699–1700.

Gemelli Careri, Giovanni Francesco. "A Voyage round the World, by Dr. John Francis Gemelli Careri." In *A Collection of Voyages and Travels, Some Now First Printed from Original Manuscripts, Others Translated out of Foreign Languages, and Now First Publish'd in English,* edited by Awnsham Churchill and John Churchill, 1–606. London: Awnsham and John Churchill, 1704.

Gerstmeier, August. "Beethoven: Ein europäischer Komponist." In *Europäische Musik— Musik Europas,* edited by Otfried Höffe and Andreas Kablitz, 91–106. Paderborn: Wilhelm Fink, 2017.

Gianturco, Carolyn. "'Cantate spirituali e morali,' with a Description of the Papal Sacred Cantata Tradition for Christmas 1676–1740." *Music & Letters* 73, no. 1 (1992): 1–31.

Giddens, Anthony. *The Constitution of Society: Outline of the Theory of Structuration.* Berkeley: University of California Press, 1984.

Gild, Gerlinde [as Gerlinde Gild-Bohne]. *Das Lü Lü Zheng Yi Xubian: Ein Jesuitentraktat über die europäische Notation in China 1713.* Göttingen: Re, 1991.

Gild, Gerlinde. "The Introduction of European Musical Theory during the Early Qing Dynasty: The Achievements of Thomas Pereira and Theodorico Pedrini." In *Western Learning and Christianity in China: The Contribution and Impact of Johann Adam Schall von Bell, S.J. (1592–1666),* edited by Roman Malek, SVD, 1189–1200. Nettetal: Steyler Verlag, 1998.

Gild, Gerlinde. "Mission by Music: The Challenge of Translating European Music into Chinese in the Lülü Zuanyao." In *In the Light and Shadow of an Emperor: Tomás Pereira, SJ (1645–1708), the Kangxi Emperor and the Jesuit Mission in China,* edited by Artur K. Wardega, and António Vasconcelos de Saldanha, 532–545. Newcastle upon Tyne: Cambridge Scholars, 2012.

Ginestet, Gaëlle. "'She, Whom Jove Transported into Crete': Europa, between Consent and Rape." In *Interweaving Myths in Shakespeare and His Contemporaries,* edited by Janice Valls-Russell, Agnès Lafont, and Charlotte Coffin, 149–172. Manchester: Manchester University Press, 2017.

Gjerdingen, Robert O. "Partimento, que me veux-tu?" *Journal of Music Theory* 51, no. 1 (2007): 85–135.

Gligo, Nikša. "Integration vs Assimilation: European 'Musics' Do Exist!" *History of European Ideas* 20, no. 1–3 (1995): 477–481.

Gletle, Johann Melchior. *Expeditionis musicae classis III: Missae concertatae a V. Vocibus Concertantibus Necessarijs: V. Instrumentis Concertantibus ad libitum: V. Ripienis, seu*

Pleno Choro, addita una ab 8 Vocibus, & 7 Instrumentis. Cum Duplici Basso Continuo pro Organo, Violone, &c. Augsburg: Johann Melchior Gletle, 1670.

Glowotz, Daniel. "Die musikalische Konfrontation der Ost- und Westkirche auf dem Konzil von Ferrara-Florenz (1438–1439)." *Die Musikforschung* 59, no. 1 (2006): 1–16.

Gluck, Christoph Willibald. "Lettre de M. le Chevalier Gluck, sur la musique." *Mercure de France*, February 1773, 182–184.

Goehr, Lydia. *The Imaginary Museum of Musical Works: An Essay in the Philosophy of Music*. Rev. ed. Oxford: Oxford University Press, 2007.

Goethe, Johann Wolfgang von. *Goethe's West-Easterly Divan*. Translated by John Weiss. Boston: Roberts Brothers, 1877.

Goethe, Johann Wolfgang von. *West-oestlicher Divan*. Stuttgart: Cottaischen Buchhandlung, 1819.

Golvers, Noël. *Ferdinand Verbiest, S.J. (1623–1688) and the Chinese Heaven: The Composition of the Astronomical Corpus, Its Diffusion and Reception in the European Republic of Letters*. Leuven: Leuven University Press, 2003.

Golvers, Noël. "Ferdinand Verbiest on European Astronomy in China: From the Compendia to the Astronomia Europaea (1687), a Historical Philological Analysis." In *Ferdinand Verbiest (1623–1688): Jesuit Missionary, Scientist, Engineer and Diplomat*, edited by John W. Witek, 65–83. Nettetal: Steyler, 1994.

Golvers, Noel, and Ferdinand Verbiest. *The* Astronomia Europaea *of Ferdinand Verbiest, S.J. (Dillingen, 1687): Text, Translation, Notes and Commentaries*. Nettetal: Steyler Verlag, 1993.

Gommers, Peter H. *Europe—What's in a Name*. Leuven: Leuven University Press, 2001.

Gong, Hong-yu. "Review of Ching-wah Lam, *The Idea of Chinese Music in Europe up to the Year 1800*." *New Zealand Journal of Asian Studies* 16, no. 1 (2014): 151–154.

Good, Anne. "The Construction of an Authoritative Text: Peter Kolb's Description of the Khoikhoi at the Cape of Good Hope in the Eighteenth Century." In *Bringing the World to Early Modern Europe: Travel Accounts and Their Audiences*, edited by Peter Mancall, 61–94. Leiden: Brill, 2007.

Goodman, Dena. *The Republic of Letters: A Cultural History of the French Enlightenment*. Ithaca, NY: Cornell University Press, 1994.

Gordon, Bonnie. *Monteverdi's Unruly Women: The Power of Song in Early Modern Italy*. Cambridge: Cambridge University Press, 2004.

Gordon, Bonnie. "Nuptial Voices: The Power of Song in the 1608 Mantuan Wedding Festivities." *Journal of Medieval and Early Modern Studies* 35, no. 2 (2005): 349–384.

Gordon, Bonnie. "What Mr Jefferson Didn't Hear." In *Rethinking Difference in Music Scholarship*, edited by Olivia Ashley Bloechl, Melanie Lowe, and Jeffrey Kallberg, 108–132. Cambridge: Cambridge University Press, 2015.

Govor, Elena. *Twelve Days at Nuku Hiva: Russian Encounters and Mutiny in the South Pacific*. Honolulu: University of Hawai'i Press, 2010.

Grafton, Anthony, with April Shelford and Nancy Siraisi. *New Worlds, Ancient Texts: The Power of Tradition and the Shock of Discovery*. Cambridge, MA: Belknap Press, 1992.

Grainger, Percy. "The Impress of Personality in Unwritten Music." *Musical Quarterly* 1, no. 3 (1915): 416–435.

Grégoire, Henri Jean-Baptiste. *De la littérature des Nègres, ou, Recherches sur leurs facultés intellectuelles, leurs qualités morales et leur littérature: Suivies de notices sur la vie et les ouvrages des Nègres qui se sont distingués dans les sciences, les lettres et les arts*. Paris: Maradan, 1808.

Grelot, Guillaume-Joseph. *A Late Voyage to Constantinople: Containing an Exact Description of the Propontis and Hellespont, with the Dardanels, and What Else is Remarkable in Those Seas; as Also of the City of Constantinople, Wherein is Particularly Describ'd the Grand Seraglio and Chief Mosquees. Likewise an Account of the Ancient and Present State of the Greek Church; With the Religion and Manner of Worship of the Turks, their Ecclesiastical Government, Their Courts of Justice, and Civil Employments*. Translated by J. Philips [John Phillips]. London: John Playford, 1683.

Grelot, Guillaume-Joseph. *Relation nouvelle d'un voyage de Constantinople: Enrichie de plans levez par l'auteur sur les lieux, et des figures de tout ce qu'il y a de plus remarquable dans cette ville. Presentée au roy*. Paris: la Veuve de Damien Foucault, 1680.

Grig, Lucy, and Gavin Kelly, eds. *Two Romes: Rome and Constantinople in Late Antiquity*. New York: Oxford University Press, 2012.

Grimal, Pierre. *The Penguin Dictionary of Classical Mythology*. Edited by Stephen Kershaw from the translation by A. R. Maxwell-Hislop. London: Penguin, 1991.

Grimm, Friedrich-Melchior, Denis Diderot, Maurice Tourneux, Abbé Raynal, and Jacques-Henri Meister. *Correspondance littéraire, philosophique et critique par Grimm, Diderot, Raynal, Meister, etc.: Revue sur les textes originaux, comprenant outre ce qui a été publié à diverses époques les fragments supprimés en 1813 par la censure, les parties inédites conservées à la Bibliothèque ducale de Gotha et à l'Arsenal à Paris*. 16 vols. Paris: Garnier, 1877–1882.

Gruzinski, Serge. *The Mestizo Mind: The Intellectual Dynamics of Colonization and Globalization*. Translated by Deke Dusinberre. New York: Routledge, 2002.

Guénoun, Denis. *About Europe: Philosophical Hypotheses*. Translated by Christine Irizarry. Stanford, CA: Stanford University Press, 2013.

Guerrero, Francisco. *El viage de Hierusalem*. Seville: Juan de Leon, 1592.

Guertin, Ghyslaine. "La reconstruction d'un savoir musical: L'esthétique de Michel-Paul-Guy de Chabanon." In *Construire le savoir musical: Enjeux épistémologiques, esthétiques et sociaux*, edited by Monique Desroches and Ghyslaine Guerti, 263–282. Paris: L'Harmattan, 2003.

Guertin, Ghyslaine. "The Universal and the Particular: The Aesthetics of Michel Paul Guy de Chabanon." In *Musicology and Globalization: Proceedings of the International Congress in Shizuoka 2002, in Celebration of the 50th Anniversary of the Musicological Society of Japan*, edited by Yoshio Tozawa et al., 203–206. Tokyo: Tokyo National University of Fine Arts and Music, 2004.

Guillo, Laurent. "Legal Aspects." Translated by Joop Beusekamp and Rudolf Rasch. In *Music Publishing in Europe 1600–1900: Concepts and Issues, Bibliography*, edited by Rudolf Rasch, 116–138. Berlin: Berliner Wissenschafts-Verlag, 2005.

Gulliver, Katrina. "Intercultural Exchange in the City of Malacca." In *Intercultural Exchange in Southeast Asia: History and Society in the Early Modern World*, edited by Tara Alberts and D. R. M. Irving, 236–254. London: I. B. Tauris, 2013.

Guzy-Pasiak, Jolanta, and Aneta Markuszewska, eds. *Music Migration in the Early Modern Age: Centres and Peripheries—People, Works, Styles, Paths of Dissemination and Influence*. Warsaw: Liber Pro Arte, 2016.

Gyekye, Kwame. *Tradition and Modernity: Philosophical Reflections on the African Experience*. New York: Oxford University Press, 1997.

Haar, James, ed. *European Music, 1520–1640*. Woodbridge, UK: Boydell Press, 2006.

Haar, James. "Preface." In *European Music, 1520–1640*, edited by James Haar, vii–viii. Woodbridge, UK: Boydell Press, 2006.

Hachenberg, Paulus. *Pauli Hachenbergi P.P. Germania media: Publicis dissertationibus in Academia Heidelbergensi proposita, in qua res mediorum seculorum, quae à Trajano ad Maximilianum I. fluxére, ex priscis autoribus recensentur, mores, ritus, leges sacrae, profanaeq́[ue] ceremoniae illustrantur, dubia obscuraq́[ue] scriptorum Germanicorum loca explicantur.* Heidelberg: Wilhelmi Walteri, 1675.

Hachenberg, Paulus. *Pauli Hachenbergi summi viri Germania media: Publicis dissertationibus in Acad. Heidelbergensi proposita, in qua res mediorum seculorum, quæ à Trajano ad Maximilianum I. fluxêre, ex priscis autoribus recensentur, mores, ritus, leges sacrae, profanaeque ceremoniae illustrantur, dubia obscuraque scriptorum germanicorum loca explicantur.* 3rd ed. Magdeburg: Officina Libraria Rengeriana, 1709.

HaCohen, Ruth. *The Music Libel against the Jews.* New Haven, CT: Yale University Press, 2011.

Haines, John. "The Arabic Style of Performing Medieval Music." *Early Music* 29, no. 3 (2001): 369–378.

Hall, Stuart. *Selected Writings on Race and Difference.* Edited by Paul Gilroy and Ruth Wilson Gilmore. Durham, NC: Duke University Press, 2021.

Hamilton, John T. "Torture as an Instrument of Music." In *Thresholds of Listening*, edited by Sander van Maas, 143–152. New York: Fordham University Press, 2015.

Hansen, Thorkild. *Arabia Felix: The Danish Expedition of 1761–1767.* Translated by James McFarlane and Kathleen McFarlane. New York: Harper & Row, 1964.

Harrán, Don. "Madama Europa, Jewish Singer in Late Renaissance Mantua." In *Festa musicologica: Essays in Honor of George J. Buelow*, edited by Thomas J. Mathiesen and Benito V. Rivera, 197–231. Stuyvesant, NY: Pendragon Press, 1995.

Harich-Schneider, Eta. *A History of Japanese Music.* London: Oxford University Press, 1973.

Harich-Schneider, Eta. "Renaissance Europe through Japanese Eyes." *Early Music* 1, no. 1 (1973): 19–25.

Harrán, Don. *Salamone Rossi: Jewish Musician in Late Renaissance Mantua.* Oxford: Oxford University Press, 1999.

Harrán, Don. *Three Early Modern Hebrew Scholars on the Mysteries of Song.* Leiden: Brill, 2015.

Harrán, Don. "Tradition and Innovation in Jewish Music of the Later Renaissance." *Journal of Musicology* 7, no. 1 (1989): 107–130.

Harrison, Frank Llewellyn. "Observation, Elucidation, Utilization: Western Attitudes to Eastern Musics, ca.1600–ca.1830." In *Slavonic and Western Music: Essays for Gerald Abraham*, edited by Malcolm Hamrick Brown and Roland John Wiley, 5–31. Ann Arbor, MI: UMI Research Press, 1985.

Harrison, Frank Llewellyn, ed. *Time, Place and Music: An Anthology of Ethnomusicological Observation c. 1550 to c. 1800.* Amsterdam: Frits Knuf, 1973.

Hartley, Janet M. "Is Russia Part of Europe? Russian Perceptions of Europe in the Reign of Alexander I." *Cahiers du Monde Russe et Soviétique* 33, no. 4 (1992): 369–385.

Hasselquist, Fredrik. *Voyages and Travels in the Levant; in the years 1749, 50, 51, 52. Containing Observations in Natural History, Physick, Agriculture, and Commerce: Particularly on the Holy Land, and the Natural History of the Scriptures.* London: L. Davis and C. Reymers, 1766.

Hawkins, Sir John. *A General History of the Science and Practice of Music.* 5 vols. London: T. Payne, 1776.

Hayes, Jeremy. "Orfeo ed Euridice [*Orphée et Eurydice* ('Orpheus and Eurydice')] (i)." *Oxford Music Online/Grove Music Online*, 2002. https://www.oxfordmusiconline.com/grovemusic/view/10.1093/gmo/9781561592630.001.0001/omo-9781561592630-e-5000008226

Hayes, William. *Vocal and Instrumental Musick, in Three Parts*. [Oxford]: William Hayes, 1742.

Haynes, Bruce, and Geoffrey Burgess. *The Pathetick Musician: Moving an Audience in the Age of Eloquence*. New York: Oxford University Press, 2016.

Head, Matthew. "Music with 'No Past'? Archaeologies of Joseph Haydn and *The Creation*." *19th-Century Music* 23, no. 3 (2000): 191–217.

Head, Raymond. "Corelli in Calcutta: Colonial Music-Making in India during the 17th and 18th Centuries." *Early Music* 13, no. 4 (1985): 548–553.

Heckmann, Ruth. "Mann und Weib in der 'musicalischen Republick': Modelle der Geschlechterpolarisierung in der Musikanschauung 1750–1800." In *Geschlechterpolaritäten in der Musikgeschichte des 18. bis 20. Jahrhunderts*, edited by Rebecca Grotjahn and Freia Hoffmann, 19–30. Herbolzheim: Centaurus, 2002.

Heer, Friedrich. *The Intellectual History of Europe*. Translated by Jonathan Steinberg. London: Weidenfeld & Nicolson, 1966.

Hegel, Georg Wilhelm Friedrich. *Lectures on the Philosophy of World History, Introduction: Reason in History*. Translated by H. B. Nisbet. Cambridge: Cambridge University Press, 1975.

Heighes, Simon. *The Lives and Works of William and Philip Hayes*. New York: Garland, 1995.

Hensel, Gottfried. *Europa polyglotta*, 1741. Map. P. J. Mode Collection of Persuasive Cartography (8548). Division of Rare and Manuscript Collections, Cornell University Library. https://www.jstor.org/stable/community.3293755

Henzel, Christoph. "Graun, Carl Heinrich." *Oxford Music Online/Grove Music Online*, 2001. https://www.oxfordmusiconline.com/grovemusic/view/10.1093/gmo/9781561592630.001.0001/omo-9781561592630-e-90000380274

Herczog, Johann. *Orfeo nelle Indie: I gesuiti e la musica in Paraguay (1609–1767)*. [Galatina]: M. Congedo, 2001.

Herder, Johann Gottfried. *Briefe zur Beförderung der Humanität*. 10 vols. Riga: Johann Friedrich Hartknoch, 1793–1797.

Herder, Johann Gottfried, and Philip V. Bohlman. *Song Loves the Masses: Herder on Music and Nationalism*. Berkeley: University of California Press, 2017.

Hernández, Pablo. *Misiones del Paraguay: Organización social de las doctrinas guaraníes de la Compañía de Jesús*. 2 vols. Barcelona: G. Gili, 1913.

Hernández Araico, Susana. "El código festivo renacentista barroco y las loas sacramentales de Sor Juana: Des/re/construcción del mundo europeo." In *El escritor y la escena: Actas del II Congreso de la Asociación Internacional de Teatro Español y Novohispano de los Siglos de Oro (17–20 de marzo de 1993, Ciudad Juárez)*, edited by Ysla Campbell, 75–93. Ciudad Juárez: Universidad Autónoma de Ciudad Juárez, 1994.

Herodotus. *The Histories*. Translated by Robin Waterfield with introduction and notes by Carolyn Dewald. Oxford: Oxford University Press, 2008.

Herresthal, Harald. *Carl Arnold (1794–1873): Ein europäischer Musiker des 19. Jahrhunderts: Eine Dokumentarbiographie mit thematischen Werkverzeichnis*. Wilhelmshaven: Noetzel, 1993.

Higgins, Geoffrey. "Old Sluts and Dangerous Minuets: Or, the Underlying Musical Tensions of the *Querelle des Bouffons*." *Eighteenth-Century Studies* 45, no. 4 (2012): 549–563.

Hince, Bernadette, Rupert Summerson, and Arnan Wiesel, eds. *Antarctica: Music, Sounds and Cultural Connections*. Acton: Australian National University Press, 2015.

Hippocrates. *Ancient Medicine. Airs, Waters, Places. Epidemics 1 and 3. The Oath. Precepts. Nutriment*. Edited and translated by Paul Potter. Loeb Classical Library 147. Cambridge, MA: Harvard University Press, 2022.

Histoire universelle, depuis le commencement du monde, jusqu'à present. Traduite de l'anglois d'une société de gens de lettres. 46 vols. Amsterdam: Arkstée et Merkus, 1742–1792.

"Historia general de los viages. Ciencias de los Chinos. Musica." *Diario Noticioso Universal* (Madrid), January 17, 1769, 5851–5852.

Hobson, John M. *The Eastern Origins of Western Civilisation*. Cambridge: Cambridge University Press, 2004.

Höffe, Otfried, and Andreas Kablitz, eds. *Europäische Musik—Musik Europas*. Paderborn: Wilhelm Fink, 2017.

Höft, Thomas. "L'Europa: una festa teatrale." Translated by Susan Marie Praeder. Liner notes in Alessandro Melani, *Europa; Sacred Works*. CD. CPO, 777 408-2, 2008.

Holm, Bent, and Mikael Bøgh Rasmussen, eds. *Imagined, Embodied and Actual Turks in Early Modern Europe*. Vienna: Hollitzer Verlag, 2021.

Holman, Peter. *Four and Twenty Fiddlers: The Violin at the English Court 1540–1690*. Oxford: Clarendon Press, 1993.

Horace. *Odes and Epodes*. Edited and translated by Niall Rudd. Loeb Classical Library 33. Cambridge, MA: Harvard University Press, 2004.

Horace and André Dacier. *Oeuvres d'Horace en latin et françois: Avec des remarques critiques et historiques*. 3rd ed. 10 vols. Paris: J.-B. Christophe Ballard, 1709.

Horace and André Dacier. *Remarques critiques sur les oeuvres d'Horace: Avec une nouvelle traduction*. 10 vols. Paris: Denys Thierry, 1681–1689.

Horowitz, Maryanne Cline. "Introduction (1): Rival Interpretations of Continent Personifications." In *Bodies and Maps: Early Modern Personifications of the Continents*, edited by Maryanne Cline Horowitz and Louise Arizzoli, 1–24. Leiden: Brill, 2021.

Horowitz, Maryanne Cline, and Louise Arizzoli, eds. *Bodies and Maps: Early Modern Personifications of the Continents*. Leiden: Brill, 2021.

Høst, Georg. *Efterretninger om Marókos og Fes, samlede der i landene fra ao. 1760 til 1768*. Copenhagen: N. Möller, 1779.

Høst, Georg. *Nachrichten von Marókos und Fes, im Lande selbst gesammlet, in den Jahren 1760 bis 1768*. Copenhagen: Christian Gottlob Proft, 1781.

Høst, Georg. *Relations sur les royaumes de Marrakech et Fès: Recueillies dans ces pays de 1760 à 1768*. Translated by Frédéric Damgaard and Pierre Gailhanou. Rabat: Éditions La Porte, 2002.

Howard, Deborah. *Venice and the East: The Impact of the Islamic World on Venetian Architecture 1100–1500*. New Haven, CT: Yale University Press, 2000.

Hoyt, Peter A. "On the Primitives of Music Theory: The Savage and Subconscious as Sources of Analytical Authority." In *Music Theory and Natural Order from the Renaissance to the Early Twentieth Century*, edited by Suzannah Clark and Alexander Rehding, 197–212. Cambridge: Cambridge University Press, 2001.

Hu, Zhuqing (Lester) S. "Chinese Ears, Delicate or Dull? Toward a Decolonial Comparativism." *Journal of the American Musicological Society* 74, no. 3 (2021): 501–569.

Hu, Zhuqing (Lester) S. "From Ut Re Mi to Fourteen-Tone Temperament: The Global Acoustemologies of an Early Modern Chinese Tuning Reform." PhD diss., University of Chicago, 2019.

Hu, Zhuqing (Lester) S. "A Princely Manuscript at the National Library of China—Part I: Guido's Hexachords and the 18th-Century Chinese Opera Reform." *History of Music Theory*, February 1, 2019. https://historyofmusictheory.wordpress.com/2019/02/01/a-princely-manuscript-at-the-national-library-of-china-part-i-guidos-hexachords-and-the-18th-century-chinese-opera-reform/amp/

Hudgebut, John. *Thesaurus Musicus: Being, a Collection of the Newest Songs Performed at Their Majesties Theatres; and at the Consorts in Viller-Street in York-Buildings, and in Charles-Street Covent-Garden . . . The Third Book*. London: John Hudgebutt, 1695.

Hughes, Lindsey. *Russia in the Age of Peter the Great*. New Haven, CT: Yale University Press, 1998.

Hughes, Rosemary S. M. "Dr. Burney's Championship of Haydn." *Musical Quarterly* 27, no. 1 (1941): 90–96.

Hume, David. *Essays and Treatises on Several Subjects. By David Hume, Esq; in Four Volumes. Vol. I. Containing Essays, Moral and Political*. 4th ed. London: A. Millar and A. Kincaid and A. Donaldson, 1753.

Hume, David. *Three Essays, Moral and Political. Never Before Published. Which Compleats the Former Edition, in Two Volumes, Octavo*. London: A. Millar and A. Kincaid, 1748.

Hyde, James H. "The Four Parts of the World: As Represented in Old-Time Pageants and Ballets Part I." *Apollo* 4, no. 24 (1926): 232–238.

Hyde, James H. "The Four Parts of the World: As Represented in Old-Time Pageants and Ballets Part II." *Apollo* 5, no. 25 (1927): 19–27.

Hyde, James H. "L'iconographie des quatre parties du monde dans les tapisseries." *Gazette des Beaux-Arts* 10 (1924): 253–272.

Irvine, Thomas. *Listening to China: Sound and the Sino-Western Encounter, 1770–1839*. Chicago: University of Chicago Press, 2020.

Irving, David R. M. "Ancient Greeks, World Music, and Early Modern Constructions of Western European Identity." In *Studies on a Global History of Music: A Balzan Musicology Project*, edited by Reinhard Strohm, 21–41. Abingdon: Routledge, 2018.

Irving, David R. M. *Colonial Counterpoint: Music in Early Modern Manila*. New York: Oxford University Press, 2010.

Irving, David R. M. "Comparative Organography in Early Modern Empires." *Music and Letters* 90, no. 3 (2009): 372–398.

Irving, David R. M. "Exchange: Musical Transactions around the World." In *A Cultural History of Music in the Age of Enlightenment*, edited by David R. M. Irving and Estelle Joubert, 101–126. London: Bloomsbury, 2024.

Irving, David R. M. "The Hearing of Humanity: Music, Colonialism, and Bartolomé de Las Casas' Philosophical Defense of Indigenous Americans." In *The Oxford Handbook of Music Colonialism*, edited by Erin Johnson-Williams, Roe-Min Kok, and Yvonne Liao. New York: Oxford University Press, forthcoming.

Irving, David R. M. "Interpreting Non-European Perceptions and Representations of Early Modern European Music." In *The Historiography of Music in Global Perspective*, edited by Sam Mirelman, 43–50. Piscataway, NJ: Gorgias Press, 2010.

Irving, David R. M. "The Pacific in the Minds and Music of Enlightenment Europe." *Eighteenth-Century Music* 2, no. 2 (2005): 205–229.

Irving, David R. M. "Psalms, Islam, and Music: Dialogues and Divergence about David in Christian–Muslim Encounters of the Seventeenth Century." *Yale Journal of Music and Religion* 2, no. 1 (2016): 53–78. https://elischolar.library.yale.edu/yjmr/vol2/iss1/3/

Irving, David R. M., and Estelle Joubert. "Introduction: Musicking in the Age of Enlightenment." In *A Cultural History of Music in the Age of Enlightenment*, edited by David R. M. Irving and Estelle Joubert, 1–37. London: Bloomsbury, 2024.

Irving, David R. M., and Alan Maddox. "Towards a Reflexive Paradigm for the Study of Musics in Australian Colonial Societies (1788–1900)." *Context: A Journal of Music Research* 46 (2020): 51–73. https://contextjournal.music.unimelb.edu.au/no-46-2020/.

Isherwood, Robert M. "The Festivity of the Parisian Boulevards." In *Edo and Paris: Urban Life and the State in the Early Modern Era*, edited by James L. McClain, John M. Merriman, and Kaoru Ugawa, 292–309. Ithaca, NY: Cornell University Press, 1994.

"Itinerant Musicians." *Saturday Magazine*, December 13, 1834, 226–229.

Jackson, Ashley. *The British Empire: A Very Short Introduction*. Oxford: Oxford University Press, 2013.

Jami, Catherine. "Tomé Pereira (1645–1708), Clockmaker, Musician and Interpreter at the Kangxi Court: Portuguese Interests and the Transmission of Science." In *The Jesuits, the Padroado and East Asian Science (1552–1773)*, edited by Luís Saraiva and Catherine Jami, 187–204. Singapore: World Scientific, 2008.

Janz, Tobias, and Chien-Chang Yang. "Introduction: Musicology, Musical Modernity, and the Challenges of Entangled History." In *Decentering Musical Modernity: Perspectives on East Asian and European Music History*, edited by Tobias Janz and Chien-Chang Yang, 9–39. Bielefeld: Transcript Verlag, 2019.

Jaucourt, Louis, Chevalier de. "Europe." In *Encyclopédie, ou dictionnaire raisonné des sciences, des arts et des métiers*, edited by Denis Diderot and Jean le Rond d'Alembert, Vol. 6 (1756), 211–212. Paris: Briasson, David, Le Breton, and Durand, 1751–1765.

Jaucourt, Louis, Chevalier de. "Europe." In *Encyclopédie, ou dictionnaire raisonné des sciences, des arts et des métiers*. University of Chicago, ARTFL Encyclopédie Project, Autumn 2017. https://artflsrv04.uchicago.edu/philologic4.7/encyclopedie0922/navigate/6/476.

Jenkinson, Matthew. "John Crowne, the Restoration Court, and the 'Understanding' of *Calisto*." *Court Historian* 15, no. 2 (2010): 145–155.

Jensen, Claudia R. *Musical Cultures in Seventeenth-Century Russia*. Bloomington: Indiana University Press, 2009.

Jensen, Claudia R. "A Theoretical Work of Late Seventeenth-Century Muscovy: Nikolai Diletskii's *Grammatika* and the Earliest Circle of Fifths." *Journal of the American Musicological Society* 45, no. 2 (1992): 305–331.

Jerold, Beverly. "Quantz and Agricola: A Literary Collaboration." *Acta Musicologica* 88, no. 2 (2016): 127–142.

Jia, Shubing. "The Dissemination of Western Music through Catholic Missions in High Qing China (1662–1795)." PhD diss., University of Bristol, 2012.

Jiang, Qingfan. "In Search of the 'Oriental Origin': Rameau, Rousseau and Chinese Music in Eighteenth-Century France." *Eighteenth-Century Music* 19, no. 2 (2022): 125–149.

Jiang, Qingfan, and David R. M. Irving. "Cultural Practices: Missions and Music in Multilingual Spaces." In *A Cultural History of Translation in the Construction of the Global World*, edited by Rebekah Clements. London: Bloomsbury, forthcoming.

Jones, Sir William. "On the Musical Modes of the Hindus: Written in 1784, and Since Much Enlarged—By the President." *Asiatick Researches: or, Transactions of the Society,*

Instituted in Bengal, for Inquiring into the History and Antiquities, the Arts, Sciences, and Literature of Asia 3 (1792): 55–87.
Joshi, Esha Basanti, ed. *Uttar Pradesh District Gazetteers: Meerut*. Lucknow: Government of Uttar Pradesh (Department of District Gazetteers), 1965.
Joubert, Estelle. "Analytical Encounters: Global Music Criticism and Enlightenment Ethnomusicology." In *Studies on a Global History of Music: A Balzan Musicology Project*, edited by Reinhard Strohm, 42–60. Abingdon: Routledge, 2018.
"Journal de Paris." *Le Nouveau Mercure*, April 1721, 165–176.
Juvenel de Carlencas, Félix de. *Essais sur l'histoire des belles lettres, des siences [sic] et des arts*. New augmented ed. 4 vols. Lyon: Frères Duplain, 1749.
Kafadar, Cemal. "A Rome of One's Own: Reflections on Cultural Geography and Identity in the Lands of Rum." *Muqarnas* 24 (2007): 7–25.
Kahn, Joel S. "Anthropology and Modernity." *Current Anthropology* 42, no. 5 (2001): 651–680.
Kaldellis, Anthony. "From Rome to New Rome, from Empire to Nation-State: Reopening the Question of Byzantium's Roman Identity." In *Two Romes: Rome and Constantinople in Late Antiquity*, edited by Lucy Grig and Gavin Kelly, 387–404. New York: Oxford University Press, 2012.
Kambe, Yukimi. "Viols in Japan in the Sixteenth and Early Seventeenth Centuries." *Journal of the Viola da Gamba Society of America* 37 (2000): 31–67.
Karnes, Kevin C. "Inventing Eastern Europe in the Ear of the Enlightenment." *Journal of the American Musicological Society* 71, no. 1 (2018): 75–108.
Kassler, Jamie C. "Brown, John." *Oxford Music Online/Grove Music Online*, 2001. https://www.oxfordmusiconline.com/grovemusic/view/10.1093/gmo/9781561592 630.001.0001/omo-9781561592630-e-0000004101
Katalinić, Vjera, ed. *Music Migrations in the Early Modern Age: People, Markets, Patterns and Styles*. Zagreb: Hrvatsko Muzikološko Društvo, 2016.
Katzew, Ilona. *Casta Painting: Images of Race in Eighteenth-Century Mexico*. New Haven, CT: Yale University Press, 2004.
Keefe, Simon. "Across the Divide: Currents of Musical Thought in Europe, c. 1790–1810." In *The Cambridge History of Eighteenth-Century Music*, edited by Simon P. Keefe, 663–687. Cambridge: Cambridge University Press, 2009.
Keenan, Paul. *St Petersburg and the Russian Court, 1703–1761*. Basingstoke: Palgrave Macmillan, 2013.
Keevak, Michael. *Becoming Yellow: A Short History of Racial Thinking*. Princeton, NJ: Princeton University Press, 2011.
Keevak, Michael. "How Did East Asians Become Yellow?" In *Reconsidering Race: Social Science Perspectives on Racial Categories in the Age of Genomics*, edited by Kazuko Suzuki and Diego A. Von Vacano, 204–208. New York: Oxford University Press, 2018.
Kelly, Thomas Forrest. *Early Music: A Very Short Introduction*. New York: Oxford University Press, 2011.
Kendall, Dave. "'This Is Not Filipino Music': Syncretism, Homogeneity, and the Search for Philippine-ness in Spanish Colonial Liturgical Music." *Pintacasi: A Journal of Church Cultural Heritage* 8 (2012): 13–40.
Kenyon, Nicholas, ed. *Authenticity and Early Music: A Symposium*. Oxford: Oxford University Press, 1988.
Keyser, Dorothy. "The Character of Exploration: Adrian Willaert's *Quid non ebrietas*." In *Musical Repercussions of 1492: Encounters in Text and Performance*, edited by Carol E. Robertson, 185–207. Washington, DC: Smithsonian Institution Press, 1992.

Kiesewetter, Raphael Georg. *Geschichte der europäisch-abendländischen oder unsrer heutigen Musik.* Leipzig: Breitkopf & Härtel, 1834.

Kiesewetter, Raphael Georg. *History of the Modern Music of Western Europe.* Translated by Robert Müller. London: T. C. Newby, 1848.

Kim, Jin-Ah. "'European Music' outside Europe? Musical Entangling and Intercrossing in the Case of Korea's Modern History." In *Studies on a Global History of Music: A Balzan Musicology Project*, edited by Reinhard Strohm, 177–197. Abingdon: Routledge, 2018.

Kinderman, William, and Malcolm Miller, eds. *Beethoven the European: Transcultural Contexts of Performance, Interpretation and Reception.* Turnhout: Brepols, 2022.

King's College London. "Musical Transitions to European Colonialism in the Eastern Indian Ocean." https://www.kcl.ac.uk/music/research-expertise/musical-transitions.

Kipling, Rudyard. *Rudyard Kipling's Verse.* Garden City, NY: Doubleday, 1940.

Kircher, Athanasius. "From *Musurgia universalis, or, the Great Art of Consonances and Dissonances*." Translated by Margaret Murata. In *Strunk's Source Readings in Music History*, edited by Leo Treitler, 707–711. New York: W. W. Norton, 1998.

Kircher, Athanasius. *Musurgia universalis sive ars magna consoni et dissoni in X. libros digesta.* 2 vols. Rome: Haeredum Francisci Corbelletti, 1650.

Kivelson, Valerie A. "The Cartographic Emergence of Europe?" In *The Oxford Handbook of Early Modern European History, 1350–1750*, Volume I: *Peoples and Places*, edited by Hamish Scott, 37–69. Oxford: Oxford University Press, 2015.

Klotz, Sebastian. "Tartini the Indian: Perspectives on World Music in the Enlightenment." In *The Cambridge History of World Music*, edited by Philip V. Bohlman, 277–297. Cambridge: Cambridge University Press, 2013.

Knapp, William. *New Church Melody: Being a Set of Anthems, Psalms, Hymns, etc. in Four Parts . . . With a great Variety of other Anthems, Psalms, Hymns, etc. composed after a Method Entirely New, and Never Printed Before . . . With an Anthem on Psalm cxxvii. by One of the Greatest Masters in Europe.* London: R. Baldwin, 1751.

Knapp, William. *New Church Melody: Being a Set of Anthems, Psalms, Hymns, &c. on Various Occasions. In Four Parts with a great Variety of other Anthems, Psalms, Hymns, &c. composed after a Method Entirely New, and Never Printed Before . . . With an Anthem on Psalm cxxvii. by One of the Greatest Masters in Europe.* 5th ed. London: R. Baldwin, S. Crowder, the author, and B. Collins, 1764.

Knighton, Tess. "Instruments, Instrumental Music and Instrumentalists: Traditions and Transitions." In *Companion to Music in the Age of the Catholic Monarchs*, edited by Tess Knighton, 97–144. Leiden: Brill, 2017.

Kolb, Peter. *Caput Bonae Spei hodiernum: Das ist vollständige Beschreibung des afrikanischen Vorgebürges der Guten Hofnung.* Nuremberg: Monath, 1719.

Kolb, Peter. *Description du Cap de Bonne-Espérance; où l'on trouve tout ce qui concerne l'histoire-naturelle du pays; la religion, les moeurs & les usages des Hottentots; et l'etablissement des Hollandois.* Translated by Jean Bertrand. 3 vols. Amsterdam: Jean Catuffe, 1741.

Kolb, Peter. *Naaukeurige en uitvoerige beschryving van de kaap de Goede Hoop: Behelzende een zeer omstandig verhaal van den tegenwoordigen toestant van dat vermaarde gewest, deszelfs gelegenheit, haven, sterkt, regerings-vorm, uitgestrektheit, en onlangs ontdekte aanleggende landen.* Amsterdam: Balthazar Lakeman, 1727.

Kolb, Peter. *The Present State of the Cape of Good-Hope.* Translated by [Guido] Medley. 2nd ed. 2 vols. London: W. Innys and R. Manby, 1738.

Kolb, Peter. *The Present State of the Cape of Good Hope: or, A Particular Account of the Several Nations of the Hottentots*. Translated by [Guido] Medley. 2 vols. London: W. Innys, 1731.

Koller, Markus. "Europe and the Ottoman Empire." Translated by Carol Oberschmidt and Thomas Oberschmidt. In *The Boundaries of Europe: From the Fall of the Ancient World to the Age of Decolonisation*, edited by Pietro Rossi, 157–172. Berlin: De Gruyter, 2015.

König, Daniel G. *Arabic-Islamic Views of the Latin West: Tracing the Emergence of Medieval Europe*. New York: Oxford University Press, 2015.

Koskoff, Ellen. "What Do We Want to Teach When We Teach Music? One Apology, Two Short Trips, Three Ethical Dilemmas and Eighty-Two Questions." In *Rethinking Music*, edited by Nicholas Cook and Mark Everist, 545–559. Oxford: Oxford University Press, 1999.

Kowner, Rotem. *From White to Yellow: The Japanese in European Racial Thought, 1300–1735*. Montreal: McGill-Queen's University Press, 2014.

[Kruzenshtern, Ivan Fedorovich]. "Die Insulaner non Nukahiwa." In *St. Petersburger Taschen-Kalender auf das Jahr nach Christi Geburt 1810, welches ein gemeines Jahr ist von 365 Tagen*, 181–226. St. Petersburg: Kaiserl. Akademie der Wissenschaften, 1810.

Kruzenshtern, Ivan Fedorovich. *Puteshestvie vokrug sveta v 1803, 4, 5 i 1806 godakh. Po poveleniiu ego Imperatorskogo Velichestva Aleksandra I, na korabliakh Nadezhde i Neve pod nachal'stvom Flota Kapitan-Leitenanta, nyne Kapitana vtorogo ranga, Kruzenshterna, Gosudarstvennogo Admiralteiskogo Departamenta i Imperatorskoi Akademii Nauk Chlena*. 3 vols. St. Petersburg: V Morskoi Tipografii, 1809–1813.

Kruzenshtern, Ivan Fedorovich. *Reise um die Welt in den Jahren 1803, 1804, 1805 und 1806 auf Befehl seiner Kaiserl. Majestät Alexanders des Ersten auf den Schiffen Nadeshda und Newa unter dem Commando des Capitäns von der Kaiserl. Marine A. J. von Krusenstern*. 2nd ed. 2 vols (in 3). Berlin: Haude und Spener, 1811–1812.

Kruzenshtern, Ivan Fedorovich. *Reize om de wereld gedaan in de jaren 1803, 1804, 1805 en 1806: Op bevel van Alexander den eersten keizer van Rusland*. 4 vols. Haarlem: Bij A. Loosjes Pz, 1811.

Kruzenshtern, Ivan Fedorovich. *Viaggio intorno al mondo fatto negli anni 1803-4-5 e 1806: d'ordine di sua maesta' imperiale Alessandro Primo su i vascelli la Nadeshda e la Neva sotto il comando del capitano della marina imperiale A.G. di Krusenstern*. Translated by Sig. Angiolini. 3 vols. Milan: Giambaitista Sonzogno, 1818.

Kruzenshtern, Ivan Fedorovich. *Voyage autour du monde: fait dans les années 1803, 1804, 1805, et 1806, par les ordres de sa majesté impériale Alexandre Ier, Empereur de Russie, sur les vaisseaux la Nadiejeda et la Néva commandés par M. de Krusenstern*. Translated by the author. Translation revised by M. J.-B.-B. Eyriès. 2 vols. Paris: Librairie de Gide Fils, 1821.

Kruzenshtern, Ivan Fedorovich. *Voyage round the World, in the Years 1803, 1804, 1805, & 1806: By Order of His Imperial Majesty Alexander the First, on Board the Ships Nadeshda and Neva, under Command of Captain A. J. von Krusenstern, of the Imperial Navy*. Translated by Richard Belgrave Hoppner. 2 vols. London: John Murray, 1813.

[Kruzenshtern, Ivan Fedorovich]. "O zhiteliakh ostrova Nukagivy." *Sanktpeterburgskii karmannyi mesiatsoslov* (1818): 191–256.

"Kurzer Anzeigen." *Allgemeine musikalische Zeitung* 35, no. 23 (1833): cols. 387–388.

Kusber, Jan, and Matthias Schnettger. "The Russian Experience: The Example of Filippo Balatri." In *Musicians' Mobilities and Music Migrations in Early Modern Europe:*

Biographical Patterns and Cultural Exchanges, edited by Gesa zur Nieden and Berthold Over, 241–254. Bielefeld: Transcript Verlag, 2016.

La Baume Le Blanc, Louis César de, duc de La Vallière. *Ballets, opera, et autres ouvrages lyriques, par ordre chronologique depuis leur origine; avec une table alphabetique des ouvrages et des auteurs*. Paris: Cl. J. Baptiste Bauche, 1760.

La Borde, Jean-Benjamin de. *Essai sur la musique ancienne et moderne*. 4 vols. Paris: Ph.-D. Pierres, 1780.

Lachmann, Robert. *The Oriental Music Broadcasts, 1936–1937: A Musical Ethnography of Mandatory Palestine*. Edited by Ruth Davis. Middleton, WI: A-R Editions, 2013.

Lafitau, Joseph François. *Moeurs des sauvages ameriquains, compareès aux moeurs des premiers temps*. 4 vols. Paris: Charles Estienne Hochereau, 1724.

Lafitau, Joseph François. *Customs of the American Indians Compared with the Customs of Primitive Times*. Edited and translated by William N. Fenton and Elizabeth L. Moore. 2 vols. Toronto: Champlain Society, 1974–1977.

La Loubère, Simon de. *Du royaume de Siam par Monsieur de La Loubere envoyé extraordinaire du roy auprés du roy de Siam en 1687. & 1688*. 2 vols. Paris: Jean Baptiste Coignard, 1691.

La Motte, Antoine Houdar de. *L'Europe galante, ballet en musique, representée par l'Accademie [sic] Royale de Musique*. Paris: Christophe Ballard, 1697.

Lang, Henry Paul. *Music in Western Civilization*. New York: W. W. Norton, 1941.

Lanzellotti, Federico. "Carlo Ambrogio Lonati, 'Inventor of Double Stops,' and His Reception in Britain (1676–1724)." Paper presented at the 58th Annual Conference of the Royal Musical Association, Durham University, September 8, 2022.

Laporte, Joseph de. *El viagero universal, ó, Noticia del mundo antiguo y nuevo*. Edited by D. P. E. P. [Pedro Estala]. 43 vols. Madrid: Fermin Villalpando, 1795–1801.

Laporte, Joseph de. *O viajante universal, ou Noticia do mundo antigo e moderno: Obra composta em francez por Mr. de Laporte. Traduzida em hespanhol, correcto o original, e illustrado com notas, e agora vertida em portuguez*. 51 vols. Lisbon: Typografia Rollandiana, 1798–1815.

Las Casas, Bartolomé de. *Apologética historia de las Indias*. Edited by Manuel Serrano y Sanz. Madrid: Bailly-Baillière é Hijos, 1909.

Law, Hedy, Daniel F. Castro Pantoja, and Hyun Kyong Hannah Chang, eds. "Teaching Global Music History: Practices and Challenges." *Journal of Music History Pedagogy* 13, no. 1 (2023): 45–173.

Le Brun, Antoine Louis [as Monsieur Le Br . . .]. *Théatre lyrique: avec une préface, ou l'on traite du Poëme de l'Opéra. Et la réponse à une epître satyrique contre ce spectacle*. Paris: Pierre Ribou, 1712.

Le Cerf de la Viéville, Jean Laurent. *Comparaison de la musique italienne, et de la musique Françoise*. 3 vols. Brussels: François Foppens, 1705.

Lee, Sidney. "Phillips, John (1631–1706)." *Oxford Dictionary of National Biography* [1895]. https://www.oxforddnb.com/display/10.1093/odnb/9780192683120.001.0001/odnb-9780192683120-e-22161

Leezenberg, Michiel. "The Oriental Origins of Orientalism: The Case of Dimitrie Cantemir." In *The Making of the Humanities*, Vol. 2: *From Early Modern to Modern Disciplines*, edited by Rens Bod, Jaap Maat, and Thijs Weststeijn, 243–264. Amsterdam: Amsterdam University Press, 2012.

Le Goff, Jacques. *The Birth of Europe*. Translated by Janet Lloyd. Malden, MA: Blackwell, 2005.

Lenke, Sabine. "Heil und Heilung: Krankheitsvorstellungen und Heilkunde der südamerikanischen Guaraní-Indianer, gespiegelt in den Quellen der Jesuiten." PhD diss., Freien Universität Berlin, 2012.
Leonhardt, Carlos. "El P. Antonio Sepp, S. J.: Insigne misionero de las reducciones guaraníticas del Paraguay 1691–1733 (conclusión)." *Estudios de la Academia Literaria del Plata* (November 1924): 370–376.
Lerman, Antony, ed. *Do I Belong? Reflections from Europe*. London: Pluto Press, 2017.
Lester, Joel. *Between Modes and Keys: German Theory 1592–1802*. Stuyvesant, NY: Pendragon Press, 1989.
Lewis, Bernard. *The Muslim Discovery of Europe*. London: Weidenfeld & Nicolson, 1982.
Libby, Dennis. "Balducci, Marina." *Oxford Music Online/Grove Music Online*, 2002. https://www.oxfordmusiconline.com/grovemusic/view/10.1093/gmo/9781561592630.001.0001/omo-9781561592630-e-5000900407
Limojon de Saint Didier, Ignace François de. *Le voyage du Parnasse*. Rotterdam: Fristch & Bohm, 1716.
Limor, Ora. "Sharing Sacred Space: Holy Places in Jerusalem between Christianity, Judaism and Islam." In *In Laudem Hierosolymitani: Studies in Crusades and Medieval Culture in Honour of Benjamin Z. Kedar*, edited by Iris Shagrir, Ronnie Ellenblum, and Jonathan Riley-Smith, 219–231. Aldershot: Ashgate, 2007.
Lincoln, Stoddard. "J. E. Galliard and *A Critical Discourse*." *Musical Quarterly* 53, no. 3 (1967): 347–364.
Lindorff, Joyce. "Missionaries, Keyboards and Musical Exchange in the Ming and Qing Courts." *Early Music* 32, no. 3 (2004): 403–414.
Lindorff, Joyce. "Pereira's Musical Heritage as Context for His Contributions in China." In *Europe and China: Science and Arts in the 17th and 18th Centuries*, edited by Luís Saraiva, 153–159. Singapore: World Scientific, 2013.
Locke, Ralph P. *Music and the Exotic from the Renaissance to Mozart*. Cambridge: Cambridge University Press, 2015.
Locke, Ralph P. *Musical Exoticism: Images and Reflections*. Cambridge: Cambridge University Press, 2009.
Lockwood, Lewis. "Review of *The Rise of European Music, 1380–1500* by Reinhard Strohm." *Journal of the Royal Musical Association* 120, no. 1 (1995): 151–162.
Lombardía, Ana. "From Lavapiés to Stockholm: Eighteenth-Century Violin Fandangos and the Shaping of Musical 'Spanishness.'" *Eighteenth-Century Music* 17, no. 2 (2020): 177–199.
Longino, Michèle. *French Travel Writing in the Ottoman Empire: Marseilles to Constantinople, 1650–1700*. New York: Routledge, 2015.
Longman and Broderip. *A Complete Register of All the New Musical Publications Imported from Different Parts of Europe by Longman and Broderip*. [London]: n.p., [1786].
Lowe, Kate. "Introduction." In *Black Africans in Renaissance Europe*, edited by T. F. Earle and K. J. P. Lowe, 1–14. Cambridge: Cambridge University Press, 2005.
Lowenthal, David. *The Past Is a Foreign Country*. Cambridge: Cambridge University Press, 1985.
Lowerre, Kathryn. "A *Ballet des nations* for English Audiences: *Europe's Revels for the Peace of Ryswick* (1697)." *Early Music* 35, no. 3 (2007): 419–433.
Lukin, Michael James Clifton. "Johann Melchior Gletle's *Expeditionis musicae classis II*, Op. 2: An Edition and Commentary." BMus (Hon.) thesis, Western Australian

Academy of Performing Arts, Edith Cowan University, 2020. https://ro.ecu.edu.au/theses_hons/1545

Lully, Jean-Baptiste. *Lully: Ballet Royal de Flore, LWV 40*. Sound recording. La Simphonie du Marais, directed by Hugo Reyne. Decca Records [Accord B00005AVB5], 2001. https://music.apple.com/es/album/lully-ballet-royal-de-flore-lwv-40/1452141710

MacNeil, Anne. "Weeping at the Water's Edge." *Early Music* 27, no. 3 (1999): 407–418.

Magnan, Dominique. *La città di Roma: Ovvero breve descrizione di questa superba citta*. 4 vols. Rome: Venanzio Monaldini, Gaetano Quojani, Gregorio Settari, 1779.

Magnan, Dominique. *La ville de Rome, ou, Description abrégée de cette superbe ville*. 4 vols. Rome: Venan, Monaldini, Bouchard et Gravier, Gregoire Settari, 1778.

Mahajani, Usha. "Is Australia a Part of Asia?" *Australian Quarterly* 36, no. 2 (1964): 25–34.

Mahdavi, Shireen. "Jukes, Andrew." *Encyclopædia Iranica*, September 15, 2009. https://www.iranicaonline.org/articles/jukes-andrew-british-east-india-company-surgeon

Malcolm, Alexander. *A Treatise of Musick, Speculative, Practical, and Historical*. Edinburgh: Alexander Malcolm, 1721.

Malcolm, Noel. *Agents of Empire: Knights, Corsairs, Jesuits and Spies in the Sixteenth-Century Mediterranean World*. New York: Oxford University Press, 2015.

March, Jenny. *Dictionary of Classical Mythology*. Oxford: Oxbow Books, 2014.

Marín López, Javier. "Tradición e innovación en los instrumentos de cuerda de la Catedral de México." In *Harmonia mundi: Los instrumentos sonoros en Iberoamérica, siglos XVI al XIX*, edited by Lucero Enríquez, 239–260. Mexico City: Universidad Nacional Autónoma de México, 2009.

Mariner, William, and John Martin. *An Account of the Natives of the Tonga Islands, in the South Pacific Ocean. With an Original Grammar and Vocabulary of Their Language*. 1st ed. 2 vols. London: William Mariner, 1817.

Mariner, William, and John Martin. *An Account of the Natives of the Tonga Islands, in the South Pacific Ocean. With an Original Grammar and Vocabulary of Their Language*. 2nd ed. 2 vols. London: William Mariner, 1818.

Marino, John A. "The Invention of Europe." In *The Renaissance World*, edited by John Jeffries Martin, 140–165. London: Routledge, 2007.

Markey, Lia. "Stradano's Allegorical Invention of the Americas in Late Sixteenth-Century Florence." *Renaissance Quarterly* 65, no. 2 (2012): 385–442.

Marks, Robert B. *The Origins of the Modern World: A Global and Ecological Narrative from the Fifteenth to the Twenty-First Century*. 3rd ed. Lanham, MD: Rowman & Littlefield, 2015.

Marshall, Melanie. "The Sound of Whiteness: Early Music Vocal Performance Practice in Britain." Paper presented at American Musicological Society Annual Meeting, San Francisco, November 10, 2011. https://hdl.handle.net/10468/2716

Marshall, Melanie. "*Voce Bianca*: Purity and Whiteness in British Early Music Vocality." *Women and Music: A Journal of Gender and Culture* 19 (2015): 36–44.

Martin, Nathan John. "Figures of Alterity in Rousseau's Writings on Music." Conference paper for the American Society for Eighteenth-Century Studies, St. Louis, March 19, 2020. (Rescheduled due to Covid-19 and read remotely April 7, 2021.)

Martineau du Plessis, Denis. *Nouvelle geographie, ou, Description exacte de l'univers: Tirée des meilleurs auteurs tant anciens que modernes*. 3 vols. Amsterdam: George Gallet, 1700.

Masoero, Alberto. "Russia between Europe and Asia." Translated by Jonathan Hunt. In *The Boundaries of Europe: From the Fall of the Ancient World to the Age of Decolonisation*, edited by Pietro Rossi, 192–208. Berlin: De Gruyter, 2015.

Mason, Lowell, ed. *The Boston Handel and Haydn Society Collection of Church Music: Being a Selection of the Most Approved Psalm and Hymn Tunes, Anthems, Sentences, Chants, &c.* Boston: Richardson, Lord and Holbrook, 1830.

Matar, Nabil. *An Arab Ambassador in the Mediterranean World: The Travels of Muḥammad ibn 'Uthmān al-Miknāsī, 1779–1788*. London: Routledge, 2015.

Matar, Nabil. *Europe through Arab Eyes, 1578–1727*. New York: Columbia University Press, 2009.

Matar, Nabil, ed. *In the Lands of the Christians: Arabic Travel Writing in the Seventeenth Century*. New York: Routledge, 2003.

Mathiesen, Thomas J. *Ancient Greek Music Theory: A Catalogue Raisonné of Manuscripts*. RISM B/11. Munich: Henle, 1988.

Mathiesen, Thomas J. "Hermes or Clio? The Transmission of Ancient Greek Music Theory." In *Musical Humanism and Its Legacy: Essays in Honor of Claude V. Palisca*, edited by Nancy Kovaleff Baker and Barbara Russano Hanning, 3–35. Stuyvesant, NY: Pendragon Press, 1992.

Mayes, Catherine. "Eastern European National Music as Concept and Commodity at the Turn of the Nineteenth Century." *Music & Letters* 95, no. 1 (2014): 70–91.

Mazlish, Bruce. *Civilization and Its Contents*. Stanford, CA: Stanford University Press, 2004.

McClary, Susan. "Afterword: The Politics of Silence and Sound." In Jacques Attali, *Noise: The Political Economy of Music*, translated by Brian Massumi, 149–158. Minneapolis: University of Minnesota Press, 1985.

McClary, Susan. "Cycles of Repetition: Chacona, Ciaccona, Chaconne, and the Chaconne." In *Repetition in Early Modern British and European Cultures*, edited by Lorna Clymer, 21–45. Toronto: University of Toronto Press, 2006.

MacClintock, Carol, and Iain Fenlon. "Beaujoyeux [Beaujoyeulx], Balthasar de [Belgioioso, Baldassare de; 'Baltazarini']." *Oxford Music Online/Grove Music Online*, 2001. https://www.oxfordmusiconline.com/grovemusic/view/10.1093/gmo/9781561592630.001.0001/omo-9781561592630-e-0000002430

McClymonds, Marita P. "Salieri and the Franco-Italian Synthesis: *Armida* and *Europa riconosciuta*." In *Antonio Salieri (1750–1825) e il teatro musicale a Vienna: Convenzioni, innovazioni, contaminazioni stilistiche*, edited by Rudolph Angermüller and Elena Biggi Parodi, 77–88. Lucca: Libreria Musicale Italiana, 2013.

McGuinness, Rosamund. "Gigs, Roadies and Promoters: Marketing Eighteenth-Century Concerts." In *Concert Life in Eighteenth-Century Britain*, edited by Susan Wollenberg and Simon McVeigh, 261–272. Aldershot: Ashgate, 2004.

Meares, John. *Voyages Made in the Years 1788 and 1789, From China to the North West Coast of America: To Which are Prefixed, an Introductory Narrative of a Voyage Performed in 1786, from Bengal, in the Ship Nootka: Observations on the Probable Existence of a North West Passage and Some Account of the Trade Between the North West Coast of America and China and the Latter Country and Great Britain*. London: Logographic Press, 1790.

Melani, Alessandro. *L'Europa; Sacred Works*. Sound recording. Das Kleine Konzert, directed by Hermann Max. CPO, 777 408-2, 2008. https://music.apple.com/es/album/melani-europa-l-beatus-vir-magnificat/343182293

"Memoirs of the Late Dr. Boyce." In *The Monthly Magazine, and British Register. Part II. for 1798. From July to December, Inclusive*, 262–253. London: R. Phillips, 1798.

Ménestrier, Claude François. *Des ballets anciens et modernes selon les règles du théâtre*. Paris: René Guignard, 1682.

Ménestrier, Claude François. *Des représentations en musique anciennes et modernes*. Paris: René Guignard, 1681.

Menocal, Maria Rosa. *The Arabic Role in Medieval Literary History: A Forgotten Heritage*. Philadelphia: University of Pennsylvania Press, 2004.

Menzel, Stefan. "Senatoren der 'musikalischen Republik': Johann Adam Hiller und die Anfänge des deutschen Musikjournalismus." *Die Tonkunst* 9, no. 1 (2015): 13–19.

Mercure de France, dédié au roy, Juin 1739. 2 vols. Paris: Guillaume Cavelier; Pissot; Jean de Nully, 1739.

Mersenne, Marin. *Harmonie universelle contenant la theorie et la pratique de la musique*. Paris: R. Charlemagne et P. Ballard, 1636.

Mersenne, Marin, Philippe Tamizey de Larroque, and Hilarion de Coste. *Les correspondants de Peiresc. XIX. Le père Marin Mersenne, lettres inédites écrites de Paris à Peiresc (1633–1637), publiées et annotées par Philippe Tamizey de Larroque et précédées de la vie de l'auteur par le père Hilarion de Coste*. Paris: A. Picard, 1892.

Mignolo, Walter D. *The Darker Side of Western Modernity: Global Futures, Decolonial Options*. Durham, NC: Duke University Press, 2011.

Mignolo, Walter D. *The Politics of Decolonial Investigations*. Durham, NC: Duke University Press, 2021.

Miles, James, and Lindsay Gibson. "Rethinking Presentism in History Education." *Theory & Research in Social Education* 50, no. 4 (2022): 509–529.

Miller, Peter N. *Peiresc's Mediterranean World*. Cambridge, MA: Harvard University Press, 2015.

Mish, John L. "Creating an Image of Europe for China: Aleni's *Hsi-Fang Ta-Wen* 西方答問." *Monumenta Serica* 23 (1964): 1–87.

Mitsi, Efterpi. "Lady Elizabeth Craven's Letters from Athens and the Female Picturesque." In *Women Writing Greece: Essays on Hellenism, Orientalism and Travel*, edited by Vassiliki Kolocotroni and Efterpi Mitsi, 19–38. Amsterdam: Rodopi, 2008.

The Modern Part of the Universal History, from the Earliest Account of Time. Compiled from Original Writers. By the Authors of the Antient Part. 16 vols. London: S. Richardson, T. Osborne, C. Hitch, A. Millar, J. Rivington, S. Crowder, P. Davey and B. Law, T. Longman, and C. Ware, 1759–1765.

Montagu, Jeremy. *Origins and Development of Musical Instruments*. Lanham, MD: Scarecrow Press, 2007.

Montagu, Jeremy. "Why Ethno-organology?" *European Meetings in Ethnomusicology* 10 (2003): 33–44.

Montagu, Lady Mary Wortley. "From Letters of 1717–1718." In *Strunk's Source Readings in Music History*, edited by Leo Treitler, 716–720. New York: W. W. Norton, 1998.

Montagu, Lady Mary Wortley. *Letters of the Right Honourable Lady M--y W---y M----e: Written, During Her Travels in Europe, Asia and Africa, to Persons of Distinction, Men of Letters, &c. in Different Parts of Europe*. 3rd ed. 3 vols. London: T. Becket and P. A. De Hondt, 1763.

Montaigne, Michel de. *The Complete Essays of Michel de Montaigne*. Translated and edited by M. A. Screech. London: Penguin, 2003.

Montaigne, Michel de. *Essais de messire Michel Seigneur de Montaigne*. 2 vols. Bourdeaux: S. Millanges, 1580.
Montéclair, Michel Pignolet de. *Cantates a une et a deux voix avec simphonie. Composées par Mr. Montéclair. Troisieme livre qui contient huit cantates francoises, et une cantate italienne. Dediée a Madame la Duchesse de Dura*. Paris: L'Auteur, Le Sr. Boivin, Le Sieur Le Clerc, 1728.
Montéclair, Michel Pignolet de. *Europe: Cantata for Soprano, Violin or Flute, and Continuo*. Edited by Cedric Lee. Richmond, VA: Green Man Press, 2010.
Montesquieu, Charles de Secondat, Baron de. *De l'esprit des lois: Ou du rapport que les loix doivent avoir avec la constitution de chaque gouvernement, les moeurs, le climat, la religion, le commerce, &c.: À quoi l'auteur a ajouté des recherches nouvelles sur les loix romaines touchant les successions, sur les loix françoises, & sur les loix féodales*. 2 vols. Geneva: Barrillot & Fils, 1748.
Monteverdi, Claudio, and Giulio Cesare Monteverdi. "Explanation of the Letter Printed in the Fifth Book of Madrigals." Translated by Stephen Hinton. In *Strunk's Source Readings in Music History*, edited by Leo Treitler, 536–544. New York: W. W. Norton, 1998.
Moody, Ivan. "The Compass Revisited: Rewriting Histories of Music in the South." *Muzikologija* 25 (2018): 199–206.
Moran, J. F. "The Real Author of the *De missione legatorum Iaponensium ad Romanam curiam . . . dialogus*: A Reconsideration." *Bulletin of Portuguese-Japanese Studies*, no. 2 (2001): 7–21.
Morar, Florin-Stefan. "The Westerner: Matteo Ricci's World Map and the Quandaries of European Identity in the Late Ming Dynasty." *Journal of Jesuit Studies* 6, no. 1 (2019): 14–30.
Morgan, Mr. [Thomas]. *A Collection of New Songs: With a Through Bass to Each Song, and a Sonata for Two Flutes*. London: J. Walsh and J. Hare, 1697.
Morley, Thomas. *A Plaine and Easie Introduction to Practicall Musicke: Set Downe in Forme of a Dialogue*. London: Peter Short, 1597.
Morrier, Denis, ed. *J. J. Froberger, musicien européen: Colloque organisé par la ville et l'Ecole Nationale de Musique de Montbéliard, Montbéliard, 2-4 novembre 1990*. Paris: Klincksieck, 1998.
Morton, Stephen. *Gayatri Spivak: Ethics, Subalternity and the Critique of Postcolonial Reason*. Cambridge: Polity, 2007.
Mosca, Matthew W. *From Frontier Policy to Foreign Policy: The Question of India and the Transformation of Geopolitics in Qing China*. Stanford, CA: Stanford University Press, 2013.
Moschus. "Europa." In *Theocritus, Moschus, Bion*, edited and translated by Neil Hopkinson, 450–465. Loeb Classical Library 28. Cambridge, MA: Harvard University Press, 2015.
[Motteux, Peter Anthony]. *The Rape of Europa by Jupiter. A Masque; As It Is Sung at the Queens Theatre, in Dorset-Garden. By their Majesties Servants*. London: M. Bennet, 1694.
Mozart, Leopold. *A Treatise on the Fundamental Principles of Violin Playing*. Translated by Edith Knocker. 2nd ed. Oxford: Oxford University Press, 1985.
Mozart, Wolfgang Amadeus. *The Letters of Mozart and His Family*. Chronologically arranged, translated, and edited with an introduction, notes, and indexes by Emily Anderson. 3rd ed., revised by Stanley Sadie and Fiona Smart. London: Macmillan, 1997.

Mozart, Wolfgang Amadeus, and Hans Mersmann. *Letters of Wolfgang Amadeus Mozart: Selected and Edited by Hans Mersmann*. Translated by M. M. Bozman. New York: Dover, 1972.

Muffat, Georg, and David Wilson. *Georg Muffat on Performance Practice: The Texts from Florilegium Primum, Florilegium Secundum, and Auserlesene Instrumentalmusik: A New Translation with Commentary*. Edited and translated by David K. Wilson. Bloomington: Indiana University Press, 2001.

Mugglestone, Erica M. H. "The Gora and the 'Grand' Gom-Gom." *African Music* 6, no. 2 (1982): 94–115.

Müller, Johann Sebastian. "Reiße-Diarium bey Kayserlicher Belehnung des Chur und Fürstl. Hauses Sachsen." In *Entdecktes Staats-Cabinet, darinnen so wohl das Jus Publicum, Feudale und Ecclesiasticum, nebst dem Ceremoniel- und Curialien-Wesen, als auch die Kirchen- und Politische Historie*, edited by Johann Joachim Müller, 83–314. Jena: Verlegts Christian Pohl, 1714.

Müller, Johann Sebastian, and Martin Scheutz. "Reiße-Diarium von Johann Sebastian Müller: Bearbeitet von Martin Scheutz." In *Einmal Weimar-Wien und retour: Johann Sebastian Müller und sein Wienbericht aus dem Jahr 1660*, edited by Katrin Keller, Martin Scheutz, and Harald Tersch, 17–140. Vienna: Oldenbourg, 2005.

Müller-Wille, Staffan. "Linnaeus and the Four Corners of the World." In *The Cultural Politics of Blood, 1500–1900*, edited by Kimberly Anne Coles, Ralph Bauer, Zita Nunes, and Carla L. Peterson, 191–209. Basingstoke: Palgrave Macmillan, 2015.

Murata, Margaret. "Music History in the *Musurgia universalis* of Athanasius Kircher." In *The Jesuits: Cultures, Sciences and the Arts, 1540–1773*, edited by John W. O'Malley et al., 190–207. Toronto: University of Toronto Press, 1999.

Murillo Velarde, Pedro. *Geographia historica, donde se describen los reynos, provincias, ciudades, fortalezas, mares, montes, ensenadas, cabos, rios, y puertos, con la mayor individualidad, y exactitud, etc*. 10 vols. Madrid: Gabriel Ramírez, 1752.

Murillo Velarde, Pedro. *Historia de la Provincia de Philipinas de la Compañía de Jesús. Segunda parte, que comprehende los progresos de esta provincia desde el año de 1616 hasta el de 1716*. Manila: Imprenta de la Compañía de Jesús, 1749.

Muthu, Sankar. *Enlightenment against Empire*. Princeton, NJ: Princeton University Press, 2003.

Napoli Signorelli, Pietro. *Storia critica de' teatri antichi e moderni*. 6 vols. Naples: Vincenzo Orsino, 1787.

National Indigenous Australians Agency. "Referendum on an Aboriginal and Torres Strait Islander Voice." 2023. https://www.niaa.gov.au/indigenous-affairs/referendum-aboriginal-and-torres-strait-islander-voice

Nawrot, Piotr. *Indígenas y cultura musical de las reducciones jesuíticas: Guaraníes, Chiquitos, Moxos*. Monuménta Música in Chiquitórum Reductiónibus Bolíviae 1. Cochabamba, Bolivia: Editorial Verbo Divino, 2000.

Nettl, Bruno. "Have You Changed Your Mind? Reflections on Sixty Years in Ethnomusicology." *Acta Musicologica* 89, no. 1 (2017): 45–65.

Nettl, Bruno. *Nettl's Elephant: On the History of Ethnomusicology*. Urbana: University of Illinois Press, 2010.

Nettl, Bruno. "On World Music as a Concept in the History of Music Scholarship." In *The Cambridge History of World Music*, edited by Philip V. Bohlman, 23–54. Cambridge: Cambridge University Press, 2013.

Nettl, Bruno. *The Western Impact on World Music: Change, Adaptation, and Survival*. New York: Schirmer Books, London: Collier Macmillan, 1985.

Nettl, Paul. "Die Wiener Tanzkomposition in der zweiten Hälfte des siebzehnten Jahrhunderts." *Studien zur Musikwissenschaft*, no. 8 (1921): 45–175.

Neubauer, Eckhard. "Der *Essai sur la musique orientale* von Charles Fonton mit Zeichnungen von Adanson." *Zeitschrift für Geschichte der Arabisch-Islamischen Wissenschaften* 3 (1986): 335–376.

Neubauer, Eckhard. "New Light on Cantemir." Translated by Lucy Baxandall. In *Theory and Practice in the Music of the Islamic World: Essays in Honour of Owen Wright*, edited by Rachel Harris and Martin Stokes, 3–21. Abingdon: Routledge, 2017.

Neubaur, Caroline. "*Europa riconosciuta*: Ovvero addio all'assolutismo." Translated by Barbara Agnese. In *Salieri sulle tracce di Mozart: Catalogo della mostra in occasione della riapertura del Teatro alla Scala il 7 Dicembre 2004*, edited by Herbert Lachmayer, Theresa Haigermoser, and Reinhard Eisendle, 63–71. Kassel: Bärenreiter-Verlag, 2004.

Ng, Su Fang. "Global Renaissance: Alexander the Great and Early Modern Classicism from the British Isles to the Malay Archipelago." *Comparative Literature* 58, no. 4 (2006): 293–312.

Niebuhr, Carsten. *Travels through Arabia, and Other Countries in the East*. Translated by Robert Heron. 2 vols. Edinburgh: R. Morison, G. Mudie, and T. Vernor, 1792.

Nieden, Gesa zur, and Berthold Over, eds. *Musicians' Mobilities and Music Migrations in Early Modern Europe: Biographical Patterns and Cultural Exchanges*. Bielefeld: Transcript Verlag, 2016.

Niemetschek, Franz Xaver. *Lebensbeschreibung des K. K. Kapellmeisters Wolfg. Amad. Mozart, aus Originalquellen*. 2nd ed. Prague: Herrlin, 1808.

Nooshin, Laudan, ed. *The Ethnomusicology of Western Art Music*. Abingdon: Routledge, 2014. [Originally published in *Ethnomusicology Forum* 20, no. 3 (2011): 285–451.]

Nordera, Marina. "The Exchange of Dance Cultures in Renaissance Europe: Italy, France and Abroad." In *Cultural Exchange in Early Modern Europe*, Vol. 4: *Forging European Identities, 1400–1700*, edited by Herman Roodenburg, 308–328. Cambridge: Cambridge University Press, 2007.

"Noticias extrangeras. Egipto. Alejandría 7 de julio." *Gaceta de Madrid*, no. 137, September 22, 1829, 499.

Novelle della repubblica delle lettere per l' anno MDCCLIV. 33 vols. Venice: Domenico Occhi, 1754.

Oakley, Howard. "Changing Stories: Ovid's Metamorphoses on Canvas, 9—The Abduction of Europa." *The Eclectic Light Company: Macs, Painting, and More*, March 10, 2017. https://eclecticlight.co/2017/03/10/changing-stories-ovids-metamorphoses-on-canvas-9-the-abduction-of-europa/

O'Connell, John Morgan. "In the Time of Alaturka: Identifying Difference in Musical Discourse." *Ethnomusicology* 49, no. 2 (2005): 177–205.

O'Donnelly, Terence Joseph. *Academy of Elementary Music*. London: n.p., 1841.

O'Donnelly, Terence Joseph. *Académie de musique élémentaire*. Translated by A. D. de Cressier. Paris: Olivier-Fulgence; Richault, 1842.O'Loghlin, Michael. *Frederick the Great and His Musicians: The Viola da Gamba Music of the Berlin School*. Aldershot: Ashgate, 2008.

Olleson, Philip. *Samuel Wesley: The Man and His Music*. Woodbridge, UK: Boydell Press, 2003.

Oppenheimer, Stephen. "Out-of-Africa, the Peopling of Continents and Islands: Tracing Uniparental Gene Trees across the Map." *Philosophical Transactions of the Royal Society of London, Series B, Biological Sciences* 367 (2012): 770–784.

Orléans, Pierre-Joseph d'. *Histoire des deux conquerans tartares qui ont subjugué la Chine*. Paris: Claude Barbin, 1688.

Orléans, Pierre Joseph d'. *History of the Two Tartar Conquerors of China: Including the Two Journeys into Tartary of Father Ferdinand Verbiest, in the Suite of the Emperor Kanh-Hi*. Translated and edited by the Earl of Ellesmere, introduction by R. H. Major. London: Hakluyt Society, 1854.

Oschema, Klaus. *Bilder von Europa im Mittelalter*. Ostfildern: Jan Thorbecke, 2013.

Oschema, Klaus. "How Does Medieval Historians' Use of the Notion of 'Europe' Compare to Its Use in the Middle Ages?" *Latest Thinking*, 2013. https://lt.org/publication/how-does-medieval-historians-use-notion-europe-compare-its-use-middle-ages

Oschema, Klaus. "L'idée d'Europe et les croisades (XIe–XVe siècles)." In *Relations, échanges et transferts en Occident au cours des derniers siècles du moyen âge: Hommage à Werner Paravicini*, edited by Bernard Guenée and Jean-Marie Moeglin, 51–86. Paris: Académie des Inscriptions et Belles-Lettres, 2010.

Oschema, Klaus. "No 'Emperor of Europe': A Rare Title between Political Irrelevance, Anti-Ottoman Polemics and the Politics of National Diversity." *Medieval History Journal* 20, no. 2 (2017): 411–446.

Osterhammel, Jürgen. *The Transformation of the World: A Global History of the Nineteenth Century*. Translated by Patrick Camiller. Princeton, NJ: Princeton University Press, 2014.

Osterhammel, Jürgen. *Unfabling the East: The Enlightenment's Encounter with Asia*. Translated by Robert Savage. Princeton, NJ: Princeton Unviersity Press, 2018.

Osterhout, Paul R. "Andrew Wright: Northampton Music Printer." *American Music* 1, no. 4 (1983): 5–26.

Otterstedt, Annette. *The Viol: History of an Instrument*. Translated by Hans Reiners. Kassel: Bärenreiter, 2002.

Ovid. *Fasti*. Translated by James G. Frazer. Revised by G. P. Goold. Loeb Classical Library 253. Cambridge, MA: Harvard University Press, 1931.

Ovid. *Metamorphoses*. Translated by Frank Justus Miller. Revised by G. P. Goold. Loeb Classical Library 42. New ed. Cambridge, MA: Harvard University Press, 2014.

Padrón, Ricardo. *The Indies of the Setting Sun: How Early Modern Spain Mapped the Far East as the Transpacific West*. Chicago: University of Chicago Press, 2020.

Paer, Ferdinando. *Europa in Creta. Cantata a voce sola accomp. con 2 Violini, Viola, 2 Clarinetti, 2 Flauti, 2 Oboi, 2 Fagotti, 2 Corni e Basso*. Leipzig: A. Kühnel (Bureau de Musique), 1810.

Pagden, Anthony. "Europe: Conceptualizing a Continent." In *The Idea of Europe: From Antiquity to the European Union*, edited by Anthony Pagden, 33–54. Cambridge: Cambridge University Press, 2002.

Pagden, Anthony. *The Fall of Natural Man: The American Indian and the Origins of Comparative Ethnology*. Cambridge: Cambridge University Press, 1986.

Pagden, Anthony, ed. *The Idea of Europe: From Antiquity to the European Union*. Cambridge: Cambridge University Press, 2002.

Pagden, Anthony. *The Pursuit of Europe: A History*. Oxford: Oxford University Press, 2022.

Page, Christopher. "Around the Performance of a 13th-Century Motet." *Early Music* 28, no. 3 (2000): 343–357.

Page, Christopher. *The Christian West and Its Singers: The First Thousand Years*. New Haven, CT: Yale University Press, 2010.

Page, Christopher. "The Geography of Medieval Music." In *The Cambridge Companion to Medieval Music*, edited by Mark Everist, 320–334. Cambridge: Cambridge University Press, 2011.

Page, Christopher. "Towards: Music in the Rise of Europe." *Musical Times* 136, no. 1825 (1995): 127–134.

Painter, Nell Irvin. *The History of White People*. New York: W. W. Norton, 2010.

Palisca, Claude V. *The Florentine Camerata: Documentary Studies and Translations*. New Haven, CT: Yale University Press, 1989.

Palisca, Claude V. *Humanism in Italian Renaissance Musical Thought*. New Haven, CT: Yale University Press, 1985.

Palomino, Pablo. *The Invention of Latin American Music: A Transnational History*. New York: Oxford University Press, 2020.

Panov, Alexei, and Ivan Rosanoff. "Sébastien de Brossard's *Dictionnaire* of 1701: A Comparative Analysis of the Complete Copy." *Early Music* 43, no. 3 (2015): 417–430.

Parker, William Henry. "Europe: How Far?" *Geographical Journal* 126, no. 3 (1960): 278–297.

Parr, Adam. *The Mandate of Heaven: Strategy, Revolution, and the First European Translation of Sunzi's Art of War (1772)*. Leiden: Brill, 2019.

[Pasquier], Alexandre. *Concert françois: Europe et Jupiter. A deux voix, avec symphonie et la basse continüe, composée par Mr. Alexandre*. Paris: Foucault, 1715.

Passerini, Luisa. *Il mito d'Europa: Radici antiche per nuovi simboli*. Florence: Giunti, 2002.

Pastells, Pablo, and Francisco Mateos. *Historia de la Compañía de Jesús en la Provincia del Paraguay (Argentina, Paraguay, Uruguay, Perú, Bolivia y Brasil) según los documentos originales*. 8 vols. Madrid: Librería General de Victoriano Suárez, 1912–1949.

Pelizäus, Niklas. "Musikalische Mission in den Jesuitenreduktionen Südamerikas: Musik als Mittel zur Christianisierung und Europäisierung der Indios in der jesuitischen Missionspraxis." MA seminar paper, Westfälische Wilhelms-Universität Münster, 2015. https://www.academia.edu/13744317/Musikalische_Mission_in_den_Jesuitenreduktionen_Südamerikas_Musik_als_Mittel_zur_Christianisierung_und_Europäisierung_der_Indios_in_der_jesuitischen_Missionspraxis

Pelliccia, Carlo. "Representing Catholic Europe: Alessandro Valignano and *De Missione* (1590)." *CECIL* 8 (2022). http://journals.openedition.org/cecil/335

Perea, Jessica Bissett. *Sound Relations: Native Ways of Doing Music History in Alaska*. New York: Oxford University Press, 2021.

Pereira, Tomás. *Tomás Pereira: Obras*. Translated from Latin to Portuguese by Arnaldo do Espírito Santo. Transcription and notes by Ana Cristina da Costa Gomes, Isabel Murta Pina, and Pedro Lage Correia. Edited by Luís Filipe Barreto. 2 vols. Lisbon: Centro Científico e Cultural de Macau, Ministério de Educação e Ciência, 2011.

Perkins, Charles Callahan. *History of the Handel and Haydn Society (founded A.D. 1815): Prefaced with a Brief Account of Puritan Psalmody in Old and New England*. Vol. 1, no. 1. Boston: Alfred Mudge & Son, 1883.

Péron, François. *Voyage de découvertes aux Terres Australes, exécuté par ordre de sa majesté l'empereur et roi sur les corvettes le Géographe, le Naturaliste, et la Goelette le Casuarina pendant les années 1880, 1801, 1802, 1803 et 1804*. 2 vols. Paris: Imprimerie Impériale, 1807.

Péron, François. *A Voyage of Discovery to the Southern Hemisphere: Performed by Order of Emperor Napoleon, During the years 1801, 1802, 1803, and 1804*. Translated from the French [translator not named]. London: Richard Phillips, 1809.

Perrault, Charles. *Paralelle des anciens et des modernes*. 2nd ed. 4 vols. Paris: la Veuve de Jean Bapt. Coignard, and Jean Baptiste Coignard Fils, 1692.

Picard, François. "Music." In *Handbook of Christianity in China, Vol 1: 635–1800*, edited by Nicolas Standaert, 851–860. Leiden: Brill, 2001.

Picard, François, and Fañch Thoraval. "*Musica mecanica, practica & speculativa*: De Pereira à Pedrini, la musique européenne à la cour de Kangxi." In *Musica, sive liber amicorum Nicolas Meeùs*, edited by Luciane Beduschi, Anne-Emmanuelle Ceulemans, and Alice Tacaille, 453–492. Paris: PUPS, 2014.

Piccardo, Lara. "Lorsque la Russie 'entra' en Europe." In *L'idée d'Europe au XVIIIe siècle: Actes du Séminaire international des jeunes dix-huitiémistes, Gênes, 24–29 octobre 2005*, edited by Lara Piccardo, 93–106. Paris: Honoré Champion, 2009.

Piechocki, Katharina. *Cartographic Humanism: The Making of Early Modern Europe*. Chicago: Chicago University Press, 2019.

Pisani, Michael V. *Imagining Native America in Music*. New Haven, CT: Yale University Press, 2005.

Piso, Willem, and Georg Marcgrave. *Historia naturalis brasiliae*. Amsterdam: Lud. Elzevirius, 1648.

Playford, Henry, ed. *Deliciae musicae: Being, a Collection of the Newest and Best Songs Sung at Court and at the Public Theatres*, Vol. 1, in four books. London: Henry Playford, 1695–1696.

Playford, Henry, ed. *Deliciae musicae: Being, a Collection of the Newest and Best SONGS*, Vol. 2, Book 1. London: Henry Playford, 1696.

Playford, Henry, ed. *Deliciae musicae: Being, a Collection of the Newest and Best SONGS*, Vol. 2, Book 2. London: Henry Playford, 1696.

[Playford, Henry]. *A General Catalogue of All the Choicest Musick-books in English, Latin, Italian and French, Both Vocal and Instrumental. Compos'd by the Best MASTERS in Europe, that Have Been from these Thirty Years Past, to this Present Time: With All the Plainest and Easiest Instructions for Beginners on Each Particular Instrument*. [London]: Henry Playford, 1695.

Playford, Henry, ed. *Harmonia sacra; or Divine Hymns and Dialogues*. [London]: Henry Playford, 1688.

Playford, Henry, ed. *The Theater of MUSIC: or, A Choice Collection of the Newest and Best SONGS Sung at the Court, and Public Theaters. The Words Composed by the Most Ingenious Wits of the Age, and Set to Music by the Greatest Masters in that Science. With a Thorow-Bass to each SONG for the Theorbo or Baß-Viol. Also Symphonies and Retornels in 3 Parts to Several of Them, for the Violins and Flutes. The Third Book*. London: Henry Playford, 1686.

Playford, John [senior], ed. *The Second Book of the Pleasant Musical Companion*. 2nd "corrected and much enlarged" ed. London: John Playford, 1686.

Playford, John [senior], Thomas Campion, and Christopher Simpson. *A Brief Introduction to the Skill of Musick: In Three Books*. London: John Playford, 1670.

Pollard, Lucy. "'Every Stone Tells a Story': The Uses of Classical Texts by Seventeenth-Century English Visitors to Greece and Asia Minor." *Classical Receptions Journal* 4, no. 1 (2012): 48–65.

Pollens, Stewart. *A History of Stringed Keyboard Instruments*. Cambridge: Cambridge University Press, 2022.

Polzonetti, Pierpaolo. "Oriental Tyranny in the Extreme West: Reflections on *Amiti e Ontario* and *Le gare generose*." *Eighteenth-Century Music* 4, no. 1 (2007): 27–53.

Pooley, Thomas Mathew. "Continental Musicology: Decolonising the Myth of a Singular 'African Music.'" *African Music* 10, no. 4 (2018): 177–193.
Popescu-Judetz, Eugenia. *Prince Dimitrie Cantemir: Theorist and Composer of Turkish Music*. Istanbul: Pan, 1999.
Porter, David. "Sinicizing Early Modernity: The Imperatives of Historical Cosmopolitanism." *Eighteenth-Century Studies* 43, no. 3 (2010): 299–306.
Powell, John S. *Music and Theatre in France, 1600–1680*. New York: Oxford University Press, 2000.
Praetorius, Michael. *Syntagma musicum, II, De organographia, Parts I and II*. Translated and edited by David Z. Crookes. Oxford: Clarendon Press, 1986.
Pratt, Mary Louise. *Imperial Eyes: Travel Writing and Transculturation*. London: Routledge, 1992.
Prévost, Abbé [Antoine François]. *Histoire générale des voyages, ou, Nouvelle collection de toutes les relations de voyages par mer et par terre, qui ont été publiées jusqu'à présent dans les différentes langues de toutes les nations connues*. 20 vols. Paris: Didot, 1746–1789.
Prévost, Abbé [Antoine François], ed. *Storia generale de' viaggi: O nuova raccolta di tutte le relazioni de' viaggi per mare, e per terra, state pubblicate fino al presente nelle diverse lingue di tutte le nazioni cognite*. 30 vols. Translated by Gaspare Gozzi. Venice: Pietro Valvasense, 1751–1764.
Prior, Roger. "Jewish Musicians at the Tudor Court." *Musical Quarterly* 69, no. 2 (1983): 253–265.
Prividali, Luigi, and Ferdinando Paer. *Arianna consolata: Accademia per musica*. Vienna: Gio. Vincenzo Degen, 1803.
Prividali, Luigi, and Ferdinando Paer. *Arianna consolata: Accademia per musica*. Vienna: n.p., 1806.
Proctor, William. *A Short Journal of his Polish Majesty's Camp of Radewitz, in Saxony, in the Year 1730*. London: L. Gilliver, 1733.
Provedi, Francesco. *Paragone della musica antica, e della moderna: Ragionamenti IV*. [Siena]: [n.p.], 1752.
Provedi, Francesco. "Paragone della musica antica e della moderna: Ragionamenti IV." In *Raccolta d'opuscoli scientifici, et filologici*, edited by Angelo Calogerà, 345–451. Venice: Cristoforo Zane [et al.], 1754.
Psychoyou, Théodora. "Latin Musical Practices in the Greek Isles: Mapping Early Modern Confessional Plurality in the Eastern Mediterranean." In *Seachanges: Music in the Mediterranean and Colonial Worlds, 1550–1880*, edited by Kate van Orden, 69–106. Florence: I Tatti Studies, 2021.
Purchas, Samuel. *Purchas his Pilgrimes, in Five Bookes*. 4 vols. London: Henrie Fetherstone, 1625.
Quantz, Johann Joachim. *Essai d'une méthode pour apprendre à jouer de la flûte traversière, avec plusieurs remarques pour servir au bon goût dans la musique le tout eclairci par des exemples et par XXIV. tailles douces*. Berlin: Chrétien Frédéric Voss, 1752.
Quantz, Johann Joachim. *On Playing the Flute: A Complete Translation with an Introduction and Notes*. Translated by Edward R. Reilly. London: Faber, 1966.
Quantz, Johann Joachim. *Versuch einer Anweisung die Flötetraversiere zu spielen: Mit verschiedenen, zur Beförderung des guten Geschmackes in der praktischen Musik dienlichen Anmerkungen begleitet, und mit Exempeln erläutert. Nebst XXIV. Kupfertafeln*. Berlin: Johann Friedrich Voss, 1752.

Quijano, Aníbal. "Coloniality and Modernity/Rationality." *Cultural Studies* 21, nos. 2–3 (2007): 168–178.
Radano, Ronald, and Philip V. Bohlman, eds. *Music and the Racial Imagination*. Chicago: University of Chicago Press, 2000.
Raguenet, François. *Paralele des italiens et des françois en ce qui regarde la musique et les opéra*. Paris: Jean Moreau, 1702.
Raguenet, François, and [John Ernest Galliard]. *A Comparison Between the French and Italian Musick and Opera's. Translated from the French; With Some Remarks. To Which is Added A Critical Discourse upon Opera's in England, and a Means Proposed for their Improvement*. Translated by [John Ernest Galliard?]. London: William Lewis, 1709.
Rameau, Jean-Philippe. *Traité de l'harmonie*. Paris: Jean-Baptiste-Christophe Ballard, 1722.
Rameau, Jean-Philippe. *Treatise on Harmony*. Translated by Philip Gossett. New York: Dover, 1971.
Ramel, Frédéric. "Perpetual Peace and the Idea of 'Concert' in Eighteenth-Century Thought." In *Music and Diplomacy from the Early Modern Era to the Present*, edited by Rebekah Ahrendt, Mark Ferraguto, and Damien Mahiet, 125–145. Basingstoke: Palgrave Macmillan, 2014.
Ramiger. "Number CLXXIV. Public Advertiser. Saturday, April 14, 1770. No. 11040." In *The Repository: or Treasury of Politics and Literature, for MDCCLXX*, Vol. 1, 434–436 [433–434 are paginated twice]. London: J. Murray, 1771.
Ramos-Kittrell, Jesús A. *Playing in the Cathedral: Music, Race, and Status in New Spain*. New York: Oxford University Press, 2016.
Raynal, Guillaume Thomas (Abbé). *Histoire philosophique et politique, des établissemens & du commerce des européens dans les deux Indes*. 6 vols. Amsterdam: n.p., 1770.
Reeves, Bridget T. "The Rape of Europa in Ancient Literature." PhD diss., McMaster University, 2003.
Rehding, Alexander. "Can the History of Theory Be Decentered?" History of Music Theory, SMT Interest Group & AMS Study Group, April 3, 2020. https://historyofmusictheory.wordpress.com/2020/04/03/can-the-history-of-theory-be-decentered-part-i-prequel-five-classics/
Reid, Anthony. "Early Southeast Asian Categorizations of Europeans." In *Implicit Understandings: Observing, Reporting, and Reflecting on the Encounters between Europeans and Other Peoples in the Early Modern Era*, edited by Stuart B. Schwartz, 268–294. Cambridge: Cambridge University Press, 1994.
Reinert, Stephen W. "Fragmentation (1204–1453)." In *The Oxford History of Byzantium*, edited by Cyril A. Mango, 248–283. New York: Oxford University Press, 2002.
Renger, Almut-Barbara, and Roland Alexander Ißler. *Europa—Stier und Sternenkranz: Von der Union mit Zeus zum Staatenverbund*. Göttingen: V&R Unipress; Bonn: Bonn University Press, 2009.
Rentsch, Ivana. "Europa als künstlerische Suggestion: Die Inszenierung des Friedens im französischen Ballett des 17. Jahrhunderts." In *Europa—Stier und Sternenkranz: Von der Union mit Zeus zum Staatenverbund*, edited by Almut-Barbara Renger and Roland Alexander Ißler, 291–304. Göttingen: V&R Unipress, 2009.
"Review of *Observations on the Present State of Music, in London*. By William Jackson, of Exeter. 8vo. 1s. 6d. Harrison and Co. 1791." In *The Monthly Review, Or, Literary Journal, Enlarged: from September to December, inclusive, M,DCC,XCI. With an Appendix*, edited by Ralph Griffiths, 196–202. London: R. Griffiths, 1791.

Revuluri, Sindhumathi K. "On Anxiety and Absorption: Musical Encounters with the *Exotique* in Fin-de-Siècle France." PhD diss., Princeton University, 2007.
Rhodes, Willard. "To the Reader." *Asian Music* 1, no. 1 (1968): 2.
Ricci, Matteo, and Nicolas Trigault. *China in the Sixteenth Century: The Journals of Matthew Ricci: 1583–1610*. Translated by Louis J. Gallagher. New York: Random House, 1953.
Ricci, Matteo, and Nicolas Trigault. *De christiana expeditione apud Sinas suscepta ab Societate Jesu: ex P. Matthaei Ricii eiusdem societatis com[m]entariis libri V*. Augsburg: Apud Christoph Mangium, 1615.
Rice, John A. *Antonio Salieri and Viennese Opera*. Chicago: University of Chicago Press, 1998.
Riethmüller, Albrecht, ed. *The Role of Music in European Integration: Conciliating Eurocentrism and Multiculturalism*. Berlin: De Gruyter, 2017.
Rife, Ellen O'Neil. "The Exotic Gift and the Art of the Seventeenth-Century Dutch Republic." PhD diss., University of Kansas, 2013.
Ripa, Cesare. *Iconologia, overo, descrittione dell'imagini universali cavate dall'antichita et da altri luoghi*. Rome: Heredi di Gio. Gigliotti, 1593.
Ripa, Cesare. *Iconologia, overo, Descrittione di diverse imagini cavate dall'antichità, & di propria inventione. Di nuovo revista, & dal medesimo ampliata di 400 & più imagini, et di figure d'intaglio adornata ed*. Rome: Lepido Facii, 1603.
Ripa, Cesare. *Iconologia di Cesare Ripa perugino, cavre. de' sti. Mauritio, e Lazzaro*. Siena: Matteo Florimi, 1613.
Ripa, Cesare, and George Richardson. *Iconology; or, a Collection of Emblematical Figures: Containing Four Hundred and Twenty-four Remarkable Subjects, Moral and Instructive; in Which are Displayed the Beauty of Virtue and Deformity of Vice. The Figures are Engraved by the Most Capital Artists, from Original Designs; with Explanations from Classical Authorities. By George Richardson, architect*. 2 vols. London: Cesare Ripa, 1779.
Ritzarev, Marina. *Eighteenth-Century Russian Music*. Aldershot: Ashgate, 2006.
Robertson, Martin. "Europe I." In *Lexicon Iconographicum Mythologiae Classicae (LIMC) IV/1: Eros–Herakles*, edited by Jean Ch. Balty et al., 76–92. Zurich: Artemis Verlag, 1998.
Robinson, Dylan. *Hungry Listening: Resonant Theory for Indigenous Sound Studies*. Minneapolis: University of Minnesota Press, 2020.
Rocchi, Girolamo, Pietro della Valle, and Bartolomeo Zanetti. *Funerale della signora Sitti Maani Gioerida della Valle: Celebrato in Roma l'anno 1627*. Rome: Erede di Bartolomeo Zannetti, 1627.
Roche, Jerome. "Vernizzi [Vernici, Invernizzi, Invernici], Ottavio." *Oxford Music Online/ Grove Music Online*, 2001. https://www.oxfordmusiconline.com/grovemusic/view/10.1093/gmo/9781561592630.001.0001/omo-9781561592630-e-0000029225.
Roger, Eugène. *La terre saincte, ou description topographique tres-particuliere des saincts lieux, & de la terre de promission*. Paris: Antoine Bertier, 1646.
Roman, Hieronymo. *Republicas del mundo*. Medina del Campo: Francisco del Canto, 1575.
Romanou, Katy. "The Music of the Modern Greeks in Western and Eastern Music Literature, from the 9th to the 19th Centuries." In *The Music Road: Coherence and Diversity in Music from the Mediterranean to India*, edited by Reinhard Strohm, 257–278. Oxford: Oxford University Press, 2019.

Romanou, Katy, ed. *Serbian and Greek Art Music: A Patch to Western Music History*. Bristol: Intellect Books, 2009.
Romberg, Marion. "Continent Allegories in the Baroque Age—A Database." *Journal18: A Journal of Eighteenth-Century Art and Culture* 5 (2018). https://www.journal18.org/2412.
Rose, Stephen. "The Musical Map of Europe *c*. 1700." In *The Cambridge History of Eighteenth-Century Music*, edited by Simon P. Keefe, 1–26. Cambridge: Cambridge University Press, 2009.
Rosenmeyer, Patricia A. *The Poetics of Imitation: Anacreon and the Anacreontic Tradition*. Cambridge: Cambridge University Press, 1992.
Ros-Fábregas, Emilio. "Cristóbal de Morales: A Problem of Musical Mysticism and National Identity in the Historiography of the Renaissance." In *Cristóbal de Morales: Sources, Influences, Reception*, edited by Owen Rees and Bernadette Nelson, 215–233. Woodbridge, UK: Boydell Press, 2007.
Rosow, Lois. "Lully's *Armide* at the Paris Opera: A Performance History: 1686–1766." PhD diss., Brandeis University, 1981.
Rossi, Pietro, ed. *The Boundaries of Europe: From the Fall of the Ancient World to the Age of Decolonisation*. Berlin: De Gruyter, 2015.
Rousseau, Jean. *Traité de la viole*. Paris: Christophe Ballard, 1687.
Rousseau, Jean-Jacques. *Considérations sur le gouvernement de Pologne et sur sa réformation projettée*. [Paris]: n.p., 1782.
Rousseau, Jean-Jacques. *A Dictionary of Music*. Translated by William Waring. London: J. French, 1779.
Rousseau, Jean-Jacques. *Dictionnaire de Musique*. Paris: la Veuve Duchesne, 1768.
Rousseau, Jean-Jacques. "Essai sur l'origine des langues." In *Collection complète des oeuvres de J. J. Rousseau, citoyen de Geneve*, 17 vols., edited by Pierre Alexandre Du Peyrou, , Vol. 8, 355–434. Geneva: n.p., 1780–1789. http://www.rousseauonline.ch/Text/essai-sur-l-origine-des-langues.php.
Rousseau, Jean-Jacques. *Essay on the Origin of Languages and Writings Related to Music*. Translated and edited by John T. Scott. Hanover, NH: University Press of New England, 1998.
Rousseau, Jean-Jacques. *Lettre sur la musique françoise*. Paris: n.p., 1753.
Rousseau, Jean-Jacques. *The Social Contract and Other Later Political Writings*. Edited and translated by Victor Gourevitch. 2nd ed. Cambridge: Cambridge University Press, 2019.
Roussier, Pierre-Joseph. *Observations sur différens points d'harmonie*. Geneva: n.p., 1755.
Rowland-Jones, Anthony. "The Minuet: Painter-Musicians in Triple Time." *Early Music* 26, no. 3 (1998): 415–431.
Rubiés, Joan-Pau. "Comparing Cultures in the Early Modern World: Hierarchies, Genealogies and the Idea of European Modernity." In *Regimes of Comparatism: Frameworks of Comparison in History, Religion and Anthropology*, edited by Renaud Gagné, Simon Goldhill, and Geoffrey E. R. Lloyd, 116–176. Leiden: Brill, 2019.
Rubiés, Joan-Pau. "The Discovery of New Worlds and Sixteenth-Century Philosophy." In *Routledge Companion to Sixteenth-Century Philosophy*, edited by Henrik Lagerlund and Benjamin Hill, 54–82. New York: Routledge, 2017.
Rubiés, Joan-Pau. "Ethnography, Philosophy and the Rise of Natural Man 1500–1750." In *Encountering Otherness: Diversities and Transcultural Experiences in Early Modern*

European Culture, edited by Guido Abbatista, 97–130. Trieste: Edizioni Università di Trieste, 2011.
Rubiés, Joan-Pau. "The Spanish Contribution to the Ethnology of Asia in the Sixteenth and Seventeenth Centuries." *Renaissance Studies* 17, no. 3 (2003): 418–448.
Rubiés, Joan-Pau. "Were Early Modern Europeans Racist?" In *Ideas of "Race" in the History of the Humanities*, edited by Amos Morris-Reich and Dirk Rupnow, 33–87. London: Palgrave Macmillan, 2017.
Rubin, Miri. "Presentism's Useful Anachronisms." *Past & Present* 234, no. 1 (2017): 236–244.
Ruetz, Caspar. *Widerlegte Vorurtheile von der Beschaffenheit der heutigen Kirchenmusic und von der Lebens-Art einiger Musicorum*. Lübeck: Peter Böckmann, 1752.
Russell, Alexander. *The Natural History of Aleppo: Containing a Description of the City, and the Principal Natural Productions in Its Neighbourhood. Together with an Account of the Climate, Inhabitants, and Diseases; Particularly of the Plague*. 2nd ed. Revised, enlarged, and illustrated edition with notes by Patrick Russell. 2 vols. London: G. G. and J. Robinson, 1794.
Russell, Alexander. *The Natural History of Aleppo, and Parts Adjacent: Containing a Description of the City, and the Principal Natural Productions in its Neighbourhood; Together with an Account of the Climate, Inhabitants, and Diseases; Particularly of the Plague, with the Methods Used by the Europeans for Their Preservation*. London: A. Millar, 1756.
Sachs, Curt. *The Rise of Music in the Ancient World: East and West*. Mineola, NY: Dover, 2008. [New York: W. W. Norton, 1943.]
Sachsenmaier, Dominic. *Global Entanglements of a Man Who Never Traveled: A Seventeenth-Century Chinese Christian and His Conflicted Worlds*. New York: Columbia University Press, 2018.
Sadie, Julie Anne. "Devils and Archangels: The French Fascination with Ultramontane Music." In *François Couperin: Nouveaux Regards*, edited by Huguette Dreyfus and Orhan Memed, 149–162. Paris: Klincksieck, 1998.
Said, Edward W. *Orientalism*. Reprinted with a new preface. London: Penguin, 2003.
Saint-Pierre, Charles-Irénée Castel de. *Projet pour rendre la paix perpetuelle en Europe*. Utrecht: Schouten, 1713.
Salgó, Eszter. *Images from Paradise: The Visual Communication of the European Union's Federalist Utopia*. New York: Berghahn Books, 2017.
Samson, Jim. *Music in the Balkans*. Leiden: Brill, 2013.
Samson, Jim. "A View from Musicology." In *The New (Ethno)musicologies*, edited by Henry Stobart, 23–27. Lanham, MD: Scarecrow Press, 2008.
Sancho, Ignatius. *Letters of the late Ignatius Sancho, an African: To Which are Prefixed Memoirs of His Life*. London: J. Nichols, 1782.
Sancho, Ignatius, and Josephine R. B. Wright. *Ignatius Sancho (1729–1780): An Early African Composer in England; The Collected Editions of His Music in Facsimile*. New York: Garland, 1981.
Sande, Duarte de. *Japanese Travellers in Sixteenth-Century Europe: A Dialogue Concerning the Mission of the Japanese Ambassadors to the Roman Curia*. Translated by J. F. Moran. Edited and annotated with an introduction by Derek Massarella. Farnham: Ashgate, 2012.
Sandri, Elvezio, and Francesco Manelli. *Il ratto d'Europa dramma per musica del signor Elvezio Sandri musica del signor Francesco Manelli*. Parma: Erasmo Viotti, 1653.

Sandu-Dediu, Valentina. "The Beginnings of Romanian Composition: Between Nationalism and the Obsession with Synchronizing with the West." *Nineteenth-Century Music Review* 14, no. 3 (2017): 315–337.
Sarreal, Julia J. S. *The Guaraní and Their Missions: A Socioeconomic History.* Stanford, CA: Stanford University Press, 2014.
Sarris, Peter. "The Eastern Roman Empire from Constantine to Heraclius (306–641)." In *The Oxford History of Byzantium*, edited by Cyril A. Mango, 19–70. New York: Oxford University Press, 2002.
Savage, Roger. "Rameau's American Dancers." *Early Music* 11, no. 4 (1983): 441–452.
Savall, Jordi. "Istanbul: Dimitrie Cantemir, 1673–1723." In *Seachanges: Music in the Mediterranean and Colonial Worlds, 1550–1880*, edited by Kate van Orden, 125–129. Florence: I Tatti Studies, 2021.
Schaub, Jean-Frédéric, and Silvia Sebastiani. *Race et histoire dans les sociétés occidentales (XVe–XVIIIe siècle)*. Paris: Albin Michel, 2021.
Schmale, Wolfgang. "Continent Allegories and History of Mankind in the 18th century." In *The Language of Continent Allegories in Baroque Central Europe*, edited by Wolfgang Schmale, Marion Romberg, and Josef Köstlbauer, 31–43. Stuttgart: Franz Steiner, 2016.
Schmale, Wolfgang. "Europe: Eighteenth-Century Definitions." In *Bordering Early Modern Europe*, edited by Maria Baramova, Grigor Boykov, and Ivan Parvev, 79–94. Wiesbaden: Harrassowitz Verlag, 2015.
Schmale, Wolfgang. *Gender and Eurocentrism: A Conceptual Approach to European History.* Translated by Bernard Heise. Stuttgart: Franz Steiner Verlag, 2016.
Schmale, Wolfgang. "'Ihr redet Euch die Geschichte schön!': Frau Europa im Gespräch." In *Resonanzen Eurovisionen: 20. bis 28. Jänner 2018, Wiens Festival der Alten Musik*, edited by Internationale Musikforschungsgesellschaft, with collaboration of Isabel Neudecker, Peter Reichelt, Alexandra Ziane, and Carlos Suárez, 9–17. Vienna: Internationale Musikforschungsgesellschaft, 2018.
Schmale, Wolfgang, Rolf Felbinger, Günter Kastner, and Josef Köstlbauer. *Studien zur Europäischen Identität im 17. Jahrhundert.* Bochum: Winkler, 2004.
Schmale, Wolfgang, Marion Romberg, and Josef Köstlbauer, eds. *The Language of Continent Allegories in Baroque Central Europe.* Stuttgart: Franz Steiner, 2016.
Schnapper, Laure. *L'ostinato, procédé musical universel.* Paris: H. Champion, 1998.
Schofield, Katherine Butler [as Katherine Butler Brown]. "Evidence of Indo-Persian Musical Synthesis? The Tanbur and Rudra Vina in Seventeenth-Century Indo-Persian Treatises." *Journal of the Indian Musicological Society* 36–37 (2006): 89–103.
Schofield, Katherine Butler. *Music and Musicians in Late Mughal India: Histories of the Ephemeral, 1748–1858.* Cambridge: Cambridge University Press, 2024.
Schofield, Katherine Butler. "Musical Transitions to European Colonialism in the Eastern Indian Ocean." CORDIS—European Commission, August 1, 2019. https://cordis.europa.eu/project/id/263643/reporting
Schofield, Katherine Butler [as Katherine Brown]. "Reading Indian Music: The Interpretation of Seventeenth-Century European Travel-Writing in the (Re)construction of Indian Music History." *British Journal of Ethnomusicology* 9, no. 2 (2000): 1–34.
Schott, Howard. "National Styles." In *Companion to Baroque Music*, edited by Julie Anne Sadie, 409–416. Berkeley: University of California Press, 1990.
Schubart, Christian Friedrich Daniel. *C. F. D. Schubart's Ideen zu einer Ästhetik der Tonkunst.* Edited by Ludwig Albrecht Schubart. Vienna: J. V. Degen, 1806.

Schwartz, Stuart B., ed. *Implicit Understandings: Observing, Reporting, and Reflecting on the Encounters between Europeans and Other Peoples in the Early Modern Era*. Cambridge: Cambridge University Press, 1994.

Schwoebel, Robert. *The Shadow of the Crescent: The Renaissance Image of the Turk (1453–1517)*. New York: St. Martin's, 1967.

"Scientific Intelligence: Willard's Treatise on the Music of Hindustan." *Journal of the Asiatic Society of Bengal* 3 (1834): 247–250.

Scott, Derek B. "'I Changed My Olga for the Britney': Occidentalism, Auto-Orientalism and Global Fusion in Music." In *Critical Music Historiography: Probing Canons, Ideologies and Institutions*, edited by Vesa Kurkela and Juha Markus Mantere, 141–158. Farnham: Ashgate, 2015.

Scott, Hamish. "Diplomatic Culture in Old Regime Europe." In *Cultures of Power in Europe during the Long Eighteenth Century*, edited by Hamish Scott and Brendan Simms, 58–85. Cambridge: Cambridge University Press, 2007.

Scott, Hamish. "Introduction: 'Early Modern' Europe and the Idea of Early Modernity." In *The Oxford Handbook of Early Modern European History, 1350–1750*, Vol. 1: *Peoples and Place*, edited by Hamish Scott, 1–33. Oxford: Oxford University Press, 2015.

Sebastiani, Silvia. "National Characters and Race: A Scottish Enlightenment Debate." In *Character, Self, and Sociability in the Scottish Enlightenment*, edited by Thomas Ahnert and Susan Manning, 187–205. New York: Palgrave Macmillan, 2011.

Semi, Maria. "Writing about Polyphony, Talking about Civilization: Charles Burney's Musical 'Corns and Acorns.'" *Music and Letters* 103, no. 1 (2021): 60–87.

Sepp [von Reinegg], Anton. "An Account of a Voyage from Spain to Paraquaria; Performed by the Reverend Fathers, *Anthony Sepp* and *Anthony Behme*, Both *German* Jesuits, The First of *Tyrol* upon the River *Eth*, the Other of *Bavaria*. Containing a Description of all the remarkable Things, and the Inhabitants, as well as of missionaries residing in that country. Taken from the Letters of the said *Anthony Sepp*, and Publish'd by his own Brother *Gabriel Sepp*. Translated from the High Dutch Original, Printed at Nurenberg [sic], 1697." In *A Collection of Voyages and Travels, Some Now First Printed From Original Manuscripts. Others Translated Out of Foreign Languages, and Now First Publish'd in English*, edited by Awnsham Churchill and John Churchill, 633–664. London: Awnsham and John Churchill, 1704.

Sepp [von Reinegg], Anton. *Continuatio laborum apostolicorum: quos R. P. Antonius Sepp, Soc. Jesu missionarius apostolicus in Paraquaria ab anno Christi 1693. usque ad annum 1701. Exantlavit. Ubi describuntur illius barbarae gentis mores, ingenium, & docilitas in rebus practicis, & mechanicis, &c. Contrà in speculativis, & metaphysicis, ruditas; aliáque plurima Europaeis admiranda*. Ingolstadt: Joannis Andreae de la Haye, 1709.

Sepp [von Reinegg], Anton, and Antonius Böhm. *RR. PP. Antonii Sepp, und Antonii Böhm, der Societät Jesu Priestern Teutscher Nation deren der erste aus Tyrol an der Etsch zu Caltern der ander aus Bayrn Gebürtig Reiß-Beschreibung wie dieselben aus Hispanien in Paraquarien kommen. Und kurzer Bericht der denckwürdigsten Sachen selbiger Landschafft Völckeren und Arbeitung der sich alldort befindeten PP. Missionariorum*. Edited by Gabriel Sepp von Rechegg. Brixen: Paul Niclaus Führ, 1696.

Sepp [von Reinegg], Antonio, and Werner Hoffmann. *Continuación de las labores apostólicas: Edición crítica de las obras del padre Antonio Sepp, misionero en la Argentina desde 1691 hasta 1733*. Vol. 2. Translated and edited by Werner Hoffmann. Buenos Aires: EUDEBA, Editorial Universitaria de Buenos Aires, 1973.

Sepp [von Reinegg], Antonio, and Werner Hoffmann. *Relación de viaje a las misiones jesuíticas: Edición crítica de las obras del padre Antonio Sepp, misionero en la Argentina desde 1691 hasta 1733*. Vol. 1. Translated by Werner Hoffmann and Mónica Wrang. Edited by Werner Hoffmann. Buenos Aires: Editorial Universitaria de Buenos Aires, 1971.

Sepp [von Reinegg], Anton, and Alphonsus Sepp. *Continuation oder Fortsetzung der Beschreibung, deren denckwürdigeren Paraquarischen Sachen, selbiger Landschafft, Völckern, und Arbeit deren sich alldort befindenden RR.um PP. Missionariorum Soc. Jesu*. Ingolstadt: Joh. Andreas de la Haye, 1710.

Seroussi, Edwin. "In Search of Jewish Musical Antiquity in the 18th-Century Venetian Ghetto: Reconsidering the Hebrew Melodies in Benedetto Marcello's *Estro Poetico-Armonico*." *Jewish Quarterly Review* 93, nos. 1–2 (2002): 149–200.

Shaw, Watkins. "Staggins, Nicholas." *Oxford Music Online/Grove Music Online*, 2001. https://www.oxfordmusiconline.com/grovemusic/view/10.1093/gmo/9781561592 630.001.0001/omo-9781561592630-e-0000026523

Shelemay, Kay Kaufman. "Toward an Ethnomusicology of the Early Music Movement: Thoughts on Bridging Disciplines and Musical Worlds." *Ethnomusicology* 45, no. 1 (2001): 1–29.

Shiloah, Amnon. "An Eighteenth-Century Critic of Taste and Good Taste." In *Ethnomusicology and Modern Music History*, edited by Stephen Blum, Philip V. Bohlman, and Daniel M. Neuman, 181–189. Urbana: University of Illinois Press, 1991.

Shilsbury, R. "R. Shilsbury." *Calcutta Gazette*, October 20, 1786, [2].

Shirley, Rodney. "Allegorical Images of Europe in Some Atlas Titlepages, Frontispieces, and Map Cartouches." *Belgeo: Revue Belge de Géographie* 3–4 (2008): 341–354. https://journals.openedition.org/belgeo/8811

Shull, Jonathan. "Locating the Past in the Present: Living Traditions and the Performance of Early Music." *Ethnomusicology Forum* 15, no. 1 (2006): 87–111.

Simonsen, Jørgen Bæk. "Georg Hjersing Høst." In *Christian-Muslim Relations. A Bibliographical History*, Vol. 13: *Western Europe (1700–1800)*, edited by David Thomas and John A. Chesworth, 420–425. Leiden: Brill, 2019.

Skinner, Graeme. "The Invention of Australian Music." *Musicology Australia* 37, no. 2 (2015): 289–306.

Skinner, Graeme. *Peter Sculthorpe: The Making of an Australian Composer 1929–74*. Sydney: UNSW Press, 2015.

Skott, Christina. "Linnaeus and the Troglodyte." *Indonesia and the Malay World* 42, no. 123 (2014): 141–169.

Skyllstad, Kjell. "Report from Aalborg: A European Music: Fact or Fiction, 24–29 August 1992." *Current Musicology* 54, no. 1 (1993): 104–105.

Small, Christopher. *Musicking: The Meanings of Perfoming and Listening*. Middletown, CT: Wesleyan University Press, 1998.

Smith, Ayana O. "Editorial." *Eighteenth-Century Music* 18, no. 2 (2021): 245–251.

Smith, Caspar Llewellyn. "'World Music' Is Invented in a North London Pub." *The Guardian*, June 16, 2011. https://www.theguardian.com/music/2011/jun/16/world-music-term-invented

Smith, Ruth. "Early Music's Dramatic Significance in Handel's *Saul*." *Early Music* 35, no. 2 (2007): 173–189.

Snyder, Kerala J. *Dieterich Buxtehude: Organist in Lübeck*. Revised ed. Rochester, NY: University of Rochester Press, 2007.

Solie, Ruth A., ed. *Musicology and Difference: Gender and Sexuality in Music Scholarship*. Berkeley: University of California Press, 1995.
Sorba, Leonardo Mariano, and Giuseppe Ottavio Pitoni. *Il mondo riparato. Concerto Musicale à cinque voci da cantarsi nel Palazzo Apostolico la notte del santissimo natale. Poesia di Leonardo Mariano Sorba musica di Giuseppe Ottavio Pitoni maestro di cappella di S. Lorenzo in Damaso*. Rome: Stamperia della Rev. Camera Apostolica, 1693.
Sorce Keller, Marcello. *What Makes Music European: Looking beyond Sound*. Lanham, MD: Scarecrow Press, 2012.
Sparrman, Anders. *Reise nach dem Vorgebirge der guten Hoffnung, den südlischen Polarländern und um die Welt, hauptsächlich aber in den Ländern der Hottentotten und Kaffern in den Jahren 1772 bis 1776*. Translated by Christian Heinrich Groskurd. Edited and with a foreword by Georg Forster. Berlin: Haude und Spener, 1784.
Sparrman, Anders. *Resa till Goda Hopps-Udden, Sodra Pol-kretsen och omkring Jordklotet, samt till Hottentott-och Caffer-Landen, Åren 1772–76*. Stockholm: Anders J. Nordstrom, 1783.
Sparrman, Anders. *Voyage au Cap de Bonne-Espérance: Et autour du monde avec le capitaine Cook, et principalement dans le pays des Hottentots et des Caffres*. Translated by [Pierre] Le Tourneur. 3 vols. Paris: Buisson, 1787.
Sparrman, Anders. *A Voyage to the Cape of Good Hope, towards the Antarctic Polar Circle, and Round the World: but Chiefly into the Country of the Hottentots and Caffres, from the Year 1772, to 1776*. 2 vols. London: G. G. J. and J. Robinson, 1785.
"Spectacles." *Chronique de Paris* 88 (November 19, 1789): 352.
Les spectacles de Paris, ou calendrier historique & chronologique des théatres. 29 vols. Paris: Duchesne, 1763–1791.
Spinks, Ian. "Morgan, Thomas." *Oxford Music Online/Grove Music Online*, 2001. https://www.oxfordmusiconline.com/grovemusic/view/10.1093/gmo/9781561592 630.001.0001/omo-9781561592630-e-0000019129
Spira, Freyda. "Allegories of the Four Continents." *Heilbrunn Timeline of Art History*, March 2021. https://www.metmuseum.org/toah/hd/alfc/hd_alfc.htm.
Spohr, Arne. "'Mohr und Trompeter': Blackness and Social Status in Early Modern Germany." *Journal of the American Musicological Society* 72, no. 3 (2019): 613–663.
Springer-Dissmann, Käthe. "Gluck the Wanderer: Travels of a European Composer (1734–1779)." In *Ottoman Empire and European Theatre V: Gluck and the Turkish Subject in Ballet and Dance*, edited by Michael Hüttler and Hans Ernst Weidinger, 61–84. Vienna: Hollitzer Verlag, 2019.
Staunton, Sir George. *An Authentic Account of an Embassy from the King of Great Britain to the Emperor of China: Including Cursory Observations Made, and Information Obtained, in Travelling Through that Ancient Empire, and a Small Part of Chinese Tartary*. 3 vols. London: G. Nicol, 1797.
Stein, Louise K. "Festivity and Spectacle at the Spanish Royal Court." In *A Companion to Music at the Habsburg Courts in the Sixteenth and Seventeenth Centuries*, edited by Andrew H. Weaver, 273–307. Leiden: Brill, 2021.
Stendhal [under pseudonym Louis-Alexandre-César Bombet]. *Lettres écrites de Vienne en Autriche: Sur le célèbre compositeur Jh. Haydn, suivies d'une vie de Mozart, et de considérations sur Métastase et l'état présent de la musique en France et en Italie*. Paris: P. Didot l'Aîné, 1814.
Stendahl. *The Life of Haydn, in a Series of Letters Written at Vienna: Followed by the Life of Mozart, with Observations on Metastasio, and on the Present State of Music in France and Italy*. Translated by William Gardiner. London: John Murray, 1817.

Stendhal. *Memoirs of Rossini*. London: T. Hookham, 1824.
Sterba, Katrin. "From Conversion to Adoration: The Depiction of the Four Continents in Prints and Baroque Paintings in Jesuit Buildings in the German and Bohemian Provinces." In *The Language of Continent Allegories in Baroque Central Europe*, edited by Wolfgang Schmale, Marion Romberg and Josef Köstlbauer, 175–190. Stuttgart: Franz Steiner, 2016.
Stevenson, Robert Murrell. *Juan Bermudo*. The Hague: Nijhoff, 1960.
Stobart, Henry, ed. *The New (Ethno)musicologies*. Lanham, MD: Scarecrow Press, 2008.
Stockigt, Janice B. "The Court of Saxony-Dresden." In *Music at German Courts, 1715–1760: Changing Artistic Priorities*, edited by Samantha Owens, Barbara M. Reul and Janice B. Stockigt, 17–49. Woodbridge: Boydell, 2015.
Stöcklein, Joseph, ed. *Der neue Welt-Bott mit allerhand Nachrichten deren Missionarien Soc. Jesu. Allerhand so lehr- als geist-reiche Brief Schrifften und Reis-Beschreibungend: Welche von denen Missionariis der Gesellschaft Jesu aus beyden Indien und andern über Meer gelegenen Landern: seit An. 1642. bis auf das Jahr 1726. in Europa angelangt seynd: jetzt zum erstenmal Theils aus denen Französischen* Lettres Edifiantes. Augsburg and Graz: Philips, Martins und Joh. Veith seel. Erben, 1726.
Stoessel, Jason. "Editor's Introduction." In *Identity and Locality in Early European Music, 1028–1740*, edited by Jason Stoessel, 1–10. Farnham: Ashgate, 2009.
Stoessel, Jason. "Howling Like Wolves, Bleating Like Lambs: Singers and the Discourse of Animality in the Late Middle Ages." *Viator* 45, no. 2 (2014): 201–235.
Stoessel, Jason. "Voice and Song in Early Encounters between Latins, Mongols, and Persians, ca. 1250–ca. 1350." In *Studies on a Global History of Music: A Balzan Musicology Project*, edited by Reinhard Strohm, 83–113. Abingdon: Routledge, 2018.
Stokes, Ellen. "Antonio Salieri's Musical Recycling: *Europa Riconosciuta*, *Tarare*, and *Cesare in Farmacusa*." *Musicology Review* 10 (2021): 31–54.
Stokes, Martin, ed. *Ethnicity, Identity, and Music: The Musical Construction of Place*. Oxford: Berg, 1994.
Stokes, Martin. "Globalization and the Politics of World Music." In *The Cultural Study of Music: A Critical Introduction*, edited by Martin Clayton, Trevor Herbert, and Richard Middleton, 107–116. New York: Routledge, 2012.
Stokes, Martin. "Introduction: Ethnicity, Identity and Music." In *Ethnicity, Identity and Music: The Musical Construction of Place*, edited by Martin Stokes, 1–27. Oxford: Berg, 1994.
Stokes, Martin. "Music and the Global Order." *Annual Review of Anthropology* 33 (2004): 47–72.
Strahlenberg, Philipp Johann von. *An Histori-Geographical Description of the North and Eastern Part of Europe and Asia; But More Particularly of Russia, Siberia, and Great Tartary*. London: W. Innys and R. Manby and L. Gilliver, 1736.
Strasser, Ulrike. "*Welt-Bott*." In *The Cambridge Encyclopedia of the Jesuits*, edited by Thomas Worcester, 840–841. Cambridge: Cambridge University Press, 2017.
Stråth, Bo. "The Conquest of the North." In *The Boundaries of Europe: From the Fall of the Ancient World to the Age of Decolonisation*, edited by Pietro Rossi, 95–109. Berlin: De Gruyter, 2015.
Strohm, Reinhard. "The Difference of Early European Music." In *Essays on Renaissance Music in Honour of David Fallows*, edited by Fabrice Fitch and Jacobijn Kiel, 380–387. Woodbridge, UK: Boydell Press, 2011.
Strohm, Reinhard. "'Medieval Music' or 'Early European Music'?" In *The Cambridge History of Medieval Music*, edited by Mark Everist and Thomas Forrest Kelly, 1177–1200. Cambridge: Cambridge University Press, 2018.

Strohm, Reinhard. "The Balzan Musicology Project: Towards a Global History of Music, the Study of Global Modernisation, and Open Questions for the Future." *Musicology: Journal of the Institute of Musicology SASA* 27 (2019): 15–29.

Strohm, Reinhard, ed. *The Music Road: Coherence and Diversity in Music from the Mediterranean to India*. Oxford: Oxford University Press, 2019.

Strohm, Reinhard. *The Rise of European Music, 1380–1500*. Cambridge: Cambridge University Press, 1993.

Strohm, Reinhard. "The 'Rise of European Music' and the Rights of Others." *Journal of the Royal Musical Association* 121, no. 1 (1996): 1–10.

Strohm, Reinhard, ed. *Studies on a Global History of Music: A Balzan Musicology Project*. London: Routledge, 2018.

Strohm, Reinhard, ed. *Transcultural Music History: Global Participation and Regional Diversity in the Modern Age*. Berlin: Verlag für Wissenschaft und Bildung, 2020.

Subrahmanyam, Sanjay. "On the Hat-Wearers, Their Toilet Practices, and Other Curious Usages." In *Europe Observed: Multiple Gazes in Early Modern Encounters*, edited by Kumkum Chatterjee and Clement Hawes, 45–81. Lewisburg, PA: Bucknell University Press, 2008.

Subrahmanyam, Sanjay. "Taking Stock of the Franks: South Asian Views of Europeans and Europe, 1500–1800." *Indian Economic & Social History Review* 42, no. 1 (2005): 69–100.

Sulzer, Franz Josef. *Geschichte des transalpinischen Daciens*. 3 vols. Vienna: Rudolph Gräffer, 1781.

Sykes, Jim, and Julia Byl, eds. *Sounding the Indian Ocean: Musical Circulations in the Afro-Asiatic Seascape*. Berkeley: University of California Press, 2023.

Tagore, Sourindro Mohun. *Six Principal Ragas, with a Brief View of Indian Music*. Calcutta [Kolkata]: Calcutta Central Press, 1876.

Takao, Makoto Harris. "Encounters in the Glocal Mirror: The Role of the Performing Arts in Japan's Christian Century and Its Reflection in Early Modern Europe, 1549–1783." PhD diss., University of Western Australia, 2017.

Takao, Makoto Harris. "Global Music History." *Oxford Bibliographies*, August 23, 2022. https://www.oxfordbibliographies.com/display/document/obo-9780199757824/obo-9780199757824-0317.xml.

Takao, Makoto Harris. "Towards a Global Baroque: Unbinding Time, Temporality, and the 'European' Tradition." *Journal of Music History Pedagogy* (2024): forthcoming.

Talbot, Michael, ed. *The Musical Work: Reality or Invention?* Liverpool: Liverpool University Press, 2000.

Tartini, Giuseppe. *L'arte dell'arco*. Naples: Luigi Marescalchi, n.d.

Taruskin, Richard. *Defining Russia Musically: Historical and Hermeneutical Essays*. Princeton, NJ: Princeton University Press, 1997.

Taruskin, Richard. "Is There a Baby in the Bathwater? (Part I)." *Archiv für Musikwissenschaft* 63, no. 3 (2006): 163–185.

Taruskin, Richard. *The Oxford History of Western Music*. 6 vols. Oxford: Oxford University Press, 2005.

Taruskin, Richard. "Review of Claudia R. Jensen, *Musical Cultures in Seventeenth-Century Russia* (Bloomington: Indiana University Press, 2009)." *Notes* 67, no. 2 (2010): 295–298.

Taylor, Timothy D. *Beyond Exoticism: Western Music and the World*. Durham, NC: Duke University Press, 2007.

Taylor, Timothy D. *Global Pop: World Music, World Markets*. New York: Routledge, 1997.

Taylor, Timothy D. "Peopling the Stage: Opera, Otherness, and New Musical Representations in the Eighteenth Century." *Cultural Critique* 36 (1997): 55–88.

Televave, Su'eina Sharon, and Kirsten Zemke. "Pasifika R&B Divas: Gender, Culture and Identity in Pacific Pop Music." In *Home, Land and Sea: Situating Music in Aotearoa, New Zealand*, edited by Glenda Keam and Tony Mitchell, 21–30. Rosedale: Pearson, 2011.

Temple, Sir Richard Carnac. "The Travels of Richard Bell (and John Campbell) in the East Indies, Persia and Palestine, 1654–1670." *Indian Antiquary* 36 (1907): 125–134.

Terrasson, Jean. *Dissertation critique sur l'Iliade d'Homere, où à l'occasion de ce poëme on cherche les regles d'une poëtique fondée sur la raison, & sur les exemples des anciens & des modernes*. Paris: François Fournier & Antoine-Urbain Coustelier, 1715.

Tinctoris, Johannes. *De inventione et usu musice. Johannes Tinctoris: Complete Theoretical Works*, 2013. http://earlymusictheory.org/Tinctoris/texts/deinventioneetusumusice/#pane0=Translation

Titon du Tillet, Évrard. *Le Parnasse françois, dedié au roi*. Paris: Jean-Baptiste Coignard, 1732.

Todorova, Maria. *Imagining the Balkans*. Updated ed. New York: Oxford University Press, 2009.

Toelle, Jutta. "'Was michs kostet, die Indianer in unserer Europäischen Music zu instruiren, ist dem lieben Gott allein bekannt': Kircher und die jesuitische Mission durch Musik in Paraquaria." In *Steinbruch oder Wissensgebäude? Zur Rezeption von Athanasius Kirchers "Musurgia universalis" in Musiktheorie und Kompositionspraxis*, edited by Melanie Wald-Fuhrmann, 93–105. Basel: Schwabe, 2013.

Tolley, Thomas. *Painting the Cannon's Roar: Music, the Visual Arts and the Rise of an Attentive Public in the Age of Haydn*. Aldershot: Ashgate, 2001.

Tomlinson, Gary. "Musicology, Anthropology, History." In *The Cultural Study of Music: A Critical Introduction*, 2nd ed., edited by Martin Clayton, Trevor Herbert, and Richard Middleton, 59–72. New York: Routledge, 2012.

Tomlinson, Gary. *The Singing of the New World: Indigenous Voice in the Era of European Contact*. Cambridge: Cambridge University Press, 2007.

Tomlinson, John. *Globalization and Culture*. Cambridge: Polity, 1999.

Toscani, Claudio. "Europa riconosciuta. Opera di Verazi e Salieri: Una rivisitazione moderna del mito antico." *Materiali di Estetica* 6, no. 2 (2019): 19–29.

Touzard, Anne-Marie. "Un drogman musicien: Coup d'oeil sur la vie et les oeuvres de Charles Fonton." In *Istanbul et les langues orientales: Actes du colloque organisé par l'IFEA et l'INALCO à l'occasion du bicentenaire de l'Ecole des Langues Orientales, Istanbul, 29–31 mai 1995*, edited by Frédéric Hitzel, 197–214. Paris: L'Harmattan, 1997.

Tragaki, Dafni. "Introduction." In *Empire of Song: Europe and Nation in the Eurovision Song Contest*, edited by Dafni Tragaki, 1–34. Lanham, MD: Scarecrow Press, 2013.

Treitler, Leo. "Gender and Other Dualities of Music History." In *Musicology and Difference: Gender and Sexuality in Music Scholarship*, edited by Ruth A. Solie, 23–45. Berkeley: University of California Press, 1993.

Treitler, Leo. "Inventing a European Music Culture—Then and Now." In *The Past and Future of Medieval Studies*, edited by John Van Engen, 344–361. Notre Dame, IN: University of Notre Dame Press, 1994.

Treitler, Leo. "Toward a Desegregated Music Historiography." *Black Music Research Journal* 16, no. 1 (1996): 3–10.

Trottier, Danick. "L'Arménien de Venise: Validation sémiologique ou ethnomusicologique?" In *Musique et langage chez Rousseau*, edited by Claude Dauphin, 93–99. Oxford: Voltaire Foundation, 2004.

Trump, Donald J. "Remarks by President Trump to the People of Poland," July 6, 2017. https://trumpwhitehouse.archives.gov/briefings-statements/remarks-president-trump-people-poland/

"Türkei." *Beilage zur Allgemeinen Zeitung*, September 6, 1829, 993–994.

"Turquie." *Le Courrier de Smyrne*, August 2, 1829, 94–95.

Twiss, Richard. *Travels through Portugal and Spain in 1772 and 1773*. London: Richard Twiss, 1775.

Urrows, David Francis. "The Pipe Organ of the Baroque Era in China." In *China and the West: Music, Representation, and Reception*, edited by Hon-Lun Yang and Michael Saffle, 21–48. Ann Arbor: University of Michigan Press, 2017.

Urrows, David Francis. "The Wind Qin: Hearing and Reading Chinese Reactions to the Pipe Organ." In *Reshaping the Boundaries: The Christian Intersection of China and the West in the Modern Era*, edited by Gang Song, 48–58. Hong Kong: Hong Kong University Press, 2016.

Valignano, Alessandro, and Eduardus de Sande. *De missione legatorum Iaponensium ad Romanam curiam, rebusq[ue] in Europa, ac toto itinere animadversis dialogus*. Macau: Domo Societatis Iesu, 1590.

Valls, Francesc. *Mapa armónico práctico*. 1742. Transcribed by Mariano Lambea with Bernat Cabré. [Barcelona]: Consejo Superior de Investigaciones Científicas, 2017. https://digital.csic.es/handle/10261/144450

van Orden, Kate. "Hearing Franco-Ottoman Relations circa 1600: The *Chansons Turcquesques* of Charles Tessier (1604)." In *Seachanges: Music in the Mediterranean and Atlantic Worlds, 1550–1880*, edited by Kate van Orden, 33–68. Florence: I Tatti Studies, 2021.

Varwig, Bettina. *Histories of Heinrich Schütz*. Cambridge: Cambridge University Press, 2011.

Vasileanu, Monica. "What Was a Relevant Translation in the 18th Century?" *Research in Language* 15, no. 1 (2017): 79–96.

Verazi, Mattia. *Europa riconosciuta: Dramma per musica da rappresentarsi nel Nuovo Regio Ducal Teatro di Milano nella solenne occasione del suo primo aprimento nel mese d' Agosto dell' anno 1778*. Milan: Gio. Batista Bianchi Regio Stampatore, 1778.

Verbiest, Ferdinand. *Astronomia europaea sub imperatore Tartaro Sinico Cám Hy'*. Dillingen: Joannis Caspari Bencard, 1687.

Verbiest, Ferdinand, and Noël Golvers. *Letters of a Peking Jesuit: The Correspondence of Ferdinand Verbiest SJ (1623–1688)*. Rev. and expanded ed. Leuven: Ferdinand Verbiest Stichting, 2017.

Veryard, Ellis. *An Account of Divers Choice Remarks, as well Geographical, as Historical, Political, Mathematical, Physical, and Moral*. London: S. Smith and B. Walford, 1701.

Vicentino, Nicola. *Ancient Music Adapted to Modern Practice*. Translated by Maria Rika Maniates. Edited by Claude V. Palisca. New Haven, CT: Yale University Press, 1996.

Vicentino, Nicola. *L'antica musica ridotta alla moderna prattica: Con la dichiaratione, et con gli essempi de i tre generi, con le loro spetie. Et con l'inventione di uno nuovo stromento, nelquale si contiene tutta la perfetta musica, con molti segreti musicali*. Rome: Antonio Barre, 1555.

[Villati, Leopoldo de]. *L'Europa galante, festa teatrale per musica da rappresentarsi nel regio teatro di Berlino per il felicissimo giorno natalizio della sacra real maestà di Sofia Dorotea, regina madre = Das galante Europa, ein Singespiel welches auf allergnädigsten Befehl Sr. Königl. Majestät von Preussen an dem höchsterfreulichen Geburts-Feste Ihro Majestät der Königl. Frau Mutter frauen Sophien Dorotheen Königinn von Preussen.* Berlin: A. Hande and J. C. Spener, 1748.

Villoteau, Guillaume André. "De l'état actuel de l'art musical en Égypte, ou relation historique et descriptive des recherches et observations faites sur la musique en ce pays." In *Description de l'Egypte, ou recueil des observations et recherches qui ont été faites en Egypte pendant l'expedition de l'armée française, État moderne*, Vol. 1, 607–846. Paris: Imprimerie Impériale, 1809.

Villoteau, Guillaume André. *Recherches sur l'analogie de la musique avec les arts, qui ont pour objet l'imitation du langage, pour servir d'introduction à l'étude des principes naturels de cet art*. 2 vols. Paris: Imprimerie Impériale, 1807.

Voltaire. *Collection complette des oeuvres de M. de Voltaire*. 30 vols. Geneva: n.p., 1768–1777.

Voltaire. "Rescrit de l'empereur de la Chine." In *Extrait du Projet de paix perpetuelle de Monsieur l'abbé de Saint-Pierre*, edited by Jean-Jacques Rousseau, 79–84. [Paris]: n.p., 1761.

Voltaire. *The Works of M. de Voltaire*. Translated by T. Smollet, T. Franklin, et al. 35 vols. London: J. Newbery, R. Baldwin, W. Johnston, S. Crowder, T. Davies, J. Coote, G. Kearsley, and B. Collins, 1761.

Waeber, Jacqueline. "Opera and Ballet to the Death of Gluck." In *The Cambridge Companion to French Music*, edited by Simon Tresize, 201–220. Cambridge: Cambridge University Press, 2015.

Wahnon de Oliveira, Olivia. "Publishing and Selling Music in Eighteenth-Century Liège." Translated by Joop Beusekamp and Rudolf Rasch. In *The Circulation of Music in Europe 1600–1900: A Collection of Essays and Case Studies*, edited by Rudolf Rasch, 107–119. Berlin: Berliner Wissenschafts-Verlag, 2008.

Walker, Margaret E. "Towards a Decolonized Music History Curriculum." *Journal of Music History Pedagogy* 10, no. 1 (April 2020): 1–19.

Walkling, Andrew R. "Masque and Politics at the Restoration Court: John Crowne's *Calisto*." *Early Music* 24, no. 1 (1996): 27–62.

Wallaschek, Richard. *Primitive Music: An Inquiry into the Origin and Development of Music, Songs, Instruments, Dances, and Pantomimes of Savage Races*. London: Longmans, Green, 1893.

Walsdorf, Hanna. *Ritual Design for the Ballet Stage: Revisiting the Turkish Ceremony in* Le bourgeois gentilhomme *(1670)*. Berlin: Frank & Timme, 2019.

Walser-Bürgler, Isabella. *Europe and Europeanness in Early Modern Latin Literature: Fuitne Europa tunc unita?* Leiden: Brill, 2021.

Walsh, John (the elder). *Choice Musick by the Most Celebrated Authors in Europe*. [London: John Walsh, 1731.]

Walsh, John (the elder), and John Hare, eds. *Select Preludes & Vollentarys for the Violin, being Made and Contrived for the Improvement of the Hand with Variety of Compositions by all the Greatest Masters in Europe for that Instrument*. London: J. Walsh and J. Hare, 1705.

Walsh, John (the younger), ed. *The British Musical Miscellany: Or, the Delightful Grove: Being a Collection of Celebrated English, and Scotch Songs. By the Best Masters. Set for the Violin, German Flute, the Common Flute, and Harpsicord* [sic]. 6 vols. London: John Walsh, [1734–1737].

Walsh, John (the younger). *A Cattalogue* [sic] *of Musick: Containing all the Vocal, and Instrumental Musick Printed in England. For John Walsh. Where May Be Had, Variety of English, and Italian Songs, Also Musical Instruments of All Sorts, and Variety of Curious Pieces of Musick Printed Abroad*. London: J. Walsh, [1741].

Walsham, Alexandra. "The Reformation and 'the Disenchantment of the World' Reassessed." *Historical Journal* 51, no. 2 (2008): 497–528.

Walsham, Alexandra. "Introduction: Past and . . . Presentism." *Past & Present* 234, no. 1 (2017): 213–217.

Walther, Johann Gottfried. *Musicalisches Lexicon: oder, Musicalische Bibliothec, darinnen nicht allein die Musici, welche so wol in alten als neuern Zeiten, ingleichen bey verschiedenen Nationen, durch Theorie und Praxis sich hervor gethan, und was von jedem bekannt worden, oder er in Schrifften hinterlassen, mit allem Fleisse und nach den vornehmsten Umständen angeführt, sondern auch die in Griechischer, Lateinischer, Italiänischer und Französischer Sprache gebräuchliche Musicalische Kunst- oder sonst dahin gehörige Wörter, nach alphabetischer Ordnung vorgetragen und erkläret, und zugleich die meisten vorkommende Signaturen erläutert werden*. Leipzig: W. Deer, 1732.

Walton, Benjamin. "Quirk Shame." *Representations* 132, no. 1 (2015): 121–129.

Waterhouse, David B. "Southern Barbarian Music in Japan." In *Portugal and the World: The Encounter of Cultures in Music*, edited by Salwa El-Shawan Castelo-Branco, 351–377. Lisbon: Publicações Dom Quixote, 1997.

Watkins, Timothy D. "Musical Instruments and Instrumental Music in the Jesuit Reductions." In *"Hands-on" Musicology: Essays in Honor of Jeffery Kite-Powell*, edited by Allen Scott, 291–308. Ann Arbor, MI: Steglein, 2012.

Weaver, Robert Lamar. "Materiali per le biografie dei Fratelli Melani." *Rivista Italiana di Musicologia* 12, no. 2 (1977): 252–295.

Weaver, Robert Lamar. "Melani Family (Opera)." *Oxford Music Online/Grove Music Online*, 2002. https://www.oxfordmusiconline.com/grovemusic/view/10.1093/gmo/9781561592630.001.0001/omo-9781561592630-e-5000009871

Weber, Max. *The Protestant Ethic and the Spirit of Capitalism*. Translated by R. H. Tawney Talcott Parsons. Mineola, NY: Dover, 2003.

Weber, Max. *The Rational and Social Foundations of Music*. Translated by Don Martindale, Johannes Riedel, and Gertrude Neuwirth. Carbondale: Southern Illinois University Press, 1958.

Weber, William. "Redefining the Status of Opera: London and Leipzig, 1800–1848." *Journal of Interdisciplinary History* 36, no. 3 (2006): 507–532.

Weber, William. *The Rise of Musical Classics in Eighteenth-Century England: A Study in Canon, Ritual, and Ideology*. Oxford: Clarendon Press, 1992.

Weiss, Susan Forscher. "Vandals, Students, or Scholars? Handwritten Clues in Renaissance Music Textbooks." In *Music Education in the Middle Ages and the Renaissance*, edited by Russell Eugene Murray, Susan Forscher Weiss, and Cynthia J. Cyrus, 207–246. Bloomington: Indiana University Press, 2010.

Welch, Ellen R. *A Theater of Diplomacy: International Relations and the Performing Arts in Early Modern France*. Philadelphia: University of Pennsylvania Press, 2017.

Wells, Graham. "Jeremy Montagu (1927–2020)." *Early Music* 49, no. 1 (2021): 166–167.

Whaples, Miriam K. "Early Exoticism Revisited." In *The Exotic in Western Music*, edited by Jonathan Bellman, 3–25. Boston: Northeastern University Press, 1998.

Whaples, Miriam K. "Exoticism in Dramatic Music, 1660–1800." PhD diss., Indiana University, 1958.

Whenham, John. "Manelli [Mannelli], Francesco." *Oxford Music Online/Grove Music Online*, 2001. https://www.oxfordmusiconline.com/grovemusic/view/10.1093/gmo/9781561592630.001.0001/omo-9781561592630-e-0000017616

"White, Adj. (and Adv.) and N." *OED Online*, March 2023. https://www.oed.com/view/Entry/228566.

White, Arthur Franklin. *John Crowne: His Life and Dramatic Works*. Cleveland: Western Reserve University Press, 1922.

White, Bryan. "'Brothers of the String': Henry Purcell and the Letter-Books of Rowland Sherman." *Music & Letters* 92, no. 4 (2011): 519–581.

White, Harry. *The Musical Discourse of Servitude: Authority, Autonomy, and the Work-Concept in Fux, Bach, and Handel*. New York: Oxford University Press, 2020.

Wierzbicki, James. "Max Weber and Musicology: Dancing on Shaky Foundations." *Musical Quarterly* 93, no. 2 (2010): 262–296.

Wilbourne, Emily. "'. . . La curiosità del personaggio': *Il Moro* on the Mid-Century Operatic Stage." In *Seachanges: Music in the Mediterranean and Colonial Worlds, 1550–1880*, edited by Kate van Orden, 133–148. Florence: I Tatti Studies, 2021.

Wilbourne, Emily. "Little Black Giovanni's Dream: Black Authorship and the 'Turks, and Dwarves, the Bad Christians' of the Medici Court." In *Acoustemologies in Contact: Sounding Subjects and Modes of Listening in Early Modernity*, edited by Emily Wilbourne and Suzanne G. Cusick, 135–165. Cambridge: Open Book, 2021.

Wilbourne, Emily. *Voice, Slavery, and Race in Seventeenth-Century Florence*. New York: Oxford University Press, 2024.

Willard, N. Augustus. *A Treatise on the Music of Hindoostan, Comprising a Detail of the Ancient Theory and Modern Practice*. Calcutta [Kolkata]: Baptist Mission Press, 1834.

Wilson, David K., and Georg Muffat. *Georg Muffat on Performance Practice: The Texts from* Florilegium primum, Florilegium secundum, *and* Auserlesene Instrumentalmusik: *A New Translation with Commentary*. Bloomington: Indiana University Press, 2001.

Wilson, Nick. *The Art of Re-Enchantment: Making Early Music in the Modern Age*. New York: Oxford University Press, 2013.

Winterbotham, William. *An Historical, Geographical, and Philosophical View of the Chinese Empire: Comprehending a Description of the Fifteen Provinces of China, Chinese Tartary, Tributary States; Natural History of China; Government, Religion, Laws, Manners and Customs, Literature, Arts, Sciences, Manufactures, &c*. London: J. Ridgway and W. Button, 1795.

Wintle, Michael. *Europa and the Bull, Europe, and European Studies: Visual Images as Historical Source Material*. Amsterdam: Amsterdam University Press, 2004.

Wintle, Michael. "Gender and Race in the Personification of the Continents in the Early Modern Period: Building Eurocentrism." In *Bodies and Maps: Early Modern Personifications of the Continents*, edited by Maryanne Cline Horowitz and Louise Arizzoli, 39–66. Leiden: Brill, 2021.

Wintle, Michael. *The Image of Europe: Visualizing Europe in Cartography and Iconography*. New York: Cambridge University Press, 2009.

Wiora, Walter. *The Four Ages of Music*. Translated by M. D. Herter Norton. London: Dent, 1966.
Wiora, Walter. *Die vier Weltalter der Musik*. Stuttgart: W. Kohlhammer, 1961.
Wiseman, Susan. *Drama and Politics in the English Civil War*. Cambridge: Cambridge University Press, 1998.
Wistreich, Richard. "'La voce è grata assai, ma . . .': Monteverdi on Singing." *Early Music* 22, no. 1 (1994): 7–19.
Wolff, Larry. *Inventing Eastern Europe: The Map of Civilization on the Mind of the Enlightenment*. Stanford, CA: Stanford University Press, 1994.
Wollny, Peter. "Johann Sebastian Bach, ein Europäer." In *Europäische Musik—Musik Europas*, edited by Otfried Höffe and Andreas Kablitz, 61–75. Paderborn: Wilhelm Fink, 2017.
Woodfield, Ian. *The Early History of the Viol*. Cambridge: Cambridge University Press, 1984.
Woodfield, Ian. *English Musicians in the Age of Exploration*. Stuyvesant, NY: Pendragon Press, 1995.
Wright, Owen. "How French Is Frenkçin?" *Journal of the Royal Asiatic Society* 21, no. 3 (2011): 261–281.
Wright, Owen. "Music in Muslim Spain." In *The Legacy of Muslim Spain*, edited by Salma Khadra Jayyusi, 555–579. Leiden: Brill, 1992.
Wright, Owen. "Turning a Deaf Ear." In *The Renaissance and the Ottoman World*, edited by Anna Contadini and Claire Norton, 143–165. Farnham: Ashgate, 2013.
Yang, Hon-Lun. "Music, China, and the West: A Musical-Theoretical Introduction." In *China and the West: Music, Representation, and Reception*, edited by Hon-Lun Yang and Michael Saffle, 1–17. Ann Arbor: University of Michigan Press, 2017.
Yepes, Victoria, and Francisco Ignacio Alzina. *Una etnografía de los indios bisayas del siglo XVII*. Madrid: Consejo Superior de Investigaciones Científicas, 1996.
Yirmisekiz Mehmed Çelebi and Gilles Veinstein. *Le paradis des infidèles: Relation de Yirmisekiz Çelebi Mehmed Efendi, ambassadeur ottoman en France sous la régence*. Translation of Ottoman text by Julien-Claude Galland; introduction, notes, and additional texts by Gilles Veinstein. Paris: François Maspero, 1981.
Yri, Kirsten. "Thomas Binkley and the Studio der Frühen Musik: Challenging 'the Myth of Westernness.'" *Early Music* 38, no. 2 (2010): 273–280.
Yu, Siu-Wah. "The Meaning and Cultural Functions of Non-Chinese Musics in the Eighteenth-Century Manchu Court." PhD diss., Harvard University, 1996.
Zarlino, Gioseffo. *The Art of Counterpoint: Part Three of* Le istitutioni harmoniche, *1558*. Translated by Guy A. Marco and Claude V. Palisca. New Haven, CT: Yale University Press, 1968.
Zarlino, Gioseffo. *Dimostrationi harmoniche*. Venice: Francesco dei Franceschi Senese, 1571.
Zarlino, Gioseffo. *On the Modes: Part Four of* Le istitutioni harmoniche, *1558*. Translated by Vered Cohen. Edited by Claude V. Palisca. New Haven, CT: Yale University Press, 1983.
Zayas, Rodrigo de. *Los moriscos y el racismo de estado: Creación, persecución y deportación (1499–1612)*. Córdoba: Editorial Almuzara, 2006.
Zernov, Nikolai Mikhailovich. *Moscow, the Third Rome*. London: S. P. C. K, 1937.
Zhang, Qiong. *Making the New World Their Own: Chinese Encounters with Jesuit Science in the Age of Discovery*. Leiden: Brill, 2015.

Zohn, Steven. *Music for a Mixed Taste: Style, Genre, and Meaning in Telemann's Instrumental Works*. New York: Oxford University Press, 2008.

Żórawska-Witkowska, Alina. "Eighteenth-Century Warsaw as a Musical Centre between Western and Eastern Europe: 1731–1794." Translated by Wojciech Bońkowski. In *Glazbene migracije u rano moderno doba: Ljudi, tržišta, obrasci i stilovi/Music Migrations in the Early Modern Age: People, Markets, Patterns and Styles*, edited by Vjera Katalinić, 177–190. Zagreb: Hrvatsko Muzikološko Društvo, 2016.

Index

For the benefit of digital users, indexed terms that span two pages (e.g., 52–53) may, on occasion, appear on only one of those pages.

Figures are indicated by an italic *f* following the page number.

Aaron, Pietro, 165
Académie des Inscriptions et Belles-Lettres, 209–10
Académie Française, 160, 169
Acosta, José de, 184–85, 197–98
acrobats, 49–50
Adams, John, 97–98
Addison, Joseph, 195–96
adjectival anachronism, 8–9, 14, 25, 93n.107, 231, 247–48
adjectives, 1–2, 3–4, 98, 99–100, 139–40, 155–61
Adler, Guido, 238–39
Adrianople (Edirne), 194–95
aesthetics, 236. *See also* romantic aesthetics and ideas
Afghani music, 108–9
Africa, 33, 116–17, 213
   allegorical representations of, 52–67
   Cape of Good Hope, 127
   map of, 73n.16
   North, 116–17, 205
   northern, 73n.16, 202–3n.89, 224–25
   southern, 127
   sub-Saharan, 116–17
African music, 1, 100–2, 100n.4, 115, 129–30
African people, 17, 62, 109–10, 114–17, 118–19, 211, 226–27
   musicians, 115–17, 127, 128, 209–10
   See also Black people; Khoikhoi people
Agawu, Kofi, 1
Agenor, 37–38, 45, 158
Agnew, Vanessa, 162, 193–94, 208–9
Ahrendt, Rebekah, 86
Ahsan, Hamja, 27–28

Airs, Waters, Places (Hippocratic treatise), 107
Al-Farabi, 100–1
Ala-ud-din Barnawi, 108–9
Albinoni, Tomaso Giovanni, 93
Alembert, Jean le Rond d', 158, 233–34
Aleni, Giulio, 229
Aleppo, 78, 100–1, 112–14, 152–53
   Sayf al-Dawla, 100–1
Alexander the Great, 222
Alexandria, 131–32
allegories. *See* continents, allegories of the; "four parts of the world"
Allsop, Peter, 141–42
almanacs, journals, newspapers, and periodicals (historical)
   Allgemeine musikalisches Zeitung, 237
   Almanach royal, 84
   Asiatic Annual Register, 131–32
   Chronique du Paris, 49–50
   Courier de l'Europe, 94–95
   Courier de Smyrne, 131–32
   Diarium europäum, 91n.99
   L'écho, ou Journal de musique françoise, italienne, 94–95
   European Magazine, and London Review, 131–32
   Mercure de France, 44–45
   Novelle della repubblica delle lettere, 88–89
   Revue et Gazette Musicale de Paris, 152–53
Alzina, Francisco Ignacio, 199–200
ambassadors, embassies, and emissaries, 131–32, 133–34, 148–50, 223–24
Ambros, August Wilhelm, 238–39

America/Americas, 33, 105, 144–45, 197–98, 199, 200–1, 203, 218
  allegorical representations of, 52–67
  see also Latin America; North America; South America
American (adjective), 93–94
American music, 1, 99, 100–2
American people, 17, 62, 118–19, 173, 197–98, 205–6, 209–10
  musicians 94–95
  See also Cherokee people; Guaraní people; Tupinambá people
Amiot, Jean-Joseph-Marie, 124–25, 128–29, 160, 173, 206–7, 229
Amphion, 187–88
anachronism, 2, 8–14
Anacreon, 198
anacreontic poetry, 197–99
analytical encounters (concept of Estelle Joubert), 185–86
Anatolia, 73–76, 78, 217
ancient music, 183–216. *See also* musical instruments
ancient writers and scholars. *See* Anacreon; Aristotle; Aristoxenus; Euripides; Hermippus; Herodotus; Homer; Horace; Lactantius; Moschus; Ovid; Plato (comic poet); Plato (philosopher); Ptolemy; Pythagoras; Socrates; Suetonius
Andalusia, 202
Andrez, Benoît, 94–95
animals, 165, 226–27
  birds, 123–24, 208
  bull, metaphor in singing, 165
  bull, Zeus/Jupiter disguised as. *See* Zeus/Jupiter
  camel, 54–58
  crocodile, 54–58
  donkey (metaphor), 204–5
  eagle, 39, 43
  elephant, 54–58
  horse, 52–54
  lion, 58n.87
  monkey, 58–61, 60f
  owl, 52–54
  parrot, 58–61
  squirrels, 123–24
  wolves (metaphor), 88, 165
Anna, tsarina of Russia, 84–85
Antarctica, 1
anthropology, 9–10, 12–13, 27–28, 35–36, 52n.75, 185
Aphrodite, 45
Apollo, 103–4n.21, 201
Appadurai, Arjun, 185–86
Appiah, Kwame Anthony, 121–22, 222
Appius Claudius, 199
Arab people, 78, 107–8, 119, 214–15
  musicians, 131–32, 135, 214–15
Arabia, 3–4, 82–83, 203
Arabic
  civilization, 222
  language, 125–26, 135, 202–3n.89, 204
  music, 18
  music theory, 111–12, 173
  script, 204
Aragon, 223–24
Arbeau, Thoinot, 199
archaeomusicology. *See* music, academic study of
Archivum Romanum Societatis Iesu, 136
Argentina, 142–43
Argonauts, 145
Ariadne, 51–52
Arion, 41–42
Aristotle, 184–85
Aristoxenus, 189–90
Armenia, 162–63
Armenian Christians, 227–28
armies, 107–8, 129–30. *See also* military musicians
Armitage, David, 13n.53
Arnold, Carl, 126–27
Arnold, Samuel, 93–94
artists. *See* Correa, Juan; Pozzo, Andrea; Rembrandt; Ripa, Cesare; Rubens, Peter Paul; Tiepolo, Giovanni Battista; Titian
art works
  de Pas, *Europe en avant*, 38–39
  Oudry, *L'allégorie de l'Europe*, 58–61, 60f
  Pozzo, *Gloria di Sant'Ignazio*, 54
  Tiepolo, *Allegory of the Planets and Continents*, 54–58, 57f

Tiepolo, fresco in Würzburg Residence, 54–58, 55f, 56f
Tiepolo, *Il ratto di Europa*, 39, 40f
See also *biombo*; continents, allegories of; Europe, allegorical representations of; fresco; iconography; mural; porcelain figurines; sculptures and statues; tapestry
Asia, 33, 71
  allegorical representations of, 52–67
  maps of, 73n.16
  frontiers/boundaries (conceptual, cultural, geographical), 76–81, 84, 230–31, 234–36
  northern, 197–98
  See also Asia Minor; East Asia; Middle East; South Asia; Southeast Asia
Asia Minor, 203
Asian Music (journal), 1
Asian music, 1, 7–8, 100–2, 154–55
  ancient, 237–38
  See also "Eastern music"/"Oriental music" (term and concept)
Asian people, 62, 118–19, 211
Asterion, 37–38, 50–51
astronomy, 136, 140n.28, 217, 233–34. See also Verbiest, Ferdinand
Athens, 221n.18
Atlantic Ocean, 73–76, 184–85, 242
  North Atlantic Ocean, 228–29
Augsburg, 143–44, 146–47
Augustine of Hippo, 224–25
Augustus II, elector of Saxony and king of Poland, 63
Australia, 28–29, 119n.81, 176, 219
Australian Aboriginal peoples, 28–29
  singing, 176
Australian music, 1, 28–29
Australian people, 28–29, 176. See also Australian Aboriginal peoples; Torres Strait Islander peoples
Austria. See Holy Roman Empire; Vienna
Aversano, Luca, 94n.117

Bach, Johann Sebastian, 17–18, 90, 166n.135, 242
Bacon, Francis, 110

Badawi, Zeinab, 28n.111
Bahía, 63n.107
Balatri, Filippo, 83–84
Balducci, Marina, 50
Balkans, 82–83, 86, 163, 234–36
  Balkan Peninsula, 71–72, 73–76
Baltic, 83–84, 86, 236n.83
Banerji, Ritwik, 23n.97
Banks, Sir Joseph, 80f
barbarian/barbarism (concept), 151–52, 166, 185–86, 201–10
Baron, Ernst Gottlieb, 230–31
Barrow, Sir John, 175–76
Bastille, 49–50
Battle of Tours and Poitiers, 107–8
Beatles, The, 28–29
Beattie, James, 115
Beaujoyeux, Balthasar de, 91–92
Beethoven, Ludwig van, 17–18, 126–27, 186–87
Beijing, 4, 228–29
Bell, John, 124
Belon, Pierre, 193–94, 203
Bengal, 131. See also Calcutta (Kolkata)
Benjamin, Jonathan, 93–94
Benserade, Isaac de, 44, 62
Berger, Karol, 187
Berger, Louis, 142n.41
Bering Strait, 197–98
Berlin, 70
  Berlin Wall, 218
Berlin-Brandenburg Academy of Sciences and Humanities, 17–18
Berlin Opera (Hofoper Berlin), 70, 96–97
Bermúdez, Egberto, 61–62, 63n.107
Bermudo, Juan, 202
Bernal, Martin, 182
Bernier, Nicolas, 48–49
Bernstein, Leonard, 1
Bertoglio, Chiara, 165
Bertozzi, Carolyn R., 28n.111
Bessarion, Cardinal, 222–23
Béthizy, Jean-Laurent de, 44–45
Bethlehem, 180
Bevilacqua, Alexander, 181
Bianchi, Francesco, 51–52
Bible, 71, 73–76, 196–97, 199, 230

biblical figures. *See* David, king of Israel; Jesus Christ; Jubal; Moses; Noah; Solomon, king of Israel
Bibliothèque de l'Opéra, Paris, 159–60
Bibliothèque Nationale de France, 152–53
bicontinentalism, 76–77, 83, 86
Bignon, Armand-Jérôme, 155n.101
binaries, 187–88, 237–38, 242
Binkley, Thomas, 179–80
biological old regime, 187n.17, *See also* climate
biombo, 58
Bisaha, Nancy, 201–2
Black, David, 127n.112
Black Athena (Bernal), 182
Black Music Research Journal, 16–17
Black musicians, 115–17, 223
    Bologne, Joseph, Chevalier de Saint-Georges, 97–98, 115, 116–17
    Buonaccorsi, Giovanni, 116–17
    Lusitano, Vicente, 116–17
    Sancho, Ignatius, 115–16, 132
    trumpeters, 116–17
Black people, 114–17, 158. *See also* race
Blackness, 39, 116–17. *See also* race
Blavet, Michel, 46
Bloechl, Olivia, 1, 9–10, 17, 21, 25–26, 98n.140, 117, 121
Blumenbach, Johann Friedrich, 121–22
Boccaccio, Giovanni, 50–51
Bodrum. *See* Halicarnassus (Bodrum)
Boethius, 186–88, 189–91, 229–30
Bogotá (Santa Fé), 63n.107
Bohemia, 126n.111
Bohlman, Philip V., 19, 198, 200–1, 243–44
Boisgelou, Paul Louis Roualle de, 159*f*
Bolivia. *See* Potosí
Bologna, 41–42, 90–91
Bologne, Joseph, Chevalier de Saint-Georges, 97–98, 115, 116–17
Bonaparte, Napoleon 171
Boncampus of Signa, 165
Bonnet-Bourdelot, Jacques, 92–93, 200
Bonnet-Bourdelot, Pierre, 92–93, 200
Bordier, René, 62
Borheck, August Christian, 174–75
Born, Georgina, 15, 218–19

Bosphorus, 73–76, 78, 107
Boston, Massachusetts, 65, 171–72
botanists. *See* naturalists and botanists
botany, 61
Bougainville, Louis Antoine de, 198–99
Bourdelot, Pierre, 92–93, 200
Bourdieu, Pierre, 88
Boyce, William, 90
Boym, Svetlana, 112–13
Bracegirdle, Anne, 43n.31
Branchi, Silvestro, 41–42
Brazil, 64n.110, 119–20, 197–98. *See also* Bahía; Tupinambá people
Breitkopf, 94–95
Britain, 64–67, 217
Britannia (allegorical figure), 64
British Empire, 217
British Isles, 73–76, 96–97
Brixen, 144
Brook, Timothy, 111–12
Brossard, Sébastien de, 87–88
Brown, John, 124–25, 205–7
Brussels, 38–39
Buca, Turkey, 112–13
Budasz, Rogério, 198n.71, 199–200
Bulgaria, 73–76, 82–83
Buonaccorsi, Giovanni, 116–17
Burden, Michael, 43n.32
Burette, Pierre-Jean, 209–10
Burke, Edmund, 170–71
Burke, Peter, 26–27, 71, 100, 110
Burney, Charles, 89–90, 94–95, 96–97, 121, 130, 132, 162–63, 173, 174–75, 190–91, 207, 208–10, 211–12
Byzantine Empire (Byzantium), 71–73, 220–21, 223–24, 225
    John VIII Palaiologus, 223–24

Caccini, Giulio, 186–87
Cádiz, 143–44, 146, 147n.69, 164
Cadmus, 158
Cairo, 135, 152–53, 213
Calcutta (Kolkata), 171–72
Calmet, Antoine Augustin, 211–12
Cambridge, University of, 65
Campra, André, 68–69, 70, 152n.86
Cândea, Virgil, 150n.79
Canova-Green, Marie-Claude, 68

Cantemir, Dimitrie, 77–78, 150–52, 230
Canton (Guangzhou), 112
Cape of Good Hope, 127
capitalism, Western, 239
Capponi, Giovanni, 41–42
Capuchins, 112–13, 152–53
Caribbean, 97–98, 168
Carolingian dynasty, 107–8
Carolingian era, 16–17
Carpani, Giuseppe, 171–72
cartography and maps, 71, 111–12
    Hensel, *Europa polyglotta*, 73–76
    Martineau du Plessis, *Nouvelle geographie*, 73, 74f
    orbis terrarum (T-O) maps, 71, 78
    Ricci, *Kunyu Wanguo Quantu*, 111–12
Castile, 223
castrati, 67, 83–84, 119–20
Castro-Gómez, Santiago, 9–10
Catalonia, 164
cathedrals, 96–97
    Augsburg, 143
    Lincoln, 94n.114
    London, 94n.114
    Mexico City, 164–65
    Seville, 146
    St. Petersburg, 73–76
    Vienna, 143
Catherine the Great, tsarina of Russia, 85–86
Catholicism. *See* Christianity
Caucasian (term and concept), 121–22. *See also* race; white people; whiteness
Caus, Salomon de, 135, 183–84
Cavicchi, Camilla, 100n.4
Cem, Ottoman prince, 223–24
Cerone, Pietro, 187–88, 204–5
Chabanon, Michel-Paul Guy de, 168–69
Chakrabarty, Dipesh, 11, 247–48
chant, liturgical, 226–28. *See also* plainchant; Gregorian chant
Chapin, Keith, 86
Chardin, Jean, 79–81
Charlemagne, 107–8. *See also* Carolingian era
Charles II, king of England, Scotland, and Ireland, 65

Charles Frederick, Duke of Schleswig-Holstein-Gottorp, 84–85
Charlevoix, François-Xavier de, 118–19
Chatterjee, Kumkum, 102–3
Chen, Jen-yen, 23–24
Cherokee people, 209–10
Chetwood, William Rufus, 119–20
Chevalier de Saint-Georges. *See* Bologne, Joseph, Chevalier de Saint-Georges
Chiabrera, Gabriello, 41–42
China, 3–4, 6, 105, 110–12, 124–25, 128–29, 136–42, 160–61, 228–29
    Kangxi emperor, 124, 136–38, 139–42, 173–74
    Qianlong emperor, 131
    Wanli emperor, 111–12
    See also Beijing; Canton (Guangzhou); Macau
Chinese
    drum, 129n.125
    geographical concepts, 6, 110–12, 228–29
    knowledge, antiquity of, 229
    language, 141
    listening, 174–75
    music, 101–2, 124–25, 136–38, 173
    music theory, 140–41
Chinese people
    ancient, 124–25
    early modern, 124–26, 140–41
    nineteenth century, 214–15
Chios, 81–82
Christendom, 76–77, 135, 139, 151–52, 170–71, 234–36
Christianity, 67, 71–73, 121–22, 179, 224–29, 233–36
    Catholicism, 54, 112–14, 202–3n.89
    Eastern Christians, 128–29, 226–28, 233–34
    Orthodox Christianity, 3–4, 82–83, 225–28, 233–34
    Reformation, 3n.14, 225–26
    Schism of 1054, 6n.22, 71–72, 225
    see also Christendom; Jesuits (Society of Jesus); missions and missionaries
Christine Marie of France, 41–42
Christmas, 67, 107–8
Churchill, Awnsham, 146–47

Churchill, John, 146–47
Cibber, Catherine, 43n.31
Cimarosa, Domenico, 85–86
circumnavigation, 176, 217
civilization, 54–58, 99n.1, 168, 185–86, 207–10
    classical, 182, 193–94, 196–97, 221–22, 243
    Islamic, 222
    Western, 190, 239, 241, 243–44
class distinctions, 42–43, 68
    elite, 35, 42–43, 46–48, 97–98, 102–3, 116–17, 194–95, 204–5, 236
    peasant class, 236
classical authors. *See* ancient writers and scholars
Clement VIII, pope, 223–24
Clements, Sir Ernest, 2n.7
climate, 107, 166–67, 226–27. *See also* biological old regime
Clossey, Luke, 54, 112
clothes and costuming, 64–65, 66
coats of arms, 73
Cobston, Mr., 43n.34
Cochinchina (Vietnam), 175–76
    people of, 175–76
Cohen, Mitchell, 88n.82
Cold War, 218, 234, 245
Cole, Janie, 100n.4
Colista, Lelio, 48
collegium musicum, 86
Collin de Blamont, François, 48–49
Colombia, 63n.107, 129–30
Columbus, Christopher, 190
colonialism, 1, 5–6, 5n.18, 27–28, 31, 66, 110–11, 120–21, 180–81, 190, 216, 233–34, 245. *See also* decolonial thinking and decolonization; postcolonialism
coloniality, 190. *See also* decolonial thinking and decolonization
colonies, 21, 23–24, 63, 97–98, 102–3, 119–21, 143–44, 164–65, 168, 219
color. *See* Blackness; race; skin color; timbre; whiteness
comparative musicology. *See* music, academic study of

comparison and comparitivism, 4, 12–13, 18, 101, 102, 133, 138, 153–54, 164, 172–73, 178, 185–216, 246
competitive distancing, 171–73
composers, 204–5, 240–41. *See also* Albinoni, Tomaso Giovanni; Arnold, Carl; Arnold, Samuel; Bach, Johann Sebastian; Beethoven, Ludwig van; Bernier, Nicolas; Béthizy, Jean-Laurent de; Bianchi, Francesco; Blavet, Michel; Boyce, William; Campra, André; Collin de Blamont, François; Capponi, Giovanni; Cimarosa, Domenico; Cobston, Mr.; Colista, Lelio; Couperin, François; Dugué, Alexandre Julien; Du Mont, Henry; Duport, Nicolas; Eccles, John; Fiorillo, Federigo; Froberger, Johann Jakob; Galliard, John Ernest; Galuppi, Baldassare; Gastoldi, Giovanni Giacomo; Giardini, Felice; Gluck, Christoph Willibald Ritter von; Graun, Carl Heinrich; Handel, George Frideric; Hasse, Johann Adolph; Haydn, Joseph; Haydn, Michael; Hayes, William; Heinichen, Johann David; Hucbald of St. Amand; Lully, Jean-Baptiste; Madan, Martin; Manelli, Francesco; Marcello, Benedetto; Martín y Soler, Vicente; Melani, Alessandro; Milgrove, Benjamin; Mondonville, Jean-Joseph Cassanéa de; monodists; Montéclair, Michel Pignolet de; Monteverdi, Claudio; Morgan, Thomas; Mozart, Wolfgang Amadeus; Muffat, Georg; Paer, Ferdinando; Paisiello, Giovanni; Pasquier, Alexandre; Purcell, Henry; Rameau, Jean-Baptiste; Rochefort, Jean-Baptiste; Romberg, Andreas Jakob; Romberg, Bernhard Heinrich; Rossini, Gioachino; Salieri, Antonio; Scarlatti, Alessandro; Sorba, Mariano; Staggins,

INDEX 311

Nicholas; Tartini, Giuseppe; Telemann, Georg Philipp; Traetta, Tommaso; Vernizzi, Ottavio; Wesley, Samuel; Woodcock, Robert; Ziani, Marc'Antonio
composition, 144–45, 239–40
　counterpoint, 163, 239–40
　minimalism, 187n.20
　ostinato, 187
　principles and practices of, 163–64, 187
　See also genres and types of music and dance; harmony; monodists
compositions. *See* genres and types of music and dance; musical works (named)
"conceptual imperialism" (concept of Lydia Goehr), 8, 10, 14, 25, 246–47
concerts, public, 96–97
Conomos, Dimitri, 226
Constantine, Roman emperor, 71–72
Constantinople (Istanbul), 71–76, 79–81, 82–83, 125–26, 152–53, 180, 183–84, 193–94, 201–2, 220–22, 226, 233–34. *See also* Pera
continents. *See* Africa; America/Americas; Antarctica; Asia; Australia Europe
continents, allegories of, 33, 52–67
Cook, Nicholas, 7–8, 21, 220
Coptic Christians, 227–28. *See also* Christianity; Eastern Christians
copyright, 95–96
Córdoba (Cordova), 206–7
Corelli, Arcangelo, 90–91, 97n.137, 103–4n.21, 126–27
Correa, Juan, 58
costumes. *See* clothes and costuming
Couperin, François, 68–69, 87–88, 103–4
Coussemaker, Edmond de, 237–38
Covel, John, 193–94
Covid pandemic, 24–25
Crete, 37–38, 50–52, 82–83
Crowne, John, 65
Crusades, 71–72, 108–9, 110–11, 206–7, 212–13, 225
cultural appropriation, 34
cultural capital, 66–67
Cupid, 39, 42–43
cycles (in music and time), 187

Cypess, Rebecca, 115–16

Dacier, André, 158
Dampier, William, 119–20
dance types and genres. *See* genres and types of music and dance
dancers. *See* Noverre, Jean-Georges; Souville, Monsieur de
dancing, 61–64, 68, 97–98, 115, 133, 199
David, king of Israel, 71, 211–12
Davies, Norman, 170–71, 234, 235*f*
decentering knowledge, 244–45
decolonial thinking and decolonization, 26, 27–28, 247–48
Denmark, 63, 73–76, 82–83, 175n.170
　Frederik IV, 63
Dennis, Flora, 189–90
de Pas, Léon, 38–39
diasporic intimacy (concept of Svetlana Boym), 112–13, 139
Diderot, Denis, 158
digital methodologies and resources
　Biblioteca Digital Hispánica, 24–25
　Gallica, 24–25
　Google Books, 24–25
Diletsky, Nikolay, 218
Dillingen, 136, 146–47
diminutions, 193
Dingle, Christopher, 98n.139
Dionysius, 201n.83
diplomacy, 152–53. *See also* ambassadors, embassies, and emissaries
discourse, 1–2, 4–6, 8, 11–12, 13–14, 19–20, 29–30, 41n.22, 51–52, 97–98, 102, 109–10, 121, 122n.99, 180–81, 185, 188, 202, 205, 213–14, 245, 247–48
disenchantment (concept of Max Weber), 3n.14
Dolmetsch, Arnold, 7–8
Doni, Giovanni Battista, 204
dragon, 73
Dresden, 96, 126n.111
Dreyfus, Laurence, 180–81
Drury Lane (theater), 43
Du Halde, Jean-Baptiste, 124, 140–41
Du Mont, Henry, 112–13
Dugué, Alexandre Julien, 46, 47*f*

Dunbar, James, 166–67
Dunstaple, John, 164
Duport, Nicolas, 46, 47f
Dutch language, 127, 128, 176–77
Dutch people, 68–69, 102–3, 112–14, 120

early music (historically informed performance), 7–8, 14, 179–81. *See also* Binkley, Thomas; Dolmetsch, Arnold; Frisch, Jean-Christophe; Max, Hermann; Savall, Jordi
Eanes, Christopher, 67n.126
ears
   Chinese, 124–25
   Egyptian, 124–25
   European, 123–26, 129–30, 132
   French, 125–26
   Greek, 124–25, 162–63
   Italian, 124, 125–26
   modern, 240–41
   Turkish, 167
East (Orient), the, 71–73
   and West, 220–24
   "peoples of the," 226–27
   see also Europe, eastern; West (Occident), the
East Asia, 4n.15, 104–5. *See also* China; Japan
Eastern Christians. *See* Christianity
Eastern Europe. *See* Europe
Eastern languages, 234
"Eastern music"/"Oriental music" (term and concept), 125–26, 152–60, 178, 230, 237
   disuse of term in academic studies, 220, 247
   social functions, 242
"Eastern world," 230
Eccles, John, 43, 68–69
economics, 28–29, 30–31, 247–48
Edinburgh, University of, 114–15
Edirne. *See* Adrianople (Edirne)
education. *See* music teaching
Egypt
   ancient, 183–84, 229, 230–31, 237–38
   early modern and nineteenth-century, 171, 173, 183–84
   See also Alexandria; Cairo

Egyptian musicians, 135
Egyptian mythology, 45n.40
Egyptian people
   ancient, 124–25, 212, 230–31
   early modern, 93–94, 226–27
   See also Rifa'a Al-Tahtawi
elite. *See* class distinctions
Ellis, Alexander J., 238–39
embassies. *See* ambassadors, embassies, and emissaries
empires. *See* British Empire; Byzantine Empire (Byzantium); European empires; Holy Roman Empire; Islamic empires; Mughal Empire; Ottoman Empire; Roman Empire; Spanish Empire
enchantment, 3–4
Encyclopédie ou Dictionnaire raisonné des sciences, des arts et des métiers (Diderot and d'Alembert), 158, 233–34
Engel, Carl, 237–38
England, 64–67, 90, 96–97, 143, 223. *See also* Britain; London
   Charles II, king, 65
   Henry VIII, king, 223
English
   language, 5, 127, 129–30, 140–41, 176–77
   style in music, 164
   taste, 154–55
   taste in music, 88
English people, 68–69, 102–14, 120, 194–96, 212
   musicians, 163
Enlightenment, 30, 31
enslavement and slavery, 17, 39, 66–67, 97–98, 115–16, 119–20
environmental conditions, 166–67. *See also* biological old regime; climate
epyllion (narrative poem), 37–38
essentialism, 2, 4–5, 11, 13–14, 97–98, 99–100, 220, 245, 247
   "strategic essentialism" (concept of Gayatri Spivak), 19–20
Estienne, Henri, 198
ethics, 3
Ethiopian Christians, 227–28

Ethiopian people, 193
ethnicity, 97–98
ethnocentrism, 153
ethnographic texts, 23–24
ethnomusicology. *See* music, academic study of
ethnonationalism, 99–100, 247–48
ethnoregionalism, 247–48
etymology, 24, 158
Euripides, 37–38
Eurocentrism, 11, 52–54, 102, 170–71, 194–95, 239, 246
Europa (allegorical representation of Europe), 52–67, 70
Europa (mythological figure), 33–34, 37–38, 52–54, 65–66, 70, 158
    iconography of, 39, 40*f*, 44, 73
    musical settings of the story of her abduction, 40–52
Europaeology (concept of Timothy Brook), 111–12
Europe, 33, 144–45, 218
    allegorical representations of, 52–70
    as "Frangistan," 108–9
    central, 241–42
    concepts of, 3–4, 72–73, 83
    description in Chinese, 228–29
    eastern, 72–73, 84, 234–36, 235*f*, 236n.83
    eastern and western, boundaries between, 234, 235*f*
    frontiers/boundaries (conceptual, cultural, geographical), 73–84, 230–31, 234–36
    mainland, 95–96
    map of, 73–76, 74*f*
    name/naming of, 38–39, 42–43, 46–49, 68–69, 71
    nations of, 16–17, 68–70, 73, 143–44, 233–34
    northern, 231–32, 234–36
    Ottoman concepts of, 78
    "part(s) of," 183–86
    "rise of," 16–17, 243–44
    southern, 204, 235n.78
    western, 84, 234–36, 235*f*, 241–42
    See also europoiesis; European; European music; European Union; Eurovision

European
    adjective, 3–4, 98, 155–61
    composer (concept), 130–31
    ears (concept), 123–26, 132
    geographical concepts, 6
    integration, 15–16, 30–31
    musician (concept), 126–32
    organ, 147–48
    organists, 148
    parliament or Diet, 30–31, 160–61
    singing, 134–35, 166
    see also European people
"European Band" (ensemble), 131
European identity, 2–4, 17, 18, 38–39, 51–52, 72–73, 107–8, 110, 116–17, 133, 135, 161, 170, 171, 199
    musical 2–3, 19–20, 25, 102, 187–88, 216
European music
    as a compound term, 1–6, 99–102, 133–78
    conflation with modernity, 182, 183–84, 213–16
    conflation with Western music, 178, 182, 237, 238–39, 246
    death of, 28–29
    first known use in title of a theoretical text, 155–58
    first known use in title of sheet music, 172–73, 172*f*
    scales and modes, 215n.146
    social functions, 242
    theory, 111–12, 140–42
European people, 62, 78, 107–32, 170–71
    ancient inhabitants of Europe, 229
    as barbarous/barbaric, 205, 206–7, 229
    as "Franks," 107–9, 110–11, 112–14
    as "Homo Europaeus," 117–18, 121, 122–23
    in nineteenth century, 215
    peoples of Europe, 154–55
European Union, 28–29, 38–39
Europeanization, 78, 83–86, 177–78
europoiesis (concept of Katharina Piechocki), 109–10
Eurovision Song Contest, 19–20, 28n.113
Eurydice, 167–68
Ewell, Philip, 21–22

exceptionalism, 4–5, 8–9, 123, 130, 182, 183, 184–85, 214–16, 239–40
Eximeno y Pujades, Antonio, 88–89
exoticism
　auto-exoticization, musical, 20n.84
　musical, 12–13
　of the canon, 180–81
　of the past, 23–24
extractivism, 5n.18, 23–24, 30, 66–67, 219

Fabian, Johannes, 185
Fabris, Dinko, 228n.51
fairy tales, 183
fame, musical, 90–98, 145
fan, 58, 59*f*
Fantuzzi, Paolo Emilio. *See* Sandri, Elvezio (Paolo Emilio Fantuzzi)
Farmer, Henry George, 182
Fatḥ-ʻAli Shah, shah of Persia, 131–32
Felipe II, king of Spain, 202–3n.89
Felipe III, king of Spain, 202–3n.89
Felipe Próspero, Prince of Asturias, 63
females and femaleness. *See* gender
femininity. *See* gender
Ferrara, 223, 225–26
Ferrari, Domenico, 96–97
Fétis, François-Joseph, 215, 237–38
Finck, Heinrich, 165
Fioravanti, Leonardo, 189–90
Fiorillo, Federigo, 96n.125
Fleckno, Richard, 64
Fleming, Simon, 95–96
Flemish music, 163
Flemish people, 139
Flora, 62
Florence, 225–26
Florentine Camerata, 189, 192–93
flowers, 41–42, 44, 73, 180
Floyd, George, 114–15
Follino, Federico, 41n.25
Fonton, Charles, 125–26, 151–60, 168, 210–11, 237
Forkel, Johann Nikolaus, 130–31, 173–74, 211, 213
Forrest, Thomas, 175–76
"four parts of the world" ("four continents"), 33, 52–67, 117, 148, 154–55, 211

France, 68–69, 90–91, 97–98, 202–3n.89
　Bonaparte, Napoleon, 171
　Charlemagne, 107–8
　Christine Marie, 41–42
　François I, king, 223
　Louis XIII, king, 62
　Louis XIV, king, 46
　Louis XV, king, 46
　Louis Auguste de Bourbon, prince, 46
　See also Lorient; Lyon; Paris; Versailles
Franciscans, 180, 228n.51
François I, king of France, 223
"Frangistan," 108–9. *See also* Europe
Frankish church, 231
"Franks" (historical term), 107–9, 110–11, 112–14. *See also* Charlemagne; European people
Frederick II "the Great," king of Prussia, 231–32
Frederik IV, king of Denmark, 63
French
　dictionaries, 169
　ears (concept), 125–26
　language, 5, 87–88, 91–92, 127, 128, 129–30, 131–32, 140–41, 175–77, 231–32
　music, 50–51, 135n.12, 149
　music theory, 141–42
　style in music, 4–5, 92–93, 94–95, 103–4, 135, 161–62, 166–67, 170, 205–6
　taste, 154–55
　taste in music, 87–88
French people, 68–69, 102–3, 112–14, 120, 154, 212
　musicians, 163, 223
fresco, 54–58, 55*f*–56*f*. *See also* mural
Frisch, Jean-Christophe, 179–80
Froberger, Johann Jakob, 126–27
Fróis, Luís, 133
Fulcher of Chartres, 225
Fuzelier, Louis, 46, 47*f*, 70

Gaffurius, Franchinus, 165, 189–90
Galilei, Vincenzo, 189–90, 204–5
Gallet, Georges, 73, 74*f*
Galletti (cornettist), 97n.137
Galliard, John Ernest, 43–44, 88
Galuppi, Baldassare, 67, 85–86

gamut, 226. *See also* music theory
Ganassi, Silvestro, 212–13
Garrett, Aaron, 114–15
Gastoldi, Giovanni Giacomo, 41–42
Geanakoplos, Deno John, 221–22
Geertz, Clifford, 12–13
Gelbart, Matthew, 5–6, 11–12
Gembero-Ustárroz, María, 140n.29
Gemelli Careri, Giovanni Francesco, 139–40
gender, 65–66, 246
    men and maleness, 25–26, 39–41, 42–43, 52n.74
    women and femaleness, 33, 39, 45n.40, 66, 67, 133
    See also matriarchy; patriarchy
Genoa, 143–44
genres and types of music and dance
    allemande, 46–48
    ballet, 33, 41–42, 62–63, 68, 152–53
    ballet des nations, 68, 69n.136
    ballet héroïque, 70
    canon, musical, 9–10, 90, 96–97
    cantata, 48–49, 51–52, 242
    cantatille, 46–48
    capriccio, 96n.125
    chamber music, 95–96
    chanson, 193
    comédie-ballet, 68
    concerto, 95–96
    concerto musicale, 67
    contredanse. *See* Sancho, Ignatius
    cotillon. *See* Sancho, Ignatius
    divertissement, 46
    duo, 95–96
    festa teatrale (theatrical festive piece), 42–43, 70
    Hungarian dances, 236
    hymns, 178, 224–25
    litany, 144
    march, 46–48
    masque, 64
    mass, 144, 145
    monody, 186–87, 193
    motet, 112–13, 144, 145
    offertory, 144
    opera. *See separate entry for* opera
    oratorio, 33, 90
    overture, 95–96
    pantomime, 43–44
    pantomime héroïque, 49–50
    passepied, 46–48
    psalms, 178
    quintet, 95–96
    sonata, 239–40
    songs, 224–25
    symphony, 94–96, 239–40
    tragédie en musique, 44–45
    trio sonata, 103–4n.21
    vespers, 144
    See also chant, liturgical; plainchant; Gregorian chant; poetry
geography and geographical concepts, 6, 34–35, 73, 83, 84, 102–3, 107, 108–9n.14, 110–12, 218–19, 228–29, 233–34. *See also* cartography and maps
geology, 73, 84
Gerbillon, Jean-François, 140n.28
German
    language, 5, 70, 91–92, 127, 128, 129–30, 131–32, 176–77, 231–32
    style in music, 100–1, 146–47
    taste, 154–55
German people, 112–13, 120, 212
    composers, 205–6
    musicians, 84–85, 126n.111, 163
German Province (Jesuit), 146
Germany, 143–44, 145
    East Germany, 218
    See also Berlin; Dillingen; Holy Roman Empire; Nuremberg; Potsdam Prussia; Würzburg
Giardini, Felice, 93–94, 96–97
Giove. *See* Zeus/Jupiter
Glareanus, Heinrich, 17
Gletle, Johann Melchior, 143, 144–45
global music history. *See* music, academic study of. *See also* Bloechl, Olivia; Schofield, Katherine Butler; Strohm, Reinhard
Global North, 20, 28–29, 218–19
Global South, 28n.113, 218–19
Glowotz, Daniel, 226
Gluck, Christoph Willibald Ritter von, 126–27, 167–68

Goa, 63n.107
Goehr, Lydia, 9–12, 25, 206–7
Goethe, Johann Wolfgang von, 220–21n.16
Golvers, Noël, 138–39, 141
Gonzaga, Francesco, 41–42
Good, Anne, 128
Gordon, Bonnie, 41–42, 121–22
Götz, Johann Michael, 95–96
Grainger, Percy, 240–41
Granada, 206–7. *See also* Spain
Graun, Carl Heinrich, 70
Greece
  ancient, 9–10, 38–39, 183–84, 214, 229, 230–31, 237–38
  early modern, 72–73, 162–63, 193–94, 203, 226–27
  modern-day, 38–39
  relationship with Europe, 38–39, 72–73, 82–83, 99, 162–63, 183–84, 193–94, 214, 222–23, 230
  See also Athens; Chios; Crete; Peloponnese; Rhodes; Zante (Zakynthos)
Greek
  civilization and culture, ancient, 107, 182, 193–95
  dance, 195–96
  lands, 72–73, 82, 195–96
  language, 71–72, 73–76, 192–93, 198, 221–22
  learning, 222
  literature (ancient), 221–22
  music (ancient), 204, 214, 237–38
  music theory (ancient), 221–23
  music theory (nineteenth-century), 82–83
  mythology, 37–38, 44–45, 51–52
  singing, 173–74
  statuary (ancient), 194–95
Greek church, 81, 233–34
  music, 81–82, 165, 196–97
Greek people
  ancient, 38–39, 121, 124–25, 183–216, 230–31
  early modern, 72–73, 124–25, 162–63, 173–75, 183–84, 193–97, 210–11, 226–27
  musicians, 82–83, 208–9, 226

Greenland, 62, 73–76
Grégoire, Henri Jean-Baptiste (Abbé Grégoire), 115, 121–22
Gregorian chant, 214–15, 227–28
Grelot, Guillaume-Joseph, 78–82, 80*f*
Grimaldi, Filippo, 136–38, 139–41
Grimm, Friedrich-Melchior, Baron von, 161n.111
Gruzinski, Serge, 14
Guadeloupe, 97–98
Guangzhou. 112, *See* Canton (Guangzhou)
Guaraní people, 142–43, 144–45, 146–48
Guerrero, Francisco, 226–27
Guido of Arezzo, 186–87, 189–91, 226
Gulliver, Katrina, 102–3
Gyekye, Kwame, 185–86

Haar, James, 17
habitus, 88
Hachenberg, Paul, 231
Haenke, Thaddeus Xaverius Peregrinus, 127n.113
Haines, John, 179–80
Haiti. *See* Saint-Domingue (Haiti)
Halicarnassus (Bodrum), 107n.2
Hall, Stuart, 27n.108, 38–39
Hamilton, John T., 37–38
Handel, George Frideric, 93–94, 96–97, 127n.113, 190–91
Handel and Haydn Society, Boston, 171–73
Hara, Martinho, 133–34. *See also* Japan
Hare, John, 93–94
harmonics, 208–9
harmony, 134–35, 161, 183, 196–97, 207–10, 215, 239–40, 242. *See also* polyphony
Harrán, Don, 41n.25, 182
Harris, James, 93–94
Hartley, Janet, 83, 84
Harvard College (Harvard University), 65, 150n.79
Hasse, Johann Adolph, 96
Hasselquist, Fredrik, 112–13, 195–96
Hawes, Clement, 102–3
Hawkins, Sir John, 43–44, 90–91, 96–97, 162–64, 173, 205, 211, 212–13
Haydn, Joseph, 94–95, 171–72, 176–77
Haydn, Michael, 176–77

Hayes, William, 49
Head, Matthew, 90
Head, Raymond, 131
Hebenstreit, Pantaleon, 89–90
Hegel, Georg Wilhelm Freidrich, 230–31, 237–38
Heidelberg, 231
Heinichen, Johann David, 86, 218
Hellenic. *See* Greek
Hellespont (Dardanelles), 79–81, 80*f*
Helmholtz, Hermann von, 238–39
Henry VIII, king of England, 223
Hensel, Gottfried, 73–76
Herder, Johann Gottfried, 34, 73, 236
Hermippus, 37–38
Herodotus, 38–39, 107
Hesmondhalgh, David, 15, 218–19
Hikayat Iskandar Zulkarnain, 222
Hindustani music, 1–2, 108–9, 214–15
Hippo, 224–25
Hippocrates, 107, 118–19
Hippocratic tradition, 118–19
  Airs, Waters, Places, 107
historical musicology. *See* music, academic study of
historically informed performance. *See* early music (historically informed performance)
histories, chronicles, descriptive works, and ethnographies (historical)
  Cantemir, "Incrementorum et decrementorum aulae othman[n]icae sive aliothman[n]icae," 77–78, 150–52
  Cantemir, *The History of the Growth and Decay of the Othman Empire*, 77–78, 150–52, 230
  Du Halde, *Description géographique, historique, chronologique, politique, et physique de l'empire de la Chine*, 124, 140–41
  Hachenberg, *Summi viri Germania media*, 231
  Herodotus, *Histories*, 38–39
  Historia Augusta, 107n.6
  Isidore of Beja (attrib.), *Mozarabic Chronicle/Continuatio hispanica*, 107–8
  Kaempfer, *History of Japan*, 119

  Lafitau, *Moeurs des sauvages américains comparées aux moeurs des premiers temps*, 200–1
  Marcgrave, *Historia naturalis brasilae*, 120
  Roman, *Republicas del mundo*, 226–27
  Russell, *The Natural History of Aleppo* (1756 ed.), 113–14
  Russell, *The Natural History of Aleppo* (1794 ed.), 113–14, 125–26
  Villoteau, *Description de l'Égypte*, 173
  See also music histories
historiography, 2–3, 6–9, 11–13, 16–17, 21, 25–26, 107, 108–9, 112, 117, 122–23, 130, 132, 133–78, 182, 186, 193–94, 216, 237, 245, 246–47. *See also* music histories; primary sources
History of European Ideas (journal), 15–16
history of ideas, 25
Hobson, John M., 221–22
Hodgson, Mary, 43n.31
Höffer, Otfried, 17–18
Hofoper, Berlin. *See* Berlin Opera
Holy Roman Empire, 54, 107–8, 233–34. *See also* Germany; Vienna
Homer, 191–92
"Homo Europaeus," 117–18, 121, 122–23
homogeneity and homogenization, 2, 9–10, 14, 99–100, 108–10, 179–80, 220, 247
Horace, 37–38, 49, 158
Høst, Georg, 175n.170
Hove, Frederick Hendrick van, 78–79, 80*f*
Hu, Lester, 124–25
Hucbald of St. Amand, 237–38
humanism. *See* Renaissance humanism
Hume, David, 114–15
humors and humoral theory, 117–19
Hungary, 160–61, 223, 236
hybridity, 38–39, 99–100, 122n.99
Hyde, James Hazen, 61–62

Iberian
  conservatism in music, 164
  music theory, 164
  organ, 147–48
  style in music, 147–48
Iceland, 73–76

iconography, 117
　Ripa, *Iconologia*, 52–54, 53*f*
　See also art works; continents, allegories of; Europa (mythological figure)
identity, 2–4, 8–9, 14–15, 23n.97, 29–30, 77–78, 87–88, 110, 120–21, 127, 135, 225
　American, 172–73
　Greek, 107n.2
　Western, 222
　See also European identity; oppositional self-definition
ideology, 8, 11–12, 17, 107–8, 110, 181, 194–95, 240, 247–48. *See also* Eurocentrism; identity; politics
Ignatius of Loyola, 54, 62–63. *See also* Jesuits (Society of Jesus)
"Imaginary Museum of Musical Works" (concept of Lydia Goehr), 9–10
improvisation, musical, 193
India, 3–4, 102–3, 105, 108–9, 110–11, 203, 222, 228–29
　northern, 214–15
　See also Bengal; Calcutta (Kolkata); Goa
Indian music, 1–2, 214–15
　musical contexts, 244
Indian Ocean, 228–29
Indian people, 125–26, 131
　musicians. *See* Ala-ud-din Barnawi; Tagore, Sourindro Mohun
"Indies, the," 3–4, 70, 135, 200
　East and West, 233–34 (*see also* Raynal, Guillaume Thomas (Abbé))
indigenous (concept discussed by Chabanon), 168–69
Indigenous peoples, 185, 197–200
Ingolstadt, 143
Innocent XII, pope, 67
instruments. *See* musical instruments
interpreters, 152–53. *See also* translation
intertextuality, 37–38, 129–30, 132, 146–47
Io, 45n.40
Irish rapparee, 69n.136
Irish songs, 163
Iron Curtain, 234
Irvine, Thomas, 6
Isfahan, 223

Isidore of Beja, 107n.7
Isidore of Seville, 71
Islam, 73, 76–77, 112n.35, 131–32, 179–81, 202–3n.89, 203. *See also* muezzins; Muslims
Islamic empires, 225. *See* Mughal empire; Ottoman empire
Islamic scholars and scholarship, 181, 204, 222. *See also* Ala-ud-din Barnawi; Al-Farabi
Israel, 183–84. *See also* David, king of Israel; Jerusalem; Palestine; Solomon, king of Israel
Istanbul. *See* Constantinople (Istanbul)
Italian
　ears (concept), 124, 125–26
　language, 5, 87–88, 91–92, 140–41, 176–77, 192–93
　music, 50–51, 149
　music theory, 141–42
　musical contexts, 244
　style in music, 4–5, 92–93, 94–95, 103–4, 135, 161–62, 166–67, 170, 205–6
　taste, 154–55
　taste in music, 87–88
Italian people, 112–14, 139–40, 154, 212
　musicians, 41–43, 48, 51–52, 70, 83–84, 85–86, 91–92, 93, 126n.111, 162, 163, 190
Italy, 68–69, 90–92, 133–34, 183–84, 230–31. *See also* Bologna; Brixen; Ferrara; Florence; Genoa; Kaltern; Naples; Rome; Savoy; Trent; Turin; Tyrol; Venice
Itapúa, Paraguay, 148
İzmir. *See* Smyrna (İzmir)

Jackson, William, 89–90
Jacob, Benjamin, 90
Jahangir, Mughal emperor, 223
janissary band, 100–1
Japan, 58, 119, 133–35, 219. *See also* Tokyo
Japanese people, 119, 133–35
　musicians (*see Tenshō shōnen shisetsu*)
Jason, 145
Jaucourt, Chevalier Louis de, 158
Jefferson, Thomas, 121–22
Jensen, Claudia, 218

Jerusalem, 71, 180, 225, 226–28, 241–42
  Church of the Holy Sepulchre, 227–28
Jesuits (Society of Jesus), 4, 54, 64, 110–12, 133–35, 136–48, 164–65, 228–29
  College of Louis-le-Grand, Paris, 152–53, 158, 168, 210–11
  De missione legatorum iaponensium ad romanam curiam, 133–35
  in China, 4, 110–12, 136–42, 228–29
  in Japan, 4n.15, 133–35
  in Paraguay, 4, 142–48
  See also Acosta, José de; Aleni, Giulio; Alzina, Francisco Ignacio; Amiot, Jean-Joseph-Marie; Berger, Louis; Charlevoix, François-Xavier de; Du Halde, Jean-Baptiste; Eximeno y Pujades, Antonio; Fróis, Luís; Grimaldi, Filippo; Ignatius of Loyola; Lafitau, Joseph-François; Ménestrier, Claude François; Murillo Velarde, Pedro; Núñez, Lauro; Orléans, Pierre-Joseph d'; Pereira, Tomé; Ricci, Matteo; Sande, Duarte de; Sepp von Reinegg, Anton; Ströbel, Matthäus; Trigault, Nicolas; Vaisseau, Jean; Valignano, Alessandro; Verbiest, Ferdinand
Jesus Christ, 67
Jewish music, 211–12
  ancient Hebrew music, 101–2, 187–88, 211–12, 230
  cantillation, 211–12
  instruments, 211–12
  traditions, 18
  See also Jewish people; Judaism
Jewish people, 180–81
  ancient, 101–2, 230
  early modern, 181, 202–3n.89
  musical instrument makers, 202–3n.89
  musicians, 41n.25, 181, 211–12, 223
  Sephardic, 223
  See also Judaism; Lachmann, Robert; Sachs, Curt
Jiang, Qingfan, 138, 229
John VIII Palaiologus, Byzantine emperor, 223–24
Jones, Sir William, 215n.146

Joubert, Estelle, 185–86
journals. *See* almanacs, journals, newspapers, and periodicals (historical)
Jove. *See* Zeus/Jupiter
Jubal, 187–88, 230
Judaism, 180–81, 211–12. *See also* Jewish music; Jewish people
Juvenel de Carlencas, Félix de, 100–1, 155n.100

Kablitz, Andreas, 17–18
Kaempfer, Engelbert, 119
Kahn, Joel, 27–28
Kaltern, 143
Kangxi, emperor of China, 124, 136–38, 139–42, 173–74
Kant, Immanuel, 119
Karnes, Kevin, 236
Kashmiri music, 108–9
Kazan, 73–76
Keevak, Michael, 119
Kiesewetter, Raphael Georg, 214
Khoikhoi people, 127, 209–10
Kim, Jin-Ah, 99–100
Kipling, Rudyard, 220–21
Kircher, Athanasius, 90–91, 141, 166, 226–27
Kissin, Yevgeny, 218
Kivelson, Valerie, 85–86
Knapp, William, 93–94
Knighton, Tess, 116n.60
Kolb, Peter, 127–28
König, Daniel, 108–9
Koskoff, Ellen, 244
Kowner, Rotem, 119
Kruzenshtern, Adam Johann von, 176–78
Kusber, Jan, 83–84

La Baume Le Blanc, Louis César de (Duke of La Vallière), 45, 68–69
La Borde, Jean-Benjamin de, 84–86, 128–29, 173–74, 213
La Loubère, Simon de, 164–65
La Motte, Antoine Houdar de, 68–69
La Salle, Marquis de (Marie-Louis Caillebot), 46

La Scala (Nuovo Regio Ducale Teatro alla Scala), 50
Lachmann, Robert, 241–42
Lactantius, 38n.9
Lafitau, Joseph-François, 118–19, 200–1, 205–6
Landsberg, 143–44
Lang, Paul Henry, 241
Lanzellotti, Federico, 93n.111
Las Casas, Bartolomé de, 197–98
Latin America, 129–30. *See also* Argentina; Brazil; Colombia; Mexico; Paraguay; Peru; Uruguay
Latin American music, 1–2
Latin language, 71–72, 77–78, 87–88, 91–92, 141, 202, 217
  neo-Latin neologisms, 138–39
Latins (people, implying Catholics), 79–81, 128–29, 226, 227n.48
laughter, 184–85, 193
law, 35. *See also* copyright
Lazarists, 141–42
Le Brun, Antoine-Louis, 45
Le Cerf de la Viéville, Jean-Louis, 154
Lebanon, 37–38
Leduc, 94–95
Leipzig, 51–52, 94–95
Lemaire de Belges, Jean, 110
Levant Company, 193–94. *See also* Sherman, Rowland
Leveridge, Richard, 43
Lewis, Bernard, 108–9
liberal arts, 52–54, 203. *See also* astronomy; metaphysics; music; philosophers; rhetoric
librettists, playwrights, and poets. *See* ancient writers and scholars; Benserade, Isaac de; Boccaccio, Giovanni; Bordier, René; Branchi, Silverstro; Chiabrera, Gabriello; Crowne, John; Fuzelier, Louis; La Motte, Antoine Houdar de; Le Brun, Antoine-Louis; Limojon de Saint-Didier, Ignace François de; Pitoni, Giuseppe Ottavio; Prividali, Luigi; Quinault, Philippe; Rousseau, Jean-Baptiste; Striggio, Alessandro the younger; Sandri, Elvezio (Paolo Emilio Fantuzzi); Tate, Nahum; Verazi, Mattia; Villati, Leopoldo de
Libya (Africa), 71. *See also* Africa
Licin (eunuch in Chinese imperial court), 228–29
Liège, 94–95
liminality, 77–78, 82–83, 150, 151–52
Limojon de Saint-Didier, Ignace François de, 48n.53
Lindorff, Joyce, 138n.17, 141–42
Linnaeus, Carl, 112–13, 117–19, 120, 129–30
Linné, Carl von. *See* Linnaeus, Carl
Lisbon, 62–63
"Little Red Riding Hood," 183
Locke, Ralph, 12–13, 21–22
Lockwood, Lewis, 16–17
Lolli, Antonio, 96–97
London, 64, 77–79, 88, 90, 93, 95–97, 169, 171–72. *See also* British Empire; British Isles; England
Longman and Broderip, 95–96
Lorient, 97–98
Los Angeles, 22, 220–21
Louis XIII, king of France, 62
Louis XIV, king of France, 46
Louis XV, king of France, 46
Louis Auguste de Bourbon, prince de Dombes, 46
Louis-le-Grand, Jesuit college of (Paris), 152–53, 158, 168
Low Countries, 144
Lowe, Kate, 109–10
Lowe, Melanie, 9–10
Lowerre, Kathryn, 69n.136
Lucerne, 143–44
Lully, Jean-Baptiste, 44, 62, 68, 91–93, 103–4n.21, 151–52
Lusitano, Vicente, 116–17
Luxembourg, 126n.111
Lyon, 69n.137

Macartney, Lord (George Macartney), 131. *See also* ambassadors, embassies, and emissaries
Macau, 4n.15, 133–34
McClary, Susan, 187, 192–93

McClymonds, Marita P., 50–51
Madan, Martin, 93–94
Madrid, 169
Magellan, Ferdinand, 217
Maghreb, 217. *See also* Africa
Magnan, Dominique, 128–29
Malaspina, Alessandro, 127n.113
Malay literature. *See Hikayat Iskandar Zulkarnain*; *Sejarah melayu*
Malcolm, Alexander, 229–31
males and maleness. *See* gender
Malta, 90–91
Manelli, Francesco, 41–42
Mantua, 41–42
maps. *See* cartography and maps
Maracaibo, Colombia, 129–30
Marcello, Benedetto, 211–12
Marcgrave, Georg, 120
Marescalchi, Luigi, 95–96
Margherita of Savoy, 41–42
Maria Theresa, Holy Roman Empress, 50–51
Mariner, William, 175–76
Marino, John A., 72–73
Marquesas Islands, 176
Marshall, Melanie, 121
Martin, John, 175–76
Martin, Nathan, 163n.120
Martín y Soler, Vicente, 85–86
Martineau du Plessis, Denis, 73, 74f
masculinity. *See* gender
Mason, Lowell, 172–73
mathematics, 140n.28
Matar, Nabil, 108–9
Mattheson, Johann, 90–91, 190–91
matriarchy, 45n.40
Mayes, Catherine, 236
Mattheson, Johann, 90–91
Max, Hermann, 42n.30
Meares, John, 112, 127n.113
Mediterranean, 71, 73–76, 193, 202, 223–24, 225
Medley, Guido, 128
Mehmed II, Ottoman sultan, 72–73, 223–24
Melaka, 111–12
Melani, Alessandro, 42–43
men. *See* gender

Ménestrier, Claude François, 62–63, 166
Menocal, María Rosa, 181
Mercury, 187–88, 200, 201
Mersenne, Marin, 135, 204, 226–28
metaphysics, 3–4
Metropolitan Museum, 54–58, 61–62
Mexico, 58, 120–21, 171–72, 219
Mexico City, 164–65
Middle Ages, 1, 3–4, 18, 100, 181, 190–91, 223
Middle East, 242
Mignolo, Walter, 190
Milan, 50, 51–52, 224–25
Milgrove, Benjamin, 93–94
military musicians, 129–30, 131–32. *See also* armies
Millefonti (Turin), 41–42. *See also* Savoy
Miller, Peter, 227–28
Minerva, 58–60
mining. *See* extractivism
Minos, 37–38, 51–52
Minuti, Théophile, 227–28
missions and missionaries, 141–42, 185–86, 197–98. *See also* Capuchins; Franciscans; Jesuits (Society of Jesus); Lazarists; *Der neue Welt-Bott*, 146–47
Mitsi, Efterpi, 194–96
modern, as adjective, 246–47
modernity, 180–81, 183–216
"modern European music" (term), 213–16
See also European music (compound term)
modes. *See* musical modes and scale systems
Moḥammad Nabi Khan, 131–32. *See also* ambassadors, embassies, and emissaries
Mohammed ben Abdallah, sultan of Morocco, 175n.170
Moisiodax, Iosipos, 82–83
Moldavia, 77–78. *See also* Cantemir, Dimitrie
Molière (Jean-Baptiste Poquelin), 68
Mondonville, Jean-Joseph Cassanéa de, 46
monodists, 186–87, 193
Montagu, Jeremy, 22–23, 220–21

Montagu, John, 115–16
Montagu, John, fourth earl of Sandwich, 208–9
Montagu, Mary, 115–16
Montagu, Mary Wortley, 194–96
Montaigne, Michel de, 197–98
Montéclair, Michel Pignolet de, 48–49
Montesquieu, 166–67, 226–27
Monteverdi, Claudio, 17, 41–42, 166
Monteverdi, Giuliio Cesare, 192
Moody, Ivan, 82–83
"moor" (historical term), 116–17, 193, 212–13. *See also* Morisco people
"Moorish" (historical term)
    culture (manners, customs), 211, 212–13
    music, 163, 202, 212–13
Morales, Cristóbal de, 130, 132
Morar, Floran-Stefan, 110–12
Morisco people, 202–3n.89
Morley, Thomas, 189–90, 229–30
Morocco, 174–75
    Mohammed ben Abdallah, 175n.170
Moschus, 37–38
Moscow, 73–76, 83–84, 171–72
Moses, 187–88
Motteux, Peter Anthony, 43, 68–69
Mount Athos, 226
Mozart family, 96
Mozart, Leopold, 85–86, 190–91
Mozart, Wolfgang Amadeus, 17–18, 94–95, 96, 126–27, 171
muezzins, 76–77, 81
Muffat, Georg, 91–92
Mugglestone, Erica, 128
Mughal Empire, 102–3, 108–9
    Jahangir, emperor, 223
    music theory, 108–9
    See also India
Muhammad, Praetorius's description of, 203
Müller, Johann Sebastian, 90–91
Müller, Robert, 237n.89
Müller-Wille, Staffan, 117–19, 120
multiculturalism, 244
Munrow, David, 179–80
mural, 63n.107, *See also* fresco
Murillo Velarde, Pedro, 63, 141–42
Muscovy, 73–76, 83–84, 85–86, 203. *See also* Moscow; Russia

Muses, 183–84, 201
music
    art music, 5–6, 11, 19, 28–29, 236
    Christian liturgical, 5–6, 17, 145, 154–55, 178, 179, 220, 224–25, 227–28, 231
    classical music (general contemporary concept), 19–20, 220
    criticism, reception, and appreciation, 90
    domestic performance, 236
    folk music, 5–6, 11, 19
    folk-songs, 236, 240–41
    melody and melodic style, 174–75, 192, 205–6, 208–10, 227–28, 242
    metaphysics of, 3–4
    musical canon, 90
    popular music, 19–20, 193, 215, 220
    sacred, 17, 172–73, 215, 246–47
    universal language concept, 168–69, 173
    See also Afghani music; African music; American music; ancient music; Asian music; Australian music; composition; genres and types of music and dance; European music; fame, musical; Hindustani music; improvisation, musical; Indian music; Kashmiri music; Latin American music; national styles in music; ornamentation, musical; Pasifika music; printing and publishing of music; Provençal music; Western art music; Western music; world music
music, academic study of
    archaeomusicology, 194–95
    comparative musicology, 122n.99, 215, 243–44
    critical musicology, 20
    ethnomusicology, 7–8, 12–13, 15, 17, 19–21, 153, 243–44
    global music history, 15n.62, 20, 25, 29, 31, 244, 247–48
    historical musicology, 7–8, 12–13, 15–22, 220, 243–44, 247–48
    music theory, 21–22, 244
    organology, 22, 195
    postcolonial musicology, 20
    see also composition

INDEX 323

music catalogues
   Longman and Broderip, *Complete Register of All the New Musical Publications Imported*, 95–96
   Playford, H., *A General Catalogue of all the Choicest Musick-Books*, 93
   Walsh (the younger), *A Cattalogue* [*sic*] *of Musick*, 130–31
music education, 6–7, 146, 247–48
music genres. *See* genres and types of music and dance
music history
   as myth, 15–16, 243–44
   diasporic, 20
   used in politics, 240, 247–48
   See also anachronism; "conceptual imperialism" (concept of Lydia Goehr)
music histories
   Bonnet-Bourdelot and Bourdelot, *Histoire de la musique et de ses effets*, 92–93
   Burney, *General History of Music*, 130, 173–74, 190–91, 207
   Forkel, *Allgemeine Geschichte der Musik*, 173–74, 213–14
   Hawkins, *General History of the Science and Pratice of Music*, 173–74
   Kiesewetter, *Geschichte der europäisch-abendländischen oder unsrer heutigen Musik*, 214
   Lang, *Music in Western Civilization*, 241
   Montagu, *Origins and Development of Musical Instruments*, 22
   Taruskin, *Oxford History of Western Music*, 218
   Wiora, *Die vier Weltalter der Musik/The Four Ages of Music*, 243
music journals and periodicals. *See* journals, newspapers, periodicals, and almanacs (historical)
music, national styles in, 5, 34, 103–4, 163–69, 246
   in singing, 165–66
   synthesis of, 50–51, 167–70
music, progress in. *See* progress (in music)
music notation, 52–54, 58, 81–82, 107–8, 128–29, 138, 146, 149
   ancient Greek, 210–11

   clef, 172–73
   Greek ecclesiastical (reformed), 82–83
   neumes, 237–38
   of Eastern Christians in Jerusalem, 227–28
   staff notation, 81–82, 128–29, 138, 172–73, 175–76, 186–87, 226, 227–28
   Western exceptionalism and, 239–40
music societies, 94–95
music teaching, 139–40, 141, 144–45, 146, 247–48. *See also* solmization
music theory
   Arabic, 111–12, 135, 173
   Chinese, 140–41
   elementary, 214–15
   European, 111–12, 140–42
   French, 141–42
   Greek (ancient), 204, 221–23
   Greek (nineteenth-century), 82–83
   Iberian, 164
   Italian, 141–42
   Mughal, 108–9
   Ottoman/Turkish, 150–51, 153
   Spanish, 164–65
   See also music, academic study of; music notation; music treatises, periodicals, and reference works (including dance); solmization
music trade, 94–96, 152–53n.90, *See also* printing and publishing of music
music treatises, 85–86, 135
music treatises, periodicals, and reference works (including dance)
   Amiot, *Mémoire sur la musique des Chinois*, 173, 206–7
   Amiot, "De la musique moderne des Chinois," 160
   Arbeau, *Orchésographie*, 199
   Baron, *Historisch-Theoretisch und Practische Untersuchung des Instruments der Lauten*, 230–31
   Bermudo, *Declaracion de instrumentos musicales*, 202
   Brossard, *Dictionnaire de musique*, 87–88
   Brossard, *Dictionnaire des termes*, 87–88
   Brown, *A Dissertation on . . . Poetry and Music*, 124–25, 205
   Chabanon, *De la musique considérée en elle-même*, 168

324 INDEX

music treatises, periodicals, and reference works (including dance) (*cont.*)
  Clements, *Introduction to the Study of Indian Music*, 2n.7
  Galilei, *Dialogo della musica antica et della moderna*, 189–90
  Galliard, "A Critical Discourse upon Opera's in England," 88
  Ganassi, *Regola Rubertina*, 212–13
  Jones, "On the Musical Modes of the Hindus," 215n.146
  Kircher, *Musurgia universalis*, 90–91, 141
  L'écho, ou journal de musique françoise, italienne, 94–95
  La Borde, *Essai sur la musique ancienne et moderne*, 128–29, 173–74
  Le Cerf de la Viéville, *Comparaison de la musique italienne et . . . françoise*, 154
  Ménestrier, *Des ballets anciens et modernes*, 62–63
  Mozart, L., *Versuch einer gründlichen Violinschule*, 190–91
  Praetorius, *Syntagma musicum*, 203
  Provedi, *Paragone della musica antica, e della moderna*, 88–89
  Quantz, *Essai d'une méthode pour apprendre à jouer de la flûte traversière*, 231–32, 233*f*
  Quantz, *Versuch einer Anweisung die Flötetraversiere zu spielen*, 205–6, 231–32, 233*f*
  Raguenet, *Paralele* [sic] *des Italiens et des François*, 154
  Rameau, *Traité de l'harmonie*, 191–92, 210–11
  Rousseau, *Dictionnaire de musique*, 96, 161, 206–8
  Rousseau, *Lettre sur la musique françoise*, 162
  Ruetz, *Widerlegte Vorurtheile von der Beschaffenheit der heutigen Kirchenmusic*, 101–2
  Scacchi, *Breve discorso sopra la musica moderna*, 190
  Tagore, *Six Principal Ragas*, 2n.7
  Tinctoris, *De inventione et usu musicae*, 224–25
  Titon du Tillet, *Le Parnasse françois*, 91–92
  Valls, *Mapa armónico práctico*, 164
  Vicentino, *L'antica musica ridotta alla moderna prattica* 189, 195
  Villoteau, *Recherches sur l'analogie de la musique avec les arts*, 171, 213–14
  Walther, *Musicalisches Lexicon*, 231, 232*f*
  Willard, *Treatise on the Music of Hindoostan*, 237
  Zarlino, *Dimostrazioni harmoniche*, 204
  Zarlino, *Istitutioni harmoniche*, 191–92
  Zarlino, *Sopplimenti musicali*, 192
musical instruments, 54–61, 83–84, 140–41, 142–43, 153, 194–96, 200–1, 203–4, 239, 242
  ancient, 194–96, 203
  aulos, 195–96
  automatic mechanism for organ, 138
  bassoon, 46, 148
  bells, 76–77, 81, 123, 203
  bows for string instruments, 237–38
  castanets, 64–65
  clavichord, 189–90, 229
  cornett (cornetto), 97n.137, 148, 223
  crwth, 237–38
  cymbals, 63n.106
  drums, 39, 63n.106, 129n.125, 203, 213
  fiddle, 64n.110, 201. *See also* violin
  flageolet, 213
  flute, 46, 48–49, 143, 213, 231–32, 233*f*
  gom gom, 127–28
  gora, 127n.115
  guitar, 58–60, 63n.107, 213
  harp, 195–96
  harpsichord, 48n.53, 58n.88, 96–97, 136–38, 139, 189–90, 229
  Hebrew instruments (ancient), 211–12
  history of, 22, 195–96, 237–38
  horn, 226
  keyboard instruments, 112–13, 143
  lute, 212–13, 223–24, 230–31
  lyre, 58, 201
  musette, 58–60
  musical bow, 127n.113
  noseflute, 198–99
  organ, 90, 136–38, 139, 147–48, 149, 180, 213, 226

'ūd (oud), 223–24
pandura, 213
panpipe (*fistula*, syrinx), 194–96
pantaleon, 89–90
Persian chordophone, 223–24
piano, 239–40
rebab, 212–13
rebec, 212–13
recorder, 42–43, 58–60, 212–13
regal organ, 180
rhombus, 201
ribible, 212–13
sackbut (trombone), 211–12, 226
shawm, 63n.106, 143, 148, 164–65, 203
simandron, 81
sistrum, 201
spinet, 213
string instruments, 42–43, 203
theorbo, 96–97, 143, 212–13
timbrel, 211–12
timpani, 63n.106
trombone (sackbut), 211–12, 226
trumpet, 64n.110, 116–17, 143, 148, 213, 223
trumpet marine, 143, 147n.69
tubalcain, 211–12
Turkish monochord, 222–23
viol, 48n.53, 143, 212–13, 223
viola, 103–4
violin, 46, 48–49, 58–60, 63n.107, 93–94, 96–97, 103–4, 124–25, 190–91, 223
violoncello, 96–97
wind instruments, 239–40
See also music histories; orchestras; organology; singers; singing; violinists; voice
musical modes and scale systems, 153, 188–89, 199–200, 214–15, 240–41
musical pitch, 134–35
Musical Quarterly (journal), 240
musical staff (invention of), 186–87, 226. *See also* music notation
"musical works, modern," 239–40
musical works (named)
 Beethoven, Symphony No. 3 ("Eroica"), 186–87
 Benjamin, *Harmonia Coelestis*, 93–94

Bernier/J.-B. Rousseau, *Jupiter et Europe*, 48–49
Béthizy, *L'enlèvement d'Europe*, 44–45
Bianchi, *Europa rapita*, 51–52
Bordier (text), *Ballet du grand bal de la douairière de Billebahault*, 62
Boston Handel and Haydn Society Collection of Church Music, The, 172–73
Campra/La Motte, *L'Europe galante*, 68–70
Colista or Scarlatti, *Europa rapita da Giove in forma di toro*, 48
Collin de Blamont/Limojon de Saint-Didier, *Europpe*, 48–49
Couperin, *Apothéose [de] . . . Lully*, 103–4n.21
Couperin, *Apothéose de Corelli*, 103–4n.21
Couperin, *Les goûts-réünis*, 87–88, 103–4n.21
Duport and Dugué/Fuzelier, *Jupiter et Europe*, 46, 47f
Eccles/Motteux, *Europe's Revels for the Peace of Ryswick*, 68–69
Eccles/Motteux, *The Rape of Europa by Jupiter*, 43
Fleckno, *The Mariage of Oceanus and Brittania*, 64–65
Galliard, Cobston, and Leveridge, *Jupiter and Europa*, 43–44
Galliard, Cobston, and Leveridge, *The Royal Chace, or Merlin's Cave*, 43–44
Galuppi, *Mundi salus*, 67
Gletle, *Expeditionis musicae*, 145
Graun/Villati after La Motte, *L'Europa galante / Das Galante Europa*, 70
Handel/Jennens, *Saul*, 211–12
Herder, *Volkslieder*, 236
Hayes, *Jupiter and Europa*, 49
Knapp, *New Church Melody*, 93–94
Le Brun, *Europe*, 45
Lully/Benserade, *Ballet royal de Flore*, 62
Lully/Benserade, *La naissance de Venus*
Lully/Molière, *Le Bourgeois gentilhomme*, 68

works (named) (*cont.*)
- Manelli/Sandri, *Il ratto d'Europa*, 41–42
- Melani, *L'Europa*, 42–43
- Montéclair, *Europe*, 48–49
- Monteverdi/Striggio, *L'Orfeo*, 41–42
  - Mozart, W. A., Symphony No. 31 ("Paris"), 94–95
- Muffat, *Florilegium secundum*, 91–92
- *Newburyport Collection of Sacred, European Musick, The*, 172–73
- Paer/Prividali, *Arianna consolata*, 51–52
- Paer/Prividali, *Europa in Creta*, 51–52
- Pasquier, *Concert françois: Europe et Jupiter*, 48–49
- Pergolesi, *La serva padrona*, 89–90, 162
- Pitoni/Sorba, *Il mondo riparato*, 67
- Purcell/Tate, *Dido and Aeneas*, 43n.31
- Rameau/Fuzelier, *Les Indes galantes*, 70
- Rochefort, *L'enlèvement d'Europe*, 49–50
- Salieri/Verazi, *Europa riconosciuta*, 50–51
- Sancho, *Cotillons &c.*, 115–16
- Sancho, *Twelve Country Dances for the Year 1779*, 115–16
- Scarlatti or Colista, *Europa rapita da Giove in forma di toro*, 48
- Staggins/Crowne, *Calisto: Or, the Chaste Nimph*, 65–67
- Walsh and Hare, eds., *Select Preludes & Vollentarys for the Violin*, 93–94
- Walsh, ed., *Choice Musick by the Most Celebrated Authors in Europe*, 93

musicians. *See* European musician (concept); military musicians; singers; violinists
musicking (concept of Christopher Small), 4–5, 30–31, 35–36, 42–43, 246, 247
musicology. *See* music, academic study of
Muslims, 107–9, 110–11, 202–3
- instrument makers, 202–3n.89
- Sufi, 180
- *See also* Spain

mythological figures. *See* Agenor; Amphion; Aphrodite; Apollo; Argonauts; Ariadne; Arion; Asterion (Asterius); Cadmus; Cupid; Dionysius; dragon; Europa; Eurydice; Flora; Io; Jason; Zeus/Jupiter; Mercury; Minerva; Minos; Muses; Narbal; nymphs; Orpheus; Pan; Polyhymnia; Rhadamanthys; Sarpedon; Syrinx (Siringa); Urania; Venus

Nakaura, Julião, 133–34
Naples, 63, 95–96, 171–72, 202
Napoleon. *See* Bonaparte, Napoleon
Narbal, 45
Nardini, Pietro, 96–97
nationalism, 28–29, 99–100, 130. *See also* ethnonationalism
nations, allegorical representations of, 68–70
naturalists and botanists. *See* Dampier, William; Haenke, Thaddeus Xaverius Peregrinus; Hasselquist, Fredrik; Linnaeus, Carl; Russell, Alexander; Sparrman, Anders
Nenita, town on Chios, 81–82
Nero, emperor of Rome, 121
Netherlands, 147–48
Nettl, Bruno, 7–8, 243–44
networks, 86, 90, 95–96
Neubauer, Eckhard, 152n.85
Neubaur, Caroline, 50–51
"New World," 241. *See also* America/Americas
New Zealand, 28–29, 219
newspapers. *See* almanacs, journals, newspapers, and periodicals (historical)
Ng, Su Fang, 222
Nicholas, Saint, 73–76
Nicolet, Jean-Baptiste, 49–50
Niebuhr, Carsten, 82–83, 213
Niemetschek, Franz Xaver, 126–27
Noah, 73–76, 144
Nooshin, Laudan, 20
North, the, 73n.16, 84, 231–32, 234–36. *See also* Global North; Europe, northern
North America, 70, 218–19
- map of, 73n.16
- *See also* American people; Boston; Los Angeles; Mexico; Nova Scotia; United States of America

INDEX 327

notation. *See* music notation
Nova Scotia, 65
novel, 119–20
Noverre, Jean-Georges, 152n.86
Nuku Hiva, Marquesas Islands, 176
Núñez, Lauro, 148
Nuremberg, 4
nymphs, 66, 194–95

Occident, the. *See* West (Occident), the
Occidental music. *See* Western music
Ockley, Simon, 181
odes. *See* Horace
O'Donnelly, Abbé Terence Joseph, 214–15
Ōmura Suminobu, 134
opera, 33, 43–44, 50–51, 84–86, 88, 103–4, 116–17, 192–93, 239–40
   French, 44–45, 162
   Italian, 162–63
   in Berlin, 70
   in Dresden, 96–97
   in Paris, 96, 162–63, 174–75
   in St. Petersburg, 84–86
   in Venice, 162–63
   See also musical works (named)
oppositional self-definition, 4, 31, 107–8, 201–2, 236. *See also* identity
orchestra, 239–40
   Berlin Opera, 96–97
   Dresden Opera, 96–97
   Naples, 96
   Paris Opéra, 96
   See also Vingt-quatre Violons du Roy
organology. *See* music, academic study of; musical instruments
"Oriental music." *See* "Eastern music"/ "Oriental music"
Orientalism, 5–6, 174–75, 242, 245
"Orientals" (people, historical term), 210
Orléans, Pierre-Joseph d', 141
ornamentation, musical, 37–38, 40–42, 193
   garganta, 133
   gorgie, 193
Ornitoparchus, Andreas, 165
Orpheus, 167–68, 187–88, 195–96
Orthodox Christianity. *See* Christianity
orthography, 155–58

Oschema, Klaus, 71, 100
Ospedale degl'Incurabili (Venice), 67
Osterhammel, Jürgen, 76–77, 205
Ottoman
   culture, 223
   elite, 114n.47, 149, 150
   Ottoman Empire, 3–4, 69n.137, 71–73, 77–78, 90–91, 110, 125–26, 131–32, 149, 152–53, 183–85, 193–95, 221–23
      Cem, prince
      Mehmed II, sultan
      Selim III, sultan, 131–32
      Suleiman the Magnificent, sultan, 223
      sultan and sultana, 69n.135
      See also Aleppo; Greece; Moldavia; Rhodes; Syria; Turkey; Turkish
   Ottoman music
      court music, 150
      janissary band, 100–1
      theory, 150–51, 153
   Ottoman musicians
      Buhurî-zâde Itrî, 150–51n.80
      Hafız Post, 150–51n.80
      Nayî Osman Dede, 150–51n.80
      See also Cantemir, Dimitrie
Oudry, Jean-Baptiste, 58–60
Ovid, 37–38
Oxford, University of, 49

Pacific Ocean, 127n.113, 175–76, 217. *See also* Nuku Hiva, Marquesas Islands; Pasifika music; Polynesia; Polynesian peoples; Tahiti; Tonga
Padrón, Ricardo, 217
Paer, Ferdinando, 51–52
Pagden, Anthony, 72–73
Page, Christopher, 16–17, 165
Painter, Nell Irvin, 121–22
painters. *See* artists
Paisiello, Giovanni, 85–86
Palestine, 77n.21, 203. *See also* Bethlehem
Palisca, Claude, 193–94
Palmas del Socorro (Colombia), 63n.107
Palomino, Pablo, 1–2
Pan, 51–52
Panov, Alexei A., 87n.79
Paraguay, 4, 142–48

Paris, 4, 44, 49–50, 78–81, 82–83, 87–88, 94–95, 96, 124–25, 135, 141, 149, 152–53, 162–63, 167–68, 169, 171–72, 173, 174–75, 210–11, 214–15, 229. *See also* France
Parr, Adam, 155n.101
Pasifika music, 1–2. *See also* Pacific Ocean; Polynesia
Pasquier, Alexandre, 48–49
patriarchy, 33–34, 42–43, 45n.40, 246
Peace of Ryswick, 43
peasants. *See* class distinctions
Pedrini, Teodorico, 141–42
Peiresc, Nicolas-Claude Fabri de, 135, 204, 223–24, 227–28
Peloponnese, 198–99
people of color, 27–28, 116–17, 122n.99
Pera, 171–72
Pereira, Tomé, 136, 138, 139–42, 149
perfection in music, 209–16
performance practice (early modern), 166, 169, 192–93, 202, 204–5. *See also* early music (historically informed performance); concerts, public
Pergolesi, Giovanni Battista, 89–90, 162
Peri, Jacopo, 193
periodicals, 90. *See also* journals, newspapers, periodicals, and almanacs (historical)
Péron, François, 176
Perrault, Charles, 183, 185–86
Persia, 70, 124, 131–32
  Suleiman I, shah, 223
Persian
  emissary, 223–24
  music, 108–9
Persian people, 62, 107
  musicians, 223–24
Peru, 70, 184–85
Peter I, tsar of Russia, 83–85
Peter II, tsar of Russia, 84–85
Peter III, tsar of Russia, 85–86
Philippines, 63, 117n.62, 126–27, 171, 175–76, 199–200. *See also* Sulu Archipelago; Tausug people; Visayan people
Phillips, John, 78–79
philosophers. *See* Al-Farabi; Alembert, Jean le Rond d'; Aristotle; Aristoxenus; Augustine of Hippo; Bacon, Francis; Beattie, James; Burke, Edmund; Diderot, Denis; Voltaire; Hegel, Georg Wilhelm Freidrich; Herder, Johann Gottfried; Plato (philosopher); Pythagoras; Rousseau, Jean-Jacques; Socrates
Phoinix (Phoenix), 37n.1
Picard, François, 155n.101
Piccardo, Lara, 83
Piccolomini, Silvio (Pope Pius II), 72–73, 109–10
Piechocki, Katharina, 109–10
pitch, musical. *See* musical pitch
Pitoni, Giuseppe Ottavio, 67
Pius II, pope (Piccolomini, Silvio), 72–73, 109–10
plainchant, 178, 179, 193–94, 206–7, 214–15, 226, 245. *See also* Gregorian chant
plants, 58–61, 169
Plato (comic poet), 37–38
Plato (philosopher), 35
Platonic ideas, 35
Playford family (firm), 78–79
Playford, Henry, 78–79n.28, 93
Playford, John junior, 78–79. *See also* Grelot, Guillaume-Joseph
Playford, John senior, 78–79
playwrights. *See* librettists, playwrights, and poets
Plesch, Melanie, 219n.12
poetry. *See* anacreontic poetry; epyllion (narrative poem)
poets. *See* librettists, playwrights, and poets
Poland, 63, 84, 170–71, 218
  Augustus II, king, 63
  See also Warsaw
political events. *See* Peace of Ryswick; wars
politics, 28–29, 48, 89–90, 160–61, 240, 247–48. *See also* discourse; public sphere
Pollard, Lucy, 193–94
Polyhymnia, 184n.3
Polynesia, 1–2, 162, 198–99
Polynesian peoples, 208–9
polyphony, 133–35, 217, 239

contrapuntal, 16–17, 99, 135, 174–75, 226
  throughout world, 239
Pompadour, Madame de (Jeanne Antoinette Poisson), 46
Popayán, 63n.107
Pope, Alexander, 194–95
popes. *See* Clement VIII; Innocent XII; Pius II
Popescu-Judetz, Eugenia, 150–51n.80
Poquelin, Jean-Baptiste. *See* Molière (Jean-Baptiste Poquelin)
porcelain figurines, 58
Porter, David, 15
Portugal, 63, 102–3, 110–12, 133–34
Portuguese Empire, 110–11, 119–20
Portuguese language, 129–30
Portuguese people, 119–20, 139
  musicians. *See* Lusitano, Vicente
positionality (of the researcher), 22–29. *See also* reflexivity
postal service, 86n.72, 94–95
postcolonialism, 11, 20
Potosí, 63n.107
Potsdam, 162–63
Pozzo, Andrea, 54
Praetorius, Michael, 203, 223
Pratt, Mary Louise, 102, 127
presentism, 13–14, 29n.117
primary sources, 14, 26–27. *See also* digital methodologies and resources
primitive (idea), as related to music, 122n.99, 236, 240–41. *See also* barbarian/barbarism (concept)
printing and publishing of music, 93, 94–96, 172–73
  piracy, 95–96
  simultaneous publishing, 95–96
  subscription, 94–95
  see also Breitkopf; Hare, John; Leduc; Longman and Broderip; Marescalchi, Luigi; music trade; Playford family (firm); Walsh, John
Prividali, Luigi, 51–52
processions, 33, 63
progress (in music), 8–9, 10–11, 185–86, 207–8, 209–16
Provedi, Francesco, 88–89
Provençal music, 163
Prussia, 85–86, 231–32

Frederick II "the Great," 231–32
  See also Potsdam
Psellus, Michael, 189–90
Psychoyou, Théodora, 82n.42
Ptolemy, 189–90
public sphere, 28–29, 247–48. *See also* discourse; politics
publishing. *See* printing and publishing of music
Purcell, Henry, 93. *See also* musical works (named); Tate, Nahum
Purchas, Samuel, 123, 125–26
"Puss in Boots," 183
Pythagoras, 187–88

Qianlong, emperor of China, 131
Quantz, Johann Joachim, 170, 205–6, 231–32, 233f
querelle des anciens et modernes, 183
querelle des bouffons, 162
Quijano, Aníbal, 219
Quinault, Philippe, 44–45, 92–93

race, 25–26, 27–28, 97–98, 114–23. *See also* Black people; Blackness; white people; whiteness
racism, 27–28, 114–23
radio, 241–42
Raguenet, François, 154
Rameau, Jean-Bapiste, 70, 166, 173–74, 191–92, 207–8, 210–11
Ramos-Kittrell, Jesús, 120–21
rape of Europa, 37–52. *See also* Europa (mythological figure); musical works (named); Zeus/Jupiter
rapparee. *See* Irish rapparee
Raynal, Guillaume Thomas (Abbé), 234n.75
reciting style, ancient, 192–93. *See also seconda pratica*; singing
recycling
  of modernity, 180–81, 187–88, 189, 212
  of otherness (concept of Rogério Budasz), 198n.71, 199–200
Rees, Abraham, 130n.131
reflexivity, 12–13, 23–24, 27–28, 246–47. *See also* positionality
Reiske, Johann Jacob, 181
relativism, 12–13, 23–24, 125–26

religion, 102–3, 121–22, 246. *See also* Christianity; Islam; Judaism
Rembrandt, 39
Renaissance, 1, 181, 184–85, 187–88, 239–40
Renaissance humanism, 109–10, 189, 193–94, 201–2
Répertoire International des Sources Musicales (RISM), 69n.137, 94n.114, 145n.59
Republic of Letters, 4–5, 35, 86–89, 102, 127
Republic of Music, 4–5, 35, 86–90, 95–96, 127, 246
Rhadamanthys, 37–38
rhetoric, 221–22
Rhodes, 223–24
Rhodes, Willard, 1n.3
Ricci, Matteo, 110–12, 228–29
Rice, John, 50
Rifa'a Al-Tahtawi, 108–9n.14
Ripa, Cesare, 52–53*f*
RISM. *See* Répertoire International des Sources Musicales (RISM)
rivers
  fluvial metaphor, 153–54
  Nile, 71
  Ob, 73–76
  Phasis (Rioni), 71
  Tanais (Don), 71, 78
  Thames, 65–66
Rochefort, Jean-Baptiste, 49–50
Roger, Eugène, 180
Rognoni, Francesco, 193
Roman, Hieronymo, 226–27
Roman Empire, 71–73, 204, 225
  Constantine, 71–72
  eastern, 72–73, 220–22, 225
  limes (frontiers), 234
  Nero, 121
  western, 107–8, 220–21
  See also Rome, ancient
Roman music (early modern), 67, 135, 226–27
  style, 146–47
Roman people (ancient), 107–8, 121
Romania, 73–76, 82–83
romantic aesthetics and ideas, 10, 11–12, 28–29
Romberg, Andreas Jakob, 176–77
Romberg, Bernhard Heinrich, 176–77

Rome, 54, 67, 71–73, 90–91, 128–29, 133–34, 135, 136, 169, 195, 203–4, 204n.94, 223–24, 226–27
Rome, ancient, 65, 121, 185–86, 199
  statuary (ancient), 194–95
  See also Appius Claudius; Roman Empire; Roman people (ancient)
Rore, Cipriano de, 192
Rosanoff, Ivan V., 87n.79
Rose, Stephen, 166–67
Rosenmeyer, Patricia, 198
Ros-Fábregas, Emilio, 130
Rossi, Europa, 41n.25
Rossi, Salamone, 41n.25
Rossini, Gioachino, 131–32, 171–72
Rouen, 197–98
Rouillé, Antoine-Louis, 152–53
Rousseau, Jean, 212
Rousseau, Jean-Baptiste, 48–49
Rousseau, Jean-Jacques, 96, 154, 160–62, 167–68, 170–71, 173–74, 206–8, 231–32
  Considérations sur le gouvernement de Pologne, 170–71
  Dictionnaire de musique, 96, 161, 173, 207–8
  Essai sur l'origine des langues, 173, 207–8, 209–10
  Lettre sur la musique françoise, 162
Roussier, Pierre-Joseph, 160
Rowland-Jones, Anthony, 58n.88
Rubens, Peter Paul, 39
Rubiés, Joan-Pau, 128n.121
Rubin, Miri, 13–14
Ruetz, Caspar, 101–2, 211–12
Russell, Alexander, 113–14, 125–26
Russell, Patrick, 113–14, 125–26
Russia, 78, 83–86
  and "European music" term, 176–78
  Anna, tsarina, 84–85
  Catherine the Great, tsarina, 85–86
  Europeanization of, 83–86
  Peter I, tsar, 83–85
  Peter II, tsar, 84–85
  Peter III, tsar, 85–86
  relationship with Europe, 83–86, 177–78
  See also Moscow; Muscovy; St. Petersburg

Russian
　language, 176–78
　music, 83–84, 85n.67
Russian Orthodox Church, 225–26
Russian people, 85–86

Sachs, Curt, 122n.99, 238–39, 242
Said, Edward W., 5–6
Saint-Domingue (Haiti), 168
St. Petersburg, 73–76, 83–86, 94n.117, 176
Saint-Pierre, Abbé de (Charles-Irénée Castel de Saint-Pierre), 160–61
Salazar, Diego José de, 146
Salgó, Eszter, 38–39
Salieri, Antonio, 50–51
Salinas, Francisco de, 130
Salvador, Brazil, 119–20
Samson, Jim, 21, 234–36
Sancho, Ignatius, 115–16, 132
Sande, Duarte de, 133–34
Sandri, Elvezio (Paolo Emilio Fantuzzi), 41–42
"Saracens" (historical term), 107–8, 212–13
Sarpedon, 37–38
Savage, Roger, 70
savagery and "savages," 185–86, 199
Savall, Jordi, 151–52, 179–80
Savoy, 41–42
Savoyard, 69n.136
Saxony, 63
　Augustus II, elector, 63
　See also Leipzig
Sayf al-Dawla, 100–1
Scacchi, Marco, 190
scales, musical. See musical modes and scale systems
Scarlatti, Alessandro, 48
Scheibe, Johann Adolph, 86
Schmale, Wolfgang, 25n.101, 35–36, 54–58, 119, 121
Schmelzer, Johann Heinrich, 90–91
Schnettger, Matthias, 83–84
Schofield, Katherine Butler, 21, 26–27, 108–9, 121
Schubart, Christian Friedrich Daniel, 89–90, 96, 183–84
Schubert, Franz, 220–21n.16

Scott, Derek, 20n.84
Scottish songs, 163
sculptures and statues, 38–39, 194–96
Sculthorpe, Peter, 28–29
seas, 73–76. See also Baltic; Mediterranean
Sebastiani, Silvia, 114–15
seconda pratica, 166, 192, 204–5
Seizaemon, Miguel (Michael) Chijiwa, 133–35
Sejarah melayu, 111n.28
Selim III, Ottoman sultan, 131–32
Semi, Maria, 205–6
Sepp von Reinegg, Anton, 142–48, 164–65
Sepp von Rechegg [sic], Gabriel, 144
Seroussi, Edwin, 211–12
Seven Years War, 96–97
Sevilla, Juan Alfonso de, 223–24
Seville, 143–44, 146, 164. See also Spain
S. Giovanni del Collegio de' Maroniti (Rome), 128–29
sheet music. See music notation; printing and publishing of music
Shelemay, Kay Kaufman, 180–81
Sherman, Rowland, 112–13
Shiloah, Amnon, 153
Shull, Jonathan, 179–80
Siam (Thailand), 164–65
Siberia, 73–76
singers, 67, 87–88, 202. See also Balducci, Marina; Bracegirdle, Anne; Cibber, Catherine; Hodgson, Mary; La Salle, Marquis de (Marie-Louis Caillebot); Leveridge, Richard; Pompadour, Madame de (Jeanne Antoinette Poisson)
singing
　Aboriginal Australian, 176
　Christian liturgical, 5–6
　of Eastern Christians, 226–28
　Greek, 81–82, 173–74
　"Moorish style," 193
　national styles of, 165
　Tongan, 175–76
　Nuku Hiva, 176–77
　See also reciting style, ancient; seconda pratica; vocal timbre; voice
skin color, 117–21, 158. See also race
Skinner, Graeme, 1

Skott, Christina, 118–19, 129n.129
slavery. *See* enslavement and slavery
Small, Christopher, 6–7, 12–13, 30–31, 42–43, 247
Smith, Ayana O., 27n.109
Smith, Ruth, 211–12
Smyrna (İzmir), 112–13, 131–32, 152–53
Society of Jesus. *See* Jesuits (Society of Jesus)
sociology, 20, 38–39, 239. *See also* Weber, Max
Socrates, 199
solmization, 141–42, 146, 186–87, 226
Solomon, king of Israel, 211–12
Sorba, Mariano, 67
Sorce Keller, Marcello, 11–12, 17, 28–29
sources. *See* digital methodologies and resources; primary sources
South, 73n.16, *See also* Global South
South America, 143–44
  map of, 73n.16
South Asia, 175–76
South Asian people, 102–3
Southeast Asia, 222. *See also* Melaka; Philippines
Souville, Monsieur de, 44
space, 2
Spain, 63, 68–69, 90–91, 133–34, 143–44, 146, 184–85, 202, 206–7, 211, 217
  and "music of the West," 219n.11
  Felipe II, 202–3n.89
  Felipe III, 202–3n.89
  Felipe Próspero, 63
  Muslim societies in, 202–3n.89, 212
  See also Andalusia; Aragon; Cádiz; Castile; Catalonia; Córdoba; Granada; Madrid; Seville; Spanish Empire
Spanish
  language (Castilian), 5, 129–30, 131–32, 140–41, 223–24
  music theory, 164–65
  musical conservatism, 164–65
  progress in music, 211
  style in music, 164–65
Spanish Empire, 63, 120–21, 217
Spanish people, 68–69, 120–21, 206–7, 212
  musicians, 130

Sparrman, Anders, 129–30
Spengler, Oswald, 241
Spivak, Gayatri, 19–20, 102
  "strategic essentialism," 19–20
Spohr, Arne, 116–17
staff, musical. *See* musical staff (invention of); music notation. *See also* Guido of Arezzo
Staggins, Nicholas, 65
Staunton, Sir George, 131
Stefansdom, Vienna, 143
Stein, Louise, 63
Stendhal, 171–72, 205–6
Stockigt, Janice, 126n.111
Stoessel, Jason, 165
Stokes, Martin, 19
Strahlenberg, Philipp Johann von, 84
Striggio, Alessandro the younger, 41–42
Ströbel, Matthäus, 145
Strohm, Reinhard, 1, 16–17, 18, 21, 99, 164, 188–89
  The Rise of European Music, 16–17, 99, 164, 226
Studio der Früher Musik, 179–80
Stumpf, Carl, 238–39
Subrahmanyam, Sanjay, 102–3
Suetonius, 121
Sufi Muslims, 180. *See also* Islam; Muslims
Sukemasu, Mancio Itō, 133–34
Suleiman I, shah of Persia, 223
Suleiman the Magnificent, Ottoman sultan, 223
Sulu Archipelago, 175–76. *See also* Philippines
Sulzer, Franz Joseph, 174–75
Sulzer, Johann Georg, 174–75
sun, 67, 184–85, 217
superlatives, 90–98
Sweden, 84, 145
Swedish language, 129–30
Swedish people, 84, 112–13, 129–30, 195–96
Switzerland, 143
Syria, 77n.21, 112–13
Syriac Rite, 128–29
Syrian music, 18
Syrian people, 109n.16, 203–4, 226–27
  musicians, 203–4, 226–27

Syrinx (Siringa), 51–52
Systema naturae (Linnaeus), 117–19, 120

T-O maps. *See* cartography and maps
Tagore, Sourindro Mohun, 2n.7
Tahiti, 198–99. *See also* Pacific Ocean
Takao, Makoto Harris, 54
tapestry, 58
Tartini, Giuseppe, 96n.125, 151–52
Taruskin, Richard, 85n.67, 218, 234
taste, 154–55, 177–78
  universal taste in music, 170
  See also English; French; German; Italian
Tate, Nahum, 43n.31
Tausug people, 175–76
taxonomies, 9–10, 117–18. *See also* Linnaeus, Carl
Taylor, Timothy D., 21–22, 121–22
Telemann, Georg Philipp, 86
teleology, 8–9, 10–11, 30, 54–58, 207–8, 213, 216
temperaments (behavior/nature), 118–19
Tenshō shōnen shisetsu, 133–35. *See also* ambassadors, embassies, and emissaries; Japan; Jesuits (Society of Jesus)
Terrasson, Jean, 191–92
Thailand. *See* Siam (Thailand)
Thamyris, Athanase, 82–83
theorists of and writers on music. *See* music histories; music treatises, periodicals, and reference works (including dance)
theory. *See* music theory
Tiepolo, Giovanni Battista, 39, 40*f*, 54–58, 55*f*–56*f*, 57*f*
timbre. *See* vocal timbre
Tinctoris, Johannes, 165, 202, 224–25
Tindal, Nicholas, 150n.79
Titian, 39
Titon du Tillet, Évrard, 91–92
Tokyo, 218, 220–21. *See also* Japan
Tonga, 175–76. *See also* Pacific Ocean
Torres Strait Islander peoples, 28–29. *See also* Australia
Toscani, Claudio, 50–51
Tosi, Pier Francesco, 85–86

Traetta, Tommaso, 85–86
Tragaki, Dafni, 19–20
transculturation, 122n.99, 125–26
translation, 70, 77–79, 81n.38, 85–86, 88–89, 92–93, 127–30, 131–32, 139–40, 146–47, 152–53, 175–78, 231–32, 237
travelogues and travel writing, 78–82, 102, 119–20, 123, 127n.113, 175–78, 193, 234–36
treatises, musical. *See* music treatises
Treitler, Leo, 16–17, 182, 243–44
Trent, 143–44. *See also* Italy
Trigault, Nicolas, 112, 228–29
Trully, Robert, 223
Trump, Donald J., 240n.101
Tupinambá people, 197–98. *See also* Brazil
Turin, 41–42. *See also* Italy
Turkey, 3–4, 68–69, 70, 73–76, 112–13, 124, 149–60, 193–94, 195–96, 203, 222–23. *See also* Adrianople (Edirne); Anatolia; Buca; Constantinople (Istanbul); Halicarnassus (Bodrum); İzmir; Ottoman Empire
Turkish
  composers, 174–75
  language, 72–76, 193
  music, 63n.106, 135, 150–52, 210–11
  singing, 166
Turkish people, 78, 119, 131–32, 167, 201–2
  musicians. *See* Ottoman musicians
Tuscan people, 113–14
Twiss, Richard, 206–7
Tyre, 37–38
Tyrol, 4, 143. *See also* Brixen

Ukraine, 218
uniqueness, cultural. *See* exceptionalism
United States of America, 1, 28–29, 219. *See also* Boston; Los Angeles
"universal language," music as a, 168–69, 173, 185–86, 246
universalism, 30, 185–86
Universität Bern, 17–18
Ural Mountains, 84
Urania, 184n.3

Urrows, David, 23–24
Uruguay, 142–43

Vaisseau, Jean, 142n.41
Valignano, Alessandro, 133–34
Valle, Pietro della, 203–4
Valle, Sitti Maani (al Jaïruda), 203–4
Valls, Francesc, 164
van Orden, Kate, 193
Varwig, Bettina, 190
Vasileanu, Monica, 150n.79
Vendrix, Philippe, 100n.4
Venetian people, 113–14
Venice, 67, 72–73, 82–83, 88–89, 193, 211–13, 221–23, 226–27
Venus, 37–38, 44, 45, 49, 198–99
Verazi, Mattia, 50
Verbiest, Ferdinand, 136–39, 140n.28, 141–42, 146–48
  Astronomia europaea, 136–39, 146–48
Vernizzi, Ottavio, 41–42
Versailles, 44–45, 46
Veryard, Ellis, 90–91
Vicentino, Nicola, 189, 195
Vienna, 143, 171–72, 223, 236. *See also* Stefansdom, Vienna
Vietnam. *See* Cochinchina (Vietnam)
Villati, Leopoldo de, 70
Villoteau, Guillaume André, 171, 173, 213–14
Vingt-quatre Violons du Roy, 91–92
violinists. *See* Beaujoyeux, Balthasar de; Bologne, Joseph, Chevalier de Saint-Georges; Corelli, Arcangelo; Ferrari, Domenico; Fiorillo, Federigo; Giardini, Felice; Lolli, Antonio; Mozart, Leopold; Nardini, Pietro; Schmelzer, Johann Heinrich; Tartini, Giuseppe
Visayan people, 175–76, 199–200. *See also* Philippines
Vittorio Amedeo I, Duke of Savoy, 41–42
vocal timbre, 121
voice, 140–41
  Eastern, 226–27
  types/ranges, 67, 134–35
  see also singers; singing; vocal timbre

Voltaire (François-Marie Arouet), 160–61, 191–92, 233–34
voyage accounts. *See* travelogues and travel writing

Wagner, Richard, 17–18
Wallaschek, Richard, 238–39
Walser-Bürgler, Isabella, 107–8
Walsh, John the elder, 93–94
Walsh, John the younger, 130–31
Walsham, Alexandra, 13–14
Walther, Johann Gottfried, 231, 232*f*
Walton, Benjamin, 24–25
Wanli, emperor of China, 111–12
War of the Spanish Succession, 143–44
wars. *See* Cold War; World War I; World War II; Seven Years War; War of the Spanish Succession
Warsaw, 86n.68, 240n.101
Watkins, Timothy D., 145
Weber, Max, 3n.14, 239, 240
Weber, William, 88n.85
weddings, 41–43, 45
Welch, Ellen R., 61–62, 68
Wesley, Samuel, 90
West (Occident), the, 6, 17–18, 110–12, 217–45
  and East, 220–24
  as seen in China, 228–29
  geographical definitions, 218–19, 233–34
  Latin West (Latin Occident), 225
  "Western civilization," 190, 222, 239, 241, 243–44
  "Western world," 229–30
  westerners (occidentals), 224–25
  See also identity
Western art music, 6
  early printed use of term, 240–41
  studies of in twentieth and twenty-first centuries, 241
  "WEAM" (Western European Art Music), 243–44
  "WECT" (Western European Classical Tradition), 243–44
Western music, 179–82, 237–44
  as a unified system, 243

as sacred music of Catholic and
   Protestant churches, 178, 179, 220,
   231, 246–47
changing meanings of, 2–3, 237–39
conflation with "European music," 182,
   237, 238–39, 246
Eastern origin of, 237–38
exceptionalism of, 239–40
Westminster Abbey, 96–97
White, Bryan, 112–13
white people, 114–15, 118–20, 121–22
   men, 11, 25–26, 27–28, 122n.99
   musician(s), 122n.99
   See also race
white voice, 121
whiteness, 26, 27–28, 97–98, 117, 119–20,
   121, 122–23, 158. *See also* race
Wilbourne, Emily, 116–17
Willard, N. Augustus, 214–15, 237
Winckelmann, Johann
   Joachim, 121–22
Wintle, Michael, 66
Wiora, Walter, 243
Wolff, Larry, 234–36
Wolkowicz, Vera, 219n.12
Wollny, Peter, 126n.110
women. *See* gender
Woodcock, Robert, 93

Woodfield, Ian, 212–13
work-concept (concept of Lydia
   Goehr), 9–10, 11–12. *See also*
   musical works
works, musical. *See* musical works;
   musical works (named)
world music, 1, 7–8, 220
World War I, 19
World War II, 19, 218, 243
writers on and theorists of music. *See*
   music histories; music treatises,
   periodicals, and reference works
   (including dance)
Würzburg, 54–58

Yapeyú, Argentina, 142–43, 145
Yri, Kirsten, 179–80, 181

zambra, 202–3n.89
Zante (Zakynthos), 226–27
Zarlino, Gioseffo, 166, 186–87, 191–92,
   196–97, 204
Zeus/Jupiter, 33–34, 37–39, 40*f*, 42–43, 44,
   45, 46–50, 51–52, 54–58, 65–66,
   73. *See also* Europa; mythological
   figures; musical works (named)
Zhang, Qiong, 111–12
Ziani, Marc'Antonio, 93

www.ingramcontent.com/pod-product-compliance
Lightning Source LLC
Chambersburg PA
CBHW072054290825
31867CB00004B/369